Developing Management Skills

for Europe

Pearson Education

We work with leading authors to develop the strongest educational materials in Management, bringing cutting edge thinking and best learning practice to a global market.

Under a range of well-known imprints, including Financial Times Prentice Hall, we craft high quality print and electronic publications which help readers to understand and apply their content, whether studying or at work.

To find out about the complete range of our publishing please visit us on the World Wide Web at:

http://www.pearsoneduc.com

Developing Management Skills

for Europe

Second Edition

DAVID A. WHETTEN

KIM S. CAMERON

MIKE WOODS

FINANCIAL TIMES
Prentice Hall

An imprint of **Pearson Education**

Harlow, England • London - New York • Reading, Massachusetts • San Francisco
Toronto • Don Mills, Ontario - Sydney • Tokyo • Singapore - Hong Kong • seoul
Taipel • Cape Town • Madrid • Mexico City • Amsterdam • Munich - Paris • Milan

Pearson Education Limited
Edinburgh Gate
Harlow
Essex CM20 2JE
England

and Associated Companies throughout the world

Visit us on the World Wide Web at:
http://www.pearsoneduc.com

First published 1994
Second edition 2000

© Pearson Education Limited 2000

First adapted edition [Developing Management Skills for Europe, First Edition],
© Harper Collins Publishers Ltd, 1994

Original American second edtion [Developing Management Skills], © David A. Whetten
and Kim S. Cameron, 1991

The right of Mike Woods to be identified as author of this adapted Work has been
asserted by him in accordance with the Copyright, Designs and Patents Act 1988.

ISBN 0–201–34276–6

British Library Cataloguing-in-Publication Data
A catalogue record for this book can be obtained from the British Library

Library of Congress Cataloging-in-Publication Data
Whetten, David A (David Alfred), 1946–
    Developing management skills for Europe / David A. Whetten, Kim S.
Cameron, Mike Woods. – 2nd ed.
        p.   cm.
Includes bibliographical references and index.
ISBN 0–201–34276–6 (alk. paper)
    1. Management – Europe. I. Cameron, Kim S. II. Woods, Mike.
III. Title.
HD70.E8W49 1999   99–28699
658'.0094 – dc21   CIP

10   9   8   7   6   5   4
05   04   03   02   01

Text design by Claire Brodman
Typeset in Stone Serif 9/12pt by 35
Produced by Pearson Education Asia Pte Ltd
Printed in Singapore (KKP)

Contents

Preface to the Fourth American Edition

Preparing to meet the challenges of the new millennium

As you prepare for or develop your managerial careers in the new millennium, the environment that you will face will undoubtedly be very different from that faced a decade ago, when we first developed this book. Globalisation, impacting on businesses great and small, is presenting new challenges to our skills and our professionalism. The increased diversity in the workplace at home and abroad requires refined communication skills. The business pressures that lead to a wave of re-engineering and downsizing have caused a radical transformation in the way business appears to function and the importance of personal, interpersonal, and group skills of all our staff – white or blue collar – has become more crucial.

Today's business students are learning the latest tools for analysing their specialised fields of study. Accounting and operations management specialists learn how computing power has given them the ability to analyse financial information that provides new insights into operational and financial performance. Finance specialists learn to appreciate the latest trading techniques in derivative markets. Marketing specialists learn how to use the astounding growth of available data to serve new market segmentations. The greatest change, in our opinion, is being felt by the human resource management (HRM) specialists who have found themselves in the cornerstone position of having to match the latest concepts with the new needs of the planned global economy with the human resource, in its widest concept. The HRM specialist has, for the first time, had to truly deliver the 'people resource' to meet the present and future strategic needs of the new organisations. The application of new techniques and understandings, and the frenetic pace of work, have created a dynamic, constantly changing work environment that continually challenges individuals to adapt and learn new methods of accomplishing objectives.

The new challenges do not obliterate the old. The business landscape painted by the changing workplace does not absolve managers of the need to acquire, practise, and utilise a set of managerial skills that allow them to work effectively. 'How do I get my people to accept this idea?' 'How do I explain the need for change to people who are set in their ways?' 'When redundancies are inevitable, how do I help the "survivors" of downsizing to manage with their sense of loss, grief, and guilt?' and 'How do I use existing structures and rewards to encourage the need for change?' are just some of the questions that managers need to address on a daily basis.

A wave of downsizing and re-engineering has created flatter workplaces with less formal hierarchies. Companies that have adopted fluid, project-based team approaches to organising their workforces have found that the requisite personal, interpersonal and group skills are still vital as the mantle of leadership is passed from one team member to another.

Will Rogers, the American sage and comic, came up with the dictum that 'Common sense ain't necessarily common practice' and this underscores the problem with most content-based discussions of management. It is one thing to catalogue the 'best practices' associated with world-class quality, efficiency or customer satisfactions; it is far more challenging to prepare the members of an organisation to accept the need for change, to help them to understand the new approach. Once this understanding is reached we need to obtain commitment to implement and manage the transition period effectively, and to institutionalise the new approach by 'hard wiring' it into the organisation's communication, evaluation and reward systems. As one experienced manager noted, 'Good ideas are not in scarce supply. What is rare is the ability to translate a good idea into accepted practice.'

The goal of this book is to provide current and prospective managers with the personal, interpersonal and group skills necessary to reduce the gap between good ideas and accepted practice. Managers can hire technical expertise, but they cannot hire stand-ins to represent them in critical staff meetings, conversations with angry customers, scheduling discussions with their secretaries, counselling sessions with troubled employees, or performance evaluations. Skilful performance in these settings has been documented by literally dozens of studies as the essential and indispensable foundation of effective management practice.

Background of this book

We have been convinced for a decade or so that management skills must be a crucial part of the business school and corporate training curricula, and this view is now being supported by academic research. Our experience with business school students and managers in executive education seminars has continually reaffirmed our commitment to the skill development approach.

Originally, the motivation for writing *Developing Management Skills* grew out of our frustration with teaching management courses following conventional methods. When we used texts based on the traditional 'principles of management' framework, we felt uncomfortable with their lack of theoretical and research grounding. Because principles of management have been generally derived from recollections and interpretations of practising managers, empirical research and theory regarding their validity in modern organisations is limited.

When we used an organisation and management theory approach, students complained that the practical relevance of the material was difficult to discern. Not enough 'hows' were included to be useful to students who aspired to the practising managers.

When we used a traditional 'organisational behaviour' approach, colleagues teaching the elective organisational behaviour courses reported that students complained about overlap. It became increasingly difficult to differentiate among topics covered by organisational behaviour and management books.

When we emphasised the 'experiential learning' approach, centred around simulations, case discussions and games, students complained that they weren't gaining enough substantive knowledge about how to be effective managers. Few students brought enough practical experience, theoretical knowledge or self-analytic skills to those exercises to get much benefit from them. As a result, the exercises were entertaining but not very useful.

After years of experimentation, we determined that while each approach had its place in a management programme and each could contribute to a student's education, none, taken alone, could help students to develop into competent managers.

In our search for alternatives, we asked recent graduates and senior executives to evaluate the organisational behaviour and management curricula in terms of their experiences as managers. In general, they criticised behavioural science courses for not teaching them job-relevant skills. They were acutely aware of the challenges posed by 'people problems' in their work, and they felt that their education had not prepared them for that component of their job.

Based on this feedback, we began formulating the teaching methodology, and we examined the way such skills as education, social work, engineering, medicine and law are taught in other professional schools. We also drew heavily on recent innovations in training programmes for practising managers that emphasise behaviour modification through role modelling. To identify the relevant management skills, we surveyed over 400 managers in public and private organisations and combed the professional literature for statements by management experts identifying the characteristics of effective managers. As our teaching model began to evolve, it became apparent that a supporting textbook would need to be developed. Further, it would necessarily have to be a hybrid, containing diverse teaching methods and material that would give equal emphasis to concept acquisition and skill practice.

Early in this project it was clear that our text would be at variance with prevailing views regarding what behavioural science courses should offer management students. Typically, these courses either present an array of general principles and concepts derived from research in industrial/organisational psychology, sociology, OB, industrial administration, and so on, or they rely heavily on group exercises, games or cases to illustrate certain management activities. They either describe management practice or provide students with theories for analysing common problems encountered by managers, or they eschew theory and research in favour of activity and involvement. Through our experience we became convinced that the strengths of each approach, used in combination, were needed for students to develop and not just hear about management skills. Therefore, the hallmark of this text is a balanced integration of theory and practice, understanding and application.

We have found that using theories of behaviour as a means to the end of developing behavioural skills not only increases students' interest in and acceptance of the conceptual material in our field, but it also significantly increases their ability to apply the concepts they have learned. Overall, the preparation of students to become productive members of organisations is markedly improved by participation in a management skills course. In fact, the research cited in the Introduction makes it clear that personal and interpersonal skill competence contributes more to the long-term success of managers than does their proficiency in analytic and quantitative skills.

Preface to the First European Edition

Readers of the American edition of *Developing Management Skills* will find much that is familiar in this edition for Europe and many changes. Some of the changes are very obvious – the American spelling and grammar have gone and many of the case studies and examples have been replaced with European ones. On a higher level I have accepted that American managerial culture differs from that of the UK and continental Europe. The most contentious chapter in this cultural divergence was that on 'Gaining Power and Influence', and the restructuring of this chapter owes considerable credit to Alasdair Galloway and the ideas of Charles Handy, which I gratefully acknowledge.

I have also found through talking to lecturers who had used the original American edition in their teaching, the book assumed a certain managerial competence and understanding in their students which was not always there. Key words such as 'communication' and 'problem solving' have developed specialised meaning for practising managers and I felt that it was not useful to allow those students learning the skills of management to struggle with such 'trade jargon'. For this reason I have provided an introduction to each chapter, designed to allow students of management to understand what is to follow in a more familiar context.

In preparing the European edition, I would like to acknowledge the valuable contributions made by Alasdair Galloway (University of Paisley), Jim Stewart (Nottingham Trent University), Nadine Vokins (University of West of England) and Lesley Whittaker (Leeds Metropolitan University). In addition, I would like to thank Elwyn Thomas for his help with the general text and case studies, Jackie Whitehead for her work on Chapter 2 and her general advice on stress management, and Jennie Finder of Bradford University Library for her support and assistance with the case studies.

Preface to the Second European Edition

The American third edition and the first European editions appeared almost simultaneously, and the second European edition was being prepared as the fourth American edition arrived. It would be perhaps an easy point to make that the American and European editions have diverged even further. This, in my opinion, is not true. Reading the new preface from David Whetton and Kim Cameron, I note the same changes that they see from their side of the 'pond'. Life is getting more hectic and the role of the human resource manager is changing, but in spite of the immense growth of the 'technology' of management, people skills have become more important, not less. The only increased divergence was the decision to remove the chapter on 'Gaining Power and Influence' and incorporate the material elsewhere in the book.

The other change is one of methodology, and for this I have to thank my original co-author, Jennie Finder of Bradford University Library. Jennie, for personal and pressing reasons, has ceased to be a proactive co-worker but continued to provide essential and generous help, including a supplement on the use of IT to maintain up-to-date references on management topics. The method she discusses in the technology was used to obtain what we hope is a useful but not overwhelming bibliography and set of references.

In my work with managers and MBA students in the UK and the Middle East, I entirely endorse David and Kim's view of the changes that shape our lives. I go further in believing that management and management training are undergoing a sea of change in Europe. Predicting what we will be teaching and operating in another 10 years is, for me, an interesting speculation – but not much more than that. I wish our readers the best of luck and believe that what we have included will help them to face the new and growing uncertainties. The only certainty is that skilled people will increase in importance.

Acknowledgements

The publishers wish to thank the following for permission to reproduce material:

Case Study 2.1, Mr A. Gordon for the excerpt from *The Day at the Beach*.

Survey 2.4, Social Readjustment Rating Scale, reprinted from the *Journal of Psychosomatic Research*, Holmes, T.H. & Rahe, R.H., The Social Readjustment Rating Scale, 1967, with permission from Elsevier Science.

Case Study 3.1, The Sony Walkman, used with permission of Arthur D. Little Inc.

Survey 3.3, Innovative Attitude Scale, used with permission of Blackwell Publishers Ltd.

Figure 6.3, copyright 1979 by The Regents of the University of California. Reprinted from the *California Management Review*, Vol. 21, No. 4. By permission of The Regents.

Financial Times Ltd for the Ciba extract in Chapter 7.

Though every effort has been made to trace the owners of copyright material, in a few cases this has proved impossible and we take this opportunity to apologise to any copyright holders whose rights may have been unwittingly infringed.

Introduction

This book is designed to help to guide individuals in improving their own personal management competencies. It is a practical guide to effective managerial behaviour and not a discussion of how some prominent industrialist has turned round a specific organisation. Unlike many 'airport' guides to successful management it is based on sound research and is designed along accepted teaching principles.

Management into the twenty-first century

Managers need to apply certain competencies backed by developable skills to perform effectively in the changing world of organisations. These competencies are in addition to their own functional expertise, they are about people skills. As Meredeth Belbin, management guru, often says in his lectures: *You are hired for what you are and fired for who you are.* This book is about developing these skills, but before we begin we need to say something about the word 'competence', which has acquired an almost mythical status in the past decade and, of course, the changing world of organisations.

Competency

There are as many definitions of competency as there are consultants attempting to sell competency training.

At a workshop organised by the British Psychological Society in 1989, a group of six human resource specialists were asked to come up with an agreed definition of competency. The chair of the group opened his report to the plenary meeting with the words: *Before presenting my report from all six of us I have to tell you that there are five minority reports!* The laughter was from understanding, relief and sympathy.

We are going to take our definition from the Cannon Working Party Report: *Progress and Change, 1987–94* (1994):

> The term competency is taken to mean the ability to perform effectively functions associated with management in a work-related situation.

1

Table 0.1 Skills required in the millennium – Ashridge survey, quoted by Colin Coulson-Thomas

	Ranking (%)
Strategic thinking, e.g., longer, broader, perspective, anticipating	78
Responding to and managing change	75
An orientation towards total quality/customer satisfaction	67
Financial management, e.g., role and impact of key indicators	46
Facilitating others to contribute	44
Understanding the role of information and IT	42
Verbal communication, e.g., coherent, persuasive	38
Organisational sensitivity, e.g., cross-functional understanding	37
Risk assessment in decision making	35

Quoted by Watson from an Ashridge Management Research Group Questionnaire (1994)

James Watson, also reporting to the Cannon Working Party, quoted from earlier work by Constable that the number of managers (and here he was speaking of the UK alone) would shrink overall by the year 2000 from 2.5–3.0 million to 2–2.25 million. Watson lists the skills needed for this new brand of manager (see Table 0.1). Colin Coulson-Thomas (1992), in a then British Institute of Management survey, came to similar conclusions.

Allred *et al.* (1996) looked at the changes in organisations and their demands on managers. Their premise was that 'organisational structure dictates core managerial competencies'. They then list the fashionable organisational structures since the First World War to one they predict for the immediate future, giving the core managerial competencies required with each development:

1. The traditional military style organisation where technical and commercial competencies predominated.

2. The matrix organisation appearing in the late 1950s and early 1960s:

   In trying to keep clients satisfied by effectively managing multifunctional resources and meeting budgets, project and brand managers in matrix organisations developed and used many of the same general management skills exercised by division managers in a diversified firm. In the global matrix organisations that appeared in the 1970s, country managers played the project management role through interactions with global functional and product divisions, responding to local needs by drawing on the resources of company-wide units. Thus country managers tended to develop a complete repertoire of technical, commercial and self-governance competencies. (Allred *et al.*, 1996)

3. The current evolution – the networked firm.

   To become more competitive, organisations downsized, delayered and outsourced many functions during the 1980s. In addition to the technical and commercial and competencies of the previous organisations, they need a raft of communications, collaborative and conflict competencies with their associated management skills. They demanded the competencies of self-learning and development.

4. Future developments – the cellular organisation.

Allred *et al.* (1996) foresee a developing organisation where hierarchy has no part and 'managers and leaders' have to survive in an organic 'pond'. Here the interpersonal skills discussed in this book will predominate and the technical competencies will largely be replaced by technologies.

Greg Boudreux (1997) helpfully distinguishes between competencies and skills – confirming the usage of our book – and lists the competencies needed in the millennium.

- Skills are specific job-related abilities that can be developed through training.
- Competencies, acquired by constant practice of the relevant skills, are the habit of doing or saying the right things at the right time.

This book will help you acquire, develop and hone skills – turning these into competencies has to be left to you, and time.

The skills of the new organisations

As Allred *et al.* (1996) have pointed out, the new organisations will call upon more and more interpersonal skills. These skills need to be discussed.

The skills are behavioural. They are not personal attributes or stylistic tendencies. They consist of an identifiable set of actions that individuals perform and that lead to certain outcomes. An important implication, therefore, is that individuals can learn to perform these actions and can improve their current level of performance. People with different styles and personalities may apply the skills differently, but there is a core set of observable attributes of effective skill performance that are common across a range of individual differences.

The skills seem, in several cases, to be contradictory or paradoxical. For example, they are neither all soft nor humanistic in orientation, nor all hard driving and directive. They are oriented neither towards teamwork and interpersonal relations nor towards the individualism of an entrepreneur exclusively. A variety of types of skills are present. This was also in the findings of the Ashridge Managerial Research Group (1994), as quoted in the Cannon Report (1994).

For example, Cameron and Tschirhart (1988) assessed the skill performance of over 500 mid-level and upper-middle managers in about 150 organisations. They used the 25 most frequently mentioned management skills taken from those in Tables 0.2 and 0.3 as well as from research by Ghiselli (1963), Livingston (1971), Miner (1973), Katz (1974), Mintzberg (1975), Flanders (1981) and Boyatzis (1982).

In an analysis of the data we found that the skills could be sorted into four main groups. The first group focused on participative and human relations skills (for example, constructive communication and team building), while the second group focused on just the opposite, that is, on competitiveness and control (for example,

Table 0.2 The most frequently discussed skills of effective managers

1. Verbal communication – including listening
2. Managing time and stress
3. Managing individual decisions
4. Recognising, defining and solving problems
5. Motivating and influencing others
6. Delegating
7. Setting goals and articulating a vision
8. Self-awareness
9. Team building
10. Managing conflict

assertiveness, power and influence skills). A third group focused on innovativeness and entrepreneurship (such as creative problem solving), while a fourth group emphasised quite the opposite type of skills, namely maintaining order and rationality (for example, managing time and rational decision making).

One conclusion from the study was that effective managers are required to demonstrate paradoxical skills – that is, the most effective managers can be both participative and hard driving, both nurturing and competitive. These people were able to be flexible and creative while also being controlled, stable and rational. The second characteristic associated with effective management, then, is the mastery of diverse and seemingly contradictory skills.

Third, these critical skills were interrelated and overlapping. No effective manager performed one skill or one set of skills independent of others. For example, in order to motivate others effectively, skills such as supportive communication, influence and delegation were also required. Effective managers, therefore, develop a constellation of skills that overlap and support one another and allow flexibility in managing diverse situations.

Improving management skills

Successful management is more than just following a cookbook list of sequential behaviours. Developing highly competent management skills is much more complicated than developing skills such as those associated with a trade (e.g., welding) or a sport (e.g., scoring goals). Management skills are:

- Linked to a more complex knowledge base than other types of skills.
- Inherently connected to interaction with other (frequently unpredictable) individuals.

A standardised approach to welding or scoring goals may be feasible, but no standardised approach to managing human beings is possible.

Table 0.3 Identifying critical management skills: a sample of studies

1 – Study 2 – Respondents 3 – Focus	Results	
1. **Prentice** (1984) 2. 230 executives in manufacturing, retail and service firms 3. Critical skills for managing organisations	• Listening • Communication • Leadership • Problem solving • Time management • Adaptability to change	• Interpersonal relations • Formal presentations • Stress management
1. **Margerison and Kakabadse** (1984) 2. 721 CEO's in US corporations 3. Most important things you've learned in order to be a CEO	• Communication • Managing people • Delegation • Patience • Respect • Control • Understanding people • Evaluating personnel • Tolerance • Team spirit	• Strategic planning • Decision making • Self-discipline • Analytical ability • Hard work • Flexibility • Financial management • Time management • Knowledge of the business • Clear thinking
1. **Margerison and Kakabadse** (1984) 2. 721 CEO's in US corporations 3. Key management skills to develop in others to help them become senior executives	• Human relations • Communication • Planning and goal setting • People management and leadership	• Decision making • Financial management • Entrepreneurial skills • Delegating • Broad experience • Teamwork
1. **Cameron** (1984) 2. 50 consultants, professors, management development experts and public administrators 3. Critical management skills needed by state government managers	• Managing conflict • Motivating others • Managing stress and time • Decision making • Delegation	• Leadership • Knowledge and experience
1. **Hunsicker** (1978) 2. 1,845 US Air Force officers 3. Skills that most contribute to successful management	• Communication • Human relations • General management ability • Technical competence	

Table 0.3 (Cont'd)

1 – Study
2 – Respondents
3 – Focus   *Results*

1. **Luthans** *et al.* (1985)
2. 52 managers in 3 organisations
3. Participant observation of skills demonstrated by most effective managers versus least effective managers

- Managing conflict
- Communicating with outsiders

- Decision making
- Communicating with insiders
- Developing subordinates
- Processing paperwork
- Planning and goal setting

1. **Benson** (1983)
2. A survey of 25 studies in business journals
3. A summary of the skills needed by students entering the profession

- Listening
- Written communication
- Oral communication
- Motivating/persuading

- Interpersonal skills
- Informational interviewing
- Group problem solving

1. **Curtis** *et al.* (1989)
2. 428 members of the American Society of Personnel Administrators in the US
3. (a) Skills needed to obtain employment
   (b) Skills important for successful job performance
   (c) Skills needed to move up the organisation

(a)
- Verbal communication
- Listening
- Enthusiasm
- Written communications
- Technical competence
- Appearance

(c) Ability to:
- work well with others one-to-one
- gather information and make a decision
- work well in groups
- listen and give counsel
- give effective feedback
- present a good image of the firm
- use computers and business machines

(b)
- Interpersonal skills
- Verbal and written communication
- Persistence/ determination
- Enthusiasm
- Technical competence

(d) Knowledge of:
- the job
- management theory
- finance
- marketing
- accounting

Skills have a potential for improvement through practice. Any approach to developing management skills, therefore, must involve practical applications. At the same time, practice without the necessary conceptual knowledge is sterile and ignores the need for flexibility and adaptation to different situations. Therefore, developing skill competency is inherently tied to both conceptual learning and behavioural practice.

The method we have found to be most successful in helping individuals develop management skills is based on social learning theory (Bandura, 1977a; Davis and Luthans, 1980). This approach marries rigorous conceptual knowledge with opportunities to practise and apply observable behaviours. Variations on this general approach have been used widely in on-the-job supervisory training programmes (Goldstein and Sorcher, 1974), as well as in allied professional education classrooms such as teacher development and social work (Rose *et al.*, 1977; Singleton *et al.*, 1980).

The original learning model consisted of four steps:

1. The presentation of behavioural principles or action guidelines, generally using traditional instruction methods.

2. Demonstration of the principles by means of cases, films, scripts or incidents.

3. Opportunities to practise the principles through role plays or exercises.

4. Feedback on performance from peers, instructors or experts.

Our own experience in teaching complex management skills has convinced us that three important modifications are necessary in order for this model to be most effective:

- The behavioural principles must be grounded in social science theory and in reliable research results and not the generalisations and panacea prescriptions that appear regularly in the popular management literature. To ensure the validity of the behavioural guidelines being prescribed, the learning approach must include scientifically based knowledge about the effects of the management principles being presented.

- Individuals must be aware of their current level of skill competency and be motivated to improve upon that level in order to benefit from the model. Most people receive very little feedback about their current level of skill competency. Most organisations provide some kind of annual or semi-annual evaluation (for example, exams in colleges or performance appraisal interviews in firms), but these evaluations are almost always infrequent and narrow in scope, and they fail to assess performance in the most critical skill areas. To help people to understand what skills to improve and why, therefore, a pre-assessment activity must be part of the model. In addition, most people find change rather uncomfortable and therefore avoid taking the risk to develop new behaviour patterns. A pre-assessment activity in the learning model helps to encourage these people to change by illuminating their strengths and weaknesses. Individuals then know where their own weaknesses lie and the areas that need to be improved. Pre-assessment activities generally take the form of self-evaluation instruments, case studies or problems that help to highlight personal strengths and weaknesses in a particular skill area.

Table 0.4 A system for developing management skills

Steps	Contents	Objectives
1. Skill pre-assessment	Survey instruments Role plays	Assess current level of skill competence and knowledge; create readiness to change
2. Skill learning	Written text Behavioural guidelines	Teach correct principles and present a rationale for behavioural guidelines
3. Skill analysis	Case studies	Provide examples of appropriate and inappropriate skills performance; analyse behavioural principles and the reason that they work
4. Skill practice	Exercises Simulations Role plays	Practise behavioural guidelines; adapt principles to personal style; receive feedback and assistance
5. Skill application	Assignments (behavioural and written)	Transfer classroom learning to real-life situations; foster ongoing personal development

- An application component is needed in the learning model. Most management skill training takes place in a classroom setting where feedback is immediate and it is relatively safe to try out new behaviours and make mistakes. Therefore, transferring learning to an actual job setting is often problematic. Application exercises help to apply classroom learning to examples from the real world of management. Application exercises often take the form of an outside-of-class intervention, or a consulting assignment, or a problem-centred intervention, which the student then analyses to determine its degree of success or failure.

In summary, evidence suggests that a five-step learning model is most effective for helping individuals develop management skills (see Cameron and Whetten, 1984). Such a model is outlined in Table 0.4.

- Step 1 involves the pre-assessment of current levels of skill competency and knowledge of the behavioural principles.
- Step 2 consists of the presentation of validated, scientifically based principles and guidelines for effective skill performance.
- Step 3 is an analysis step in which models or cases are made available in order to analyse behavioural principles in real organisational settings. This step also helps to demonstrate how the behavioural guidelines can be adapted to different personal styles and circumstances.

- Step 4 consists of practice exercises in which experimentation can occur and immediate feedback can be received in a relatively safe environment.
- Step 5 is the application of the skill to a real-life setting outside the classroom with follow-up analysis of the relative success of that application.

Research on the effectiveness of training programmes using this general learning model has shown that it produces results superior to those based on the traditional lecture and discussion approach (Moses and Ritchie, 1976; Burnaska, 1976; Smith, 1976; Latham and Saari, 1979; Porras and Anderson, 1981). In addition, evidence suggests that management skill training can have significant impact on the financial performance of a firm.

> The US Postal Service completed a study a few years ago in which 49 of the largest 100 post offices in America were evaluated. An important question in the study was, 'How can we make post offices more effective?' Productivity and service quality were both monitored over a five-year period. The two major factors that had impact on these effectiveness measures were:
>
> **1.** Degree of mechanisation (automation)
> **2.** Investment in training.
>
> Two kinds of training were provided:
>
> (a) maintenance training (training in operating and maintaining the equipment)
> (b) management training (training in developing management skills).
>
> The overall conclusion of the study was: 'Performance levels in these organisations vary systematically and predictably as training levels vary. The training/performance relationship is positive and statistically significant.' More specifically, the study found that:
>
> - providing management training was more important than providing maintenance training in accounting for improved productivity and service in the post offices;
> - both kinds of training were more important than having automated or up-to-date equipment in the post office (mechanisation);
> - low-tech offices outperformed high-technology offices when managers were provided with management skill training.
>
> In short, its five-year study convinced the US Postal Service that helping employees to develop management skills was the best way to improve organisational effectiveness.

Successful managers must be able to work effectively with people. Unfortunately, interpersonal and management skills have not always been a high priority for business school students and aspiring executives. In a survey of 110 Fortune 500 CEOs, 87 per cent were satisfied with the level of competence and analytic skills of business school graduates, 68 per cent were satisfied with conceptual skills of graduates, but only 43 per cent of the CEOs were satisfied with graduates' management skills, and only 28 per cent were satisfied with their interpersonal skills!

To assist you in improving your own management skills, this book emphasises practising management skills, rather than just reading about them. We have organised the book with this specific approach in mind.

Organisation of the book

This book focuses on the management skill areas that research has identified as most important. Part 1, comprising the first three chapters of the book, focuses on intrapersonal skills: developing self-awareness, managing stress, and effective problem solving – each skill overlapping with other skills. No skill stands alone. Part 2 concentrates on the interpersonal skills of management – constructive communication, effective motivation, and constructive conflict management – while Part 3 deals with the hard management skills of effective empowerment and delegation and the issues of teams, leaders and managers. These skill areas also overlap with managers having to rely on combinations of skills taken from all areas to function effectively. As one progresses from personal to interpersonal to group skills, the core competencies developed in the previous area help to form a foundation for successful performance of the new skill area.

The final parts of the book are supplements and appendices, one of which covers the scoring procedures for the exercises, etc., in the text.

The supplements are devoted to specific skill areas that we have found in practice to require special attention:

- Conducting meetings
- Making oral presentations
- Interviewing
- Management of information.

We make no apology for including a section on data management. As we produce this book we find that its references become out of date and any practising manager needs to be up to date. The new technologies that are clumped under the word 'Internet' allow managers to be up to date in a way that their predecessors were never able to envisage – unless they wished to become academics and forget their management duties entirely. Using these new resources involves a new set of skills that fit happily under our title – *Developing Management Skills for Europe*.

Each chapter is organised on the basis of a cyclic learning model that allows the reader a measure of control over his or her learning. The chapters begin with questionnaires that allow you, the reader and learner, to find out your current level of skills in the area to be covered. After completing the questionnaires you will be able to focus your attention on areas of personal competence as well as areas needing improvement in both knowledge and performance – develop your own learning objectives. The body of each chapter will bring the reader up to speed on current thinking in the area and quote key references for further study if required. In practice we find that we have two clusters of readers: students and working managers who wish to improve the skills they are already using and perhaps give legitimacy to practices they have developed for themselves. The references and further reading provide a good starting point for projects and examination assessment. The summaries at the end of each chapter list the key behavioural guidelines.

Since we believe that *'When all is said and done, more is said than done'*, we now ask you to practise your newly considered skills, initially on graded case studies and finally on real-life assignments based at home and at work. The purpose of these assignments is to help you to transfer behavioural guidelines into everyday practice now or later. You may be asked to teach the skill to someone else, to consult with another manager to help to resolve a relevant problem, or to apply the skill in an organisation or your home life. Having finished each chapter we invite you to go back to the questionnaires and see how your answers and behavioural application may have changed.

Practice and application

The last section of each chapter (Skill Application) contains exercises for practice and application. As we have said before, we consider that improvement in management skills is primarily the responsibility of the learner. If the application of the principles covered in this book is not conscientiously applied within the real world, then little or nothing will have been achieved. Effective management is no different from effectiveness in most other human enterprises. It requires the same kind of skills to live a productive and successful life as it does to manage people effectively. That is why, even though some readers may have responsibility for others at work, and indeed may never become managers, they should neither dismiss these skills as irrelevant nor wait until they become managers before attempting to practise them.

The researchers Staw, Sandelands and Dutton claimed in 1981 that people under stress revert to a 'dominant response pattern' – that is, they rely on behaviour patterns that are most deeply ingrained and may not be the most appropriate in the exact, new and novel circumstances. For example, if a person who has been accustomed to responding to conflict aggressively, but who has recently begun practising a more constructive mode is faced with an intense, emotional confrontation, that person may begin by reacting supportively. But as pressure mounts, he or she is likely to revert to the more practised, combative style: *we do what we do because that is always what we have done – forget all these new fangled theories.* The only way of adopting appropriate actions is practice and it is never too early to begin that practice. Whatever stage of our careers we find ourselves in, we should practise and apply the skills we are about to learn even if it is in our friendships, student organisations, families or social groups. With conscientious practise, following the behavioural guidelines will become second nature.

People learn best that which affects them, and they feel affected by something if they see an immediate effect on their lives. The converse is also true – if you do not practise the skills we are about to work on together, they will not be available for later, and perhaps vital, applications. Think about learning an unfamiliar language – practise among those actually speaking it is much more effective than any amount of study in isolation. Application is a crucial component of the skill development process, but it generally takes extra effort and ingenuity to make application exercises effective and worth while. We would encourage you to put that extra effort.

We are not entirely writing for practising managers and would-be managers. It is intended to help people in general to improve the management of many aspects of their lives and relationships. In fact, John Holt (1964, p. 165) put it in a way we do not wish to improve on. He equated management skill to intelligence:

> When we talk about intelligence, we do not mean the ability to get a good score on a certain kind of test or even the ability to do well in school; these are at best only indicators of something larger, deeper and far more important. By intelligence we mean a style of life, a way of behaving in various situations. The true test of intelligence is not how much we know what to do, but how we behave when we don't know what to do.

Fostering this intelligence is the purpose of our book.

So let's begin. This time we will close our Introduction with our skill assessment questionnaire and this time the questionnaire will cover the contents of the whole book and not just a single chapter.

Personal assessment of management skills

The questionnaires are designed to let you, our readers, understand where you rate now and where you rate when you have finished the book, on the key skill areas we are about to cover. There are a series of statements of behaviour and you should rate how well this behaviour fits you now, not how you would like it to be or how you think we would like it to be. Some of the statements may well relate to activities of which you have no experience. If this is the case, think about them and try to answer honestly 'How I would if I were . . .'. A scoring key in Appendix 1 at the end of the book will help you generate an overall profile of your management skill strengths and weaknesses.

RATING SCALE

1 = strongly disagree   **2** = disagree   **3** = slightly disagree
4 = slightly agree   **5** = agree   **6** = strongly agree

	Assessment Pre-	Post-
In regard to my level of self-knowledge		
1. I seek information about my strengths and weaknesses so that I can improve myself.	____	____
2. I am willing to share my beliefs and feelings to others so that I can improve myself.	____	____
3. I am fully aware of how I prefer to gather information and make decisions.	____	____
4. I understand how I cope with ambiguous and uncertain situations.	____	____
5. I have a well-developed set of personal standards and principles that guide my behaviour.	____	____

These issues will be discussed in Chapter 1: Developing Self-awareness

When faced with stressful or time-pressured situations

6. I use effective time-management methods such as keeping track of my time, making action lists and prioritising tasks.   ____ ____

7. I frequently check my priorities so that less important things don't drive out the more important.   ____ ____

8. I work to keep myself fit.   ____ ____

9. I maintain an open, trusting relationship with someone with whom I can share my frustrations.   ____ ____

10. I know and practise several temporary relaxation techniques such as deep breathing and muscle relaxation.   ____ ____

11. I strive to redefine problems as opportunities for improvement.   ____ ____

These and issues 12 and 13 will be discussed in Chapter 2: Managing Stress

When I delegate tasks to others

12. I specify the level of performance I expect and the degree of initiative the other person should assume.   ____ ____

13. I follow up and maintain accountability for delegated tasks on a regular basis.   ____ ____

When I approach a typical, routine problem

14. I always attempt to define problems clearly and explicitly.   ____ ____

15. I always generate more than one alternative solution to the problem.   ____ ____

16. I keep problem-solving steps distinct; that is, I make sure that the processes of formulating definitions, generating alternatives and finding solutions are separated.   ____ ____

When faced with a complex or difficult problem that does not have a straightforward solution

17. I try to be flexible in the way I approach the problem; I don't just rely on conventional wisdom or past practice.   ____ ____

18. I try to unfreeze my thinking by asking lots of questions around the issue.   ____ ____

19. I often use metaphors or analogies to help me see issues differently.   ____ ____

20. I strive to look at problems from different perspectives so as to generate multiple definitions.   ____ ____

21. I only evaluate potential solutions when I have completed a list of alternatives – however bizarre some of them may seem.   ____ ____

When trying to foster more creativity and innovation among those with whom I work

22. I make sure there are divergent points of view represented in every problem-solving group.   ____ ____

23. I try to acquire information from customers regarding their preferences and expectations. ____ ____

24. I recognise that those who support ideas and those involved with the implementation need recognition along with the 'idea people'. ____ ____

25. I encourage informed rule-breaking in pursuit of creative solutions. ____ ____

Issues 14–25 will be discussed in Chapter 3: Effective Problem Solving

In situations where I have to provide negative feedback or offer corrective advice

26. When I counsel others I help them to their own solutions. ____ ____

27. I know when it is correct to offer advice and direction and when it is not. ____ ____

28. I attempt to give feedback focused on tasks and not personalities. ____ ____

29. My feedback is specific and to the point, rather than general or vague. ____ ____

30. When I have to give negative feedback I describe the events objectively, their consequences and my feelings about them. ____ ____

31. I take responsibility for my statements and views by using 'I' statements and avoid attributing things to 'them'. ____ ____

32. I convey flexibility and openness to conflicting opinions when presenting my point of view, even when I feel strongly about it. ____ ____

33. I do not patronise those who happen to have less authority or knowledge. ____ ____

34. I attempt not to dominate conversations. ____ ____

Issues 26–34 will be discussed in Chapter 4: Constructive Communication

When another person needs to be motivated

35. I always determine if a person has the necessary resources and support to succeed in a task. ____ ____

36. I use a variety of rewards to reinforce exceptional performances. ____ ____

37. I design task assignments to make them interesting and challenging. ____ ____

38. I make sure to give timely and focused feedback. ____ ____

39. I always help to establish performance goals that are challenging, specific and time-bound. ____ ____

40. I regard getting rid of staff as a last resort, however poorly I judge their performance. ____ ____

41. I maintain consistent feedback when I feel effort is below expectations and capabilities. ____ ____

42. I make sure that people feel fairly and equitably treated. ____ ____

43. I provide immediate and appropriate praise for effective effort. ____ ____

Issues 35–43 will be covered in Chapter 5: Effective Motivation

When I see someone doing something that needs correcting

44. I avoid making personal accusations and attributing self-serving motives to the other person. ____ ____

45. I accept the need for two-way communication by encouraging questions and the expression of alternative views. ____ ____

46. I make a specific request, detailing what I see as preferred option. ____ ____

When someone complains about something I've done

47. I show genuine concern and interest, even when I disagree. ____ ____

48. I seek additional information by asking questions that provide specific and descriptive information. ____ ____

49. I ask the other person to suggest more acceptable behaviours. ____ ____

When two people are in conflict and I am the mediator

50. I do not take sides but remain neutral. ____ ____

51. I help the parties generate multiple alternatives. ____ ____

52. I help the parties find areas on which they agree. ____ ____

Issues 44–52 are discussed in context in Chapter 6: Effective Conflict Management

Where I have an opportunity to empower others

53. I help people feel competent in their work by recognising and celebrating any small successes. ____ ____

54. I provide regular feedback and needed support. ____ ____

55. I try to provide all the information required to accomplish their tasks. ____ ____

56. I am genuinely concerned for those I work with. ____ ____

When delegating work to others

57. I specify clearly the results I desire. ____ ____

58. I specify clearly the level of initiative I want others to take (e.g. wait for directions, do part of the task and then report, do the whole task and then report, etc.). ____ ____

59. As far as possible, I let the people actually doing the work develop, with my assistance and understanding, how work will be done. ____ ____

60. I avoid upward delegation by asking people to recommend solutions, rather than merely asking for advice or answers, when a problem is encountered. ____ ____

Issues 53–60 will be covered in Chapter 7: Effective Empowerment and Delegation

When working in a team

61. I like to be comfortable with my co-workers, understand my function and role as well as making close contacts. ____ ____

62. I accept responsibility and do not expect to be told everything. ____ ____

When leading a team

63. I specify why things need to be done and what needs to be done and work towards the team, taking responsibility for the actual task. ⎯⎯ ⎯⎯

64. I accept that teams and individuals need developing. ⎯⎯ ⎯⎯

65. I see my job as facilitating the work, in every respect, monitoring the output and communication to authority and other teams. ⎯⎯ ⎯⎯

66. I accept that I need to be flexible in my management and leadership style. ⎯⎯ ⎯⎯

67. As a leader I maintain my position by modelling the behaviour I need and not by exercising power. ⎯⎯ ⎯⎯

68. I see the role of team leader as a privilege and not a right. ⎯⎯ ⎯⎯

Issues 61–68 will be developed in Chapter 8: Teams, Leaders and Managers

When communicating or requiring information

69. I keep myself up to date with my own area of expertise. ⎯⎯ ⎯⎯

70. I read generally about management – maybe a book a month. ⎯⎯ ⎯⎯

71. I have access to the Internet. ⎯⎯ ⎯⎯

72. I use e-mail and similar means to communicate with people. ⎯⎯ ⎯⎯

73. I use the Internet as a source of information about my job, including the business of my customers, clients, etc. ⎯⎯ ⎯⎯

Issues 69–72 will be developed in Supplement D: Management of Information

---

EXERCISE **0.1**

WHAT DOES IT TAKE TO BE AN EFFECTIVE MANAGER?

The purpose of this exercise is to help you to find out for yourself the role of a manager and the skills required to perform that job successfully.

Your assignment is to interview at least three full-time managers using the questions we list as a starting point. Treat the interviews as confidential and do not allow your notes to identify individual managers. Tell the managers that no one will be able to identify them from their responses.

Your notes should be as detailed as possible so that you can reconstruct the interviews for use later – if you are a student, to your class. The notes should include each person's job title and a brief description of his or her organisation.

Discussion questions

1. What would be a typical day at work?

2. What are the most critical problems you face as a manager?

3. What are the most critical skills needed to be a successful manager in your area?

4. What are the major reasons that some managers are less successful than others?

5. What are the outstanding skills or abilities of other effective managers you have known?

6. If you had to train someone to replace you in your current job, what key abilities would you focus on?

On a scale of 1 (very rarely) to 5 (constantly), can you rate the extent to which you use the following skills or behaviours during your workday?

Managing personal stress	____	Managing time	____
Facilitating group decision making	____	Orchestrating change	____
Making private decisions	____	Appraising others, formally or informally	____
Recognising or defining problems	____	Goal setting	____
Using verbal communication skills	____	Listening and counselling	____
Delegating	____	Disciplining	____
Motivating others	____	Self-learning	____
Managing conflict	____	Team building	____
Interviewing	____	Problem solving	____
Negotiation	____	Conducting or attending meetings	____

EXERCISE **0.2**

USING YOUR MANAGEMENT SKILLS

Another way to assess your own strengths and weaknesses in management skills is to engage in an actual managerial work experience. Some companies in developing their managers use this process. Trainee managers of any seniority are sent into 'strange' departments inside their own organisation or outside into 'sister' organisations and given an actual project to complete. Such action learning, pioneered by Enid Mumford of Manchester Business School, is outside the scope of our book.

A further technique, taking less resources but with an action learning element, is the simulation or management 'game' – either indoors or on occasion out of doors. Since this is a book, we have to chose an even simpler course of action – we would like you to work on a case study from the point of view of a manager faced with the issues.

Complete the exercise and assignments and then compare your own decisions with those of other class mates. Ideally the discussions should then be taken to plenary with a tutor for further analysis and discussion.

If you have not been given a case study before we would suggest a way of proceeding. Read it all through quickly and then go through it again, highlighting the main points. Although we hate to say it, this case study, as all the other case studies we have met, is full of packing and finding the key points at the beginning helps a lot.

CASE STUDY **0.1**

THE THAMES PUMP & VALVE COMPANY

The Thames Pump & Valve Company, whose managing director is John Manners, is a subsidiary of Arnold Chemicals & Equipment Ltd. Its operations have been quite successful. Beginning with a capital investment of slightly less than £750,000 in 1947, its capital investment today is in excess of £500 million. Thames Pump & Valve own a newly constructed office building in Slough and a manufacturing and assembly plant, also in Slough. There are two sales outlets in the UK in Reading and one in Henley. The mainland Europe sales are through strategically placed agents.

The company, excluding top management, employs 60 engineers and 32 technicians, and about 1,000 people in the production. The production unit works two 38-hour shifts a week.

John Dunn is the production manager. All valves and pump assemblies and components are either manufactured or assembled in the production department according to detailed specifications. The specifications are distributed to various sites and locations according to set procedures or are stored in the company's warehouses in Reading and Henley. Centralised product and planning enables the company to maintain rigid production and quality controls over all units that become a part of completed products. In addition, carefully planned production and shipping schedules reduce the amount of time that completed units must be stored at production points. As a result, distribution costs are reduced and the company is better able to ensure that contracted completion dates are met.

The research and development division, currently under the direction of Tom Evans, has grown from two engineers to its present size of 30 engineers and 12 technicians and draftsmen. Partly because of the plant manager's intense interest, 10 per cent of the company's profits are allocated to research and development. The research division has developed, among other things, a less expensive and longer lasting rust inhibitor system, a rotary arc-welding unit for the plant and a new method for testing the strength and quality of welded unions. Also, the division was responsible for the design of expansion joints which are formed and assembled in the company's plant, ready for immediate installation at construction sites.

Bill Marshall is the financial controller and has approximately 15 people in the accounts department. Alan Cushwell's personnel department is also staffed by 15 people, while there is a total of 82 employees in the marketing department headed by James Barber.

John Manners, the managing director, suffered a severe heart attack on 12 April and died. It had been noticed that he appeared tired and overworked recently but nothing was done about it. His place has been taken by Richard West, transferred from Kent Pump & Valve, a slightly smaller subsidiary of the Arnold Group.

Assignment

Today is Sunday, 11 April 1999. Richard West has just come into the office, for the first time at 17.45 p.m. He must leave in time to catch the midnight plane for an important meeting in Cologne. He will not be back until next Monday, 20 April. His secretary is Doreen Powell, who was secretary to John Manners before he died.

Doreen Powell has left a number of letters in Richard West's in-tray (Items 0.1–0.11 below). You are to assume the role of Richard West and go through all the material, taking whatever action you deem appropriate for each item and prioritising your actions. Every action you wish to take should be written down, including memos to the secretary, memos to 'yourself' (Richard West), etc. Draft letters where appropriate, and write out any plans or agendas for meetings or conferences that you plan. These letters, memos, notes, etc., may be in 'rough draft' form.

---

10 April 1999

OFFICE MEMORANDUM
TO: Richard West
FROM: Doreen Powell
SUBJECT: SAM Presentation (See attached)

Mr West:

Just a note to let you know that Mr Manners did nothing towards developing the programme scheduled for 24 April, except to send the title to Mr Johnson via E-Mail. The title was announced to members some time ago. I don't think Mr Manners discussed the matter with any of the department heads.

Doreen

Item 0.1 A

THE SOCIETY FOR THE ADVANCEMENT OF MANAGEMENT
Berkshire Branch
PO Box 106
Windsor, Berks

1 April 1999

Mr John Manners
Managing Director
Thames Pump & Valve Ltd
Wokingham Road
Slough
Berks

Dear John

This is a reminder that we are counting on you and on the Thames Pump & Valve Company to provide us with the three-hour evening programme for our meeting on 24 April.

I know you and your team will provide a stimulating and worthwhile programme. The title of the programme you are to present, 'The Image of Today's Executive', sounds very interesting and already the dinner and programme is a 'sell out'. It means you can look forward to a full house on the night of your presentation.

Could you prepare a brief outline of the programme and text of any speeches that will be presented, indicating who will present them so we can go ahead with the programme and press releases?

We are all looking forward to seeing you on 24 April.

Best regards

Paul Johnson
Secretary, Berkshire Branch.

Item 0.1 B

PERSONAL

7 April 1999

OFFICE MEMORANDUM
TO: John Manners
FROM: Alan Cushwell, Industrial and Employee Relations
SUBJECT: Frank Munro

I have been told confidentially from an unimpeachable source that Frank Munro has been offered a job with N.C.A. and he is going to give a firm answer next week. I don't think anyone else knows this yet, I just stumbled onto the information. I understand that he has been offered more money than we can offer him now based on present wage and salary policy. As you know, Munro has only been with the company a short time and is already earning somewhat more than others at his level. This presents a problem which needs to be ironed out. I'm afraid I mentioned the possibility of just such an eventuality when you instituted the plan last November. Perhaps we need to reconsider some of the aspects of your plan before we make offers to June graduates.

I know that you and Tom Evans feel that Munro is one of the most valuable men in research and development. It's not certain that Munro will take the job but I thought I'd better give you advance warning in case he does leave us. Please let me know what action you are likely to take on this matter.

Alan Cushwell

Item 0.2

---

3 April 1999

OFFICE MEMORANDUM
TO: John Manners
FROM: Alan Cushwell, Industrial and Employee Relations
SUBJECT: Testing Programme

I feel it is essential that we institute a professional and systematic testing programme for recruiting secretarial and clerical personnel. The following are some suggested tests and other criteria we might want to consider. Do you have any suggestions for types of tests or other selection procedures which we might want to look at before we finalise the programme?
(1) Clerical Personnel:
    (a) Saville and Holdsworth's Aptitude Test (including measurements on spelling, arithmetic and general aptitude)
    (b) Mann-Watson Typing Test
    (c) Age to 40
(2) Secretarial Personnel:
    (a) Saville and Holdsworth's Aptitude Test
    (b) Mann-Watson Typing Test
    (c) Collins Shorthand Skill Inventory (via recording)
    (d) College diploma
    (e) Age to 40

Alan Cushwell

Item 0.3

7 April 1999

OFFICE MEMORANDUM
TO: John Manners
FROM: Bill Marshall, Finance
SUBJECT: Dismissal of Robert Roberts

This is a summary of my reasons for dismissing Robert Roberts. As you know, Mr Roberts was employed as an assistant credit controller on 4 March, 1997. For the two years he has been working with us on a full-time basis while attending the technical college at night. He has continually been a source of irritation to those who have been working closely with him. The main problem is that he often oversteps his authority. He has frequently been involved in controversies with the sales staff over problems which were not his concern. In general he did an adequate job on the work he was assigned but many of the accounts staff felt he wasn't putting enough effort into the job. He seemed to have a lot of free time which he spent in the canteen or gossiping with others in the department. The final straw came when he was told to pick up a cheque from Gavins, who have always been a good account in the past. He returned without the cheque, claiming that the amount owed was disputed. But in the meantime Gavins' boss George Thomas had been on the phone complaining about Roberts's attitude. He said Roberts was arrogant, off-hand and highly sarcastic about the outstanding debt, so much so that Gavins are now refusing to pay the invoice until we have formally apologised for Roberts's behaviour.

Bill

Item 0.4

---

3 April 1999

OFFICE MEMORANDUM
TO: John Manners
FROM: James Barber, Marketing
SUBJECT: Sales Promotion of Rust

As you know, we are moving into our campaign to push the new rust inhibitor. I would like to have your permission to set up a contest among our sales representatives with a trip to Hong Kong for the sales rep with the best sales figures in the next six-month period. I want to make the prize good enough to tempt the sales force to push this launch as hard as they can.

Jim

Item 0.5

8 April 1999

OFFICE MEMORANDUM
TO: John Manners
FROM: Alan Cushwell, Industrial and Employee Relations
SUBJECT: Employment of John Jones, Engineer

I would like to bring you up to date on my feelings concerning the engineer, John Jones, whom Evans wishes to employ. Evans is from Birmingham and I don't think that he fully understands the morale problems we would have if we recruited a black engineer who would have supervision over several white assistants. I realise that we are going to have to protect our interests in local authority contracts, but I think we can find a better way to do so than starting at this level. I would suggest that you talk with Evans about this problem and the possible complications that could arise.

Alan Cushwell

Item 0.6

3 April 1999

OFFICE MEMORANDUM
TO: John Manners
FROM: Bill Marshall, Finance
SUBJECT: Annual Budget Request

We are late in turning in our budget request to Arnold Chemical and Equipment Ltd for the next fiscal year since the report from R & D is still not in. All other department heads have turned in sound budgets which, if approved, should greatly facilitate the cutting of costs next year. Can you do something to speed up action?

Bill Marshall

Item 0.7

3 April 1999

OFFICE MEMORANDUM
TO: John Manners
FROM: Bill Marshall, Finance
SUBJECT: Coffee breaks

This morning I timed a number of people who took 40 minutes drinking their coffee during the mid-morning break. These people were mainly from the production and research department. I am able to control this in my department and I feel you should see that this matter is taken care of by the heads of the other departments. I estimate that the waste amounts to 125,000 man hours (in excess of £1 million) a year.

Bill Marshall

item 0.8

---

6 April 1999

OFFICE MEMORANDUM
TO: John Manners
FROM: Tom Evans, Research and Development
SUBJECT: Allocation for Research

This department has been successful in developing an efficient method for extracting certain basic compounds from slag and other similar by-products that are currently classified as waste by a large number of chemical plants within this area.

It is my recommendation that this company take every step necessary to commercially develop this extraction method. I have brought this matter to Bill Marshall's attention on two separate occasions, requesting that the necessary funds be allocated to fully develop this programme. He has advised me on both occasions that the funds could not possibly be made available within the next fiscal year. He has also indicated that we should reduce the emphasis on research in the chemical area, since this is an unnecessary duplication of functions within the Gateshead and Carlisle plants which the Arnold group own.

It is my opinion that Thames Pump & Valve Company should capitalise on its advantageous position now, before our competitors are able to perfect a similar method.

The above is for your consideration and recommendations.

Tom Evans

cc: Mr O J Thompson, Director
    Research & Development

Item 0.9

BRITISH FEDERATION OF FOUNDRY WORKERS
Erdington Road
Solihull
Near Birmingham

3 April 1999

Mr John Manners
Managing Director
Thames Pump & Valve Ltd
Wokingham Road
Slough
Berks

Dear Sir

On several occasions I have noticed that you and your staff have used your company newspaper as a vehicle for undermining the present union leadership.

In addition, a series of supervisory bulletins have been circulated that were designed to cause supervisory personnel to influence the thinking of union members in the forthcoming union elections. I am also aware of your 'support' for Brendan Sullivan and others who have been more than sympathetic towards company management.

As you know, such behaviour as I have described is in direct breach of Article 21 of our contract with the Arnold group. I am sure you are also aware of the potential damage that a charge of unfair management practices could have on future elections and negotiations.

I trust such action will not become necessary and that you will take steps to prevent any further discrimination against this union administration.

Yours sincerely

Humphrey Swindells
Branch secretary

cc: Mr A Cushwell

Item 0.10

7 April 1999

OFFICE MEMORANDUM
TO: John Manners
FROM: John Dunn, Production
SUBJECT: Quality Control

The Marketing Department has put pressure on us to increase production for the next two months so that promised deliveries can be made. At the present time we cannot increase production without taking some risks in terms of quality. The problem is that marketing does not check with us before committing us to specific delivery dates. This problem has come up before, but nothing has been done. Could we meet in the near future to discuss the situation?

John

Item 0.11

Intrapersonal Skills

The book is divided into three parts and a series of supplements. This first part is devoted to a study of intrapersonal skills. It is our contention that developing the craft of management must begin with an understanding of ourselves; without such an understanding we are nowhere. A piece a graffiti we have on the wall of our office puts the point succinctly: *A map is useless unless you know where you are now.*

Once we have established our starting point we can move on to Part 2, working with others – interpersonal skills – and finally the issues of leading others – the ultimate interpersonal skills.

We see intrapersonal skills as having three components, the first being introspective: **Developing Self-awareness**. With self-awareness we can begin to understand how to survive and grow through the pressures that are inevitable as we take on the managerial role: **Managing Stress**. Knowing ourselves and how to survive, we can learn to prosper by developing skills for solving problem issues: **Effective Problem Solving**.

CHAPTER 1
Developing Self-awareness

- Determining values and priorities
- Identifying cognitive style
- Assessing attitudes to change

CHAPTER 2
Managing Stress

- Stress at work
- Stress and the individual
- Stress factors
- Time management
- Developing resilience

CHAPTER 3
Effective Problem Solving

- Rational problem solving
- The creative approach
- Fostering creativity

Developing Self-awareness

SKILL DEVELOPMENT OUTLINE

Skill Pre-assessment surveys

- Self-awareness
- Defining issues test
- Learning Style Indicator
- Cognitive style instrument
- Locus of control scale
- Tolerance or ambiguity scale
- Interpersonal orientations and needs (Firo-B)

Skill Learning material

- Key dimensions of self-awareness
- The sensitive line
- Cognitive styles
- Learning styles
- Personal values
- Ethical decision making

- Attitudes towards change
- Interpersonal needs
- Summary
- Behavioural guidelines

Skill Analysis case studies

- The Communist prison camp
- Decision dilemmas

Skill Practice exercises

- Improving self-analysis through self-disclosure
- Identifying aspects of personal culture

Skill Application activities

- Suggested assignments
- Application plan and evaluation

LEARNING OBJECTIVES

- Understanding of one's self as a starting point for working with others
- An ability to look at values and beliefs analytically

- Understanding the process of learning and the adaptation to change
- The acceptance of psychological needs as a prime source of motivation in management

INTRODUCTION

The starting point of this book is you. Our aim in this first chapter is to help you to develop a greater knowledge of yourself, so that when we begin to explore the skills of working with and managing other people, you understand something about our starting point.

> Two managers were working together on the design of a new working area. There was no argument about the specification to which they were working – the size of each employee's working area was tightly laid down, as was the lighting and ventilation plan. The desks and fittings would conform to company standards and the computer screens would conform to health and safety regulations.
>
> These things brought no problems. What did bring problems was finishing the project off with discretionary items – 'accessories'. One manager was keen on plants and the other on partitions – each saw the other's ideas as a waste of time. Discussion showed that they were 'coming from different directions'. One manager, brought up as an only child, attached great importance to privacy – he wanted the partitions. The other manager, brought up with a large number of siblings, liked the comfort of being able to see others about him, and preferred the plants. Once they accepted that what they wanted for others reflected what they wanted for themselves, a compromise was reached. The working area contained partitioned areas and open plant-ornamented areas and the people using the area were encouraged to choose where they wanted to work.

Some of the ways we will look at ourselves may need some defending, and you may feel that questioning values is a trifle intrusive. We can only say that the values we bring to the job are becoming increasingly important. In 1996 we took one week's newspapers and listed the cases of dysfunctional values operating in European business – frauds leading to corporate embarrassment of various degrees. One airline was being accused of tapping into a competitor's database and using the information to 'poach' passengers from a rival airline. An Italian computer company was being accused of using bribes to obtain contracts, and Europe's largest car manufacturer was alleged to be using industrial espionage in a way that would have made a writer of spy fiction blush. There were many other 'less important' cases. In 1998 these particular issues are still bringing problems to their 'originators'. Values are important.

Collins and Porras (1995) studied the habits of several exceptional companies and discovered a common feature. They all had clear core ideologies reflecting issues beyond being profitable and reflecting real values. It was these core ideologies that shaped management practice. However, we will begin with one of the most fundamental ways in which our behaviour is formed: how we take on and assimilate data.

Skill pre-assessment

SURVEY **1.1**

SELF-AWARENESS

The first survey is designed to explore your view of yourself and how you can tailor your learning to your specific needs. When you have completed the survey, use the scoring key at the end of the book to identify the skills that are most important for you to master.

Step 1   For each statement circle a number on the rating scale in the Pre-assessment column. Your answers should reflect your attitudes and behaviour as they are now, not as you would like them to be. Be honest. When you have completed the survey, use the scoring key in Appendix 1 to identify the skill areas discussed that are most important for you to master. The process of improving these skill areas should help you with your learning objectives.

Step 2   When you have completed the chapter and the Skill Application assignments, record your responses in the Post-assessment column then use the scoring key in Appendix 1 to measure your progress. If your score remains low in specific skill areas, use the behavioural guidelines at the end of the Skill Learning section to guide your Application Planning.

RATING SCALE

1 = Strongly disagree   **2** = Disagree   **3** = Slightly disagree
4 = Slightly agree   **5** = Agree   **6** = Strongly agree

	Assessment	
	Pre-	Post-
1. I seek information about my strengths and weaknesses from others as a basis for self-improvement.	____	____
2. When I get negative feedback about myself, I do not get angry or defensive.	____	____
3. In order to improve, I am willing to share my beliefs and feelings with others.	____	____
4. I am very much aware of my personal style of gathering information and making decisions.	____	____
5. I am very much aware of my own interpersonal needs when it comes to forming relationships with other people.	____	____
6. I understand how I cope with situations that are ambiguous and uncertain.	____	____
7. I have a well-developed set of personal standards and principles that guide my behaviour.	____	____
8. I feel very much in charge of what happens to me, good and bad.	____	____
9. I seldom, if ever, feel angry, depressed, or anxious without knowing why.	____	____

10. I am conscious of the areas in which conflict and friction most frequently arise in my interactions with others. ___ ___

11. I have a close relationship with at least one other person in whom I can share personal information and personal feelings. ___ ___

SURVEY **1.2**

DEFINING ISSUES TEST

This second survey is designed to look at your approach to controversial social issues. Complete the survey by yourself before discussing it with others – the differences between your approach and that of others may be revealing. The survey seeks to investigate two points:

- In making a decision about these social problems, what are the most important questions one should ask oneself?
- On what principles would you want people to base the decisions?

You are presented with three problem stories. Following each problem story there are 12 statements (or questions). Read each story and rate each statement (question) in terms of its importance in making a decision. Take your top 4 and rank these from the most to the least crucial for making a quality decision. Some statements will raise important issues, but you should ask yourself: Are these relevant to the decision in hand? Some statements may sound impressive but are non-sensical while others are confused or confusing – these are 'of no importance' to you and rate a score of 0.

Use the following rating scale for your responses to the statements of questions:

4. Of great importance – something that is absolutely crucial.

3. Very important – something that one should clearly take notice of before making the decision.

2. Important – something that concerns you but will not sway the decision.

1. Of little importance.

0. Of no importance – a waste of time to consider, nonsense or confused.

The analysis of the scoring is given in Appendix 1.

The escaped prisoner

A man had been sentenced to prison for 10 years. After one year, however, he escaped from prison, moved to a new area, and adopted the name of Thompson. For eight years he worked hard, and gradually he saved enough money to buy his own business. He was fair to his customers and his staff, as well as being an active and worthwhile member of the community. Then one day, Mrs Jones, an old neighbour, recognised Thompson from an old newspaper photograph as a man who had escaped from prison eight years previously. Should Mrs Jones report Mr Thompson to the police and have him sent back to prison? (*Tick one.*)

____ Should report him
____ Can't decide
____ Should not report him.

Importance in Mrs Jones's decision (1 to 5)

1. Hasn't Mr Thompson proved that he is not really bad by being good for so long? ____

2. Every time someone escapes punishment for a crime, doesn't that just encourage more crime? ____

3. Wouldn't we be better off without prisons and the oppression of our legal systems? ____

4. Has Mr Thompson really paid his debt to society? ____

5. Would society be failing if it did not deliver what Mr Thompson should fairly expect? ____

6. Leaving out the obvious fact that he has broken the rules, what benefit would prison be to someone who is evidently a good man? ____

7. How could anyone be so cruel and heartless as to send Mr Thompson back to prison? ____

8. Would it be fair to all the prisoners who had to serve their full sentences if Mr Thompson was let off? ____

9. Was Mrs Jones a good friend of Mr Thompson? ____

10. Wouldn't it be a citizen's duty to report an escaped criminal, regardless of the circumstances? ____

11. How would the will of the people and the public good best be served? ____

12. Would going to prison do any good for Mr Thompson or protect anybody? ____

From the list of 12 questions, select the four most important and rank these from most to least important.

The doctor's dilemma

A woman had an incurable cancer and was told that she had a maximum of six months to live. She was in terrible pain and very weak, so weak that a medium dose of morphine would accelerate her death. She was delirious in her pain but, in her calm periods, she would ask the doctor to give her enough morphine to kill her. She argued that she had nothing to live for and that she was going to die in a few months anyway. What should the doctor do? (*Tick one.*)

____ He should give the overdose
____ Can't decide
____ Should not give the overdose.

Importance in the doctor's decision (1 to 5)

1. Whether the woman's family is in favour of giving her the overdose or not. ____

2. Does the doctor work to the same set of laws as everybody else if giving her an overdose would be the same as killing her? ____

3. Whether people would be much better off without society regimenting their lives and even their deaths. ____

4. Whether the doctor could make it appear like an accident. ____

5. Does the government have the right to force continued existence on those who don't want to live? ____

6. What is the value of death prior to society's perspective on personal values? ____

7. Whether the doctor has sympathy for the woman's suffering or cares more about what society might think. ____

8. Is helping to end another's life ever a responsible act of co-operation? ____

9. Whether only God should decide when a person's life should end. ____

10. What values the doctor has set for himself in his own personal code of behaviour. ____

11. Can society afford to let everybody end their lives when they want to? ____

12. Can society allow suicides or mercy killings and still protect the lives of individuals who want to live? ____

From the list of questions above, select the four most important and rank them from the most crucial to the least.

The newspaper

Frank wanted to produce a newspaper at his school to act as a platform on which he could express his views on a number of controversial issues. In particular, he wanted to speak out about waste, environmental pollution and also about the pettiness of some of the school's rules. He had been very proud of growing a pigtail but had been told to stay at home until he cut it off.

When he started his newspaper, he asked his headmaster for permission and the head responded very positively: he could produce his newspaper provided he sent in his articles for the head's approval before publication. Frank agreed and duly submitted the first two issues for approval, which was granted. The head had not expected Frank's newspaper to receive so much attention. Pupils were so excited by the paper that they began to organise protests against the 'petty rules' – 'petticoat rules' as they had begun to call them. Several vocal parents phoned the head objecting to everything about the newspaper and insisting that it be banned. What should the head do? (*Choose one.*)

____ Should stop it
____ Can't decide
____ Should not stop it.

Importance in the head's decision (1 to 5)

1. Is the head more responsible to the pupils or to the parents? _____

2. Did the head give her word that the newspaper could be published for a long time, or did she just promise to approve the newspaper one issue at a time? _____

3. Would the pupils start protesting even more if the head stopped the newspaper? _____

4. When the good name of the school is threatened, does the head have the right to tell the pupils what to do? _____

5. Does the head have the freedom of speech to say 'no' in this case? _____

6. If the head stopped the newspaper, would she be preventing full discussion of important problems? _____

7. Would the head's order make Frank lose respect for her? _____

8. Was Frank really loyal to his school? _____

9. What effect would stopping the paper have on the pupils' education in critical thinking and judgements? _____

10. Was Frank in any way violating the rights of others in publishing his own opinions? _____

11. Should some angry parents be allowed to influence the head when she knows best what is going on in the school? _____

12. Was Frank using the newspaper to stir up hatred and discontent? _____

From the list of questions above, select the four most important, ranking them from most to least crucial.

Source: Rest (1979)

SURVEY **1.3**

LEARNING STYLE INDICATOR

We are presenting six sets of views on management. You have 10 points to distribute within each set. For instance, you could give all 10 points to one statement that you feel completely reflects your views, or perhaps distribute the 10 points more evenly. At the end of the exercise, you should have a total of 60 points in six batches of 10. There is no right or wrong view and the questions are intended to illustrate differences between effective managers in the field. If you have no managerial experience, try to see yourself as a manager and how you would feel about the various issues.

Score

1. My personal aim as a manager in an organisation is:

   a. To extend knowledge or understanding in my area _____
   b. To be useful _____
   c. To solve problems _____
   d. To keep the organisation on a moral basis. _____

2. I am proud of:

   a. My staff or peers as people _____
   b. What we have/will have achieved _____
   c. Our abilities to solve problems _____
   d. My department or discipline. _____

3. I feel we should be judged on:

   a. Our useful contacts _____
   b. The stimulus provided to the organisation _____
   c. Things that we have actually done which can be of use _____
   d. Our reputation as a centre of excellence. _____

4. I get my personal job rewards from:

   a. Working with difficult problems _____
   b. Interacting with challenging people _____
   c. The respect from others doing similar things _____
   d. Sudden flashes of insight. _____

5. I see my job as a people manager as:

   a. Making sure that 'good people' can be effective _____
   b. Developing their analytical skills _____
   c. Developing my people _____
   d. Maintaining a 'tight ship'. _____

6. I think the best reports I produce:

   a. Excite and stimulate my readers _____
   b. Extend knowledge in some way _____
   c. Clearly recommend courses of action _____
   d. Present argued alternatives. _____

When you have completed the form, score in the following way:

Section	Why?	What?	How?	If?
1	d.	a.	c.	b.
2	a.	d.	c.	b.
3	b.	d.	a.	c.
4	b.	c.	a.	d.
5	c.	b.	d.	a.
6	a.	b.	d.	c.
Total				

Source: From *The New Manager* (Woods, 1988)

SURVEY **1.4**

COGNITIVE STYLE INSTRUMENT

The purpose of the instrument is to look at the way you view the information you use in your work. There are no right or wrong answers, and one alternative is just as good as another. Try to indicate the ways you do, or would, respond, not the ways you think you should respond. For each scenario there are three pairs of alternatives. For each pair, tick the alternative that comes closest to the way you would work. Answer each item. If you are not sure, make your best guess. When you have finished answering all the questions, use the scoring key in Appendix 1 at the end of the book to see how you rate against other people.

Suppose you are a scientist whose job it is to gather information about the moons of Saturn. Which alternative would be more interesting to you?

1. a. How the moons are similar to one another ____
   b. How the moons differ from one another ____

2. a. How the whole system of moons operates ____
   b. The characteristics of each moon ____

3. a. How Saturn and its moons differ from Earth and its moon ____
   b. How Saturn and its moons are similar to Earth and its moon. ____

Suppose you are the chief executive of a company and have asked division heads to make presentations at the end of the year. Which of the following would be more appealing to you?

4. a. A presentation analysing the details of the data ____
   b. A presentation focused on the overall perspective ____

5. a. A presentation showing how the division contributed to the company as a whole ____
   b. A presentation showing the unique contributions of the division ____

6. a. Details of how the division performed ____
   b. General summaries of performance data. ____

Suppose you are visiting a country from Eastern Europe for the first time, and you are writing home about your trip. Which of the following would be most typical of the letter you would write?

7. a. A detailed description of people and events ____
   b. General impressions and feelings ____

8. a. A focus on similarities between our culture and theirs ____
   b. A focus on the uniqueness of their culture ____

9. a. Overall, general impressions of the experience ____
   b. Separate, unique impressions of parts of the experience. ____

Suppose you are attending a concert featuring a famous symphony orchestra. Which of the following would you be most likely to do?

10. a. Listen for the parts of individual instruments ____
    b. Listen for the harmony of all the instruments together ____

11. a. Pay attention to the overall mood associated with the music ____
    b. Pay attention to the separate feelings associated with different parts of the music ____

12. a. Focus on the overall style of the conductor ____
    b. Focus on how the conductor interprets different parts of the score. ____

Suppose you are considering taking a job with a certain organisation. Which of the following would you be more likely to do in deciding whether or not to take the job?

13. a. Systematically collect information on the organisation ____
    b. Rely on personal intuition or inspiration ____

14. a. Consider primarily the fit between you and the job ____
    b. Consider primarily the politics needed to succeed in the organisation ____

15. a. Be methodical in collecting data and making a choice ____
    b. Mainly consider personal instincts and gut feelings. ____

Suppose you inherit some money and decide to invest it. You learn of a new high-technology firm that has just issued shares. Which of the following is most likely to be true of your decision to purchase the firm's shares?

16. a. You would invest on a hunch ____
    b. You would invest only after a systematic investigation of the firm ____

17. a. You would be somewhat impulsive in deciding to invest ____
    b. You would follow a pre-set pattern in making your decision ____

18. a. You could rationally justify your decision to invest in this firm and not in another ____
    b. It would be difficult to rationally justify your decision to invest in this firm and not another. ____

Suppose you are being interviewed on TV, and you are asked the following questions. Which alternative would you be most likely to select?

19. How are you more likely to cook?

    a. With a recipe ____
    b. Without a recipe. ____

How would you predict the next winner of the European Football Cup?

20. a. After systematically researching the personnel and records of the teams ____
    b. On a hunch or by intuition. ____

Which games do you prefer?

21. a. Games of chance (like bingo) ____
    b. Games of skill (like chess, draughts or Scrabble). ____

Suppose you are a manager and need to hire an executive assistant. Which of the following would you be most likely to do in the process?

22. a. Interview each applicant using a set outline of questions ____
    b. Concentrate on your personal feelings and instincts about each applicant ____

23. a. Consider primarily the personality fit between yourself and the candidates ____
    b. Consider the match between the precise job requirements and the candidates' capabilities ____

24. a. Rely on factual and historical data on each candidate in making a choice ____
    b. Rely on feelings and impressions in making a choice. ____

SURVEY **1.5**

LOCUS OF CONTROL SCALE

This survey assesses your opinions about certain issues. Each item consists of a pair of alternatives marked 'a' or 'b'. Select (*tick*) the alternative with which you most agree, forcing the choice – do make a choice. Since this is an assessment of opinions, there are obviously no right or wrong answers. When you have finished each item, turn to the scoring key in Appendix 1 for instructions on how to tabulate the results and for comparison data.

This survey is similar to, but not exactly the same as, the original locus of control scale developed by Julian Rotter, and the comparison data provided in Appendix 1 is based on the original scale. No significant differences are expected.

---

1. a. Leaders are born, not made ____
   b. Leaders are made, not born ____

2. a. People often succeed because they are in the right place at the right time ____
   b. Success is most dependent on hard work and ability ____

3. a. When things go wrong in my life it is generally because I have made mistakes ____
   b. Misfortunes occur in my life regardless of what I do ____

4. a. Whether there is war or not depends on the actions of certain world leaders ____
   b. It is inevitable that the world will continue to experience wars ____

5. a. Good children are mainly the products of good parents ____
   b. Some children turn out bad no matter how their parents behave ____

6. a. My future success depends mainly on circumstances I cannot control ____
   b. I am in charge of myself – I am 'master of my fate' ____

7. a. History judges certain people to have been effective leaders mainly because circumstances made them visible and successful ____
   b. Effective leaders are those who have made decisions or have taken actions that resulted in significant contributions ____

8. a. To avoid punishing children is to guarantee that they will grow up irresponsible ____
   b. Spanking children is never appropriate ____

9. a. I often feel that I have little influence over the direction my life is taking ____
   b. It is unreasonable to believe that fate or luck plays a crucial part in how my life turns out ____

10. a. Some customers will never be satisfied no matter what you do ____
    b. You can satisfy customers by giving them what they want when they want it ____

11. a. Anyone can get good results at school if he or she works hard enough _____
    b. Some people are never going to excel in school no matter how hard they try _____

12. a. Good marriages result when both partners continually work on the relationship _____
    b. Some marriages are going to fail because the partners are simply incompatible _____

13. a. I am confident that I can improve my basic management skills through learning and practice _____
    b. It is a waste of time to try to improve management skills in the classroom _____

14. a. More management skill courses should be taught in business schools _____
    b. Less emphasis should be put on skills in business schools _____

15. a. When I think back to the good things that have happened to me, I believe they happened mainly because of something I did _____
    b. The bad things that have happened in my life have mainly resulted from circumstances outside my control _____

16. a. Many exams I took at school were unconnected to the material I had studied, so studying hard didn't help at all _____
    b. When I prepared well for exams in school, I generally did quite well _____

17. a. 'What the Stars Say' in the papers sometimes influences me _____
    b. No matter what the stars say, I can determine my own destiny _____

18. a. Government is so big and bureaucratic that it is very difficult for any one person to have any impact on what happens _____
    b. Single individuals can have a real influence on politics if they will speak up and let their wishes be known _____

19. a. People seek responsibility at work _____
    b. People try to get away with doing as little as they can _____

20. a. Most popular people have a special, inherent charisma that attracts people to them _____
    b. People are popular because of the way they behave _____

21. a. Things over which I have little control just seem to occur in my life _____
    b. Most of the time I feel responsible for the outcomes I produce _____

22. a. Managers who improve their personal competence will succeed more than those who do not _____
    b. Management success has very little to do with the competencies possessed by individuals _____

23. a. Teams that win championships in most sports are usually the teams that have the most luck _____
    b. More often than not, the teams that win championships are those with the most talented players and those who train hardest. (Gary Player: 'The more I practice, the better my luck gets') _____

24. a. Teamwork in business is a pre-requisite of success _____
    b. Individual effort is the best hope of success _____

25. a. Some workers are just lazy and can't be motivated to work harder no matter what you do
    b. If you are a skilful manager, you can motivate almost any worker to make an effort ____

26. a. Over all, people can improve their country's economic strength by their own actions ____
    b. The economic health of a country is largely out of the control of individuals ____

27. a. I am persuasive when I know I am right ____
    b. I can persuade most people even when I'm not sure that I'm right ____

28. a. I tend to plan ahead and generate steps to accomplish the goals I have set ____
    b. I seldom plan ahead because things generally sort themselves out ____

29. a. Some things are just meant to be ____
    b. We can change anything in our lives by hard work, persistence and ability ____

SURVEY **1.6**

TOLERANCE OF AMBIGUITY SCALE

Circle the number that best represents your agreement with each statement. The scoring key is given in Appendix 1.

1 = Strongly disagree   **2** = Moderately disagree   **3** = Slightly disagree
4 = Neither agree nor disagree   **5** = Slightly agree   **6** = Moderately agree
7 = Strongly agree

1. An expert who doesn't come up with a definite answer probably doesn't know too much.   1 2 3 4 5 6 7

2. I would like to live in a foreign country for a while.   1 2 3 4 5 6 7

3. There is really no such thing as a problem that can't be solved   1 2 3 4 5 6 7

4. People who fit their lives to a schedule probably miss most of the joy of living.   1 2 3 4 5 6 7

5. A good job is one where what is to be done and how it is to be done are always clear.   1 2 3 4 5 6 7

6. It is more fun to tackle a complicated problem than to solve a simple one.   1 2 3 4 5 6 7

7. In the long run it is possible to get more done by tackling small problems rather than large and complicated ones.   1 2 3 4 5 6 7

8. Often the most interesting and stimulating people are those who don't mind being different and original.   1 2 3 4 5 6 7

9. What we are used to is always preferable to what is unfamiliar.   1 2 3 4 5 6 7

10. People who insist upon a yes or no answer just don't know how complicated things really are.   1 2 3 4 5 6 7

11. A person who leads an even, regular life in which few surprises or unexpected happenings arise ought to be grateful.   1 2 3 4 5 6 7

12. Many of our most important decisions are based on insufficient information.   **1** 2 3 4 5 6 7

13. I like parties where I know most of the people more than ones where all or most of the people are complete strangers.   **1** 2 3 4 5 6 7

14. Teachers or supervisors who hand out vague assignments give one a chance to show initiative and originality.   **1** 2 3 4 5 6 7

15. The sooner we all acquire similar values and ideals the better.   **1** 2 3 4 5 6 7

16. A good teacher is one who makes you wonder about your way of looking at things.   **1** 2 3 4 5 6 7

Source: Budner (1962)

SURVEY **1.7**

INTERPERSONAL ORIENTATIONS AND NEEDS (FIRO-B)

The surveys up to this point can be taken as learning tools and not as the basis of any true analysis of either behaviour or personality. The next instrument we want you to complete is a fully validated test used in professional counselling. For each statement below, decide which of the following answers best applies to you. Circle the number of the answer at the right of the statement. When you have finished, turn to the scoring key in Appendix 1.

For the next group of statements, choose one of the following answers:

1 = Usually   **2** = Often   **3** = Sometimes   **4** = Occasionally
5 = Rarely   **6** = Never

1. I try to be with people.   1 2 3 4 5 6

2. I let other people decide what to do.   1 2 3 4 5 6

3. I join social groups.   1 2 3 4 5 6

4. I try to have close relationships with people.   1 2 3 4 5 6

5. I tend to join social organisations when I have an opportunity.   1 2 3 4 5 6

6. I let other people strongly influence my actions.   1 2 3 4 5 6

7. I try to be included in informal social activities.   1 2 3 4 5 6

8. I try to have close, personal relationships.   1 2 3 4 5 6

9. I try to include other people in my plans.   1 2 3 4 5 6

10. I let other people control my actions.   1 2 3 4 5 6

11. I try to have people around me.   1 2 3 4 5 6

12. I try to get close and personal with people.   1 2 3 4 5 6

13. When people are doing things together I tend to join them.   1 2 3 4 5 6

14. People easily lead me.   1 2 3 4 5 6

15. I try to avoid being alone.   1 2 3 4 5 6

16. I try to participate in group activities.   1 2 3 4 5 6

For each of the next group of statements, choose one of the following answers:
1 = Most people   **2** = Many people   **3** = Some people
4 = A few people   **5** = One or two people   **6** = Nobody

17. I try to be friendly to people.	1 2 3 4 5 6
18. I let other people decide what to do.	1 2 3 4 5 6
19. My personal relations with people are cool and distant.	1 2 3 4 5 6
20. I let other people take charge of things.	1 2 3 4 5 6
21. I try to have close relationships with people.	1 2 3 4 5 6
22. I let other people strongly influence my actions.	1 2 3 4 5 6
23. I try to get close and personal with people.	1 2 3 4 5 6
24. I let other people control my actions.	1 2 3 4 5 6
25. I act cool and distant with people.	1 2 3 4 5 6
26. People easily lead me.	1 2 3 4 5 6
27. I try to have close, personal relationships with people.	1 2 3 4 5 6

For each of the next group of statements, choose one of the following answers:
1 = Most people   **2** = Many people   **3** = Some people
4 = A few people   **5** = One or two people   **6** = Nobody

28. I like people to invite me to things.	1 2 3 4 5 6
29. I like people to act close and personal with me.	1 2 3 4 5 6
30. I try to influence strongly other people's actions.	1 2 3 4 5 6
31. I like people to invite me to join in their activities.	1 2 3 4 5 6
32. I like people to act close towards me.	1 2 3 4 5 6
33. I try to take charge of things when I am with people.	1 2 3 4 5 6
34. I like people to include me in their activities.	1 2 3 4 5 6
35. I like people to act cool and distant towards me.	1 2 3 4 5 6
36. I try to have other people do things the way I want them done.	1 2 3 4 5 6
37. I like people to ask me to participate in their discussions.	1 2 3 4 5 6
38. I like people to act friendly towards me.	1 2 3 4 5 6
39. I like people to invite me to participation in their activities.	1 2 3 4 5 6
40. I like people to act distant towards me.	1 2 3 4 5 6

For each of the next group of statements, choose one of the following answers:
1 = Usually   **2** = Often   **3** = Sometimes   **4** = Occasionally
5 = Rarely   **6** = Never

41. I try to be a dominant person when I am with people.	1 2 3 4 5 6
42. I like people to invite me to things.	1 2 3 4 5 6
43. I like people to act close towards me.	1 2 3 4 5 6
44. I try to have other people do things I want done.	1 2 3 4 5 6
45. I like people to invite me to join their activities.	1 2 3 4 5 6

46. I like people to act cool and distant towards me.   **1   2   3   4   5   6**
47. I try to influence strongly other people's actions.   **1   2   3   4   5   6**
48. I like people to include me in their activities.   **1   2   3   4   5   6**
49. I like people to act close and personal with me.   **1   2   3   4   5   6**
50. I try to take charge of things when I'm with people.   **1   2   3   4   5   6**
51. I like people to invite me to participate in their activities.   **1   2   3   4   5   6**
52. I like people to act distant towards me.   **1   2   3   4   5   6**
53. I try to have other people do things the way I want them done.   **1   2   3   4   5   6**
54. I take charge of things when I'm with people.   **1   2   3   4   5   6**

When you return to the surveys after reading the chapter you may find that some of your views and opinions have changed. We would hope for some changes but suspect that the Learning Style Inventory and Firo-B will remain relatively constant.

Skill Learning

Key dimensions of self-awareness

We need to understand ourselves before we can even consider understanding other people. In this we have many sources:

The ancient dictum 'know thyself' has been variously attributed to Plato, Pythagoras and Thales, and Socrates, quoted by Plutarch, noted that this inscription was carved on the Delphic Oracle – that mystical sanctuary where kings and generals sought advice on matters of greatest importance to them.

'It matters not what you are thought to be, but what you are', as Publilius Syrus proposed in 42 BC; or, as stated by Alfred Lord Tennyson, 'Self-reverence, self-knowledge, self-control, these three alone lead to sovereign power'; or as written by Shakespeare in Polonius's advice in Hamlet: 'to thine own self be true, and it must follow, as the night the day, thou canst not then be false to any man'.

As Messinger reminded us: 'He that would govern others must first master himself.' We consider that the setting of personal priorities and goals through self-awareness allows us to direct our own lives. It is the foundation stone upon which rests the practice of the skills we will discuss later.

Figure 1.1 illustrates our point that problems of dysfunctional stress may well have their roots in a lack of self-awareness – our priorities or goals have become out of balance. Increased self-awareness and a constant review of priorities are the keys. To know one's self is a necessary starting point for working with others, and many techniques have grown up to satisfy the demand for self-knowledge. We are not attempting to summarise or indeed criticise any of these techniques; rather, we will discuss the importance of self-awareness in managerial behaviour, and we introduce several self-assessment assignments which research has shown to relate to managerial success. We will attempt in our discussions to avoid 'common sense' generalisations and work from information validated by research.

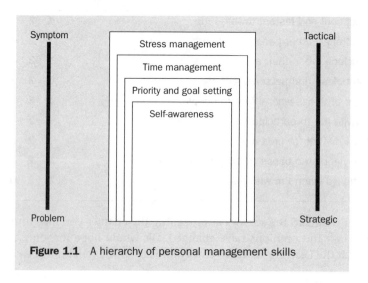

Figure 1.1 A hierarchy of personal management skills

The enigma of self-awareness

Erich Fromm (1939) was one of the first behavioural scientists to observe the close connection between one's self-concept and one's feelings about others: 'Hatred against oneself is inseparable from hatred against others.' Carl Rogers (1961) later proposed that self-awareness and self-acceptance are prerequisites for psychological health, personal growth, and the ability to know and accept others. Rogers further suggested that the basic human need is for self-regard, which he found, in his clinical cases, to be more powerful than physiological needs. Hayakawa (1962) has asserted that the first law of life is not self-preservation, but self-image-preservation.

'The self-concept,' he states, 'is the fundamental determinant of all our behaviour. Indeed, since it is an organisation of our past experiences and perceptions as well as our values and goals, it determines the character of the reality we see.' There is considerable empirical evidence that self-awareness and self-acceptance are strongly related to personal adjustment, interpersonal relationships and life success. Brouwer (1964) asserted:

> The function of self-examination is to lay the groundwork for insight, without which no growth can occur. Insight is the 'Oh, I see now' feeling which must consciously or unconsciously precede change in behaviour. Insights, real, genuine glimpses of ourselves as we really are, can be reached only with difficulty and sometimes with real psychic pain. They are, however, the building blocks of growth. Thus, self-examination is a preparation for insight, a groundbreaking for the seeds of self-understanding which gradually bloom into changed behaviour.

There is little question that the knowledge we possess about ourselves, which makes up our self-concept, is central to improving our management skills. We cannot improve ourselves or develop new capabilities unless and until we know what level of capability we currently possess. On the other hand, self-knowledge may inhibit personal improvement rather than facilitate it. The reason for this is that individuals frequently evade personal growth and new self-knowledge. They resist acquiring additional information in order to protect their self-esteem or self-respect. If they acquire new knowledge about themselves, there is always the possibility that it will be negative or that it will lead to feelings of inferiority, weakness or shame, so they avoid it. As Maslow (1962) notes,

> We tend to be afraid of any knowledge that would cause us to despise ourselves or to make us feel inferior, weak, worthless, evil, shameful. We protect our personally ideal image and ourselves by repression and similar defences. These are essentially techniques by which we avoid becoming conscious of unpleasantness or dangerous truths.

The implication is that personal growth is avoided for fear of finding out that we are not all that we would like to be. If there is a better way to be, the current state must therefore be inadequate or inferior. The realisation that one is not totally adequate or knowledgeable is difficult for many people to accept. This resistance is the 'denying of our best side, of our talents, of our finest impulses, of our highest potentialities, of our creativeness is the struggle against our own greatness' (Maslow, 1962). Freud (1956) asserted that to be completely honest with oneself is the best effort an individual can make, because complete honesty requires a continual search for more information about the self and a desire for self-improvement.

The sensitive line

Seeking knowledge of the self, therefore, seems to lead to an enigma. The very self-knowledge that must act as a starting point of self-growth may indeed prevent us from wanting to grow. We may well not wish to move forward because we fear the unknown.

How, then, can improvement be accomplished? How can management skills be developed if they are being resisted? The answer lies in understanding that there is a sensitive line beyond which all of us become defensive or protective when encountering information about ourselves that is inconsistent with our self-concept and we are under pressure to alter our behaviour. Most of us are regularly told things about ourselves that do not quite fit or are marginally inconsistent with our perceptions. For example, a friend might say, 'You look tired. Are you feeling well?' If you are feeling fine, the comment is inconsistent with how you feel about yourself at that time, but because the discrepancy is relatively minor, it would not be likely to offend or to evoke a strong defensive reaction, merely some sort of polite exchange. However, imagine a situation where you think that you are coping effectively with ageing relatives or tiresome children, and you hear a friend remark that 'you do not seem to be coping'. Most of us would find ourselves across the sensitive line and defending ourselves. The comment, if accepted, would mean a review of your perceptions and possibly a change of behaviour. Equally, having a colleague judge you incompetent as a manager may push you across your sensitive line if you think you are doing a good job, and even more so if the colleague is influential. Hayakawa (1962) stated the point differently, saying that 'the self-concept tends

to rigidify under threat', so that if an individual encounters discrepant information that is threatening, the current self-concept is reasserted with redoubled force.
Haney (1979) refers to a 'comfort zone' similar to a thermostat. When a situation
becomes too uncomfortable, protective measures are brought into play that bring
the situation back to normal. When marked discrepancies in the self-image are
experienced, either the validity of the information or its source is denied, or we
put in place other defensive mechanisms to ensure that the self-concept remains
stable.

How then, in the light of our innate defensiveness, can increased self-knowledge
and personal change ever occur? There are at least two answers.

Firstly, if the information about us can be checked, is predictable and control-
lable, then the sensitive line is less likely to be crossed than with information without those characteristics. Thus if:

- an individual can test the validity of the conflicting information and some
  objective standard exists
- the information is not unexpected or 'out of the blue' but is received at regular
  intervals and if there is some control over what, when and how much
  information is received, it is more likely to be heard and accepted.

We will deal in detail with these points in our chapters on effective communication
and constructive conflict management, when we discuss effective feedback.

We have attempted at the start of this chapter to allow you feedback from our
self-assessment surveys. Their reliability and validity have been established. Moreover, they have been found to be associated with managerial success. Therefore, in
your analysis of your scores, you can gain important insight that can prove helpful
to you.

A second answer to the problem of overcoming this resistance to self-
examination lies in the role other people can play in helping insight to occur. It is
almost impossible to increase skill in self-awareness without interacting with and
disclosing ourselves to others. Unless one is willing to open up to others, to discuss
aspects of the self that seem ambiguous or unknown, little growth can ever occur.
Self-disclosure, therefore, is a key to improvement in self-awareness and allows one
to move across the sensitive line.

Harris (1981) points out:

> In order to know oneself, no amount of introspection or self-examination will
> suffice. You can analyse yourself for weeks, or meditate for months, and you will
> not get an inch further any more than you can smell your own breath or laugh
> when you tickle yourself. You must first be open to the other person before you
> catch a glimmer of yourself. Our self-reflection in a mirror does not tell us what
> we are like; only our reflection in other people. We are essentially social creatures,
> and our personality resides in association, not in isolation.

The practice exercises at the end of this chapter will hopefully encourage you
to discuss your insights with someone else. For example, several studies have shown
that people who discuss personal matters are likely to be healthier and more socially acceptable than those who do not (Jourard, 1964). However, there is always the

caveat that self-disclosure is a game for two or more players – one who discloses and does not listen is known in technical terms as a bore.

The enigma of self-awareness can be managed, then, by exercising some control over when and what kind of information you receive about yourself, and by sharing with others your pursuit of self-understanding. The social support individuals receive from others during the process of self-disclosure is important, besides helping to increase feedback and self-awareness without crossing the sensitive line.

Important areas of self-awareness

In the remainder of this chapter we will focus on six major areas of self-awareness, found to be the key in developing successful management:

• Cognitive styles
• Learning styles
• Personal values
• Ethical decision making
• Attitudes towards change
• Interpersonal needs

Cognitive styles

The way in which we take on information and learn from it is a foundation of our behaviour. George Kelly, as described by Bannister and Fransella (1971), considered mankind as, in his metaphor, a scientist. In the Kelly model we are continually making decisions as we refine our universe. Thus when we are very young we may see our outside world as comfortable or uncomfortable. As we develop the construct of comfort is split into warm or cold and then warm is split again into inside and outside. We go on splitting our world into a massive decision tree. In practice, we have found Kelly's personal Construct Theory of less use in skill training than a series of concepts codified as Cognitive Style and Experiential Learning Theory. We will take cognitive styles first, accepting that there are many overlaps between the two.

We are all faced with an overwhelming amount of information, most of which, in order to preserve our sanity, survive or indeed do the jobs we are paid to do, we learn to ignore. No process for filtering the information is inherently good or inherently bad, and not everyone adopts an identifiable, consistent process that becomes part of his or her cognitive style. However, about 80 per cent of us do eventually develop, mostly unconsciously, a preferred process of handling information, and these make up our cognitive style.

The cognitive style instrument in the Pre-assessment section looks at the two core dimensions of the way we prefer to process information. The model upon which it is based is grounded in the work of Jung (1971). Figure 1.2 illustrates its dimensions. The vertical dimension has its poles Sensing and Intuition. Thus at its extremes one individual would physically collect information while another would rely on

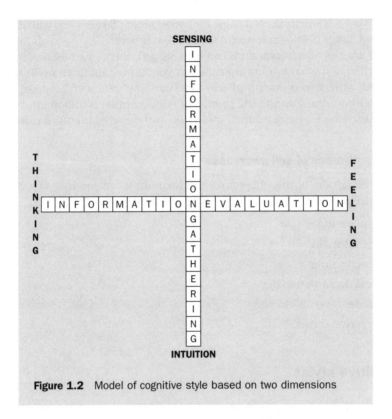

Figure 1.2 Model of cognitive style based on two dimensions

his or her intuition. In our example of the interview, one manager would check the information on the disc, go back to the candidate's application form and find out what he or she could about his present employer. The other would see the elements of the problem as a pattern and act accordingly.

The horizontal dimension is from Feeling to Thinking and is concerned with information processing. The manager on the Feeling pole would know what he or she was comfortable with while one on the Thinking pole would 'work it out'.

The various strategies we employ for internalising information lie within the vertical and horizontal axes.

Vertical axis

An **intuitive strategy** takes a holistic view and emphasises commonalities and generalisations – the perceived relationships among the elements of available data. Intuitive thinkers often have preconceived notions about what sort of information may be relevant, and they look at the information to find what is consistent with their preconceptions. They tend to be convergent thinkers in general opposed to the new.

The **sensing strategy** focuses on detail, or on the specific attributes of each element of data, rather than on relationships among the elements. Sensing thinkers are rational and have few preconceptions about what may be relevant, so they insist on a close and thorough examination of the information. They attach special importance to the unique attributes of various parts of the information they encounter, and tend to be the divergent thinkers (a term we will define in Chapter 3 when we discuss problem-solving strategies).

- An intuitive strategy focuses on the whole, a sensing strategy on the parts of the whole.
- An intuitive strategy looks for commonalities and overall categories, a sensing strategy for uniqueness, detail and exceptions to the general rule.

Horizontal axis

The horizontal axis, which is concerned with interpreting and judging information, has also two strategies.

A **thinking strategy** evaluates information using a systematic plan with specific sequential steps and logical progressions. Individuals who use a thinking style generally rely on objective data, problems are considered against known models. When managers with such a style defend their decisions they emphasise the methods and procedures they have used.

Vertinsky (1976) refers to people using the thinking strategy as 'members of a continuous culture', meaning that they operate consistently with existing patterns of thought.

A **feeling strategy** approaches a problem on the basis of 'gut feel', or an internal sense of how to respond. The problem is often defined and redefined, and approaches are tried on a trial-and-error basis rather than through a logical procedure. Feeling individuals prefer the subjective or impressionistic against the objective. They often cannot describe how they achieved their conclusions. They often use analogies and metaphors relating the problem to 'unrelated' past experiences. Vertinsky (1976) refers to these individuals as 'members of a discontinuous culture'.

Implications

These strategies have important implications for managerial behaviour, each having advantages and disadvantages. We do have to remember that very few individuals operate all the time on one of the poles of our figure. However, we can draw certain generalisations.

- **Sensing managers** find they cannot prioritise and have to give each detail attention. Thus in chaotic situations they are more likely to overload than intuitive managers, and tend to suffer from dysfunctional stress.
- **Intuitive managers**, because they focus on the relationships between elements, on the whole handle detail and confusion relatively easily. However, their stresses occur when either the information they attempt to collect is confused, or their preconceived patterns fail to work. Exceptions to the rule faze the intuitive manager where the sensing manager simply looks further into the detail.

Table 1.1 Characteristics of cognitive styles

INFORMATION GATHERING

Intuitive types	Sensing types
Like solving new problems.	Dislike new problems unless there are standard ways of dealing with them.
Dislike doing the same thing over and over again.	Like an established routine.
Enjoy learning a new skill more than using it.	Enjoy using skills already learned more than learning new ones.
Work in bursts of energy powered by enthusiasm, with slack periods in between.	Work more steadily with realistic idea of how long things will take.
Jump to conclusions frequently.	Must usually work all the way through to reach a conclusion.
Are patient with complicated situations.	Are impatient when the details are complicated.
Are impatient with routine details.	Are patient with routine details.
Follow inspirations good of bad.	Rarely trust inspirations, and don't usually feel too inspired.
Often tend to make errors of fact.	Seldom make errors of fact.
Dislike taking time for precision.	Tend to be good at precise work.

INFORMATION EVALUATION

Feeling types	Thinking types
Tend to be very aware of other people and their feelings.	Are relatively unemotional and uninterested in people's feelings.
Enjoy pleasing people even in unimportant things.	May hurt people's feelings without knowing.
Like harmony. Efficiency may be badly disturbed by office feuds.	Like analysis and putting things Into logical order. Can get along without harmony.
Often let decisions be influenced by their own or other people's personal likes and wishes.	Tend to decide impersonally, sometimes ignoring people's wishes.
Need occasional praise.	Need to be treated fairly.
Dislike telling people unpleasant things.	Are able to reprimand people or fire them when necessary.
Relate well to most people.	Tend to relate well only to other thinking types.
Tend to be sympathetic.	May seem hard-hearted.

- **Thinking managers** prefer issues where a structured approach is effective and find problems where a creative approach is needed or where there is no pool of relevant information. The reader may consider that most people problems fall into this category.

> We were working with a chemist whose job was to design and mimic flavours and aromas. His instrument was an 'aroma organ' which brought together a vast array of elements at great precision into his potions. He saw the whole world on the basis of his 'aroma organ'. We might argue that he had elements of an intuitive manager, but since his work was based on logic and theory, we would see him as 'thinking'. Whatever his psychometric profile, he found the vagaries of handling people impossible – they never fitted patterns, never reacted according to plan and never came with complete information.

- **Feeling managers** have a tendency to try new approaches, to redefine problems, and to reinvent the solution without, at least first, using the tried and tested. This generally leads to inefficient problem solving or even solving the wrong problem. Thinking and intuitive managers do not justify such criticism – perhaps to a fault.

We find that individuals are inflexible in their approach to problems – preferring their own style, whatever the problem. For example, in one study, managers who were more thinking than feeling implemented more computer-based systems and rational procedures for decision making. Managers in another study defined identical problems differently, depending on their different cognitive styles. Another study found that differences in cognitive style led to significantly different decision-making processes in managers (see Henderson and Nutt, 1980; Mulkowsky and Freeman, 1980). Of course we find successful managers moving to work that welcomes their cognitive style – thinking people working in thinking jobs.

An understanding of one's own cognitive style can help managers in many ways – in learning new skills, in choosing the right career, and even in selecting the most effective team members for difficult jobs. Table 1.1 summarises some personal characteristics associated with each of these major cognitive patterns.

Learning styles

Students with different cognitive styles have also been found to approach learning differently and different kinds of educational experiences hold meaning for different types of people. For example, individuals who emphasise intuitive strategies tend to do better in conceptual courses and learn more easily through reading and through discussing general relationships. Exams with one right answer may be easier for them than for those who emphasise sensing. Individuals who emphasise sensing strategies tend to do better in factual courses or courses in which attention to detail and dissimilarity is important. Critical and analytical learning activities (e.g., debates) facilitate their learning, and exams emphasising implications and applications may be easiest for these individuals. Individuals who emphasise a thinking strategy do best in courses that take an orderly, step-by-step approach to

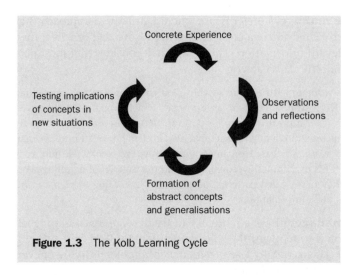

Figure 1.3 The Kolb Learning Cycle

the subject, courses in which what is learned builds on, and follows directly from, what was learned earlier (e.g., mathematics). On the other hand, feeling individuals do best in courses requiring creativity and idea generation. Learning activities in which the student must rely on a personal sense of what is appropriate (e.g., sculpting) are likely to be preferred by these individuals. Okanlawon (1989), using the Kolb Learning Style Inventory, an instrument similar to the Cognitive Style Instrument, went much further. Working with a large group of managers and students in Nigeria, his findings were that the teaching methods employed for effective learning had two dimensions – the learning style and the learning objective. He also found that the choice of method was much more critical for managers than for students. It is interesting to note that several workers, including Bernice McCarthy, have used the Kolb Inventory for career advice and for the design of teaching materials.

Kolb derives his work from many sources, but primarily the work of Jung and his ideas are introduced in this book by our first survey – the Kolb/McCarthy Learning Style Inventory. Kolb chooses to work from different axes from those used for the cognitive style (Figure 1.3) and makes the intuitive leap that they can be made into what he calls a Learning Cycle. (Note that the figure resembles a 'dartboard' with 5 rings. These rings represent the percentiles of individuals falling within each 'circle'. The percentiles were originally for a sample of 1933 individuals in the USA but Okanlawon confirmed the values for UK and Nigeria.)

Kenneth Raymont, following up the work of Reid, reviewed the current state of the debate on Kolb's work. Raymont, working with Bradford Management Centre MBA, found the concept useful but he concludes:

> On first acquaintance, Kolb's Experiential Learning Theory appears as light on murky water. It purports to explain individual learning differences by a 'type' model and seemingly explains that because individuals view the same situation differently there is an inbuilt conflict mechanism in any group venture. Indeed, it was this very aspect that attracted the writer to it. Differences in opinion and modes of working were merely an expression of the respective individuals learning style.

Table 1.2 Summary of the various notations for learning styles

Quadrants	Kolb	Lewis and Margerison (1979)	Woods (1989)
1	Diverger	Imaginatives	WHY? people
2	Assimilator	Logic	WHAT? people
3	Converger	Practical	HOW? people
4	Accommodator	Enthusiast	IF? people

The simplicity of the theory with the equally simple method of measuring an individuals learning style from which their learning type can be determined appeared an all too easy solution to what are complex problems. It was the discovery of some minor flaws in Kolb's supporting evidence that led to this more in-depth study of the underlying structure of Kolb's model.

Much of the criticism of Kolb's tool is to be found in the work of Wilson (1986) who discussed the validity of the survey itself and Stumph and Freedman (1981) who took a more theoretical approach. Woods (1989) simplified the language and discussed areas as opposed to points. Table 1.2 summarises various notations.

Kolb's first premise is that learning is cyclic and in four steps, which can be shown as right-angled axes:

1. Concrete Experience, where we 'measure' the world about us with our senses.

2. Reflective Observation, where we think about and consider what we have observed.

3. Abstract Conceptualisation, where we pattern our thoughts ready for practical application.

4. Active Experimentation, where we 'try' to apply what we have observed, considered and patterned.

Kolb's second premise is that individuals whose main energy lies between the axes have certain characteristics, and he developed a tool – the Learning Style Index (LSI) – to codify this. The LSI classifies individuals who 'specialised' in particular ways of learning. The Kolb classification titles were:

1. Divergers, who preferred the segment of the cycle involved in moving from Concrete Experience to Reflective Observation.

2. Assimilators, preferring the segment moving from Reflective Observation to Abstract Conceptualisation.

3. Convergers, preferring the segment moving from Abstract Conceptualisation to Active Experimentation.

4. Accommodators, who preferred the final segment moving Active Experimentation to new Concrete Experience.

Bernice McCarthy (1987) in the USA and, later, Woods and Okanlawon (1991) in Nigeria and the UK used the concepts to consider the teaching process. Many trainers, often working from the CCDU unit of Leeds University Psychology Department, pushed the ideas further and took Kolb's second premise to consider management style. This work was summarised by Woods (1989) who also introduced a simplified nomenclature and the short survey we found at the beginning of the chapter. (The full survey is to be found in a technical manual due to David Kolb (1978).)

The Kolb patterns

- Indicate a process of learning – asking WHY? questions, WHAT? questions, HOW? questions and finally the consequential questions, the IF? questions, in sequence.
- Accept that these profiles can correspond to behavioural patterns. The reader may like to see how his or her interpretation of the first survey fits their own behaviour as generalised in Exercise 1.1.

EXERCISE **1.1**

GENERALISED BEHAVIOURS OF THE FOUR BASIC KOLB PATTERNS

Although most of us have strength in two or more quadrants, look back at the Learning Style Indicator at the beginning of the chapter and see if your largest quadrant is WHY?, WHAT?, HOW? or IF?

The WHY? quadrant

Those with a largest WHY? quadrant are **imaginatives** who think about personal experience.

The WHY? person:

- has a clear picture of a total situation
- uses imagination and fantasy
- works in bursts of energy
- is good at imagining himself or herself in new situations
- is unhurried, casual, friendly, avoids conflict
- uses insight.

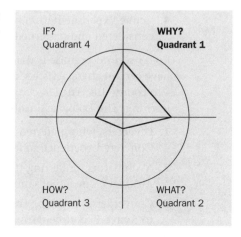

The WHY? manager:

- cannot be pushed until ready
- listens to others, shares ideas with a small number of people
- likes assurance from others, uses eyes and ears, listens, observes and asks questions
- attempts to develop his or her people.

These are the innovative learners and their strength is ideas. Their goal is self-fulfilment and bringing order to chaos. They are to be found fulfilled in careers spanning primary school teaching, counselling, the humanities, training forecasting and organisational development.

The WHAT? quadrant

Those with a predominance in the WHAT? quadrant are **logics** who think and theorise. They uses intuition plus thinking.

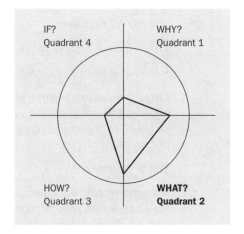

The WHAT? person:

- likes to place experience in a theoretical context
- is able to make new models mentally
- is a good synthesiser
- is precise, thorough and careful
- is organised and likes to follow a plan
- reacts slowly and wants facts
- calculates the probabilities.

The WHAT? manager:

- avoids becoming over-emotional
- analyses experiences often by writing them down
- looks for similar past experiences from which to extract learning.

These are the analytical learners. Their strength is the development of concepts and models and their goal is personal satisfaction and intellectual recognition. They are to be found in careers based on basic science, mathematics, economics, planning, etc.

The HOW? quadrant

Those with strength in the HOW? quadrant are the **practicals** who combine theory with doing things.

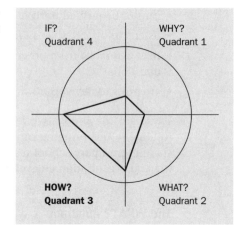

The HOW? person:

- applies ideas to solving problems
- makes theories useful
- has good detective skills
- enjoys the search and solve
- uses reason to meet goals
- likes to be in control of situations
- acts independently and then gets feedback.

The HOW? manager:

- uses factual data, books and theories
- learns by testing out new situations and assessing the results.

These are common-sense learners whose strength is the practical application of ideas and whose goal is to bring ideas into reality. People with such a profile are to be found in the engineering professions, physical science, nursing and technology.

The IF? quadrant

Strength in the IF? quadrant indicates the **enthusiast** who relies on his or her own intuition and experience.

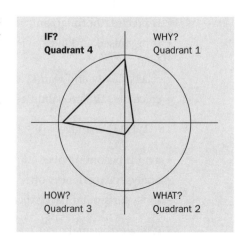

The IF? person:

- enjoys new situations often rushing in
- operates on trial and error
- uses 'gut' reactions
- gets others opinions, feelings and information
- involves other people
- likes risks, change and excitement
- adapts well and revels in new situations.

The IF? manager:

- looks to the future and the untested
- can be impulsive

- relies heavily on a support network

- likes to discharge emotion.

These are the dynamic learners and their strengths and goals are concerned with getting things done. Likely careers for people with such a pattern would be marketing, sales, 'action-centred' management jobs.

Figure 8.11 in Chapter 8 indicates how the dominant area in the profiles can correspond to particular managerial styles and indicates how individuals will relate to work situations

> The career adviser of Manchester Grammar School ran a Kolb survey with school leavers. Three students indicated that they wanted to be vets – the three students had their main energy in quadrants 2, 3 and 4 respectively. Since career advice is not about what you do but about reflecting on consequences, the adviser took the three students separately. The student predominantly in quadrant 2 would see the job as one of research. Was he good enough for this career? The quadrant 3 student would be a practical animal worker. Did he have the aptitude and the finance to work in the field – a muddy field at that? The quadrant 4 person was concerned with the glamour, and before he had had time to be interviewed, had decided he wanted to be a jet pilot.

Our first two related issues have been concerned with the way we take in information – part of the picture. The next issue is how we filter the information – our value systems.

Personal values

Personal values are considered to be: 'the core of the dynamics of behaviour, and play so large a part in unifying personality' (Allport *et al.*, 1931). That is, all other attitudes, orientations and behaviours arise out of individuals' values. Two major types of value are considered: those that are concerned with meeting our objectives and those concerned with the objective itself – instrumental and terminal (Rokeach, 1973). We present research findings that relate personal development in these two types of value to successful managerial performance. The pre-assessment instrument designed to assess your values development is discussed, along with information concerning the scores of other groups of people to enable you to compare your scores with those of more and less successful managers.

Value development is connected to ethical decision making, and its implications are direct.

The second area of self-awareness is cognitive style, which refers to the manner in which individuals gather and process information. A discussion of the critical dimensions of cognitive style is presented, based on the pre-assessment instrument that you used to assess your own style. Empirical research linking cognitive style to managerial behaviour is discussed, and your scores are compared to other successful managers in a variety of organisations.

Third, a discussion of attitudes towards change focuses on the methods people use for coping with change in their environment.

All of us, but especially managers, are faced with increasingly fragmented, rapidly changing, chaotic conditions. It is important that you become aware of how you adapt to these conditions. We have considered two dimensions – the locus of control and tolerance of ambiguity – and how these two factors relate to effective management.

Finally, we have looked at the way we relate to others, and what we need from our relationships.

These four areas of self-awareness – values, cognitive style, adaptation to change, and interpersonal orientation – constitute the very core of the self-concept.

- Values define an individual's basic standards about what is good and bad, worth while and worthless, desirable and undesirable, true and false, moral and immoral.

- Cognitive style determines individual thought processes and perceptions. It determines not only what kind of information is received by an individual, but how that information is interpreted, judged and responded to.

- Attitudes towards change identifies the adaptability of individuals. It includes the extent to which individuals are tolerant of ambiguous, uncertain conditions, and the extent to which they are inclined to accept personal responsibility for the consequences that follow from their actions.

- Interpersonal orientation determines the behaviour patterns that are most likely to emerge in interactions with others. The extent to which an individual is open or closed, assertive or retiring, controlling or dependent, affectionate or aloof, depends to a large degree on interpersonal orientation.

Figure 1.4 summarises these four aspects of self-awareness. Of course we could have looked at other aspects of self-awareness – emotions, attitudes, temperament, personality and interests – but we consider that these are all related fundamentally to our four core concepts. What we value, how we feel about things, how we behave towards others, what we want to achieve, and what we are attracted to are all strongly influenced by our values, cognitive style, orientation towards change, and interpersonal style. These are among the most important building blocks upon which other aspects of the self emerge. On the other hand, if you want to do a more in-depth analysis of multiple aspects of self-awareness there are several psychometric tests currently available. The leading European exponents are Saville and Holdsworth Ltd, who have a wide range of occupational tests and personality surveys, and Belbin Associates. Both offer computerised systems and Belbin's Interplace system has the added advantage of using the views of observers as well as self-perception. Self-knowledge is a vital key to management success.

Values

Values are the foundation stones of our lives, shaped by our upbringing and education. (Carr and Haldane, 1993). They are the basis upon which attitudes and personal preferences are formed and form the basis for crucial decisions, life directions, and personal tastes. Much of what we are is a product of the basic values we have developed throughout our lives. Organisations have values, although they

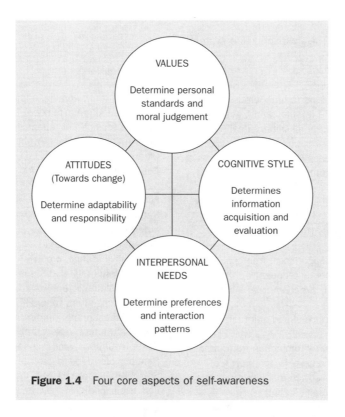

Figure 1.4 Four core aspects of self-awareness

are usually discussed as organisational culture. If individual values match organisational values, we are much more likely to be productive and satisfied workers within that organisation. The reverse is also true. Employees whose values differ from that of the organisation can be seen as 'difficult' or 'awkward'. Considerable problems arise when by design or accident individual or corporate values change. Equally unfortunate is the situation where individuals mis-read organisational values and find that their life work has been towards a personally unacceptable goal. Being aware of one's own priorities and values, therefore, is important if one expects to achieve compatibility at work and in a long-term career.

Simon (1974) and others have suggested that people sometimes lose touch with their own values, behaving in ways that are inconsistent with those values. That is, they pursue lower priorities at the expense of higher priorities, substituting goals with immediate payoffs for those with more long-term, central values. They may pursue an immediate reward or a temporary satisfaction, for example, in place of longer-term happiness and inner peace. The long-term effect of such a mismatch can be unsatisfactory for the organisation and the individual. On the whole, most people feel that they have quite a clear concept of their values, and because their values are seldom challenged they rarely review them. It is this lack of review that leads us to ignore our priorities and behave incongruously. We are inclined to reserve a review of our values to when we are threatened or are caught in a contradiction.

Table 1.3 The Rokeach value system

Terminal values	Instrumental values
A comfortable life (a prosperous life)	Ambitious (hard-working, aspiring)
An exciting life (a stimulating, active life)	Broadminded (open-minded)
A sense of accomplishment (lasting contribution)	Capable (competent, effective)
A world at peace (free of war and conflict)	Cheerful (light-hearted, joyful)
A world of beauty (beauty of nature and the arts)	Clean (neat, tidy)
Equality (brotherhood, equal opportunity for all)	Courageous (standing up for your beliefs)
Family security (taking care of loved ones)	Forgiving (willing to pardon others)
Freedom (independence, free choice)	Helpful (working for the welfare of others)
Happiness (contentedness)	Honest (sincere, truthful)
Inner harmony (freedom from inner conflict)	Imaginative (daring, creative)
Mature love (sexual and spiritual intimacy)	Independent (self-reliant, self-sufficient)
National security (protection from attack)	Intellectual (intelligent, reflective)
Pleasure (an enjoyable, leisurely life)	Logical (consistent, rational)
Salvation (saved, eternal life)	Loving (affectionate, tender)
Self-respect (self-esteem)	Obedient (dutiful, respectful)
Social recognition (respect, admiration)	Polite (courteous, well-mannered)
True friendship (close companionship)	Responsible (dependable, reliable)
Wisdom (a mature understanding of life)	Self-controlled (restrained, self-disciplined)

Rokeach (1973) claims that we all have the same small set of values, differing only in degree. For example, everyone values peace, but some make it a higher priority than others. Rokeach classifies the 'small set of values' we all choose from as being those about our goals – the 'ends' – and those about our way of achieving our goals – the 'means'. Some of us would believe, for instance, 'that the end justifies the means' while others would accept the Olympic motto that 'taking part is more important than winning'. Most of us would accept that there is some truth in both extremes. Rokeach called 'means'-orientated values *instrumental* and 'end'-orientated values *terminal*.

- Instrumental values relate to morality and competence. Violating moral values (e.g., behaving dishonestly) causes feelings of guilt, while violating competence values (e.g., behaving stupidly) brings about feelings of shame.

- Terminal values relate to the desired ends or goals for the individual and are fewer in number, according to Rokeach. Terminal values are either personal (e.g., peace of mind) or social (e.g., world peace).

Rokeach has found that when individuals become more concerned with one personal value, they increase the values of other personal values at the expense of social values, and vice versa. Thus, if one suddenly becomes particularly concerned with one's safety one is likely to find other personal goals, such as comfort, rising as well, whereas one's social concerns for fighting poverty and world peace will fall. Table 1.3 lists the 18 terminal values 'judged to represent the most important values in American society' (Rokeach, 1973).

Schmidt and Posner (1982) asked 1,460 American managers to rank the Rokeach's Terminal and Instrumental values for their importance in the workplace. 'Responsible' and 'honest' were by far the most desired value in employees (over 85 per cent of the managers selected them), followed by 'capable' (65 per cent), 'imaginative' (55 per cent) and 'logical' (49 per cent). 'Obedient', 'clean', 'polite' and 'forgiving' were the least important, being selected by fewer than 10 per cent of the managers. Different groups of people tend to differ in the values they hold. Cavanaugh (1980), also working in America, found that business school students and professors tend to rate ambition, capability, responsibility and freedom higher than the general population, and give lower concern for helpfulness to others, aesthetics and cultural values, and overcoming social injustice. Rokeach (1973), in America, compared highly successful, moderately successful, and unsuccessful managers. Highly successful managers gave significantly higher scores to values relating to economic (e.g., a comfortable life) and political values (e.g., social recognition) than less successful managers. Also in America, Clare and Sanford (1979) found that the instrumental value managers held highest for themselves was 'ambition', and their highest-held terminal value was a 'sense of accomplishment'.

In comparing the research findings from America we have two concerns. Firstly, that of taking a comparison of values across national boundaries and, secondly, the value of quoting population averages when individual differences are highly pronounced.

On the issue of national boundaries, a study of opinions organised in 1994 by *The Guardian* in the UK, *Asahi Shimun* in Japan, *Der Spiegel* in Germany and the *New York Times* brought to light some considerable differences between the UK, Japan, Germany and America. This discrepancy is illustrated in Table 1.4.

The reasons for the differences of opinions, and presumably the value systems upon which they are based, are certainly complex. Carr and Haldane (1993) cite one significant factor in the formation of values. It is concerned with education systems. These differ from country to country and within countries. European countries are inclined to train potential managers differently from those who are perceived to be potential 'shop floor workers'. This brings us onto our second concern about the direct use of research information. Individual differences can make nonsense out of average figures. (See Chapter 6 on the work of Galloway and motivation (1990).)

The reader will find it interesting to make a personal ranking of the two sets of values – as has been said many times before: If you do not know where you are going, you will end up somewhere else. What is rarely discussed are the values concerned with 'where you are going'. It is, in our opinion, valuable to review a personal value system when we are not under pressure.

Table 1.4 Percentage of respondents giving each reply to the question: 'What is the most serious problem facing the world in 1994?'

Problem	UK	Germany	Japan	US
Bosnia	0	10	8	0
Crime	7	0	0	17
Drugs	0	0	0	7
Economy	0	10	0	7
Ethnic strife	0	0	14	0
Famine	11	4	6	7
Morals	0	0	0	6
Pollution	12	11	10	0
Population	0	4	0	0
Poverty	11	0	0	0
Unemployment	6	0	0	0
War	23	40	13	8

Kohlberg (1969), Graves (1970) and Flower *et al.* (1975) all argue that the behaviour displayed by individuals (i.e., the means used to achieve their valued ends) is related to the maturity of their value system. People progress from one level of maturity to another, and, as they do, their value priorities change. Individuals who have progressed to more mature levels of values development possess a qualitatively different set of instrumental values than individuals who are at less mature levels. The maturity of value systems is therefore important if we are to relate value systems to managerial effectiveness. However, we could argue that the term 'maturity is value laden. Working with multi-ethnic groups, any codification has to be agreed and presented as culturally based.

Kohlberg's model is the best-known and most widely researched approach to the maturity of values. The model focuses on the kind of reasoning used to reach a decision about an issue that has value or moral connotations. The model consists of three major levels, each of which contains two stages. Table 1.5 summarises the characteristics of each stage. In brief, the stages are sequential (for example, a person cannot progress to stage 3 before passing through stage 2), and each stage represents a higher level of maturity.

The first level of maturity, the self-centred level, contains the first two stages of values development. Moral reasoning and instrumental values are based on personal needs or wants and on the consequences of an act. For example, something could be judged as right or good if it helped an individual to obtain a reward or avoid punishment and if the consequences were not negative for someone else. Stealing 50,000EUs is worse than stealing 500EUs in the self-centred level because the consequences are more negative for someone else.

The second level, or conformity level, contains stages 3 and 4. Moral reasoning is based on conforming to and upholding the conventions and expectations

Table 1.5 Kohlberg classification of moral judgement into levels and stages of development

Level	Basis of moral judgement	Stage of development
I	Moral value resides in external, quasi-physical happenings, in bad acts, or in quasi-physical needs, rather than in persons and standards.	1. Obedience and punishment orientation. Egocentric deference to superior power or prestige, or a trouble-avoiding set. Objective responsibility.
		2. Naively egotistic orientation. Right action is that instrumentally satisfying the self's needs and occasionally others'. Awareness of relativism of value to each actor's needs and perspectives. Naive egalitarianism and orientation to exchange and reciprocity.
II	Moral value resides in performing good or right roles, in maintaining the conventional order and the expectancies of others.	3. Good-boy orientation. Orientation to approval and to pleasing and helping others. Conformity to stereotypical images of majority or natural role behaviour, and judgement by intentions.
		4. Orientation to doing duty, 'showing respect for authority', and maintaining the social order for its own sake. Regard for earned expectations of others.
III	Moral value resides in conformity by the self to shared or shareable standards, rights or duties.	5. Contractual legalistic orientation. Recognition of an arbitrary element or starting point in rules or expectations for the sake of agreement. Duty defined in terms of contract, general avoidance of violation of the will or rights of others, and majority will and welfare.
		6. Conscience of principle orientation. Orientation not only to actually ordained social rules, but to principles of choice involving appeal to logical universality and consistency. Orientation to conscience as a directing agent and to mutual respect and trust.

Source: Kohlberg, 1969

of society. This level is sometimes referred to as the 'law and order' level because the emphasis is on conformity to laws and norms. Right and wrong are judged on the basis of whether or not behaviours conform to the rules of those in authority. Respect from others based on obedience is a prized outcome. Stealing 50,000EUs and stealing 500EUs are equally wrong at this level because both violate the law. Most adults in the Western culture function at this level of values maturity.

Third is the principled level. This contains the final two stages of maturity and represents the most mature level of moral reasoning and the most mature set of instrumental values. Right and wrong are judged on the basis of the internalised principles of the individual. That is, judgements are made on the basis of a set of principles that have been developed from individual experience. In the highest stage of maturity, this set of principles is comprehensive (it covers all contingencies), consistent (it is never violated) and universal (it does not change with the situation or circumstance). Thus, stealing 50,000EUs and stealing 500EUs are still judged to be wrong, but the basis for the judgement is not the violation of laws or rules, but the violation of a comprehensive, consistent, universal principle developed by the individuals. Few individuals, according to Kohlberg, reach this highest level of maturity. (Kohlberg uses the terms 'pre-conventional', 'conventional' and 'post-conventional' to describe the three levels. We have chosen instead to use terms that capture the dominant characteristics of each stage.)

Self-centred individuals view rules and laws as outside themselves, but they obey because, by doing so, they may be rewarded or at least avoid punishment. Conformist individuals view rules and laws as outside themselves, but they obey because they have learned and accepted those rules and laws. Principled individuals examine the rules and laws and develop a set of internal principles. If there is a choice to be made between obeying a rule or obeying a principle, they choose the principle. Internalised principles supersede rules and laws in principled individuals. Again reverting to our experience in working with multi-ethic groups we find that it is argued that retribution and conscience can be confused. The linear progression becomes a loop.

Kohlberg uses a story to explain the levels. We will do the same.

> A child was dying of a rare disease, the treatment for which could only be obtained at a clinic in the United States. The child's case was publicised on a TV programme and a public subscription allowed the child to go for what was expected to be a complete course of treatment.
>
> When the child first returned home she showed considerable improvement but then began to revert to her previous lethargic state. The American clinic was helpful and explained that they had always been aware that the child might have to return for further treatment – of course at extra cost.
>
> The sick child's father, Heinz, went back to the TV company but found that they had lost interest. He made various attempts to borrow the money, and even to start an appeal on his own. He failed. He also failed to get the bank that employed him to provide him with a loan to be paid back out of his salary.
>
> Heinz worked in the computer services department of the bank and was explaining the problem to a colleague over a coffee. The colleague was enthusiastic to help and explain a 'foolproof' scam which would use Heinz's access to the computer

system and his special knowledge to 'generate' enough money to send his child to America. Heinz was well aware that what he would have to do was stealing.

Now answer the following questions:

	Yes	No
1. Would it be wrong for Heinz to steal from his employer?	____	____
2. Was the company right in refusing to give him a loan against his salary?	____	____
3. Did Heinz have an obligation to steal for his child?	____	____
4. If the sick child was not his favourite child, did he still have the same obligations to steal for her?	____	____
5. Suppose the child was that of his best friend and not his, should he steal?	____	____
6. Suppose the child was not close to Heinz personally. Should Heinz steal?	____	____
7. Suppose Heinz read in the paper about the child. Should he steal for her?	____	____
8. Would you steal to save your own life?	____	____
9. If he were caught, should he be sent to jail?	____	____

For individuals in the self-centred level of maturity, stealing might be justified because Heinz's child had instrumental value, she could give him pleasure and perhaps look after him in old age. A stranger, however, would not have the same instrumental value for Heinz, so it would be wrong to steal for a stranger. Individuals in the conformity level would base their judgements on the closeness of the relationship and on law and authority. Heinz has an obligation to steal for family members, according to this reasoning, but not for non-family members. The governing principle is always whether it is against the law (or society's expectations) or not. Principled individuals base their judgements on a set of universal, comprehensive and consistent principles. They may answer any question yes or no, but their reasoning will be based on their own internal principles, not on externally imposed standards or expectations. (For example, they might feel an obligation to steal for anyone because they value human life more than property.)

Research on Kohlberg's model of value development has revealed some interesting findings that have relevance to managerial behaviour. For example, moral judgement stories were administered to college pupils who had earlier participated in Milgram's (1963) obedience study. Under the guise of a reinforcement-learning experiment, Milgram's subjects had been directed to give increasingly intense shocks to a person who was observed to be in great pain. Of the respondents at the principled level (stages 5 and 6), 75 per cent refused to administer the shocks, while only 12.5 per cent of the respondents at the conformity level refused. Higher levels of values development were associated with more human behaviour towards other people. Haan *et al.* (1968) found that although both principled and self-centred individuals are inclined to join in massive social protests, self-centred individuals are motivated by the desire to better themselves individually, while principled individuals are motivated by justice and the rights of the larger community.

Becoming mature in value development requires that individuals develop a set of internalised principles by which they can govern their behaviour. The development of those principles is enhanced and value maturity is increased as value-based issues are confronted, discussed and thought about. Lickona (1976) notes that 'Simply increasing the amount of reciprocal communication that occurs among people is likely to enhance moral development.'

To help you to determine your own level of values maturity an instrument, developed by James Rest at the University of Minnesota's Moral Research Center, was included in the Pre-assessment section. It has been used extensively in research because it is easier to administer than Kohlberg's method for assessing maturity. According to Kohlberg (1976), 'Rest's approach does give a rough estimate of an individual's moral maturity level.' Rather than placing a person on one single level of values maturity, it identifies the stage that the person relies on most. That is, it assumes that individuals use more than one level of maturity (or set of instrumental values), but that one level generally predominates. By completing this instrument, therefore, you will identify your predominant level of value maturity. To determine your maturity level, refer to the self-scoring instructions in Appendix 1. An exercise in the Skill Practice section will help you develop or refine principles at stages 5 and 6.

Ethical decision making

In addition to its benefits for self-understanding, awareness of your own level of values maturity also has important practical implications for ethical decision making. Unfortunately, there have been several highly publicised examples of unethical dealings in recent years in Europe. The publisher Robert Maxwell was able to ransack millions of pounds from the unsuspecting pension funds of companies he had bought in a flurry of acquisitions. At least his mysterious death prevented him from being imprisoned; not so lucky were Ernest Saunders and Gerald Ronson who were jailed for their involvement in the attempt to inflate the value of Guinness shares during its take-over bid. The magnitude of the scandal at the Bank of Credit and Commerce International (BCCI) will perhaps never be rivalled, but hundreds of investors have been ruined in the process. British Airways has paid a high price for its 'dirty tricks' campaign against Virgin Airlines, while the defence electronics group Ferranti eventually collapsed when it became the victim of a million pound fraud. Volkswagen and GM have issues of industrial espionage at the highest level. There have also been widespread accusations that French and Spanish companies have contributed to political parties in exchange for public favours, and there has been a wholesale indictment of Italy's corrupt business and political class, particularly after the Olivetti scandal. Neil Hamilton in the UK, with his alleged corruption of the British parliament, may have brought a government down. A recent cartoon summarises this state of affairs. It showed a group of executives sitting at a conference table. The leader remarked: 'Of course honesty is one of the better policies.'

Corporate behaviour that exemplifies unethical decision making is not our concern here. What is more to the point is a study by the American Management Association that included 3,000 managers in the USA. It reported that most individual managers felt that they were under pressure to compromise personal standards to meet company goals (Cavanaugh, 1980). As an illustration, consider the following incident.

> You are interviewing for a senior position and the candidate in front of you satisfies every criterion – he is perfect. Having decided, without telling the candidate that he is 'in', you begin to close the interview. At this point he says:
>
> 'You know my present employer is of course a major rival – perhaps this disc will be of use.'
>
> The disc he explains contains details of all the accounts of his present employer. The information would be VERY valuable to your company. What do you do and why?

This sort of incident is common and is described by Kenneth Blanchard and Norman Peale (1988) who, in their excellent book on ethical management, go well beyond the scope of this book. Looking at Kohlberg's Stages of Development we imagine six ways of deciding what to do:

1. If I take them I will be caught – fired.

2. I might be caught but the advantages far outweigh/are less than the risks.

3. I would get my boss's approval/disapproval if I did.

4. It would be letting the side down/help us.

5. It would be illegal.

6. It's wrong.

Managers in the real world have to resolve the conflict between commercial short- and long-term gain and their own need to 'sleep at night' on a surprisingly regular basis (Hosmer, 1987). To do so we need to understand our own values, accepting that, in the short term, trade-offs are inevitable. The stress that these trade-off's produce and the way in which individuals can cope are discussed in the next chapter. It is a great advantage to the individual if he or she can call out an absolute set of values to guide.

Working with groups of different ethnic backgrounds, Islam provides such a set of principles – a 'joke' of Islam is that when oil comes up the well Allah goes down the hole.

For those less fortunate and not possessing a guiding faith we recommend three questions, due again to Blanchard and Peale (1988):

1. Is it legal? Will I be violating either civil law, company policy or 'standard' practice?

2. Is it balanced? Is it fair to all concerned in the short term as well as the long term? Does it promote win–win relationships?

3. How will it make me feel about myself? Will it make me feel proud? Would I feel good if my decision was published in a newspaper for my family to read?

Look at the example of the candidate who was willing to 'sell' his previous employer and ask the questions. The answers you come to will be about YOU and not about the theory we can cover.

In all we have reviewed it is inevitable now that we consider your ability to cope with change. The environment we all face continues to become more chaotic, more temporary, more complex, and more overloaded with information, and you need to survive and prosper. We all have an attitude to change.

Attitudes towards change

Almost no one disagrees with the prediction that change will increase. Toffler (1980) states it this way:

> A powerful tide is surging across much of the world today, creating a new, often bizarre, environment in which to work, play, marry, raise children or retire. In this bewildering context, businessmen swim against highly erratic economic currents; politicians see their ratings bob wildly up and down; universities, hospitals, and other institutions battle desperately against inflation. Value systems splinter and crash, while lifeboats of family, church and state are hurled madly about. Many observers have suggested that we are now entering a post-industrial environment, 'characterised by more and increasing information, more and increasing turbulence, and more and increasing complexity' (Huber, 1984).

These views were from the 1980s and things have accelerated since then – the ONLY certainty is change. We are called upon to make decisions much more quickly against a rising tide of information (Cameron and Ulrich, 1986); we are only human so more and more decisions are made on the basis of incomplete and ambiguous information (Simon, 1973). We all need increasingly to function in conditions of ambiguity and turbulence, and become hostages to our attitude to change.

The first step is to be aware of our own attitude to change. Again our approach is to look at the dimensions of the system – our orientation to change. We find two dimensions: *tolerance of ambiguity* and *locus of control*.

Tolerance of ambiguity

One's personal tolerance of ambiguity is a guide to how we will function in ambiguous, chaotic situations where the data may well be confused and 'too much' is happening. Regardless of one's cognitive style, people vary in their ability to cope. Individuals who have a high tolerance of ambiguity also tend to be those who are more cognitively complex. They tend to pay attention to more information, interpret more cues, and possess more patterning capability than less complex individuals.

> Perhaps the most ambiguous work situation known to human beings is code breaking. Various writers, and most excitingly Robert Harris in his novel, *Enigma*, describes the recruitment of code breakers working against the ever-changing flood of German messages in World War II. A crossword competition was set up and the winners were recruited.

Bieri and his co-workers (1966) found that cognitively complex and tolerant individuals were better communicators, and Schneier (1979) found that they were more sensitive to the critical characteristics of others when appraising their work. Haase *et al.* (1979) showed them to be more flexible under ambiguous and over-loaded conditions than less tolerant and less complex individuals. Managers with a high tolerance of ambiguity are more likely to be entrepreneurial in their actions (Schere, 1982), to screen out less information in a complex environment (Haase *et al.*, 1979) and to choose specialities in their occupations that involve less structured tasks (Budner, 1962). However, individuals who are more tolerant of ambiguity have more difficulty focusing on important details, are inclined to pay attention to a variety of items and may have somewhat less ability to concentrate without being distracted by interruptions. This said, a high tolerance of ambiguity is an advantage in our changing world.

In the Skill Pre-assessment section of this chapter, the Tolerance of Ambiguity Scale (Budner, 1962) should help you to assess the extent to which you have a tolerance for these kinds of complex situations.

In scoring the Tolerance of Ambiguity Scale (Appendix 1, page 611), we look at three different factors:

- The *novelty* score, which relates to the extent to which you are tolerant of new, unfamiliar information or situations.

- The *complexity* score, which indicates the extent to which you are tolerant of multiple, distinctive, or unrelated pieces of information.

- The *insolubility* score, which indicates the extent to which you are tolerant of problems that are very difficult to solve, where alternative solutions are not evident, information is unavailable, or the problem's components seem unrelated to each other.

In general, the more tolerant people are of novelty, complexity and insolubility, the more likely they are to succeed as managers in information-rich, ambiguous environments. They are less overwhelmed by these ambiguous circumstances. However, cognitive complexity and tolerance for ambiguity are not related to intelligence (Smith and Leach, 1972), and your score on the Tolerance of Ambiguity Scale is not an evaluation of how smart you are. Most importantly, individuals can learn to tolerate more complexity and more flexibility in their information-processing abilities. The first step is becoming aware of where you are now.

The Skill Analysis and Skill Practice sections of this chapter, together with our chapter on effective problem solving, should continue the process. Although intelligence and a tolerance of uncertainty are not linked, a second dimension of our attitudes to change – discussed here as 'locus of control' – is.

Locus of control

Locus of control refers to the attitude people have concerning the extent to which they are in control of their own destiny. When we take any action, some actions are rewarded and others penalised – we receive positive or negative feedback and this feedback reinforces our behaviour for the 'next time'. If we interpret the feed-back as determined by, or contingent on, our actions, it is within our internal locus of control: '*I was the cause of the success or failure of the change.*'

If, however, we interpret the feedback as being determined by outside factors, we have something in an external locus of control: '*It was not my fault. I was rescued by . . .*'

Over time, people develop an overall view of where the reinforcement for their actions will come – internally or externally. Over 1,000 studies have been done using the Locus of Control Scale. Not surprisingly, the research suggests that, in American culture, internal locus of control is associated with the most successful managers (see Hendricks, 1985, and Spector, 1982, for reviews of the literature). Julian B. Rotter (1966), whose scale it was, summarised several studies and showed that people with an internal locus of control are more likely to:

- be attentive to aspects of the environment that provide useful information for the future;
- engage in actions to improve their environment;
- place greater emphasis on striving for achievement;
- be more inclined to develop their own skills;
- ask more questions;
- remember more information than people with an external locus of control (also see Seeman, 1982).

Elsewhere in the literature it is claimed that people with high internal locus of control are:

- more able to manage stress and outperform in stressful situations (Oakland, 1997; Anderson *et al.* 1977);
- less alienated from the work environment (Mitchell, 1975; Seeman, 1982; Wolf, 1972);
- more satisfied with their work (Organ and Greene, 1974; Pryer and Distefano, 1971);
- able to experience less job strain and more position mobility (promotions and job changes) than externals (Gennill and Heisler, 1972);
- more likely to act as leaders and be more effective in this role than those with a dominant external locus of control (Anderson and Schneider, 1978);
- likely to engage in more entrepreneurial activity (Durand and Shea, 1974);
- more active in managing their own careers (Hammer and Vardi, 1981), and had higher levels of job involvement than externals (Runyon, 1973).

In the leadership role, externally focused individuals tend to use coercion and threats, whereas internally focused leaders rely more on persuasion and expertise as a source of power (Goodstadt and Hjelle, 1973; Mitchell *et al.*, 1975) and are more able to use a participative management style, when relevant, than the externally focused manager (Runyon, 1973).

A study of locus of control among top executives found that the firms controlled by outside management were less likely to take risks. Sentient-controlled firms engaged in more innovative risky projects, took more leadership in the marketplace, had longer planning horizons, engaged more scanning of the environment, and demanded more highly developed technology (Miller *et al.*, 1982).

In summarising his conclusions about locus of control, McDonald (1970) stated that 'all research points to the same conclusion: "In the American culture, people are handicapped by external locus of control."'

An internal locus of control is not the panacea for all management problems and is not always a positive attribute. As leaders, those with an external locus of control are more inclined to define roles, clarify structures and show consideration. (Durand and Shea, 1974). Internally focused individuals are less likely to accept authority and provide unbiased feedback. (Cravens and Worchel, 1977). Internals also have more difficulty arriving at decisions when those decisions have serious consequences for someone else (Wheeler and Davis, 1979).

The dominant locus of control can shift over time, particularly as roles change at work (Harvey, 1971). Rothenberg in 1980 gave comfort to those with a dominant high external locus of control – they can get to the top.

People who look at change as inevitable and as an opportunity to grasp, perceiving themselves as masters of their own fate, are more likely to be effective managers in most circumstances in our culture.

Using the Locus of Control Scale at the beginning of the chapter will give you a view of your own internal/external locus ratio. Remember that whatever the value is, you can be a successful manager in the right setting, and you can alter the ratio when you like.

Summary

Two key attitudes towards change – tolerance of ambiguity and locus of control – have been found to be associated with performance in management roles. Knowing your scores on these two factors can help you capitalise on your strengths and enhance your potential. While substantial research exists associating some positive managerial behaviours with internal locus of control and tolerance of ambiguity, possessing these orientations is neither an assurance of success as a manager nor a solution to the problems that managers face. By knowing your scores, however, you will be able to choose situations in which you will more likely feel comfortable, perform effectively, and understand the point of view of those whose perspective differs from yours. Self-understanding is a prerequisite to self-improvement and change.

Interpersonal needs

Sayles (1964) suggests that management involves virtually constant contact with people, and individuals who do not enjoy such contact are likely to be ineffective, frustrated and dissatisfied. Enjoying contact with others is about satisfying certain fundamental needs and this is the fourth critical area of self-awareness we will be discussing. Although all of us need to relate to others, the quantity and quality of the relationships vary from individual to individual. Some of us require the constant buzz of the herd while others prefer the company of a few chosen friends with whom they can relate closely. Some of us need both. Some of us need to have clarity in our relationships, knowing who is in charge and who is the follower, while others prefer equality. The further complication is what we say we want for ourselves and what we want from others.

Schutz (1958) proposed a validated method of quantifying interpersonal needs. The basic assumption behind Schutz's model is that people need people and that all of us seek to establish compatible relationships with other individuals in their social interactions. He goes further in stating that three interpersonal needs must be satisfied if the individual is to function effectively and avoid unsatisfactory relationships. It is the process of striving to achieve a personal balance of these needs that determines much of our behaviour towards others.

The first interpersonal need is for inclusion. We all, at some level, need to maintain a relationship with other people, to be included in their activities, and to include them in our own activities. The personal balance is between identifying with a group and wanting to be alone. It is a trade-off between tendencies towards extroversion and introversion. We differ in the strength of their relative needs: (1) the need to include others, or expressed inclusion, and (2) the need to be included by others, or wanted inclusion.

A second interpersonal need is for control. This is the need to maintain a satisfactory balance of power and influence in relationships. We all need, in some measure, to be masters of our own fate, to exert control, direct, or structure other people while at the same time being independent of them. We also have a need to be controlled, directed, or structured by others but at the same time to maintain freedom and discretion. Essentially, this is a trade-off between authoritarianism and dependency. Individual differences arise, therefore, in the need to control others, or expressed control, and the need to be controlled by others, or wanted control.

A third need is the need for affection, or the need to form close personal relationships with others. This need is not restricted to physical affection or romantic relationships but includes needs for warmth, intimacy and love without overtones. We all need, to some measure, close personal relationships with other people, but there is a personal balance between what we see as welcome and smothering. We all need, in some measure, to have others show warmth and affection to us, while maintaining a chosen degree of distance. This is a trade-off between high affiliative needs and high independence needs. Individuals therefore vary in their needs for expressing affection towards other people and for wanting affection to be expressed towards them.

The three interpersonal needs thus have two aspects: a desire to express the need and a desire to receive the needed behaviour from others. These three needs determine an individual's interpersonal orientation. That is, individuals differ uniquely in their needs and thus their behaviours to achieve their needs.

In the Skill Pre-assessment section we provided the instrument Schutz developed to assess inclusion, control and affection needs. Ideally you should compute your score before continuing the chapter. This way you will be able to personalise the discussion. The process of answering the 54 questions and their analysis may take about 20 minutes, but it is time well spent. The template for the analysis is at the end of the book. Use the analysis instructions at the end of the book to fill in the matrix.

	INCLUSION *The need to join and belong*	CONTROL *The need for role and control*	AFFECTION *The need for individual relationships*
Expressed			
Wanted			

First, add all the figures together and come up with a grand total. The maximum points possible in each cell are 9 and with six cells we have a maximum of 54. Scores above 35 are regarded as high. If you have a high score you are best suited to a job with a high people content. Scores from 34 to 15 are regarded as average – you like contact with people, but can work effectively without such contact. Scores below 14 are regarded as low and indicate that human contact is not your primary objective at work – the task is of primary importance to you. Adding along the rows we find out more.

Score – row total	*Inclusion*	*Control*	*Affection*
High: 12–18	You need the 'buzz' of people around you – you need to be associated with teams or groups	You like to know where you are – clarity of position/ role and structure is needed for you to be effective	You like the company of intimates and probably, if your inclusion and control scores are only medium, you prefer to deal with your staff on a one-to-one basis
Average: 6–11	You are ambivalent about working in teams or groups	Although you probably prefer clarity in your role, it is not essential	You probably prefer the company of a select few, but it is not essential
Low: 0–5	You prefer your own company or that of a few friends	You are happy to function in situations of uncertainty	You may well be unhappy or embarrassed in stressed, intimate situations

We can get an even better focus by looking at the content of individual cells in the matrix. We are looking here at the difference between the expressed needs and the wanted needs – what you say you want from others and what you actually want – for each cell, 6–9 is high, 3–5 is medium and 0–2 is low.

	Inclusion	Control	Affection
High top/high bottom	Clear and expressed wish to be 'in the action'	A wish to control in a tightly controlled environment	A high and clearly expressed need for individual contacts
High top/ medium bottom	High express wish to 'be in the action' but in fact a rather ambivalent attitude when it comes time to join in	A strong wish to control with perhaps some reluctance to accept authority or procedures	A high and clearly expressed wish for intimate human contact which may on occasion be one-way
High top/ low bottom	A high expressed wish to be included as a social necessity but not as a genuine need	A wish to control but remain independent	A perhaps dangerous demand for intimacy that will not be reciprocated
Medium top/ high bottom	Some reluctance to ask to be included in things – but want to be involved	Control can be taken but regretfully	Some shyness to express real feeling
Medium top/ medium bottom	Genuine ambivalence to groups teams and their membership	Control and structures are not the major factor but accepted – weak or strong	A straightforward relationship is preferred – privacy or intimacy is acceptable
Medium top/ low bottom	Lack of clarity of messages – do you want to be involved or not – you do not!	Perhaps unassertive, wish for structures but a reluctance to accept it from others	A lack of clarity of signals – do you wish intimacy and trust – you do not!
Low top/ high bottom	A lonely position where it is difficult not to watch others from afar and hope to be invited in	A wish for other things, events of people to dominate or set rules	A shy position that once breached is inclined to surprise, if not frighten others by its intensity
Low top/ medium bottom	An only partially expressed hope to be 'let in'	Control, order and certainty are not major issues	A partially expressed hope to share with individuals
Low top/ low bottom	No need to have to face others or join in	Control, order and certainty mean very little indeed	What you see is what you get – an expressed and real need for privacy

The issue we need to pursue is the interaction between individuals, as the following story exemplifies:

Stuart Blyth was becoming exasperated. He had only been at Vulcan Computers for three months and already he was finding Helen impossible to work with. 'I've got enough problems without her rambling memos,' he muttered to his secretary. Stuart's predecessor, Duncan Johnson, had appreciated being kept in constant touch with developments by Helen. 'I really look forward to reading your personal memos,' he used to say at their weekly meetings. 'They keep me in touch with the pulse of the company.' That was why Helen was completely mystified by Stuart's reaction. Hadn't he said he wanted to be informed about staff changes when he joined the company? And now after three months he had finally snapped and had thrown back her latest memo: 'Don't keep sending me these boring reports. I haven't got time to read all this stuff – just tell me.'

Source: Thomas and Woods (1994)

The clue to the boss's personal orientation lies in the last line of the case study – 'just tell me'. Stuart probably had a high need for affection – one-to-one contact. By reporting in written format, Helen was not giving Stuart what he needed. Helen, by recognising her boss's orientation, could have saved herself a great deal of grief.

Managers with high inclusion needs will prefer to use group meetings to give information and may well find themselves damaged when they have to act in a way that alienates them from their working team.

Sam was the manager of a distribution depot and enjoyed his regular 'Saturday night out with the boys'. The company was running into financial problems and was laying off staff. During one fateful Saturday evening he was asked whether he would sack any of the team. He replied that he could never do that and he would fight for them 'come hell or high water'.

The next Monday he received orders to make 25 per cent of his team redundant. He did the job but it was made very clear to him that he would not be welcome for the next Saturday night out.

We met him in a counselling session where he was suffering from depression. His Firo-B score for inclusion was 8/7 and 'belonging' to the team was very important to him.

Managers with high affection needs may find it difficult to discipline subordinates with whom they wish to retain one-to-one relationships. Managers with a high expressed control need and a low wanted control may well find themselves in conflict with their own boss. Manager's with the reverse low expressed control and high wanted control may well be seen as unsure and lacking determination.

Individuals who have high expressed scores and low wanted scores are called 'controllers' by Ryan (1970) because they want to express but are unwilling to accept in return. The reverse pattern, high wanted scores and low expressed scores, is called a 'passive' pattern by Ryan because these individuals want to receive but are unwilling to initiate any interaction.

Knowing your interpersonal orientation, then, can be an important factor in your managerial success. Not only does it enhance good interpersonal relations by helping you diagnose potential areas of incompatibility, but it helps you generate alternatives for behaviour when you attempt to solve interpersonal difficulties. For example, some problems can be solved simply by increasing inclusion activities, by allowing someone else to express a little more control, or by redefining an issue as an affection problem instead of a control problem.

SUMMARY

Modern organisations have begun more and more to discover the power of developing self-awareness among their managers. Managers have completed instruments designed to increase self-awareness in such companies as Barclays Bank, British Gas, ICI, KLM UK, Marks and Spencer, Nissan UK, Peugeot, Unilever and Volvo.

An awareness of how individuals differ in their value priorities and values maturity, cognitive style, orientation towards change and, for example, after requiring his top 100 managers to undergo self-awareness training, the president of the computer reservations company of Hilton Hotels and Budget Rent-a-Car stated:

> We had some real morale problems. I realised I had a mixed bag of people reporting to me and that this training could help us better understand each other and also understand how we make decisions. We wouldn't have made it through [a recent company crisis] without self-awareness training.
>
> *Source*: Moore (1987)

Not only does self-awareness training assist individuals in their ability to understand, and thereby manage, themselves, but it also is important in helping individuals develop understanding of the differences in others. Most people will regularly encounter individuals who possess a different style, a different set of values and a different perspective from their own. Most workforces are becoming more, not less, diverse.

Self-awareness training, as discussed in this chapter, therefore, can be a valuable tool in helping individuals develop empathy and in understanding the expanding diversity they will face in work and school settings. The relationship between the four critical areas of self-awareness and these management outcomes is summarised in Figure 1.5.

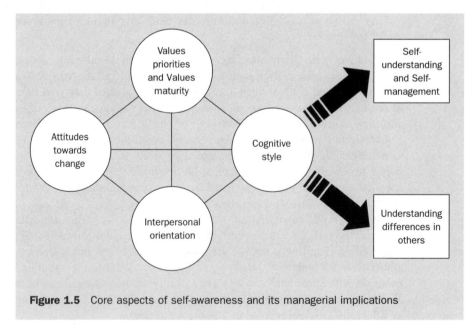

Figure 1.5 Core aspects of self-awareness and its managerial implications

Most of the following chapters relate to skills in interpersonal or group interaction, but successful skill development in those areas will occur only if individuals have a firm foundation in self-awareness. In fact, there is an interesting paradox in human behaviour: we can know others only by knowing ourselves, but we can know ourselves only by knowing others. Our knowledge of others, and therefore our ability to manage or interact successfully with them, comes from relating what we see in them to our own experience. If we are not self-aware, we have no basis for knowing certain things about others. Self-recognition leads to recognition and understanding of others. As Harris (1981) puts it: Nothing is really personal that is not first interpersonal, beginning with the infant's shock of separation from the umbilical cord. What we know about ourselves comes only from the outside, and is interpreted by the kind of experiences we have had; and what we know about others comes only from analogy with our own network of feelings.

Behavioural guidelines

The guidelines will help you develop your self-awareness:

1. Identify your sensitive line. Determine what information about yourself you are most likely to defend against.
2. Identify a comprehensive, consistent and universal set of principles on which you will base your behaviour. Identify the most important terminal and instrumental values that guide your decisions.
3. Expand your cognitive style, your tolerance of ambiguity, and your internal locus of control by increasing your exposure to new information and engaging in activities different from those you are used to. Seek ways to expand and broaden yourself.
4. Compute incompatibility scores with those you regularly interact with and identify areas in which potential incompatibilities may arise. Apply principles of constructive communication (Chapter 4) and constructive conflict management (Chapter 7) when disagreements arise.
5. Engage in honest self-disclosure with someone who is close to you and accepting of you. Investigate aspects of yourself that you are not sure of.
6. Keep a diary, and make time regularly to engage in self-analysis. Balance life's activities with some time for self-renewal.

Skill Analysis

CASE STUDY **1.1**

COMMUNIST PRISON CAMP

To find examples of a more intensive destruction of identification with family and reference groups and the destruction of social role and self-image, we must turn to the experiences of civilian political prisoners interned in Chinese communist prisons.

In such prisons the total regimen, consisting of physical privation, prolonged interrogation, total isolation from former relationships and sources of information, detailed regimentation of all daily activities, and deliberate humiliation and degradation, was geared to producing a complete confession of alleged crimes and the assumption of a penitent role preceding the adoption of a communist frame of reference. The prisoner was not informed of his crimes, nor was he permitted to evade the issue by making up a false confession. Instead, what the prisoner learned he must do was re-evaluate his past from the point of view of the communists and recognise that most of his former attitudes and behaviour were actually criminal. For example, a priest who had dispensed food to needy peasants in his mission church had to recognise that he was actually a tool of imperialism and was using his missionary activities as cover for exploitation of the peasants. Even worse, he may have had to recognise that he had used food as blackmail to accomplish his aims.

The key technique used by the communists to produce social alienation to a degree sufficient to allow such redefinition and revaluation to occur was to put the prisoner into a cell with four or more other prisoners who were somewhat more advanced in their 'thought reform' than he. Such a cell usually had one leader who was responsible to the prison authorities, and the progress of the whole cell was made contingent upon the progress of the 'least reformed' member. This condition meant, in practice, that four or more cell members devoted all their energies to getting their 'least reformed' member to recognise the truth about himself and to confess. To accomplish this they typically swore at, harangued, beat, denounced, humiliated, reviled and brutalised their victim 24 hours a day, sometimes for weeks or months on end. If the authorities felt that the prisoner was basically uncooperative, they manacled his hands behind his back and chained his ankles, which made him completely dependent on his cell mates for the fulfilment of his basic needs.

It was this reduction to an animal-like existence in front of other humans, which, I believe, constituted the ultimate humiliation, and led most reliably to the destruction of the prisoner's image of himself. Even in his own eyes he became something which was not worthy of the regard of his fellow man.

If, to avoid complete physical and personal destruction, the prisoner began to confess in the manner desired of him, he was usually forced to prove his sincerity by making irrevocable behavioural commitments, such as denouncing and implicating his friends and relatives in his own newly recognised crimes. Once he had done this he became further alienated from his former self, even in his own eyes, and could seek security only in a new identity and new social relationships.

Aiding this process of confessing was the fact that the crimes gave the prisoner something concrete to which to attach the free-floating guilt which the accusing environment and his own humiliation usually stimulated.

A good example was the plight of the sick and wounded prisoners of war who, because of their physical confinement, were unable to escape from continual conflict with their interrogator or instructor, and who therefore often ended up forming a close relationship with him. Chinese communist instructors often encouraged prisoners to take long walks or have informal talks with them and offered as incentives cigarettes, tea and other rewards. If the prisoner was willing to cooperate and become a 'progressive', he could join with other 'progressives' in an active group life.

Within the political prison, the group cell not only provided the forces towards alienation but also offered the road to a 'new self'. Not only were there available among the fellow prisoners individuals with whom the prisoner could identify because of their shared plight, but once he showed any tendency to seek a new identity by truly trying to re-evaluate his past, he received again a whole range of rewards, of which perhaps the most important was the interpersonal information that he was again a person worthy of respect and regard.

Source: Schein (1960)

Discussion questions

1. To what extent is the self-concept a product of situational factors or inherited factors?

2. What is the relationship between self-knowledge and social pressure?

3. Is self-awareness constant, or do people become more and less self-aware over time?

4. What mechanisms could have been used by prisoners of war to resist the destruction of their self-concepts?

5. What could have been done to facilitate the reform of the self-concepts of prisoners?

6. What can be done to enhance a positive self-concept?

CASE STUDY **1.2**

DECISION DILEMMAS

For each of the five scenarios below, select the choice you would make if you were in the situation.

1. A young manager in a high technology firm was offered a position by the firm's chief competitor for almost double her salary. Her firm sought to prevent her from changing jobs, arguing that her knowledge of certain specialised manufacturing processes would give the competitor an unfair advantage. Since she had acquired that knowledge through special training and unique opportunities in her current position, the firm argued that it was unethical for her to accept the competitor's offer. What should the young manager do?

Accept the offer/Reject the offer

2. A consumer organisation conducted a survey to determine whether Bene beer was really more 'thirst quenching' than any other beer. After testing a number of other popular beers, each beer brand received approximately the same number of votes for quenching thirsts. The consumer group proposed that Bene should no longer advertise its product as being 'more thirst quenching' than its rivals. The company indicated that its own tests showed different results, and that the image of the beer was the important factor, not the test results. Should the advertisements cease or not?

Cease to advertise/Continue to advertise

3. After several profitable years, the Joe Jameson Organic Vitamin Company was made available for sale. Joe's film and TV appearances prevented him from keeping control of a large company, and it became apparent that, if present trends continued, the company would either have to expand substantially or lose a large share of the market. Several firms were interested in purchasing the company for the asking price, but one firm was particularly aggressive. It sponsored several parties and receptions in Joe's honour, a 35-foot yacht was made available for his use during the summer, and several gifts arrived during the holidays for family members. His wife questioned the propriety of these activities. Was it appropriate for him to accept the gifts? Should he sell to that firm?

Proper to accept/Not proper to accept
Should not sell/Should sell

4. Keith Waller was a successful athletics coach who had helped produce several international sprinters and long-distance runners. He was very vocal about the need to clean up the sport, and in particular about drug taking. He had heard rumours that some members of his athletics club had taken performance-enhancing drugs, but after confronting those he thought were involved he was satisfied with their assurances that the rumours were unfounded. At the beginning of the next track season he received conclusive evidence that seven club members had in fact taken drugs. What should Keith do?

Report them to the National Athletics Body/
Suspend them for part of the season/Warn them but do nothing

5. Roger's company had been battered by competition from Asian firms. Not only were their products selling for less money, but the quality was substantially higher. By investing in some high-technology equipment, and by fostering better union–management relations, Roger was relatively certain that the quality gap could be overcome. But his overhead rate was more than 40 per cent above the competitor firms. He thought that the most efficient way to lower costs would be to close one of his older sites, lay off the employees, and increase production in the newer plants. He knew just which plant to close. Unfortunately, the community depended on this factory as its major employer and had recently invested a great deal of money for road repair and street light construction around the site. Many of the workforce were older people who

had lived in the area most of their lives. It was unlikely that they could obtain alternative employment in the same area. Should Roger close the plant or not?

Close the plant/Do not close

Discussion questions

Form a small group and discuss the following questions regarding the previous five scenarios:

1. Why did you make the choices you did in each case? Justify each answer.
2. What principles or basic values for decision making did you use in each case?
3. What additional information would you need in order to be certain about your choices?
4. What circumstances might arise to make you change your mind about your decision? Could there be a different answer to each case in a different circumstance?
5. What do your answers tell you about your own values, cognitive style, attitude towards change and interpersonal orientation?

Skill Practice

EXERCISE **1.2**

IMPROVING SELF-AWARENESS THROUGH SELF-DISCLOSURE

In the nineteenth century the concept of 'looking-glass self' was developed to describe the process used by people to develop self-awareness. It means simply that other people serve as a 'looking-glass' for each of us. They reflect our actions and behaviours. In turn, we form our opinions of ourselves as a result of observing and interpreting this 'mirroring'. The best way to form accurate self-perceptions, therefore, is to share with others our thoughts, attitudes, feelings, actions and plans. This exercise helps you do that by asking you to analyse your own styles and inclinations and then share and discuss them with others. They may provide insights that you hadn't thought of.

Assignment

In a group of two or three, share your scores on the Skill Pre-assessment instruments with the others. Determine what similarities and differences exist among you. Do systematic ethnic or gender differences exist? Now complete the 11 statements listed below and say them out loud. Each person should complete each statement, but take turns at going first. The purpose of completing the statements aloud is to help you articulate aspects of your self-awareness and to receive reactions to them from others.

1. In taking the instruments, I was surprised by . . .

2. Some of my dominant characteristics captured by the instruments are . . .

3. Among my greatest strengths are . . .

4. Among my greatest weaknesses are . . .

5. The time I felt most successful was . . .

6. The time I felt least competent was . . .

7. My three highest priorities in life are . . .

8. The way in which I differ most from other people is . . .

9. I get along best with people who . . .

10. The best analogy that captures how I think of myself is . . .

11. From what you've said, I have noticed that you . . .

EXERCISE **1.3**

IDENTIFYING ASPECTS OF PERSONAL CULTURE

Not only do our experiences and interactions affect our self-concept, but each person enters this world with certain inclinations and talents, sometimes called 'temperament' by psychologists. This temperament may be developed both socially by our close family interactions and as a result of genetic factors.

This exercise helps you identify and analyse the major family influences that may have had an important impact on your values, attitudes, styles and personality. Not only is each person's physiology different, but each person's family culture is different as well. This exercise can help you highlight important aspects of your family culture.

Assignment

The outcome of this exercise will be a written autobiography. In order to help you prepare such a document, the following four steps should be completed. Use the results to construct an autobiography.

Step 1 On the chart in Figure 1.6, plot the points in each area of self-awareness that correspond to where you would ideally like to have scored. The vertical axis in the figure ranges from Very Satisfied to Very Dissatisfied. Your plots will represent your level of satisfaction with the scores you received on each instrument. For example, if you are satisfied with the score on the Defining Issues Test, make a mark near the top for 1. If you are dissatisfied with your score on Firo-B, make a mark near the bottom on 5. Connect each point so you have a 'self-awareness satisfaction profile'.

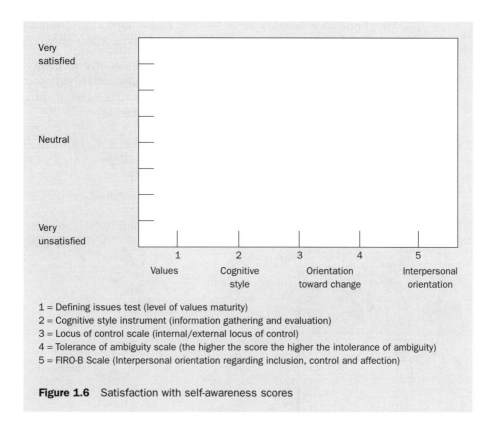

1 = Defining issues test (level of values maturity)
2 = Cognitive style instrument (information gathering and evaluation)
3 = Locus of control scale (internal/external locus of control)
4 = Tolerance of ambiguity scale (the higher the score the higher the intolerance of ambiguity)
5 = FIRO-B Scale (Interpersonal orientation regarding inclusion, control and affection)

Figure 1.6   Satisfaction with self-awareness scores

Step 2   On the chart in Figure 1.7, draw your lifeline, plotting the major activities and events of your life. The vertical axis represents the importance or significance of events in terms of their impact on who you are today and how you think. The horizontal axis represents time in years.

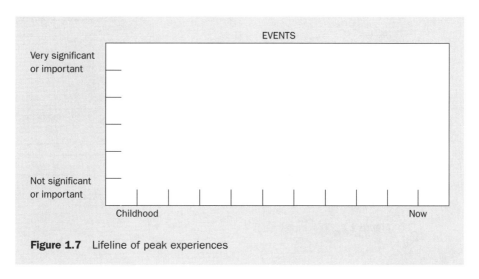

Figure 1.7   Lifeline of peak experiences

Your line should identify times that had major impact on forming your values, styles and orientations. Label each of these 'peak' experiences on your lifeline.

Step 3   On the chart in Figure 1.8, complete as much of your family tree as you can. Below each name, identify the major traits you associate with the person and the major way in which the person influenced your life. Then identify the way in which your family differs from other families you know.

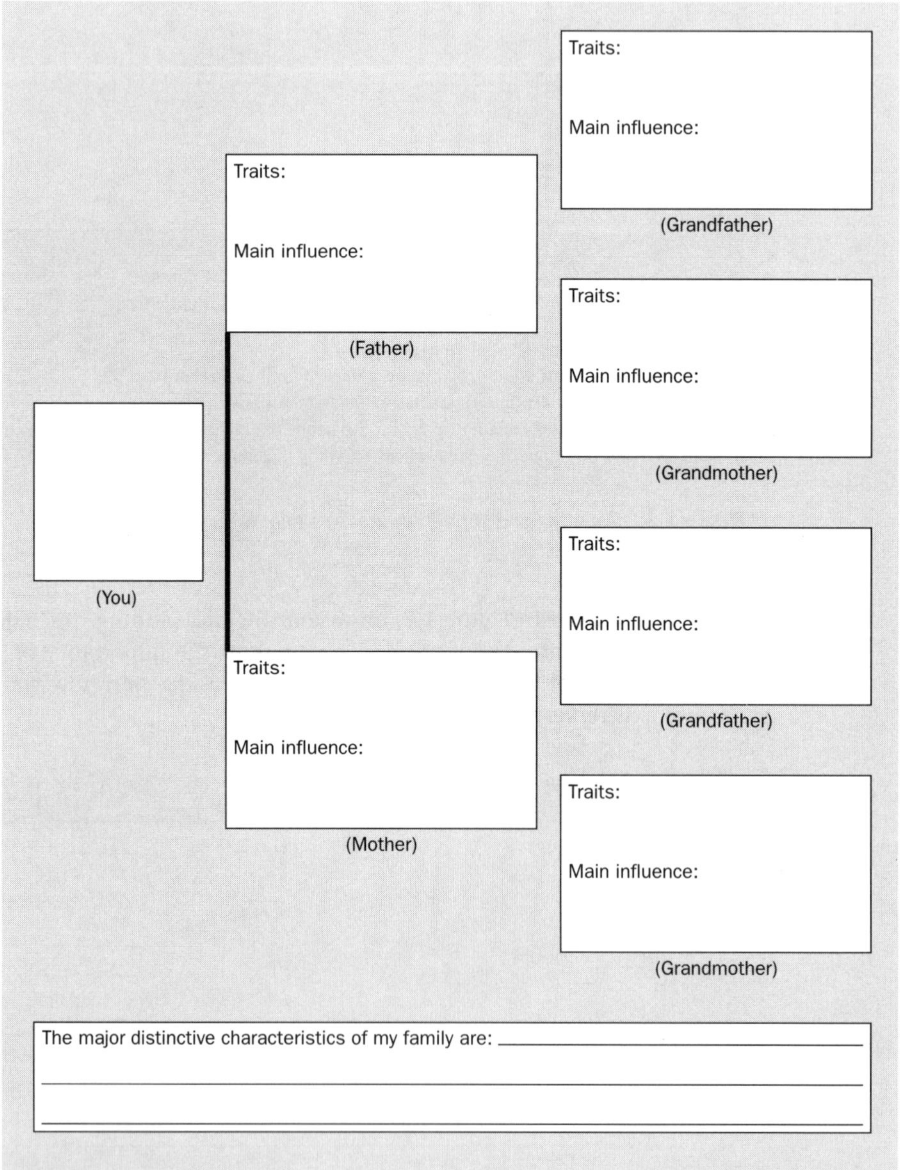

Traits:

Main influence:

(Grandfather)

Traits:

Main influence:

(Father)

Traits:

Main influence:

(Grandmother)

(You)

Traits:

Main influence:

(Grandfather)

Traits:

Main influence:

(Mother)

Traits:

Main influence:

(Grandmother)

The major distinctive characteristics of my family are: _____
_____
_____

Figure 1.8   The family tree

Step 4 Now combine all the information you have generated in steps 1, 2 and 3 and write an autobiography, essentially an answer to the question, 'Who am I?' Include in your autobiography your answers to the following five questions. Your analysis should include more than just the answers to these questions, but be sure to include them.

1. How would you describe your personal style?
2. What are your main strengths and weaknesses?
3. What behavioural principles lie at the centre of your life?
4. What do you want to achieve in the next five years?
5. What legacy do you want to leave with your life?

Skill Application

ACTIVITY **1.1**

SUGGESTED ASSIGNMENTS

1. Keep a diary for at least the remainder of this course. Record significant discoveries, insights, learning and personal recollections, not just daily activities. Write in your diary at least twice a week. Give yourself some feedback.

2. Write down the comprehensive, consistent and universal principles that guide your behaviour in all circumstances and that you will rarely violate.

3. After completing these personal assessment instruments and discussing their implications with someone else, write a statement or an essay responding to the following four questions:

   - Who am I?
   - What are my main strengths and weaknesses?
   - What do I want to achieve in my life?
   - What legacy do I want to leave?

4. Spend an evening with a close friend or relative discussing your values, cognitive style, attitude towards change and interpersonal orientation. You may want to have that person complete the instruments, giving his or her impressions of you, so you can compare and contrast your scores. Discuss implications for your future and for your relationship.

5. Teach someone else the value of self-awareness in managerial success, and explain the relevance of values maturity, cognitive style, attitudes towards change and interpersonal orientation. Describe the experience in your journal (see 2 above).

ACTIVITY **1.2**

APPLICATION PLAN AND EVALUATION

The intent of this exercise is to help you apply your skills in a real-life, out-of-class setting. Now that you have become familiar with the behavioural guidelines that form the basis of effective skill performance, you will improve the most by trying out those guidelines in an everyday context. The trouble is, unlike a classroom activity in which feedback is immediate and others can assist you with their evaluations, this skill application activity is one you must accomplish and evaluate on your own. There are two parts to this activity. Part 1 helps prepare you to apply the skill. Part 2 helps you evaluate and improve on your experience. Be sure to actually write down answers to each item. Don't short-circuit the process by skipping steps.

Part 1: Plan

1. Write down the two or three aspects of this skill that are most important to you. These may be areas of weakness, areas you most want to improve, or areas that are most salient to a problem you face currently. Identify the specific aspects of this skill that you want to apply.

2. Now identify the setting or the situation in which you will apply this skill. Establish a plan for performance by actually writing down the situation. Who else will be involved? When will you do it? Where will it be done?

3. Identify the specific behaviours you will engage in to apply this skill. Convert the theory into practice.

4. What are the indicators of successful performance? How will you know you have succeeded in being effective? What will indicate that you have performed competently?

Part 2: Evaluation

5. After you have completed your implementation, record the results. What happened? How successful were you? What was the effect on others?

6. How can you improve? What modifications can you make next time? What will you do differently in a similar situation in the future?

7. Looking back on your whole skill practice and application experience, what have you learned? What has been surprising? In what ways might this experience help you in the long term?

Further reading

Institute of Management Foundation (1998) *Test your management skills: the management self-assessment test on disk*. Oxford: Butterworth–Heinemann. (Diskette)

Norton, R. and Burt, V. (1997) *Practical self-development*. London: Institute of Management Foundation.

Palmer, S. (1998) *People and self management*. Oxford: Butterworth-Heinemann.

Pedler, M. Burgoyne, J. and Boydell, T. (1994) *A manager's guide to self-development*, 3rd edn. Maidenhead: McGraw-Hill.

Scutt, C.N. (1997) *Personal effectiveness*. Oxford: Butterworth-Heinemann.

CHAPTER 2

Managing Stress

SKILL DEVELOPMENT OUTLINE

Skill Pre-assessment surveys

- Stress management
- Time management
- Type A personality inventory
- Social Readjustment Rating Scale (SRRS)-Life Change Units (LCU)

Skill Learning material

- Stress at work
- Stress for individuals
- Stressors
- Eliminating stressors
- Developing resilience
- Temporary stress-reduction techniques
- Summary
- Behavioural guidelines

Skill Analysis cases

- The day at the beach
- The case of the missing time

Skill Practice exercises

- The small-wins strategy

Skill Application activities

- Life-balance analysis
- Deep relaxation
- Monitoring and managing Time
- Personal stressors
- Teaching others
- Implement techniques
- Application plan and evaluation

LEARNING OBJECTIVES

To increase proficiency in:

- eliminating stressors
- developing resilience
- coping with temporary stress

INTRODUCTION

Stress, like change, is an ever-present and growing element in our lives, as students and as managers. Unfortunately many books on stress tend to deal with the clinical aspects – they are not designed for 'well people'. In this book we hope to strike a balance. We accept that stress is a part of all our working lives and that without stress not only would things be intolerably dull for most of us, but also very few things would be done. Tolerable levels of stress are the winding mechanism of our world. As individuals we develop strategies to deal with accustomed levels of stress. We have simple techniques for dealing with temporary surges and stronger techniques for negotiating our way out of uncomfortable but predictable pressures. We can 'stand on the shoulders' of those before us and learn from their skills and application. However, we also need to recognise that prolonged and personally intolerable levels of stress can lead to serious illness, although we have, as a right, the alternative of engineering our lives so that this does not occur. This book does not suggest that we all take up farming in one of the remote places of the world, but that there are easily acquired skills that will make our lives easier, and more personally fulfilling and fruitful, without financial penalty. The skills we will discuss will assist us in our studies and make us more efficient and effective in our jobs. By learning about stress in what we feel is a stress-free way, we will not only help ourselves but also those around us. Stress is a contagious disease. Therefore, we are offering a diagnosis, a prognosis and helpful advice towards a cure, all of which you can practise in the safety of these pages before trying them out in what you may find to be an unforgiving world.

Skill Pre-assessment

We will begin with a number of surveys designed to:

- explore your own responses to situations you may find stressful
- look at the techniques you use to manage your own time
- help you to establish a personality *type*
- consider the factors that others find stressful and introduce you to methods of coping.

As with the rest of the book, we would like you to complete the questionnaires before starting the chapter. We feel the process will set the agenda for what is to follow. The first questionnaire is designed for acting managers but may well provide you, if you are a student, with insights of the managerial world. After completing the chapter, the readers should be able to relate what they have read, and hopefully discussed, to their own world and set about personal action planning.

SURVEY **2.1**

STRESS MANAGEMENT

Step 1 For each statement circle a number on the rating scale in the Pre-assessment column on the left. Your answers should reflect your attitudes and behaviour as they are **now**, not as you would like them to be. Be honest. When you have completed the survey, use the scoring key in Appendix 1 to identify the skill areas discussed that are most important for you to master. The process of improving these skill areas should help you with your learning objectives.

Step 2 When you have completed the chapter and the Skill Application assign-ments, review your responses in the right-hand Post-assessment column to measure your progress. If your score remains low in specific skill areas, use the behavioural guidelines at the end of the Skill Learning section to guide your Application Planning.

RATING SCALE

1 = Strongly disagree   **2** = Disagree   **3** = Slightly disagree
4 = Slightly agree   **5** = Agree   **6** = Strongly agree

	Assessment	
	Pre-	Post-
When faced with stressful or time-pressured situations		
1. I make lists, set priorities, use time diaries to manage my time well.	____	____
2. I maintain a programme of regular exercise for fitness.	____	____
3. I maintain trusting relationships with those with whom I can share my frustrations.	____	____
4. I practice relaxation techniques such as deep breathing and muscle relaxation.	____	____
5. I make sure that less important things don't drive out the more important.	____	____
6. I maintain balance in my life by pursuing interests outside of work.	____	____
7. I have a good relationship with someone who serves as mentor or adviser.	____	____
8. I use other people appropriately to complete what has to be done.	____	____
9. I encourage people who come to me with problems or concerns to consider solutions, not just questions.	____	____
10. I strive to redefine problems as opportunities for improvement.	____	____
When I get others to do things for me		
11. I check they have the means and authority to do what needs to be done.	____	____
12. I specify clearly what I want achieved and how much they can do without referring it back to me.	____	____
13. I delegate effectively passing on information and providing resources.	____	____

14. When I delegate I explain exactly what is required.   ___ ___

15. I monitor and maintain accountability for delegated tasks on a regular basis   ___ ___

SURVEY **2.2**

TIME MANAGEMENT

Students and practising managers need to manage their time. The first section of the questionnaire is universal but the second section, although it may provide insights for students, is designed specifically for working managers.

In responding to the statements, circle the number that indicates the frequency with which you do each activity. Assess your behaviour as it is, not as you would like it to be. How useful this questionnaire will be depends on your ability to assess your own behaviour.

Turn to Appendix 1 to find the scoring key and an interpretation of your scores.

RATING SCALE

0 = Never   **1** = Seldom   **2** = Sometimes   **3** = Usually   **4** = Always

---

Section I

1. I read selectively, skimming until I find what is important, then highlighting it.   0 1 2 3 4

2. I make a list of tasks to accomplish each day.   0 1 2 3 4

3. I keep everything in its proper place at work.   0 1 2 3 4

4. I prioritise the tasks I have to do according to their importance and urgency.   0 1 2 3 4

5. I concentrate on one major task at a time, but do multiple trivial tasks together.   0 1 2 3 4

6. I make a list of short five- or ten-minute tasks to do.   0 1 2 3 4

7. I divide large projects into smaller, separate stages.   0 1 2 3 4

8. I identify the 20 per cent of my tasks that will produce 80 per cent of the results.   0 1 2 3 4

9. I do the most important tasks at my best time during the day.   0 1 2 3 4

10. I arrange to have some time during each day when I can work uninterrupted.   0 1 2 3 4

11. I don't procrastinate. I do today what needs to be done.   0 1 2 3 4

12. I keep track of the use of my time with devices such as a time log.   0 1 2 3 4

13. I set deadlines for myself.   0 1 2 3 4

14. I do something productive whenever I am waiting.   0 1 2 3 4

15. I try to confine my fire-fighting to one set time during the day.   0 1 2 3 4

16. I set myself targets to finish at least one thing every day.   0 1 2 3 4

17. I set some time during the day for personal time – thinking, planning, exercise.   **0 1 2 3 4**

18. I confine my time for 'worrying' to one particular time during the day.   **0 1 2 3 4**

19. I have clearly defined long-term objectives towards which I work.   **0 1 2 3 4**

20. I always seek to find ways to use my time more efficiently.   **0 1 2 3 4**

Section II: for working managers

1. I hold routine meetings at the end of the day.   **0 1 2 3 4**

2. I hold all short meetings informally – sitting or standing appropriately.   **0 1 2 3 4**

3. I set a time limit at the outset of each meeting.   **0 1 2 3 4**

4. I cancel scheduled meetings that are not necessary.   **0 1 2 3 4**

5. I have a written agenda circulated before each meeting.   **0 1 2 3 4**

6. I stick to the agenda so that all understand their required actions for each item.   **0 1 2 3 4**

7. I ensure that someone takes minutes and watches the time.   **0 1 2 3 4**

8. I start all meetings on time wherever possible.   **0 1 2 3 4**

9. I prepare prompt action minutes of meetings and follow them through.   **0 1 2 3 4**

10. When people come with problems I listen and ask them to suggest solutions.   **0 1 2 3 4**

11. I meet visitors in the doorway.   **0 1 2 3 4**

12. I go to subordinates' offices when feasible so that I can control when I leave.   **0 1 2 3 4**

13. I leave at least one-fourth of my day free from meetings and appointments.   **0 1 2 3 4**

14. I have someone else who can answer my calls and greet visitors where possible.   **0 1 2 3 4**

15. I have one place where I can work without being interrupted.   **0 1 2 3 4**

16. I process all the papers I receive – action or ignore – nothing is 'held'.   **0 1 2 3 4**

17. I keep my workplace clear of everything except the things I am working on.   **0 1 2 3 4**

18. I work to delegate tasks where others have the background and skills to assist.   **0 1 2 3 4**

19. I define the freedom of initiative others have when I delegate a task.   **0 1 2 3 4**

20. I am happy to let others take the credit for tasks they accomplish.   **0 1 2 3 4**

SURVEY **2.3**

TYPE A PERSONALITY INVENTORY

Rate the extent to which each of the following statements is typical of you most of the time. Focus on your general way of behaving and feeling. There are no right or wrong answers. When you have finished, turn to the scoring key in Appendix 1 to interpret your scores.

RATING SCALE

The statement is:
1, not typical of me;   **2**, somewhat typical of me;   **3**, typical of me

---

1. My greatest satisfaction comes from doing things better than others.   ____

2. I tend to bring the theme of a conversation around to things I'm interested in.   ____

3. In conversations, I use strong movements to emphasise my points.   ____

4. I move, walk and eat rapidly.   ____

5. I feel as though I can accomplish more than others.   ____

6. I feel guilty when I relax or do nothing for several hours or days.   ____

7. It doesn't take much to get me to argue.   ____

8. I feel impatient with the rate at which most events take place.   ____

9. Having more than others is important to me.   ____

10. One aspect of my life (e.g. work, family care, school, etc.) dominates all others.   ____

11. I frequently regret not being able to control my temper.   ____

12. I find myself hurrying others in conversation and even finishing their sentences for them.   ____

13. People who avoid competition have low self-confidence.   ____

14. To do something well you have to concentrate and screen out all distractions.   ____

15. I feel others' mistakes and errors cause me needless aggravation.   ____

16. I find it intolerable to watch others perform tasks I know I can do faster.   ____

17. Getting ahead in my job is a major personal goal.   ____

18. I simply don't have enough time to lead a well-balanced life.   ____

19. I take out my frustration with my own imperfections on others.   ____

20. I frequently try to do two or more things simultaneously.   ____

21. When I encounter a competitive person, I feel a need to challenge him or her.   ____

22. I tend to fill up my spare time with thoughts and activities related to my work.   ____

23. I am frequently upset by the unfairness of life.   ____

24. I find it anguishing to wait in line.   ____

Source: Adapted from Friedman and Rosenman (1974)

SURVEY **2.4**

SOCIAL READJUSTMENT RATING SCALE (SRRS) — LIFE CHANGE UNITS (LCU)

Consider this table and answer the questions that follow.

Life event	Rank '65	LCU '65	Rank '95	LCU '95
Death of spouse	1	100	1	119
Divorce	2	73	2	98
Marital separation from mate	3	65	4	79
Detention in jail or other institution	4	63	7	75
Death of a close family member	5	63	3	92
Major personal injury or illness	6	53	6	77
Marriage	7	50	19	50
Losing your job	8	47	5	79
Marital reconciliation with partner	9	45	13	57
Retirement from work	10	45	16	54
Major change in the health or behaviour of a family member	11	44	14	56
Pregnancy	12	40	9	66
Sexual difficulties	13	39	21	45
Gaining a new family member	14	39	12	57
Major business readjustment	15	39	10	62
Major change in financial state	16	38	15	56
Death of a close friend	17	37	8	70
Change to a different type of work	18	36	17	51
Change in form or number of arguments with spouse	19	35	18	51
Taking out a mortgage or loan for a major purchase	20	31	23	44
Foreclosure on a mortgage or loan	21	30	11	61
Major change in responsibilities at work	22	29	24	43
Son or daughter leaving home	23	29	22	44
Trouble with in-laws	24	29	28	38
Outstanding personal achievement	25	28	29	37
Spouse beginning or ceasing work outside the home	26	26	20	46
Beginning or ending formal education	27	26	27	38
Major change in living conditions	28	25	25	42
Change in personal habits	29	24	36	27
Trouble with the boss	30	23	33	29
Major change in working hours or conditions	31	20	30	36
Moving home	32	20	26	41
Change to a new college, school, university	33	20	31	35
Major change in usual type and/or amount of recreation	34	19	34	29
Major change in outside activities – church, etc.	35	19	42	22
Major change in social activities	36	18	38	27
Taking out a mortgage or loan for a lesser purchase	37	17	35	28
Major change in sleeping habits	38	16	40	26
Major change in number of family get-togethers	39	15	39	26
Major change in eating habits	40	15	37	27
Holiday	41	13	41	25
Christmas	42	12	32	30
Minor violations of the law	43	11	43	22
Grand Mean LCU values (for all events)		**34**		**49**

Sources: Miller *et al.* (1997); Holmes and Rahe (1967)

EXERCISE BASED ON THE SRRS

SOURCES OF PERSONAL STRESS

1. Identify the factors that produced the most stress for you over the past few years. Consider whether there is a pattern?

2. Accepting that the relative value of the stressors given in the above table are based on work in the USA in 1965 and then 20 years later using samples of some 400 people, compare how seriously your 'life events' affected you on the same scale of 1 to 100. Thus 'major personal injury or illness' is sixth with a relative value as a stressor of 77 (53 in 1965) and in your view 'Personal injury' would only have an impact of say 30 – What helped you cope?

List the factors that give you most stress and keep these in your mind as you complete the chapter.

Skill Learning

Stress at work

The prevalence of stress

The problems currently associated with stress at work appear to be particularly acute and are becoming worse in Europe and the USA. Miller and Rahr (1997), working in the USA, found the top 43 stressors were now 45 per cent more stressful than they were in 1965. We will discuss the pattern of change later. Stress is not an issue for individuals in the abstract, the effects of stress are important commercially. Charlesworth (1997), working specifically with managers the Institute of Management, conducted a survey of 1,100 managers and showed that 270,000 people take time off every day through work-related stress at a total cost to the economy of £7 billion. He found that 85 per cent of the respondents reported increased workloads and 50 per cent agreed that they had a 'great increase in workload since 1994'. The Samaritans, a charity in the UK dealing with individuals considering suicide, showed stress as having more sinister consequences. This was confirmed by a study for the British Heart Foundation which has estimated that coronary heart disease costs £200 per employee per year and that some coronary heart disease can be attributable to stress. Davidson and Sutherland (1993), however, suggest an indirect linkage. Common behavioural responses to stress, such as cigarette smoking, poor dietary habits, physical inactivity and/or escapist drinking, are all risk factors for cardiovascular disease. Thus, as a consequence, stress may be both directly and indirectly implicated as a causal factor in the aetiology of heart disease.

The financial cost of stress to industry

The costs of work-related stress, however, extend beyond coronary heart disease. Kearns (1986) comments that 60 per cent of absence from work is caused by stress-related illness, while Gill (1987) reports that approximately 100 million working days are lost each year because people cannot face going to work. Additionally, Cooper *et al.* (1988) note that there is mounting evidence to suggest that days lost in British Industry due to mental and stress-related causes are on the increase. This view is further endorsed by a recent estimate completed by Summers (1990) for the Confederation of British Industry, which showed the annual cost of stress-related absenteeism in labour turnover to be around £1.5 billion. A further factor is the growing movement to litigation. Ian Campbell (1995) details recent successful compensation claims over work-related stress. His advice is that companies would be wise to introduce risk management programmes to avoid such claims in the future. He sees the programmes as having the direct effect of avoiding litigation and also of combating lost productivity.

The cost to individuals

The personal costs of job-related stress can be very high. This example is adapted from an Associated Press article.

Patrick was an ambulance attendant and the job was getting to him. He was becoming too involved in the continuous insights into personal tragedy and the personal alienation caused by the shift pattern. His marriage was in trouble and his only child was having respiratory problems that could well involve an operation. He was drinking too much. One night it all blew up.

On the way to pick up his ambulance a new manager called him over and told him that his cab was dirty and he should have it cleaned before meeting the public. Patrick dumped his frustrations and had to be restrained from hitting the 'new broom'.

His mildest comment was: 'If you came out and did the job instead of sitting at a desk you would not worry about ashtrays.' The manager was left forming a report that Patrick thought might well lose him his job. He desperately needed the money.

It was Patrick's turn to ride in the back while his partner drove. Their first call was for a man whose leg had been cut off by a train. His screaming and agony were horrifying, but the second call was worse. It was a child beating. As the attendant treated the youngster's bruised body and snapped bones, he thought of his own child. His fury grew.

Immediately after leaving the child at the hospital, the attendants were sent out to help a heart attack victim seen lying in a street. When they arrived, however, they found not a cardiac patient but a drunk who had passed out. As they lifted the man into the ambulance, their frustration and anger came to a head. They decided to give the drunk a ride he would remember.

The ambulance vaulted over railroad tracks at high speed. The driver took the corners as fast as he could, flinging the drunk from side to side in the back. To the attendants, it was a joke.

Suddenly, the drunk began having a real heart attack. The attendant in the back leaned over the drunk and started shouting. 'Die, you fool!' he yelled. 'Die!' He watched as the drunk shuddered. He watched as the drunk died. By the time they reached the hospital, they had their stories straight. Dead on arrival, they said. Nothing they could do.

Patrick talked about that night in a counselling session on 'professional burnout' – a growing problem in high-stress jobs.

As this story illustrates, stress can produce totally dysfunctional outcomes – a man in this case was killed. Less dramatically, the personal outcomes can range from the inability to concentrate, through anxiety and depression, stomach disorders and heart disease. Overall we have a loss of personal resilience to disease of all types. For organisations, consequences range from absenteeism and job dissatisfaction, to high accident and turnover rates.

The role of management

A 25-year study of employee surveys revealed that incompetent management is the largest cause of workplace stress. In three out of the four surveys employees put their relationships with their immediate supervisors as the worst aspect of the job. Research shows that stress not only affects the physical well-being of workers but also produces less visible (though equally detrimental) consequences in the workplace. Thus dysfunctionally stressed managers tend to:

- perceive information selectively and see only that which confirms their previous biases
- become very intolerant of ambiguity and demanding of right answers
- consider only a single approach to a problem
- overestimate how fast time is passing (hence, they always feel rushed)
- adopt a short-term perspective or crisis mentality and cease to consider long-term implications
- have less ability to make fine distinctions in problems, so that complexity and nuances are missed
- consult and listen to others less
- rely on old habits to cope with current situations
- have less ability to generate creative thoughts and unique solutions to problems

Sources: Staw *et al.* (1981); Weick (1984)

Stress affects employees in a personally negative way and reduces the effective behaviour – listening, making good decisions, solving problems effectively, planning, and generating new ideas. Developing the skill of managing stress therefore can have significant advantages to all concerned. The ability to deal appropriately with stress not only enhances individual self-development, but can also have an enormous financial impact on entire organisations.

Unfortunately, most of the scientific literature on stress focuses on its consequences. Too little examines how to cope effectively with stress and even less addresses how to prevent stress. We begin our discussion by presenting a framework for understanding stress and learning how to cope with it. Here we will explain the major types of stressors faced by managers, the primary reactions to stress and the reasons some people experience more negative reactions than others. In the last section, we will present principles for managing and adapting to stress, along with specific examples and behavioural guidelines.

Stress for individuals

One way to understand the dynamics of stress is to think of it as the product of a 'force field' (Lewin, 1951). Kurt Lewin suggested that all individuals and organisations exist in an environment filled with reinforcing or opposing forces (i.e., stresses). These forces act to stimulate or inhibit the performance desired by the individual. Figure 2.1 indicates this – a person's level of performance in organisation results with stress from factors that may either complement or contradict one another. Certain forces drive or motivate changes in behaviour, while other forces restrain or block those changes.

According to Lewin's theory, the forces affecting individuals are normally balanced in the force field. The strength of the driving forces is exactly matched by the strength of the restraining forces. (In the figure, longer arrows indicate stronger forces.) Performance changes when the forces become out of balance. If the driving forces become stronger than the restraining forces, or more numerous or enduring, then change occurs. Conversely, if restraining forces become stronger or more numerous than driving forces, change occurs in the opposite direction. Feelings of stress are a product of a combination of stressors from inside ourselves or from our immediate environment. These stressors are the driving forces in our model; they exert pressure on the individuals to change their existing levels of performance – physiologically, psychologically and interpersonally. Unrestrained, those forces can lead to pathological results (e.g., anxiety, heart disease and mental breakdown). However, most people have developed a certain resilience, or restraining forces, to counteract the stressors thus inhibiting their pathological effects. These restraining forces include behaviour patterns, psychological characteristics and supportive

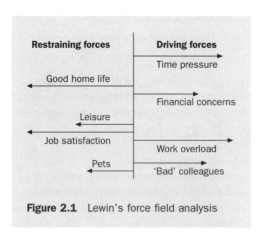

Figure 2.1 Lewin's force field analysis

social relationships. Strong restraining forces lead to low heart rates, good interpersonal relationships, emotional stability and effective stress management. Without the restraining forces, which have to be developed by individuals over time, the stressors reign.

Of course, stress produces positive as well as negative effects. In the absence of any stress, people feel completely bored and lack any inclination to act. Even when high levels of stress are experienced, equilibrium can be restored quickly if sufficient resilience is present. In the case of the ambulance driver, for example, multiple stressors overpowered the available restraining forces and burnout occurred. Before such an extreme state is reached, however, individuals typically progress through three stages of reactions: an alarm stage, a resistance stage, and an exhaustion stage.

Reactions and defence mechanisms

We all have our own first sign of being under stress – a first sign may be prickly heat in the legs, or a sudden wish to go to the toilet or perhaps a dryness of the mouth. As functioning adults we recognise these first signs and ignore them at our peril. We accept the first alarm sign as a notice of anxiety or fear, recognising that some stressor is perceived by us as a threat, or by sorrow or depression if the stressor is perceived as a loss. A feeling of shock or confusion may result if the stressor is particularly acute. Physiologically, the individual's energy resources are mobilised and heart rate, blood pressure and alertness increase – hence the prickly heat from our flooded capillaries or the dryness of the mouth. The reactions are largely self-correcting if the stressor is of brief duration, but if the stressor continues we move into a resistance stage, in which defence mechanisms predominate and the body begins to store up excess energy. In the veldt of our ancestors we were preparing for 'fight or flight', but in the office, these responses are seldom appropriate; however, our bodies do not know this.

Five types of defence mechanism are typical of most people who experience extended levels of stress.

1. Aggressive – the stressor is attacked directly. It may also involve violence against oneself, other people or even objects (e.g., kicking the table).
2. Regression – the adoption of patterns of response that were successful earlier, perhaps in childhood (childish behaviours such as sulking).
3. Denial – forgetting, avoiding or redefining the stressor.
4. Escape – in physical or psychological form including an escape to fantasy.

   > We were working with a manager whose company was taken over by a larger group and whose job was definitely at risk. He chose to take a three-week holiday in India until the 'noise' subsided. His defence mechanism was successful and against all the odds he resumed his job as Personnel Director – now of the extended group.

5. Fixation – a response repeated of its effectiveness – repeatedly redialling a phone number or rechecking that we have 'all the notes'.

If our defence mechanisms work to reduce such symptoms as high blood pressure, anxiety or other disorders the only signs of prolonged stress need be

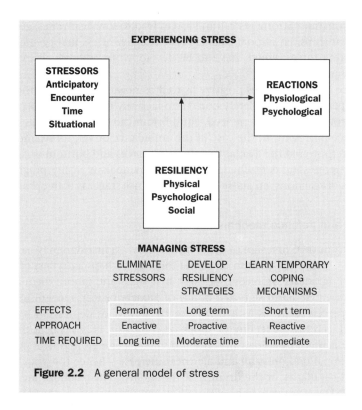

Figure 2.2 A general model of stress

an increase in apparent defensiveness. However, if the pressures overwhelm our defences, our available energy is exhausted and the body may well be defeated.

While each reaction stage may be experienced as being uncomfortable, the exhaustion stage is the most dangerous. When stressors overpower or outlast the resilient capacity of individuals, or their ability to defend against them, negative personal and organisational consequences may well occur. The consequences may be physiological (heart disease, ulcers), psychological (severe depression) or interpersonally (hostility).

Figure 2.2 identifies the major categories of stressors (driving forces) managers experience, as well as the major attributes of resilience (restraining forces) that inhibit the negative aspects of stress.

Coping with stress

Individuals vary in the extent to which they are affected by stress. Some people are what Eliot and Breo (1984) labelled 'hot reactors', meaning they have a predisposition to experience extremely negative reactions to stress. For others, stress has less serious consequences. Think in terms of some athletes who perform at their peak in 'the big game' while others are crushed. Managers are no different.

Our physical condition, personality characteristics and social support mechanisms work with us producing resiliency or the capacity to cope effectively with stress. In

Table 2.1 Coping strategies

Approach	Short term	Medium term	Long term
	Immediate Reactive Example – relaxation techniques	Delayed Proactive Examples – job redesign, life style changes. . . .	Considered Proactive – eliminate the stressor Example – divorce, quitting job . . .

effect, resiliency serves as a form of inoculation against the effects of stress. It eliminates exhaustion. One classification of those most liable to 'suffer' from dysfunctional stress reaction is the Type A Personality Inventory, the interpretation of which is given in the 'scoring key' at the end of the book.

An effective way of coping with stress can be seen through a hierarchy of strategies for personal stress management, the most effective being those concerned with managing stress.

The most obvious way to manage stress is to eliminate or minimise the stressors by simply eliminating the situations that cause them – the proactive strategy (Weick, 1979). In practice few of us have complete control over our environment or circumstances and elimination or avoidance is more easily said than done in the short or medium term. Imagine a broker on the floor of the stockmarket – the job is *about* stress and he or she can always leave if the pressure does not suit. A second approach that the broker will certainly adopt to survive, and retain the job, is to try to increase his or her personal resiliency – the proactive strategy (Table 2.1). He or she may develop ways of releasing tensions in sport, take up yoga or reduce weight. Both these strategies take time and a reactive short-term may well be the best way to handle the immediate issues. Reactive strategies such as controlled breathing can be applied on the spot as temporary remedies against the ill effects of stress when the first warning signs are recognised. Relaxation techniques are covered later in the chapter. Most people do rely first on temporary reactive methods to cope with stress because these actions can be implemented immediately. But reactive strategies also have to be repeated whenever stressors are encountered because their effects are short-lived. The unwise broker may adopt dysfunctional short-term strategies such as excessive alcohol intake, heavy smoking, sleeping pills or letting off steam through anger. All these can become habit-forming and harmful in themselves. We need to put medium-term strategies into place whenever we realise that the stressors that get to us are persistent. It takes more time and effort to develop proactive resiliency strategies, but although the payoff is delayed the effects are more long-lasting. The best and most permanent strategies are those that eliminate stressors altogether. They require the longest time to implement and may involve complex arrangements but since the stress is purged, the payoff is enduring. It is our choice whether we, as the stockbroker, wish to continue with the material rewards of weathering stress or live longer. It is no surprise that many trading floor workers plan for an early retirement. Death is God's way of saying slow down!

Stressors

In the next section we will work through the three components of the stress model shown in Figure 2.2.

Classification of stressors

Time stressors generally result from having too much to do in too little time, or the exact opposite. These are the most common and most pervasive sources of stress faced by managers in corporations (Mintzberg, 1973; Carlson, 1951; Sayles, 1964).

> In the story of the ambulance drivers presented earlier, time stressors were evidenced by the driver's work overload – the drivers felt compelled to accomplish a large number of tasks in a short time, but were not in control of the time available.
>
> Our culture seems obsessed with time and appears to grow more time conscious every year. The bleeping wrist watch alarms may have been replaced by the mobile phones, but the purpose is the same – to make use of our every moment, as if there is some great time diary in the sky. This constant concern with time is a significant source of stress. A variety of researchers, for example, have studied the relationships between being expected to take on an increasing range of potentially conflicting, ambiguous responsibilities and chronic time pressures, against the psychological and physiological dysfunctions (French and Caplan, 1972). The researchers found significant relationships between the presence of time stressors and job dissatisfaction, tension, perceived threat, heart rate, cholesterol levels, skin resistance and other factors.

The presence of temporary time stressors, however, may serve as motivators for getting work done; some individuals accomplish much more when faced with an immediate deadline than when left to work at their own pace. Against this, a constant state of time pressure – having too much to do and not enough time to do it – is usually harmful.

Encounter stressors

Encounter stressors are caused by flawed interpersonal interactions. Quarrels debilitate, be they with friends, flatmates, or one's spouse. Trying to work with an employee or supervisor with whom there has been an interpersonal conflict, or trying to accomplish a task in a group that is divided by lack of trust and cohesion, is often unproductive and usually stressful.

> For Patrick the ambulance man, the encounter stressor that 'wound him up' was the meeting with the new manager. His cab was dirty and in other circumstances he would have acknowledged the fault and the manager's right to comment. This particular night the incident was one factor that led to manslaughter.

Encounter stressors arise from three types of conflicts:

- Role conflicts, in which roles performed by group members are incompatible
- Issue conflicts, in which disagreement exists over how to define or solve a problem
- Interaction conflicts, in which individuals fail to get along well because of mutual antagonism (Hamner and Organ, 1978).

In our own research we have found that encounter stressors in organisations can reduce both work satisfaction and actual productivity (Cameron, Kim and Whetten, 1987 a & b). Other workers have found encounter stressors to be at the very heart of most organisational dysfunction (Likert, 1967), most frequently affecting managers with responsibility for people rather than for equipment. The highest levels of encounter stress exist among managers who interact frequently with other people and have responsibility for individuals in the workplace (French and Caplan, 1972). Mishra (1993), reviewer of literature on interpersonal trust, showed that a lack of trust among individuals not only blocks effective communication, information sharing, decision competence and problem-solving capabilities, but also results in high levels of personal stress. In a United States survey of workers, encounter stressors were cited as a major cause of burnout. When workers were reported as feeling not free to interact socially, experiencing workplace conflict, not being able to talk openly to managers, feeling unsupported by fellow employees, being stifled by red tape, and not feeling recognised, burnout was significantly higher than when those encounter stressors were not present. Of the ten most significant stressors associated with burnout, seven dealt with encounter stressors. The other three were situational stressors, to which we turn next.

Situational stressors

Situational stressors arise from the environment in which a person lives or from individual circumstances. One of the most common forms of situational stress is a poor working environment. For the ambulance drivers, for example, this would include continual crises, long hours and isolation from colleagues.

One of the most well-researched links between situational stressors and negative consequences involves rapid change, particularly the effects of changes in life events (Wolff *et al.*, 1950; Holmes and Rahe, 1970; Miller and Rahe, 1997). The Social Readjustment Rating Scale (SRRS) was introduced in 1967 to track the number of changes some 427 individuals had experienced over the past 12 months. Since changes in some events were thought to be more stressful than others, a scaling method was used to assign weights to each life event. Numerous studies among a variety of cultures, age groups and occupations have confirmed the relative weightings in the 1967 instrument (see Rahe *et al.*, 1980) which generally hold true regardless of culture, age or occupation. You completed this instrument in the Pre-assessment section and may like to look at your own rating now.

Statistical relationships between the amount of life-event change and physical illness and injury have been found consistently among managers (Kobasa, 1979), sports figures (Holmes and Masuda, 1974), naval personnel (Rahe, 1974), and the general population (Jenkins, 1976). For example, scores of 150 points or below result in a probability of less than 37 per cent that a serious illness will occur in the next year, but the probability increases to about 50 per cent with scores of 151–300. Those who score over 300 on the SRRS have an 80 per cent chance of serious illness (Holmes and Rahe, 1967).

Holmes and Holmes (1970) studied the extent to which daily health changes occurred as a result of life-event changes. Rather than focusing on major illness or injuries, they recorded minor symptoms such as headache, nausea, fever, backache, eyestrain, etc., over 1,300 work days. The results revealed high correlations between scores in life-event changes and the chronic presence of these symptoms. As we have pointed out earlier, a 45 per cent increase the mean value of the intensity of the events has been recorded over a 30-year period. The change of the ranking of the events may show specific changes in American society based on and not be reflected in European culture. We must caution, of course, that a high score on the SRRS does not necessarily mean that an individual is going to become ill or be injured – they are average values. A variety of coping skills and personal characteristics, to be discussed later, may counteract those tendencies. The point to be made here is that situational stressors are important factors to consider in learning to manage stress skilfully. For example, we were using the SRRS with a group of Hungarian managers, one of whom was an interpreter. She reported that in one year of her life she had a score of over 300. Wanting to talk, she explained that she had been released from Auschwitz, got married and had her first child – all in one year. In 1995 she still looked remarkably well for her years.

Anticipatory stressors

Anticipatory stressors arise from disagreeable events that we feel could occur – unpleasant things that have not yet happened, but might happen. Stress results from the anticipation or fear of the event.

Patrick, the Ambulance man, was concerned for his child and what might happen 'if she needed an operation', the boss's report and losing his job plus the consequences of having no money and the possibility of being found out about the drunk. Anticipatory stressors were probably the focus of his counselling sessions. We have met many people like Patrick in our work and getting them to face 'the worst scenario' is a great challenge.

Anticipatory stressors can be used for manipulation. Schein (1960) reported that dramatic behavioural and psychological changes occurred in American prisoners in the Korean War. He identified anticipatory stressors (e.g., threat of severe punishment) as major contributors to psychological and physiological pathology among the prisoners.

Anticipatory stressors need not be highly unpleasant or severe, however, to produce stress. For example, Schachter (1959), Milgram (1963) and others induced high levels of stress by telling individuals that they would experience a loud noise or a mild shock, or that someone else might become uncomfortable because of their actions. Fear of failure or fear of embarrassment in front of peers is a common anticipatory stressor. The middle-age anxieties about retirement and losing vitality have been identified by Levinson (1978), Hall (1976) and others as common stressors.

Table 2.2 Management strategies for eliminating stressors

Type of stressor	Elimination strategy
Time	Time Management Delegation
Encounter	Delegation Interpersonal competence
Situational	Work re-design
Anticipatory	Prioritising Planning

Eliminating stressors

Because eliminating stressors is a permanent stress-reduction strategy, it is by far the most desirable. It would be impossible, and perhaps not even an advantage, for individuals to eliminate all the stressors they encounter, but they can effectively eliminate those that are harmful. One way is to 'evolve' the environment rather than merely 'reacting' to it (Weick, 1979). Accepting that we can take control of the world around us and not merely accept 'the slings and arrows' passively, is a release in itself which leads to the elimination of the stressors. By working to create more favourable environmental circumstances we can rationally and systematically eliminate stressors.

Table 2.2 outlines several ways in which the four kinds of stressor can be eliminated.

Eliminating time stressors

Time stressors are often the greatest sources of stress for managers. Research by Mintzberg (1973) and Kotter (1987) showed, for example, that managers experience frequent interruptions (over 50 per cent of their activities last nine minutes or less); they seldom engage in long-range planning but allow fragmentation, brevity and variety to characterise their time use. On the average, no manager works more than 20 minutes without interruption, and most of a manager's time is controlled by the most tiresome, persistent and energetic people (Carlson, 1951). Junior managers can be in a worse position. Guest (1956) found that industrial foremen engage in between 237 and 1,073 separate incidents a day with no real breaks.

Effective time management can enable managers to gain control over their time and to organise their fragmented, chaotic environment.

Two different sets of skills are important for managing time effectively and for eliminating time stressors. The first focuses on efficiently using time on a daily basis while the second focuses on effectively using time over the long-term. Because the effectiveness approach to time management serves as the foundation for the efficiency approach, we will explain it first. We will then review the tools and techniques for achieving efficiency in time use.

Time management

Overload and lack of control are the greatest sources of time stress for most of us – managers or not. Somehow, no matter how much time is available, it seems to get filled up and squeezed out. Probably the most commonly prescribed solutions for attacking problems of time stress are to use diaries and planners, to generate 'to-do' lists, and to learn to say 'no'. But although almost everyone has tried such tactics, nearly all of us still claim to be under enormous time stress. This is not to say that diaries, lists and saying 'no' are not useful, but they do not eliminate the cause, they only reduce the symptoms. To reduce time stressors we must learn to be more effective and this means we:

- spend more time on important matters, not just urgent matters
- distinguish clearly between what they view as important versus what they view as urgent
- focus on outputs rather than processes
- stop feeling guilty when we say 'no'.

The 'time management matrix' (Figure 2.3) is the key to improved effectiveness (Covey, 1988). Key activities are categorised on a scale of Importance and Urgency. Important activities are those that produce a valued output or achieve a worthwhile purpose. Urgent activities are those that demand immediate attention.

		URGENCY	
		HIGH	LOW
		1	**3**
	HIGH	Crises	Developmental opportunities
		Customer complaint	Innovating
			Planning
IMPORTANCE		**2**	**4**
	LOW	Mail	Escapes
		Ringing telephone	Routines
		Unscheduled interruptions	Arguments

Figure 2.3 Time management matrix

They are associated with a need expressed by someone else, or they relate to an uncomfortable problem or situation that requires a solution as soon as possible.

Activities such as handling employee crises or customer complaints are both *urgent* and *important*. A ringing telephone, the arrival of the post or unscheduled interruptions might be examples of *urgent but potentially unimportant* activities. *Important but non-urgent* activities include developmental opportunities, innovating, planning and so on.

Unimportant and *non-urgent* activities are escapes and routines that people may pursue but which produce little valuable payoff – for example, computer games, small talk, daydreaming, shuffling paper and arguing.

Activities in the *important/urgent* quadrant (Cell 1) usually dominate the lives of managers. They are seen as activities that demand immediate attention. Attending a meeting, responding to a call or request, interacting with a customer, or completing a report might all legitimately be defined as important/urgent activities. The trouble with spending all one's time on activities in this quadrant, however, is that they all require the manager to *react*. Someone else usually controls them, and they may or may not lead to a result the manager wants to achieve.

The problem is even worse in the *unimportant/urgent* quadrant (Cell 2). Demands by others that may meet their needs but that serve only as deflections or interruptions to the manager's agenda only escalate time stressors. Because we may not achieve results that are meaningful, purposeful and valued – important to us – the stressors persist, we experience overload and a lack of control. Being purely reactive is not a solution to anything.

If the time stressors persist we generally try to escape into *unimportant/non-urgent* activities (Cell 4). We seek to escape by attempting to shut out the world or put everything on hold. Stress may be temporarily relieved but no long-term solutions are implemented, so time stress comes back with perhaps more urgency. One can spend 95 per cent of life in reactive battles with crises and 5 per cent in relieving tensions that could well be avoided in the first place.

A better alternative is to focus on activities in the *important/non-urgent* quadrant (Cell 3). These activities might be labelled *opportunities* instead of *problems*. They are oriented towards accomplishing high priority results. They prevent problems from occurring, or build systems that eliminate problems rather than just coping with them. Preparation, preventive maintenance, planning, building resiliency and organising are all activities that are crucial for long-term success. Cyert and March (1963) discuss this use of 'slack resources' as a preferred way of dealing with all organisational change. Handy uses a metaphor we will use several times in the book – 'Drinking in Davy's Bar' – once we have settled down to handling the situation, we have progressed beyond the point when we can tackle the underlying problems. *Important/non-urgent* activities should be the number one priority on the time management agenda. By making certain that these kinds of activities get priority, the urgent problems being encountered can be reduced. Time stressors can be eliminated.

One of the most difficult yet crucially important decisions one must make in managing time effectively is determining what is important and what is urgent. There are no automatic rules of thumb that divide all activities, demands or opportunities into those neat categories. Problems don't come with categorising labels attached, it's a very personal classification – one secure individual's 'non-urgent' may be another's perceived key to survival in the corporate jungle. We categorise our own activities.

> We advised a harassed chief executive to change her habits and move away from the precedent of her predecessor. Instead of leaving her appointments diary in the control of her secretary, she should spend her first moments in the office deciding what activities were her priority and allocating specific blocks of time accordingly. Only after she had made these decisions should she make the diary available to her secretary to schedule other appointments.

We still need to answer the 'How?' question – How can people make certain that they focus on activities that are important, not just urgent? The answer is to identify clear and specific personal priorities. It is important for people to be aware of their own core values and to establish a set of basic principles to guide their behaviour. In order to determine what is important in time management, those core values, basic principles and personal priorities must be clearly identified. Otherwise, individuals are at the mercy of the unremitting demands that others place upon them. 'If you don't know where you are going, you will finish somewhere else.'

Answer the following questions:

1. What do I stand for? What am I willing to die (or live) for?

2. What do I care passionately about?

3. What legacy would I like to leave? How would I like to be remembered?

4. If I could persuade everyone to follow a few basic principles, what would they be?

5. What do I want to have accomplished twenty years from now?

From these questions you can create a *personal* mission statement – an expression of what is truly important to you. With this statement you can be proactive in determining what is important to you.

> Two people aged 26 and 56 wrote their Mission Statements. The 26-year-old was concerned with learning new skills so that in four years time he and his partner could set up a business on their own. The 56-year-old was concerned with her grandchildren, and passing her skills and the progress she had made in the organisation on to a new generation of managers.

Basing time management on core principles to judge the importance of activities is also the key to being able to say 'no' without feeling guilty. When you have decided what it is that you care about passionately, what it is you most want to accomplish and what legacy you want to leave, you can more easily say 'no' to activities that don't fit these principles – provided you have time. This is why it is easier to say 'no' to *important/non-urgent* activities (Cell 3) because you have time. Unfortunately, against time pressures, we allow our goal setting to be completely reactive and pragmatic, fumbling ourselves into more stress.

Understanding, communicating and acting upon our core principle does not mean that we have to weigh and decide instantly on every action. To act in a proactive way we need to be in sympathy with the ethics of our organisation – our mission statement must match that of our employees or we have endemic personal stress. There are times when we decide that external pressures mean that we 'go with the flow', but it is our choice. Blanchard and Peale (1990) list five principles for what they term ethical power:

1. *Purpose*. The mission of our organisation is communicated from the top. Our organisation is guided by the values, hopes, and a vision that helps us to determine what is acceptable and unacceptable behaviour.
2. *Pride*. We feel proud of ourselves and of our organisation. We know that when we feel this way, we can resist temptations to behave unethically.
3. *Patience*. We believe that holding to our ethical values will lead us to success in the long term. This involves maintaining a balance between obtaining results and caring how we achieve these results.
4. *Persistence*. We have a commitment to live by ethical principles. We are committed to our commitment. We make sure our actions are consistent with our purpose.
5. *Perspective*. Our managers and employees take time to pause and reflect, take stock of where we are, evaluate where we are going and determine how we are going to get there.

Effectiveness in time management then means that you accomplish what you want to accomplish with your time. How you achieve those accomplishments relates to efficiency of time use, to which we now turn.

Pitfalls in time management

In addition to structuring our time in line with our core principles and those of the organisation we also need to think of our actual use of time. Table 2.3 lists common ways of wasting time.

Being aware of the pitfalls is often enough to reduce the stressors that following them generates. For example, if we do things that are planned before things that are unplanned, some important tasks may never get done unless they are consciously scheduled. Because many people have a tendency to do things that are urgent before things that are important, they may find themselves saying 'no' to important things in order to attend to urgent things, thereby perpetuating feelings of overload. If we do the things that are easiest before the things that are difficult, our time may be taken up dealing with mundane and easy-to-resolve issues while difficult but important problems go unresolved.

Time is such a universal stressor that time management is hugely important. The Time Management Survey at the beginning of the chapter is designed to highlight your own competencies in the area. The first section of the survey applies to everyone in his or her daily life. The second section is most applicable to individuals who have managed or worked in an organisation. The key to scoring is at the end of the book and will show you how well you manage your time. The questionnaire is derived from our Rules of Time Management. It should also be pointed out that no individual can or should implement all of these time management techniques at

Table 2.3   Potential time-management pitfalls

- We do what we like to do before we do what we don't like to do.
- We do the things we know how to do faster than the things we do not know how to do.
- We do the things that are easiest before things that are difficult.
- We do things that require a little time before things that require a lot of time.
- We do things for which the resources are available.
- We do things that are scheduled (for example, meetings) before non-scheduled things.
- We sometimes do things that are planned before things that are unplanned.
- We respond to demands from others before demands from ourselves.
- We do things that are urgent before things that are important.
- We readily respond to crises and emergencies.
- We do interesting things before uninteresting things.
- We do things that advance our personal objectives or that are politically expedient.
- We wait until a deadline before we really get moving.
- We do things that provide the most immediate closure.
- We respond on the basis of who wants it.
- We respond on this basis of the consequences to us of doing or not doing something.
- We tackle small jobs before large jobs.
- We work on things in the order of arrival.
- We work on the basis of the squeaky-wheel principle (the squeaky wheel gets the grease).
- We work on the basis of consequences to the group.

once. The amount of time spent trying to implement all the techniques would be so overwhelming that time stressors would only increase. Therefore, it is best to incorporate a few of these techniques at a time into everyday life. Implement first those hints that will lead to the most improvement in your use of time. Saving just 10 per cent more time, or using an extra 30 minutes a day more wisely, can produce astounding results over months and years. Effective time management not only helps a person to accomplish more in a typical work day, but also helps eliminate feelings of stress and overload.

The rules of effective time management

The first 20 rules are applicable to everyone; the second set relate more directly to managers and the management role.

Rule 1: Read selectively   Most of us have too much to read, ranging from unsolicited trash mail to vital instructions. Except when you read for relaxation or pleasure, most reading should be done the way you read a newspaper; skim most of it, but stop to read what seems most important. Even the most important articles don't need a thorough reading, since important points are generally at the beginnings of paragraphs or sections. Furthermore, if you underline or highlight what you find important, you can review it quickly when you need to.

Rule 2: Make a list of things to perform each day   This is a common-sense rule which implies that you need to do some advance planning each day and not rely solely on your memory. (It also implies that you should have only one list, not multiple lists on multiple scraps of paper.)

Rule 3: Have a place for everything and keep everything is its place   Letting things get out of place robs you of time in two ways: you need more time to find something when you need it, and you are tempted to interrupt the task you are doing to do something else. For example, if material for several projects is scattered on top of your desk, you will be continually tempted to switch from one project to another as you shift your eyes or move the papers.

Rule 4: Prioritise your tasks   Each day you should focus first on important tasks, then deal with urgent tasks. During the Second World War, with an overwhelming number of tasks to perform, General Eisenhower successfully managed his time by following Rule 4 strictly. He focused his attention rigorously on important matters that only he could resolve, while leaving urgent, but less important matters to be dealt with by subordinates.

Rule 5: Do one important thing at a time but several trivial things simultaneously   You can accomplish a lot by doing more than one thing at a time when tasks are routine, trivial or require little thought. This rule allows managers to get rid of multiple trivial tasks in less time – e.g., sign letters while talking on the phone.

Rule 6: Make a list of some five- or ten-minute discretionary tasks   This helps to use the small bits of time almost everyone has during his or her day (waiting for something to begin, between meetings or events, talking on the telephone, etc.). Beware, however, of spending all your time doing these small discretionary tasks while letting high-priority items go unattended.

Rule 7: Divide up large projects   This helps you avoid feeling overwhelmed by large, important, urgent tasks. Feeling that a task is too big to accomplish contributes to a feeling of overload and leads to procrastination.

Rule 8: Determine the critical 20 per cent of your tasks   Pareto's law states that 20 per cent of the tasks produce 80 per cent of the results. Therefore, it is important to analyse which tasks make up the most important 20 per cent and spend the bulk of your time on those.

Rule 9: Save your best time for important matters   Time spent on trivial tasks should not be your 'best time'. Do routine work when your energy level is low, your mind is not sharp or you aren't on top of things. Reserve your quality time for accomplishing the most important and urgent tasks. As Carlson (1951) pointed out, managers are often like puppets whose strings are being pulled by a crowd of unknown and unorganised people. Don't let others interrupt your best time with unwanted demands. Control your own time.

Table 2.4 The divisions of priority

1. Importance	**3. Delegation**
(a) Very important – a must	(a) I am the only one who can do it
(b) Important – should be done	(b) It can be delegated but requires
(c) Not so important but it would be	some authority, training or
nice if it were done	instruction
(d) Unimportant – no real point in it	(c) Virtually anyone could do it
anyway when you think	
	4. Interactions
2. Urgency	(a) I must see these people every day
(a) Very urgent – must be done NOW	(b) I need to see these people
(b) Urgent – should be done soon	frequently
(c) Not urgent – should be fitted in	(c) I should see them sometime
sometime	(d) I do not NEED to see these people
(d) Time is not a factor	at all

Rule 10: Reserve some time during the day when others don't have access to you Use this time to accomplish *important/non-urgent* tasks, or spend it just thinking. This might be the time before others in the household get up, after everyone else is in bed or at a location where no one else comes. The point is to avoid being in the line of fire all day, every day, without personal control over your time.

Rule 11: Don't put things off If you do certain tasks promptly, they will require less time and effort than if you procrastinate. Of course, you must guard against spending all your time on trivial, immediate concerns that crowd out more important tasks. The line between procrastination and time wasting is a fine one.

Rule 12: Keep track of how you use your time This is one of the best time-management strategies. It is impossible to improve your management of time or decrease time stressors unless you know how you spend your time. You should keep time logs in short enough intervals to capture the essential activities. We suggest that units of 30 minutes provide a balance between accuracy and feasibility and that you keep the time log for at least two weeks. Table 2.4 should be used to classify your activities and eliminate obvious slack.

Rule 13: Set deadlines This helps improve your efficient use of time. Work always expands to fill the time available, so if you don't specify a termination time, tasks tend to continue longer than necessary.

Rule 14: Do something productive while waiting for other jobs Up to 20 per cent of your time is likely to be spent in waiting. Use this time for reading, planning, preparing, rehearsing, reviewing, outlining or doing other things that help you to accomplish your work.

Rule 15: Do quality work at one set time during the day Because it is natural to let simple tasks drive out difficult tasks, specify a certain period of time to do quality work which fits your own personal 'clock'. Many people do their best work in the morning – if this is you, don't waste the mornings on trivia.

Rule 16: Finish at least one thing every day – set realisable targets   Reaching the end of a day with nothing completely finished, however small, serves to increase a sense of overload and time stress. Finishing a task is a reward in itself.

Rule 17: Schedule personal time   You need some time when no interruptions will occur, when you can get off the 'fast track' and be alone. This time should be used to plan, prioritise, take stock, pray, meditate or just relax. Among other advantages, personal time also helps you to maintain self-awareness.

Rule 18: Don't worry about anything on a continuing basis – if it is a continuing concern FIX IT!

> A remote village had the problem of a dog who had fallen down the well and contaminated the water. The village elders consulted the Zen priest who advise them to draw seven buckets of water before drinking again. They drew seven times seven and still the water was foul. They went back to the priest who delayed answering and then said: *Of course you have removed the dog!*

Very often we prefer to worry and go over the same thing time and time again when it is quite obvious what we need to do. Pointless worry stops us focusing on essentials.

Rule 19: Have long-term objectives   Know what you need to achieve and do not sabotage your real aims with expediency.

Rule 20: Be on the alert for ways to improve your management of time

The next set of rules cover the major managerial activities. As managers report that approximately 70 per cent of their time is spent in meetings (Mintzberg, 1973; Cooper and Davidson, 1982), rules relating to meetings are given pride of place.

Rule 21: Hold routine meetings at the end of the day   Energy and creativity levels are highest early in the day and shouldn't be wasted on trivial matters. Furthermore, close of the day meetings are inclined to be shorter and set their own priorities.

Rule 22: Hold short meetings standing up   This guarantees that meetings will be kept short. Getting comfortable helps to prolong meetings.

Rule 23: Set a time limit   This establishes an expectation of when the meeting should end and creates pressure to conform to a time boundary. Set such limits at the beginning of every meeting and appointment.

> An idea used by one organisation to make their meetings more efficient was to specify times and purposes for each item in a pre-published agenda. Thus you would book 10 minute slots and specify whether you wanted to pass information, make a decision or solve a problem. The discipline of the time/purpose agenda for a few meetings carried forward even when the rules were relaxed.

Rule 24: Cancel meetings when they are not needed   The occasional cancellation makes the meetings that are held more productive and more time efficient.

Rule 25: Have agendas; stick to them; and keep action minutes with timing and account-ability These rules help people to prepare for a meeting, stick to the subject and remain work oriented. Many things will be handled outside of meetings if they have to appear on a formal agenda to be discussed. Managers can set a verbal agenda at the beginning of even impromptu meetings. Keeping action minutes ensures that assignments are not forgotten, that follow-up and accountability occur, and that everyone is clear about responsibilities.

Rule 26: Start meetings on time This shows commitment – people who arrive on time should be rewarded, not asked to wait for laggards.

Rule 27: Prepare minutes promptly and follow them up This practice keeps items from appearing again in a meeting without having been resolved. It also creates the expectation that most work should be done outside the meeting. Commitments and expectations made public through minutes are more likely to be fulfilled.

Rule 28: Present and demand solutions, not problems

> Winston Churchill working with a committee on the issues of landing the major Allied forces on open beaches in July 1945 instructed: *'I want solutions not problems – the problems speak loudly enough for themselves.'*

Meetings can easily become forums for upward delegation and the hedging of responsibility. Problem setters are often better positioned to present solutions than the less initiated. Only when the obvious is ruled out do we need 'creative' solutions. Meetings are often to communicate proposed actions so that their wider implications can be understood by all the stakeholders.

Rule 29: Meet visitors in your doorway It is easier to keep a meeting short if you are standing in the doorway rather than sitting in your office.

Rule 30: Hold meetings in the appropriate place Often the appropriate place is the home territory of the key stakeholder. Such appropriately placed meetings can call upon extra data and unplanned 'witnesses' without formality and delay. This rule does not apply if the manager's travelling time is impracticable or where the 'home territory' cannot be protected from dysfunctional interruptions.

> We were called upon to comment on the appraisal systems of Bass Taverns. Managers used the public houses of the landlords during opening hours as sites for formal annual assessments and were finding difficulties. The idea might have been good, but in practice the interviews were interrupted. Bringing the landlords to the head office had the double benefit of uninterrupted work and of convincing the landlords that they were valued and that the process of appraisal was meaningful.

Rule 31: Use technology Telephone technology allows the re-routing of calls, conferencing systems exist, and e-mail is common place. Meetings may not be the best way of disseminating data – fax and the simple office memo are less glamorous but may fit the need more efficiently than face to face.

Rule 32: Have a place to work uninterrupted Not all of us have a 'protected' workplace but we do not have to meet in a formal office. Lawns or even canteens can allow us more confidentiality on occasion. Think always of the purpose of the meeting and the state of mind you want and expect from those present.

> Working for what became Birds Eye Walls, we had a spell in fish processing. The manager's office was halfway down the fish filleting lines, which in the 1970s was a very tough place. Anyone 'called' to the office had to face some hundred filleters who chose to humble the visitor by banging their knives on the stainless steel belts. Most visitors were severely shaken if not stirred by the time they got to the manager's office.

Rule 33: Do something definite with every piece of paperwork you handle   Either bin it or action it; never shuffle it.

Rule 34: Keep the working space clear   Those who know at least two of the authors will laugh at this rule, as our working spaces are piled high; however, it is a good rule. A hint is also to use staples and not paper clips – paper clips seem to take great delight in losing their charges and gaining sheets from other documents. However, remember that 'reorganising the paper work' is a great time-wasting game.

Rule 35: Time taken to delegate is never wasted   Delegation is such a key management skill as to merit part of its own chapter.

Remember that these rules of thumb for managing time are a means to an end, not the end itself. If the implementation of rules creates more stress rather than less, the rules should not be applied. However, research has indicated that managers who use these kinds of techniques have better control of their time, accomplish more, have better relations with subordinates and eliminate many of the time stressors that most managers ordinarily encounter. Therefore, you will find that as you select a few of these hints to apply in your own life, the efficiency of your time use will improve and your time stress will decrease.

Most time-management techniques involve single individuals changing their own work habits or behaviours by themselves. However, effective time management must often take into account the behaviour and needs of others – my time management without understanding its impact on the time management of others may well be dysfunctional. Really effective time management may require all one's management skills, and we still have encounter stressors to deal with.

Eliminating encounter stressors

Unsatisfactory personal relationships are significant stressors. Encounter stressors result directly from abrasive, non-fulfilling relationships. Even though work is going smoothly, when encounter stress is present, everything else seems wrong.

Collaboration

One important factor that helps to eliminate encounter stress is membership in a stable, closely knit group or community. Our evidence is based on anthropologists' studies of particular communities. Thirty years ago Dr Stewart Wolf found that the residents of Roseto, Pennsylvania, were completely free from heart disease and other stress-related illness. He suspected that their protection sprang from the town's uncommon social cohesion and stability.

> The town's population consisted entirely of descendants of Italians who had moved there 100 years ago from Roseto, Italy. Few married outside the community; the firstborn was always named after a grandparent; conspicuous consumption and displays of superiority were avoided; and social support among community members was a way of life.

Wolf predicted that residents would begin to display the same level of stress-related illness as the rest of the country if the modern world intruded. It did, and they did. By the mid-1970s, residents in Roseto had exotic cars, mansion-style homes, mixed marriages, new names, competition with one another and a rate of coronary disease the same as in any other town (Farnham, 1991). They had ceased to be a cohesive, collaborative clan and instead had become a community of selfishness. Self-centredness, it was discovered, was dangerous to health.

The most important psychological discovery resulting from the Vietnam and Persian Gulf wars was the strength associated with the small, primary work group. In Vietnam, unlike with Desert Storm, strong primary groups of soldiers who stayed together over time were not formed. The constant injection of new personnel into squadrons, and the constant transfer of soldiers from one location to another made soldiers feel isolated, without loyalty and vulnerable to stress-related illness. In the Gulf War, by contrast, soldiers were kept in the same unit throughout the campaign, brought home together and given lots of time to debrief together after the battle (Farnham, 1991). Professional debriefing and the use of a closely knit group to provide interpretation and social support was found to be the most powerful deterrent to post-battle trauma: Post-Traumatic Stress Disorder (PSMS). Woods and Whitehead (1993) give three examples of social support:

- the restoration of civilian morale in Darmstadt, Germany, after one of the most intensive aerial bombardments in the Second World War
- the recovery after the flooding and destruction of Les Salles in southern France
- the acceptance of the horrors of the Bradford Football Stadium fire where 55 people were burnt to death in the sight of their friends.

In all these cases the support of tight-knit communities aided recovery.

Collaborative or even clan-like relationships are a powerful deterrent to encounter stress. One way of developing this kind of relationship is by applying a concept introduced by Covey (1989) in describing habits of highly effective people. Covey used the metaphor of an emotional bank account to describe the trust or feeling of security that one person has towards another. This approach has been seen by many as being manipulative in a very obvious way, but the point is made. Covey, controversially, regards the more 'deposits' made in an emotional bank account, the stronger and more resilient the relationship becomes. He quoted going to a ball game with his son as an example – apparently Covey is indifferent to ball games. Conversely, too many 'withdrawals' from the account weakens relationships by destroying trust, security and confidence. 'Deposits' are made through treating people with kindness, courtesy, honesty and consistency. The emotional bank account grows when people feel they are receiving love, respect and caring. 'Withdrawals' are made by not keeping promises, not listening, not clarifying expectations or allowing choice – cashing in on the relationship. Relationships, according to Covey, are ruined because the account becomes overdrawn, but the mechanistic model is widely challenged.

The common-sense prescription, therefore, is to base relationships with others on mutual trust, respect, honesty and kindness. Collaborative, cohesive communities are, in the end, a product of the one-on-one relationships that people develop with each other. As Dag Hammarskjöld, former Secretary General of the United Nations, stated: 'It is more noble to give yourself completely to one individual than to labour diligently for the salvation of the masses.' Feeling trusted, respected and loved is, in the end, what each of us desires as individuals. We want to experience those feelings personally, not just as a member of a group.

Interpersonal competence

In addition to one-on-one relationship building, a second major category of encounter stress eliminators is developing *interpersonal competence*. We are discussing competencies to:

- resolve conflict
- build and manage high-performing teams
- conduct efficient meetings
- coach and counsel employees
- provide positive and constructive negative feedback
- influence
- motivate, energise and empower themselves and others.

These seven elements of interpersonal competence in a manager are about support. A survey of workers found that employees who rated their manager as supportive and interpersonally competent had lower rates of burnout, lower stress levels, lower incidence of stress-related illness, higher productivity, more loyalty to their organisations, and more efficiency in work than employees with non-supportive and interpersonally incompetent managers.

Eliminating situational stressors

Job redesign

A medium-term strategy is to redesign the work process. We have to accept that many of us report feeling stress because it seems fashionable to be stressed. 'I'm busier than you are' is a common game many of us enjoy playing. We discuss the problems of repeated reorganisations; the vulnerability of our jobs; traffic delays; and the lack of discipline in others, all in terms of our personal stresses. The whole issue is serious since the time lost through stress-related illness and its medical treatment costs twice as much as industrial injuries (Farnham, 1991). The costs are rising. A significant source of stress, as we all 'know', arises from our 'situation'.

For decades, researchers in the area of occupational health have examined the relationship between job strain and stress-related behavioural, psychological and physiological outcomes. Studies have focused on various components of job strain, including the level of task demand (e.g., the pressure to work quickly or excessively), the level of individual control (e.g., the freedom to vary the work pace), and the level of intellectual challenge (e.g., the extent to which work is interesting).

The kind of stress experienced by individuals will vary according to their culture. In a study by Cary Cooper *et al.* (1988) of nearly 1,000 senior top level executives in 10 countries it was found that each country presents its own idiosyncratic work pressures. Cooper also looked specifically at the stresses of women managers.

US executives perceived their greatest source of pressure at work to be 'the lack of power and influence', 'incompetent bosses' and 'beliefs conflicting with those of the organisation'. However, Japanese executives rated 'keeping up with new technology' as their major source of strain and job dissatisfaction, while Swedish executives cited stresses involving encroachment of work upon their private lives. German complaints were more specific; they complained of 'time pressures' and 'working with inadequately trained subordinates'.

Other research in this area, however, has challenged the common myth that job strain occurs most frequently in the executive suite (Hingley and Cooper, 1986). In a General Household Survey 1974–75, the frequency of deaths due to major causes increases as we move from professional and white collar jobs down to the unskilled. This applies both to stress-related illness and to other illness such as pneumonia and prostrate cancer. In the UK, blue-collar workers consult their doctors more often and have more days off than white-collar workers. Professional males average 12 days off per year, while unskilled manual workers average around 20 days. An explanation for this could well be that low-discretion, low-interest jobs with high demand produce at least as much stress as high-profile work. This is borne out by research. A review of this research suggests that the single most important contributor to stress is lack of freedom (Adler, 1989).

Studies throughout the Goddard Space Flight Centre showed that staff with higher discretionary decision-making power experience less from all four of the stressor classifications – time, situational, encounter and anticipatory (French and Caplan, 1972).

Cecilia Macdonald (1996) considers that managers need to manage their own stress and then 'get creative about managing the stress of their employees'. She sees the reactive policy of 'waiting for their annual vacation as being unhelpful. Positive measures are needed. Her recommendations include a 'small wins strategy' and a short time for reflection at the end of the day. Siobahn Butler (1996) explains that the stress issues of the company Cable Midlands in the UK provide enough concern for the HR department to offer stress management courses which include clinical hypnosis and aromatherapy. Sara Zeff Gerber (1996) sees an impending disaster in the growth of chronically stressed employees throughout US industry and proposes even more drastic remedies. The examples we have quoted are simply examples drawn from one year – 1997. The concerns over stress are not new but the present interest is now overwhelming.

The urgency of the problem makes us hesitate slightly to quote a key response from the 1970s. Hackman and his colleague (1975) proposed a model of job re-design that has proved effective in reducing stress and in increasing satisfaction and productivity. Hackman recommended the following policy:

1. Combine tasks When individuals are able to work on a whole project and per-form a variety of related tasks (e.g., programming all components of a computer software package), rather than being restricted to working on a single repetitive task or sub-component of a larger task, they are more satisfied and committed. In such cases, they are able to use more skills and feel a certain pride of ownership in their job.

2. Form identifiable work units When tasks are combined people feel more integ-rated, and the strain associated with repetitive work is diminished. Productivity often improves even further when groups combine and co-ordinate their tasks, making their own decisions on how to complete their work. This formation of nat-ural work units has received a great deal of attention in Japanese auto plants in America and the UK as workers have combined in teams to assemble an entire car from start to finish, rather than do separate tasks on an assembly line. Workers learn one another's jobs, rotate assignments and experience a sense of completion in their work. The process reduces work-related stress dramatically.

3. Establish customer relationships One of the most enjoyable parts of a job is see-ing the consequences of one's labour. In most organisations, producers are buffered from consumers by intermediaries, such as customer relations departments and sales personnel. The process of allowing producers to obtain first-hand unfiltered contact with customers and understand the problems, needs and expectations, is not only efficient and motivating, it also reduces situational stress.

4. Increase decision-making authority Decisions being made at the appropriate level is again both efficient, motivating and helps to reduce stress of all concerned. It allows individuals to feel that they are valued and in control of what we will call later their 'Circle of Concern'.

> Zenica, a producer of fine chemicals in Huddersfield, Yorkshire, began their empowerment programme by creating legends. One such legend took place in a working store room which the Change Manager found in partial darkness. The rea-son for the room being in darkness was a single electric bulb that had failed. The manager asked the operators why it had not be replaced and was told that a light bulb had been requisitioned but the supervisor required for the authorisation was off sick. The manager asked how much the bulb would cost in the local supermarket and was told about 60p. He fished the money out of his pocket and told the oper-ator to buy one.

The issue is about the role of management in the new world – the subject of the last chapter. New managers should understand 'why' things are to be done, explain 'what' needs to be done and allow maximum participation in 'how' things are done

– consulting and monitoring the processes on a continuous basis. Cameron *et al.* (1990) found a significant decrease in experienced stress in firms that were downsizing when workers were given authority to make decisions about how and when they did the extra work required of them.

5. Provide feedback – listen and communicate   At its simplest we need to be told how our efforts fit into the grand scheme.

> A Central Office of Information (COI) film made in Britain during the Second World War described a strike in a factory making luxury sheepskin gloves during the Battle of Britain. The women operators wanted to 'do something for the war effort and not make luxury items'. The Ministry of Aircraft Production – for whom the factory was supplying the goods – brought a wounded fighter pilot to meet the operators and show how the gloves contributed to his performance in an unheated cabin of a Spitfire warplane. The strike vanished.

Knowing your place in the 'grand scheme' is not enough – we need to know what is expected of us and how we are judged. The effective manager needs to communicate expectations clearly, giving timely and accurate feedback, these expectations need to include quality standards and achievements. Firms that allow the workers who assemble a product to test its quality, instead of shipping it off to a separate quality assurance group, find that quality increases substantially and that conflicts between production and quality control personnel are eliminated.

These practices are used widely today in all types of organisations, such as Volvo, Saab and Philips Industries. They have all undertaken extended projects of job redesign. Philips have pursued a programme of work structuring. Job enrichment and job enlargement have been attempted and greater opportunities for worker participation have been provided.

Eliminating anticipatory stressors

While redesigning work can help structure an environment where stressors are minimised, it is much more difficult to eliminate entirely the anticipatory stressors experienced by individuals. Stress associated with anticipating an event is more a product of psychological anxiety than current work circumstances. To eliminate anticipatory stressors requires a change in thought processes, priorities and plans. As we have said earlier, it is important to establish clear personal priorities – identifying long-term goals and hence what cannot be compromised or sacrificed. A personal mission statement acts as a map or guide. It makes clear where you will eventually end up, and fear of the unknown – another way of defining anticipatory stress – is thus eliminated.

Goal setting

Establishing short-term plans helps eliminate anticipatory stressors by focusing attention on immediate goal accomplishment instead of a fearful future. Short-term planning, however, implies more than just specifying a desired outcome. Several action

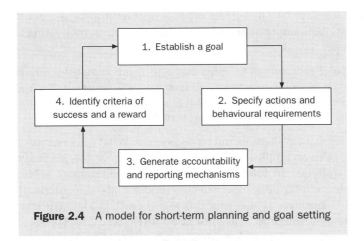

Figure 2.4 A model for short-term planning and goal setting

steps are needed if short-term plans are to be achieved. The model (Figure 2.4) illustrates the four-step process associated with successful short-term planning.

Step 1 Identify the desired goal. Most goal-setting, performance appraisal or management-by-objectives (MBO) programmes specify that step, but most also stop at that point. Unfortunately, the first step alone is not likely to lead to goal achievement or stress elimination. Merely establishing a goal, while helpful, is not sufficient.

Step 2 Identify, as specifically as possible, the tactics necessary to achieve the goal. The more difficult the goal is to accomplish, the more rigorous should be the tactic setting.

> A friend approached one of us with a problem. She was a single woman about 25 years old who had a high degree of anticipatory stress because of her size. She weighed well over 300 pounds and seemed to be unable to lose any of it. She was concerned both from the health and the social consequences of her size. She set a goal, or short-term plan, to lose 100 pounds in the next 10 months. As counsellors we saw this as a distant goal and asked her to list a dozen or so specific actions that would help her to reach that goal. Her list included: never eat alone, never carry any small change (in order to avoid the impulse buying of chocolates), exercise with friends each evening in a gym, get up 7:00 a.m., eat a controlled breakfast with a friend, cut back on television and so reduce the temptation to eat snacks and finally go to bed by 10:30 p.m. These were her tactics, and were in no way influenced by us. The tactics were rigid, but the goal was so difficult that they were necessary to ensure progress. Success came with a weight loss of 100 pounds within the 10 months. She was happy.

Step 3 Establish accountability and reporting mechanisms. The principle at the centre of this step is to make it more difficult to stay the same than to change. We do this by involving others in ensuring that we stick to the plan, establishing a social support network to obtain encouragement from others, and instituting penalties for not doing so. In addition to announcing her goal to her workmates and friends, our slimmer arranged to take up private medical treatment if she did not succeed. The treatment was both unpleasant and costly, but was a great motivating factor to success by cheaper means.

> In our change programmes we insist that participants complete a formal contract of what they are going to achieve and how they will achieve it. The contract has to be countersigned by a witness and is filed by us for the record. The contract is sent to the individuals after a specified period for comment.

Step 4 Establish an evaluation and reward system. What evidence will there be that the goal has been accomplished? In the case of losing weight, it's easily established – the scales rule OK. In softer goals – improving management skills, developing more patience, establishing more effective leadership – the criteria of success are not so easily identified. That is why this step is crucial. 'I know it when I see it' is not good enough. Our objectives must be SMART (Table 2.5): **S**pecific, **M**easurable, **A**greed, **R**ealistic and **T**imed. For our slimmer, the specific goal was to lose weight 100 pounds and this was agreed by her, her doctor and her friends. The weight loss was realistic, whereas 200 pounds would not have been, and the time scale was 'by Christmas' – ten months away. The key is making the goal specific and the purpose is to eliminate anticipatory stress by establishing a focus and direction for activity. The anxiety associated with uncertainty and potentially negative events is dissipated when mental and physical energy are concentrated on purposeful activity.

Small wins

Turning the vague goal to a series of specific goals can be described as a small wins strategy.

> We were working with a manager whose job was to make the public transport system of Miscolc, Hungary, into an effective system based on UK lines. Her problems were aged buses, demotivated staff, lack of any form of financial support, hostility of the public, political blindness. There was no possibility of **achieving** effectiveness in one stage – in fact we identified six stages for success. At each stage there was an assessible victory and no step blinded us to the next of the total objective.

By 'small wins' we mean a tiny but definite change made in a desired direction. One begins each step by changing something that is relatively easy to change. Then another 'change' is added, and so on. Each individual success may be relatively modest when considered in isolation, but the small gains mount up and show measurable progress. The progress we see helps to convince us, as well as others, of our ability to accomplish our objective. The fear associated with anticipatory change is eliminated as we build self-confidence through small wins. We also gain the support of others as they see that things are happening.

In the case of our overweight friend, one key was to begin changing what she could change, a little at a time. Tackling the loss of 100 pounds all at once would have been too overwhelming a task. But she could change the time she shopped, the time she went to bed and what she ate for breakfast. Each successful change generated more and more momentum that, when combined together, led to the

Table 2.5 The SMART system

Action	Goal			
	Improve management skills	Become more patient	Becoming a better leader	Reader's goal
Specific	Learn and practise running meetings	Learn and listen more effectively	Give instructions on a particular project to a particular subordinate	
Measurable	Reduce the business carried forward to the next meeting to two items	Get a friend to watch you in an interview – aim to speak not more than 30% of the time	Reduce the number of times he or she needs to return to you for clarification to once a week	
Agreed	Check with those attending the meeting	Check out with a friend that 30% sounds right – you are now at 80%	Explain the goal to the subordinate	
Realistic	Reduction to two items is fine – no carry forward would be unrealistic	30% is realistic from what you have read	Now we have continuous seeking of clarification – old habits die hard – once a week allows some latitude	
Timed	Our next meeting is on Friday – the plan will start then and be in action by Friday week	The next difficult meeting you will work from 80% to 60% and then by meeting three you will achieve the 30%	This is a real project with real time scales. At the end of its run – 3 months – you will have success	

larger change that she desired. Her ultimate success was a product of multiple small wins.

Similarly, Weick (1993) has described Poland's peaceful transition from a communistic command economy to a capitalistic free-enterprise economy as a product of small wins. Not only is Poland now one of the most thriving economies in eastern Europe, but it made the change to free enterprise without a single shot being fired, a single strike being called or a single political upheaval. One reason for this is that long before the Berlin Wall fell, small groups of volunteers in Poland began to change the way they lived.

Poles adopted a theme that went something like this: If you value freedom, then behave freely; if you value honesty, then speak honestly; if you desire change, then change what you can. Polish citizens organised volunteer groups to help at local hospitals, assist the less fortunate and clean up the parks. They behaved in a way that was outside the control of the central government, but reflected their free choice. Their changes were not on a large enough scale to attract attention and official opposition from the central government, but their actions nevertheless reflected their determination to behave in a free, self-determining way. They controlled what they could control, namely, their own voluntary service. These voluntary service groups spread throughout Poland; thus, when the transition from communism to capitalism occurred, a large number of people in Poland had already got used to behaving in a way consistent with self-determination. Many of these people simply stepped into positions where independent-minded managers were needed. The transition was smooth because of the multiple small wins that had previously spread throughout the country relatively unnoticed.

In summary, the rules for instituting a small wins strategy are simple:

• Identify your area of concern.
• Identify your ultimate goal.
• Look for realistic steps towards your goal.
• Take one step at a time – rewarding each step as you make it.
• Consolidate your successes and move on.

Anticipatory stressors are eliminated because the fearful unknown is replaced by a focus on immediate successes. The alternative strategy is to prepare for the worst and feel good when it does not happen.

> Douglas Construction, a Midlands-based construction company, was being acquired by Tilbury. Tilbury was an unknown to the Douglas managers who feared redundancy. What was the worst that could happen? They were all fired and lost their pension rights. OK, prepare for that but remember that Tilbury has paid a lot for Douglas. Why? The obvious answer is the skills of the Douglas managers. They are the assets that Tilbury has bought – exploit this opportunity.

Developing resilience

Some stress cannot be eliminated. People vary widely in their ability to cope with stress: some individuals seem to crumble under pressure, while others appear to thrive. Resilience is associated with balancing the various aspects of one's life.

The pie chart (Figure 2.5) represents resilience development. Each wedge in the figure identifies an important aspect of life that must be developed in order to achieve resilience. The most resilient individuals are those who have achieved life balance. If the centre of the figure represents the zero point of resilience development and the outside edge of the figure represents maximum development, shading in a portion of the area in each wedge would represent the amount of development achieved in each area. Individuals who are best able to cope with stress would shade in a majority of each wedge, indicating that they have not only spent time

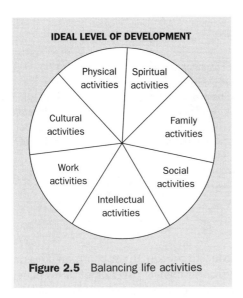

IDEAL LEVEL OF DEVELOPMENT

Physical activities · Spiritual activities · Cultural activities · Family activities · Work activities · Social activities · Intellectual activities

Figure 2.5 Balancing life activities

developing a variety of aspects of their lives, but also that the overall pattern is relatively balanced. A lopsided pattern is as non-adaptive as minimally shaded areas.

- Generally, when people are feeling stress in one area of life, such as work, they respond by devoting more time and attention to work. While this is a natural reaction, it is counterproductive for several reasons. Firstly, the more that individuals concentrate exclusively on work, the more restricted and less creative they become. As we shall see in the discussion of creativity in a later chapter, breakthroughs in problem solving come from using analogies and metaphors gathered from unrelated activities. That is why several major corporations send senior managers on high adventure wilderness retreats (Scully, 1989); invite actors to perform plays before the executive committee; require volunteer community service; or encourage their managers to engage in completely unrelated activities outside of work (*Business Week*, 30 Sept. 1985, pp. 80–4).

- Secondly, refreshed and relaxed minds think better. A bank executive commented recently during an executive development workshop that he had gradually become convinced of the merits of taking the weekend off from work. He finds that he gets twice as much accomplished on Monday as his colleagues who have been in their offices all weekend.

- Thirdly, the cost of stress-related illness decreases markedly when employees are able to receive support from occupational health services. People need to be able to obtain unbiased advice, within their place of work on stress-related problems (Woods and Whitehead, 1993).

- Well-developed individuals, who give time and attention to cultural, physical, spiritual, family, social and intellectual activities in addition to work, are more productive and less stressed than those who are workaholics.

Table 2.6 Resilience: moderating the effects of stress

Physiological resilience	Psychological resilience	Social resilience

• Cardiovascular conditioning
• Proper diet
	• Balanced lifestyle
	• Hardy personality
	   – High internal control
	   – Strong personal commitment
	   – Love of challenge
	• Small-wins strategy
	• Deep-relaxation techniques
		• Supportive social relations
		• Mentors
		• Teamwork

In this section, therefore, we concentrate on three common areas of resilience development for managers: physical resilience, psychological resilience and social resilience. Development in each of these areas requires initiative on the part of the individual and takes a moderate amount of time to achieve. These are not activities that can be accomplished by lunchtime or the weekend. Rather, achieving life balance and resilience requires ongoing initiative and continuous effort. Components of resilience are summarised in Table 2.6.

Physiological resilience

One of the most crucial aspects of resilience development involves one's physical condition, because physical condition significantly affects the ability to cope with stress. Two aspects of physical condition combine to determine physical resilience: cardiovascular conditioning and dietary control.

Cardiovascular conditioning

Henry Ford is reputed to have stated: 'Exercise is bunk. If you are healthy, you don't need it. If you are sick, you shouldn't take it.' Fortunately, European business has not taken Ford's advice; thousands of major corporations now have in-house fitness facilities. An emphasis on physical conditioning in business has resulted partly from overwhelming evidence that individuals in good physical condition are better able to cope with stressors than those in poor physical condition. Table 2.7 illustrates the benefits of regular physical exercise.

Marks & Spencer, well known for its work in this area, is one of the founder members of the Wellness Forum. One of the examples of care they give their employees is the provision of oral cancer screening. As a result of its Live for Life programme, Johnson & Johnson lowered absenteeism and sickness cost to produce a saving of about £160 per employee in 1982. Prudential Life Insurance found a 46 per cent reduction in major medical expenses over five years resulting from a workplace fitness programme. The advantages of physical conditioning, both for individuals and for companies, are irrefutable.

Table 2.7 Confirmed benefits of regular vigorous exercise

- Blood pressure is lowered.
- Resting heart rate is lowered; the heart is better able to distribute blood where needed under stress.
- Cardiac output is increased; the heart is better able to distribute blood where needed under stress.
- Number of red blood cells is increased; more oxygen can be carried per quart of blood.
- Elasticity of arteries is increased.
- Triglyceride level is lowered.

- Blood cholesterol level is decreased. High-density cholesterol, which is more protective of blood vessels than low-density cholesterol, is proportionately increased.
- Adrenal secretions in response to emotional stress are lowered.
- Lactic acid is more efficiently eliminated from the muscles. (This has been associated with decreased fatigue and tension.)
- Fibrin, a protein that aids in the formation of blood clots, is decreased.
- Additional routes of blood supply are built up in the heart.

Source: Goldberg (1976)

Psychological resilience

Three primary purposes exist for a regular exercise programme: maintaining optimal weight, increasing psychological well-being and improving the cardiovascular system. One indirect cause of stress is the sedentary lifestyle adopted by many individuals. An office worker burns up only about 1,200 calories during an eight-hour day. That is fewer calories than are contained in the typical office worker's lunch. It is little wonder that many people are overweight. The resulting excessive strain on both the heart and the self-image makes overweight individuals more vulnerable to stress (Wolman, 1982).

An advantage of regular physical exercise is that it improves mental as well as physical outlook. It increases self-esteem and gives individuals the energy to be more alert and attentive throughout the day. Episodes of depression are far less frequent. Exercise fosters the necessary energy to cope with the stresses of both unexpected events and dull routine. Physically active individuals are less prone to anxiety, have less illness and fewer days off work (Griest *et al.*, 1979). Researchers have found a chemical basis for the psychological benefit of exercise: the brain releases endorphins (similar to morphine) during periods of intense physical activity. This substance numbs pain and produces a feeling of well-being, sometimes referred to as joggers' high – a euphoric, relaxed feeling reported by long-distance runners.

Another vital benefit of exercise is a strengthened cardiovascular system (Greenberg, 1987). The best results come from aerobic exercises that do not require more oxygen than a person can take in comfortably (as compared with all-out sprinting or long-distance swimming). This type of exercise includes brisk walking, jogging, riding a bicycle or climbing stairs. However, the cardiovascular system is improved by exercise only when the following two conditions are met:

1. The target heart rate is sustained throughout the exercise. This rate is 60–80 per cent of the heart's maximum. To work your target rate, subtract your age in years from 220, then take 60–80 per cent of that number. You should begin your exercise programme at the 60 per cent level and gradually increase to the 80 per cent rate. To check your heart rate during your exercise, periodically monitor your heartbeat for six seconds and multiply by 10.

2. The exercise should be for 20–30 minutes, three or four time a week. Since cardiovascular endurance decreases after 48 hours, it is important to exercise at least every other day.

Dietary control

The adage 'You are what you eat' is sobering, especially given the fact that Americans, who are often seen as trend-setters, have developed some bad eating habits. Annually they consume approximately 100 pounds of refined sugar, 125 pounds of fat, 36 gallons of carbonated beverages, and 25 times more salt than the human body requires (Perl, 1980). Europeans, however, do seem to be eating a more healthy diet and government programmes throughout the EC are encouraging this. After years of attack by health professionals, magazines, newspapers, books and TV programmes, old eating habits are finally being swept away. It is now clearly understood that a good diet is linked to good health. A healthy diet need not be hard work, and a few simple changes can soon put you on the right road:

- Eat plenty of fresh fruit and vegetables.
- Cut down on your sugar by opting for unsweetened fruit juices or low calorie soft drinks and eating less sugary foods such as cakes, puddings, sweets and biscuits.
- Limit the quantity of salt you take by using less in cooking and at the table and by eating fresh fruit instead of salty crisps and nuts – which are also high in fat.

Source: The Flora Project for Heart Disease Prevention

Hardiness

In their book, *The Hardy Executive*, Maddi and Kobasa (1984) described three elements that characterise a hardy, or highly stress-resistant, personality. Hardiness results from feeling:

- in control of one's life, rather than powerless to shape external events
- committed to and involved in what one is doing, rather than alienated from one's work and other individuals
- challenged by new experiences rather than viewing change as a threat to security and comfort.

According to these authors, hardy individuals tend to interpret stressful situations positively and optimistically, responding to stress constructively. As a result, their incidence of illness and emotional dysfunction under stressful conditions is considerably below the norm.

Three concepts – control, commitment and challenge – are central to the development of a variety of management skills, and are crucial for mitigating the harmful effects of stress (Kobasa, 1982).

Individuals with a high degree of **internal control** feel that they are in charge of their own destinies. They take responsibility for their actions and feel they can neutralise negative external forces. They generally believe that stressors are the result of their personal choices rather than uncontrollable, capricious or even malicious external forces. The belief that one can influence the course of events is central to developing high self-esteem. Self-esteem, in turn, engenders self-confidence and the optimistic view that bad situations can be improved and problems overcome. Confidence in one's own efficacy produces low fear of failure, high expectations, willingness to take risks and persistence under adversity (Mednick, 1982; Anderson, 1977; Ivancevich and Matteson, 1980), all of which contribute to resilience under stress.

Commitment implies both selection and dedication. Hardy individuals not only feel that they choose what they do, but they also strongly believe in the importance of what they do. This commitment is both internal (that is, applied to one's own activities) and external (that is, applied to a larger community). The feeling of being responsible to others is an important buffer against stress (Antonovsky, 1979). Whereas self-esteem and a sense of purpose help to provide a psychological support system for coping with stressful events, an individual's belief that others are counting on him or her to succeed, and that he or she belongs to a larger community, fosters psychological resilience during stressful periods. Feeling part of a group, cared about and trusted by others engenders norms of co-operation and commitment, and encourages constructive responses to stress.

Hardy people also welcome **challenge**. They believe that change, rather than stability, is the normal and preferred mode of life. Therefore, much of the disruption associated with a stressful life event is interpreted as an opportunity for personal growth rather than as a threat to security. This mode of thinking is consistent with the Chinese word for crisis, which has two meanings: 'threat' and 'opportunity'. Individuals who seek challenges search for new and interesting experiences and accept stress as a necessary step towards learning. Because these individuals prefer change to stability, they tend to have high tolerance for ambiguity and high resilience under stress (Ivancevich and Matteson, 1980; Maddi and Kobasa, 1984). The three characteristics of hardy personalities – control, commitment and challenge – have been found to be among the most powerful ways of reducing the dysfunctional consequences of stress. By contrast, a different complex of personality attributes, the so-called 'Type A Syndrome', is associated with reduced hardiness and higher levels of psychological stress.

Type A personality

A second important aspect of psychological resilience relates to a personality pattern that many of us develop as we enter the competitive worlds of advanced

Table 2.8 Characteristics of the Type A personality

- Signs of personal tension, such as a clenched jaw, tight muscles, tics.
- Personal commitment to having, rather than being.
- Unawareness of the broader environment. Ignorance of elements outside the immediate task.
- Strong need to be an expert on a subject; otherwise, lack of involvement.
- Compulsion to compete with other Type A's rather than understanding and co-operate with them.
- Speech characterised by explosive accentuation, acceleration of the last few words of a sentence, impatience when interrupted.

- Chronic sense of being in a hurry.
- Polyphasic thoughts and actions, that is, a tendency to do several things simultaneously.
- Impatience with the normal pace of events. Tendency to finish others' sentences.
- Doing everything rapidly.
- Feelings of guilt when relaxing.
- Tendency to evaluate all activities in terms of measurable results.
- Belief that Type A attributes are what lead to success.
- Frequent knee-jiggling or finger-tapping.
- Determination to win every game, even when playing with those who are less skilled or experienced.

education and management. By far the most well-known connection between personality and resilience relates to a combination of attributes known as the Type A personality. For at least three decades scientists have been aware of a link between certain personality attributes and stress-related behavioural, psychological and physiological problems such as anxiety, deteriorating relationships and heart disease (Friedman and Rosenman, 1959). Table 2.8 summarises the primary attributes of Type A personalities that have emerged from the research.

The manner in which Friedman and Rosenman, both cardiologists, discovered the link between personality and heart disease is intriguing. Observing that their waiting room was becoming a bit shabby, they decided to have their chairs re-upholstered. The decorator pointed out that only the front edges of the chairs were worn. The doctors suddenly realised that their patients seemed to be 'on edge', literally sitting on the edges of their seats, prepared for action.

Following up their observations with intensive interviews, they noted that during interviews many of their patients showed signs of impatience and hostility such as fidgeting, eye-blinking, grimaces, rapid or explosive speech, interrupting, and filling in incomplete sentences during a pause. The opposite personality types – which they labelled Type B – appeared more relaxed, patient and able to listen without interrupting. Over 15 per cent of Friedman and Rosenman's Type A patients had had heart attacks, compared to 7 per cent of Type B patients. Subsequent research has found that, in America, about 70 per cent of men and 50 per cent of women exhibit Type A personality traits, such as extreme competitiveness, strong desires for achievement, haste, impatience, restlessness, hyper-alertness, explosive speech, tenseness of facial muscles, free-floating hostility and so on. Rosenman suggested that anger, impatience and competitiveness were the most debilitating factors in the Type A personality; others have proposed hostility (Greenberg, 1987) and some have blamed a feeling of urgency that keeps adrenaline constantly flowing (Kobasa, 1979). Regardless of the key ingredient, the Type A personality is certain to have a disastrous effect on well-being.

In the most extensive study of personality effects on heart disease ever conducted, an eight-year survey of 3,400 men found that Type A individuals in the 39–49 age group had approximately 6.5 times the likelihood of heart disease as Type Bs. Even when factors such as cigarette smoking, parental medical history, blood pressure and cholesterol levels were taken into account, the Type A personality still accounted for two to three times greater likelihood of heart disease. This research concluded that personality is a better predictor than physiology of cardiovascular illness (Friedman and Rosenman, 1974). Ironically, subsequent research has also found that whereas Type A personalities are more prone to experience heart attacks, they are also more likely to recover from them. Janice Ho (1995) working in Singapore, would add to this finding. Her Type A *reported* more stress but the Type B were not physiologically less healthy. Her sample from three sectors – service, financial and banking – quoted time, encounter and situational stressors but seemed well versed in coping mechanisms.

Most Type A individuals believe that it is their Type A personality that has led to their success. Many are unwilling to give up that orientation because hard-driving, intense, persistent action is generally admired and valued among managers. This has often been associated with the traditional male management role, but it has also been connected to the disproportionately high incidence of heart disease among men. In fact, Goldberg (1976) and Jourard (1964) initially linked Type A personality characteristics to certain sex-linked behaviour patterns. Specifically, males or females that follow the stereotypic views of appropriate male behaviour were found to be more likely to experience stress-related illness. They tended to equate low self-disclosure, low emotional involvement, low display of feelings, high defensiveness and high insensitivity to the acquisition of power and control – the presumed prerequisites for success. These were so typical of male behaviour in the workplace that they became known as the 'lethal aspects of the male role' (Jourard, 1964). As more women began to enter the workforce, this same pattern became less and less gender-linked. Many women also behaved as if acceptance in the workplace required 'acting as masculine', i.e., as their male counterparts. As a result, the gap between stress-related illness among professional men and women has narrowed. In recent years, female stress-related illness (e.g., heart attacks, suicides, and migraine headaches) has actually surpassed those of males in some professions. This trend is not only tragic but ironic, because corporations are spending huge amounts each year on training workshops designed to encourage their managers to become more sensitive, understanding and supportive. The folly of the Type A approach to management is illustrated in the following Zen story.

Matajura wanted to become a great swordsman, but his father said he wasn't quick enough and could never learn. So Matajura went to the famous dueller, Banzo, and asked to become his pupil. 'How long will it take me to become a master?' he asked. 'Suppose I become your servant, and spend every minute with you; how long?'

'Ten years.' said Banzo.

'My father is getting old. Before ten years have passed, I will have to return home to take care of him. Suppose I work twice as hard; how long will it take me?'

'Thirty years.' said Banzo.

'How is that?' asked Matajura. 'First you say ten years. Then when I offer to work twice as hard, you say it will take three times as long. Let me make myself clear: I will work unceasingly; no hardship will be too much. How long will it take?'

'Seventy years,' said Banzo. 'A pupil in such a hurry learns slowly.'

This Type A sense of urgency, of thinking that any obstacle can be overcome by working harder and longer, works against the ability to develop psychological hardiness. When stressors are encountered, arousal levels increase, and the tendency is to combat them by increasing arousal levels or effort even further. But at high arousal levels, coping responses become more primitive (Staw *et al.*, 1981). Patterns of response that were learned most recently are the first ones to disappear, which means that the responses that are most finely tuned to the current stressful situation are the first ones to go. The ability to distinguish among fine-grained stimuli actually deteriorates, so the extra energy expended by individuals trying to cope becomes less and less effective. Weick (1984) pointed out that highly stressed people consequently find it difficult to learn new responses, to brainstorm, to concentrate, to resist relying on old non-adaptive behaviour patterns, to perform complex responses, to delegate and to avoid the vicious spiral of escalating arousal. Resilience deteriorates.

The small-wins strategy

An effective antidote to this Type A escalation problem is working for 'small wins', as discussed earlier. When individuals work for small wins, they consciously remain sensitive to their small successes – and celebrate them – while coping with a major stressor.

A hypothetical example introduced by Kuhn and Beam (1982, pp. 249–50) illustrates the power of small wins:

Your task is to count out a thousand sheets of paper while you are subject to periodic interruptions. Each interruption causes you to lose track of the count and forces you to start over. If you count the thousand as a single sequence, then an interruption could cause you to lose count of as many as 999. If the sheets are put into stacks of 100, however, and each stack remains undisturbed by interruptions, then the worst possible count loss from interruption is 108. That number represents the recounting of nine stacks of 100 each plus 99 single sheets. Further, if sheets are first put into stacks of 10, which are then joined into stacks of 100, the worst possible loss from interruption would be 27. That number represents nine stacks of 100 plus nine stacks of 10 plus nine single sheets. With this system there is far less recounting time, but the chances of completing the count are vastly higher.

When individuals work for a small, concrete outcome, giving them a chance to enjoy visible success, there is a sense of heightened confidence, excitement and optimism. They then want to go for another 'small win'. When one solution has been identified, the next solvable problem often becomes more visible. Additional resources also tend to flow towards winners, so the probability of additional success increases.

Research clearly demonstrates that a small-wins strategy is superior to a strategy of trying to cope with stressors in large chunks. For example, successive small requests are more likely to be approved and achieve compliance than one large request (Freedman and Fraser, 1966). Positions advocated within the latitude of acceptance (i.e., that are only slightly different from current positions) modify opinions more than does advocacy of a position that exceeds those limits (i.e., large differences exist between current and proposed positions). People whose positions are close to one's own tend to be the targets of the most intensive persuasion attempts, while those whose positions are farther away are dismissed, isolated or derogated.

Cognitive therapy is most successful when the patient is persuaded to do just one thing differently that changes his or her pattern of coping up to that point. Learning tends to occur in small increments rather than in large, all-or-nothing chunks. Retention of learning is better when individuals are in an emotional state similar to the one in which they learned the original material. Over 75 per cent of the changes and improvements in both individuals and reorganisations over time can be accounted for by minor improvements, not major alterations (Hollander, 1965). The point is that the incremental approach used in a small-wins strategy is the most basic and the one most compatible with human preferences for learning, perception, motivation and change (Weick, 1984). What does this have to do with hardiness and resilience? A small-wins strategy both engenders hardiness and helps overcome the Type A personality syndrome, which is basically a winner-takes-all approach to stress. You may recall that hardiness is composed of control, commitment and challenge. The deliberate cultivation of a strategy of small wins helps to produce precisely those psychological states. Small wins reinforce the perception that individuals can influence what happens to them and it helps motivate further action by building on the confidence of past successes and produces changes of manageable size that serve as incentives to learn and seek new opportunities (Weick, 1984, p. 46).

Deep-relaxation strategies

A further medium-term strategy is the practice of deep relaxation (Curtis and Detert, 1981; Greenberg, 1987; Davis *et al.*, 1980). Deep-relaxation techniques differ from temporary, short-term relaxation techniques, which we will discuss later. Deep relaxation, like physical exercise, takes time to develop because its benefits cannot be achieved quickly, but it serves to engender resilience towards stress. Deep-relaxation techniques include meditation, yoga, autogenic training or self-hypnosis, biofeedback, and so on. Considerable evidence exists that individuals who practise such techniques regularly are able to condition their bodies to inhibit the negative effects of stress (Cooper and Aygen, 1979; Stone and Deleo, 1976; Orme-Johnson, 1973; Beary and Benson, 1977; Benson, 1975). Most of these deep-relaxation techniques must be practised over a period of time in order to develop fully, but they are not difficult to learn. Most deep-relaxation techniques require the following conditions:

1. *A quiet environment* in which external distractions are minimised.

2. *A comfortable position* so that muscular effort is minimised.

3. *A mental focus*. Transcendental meditation (TM) advocates recommend concentrating on one word, phrase or object. Benson (1975) suggests the word 'one'. Others suggest picturing a plain vase. The ancient Chinese used a carved jade object that resembled a mountain, sitting on a desktop. The purpose of focusing on a word or object is to rid the mind of all other thoughts.

4. *Controlled breathing*, i.e., deliberate breathing, with pauses between breaths. Thoughts are focused on rhythmic breathing, which helps to clear the mind and aids concentration.

5. *A passive attitude*, so that if other thoughts enter the mind they are ignored.

6. *Focused bodily changes*. While meditation uses the mind to relax the body, autogenic training used bodily sensations of heaviness and warmth to change the psychological state. Feelings of warmth and heaviness are induced in different parts of the body which, in turn, create deep relaxation (Luthe, 1962; Kamiya, 1978).

7. *Repetition*. Because physiological and psychological results depend on consistent practice, the best results occur when such techniques are practised from 20 to 30 minutes each day. (The Skill Practice section (page 149) contains an example of a deep-relaxation exercise.)

Social resilience

The third factor moderating the harmful effects of stress and contributing to resilience involves developing close social relationships. Individuals who are embedded in supportive social networks are less likely to experience stress and are better equipped to cope with its consequences (Beehr, 1976). Supportive social relations provide opportunities to share one's frustrations and disappointments, to receive suggestions and encouragement, and to experience emotional bonding. Such supportive interactions provide the empathy and bolstering required to cope with stressful events. They are formed most easily among individuals who share close emotional ties (e.g., family members) or common experiences (e.g., co-workers). Dramatic evidence for the value of social support systems during periods of high stress comes from the experiences of soldiers captured during the Second World War and the Korean and Vietnam wars. When it was possible for prisoners to form permanent, interacting groups, they maintained better health and morale and were able to resist their captors more effectively than when they were isolated or when groups were unstable. Indeed, the well-documented technique used by the Chinese during the Korean War for breaking down soldiers' resistance to their indoctrination efforts involved weakening group solidarity through planting seeds of mistrust and doubt about members' loyalty. Apart from personal friendships or family relations, two types of social support systems can be formed as part of a manager's job. One is a mentor relationship; the other is a task team. Most individuals, with the possible exception of the most senior managers, can profit from a mentoring relationship. The research is clear that career success, work satisfaction and resilience to stress are enhanced by a mentoring relationship (Hall, 1976; Kram, 1985). Individuals need someone else in the organisation who can provide a role model, from whom they can learn, and from whom they can receive personal attention and a reinforcement of self worth, especially in uncertain, crucial and stressful situations.

Many organisations formally prescribe a mentoring system by assigning a senior manager to shepherd a younger manager when he or she enters the organisation. With rare exceptions, when the contact is one-way, from the top down, these relationships do not work out (Kram, 1985). The junior manager must actively seek and foster the mentoring relationship as well. The junior manager can do this, not by demonstrating over-dependence or over-adaptation, but by expressing a desire to use the senior person as a mentor and then by making certain that the relationship does not become a one-way street. The subordinate can pass along important information and resources to the potential mentor, while both will share in working out solutions to problems. That way, the mentoring relationship becomes mutually satisfying and beneficial for both parties, and resilience to stress is enhanced because of the commitment, trust and co-operation that begin to characterise the relationship. A mentor's guidance can both help to avoid stressful situations and provide support for coping with them.

Smoothly functioning work teams also enhance social resilience. The social value of working on a team has been well-documented in the research (Dyer, 1981). The more cohesive the team, the more support it provides its members. Members of highly cohesive teams communicate with one another more frequently and positively, and report higher satisfaction, lower stress and higher performance levels than do individuals who do not feel as though they are part of a work team (Shaw, 1976).

The value of work teams has also been amply demonstrated in practice.

In the Fremont, California, plant of General Motors a dramatic change occurred when US workers came under Japanese management. In just one year, marked improvements in productivity, morale and quality occurred, due in a large part to the use of effective work teams. Relationships were formed based not only on friendship, but on a common commitment to solving work-related problems and to generating ideas for improvement. Teams met regularly during work hours to discuss ideas for improvement and to co-ordinate and resolve issues.

Similar dynamics have been fostered in many of the successful companies in Europe. Changes at British Aerospace have been attributed largely to the effective use of work teams. The marked improvements that occur in individual satisfaction and lowered stress levels suggest that the model should be followed wherever it is appropriate. The idea would be that the team, rather than independent individuals, becomes the standard unit for working.

Temporary stress-reduction techniques

So far we have emphasised eliminating sources of stress and developing resilience to stress as the most desirable stress management strategies. However, even in practical circumstances it may be impossible to eliminate all stressors, and individuals must use temporary reactive mechanisms in order to maintain more equilibrium. Although increased resilience can buffer the harmful effects of stress, people must sometimes take immediate action in the short term to cope with stress. Implementing short-term strategies reduces stress temporarily so that longer-term stress elimination or resilience strategies can be incorporated. Short-term strategies are largely reactive and must be repeated whenever stressors are encountered because, unlike other strategies, their effects are temporary. On the other hand, they are especially useful for the immediate calming feelings of anxiety or apprehension. Individuals can use them when they are asked a question they cannot answer, when they become embarrassed by an unexpected event, when they are faced with a presentation or an important meeting, or almost any time they are suddenly stressed and must respond in a short period of time. Five of the best-known and easiest to learn techniques are briefly described below. The first two are physiological; the last three are psychological.

Muscle relaxation

Muscle relaxation involves easing the tension in successive muscle groups. Each muscle group is tightened for five or ten seconds, then completely relaxed. Starting with the feet and progressing to the calves, thighs, stomach, and on to the neck and face, one can relieve tension throughout the entire body. All parts of the body can be included in the exercise. One variation is to roll the head around on the neck several times, shrug the shoulders or stretch the arms up towards the ceiling for five to ten seconds, then release the position and relax the muscles. The result is a state of temporary relaxation that helps eliminate tension and refocus energy.

> The Management Training Centre of Unilever UK Holdings in Port Sunlight, UK, was well known for promoting a particular technique of relaxation at meetings. Individuals, feeling under stress, were encouraged to push hard on the underside of the table with their little fingers. The legend was that after several years and several generations of managers had been training in this technique, the table spontaneously levitated at a Unilever Board meeting. After this incident, the legend goes, training in the technique was stopped. In fact the trainers moved on.

Deep breathing

A variation of muscle relaxation involves deep breathing. You take several successive, slow, deep breaths, holding them for five seconds and exhaling completely. You should focus on breathing itself, so that the mind becomes cleared for a brief time while the body relaxes. After each deep breath, muscles in the body should consciously be relaxed.

Imagery and fantasy

A third technique uses imagery and fantasy to eliminate stress temporarily by changing the focus of one's thoughts. Imagery involves visualising an event, using 'mind pictures'. In addition to visualisation, however, imagery also can include recollections of sounds, smells and textures. The mind focuses on pleasant experiences from the past (e.g., a fishing trip, family holiday, visit with relatives, a day at the beach) that can be recalled vividly. Fantasies, on the other hand, are not past memories but make-believe events or images. It is especially well known, for example, that children often construct imaginary friends, make-believe occurrences or special wishes that are comforting to them when they encounter stress. Adults also use daydreams or other fantasy experiences to get them through stressful situations. The purpose of this technique is to relieve anxiety or pressure temporarily by focusing on something pleasant so that other more productive stress-reducing strategies can be developed for the longer term.

Rehearsal

The fourth technique is called rehearsal. Using this technique, people work themselves through potentially stressful situations, trying out different scenarios and alternative reactions. Appropriate reactions are rehearsed, either in a safe environment before stress occurs, or 'off-line', in private, in the midst of a stressful situation. Removing oneself temporarily from a stressful circumstance and working through dialogue or reactions, as though rehearsing for a play, can help an individual to regain control and reduce the immediacy of the stressor.

Reframing

The last strategy, reframing, involves temporarily reducing stress by optimistically redefining a situation as manageable. Although reframing is difficult in the midst of a stressful situation, it can be developed using cues:

> 'I understand this situation.'
> 'I've solved similar problems before.'
> 'Other people are available to help me get through this situation.'
> 'Others have faced similar situations and made it through.'
> 'In the long run, this really isn't so critical.'
> 'I can learn something from this situation.'
> 'There are several good alternatives available to me.'

Each of these statements can assist an individual to reframe a situation in order to develop long-term proactive or evolutionary strategies.

SUMMARY

We have shown that four kinds of stressor – time, encounter, situational and anticipatory – can cause negative physiological, psychological and social reactions in individuals and that these reactions have adverse effects on organisations. Individuals adopt short-, medium- and long-term strategies to cope. The medium-term strategy is to eliminate the stress through time management, delegation, collaboration, interpersonal competence, work redesign, prioritising, goal setting and small-wins strategies. Failing this, removing oneself from the situation is a drastic but permanent solution. This is the long-term strategy.

Resistance to stress can be increased by improving one's personal resilience. Physiological resilience is strengthened through increased cardiovascular conditioning and improved diet. Psychological resilience and hardiness are improved by practising small-wins strategies and deep relaxation. Social resilience is improved by learning to work with others and fostering teamwork. However, when circumstances make it impossible to apply longer-term strategies for reducing stress, short-term relaxation techniques can temporarily alleviate the symptoms of stress.

Behavioural guidelines

Cynthia Berryman-Fink and Charles Fink (1996) suggest a series of tips for managing personal stress – practising relaxation techniques, developing an exercise programme, practising healthy eating, socialising outside work, developing social support and practising time management. We would agree, adding a clarification of personal goals and the longer-term solutions of work redesign even to the point of leaving.

1. Use effective time management practices. Make sure that you use time effectively as well as efficiently by generating your own personal mission statement. Make sure that low-priority tasks do not drive out time to work on high-priority activities.

2. Make better use of your time by using the guidelines in the Time Management Survey on page 93.

3. Build collaborative relationships with individuals based on mutual trust, respect, honesty and kindness. Make 'deposits' into the 'emotional bank accounts' of other people. Form close, stable communities among those with whom you work.

4. Consciously work to improve your interpersonal competency by learning and practising the principles discussed in other chapters of this book.

5. Redesign your work to increase its skill variety, importance, task clarity, autonomy and feedback. Make the work itself stress-reducing rather than stress-inducing.

6. Reaffirm priorities and short-term plans that provide direction and focus to activities. Give important activities priority over urgent ones.

7. Increase your general resilience by leading a balanced life and consciously developing yourself in physical, intellectual, cultural, social, family, and spiritual areas, as well as in your work.

8. Increase your physical resilience by engaging in a regular programme of exercise and proper eating.

9. Increase your psychological resilience and hardiness by implementing a small-wins strategy. Identify and celebrate the small successes that you and others achieve.

10. Learn at least one deep-relaxation technique and practise it regularly.

11. Increase social resilience by forming an open, trusting, sharing relationship with at least one other person. Facilitate a mentoring relationship with someone who can confirm your worth as a person and provide support during periods of stress.

12. Establish a teamwork relationship with those with whom you work or study by identifying shared tasks and structuring co-ordinated action among team members.

13. Learn at least two short-term relaxation techniques and practise them consistently.

Skill Analysis

CASE STUDY **2.1**

THE DAY AT THE BEACH

Not long ago I came to one of those bleak periods that many of us encounter from time to time, a sudden drastic dip in the graph of living when everything goes stale and flat, energy wanes, enthusiasm dies. The effect on my work was frightening. Every morning I would clench my teeth and mutter: 'Today life will take on some of its old meaning. You've got to break through this thing. You've got to!'

But the barren days went by, and the paralysis grew worse. The time came when I knew I had to have help. The man I turned to was a doctor. Not a psychiatrist, just a doctor. He was older than I, and under his surface gruffness lay great wisdom and compassion. 'I don't know what's wrong,' I told him miserably, 'but I just seem to have come to a dead end. Can you help me?'

'I don't know,' he said slowly. He made a tent of his fingers and gazed at me thoughtfully for a long while. Then, abruptly, he asked, 'Where were you happiest as a child?'

'As a child?' I echoed. 'Why, at the beach, I suppose. We had a summer cottage there. We all loved it.'

He looked out of the window and watched the October leaves wafting down. 'Are you capable of following instructions for a single day?' 'I think so,' I said, ready to try anything. 'All right. Here's what I want you to do.'

I was living in The Hague at the time and he told me to drive down to a quieter part of the local beach by myself the following morning, arriving not later than nine o'clock. I could take some lunch; but I was not to read, write, listen to the radio or talk to anyone. 'In addition,' he said, 'I'll give you a prescription to be taken every three hours.'

He tore off four prescription blanks, wrote a few words on each, folded them, numbered them and handed them to me.

'Take these at nine, twelve, three and six.'

'Are you serious?' I asked. He gave a short bark of laughter. 'You won't think I'm joking when you get my bill!'

The next morning, with little faith, I drove to the beach. It was lonely. A north-easter was blowing; the sea looked grey and angry. I sat in the car, the whole day stretching emptily before me. Then I took out the first of the folded slips of paper. On it was written: LISTEN CAREFULLY.

I stared at the two words. 'Why,' I thought, 'the man must be mad.' He had ruled out music, news programmes and human conversation. What else was there?

I raised my head and I did listen. There were no sounds but the steady roar of the sea, the creaking cry of a gull, the drone of some aircraft high overhead. All these sounds were familiar. I got out of the car. A gust of wind slammed the door with a sudden clap of sound.

'Was I supposed to listen carefully to things like that?' I asked myself.

I looked out over the deserted beach, it was winter and not a very nice day. Here the sea bellowed so loudly that all other sounds were lost. And yet, I thought sud-denly, there must be sounds beneath sounds – the soft rasp of drifting sand, the tiny wind whisperings in the dune grasses – if the listener got close enough to hear them. On an impulse I ducked down and, feeling fairly ridiculous, thrust my head into a clump of seaweed. Here I made a discovery: If you listen intently, there is a frac-tional moment in which everything seems to pause. In that instant of stillness, the racing thoughts halt. For a moment, when you truly listen for something outside yourself, you have to silence the clamorous voices within. The mind rests.

I went back to the car and slid behind the wheel. LISTEN CAREFULLY. As I lis-tened again to the deep growl of the sea, I found myself thinking about the white-fanged fury of its storms. I thought of the lessons it had taught us as children. A certain amount of patience: you can't hurry the tides. A great deal of respect: the sea does not suffer fools gladly. An awareness of the vast and mysterious interde-pendence of things: wind and tide and current, calm and squall and hurricane, all combining to determine the paths of the birds above and the fish below. And the cleanness of it all, with every beach swept twice a day by the great broom of the sea.

Sitting there, I realised I was thinking of things bigger than myself – and there was relief in that. Even so, the morning passed slowly. The habit of hurling myself at a problem was so strong that I felt lost without it. Once, when I was wistfully eye-ing the car radio, a phrase from Carlyle jumped into my head: '*Silence is the element in which great things fashion themselves.*'

By noon the wind had polished the clouds out of the sky, and the sea had a hard, polished and merry sparkle.

I unfolded the second 'prescription.' Again I sat there, half amused and half exas-perated. Three words this time: TRY REACHING BACK.

Back to what? To the past, obviously. But why, when all my worries concerned the present or the future?

I left the car and started tramping back to the foreshore. The doctor had sent me to the beach because it was a place of happy memories. Maybe that was what I was to reach for: the wealth of happiness that lay half-forgotten behind me. I decided to experiment: to work on these vague impressions as a painter would, retouching the colours, strengthening the outlines. I would choose specific incidents and recapture as many details as possible. I would visualise people complete with dress and gestures. I would listen carefully for the exact sound of their voices, the echo of their laughter.

The tide was going out now, but there was still thunder in the surf. So I chose to go back 20 years to the last fishing trip I made with my younger brother. (He died in the Battle of the Atlantic in the Second World War and his body was never recovered.) I found that if I closed my eyes and really tried, I could see him with amazing vividness. I could even see the humour and eagerness in his eyes that far-off morning.

I could see it all: the ivory scimitar of beach where we were fishing; the skies smeared with sunrise; the great rollers creaming in, stately and slow. I could feel the backwash swirl warm around my knees, see the sudden arc of my brother's rod as he struck a fish, hear his exultant yell. Piece by piece I rebuilt it, clear and unchanged under the transparent varnish of time. Then it was gone.

I sat up slowly. TRY REACHING BACK. Happy people were usually assured, confident people. If, then, you deliberately reached back and touched happiness, might there not be released little flashes of power, tiny sources of strength?

This second period of the day went more quickly, people appeared and seemingly resented each other, keeping in little knots of privacy. As the sun began its long slant down the sky, my mind ranged eagerly through the past, reliving some episodes, uncovering others that had been almost completely forgotten. For example, when I was around 13 and my brother 10, Father had promised to take us to the circus. But at lunch there was a phone call: some urgent business required his attention. We braced ourselves for disappointment. Then we heard him say, 'No, I won't be down. It'll have to wait.' When he came back to the table, Mother smiled. 'The circus keeps coming back, you know, she said.' 'I know,' said Father, 'but childhood doesn't.' Across all the years I remembered this and knew from the sudden glow of warmth that no kindness is ever wasted or ever completely lost.

By three o'clock the tide was out and the sound of the waves was only a rhythmic whisper, like a giant breathing. I stayed in my sandy nest, feeling relaxed and content, and a little complacent. The doctor's prescriptions, I thought, were easy to take. But I was not prepared for the next one. This time the three words were not a gentle suggestion. They sounded more like a command. RE-EXAMINE YOUR MOTIVES.

My first reaction was purely defensive. 'There's nothing wrong with my motives,' I said to myself. 'I want to be successful – who doesn't? I want to have a certain amount of recognition – but so does everybody. I want more security than I've got – and why not?'

'Maybe', said a small voice somewhere inside my head, 'those motives aren't good enough. Maybe that's the reason the wheels have stopped going around.' I picked up a handful of sand and let it stream between my fingers. In the past, whenever my work went well, there had always been something spontaneous about it, something uncontrived, something free. Lately it had been calculated, competent and dead.

Why? Because I had been looking past the job itself to the rewards I hoped it would bring. The work had ceased to be an end in itself, it had become merely a means to make money, to pay bills. The sense of giving something, of helping people, of making a contribution, had been lost in a frantic clutch at security. In a flash of certainty, I saw that if one's motives are wrong, nothing can be right. It makes no difference whether you are a postman, a hairdresser, an insurance salesman, a housewife . . . As long as you feel you are serving others, you do the job well. When you are concerned only with helping yourself, you do it less well. That is a law as inexorable as gravity. For a long time I sat there. Far out on the bar I heard the murmur of the surf change to a hollow roar as the tide turned. Behind me the spears of light were almost horizontal.

My time at the beach had almost run out, and I felt a grudging admiration for the doctor and the 'prescriptions' he had so casually and cunningly devised. I saw, now, that in them was a therapeutic progression that might well be of value to anyone facing any difficulty.

Listen carefully: To calm a frantic mind, slow it down, shift the focus from inner problems to outer things.

Try reaching back: Since the human mind can hold only one idea at a time, you blot out present worry when you touch the happiness of the past.

Re-examine your motives: This was the hard core of the 'treatment', this challenge to reappraise, to bring one's motives into alignment with one's capabilities and conscience. But the mind must be clear and receptive to do this – hence the six hours of quiet that went before.

The western sky was a blaze of crimson as I took out the last slip of paper. Six words this time. I walked slowly along the beach. A few yards below the high-water mark I stopped and read the words again: WRITE YOUR TROUBLES ON THE SAND. I let the paper blow away, reached down and picked up a fragment of shell. Kneeling there under the vault of the sky, I wrote several words on the sand, one above the other. Then I walked away, and I did not look back. I had written my troubles on the sand. And the tide was coming in.

Source: Adapted from *The Day at the Beach*, by Arthur Gordon. (© 1959 by Arthur Gordon. First published in *Reader's Digest*. Reprinted by permission of the author. All rights reserved.)

Discussion questions

1. What is effective about these strategies for coping with stress? Why did they work? Upon what principles are they based?

2. Which of these techniques can be used on a temporary basis without going to 'the beach'?

3. Are these prescriptions effective coping strategies or merely escapes?

4. What other prescriptions could the author take besides the four mentioned here? Generate your own list.

5. What do these prescriptions have to do with the model of stress management presented in this chapter?

CASE STUDY **2.2**

THE CASE OF THE MISSING TIME

At approximately 07.30 on Tuesday, 17 June 1997, Chris Craig, a senior production manager in Norris Printing Ltd, set off to drive to work. It was a beautiful day and the journey to the factory took about 20 minutes, giving Chris an opportunity to think about plant problems without interruption.

The Norris Company owned and operated three factories and had a Europe-wide reputation for quality colour printing. Three hundred and fifty people worked for the company, about half working in Chris's Belgium plant which also housed the company's headquarters.

Chris was in fine spirits as he relaxed behind the wheel. Various thoughts occurred to him, and he said to himself, 'This is going to be the day to really get things done.'

He began to run through the day's work, first one project, then another, trying to establish priorities. After a few minutes he decided that progressing with the new system of production control was probably the most important, certainly the most urgent of his jobs for the day. He frowned for a moment as he remembered that on Friday the general manager had casually asked him if he had given the project any further thought.

Chris realised that he had not been giving it much thought lately. He had been meaning to get to work on this idea for over three months, but something else always seemed to crop up. 'I haven't had much time to sit down and really work it out,' he said to himself.

'I'd better get going and sort this one out today.' With that he began to break down the objectives, procedures and installation steps of the project. He grinned as he reviewed the principles involved and calculated roughly the anticipated savings. 'It's about time,' he told himself, 'this idea should have been followed up long ago.' Chris remembered that he had first thought of the production control system nearly 18 months ago, just before leaving the Norris factory in Spain. He had spoken to his boss, Jim Quince, manager of the Spanish factory about it then, and both agreed that it was worth looking into.

The idea was temporarily shelved when he was transferred to the Belgium plant a month later. Then he started to think through a procedure for simpler transport of dies to and from the Spanish plant. Visualising the notes on his desk, he thought about the inventory analysis he needed to identify and eliminate some of the slow-moving stock items, the packing controls that needed revision, and the need to design a new special-order form. He also decided that this was the day to settle on a job printer to do the simple outside printing of office forms. There were a few other projects he couldn't remember, but he could tend to them after lunch, if not before.

When he entered the plant Chris knew something was wrong as he met Albert Marsden, the stockroom foreman, who appeared troubled.

'A great morning, Albert,' Chris greeted him cheerfully.

'Not so good, Chris; the new man isn't in this morning.'

'Did he phone in – let you know why?' asked Chris.

'No, nothing,' replied Marsden. Chris shared Albert's concern. He knew that 'the new man' had been taken on to deal with a major problem in the warehouse. Without him, and particularly without him at no notice, the whole of the new auto-mated stock delivery system could and probably would grind to a halt.

'OK, we have a problem, ask Personnel to call him and see if he intends to come in.' Albert Marsden hesitated for a moment before replying, 'Okay, Chris, but can you find me a man with real computer skills? – you know the problem as well as I do.'

'OK, Albert, I'll call you in half an hour with something, even if I have to do it myself.'

Making a mental note of the situation, Chris headed for his office. He greeted the group of workers huddled around Marie Heinlinne, the office manager, who was discussing the day's work schedule with them. As the meeting broke up, Marie picked up a few samples from the pallet, showed them to Chris, and asked if they should be sent out as they were or whether it would be necessary to inspect all of them. Before he could answer, Marie went on to ask if he could suggest another operator for the sealing machine to replace the regular operator, who was absent. She also told him that George, the industrial engineer, had called and was waiting to hear from Chris. After telling Marie to send the samples as they were, he made a note of the need for a sealer operator for the office and then called George. He agreed to go to George's office before lunch and started on his routine morning tour of the factory. He asked each team leader the types and volumes of orders they were running, the number of people present, how the schedules were coming along, and the orders to be run next. He helped the folding-room team leader find temporary storage space for consolidating a consignment; discussed quality control with a press operator who had been producing work off specification; arranged to transfer four people temporarily to different departments, including one for Albert from accounts who 'was not frightened of computers'; and talked to the shipping fore-man about collecting some urgent ink supplies and the special deliveries of the day. As he continued through the factory, he saw to it that reserve stock was moved out of the forward stock area, talked to another pressman about his holiday, had a 'heart-to-heart' talk with a press assistant who seemed to need frequent reassurance, and approved two type changes and one colour change with three press operators and their team leader.

Returning to his office, Chris reviewed the production reports on the larger orders against his initial estimates and found that the plant was running behind schedule. He called in the folding-room team leader and together they went over the production schedule in detail, making several changes. During this discussion, the composing-room foreman stopped in to note several type changes, and the routing foreman telephoned for approval of a revised printing schedule. The stock-room team leader called twice, first to inform him that two standard, fast moving stock items were dangerously low, later to advise him that the paper stock for the urgent Pitman's job had finally arrived. Chris made the necessary calls to inform those concerned. He then began to put delivery dates on important and difficult enquiries received from customers and salesmen – Marie handled the routine enquiries. While he was doing this he was interrupted twice, once by a sales rep to ask for a better delivery date than originally scheduled, and once by the personnel director asking him to set a time when he could hold an initial training and induction interview with a new employee. After sorting the customer and salesmen enquiries, Chris headed for his morning conference in the executive offices. At this meeting he answered the sales director's questions in connection with some problem orders, complaints, and the status of large-volume orders and potential new orders. He then met the general manager to discuss a few ticklish policy matters and to answer questions on several specific production and personnel problems. Before leaving the executive offices, he stopped at the office of the secretary–treasurer to enquire about delivery of cartons, paper and boxes, and to place a new order for paper.

On the way back to his own office, Chris conferred with George about the two current engineering projects that had been discussed earlier. When he reached his desk, he looked at his watch. He had five minutes before lunch – enough to make a few notes of the details he needed to check in order to answer difficult questions raised by the sales manager that morning.

After a lunch of sandwiches grabbed from the canteen, Chris started again. He began by checking the previous day's production reports, did some rescheduling to get out urgent orders, placed appropriate delivery dates on new orders and enquiries received that morning, and helped a team leader with a personal problem. He spent about 20 minutes on the phone going over routine problems with the Spanish factory.

By mid-afternoon Chris had made another tour of the site, after which he met with the personnel director to review a touchy personal problem raised by one of the clerical employees, the holiday schedules submitted by his foremen, and the pending job-evaluation programme. Following this meeting, Chris hurried back to his office to complete the special statistical report for U.W.C., one of Norris's best customers. As he finished the report, he discovered that it was 18.10 and he was the only one left in the office. Chris was tired. He put on his coat and headed for his car; on the way he was stopped by two team leaders from the incoming night shift with urgent issues needing decisions.

With both eyes on the traffic, Chris reviewed the day he had just completed. 'Busy?' he asked himself. 'Too busy – but did I actually DO anything? There was the usual routine, the same as any other day. The factory kept going and I think it must have been a good production day. Any creative or special project work done?' Chris grimaced as he reluctantly answered, 'No'. Feeling guilty, he probed further. 'Am I a senior manager – a true executive? I'm paid like one, respected like one, and have a responsible assignment with the necessary authority to carry it out. Yet an executive should be able to think strategically and creatively and not just firefight. An executive needs time for thinking. Today was typical and I did little, if any, creative work. The projects that I planned in the morning have not moved an inch. What's more, I have no guarantee that tomorrow or the next day will be any different. This is the real problem.' Chris continued talking silently to himself. 'Taking work home? Yes, occasionally, it's expected but I've been doing too much lately. I owe my wife and family some of my time. After all, they are the people for whom I'm really working. If I am forced to spend much more time away from them, am I being fair to them or myself. What about work with the Scouts? Should I stop it? It takes up a lot of my time, but I feel I owe other people some time, and I feel that I am making a valuable contribution. When do I have time for a game of squash or even a quiet drink with my friends these days? Maybe I'm just making excuses because I don't plan my time better, but I don't think so. I've already analysed my way of working and I think I plan and delegate pretty well. Do I need an assistant? Possibly, but that's a long-term project and I don't believe I could justify the additional overhead expenditure. Anyway, I doubt whether it would solve the problem.'

All the way home he was concerned with the problem – even as he pulled into the drive. His thoughts were interrupted as he saw his son running towards the car, 'Mummy, Daddy's home.'

Discussion questions

1. Which of Chris's personal characteristics inhibit his effective management of time?

2. What are his organisational problems?

3. What principles of time and stress management are violated in this case?

4. If you were hired as a consultant to Chris, what would you advise him to do?

Skill Practice

EXERCISE **2.1**

THE SMALL-WINS STRATEGY

An ancient Chinese proverb states that long journeys are always made up of small steps. In Japan, the feeling of obligation to make small, incremental improvements in one's work is known as *Kaizen*. In this chapter the notion of small wins was explained as a way to break up large problems and identify small successes in coping with them. Each of these approaches represents the same basic philosophy – to recognise incremental successes – and each helps an individual to build up psychological resilience to stress.

Answer the following questions. An example is given to help clarify each question, but your response need not relate to the example.

1. What major stressor do you currently face? What creates anxiety or discomfort for you? (For example, 'I have too much to do.')

2. What are the major components of the situation? Divide the major problem into smaller parts or sub-problems. (For example, 'I have said "yes" to too many things. I have deadlines approaching. I don't have all the resources I need to complete all my commitments right now.')

3. What are the sub-components of each of those sub-problems? Divide them into yet smaller parts. (For example, 'I have the following deadlines approaching: a report due, a large amount of reading to do, a family obligation, an important presentation, a need to spend some personal time with someone I care about, a committee meeting that requires preparation.')

4. What actions can I take that will affect any of these sub-components? (For example, 'I can engage the person I care about in helping me prepare for the presentation. I can write a shorter report than I originally intended. I can carry the reading material with me wherever I go.')

5. What actions have I taken in the past that have helped me to cope successfully with similar stressful circumstances? (For example, 'I have found someone else to share some of my tasks. I have got some reading done while waiting/travelling/eating. I have prepared only key elements for the committee meeting.')

6. What small thing should I feel good about as I think about how I have coped or will cope with this major stressor? (For example, 'I have accomplished a lot under pressure in the past. I have been able to use what I had time to prepare to its best advantage.')

Repeat this process each time you face major stressors. The six specific questions may not be as important to you as:

- Breaking the problem down into parts and then breaking those parts down again.
- Identifying alternative actions that you have previously found successful in coping with components of the stressor.

Skill Application

ACTIVITY **2.1**

LIFE-BALANCE ANALYSIS

The prescription to maintain a balanced life seems to contain a paradox:

> *It makes sense that life should have variety and that each of us should develop multiple aspects of ourselves. Narrowness and rigidity are not highly valued by anyone.*

However, the demands of work, school, or family, for example, can be so overwhelming that we don't have time to do much except respond to those demands. Work could take all of one's time. So could school. So could family. The temptation for most of us, then, is to focus on only a few areas of our lives that place a great deal of pressure on us, and leave the other areas undeveloped. Use Figure 2.5 (Balancing Life Activities) to complete this exercise. In responding to the four items in the exercise, think of the amount of time you spend in each area, the amount of experience and development you have had in the past in each area, and the extent to which development in each area is important to you.

1. In Figure 2.5 (Balancing Life Activities), shade in the portion of each section that represents the extent to which that aspect of your life has been developed. How satisfied are you that each aspect is adequately cultivated?

2. Now write down at least one thing that you can start doing to improve your development in the areas that need it. (For example, you might do more outside reading to develop culturally, invite a foreign visitor to your home to develop socially, go to Church regularly to develop spiritually, and so on.)

3. Because the intent of this exercise is not to add more pressure and stress to your life but to increase your resilience through life balance, identify the things you will stop doing that will make it possible to achieve a better life balance.

4. To make this a practise exercise and not just a planning exercise, do something today from your list for items 2 and 3 above. Write down specifically what you will do and when. Don't let the rest of the week go by without implementing something you've written.

ACTIVITY **2.2**

DEEP RELAXATION

To engage in deep relaxation, you need to reserve time that can be spent concentrating on relaxing. By focusing your mind, you can positively affect both your mental and physical states. This exercise describes one technique that is easily learned and practised. The particular technique we are presenting combines key elements of several well-known formulas. It is recommended that this technique be practised for 20 minutes a day, three times a week (Robinson, 1985; Davis *et al.*, 1980). Reserve at least 30 minutes to engage in this exercise for the first time. Find a quiet spot with your partner or a friend, and have that person read the instructions below. When you have finished, switch roles. Since you will practise this exercise later in a different setting, you may want to make a tape recording of these instructions.

Step 1   Assume a comfortable position. You may want to lie down. Loosen any tight clothing. Close your eyes and be quiet.

Step 2   Assume a passive attitude. Focus on your body and on relaxing specific muscles. Make your mind a blank – thinking of a colour such as grey often helps.

Step 3   Tense and relax each of your muscle groups for five to ten seconds, in the following order:

- *Forehead*   Wrinkle your forehead. Try to make your eyebrows touch your hairline for five seconds, then relax.

- *Eyes and nose*   Close your eyes as tightly as you can for five seconds, then relax.

- *Lips, cheeks and jaw*   Draw the corners of your mouth back and grimace for five seconds, then relax.

- *Hands*   Extend your arms in front of you. Clench your fists tightly for five seconds, then relax.

- *Forearms* Extend your arms out against an invisible wall and push forward for five seconds, then relax.
- *Upper arms* Bend your elbows and tense your biceps for five seconds, then relax.
- *Shoulders* Shrug your shoulders up to your ears for five seconds, then relax.
- *Back* Arch your back off the floor for five seconds, then relax.
- *Stomach* Tighten your stomach muscles by lifting your legs off the ground about two inches for five seconds, then relax.
- *Hips and buttocks* Tighten your hip and buttock muscles for five seconds, then relax.
- *Thighs* Tighten your thigh muscles by pressing your legs together as tightly as you can for five seconds, then relax.
- *Feet* Bend your ankles towards your body as far as you can for five seconds, then point your toes for five seconds, then relax.
- *Toes* Curl your toes as tightly as you can for five seconds, then relax.

Step 4 Focus on any muscles that are still tense. Repeat the exercise for that muscle group three or four times until it relaxes.

Step 5 Now focus on your breathing. Do not alter it artificially, but focus on taking long, slow breaths. Concentrate exclusively on the rhythm of your breathing until you have taken at least 45 breaths.

Step 6 Now focus on the heaviness and warmth of your body. Let all the energy in your body seep away. Let go of your normal tendency to control your body and mobilise it towards activity.

Step 7 With your body completely relaxed, relax your mind. Picture a plain object such as a glass ball, an empty white vase, the moon, or some favourite thing. Don't analyse it; don't examine it; just picture it. Concentrate fully on the object for at least three minutes without letting any other thoughts enter your mind. Begin now.

Step 8 Now open your eyes, slowly get up, and return to your hectic, stressful, anxiety ridden, Type A environment better prepared to cope with it effectively.

ACTIVITY **2.3**

MONITORING AND MANAGING TIME

Managers and business school students very often identify time management as their most pressing problem. They feel overwhelmed at times with the feeling of not having achieved those things that they know they could have achieved. Even when extremely busy, people experience less dysfunctional stress if they feel they are in control of their time and, in particular, in control of their ability to take time out. It is the existence of time that is under your control, which includes time out – discretionary time, that is the key to effective time management. This next activity should help you identify and better manage your discretionary time.

The exercise, in one form or another, is a key element in most time-management programmes. It takes one week to complete and requires you to keep a time diary for the whole period. Complete the following five steps, then use your partner or a friend to get feedback and ideas for improving and refining your plans.

Step 1 Beginning tomorrow, keep a time diary for a whole week. Record how you spend each 30 minutes in the next seven 24-hour periods, using the following format in a notebook you can carry with you.

Time	*Required/discretionary activity*	*Productive/unproductive*
09.00–09.30		
09.30–10.00		
10.00–10.30		
...		

Step 2 Under the heading 'Required/discretionary activity,' write whether someone required the time spent in each 30-minute block (R) or it was actually discretionary (D).

Step 3 Under the heading 'Productive/unproductive', and beside only the discretionary time blocks, rate the extent to which you used each one productively; that is, whether or not it led to improvements of some kind. Use the following scale for your rating: **4**, used productively; **3** used somewhat productively; **2**, used somewhat unproductively; **1**, used unproductively.

Step 4 Draw a plan to increase your weekly discretionary time. (The Time Management Survey earlier in the chapter may help.) Write down the things you will implement.

Step 5 How can you use your discretionary time more productively, especially any blocks of time you rated 1 or 2 in Step 3. What will you do to make sure the time you control is used for more long-term benefit? What will you stop doing that impedes your effective use of time?

ACTIVITY **2.4**

PERSONAL STRESSORS

Do a systematic analysis of the stressors you face in your job/college/family and social life – using our classification – Time, Encounter, Situational, Anticipatory. Identify strategies to eliminate or sharply reduce them. Record this analysis in your notebook.

ACTIVITY **2.5**

TEACHING OTHERS

Find someone you know well who is experiencing a great deal of stress. Teach him or her how to manage that stress better by applying the concepts, principles, techniques and exercises in this chapter. Describe what you taught and record the results in your notebook.

ACTIVITY **2.6**

IMPLEMENT TECHNIQUES

1. Implement at least three of the time-management techniques suggested in the Time Management Survey or elsewhere that you are not currently using but think you might find helpful. In your time diary, keep track of the amount of time these techniques save you over a one-month period. Be sure to use that extra time productively.

2. With a colleague or fellow student, identify ways in which your work can be redesigned to reduce stress and increase productivity.

3. Write a personal mission statement. Specify precisely your core principles; those things you consider to be central to your life and your sense of self-worth; and the legacy you want to leave. Identify at least one action you can take in order to accomplish your mission statement. Begin working on it today.

4. Establish a short-term goal or plan that you wish to accomplish this year. Make it compatible with the top priorities in your life. Specify the steps, the reporting and accounting mechanisms, and the criteria of success and rewards.

5. Share this plan with others you know so that you have an incentive to pursue it even after you finish this assignment.

6. Have a physical examination, then outline and implement a regular physical fitness and diet programme. Even if it is just regular walking, do some kind of physical exercise at least three times a week. Preferably, institute a regular, vigorous cardiovascular fitness programme. Record your progress in your diary.

7. Pick at least one long-term deep-relaxation technique. Learn it and practise it on a regular basis. Record your progress in your diary.

8. Establish a mentoring relationship with someone with whom you work or go to college. Your mentor may be a tutor, a senior manager, or someone who has been around longer than you have. Make certain that the relationship is reciprocal and that it will help you to cope with the stresses you face at work or college.

ACTIVITY **2.7**

APPLICATION PLAN AND EVALUATION

This activity is designed to help you apply your time-management skills to real life. Unlike a 'training' activity, in which feedback is immediate and others can assist you with their evaluations, this skill application activity is one you must accomplish and evaluate on your own. There are two parts to this activity.

Part 1 helps to prepare you to apply the skill. Part 2 helps you to evaluate and improve on your experience. Be sure to write down answers to each item. Don't short-circuit the process by skipping steps.

Part 1: Plan

1. Write down the two or three aspects of this skill that are most important to you. These may be areas of weakness, areas you most want to improve, or areas that are most salient to a problem you are currently facing. Identify the specific aspects of this skill that you want to apply.

2. Now identify the setting or the situation in which you will apply this skill. Establish a plan for performance by actually writing down a description of the situation. Who else will be involved? When will you do it? Where will it be done?

3. Identify the specific behaviours you will engage in to apply this skill.

4. What are the indicators of successful performance? How will you know you have been effective? What will indicate that you have performed competently?

Part 2: Evaluation

5. After you have completed your implementation, record the results. What happened? How successful were you? What was the effect on others?

6. How can you improve? What modifications can you make next time? What will you do differently in a similar situation in the future?

7. Looking back on your whole skill practice and application experience, what have you learned? What has been surprising? In what ways might this experience help you in the long term?

Further reading

Brewer, K.C. (1997) *Managing stress*. Aldershot: Gower.

Cooper, C. and Ferrario, M. (1997) *The essence of stress management*. London: Prentice Hall.

Cooper, C. and Lewis, S. (1998) *Balancing your career, family and life*. London: Kogan Page.

Handy, C. (1995) *Beyond certainty: the changing worlds of organisations*. London: Hutchinson.

Haynes, M.E. (1996) *Make every minute count: how to manage your time effectively*, 2nd edn. London: Kogan Page.

CHAPTER 3

Effective Problem Solving

SKILL DEVELOPMENT OUTLINE

Skill Pre-assessment surveys

- Problem solving, creativity and innovation
- How creative are you?
- Innovative Attitude Scale

Skill Learning material

- Problem solving, creativity and innovation
- Steps in rational problem solving
- A basis for all problem solving
- Limitations of the rational problem-solving model
- Impediments to creative problem solving
- Problems requiring a creative Input
- Conceptual blocks
- Review of conceptual blocks
- Conceptual blockbusting

- Stages in creative thought
- Methods for improving problem definition
- Generate more alternatives
- Hints for applying problem-solving techniques
- Summary
- Behavioural guidelines

Skill Analysis case

- The Sony Walkman

Skill Practice exercise

- Applying conceptual blockbusting

Skill Application activities

- Suggested further assignments
- Application plan and evaluation

LEARNING OBJECTIVES

- To allow individuals to assess their existing problem-solving skills and give them a chance to improve them.
- To provide a framework for rational problem solving and see where this framework falls down.

- To look at the blocks to creativity and how to reduce them.
- To understand how creativity can be fostered and managed in organisations.

INTRODUCTION

The words 'problem solving' are jargon, but they have become so much part of the language of managers that it is easy to forget that they imply a special meaning only to be understood by their select band. Problem solving, in the managerial context, implies a logical process which is called upon when something out of the routine occurs or when something out of the routine is needed. Handling the non-routine can be a problem in anyone's language – a challenge. The concept of 'problem solving' may well not be new to you, but, as with other parts of the book, we will discuss common sense that is not commonly applied. Let's look at a very ordinary way of handling the routine.

Every time we are faced with any form of new activity we need to be motivated – we need to be impressed by WHY things need to change. Then we need to understand WHAT has to be changed, have a practical assessment of HOW it can be changed. We then explore the consequences, IF – and if the consequences are acceptable or inevitable we proceed.

Suppose that we were told to travel to Munich to deliver some drawings to our agent tomorrow. The journey is routine and part of our job. We accept the WHYs without question – this is our job and the boss knows what he or she is doing. The WHATs are also obvious and, provided there are no politics involved, accepted without question – we will take the drawings, a clean set of underwear and revise our knowledge on the project so that we can answer questions. The fact that we need to revise our knowledge probably rules out driving to Munich and we will either go by train or plane – these are our HOWs. We may choose the train to give us more time and the consequences, our IFs, seem fine. The work in the office can be either delegated or postponed but a snag arises. Suppose just before we set out a very near and dear relative is taken ill and needs our support for the time we are to be away. This is a problem, and we will go round the cycle again, beginning with questioning the WHY. The original issue implied that we should go to Munich now with the drawings – but we now need to start asking questions.

- Do we have to be *with* the drawings?
- Could anyone else take them?
- Are *all* the drawings and instructions needed tomorrow? What is so important about tomorrow?
- Is the time so important? Could there be a delay while we sorted out day care?

Suppose in our new set of WHY questions we find that the agent could start work on some limited instructions with the ability to contact us. The drawings could be delayed because he has a lot of pre-work before the detail is required. Workings from this point our new WHATs would be to get instructions out immediately, being available for questioning, getting the drawings out as soon as possible but delaying our visit.

The HOWs would be about faxing the basic instructions and being available on an e-mail address. A commercial courier could send the drawings and we could follow at the end of the month when the agent was ready with the really deep questions.

The IFs may well be acceptable to us, the company and the agent but they need to be reviewed in the light of the present situation and previous experience.

Unfortunately, this common-sense and logical approach is rarely used rigorously although it may seem intuitive. To stick to it in simple cases we need constant encouragement, but in complex cases we need some form of detailed procedure that all the stakeholders can accept, understand and follow. There is also the point that common sense and logic will not answer all problem issues. Sometimes we need to take a lateral view and provide a creative solution. Our chapter will close with the commonly acknowledged blocks to logical and creative thinking in the real world.

Skill Pre-assessment

SURVEY **3.1**

PROBLEM SOLVING, CREATIVITY AND INNOVATION

Step 1   Before you start the chapter, please respond to the following statements by writing a number from the rating scale below in the left-hand column (Pre-assessment). The questions do prompt towards best practice but your answers should reflect your attitudes and behaviour as they are now, not as you would like them to be. Be honest. This instrument is designed to help you to discover your level of competency in problem solving and creativity so that you can tailor your learning to your specific needs. When you have completed the survey, use the scoring key at the end of the book to identify the skills that are most important for you to master.

Step 2   After you have completed the chapter, cover up your first set of answers and respond to the same statements again, this time in the right-hand column (Post-assessment). When you have completed the survey, go back to the scoring key to measure your progress. If your score remains low in specific skill areas, use the behavioural guidelines at the end of the Skill Learning section to guide your further practice.

RATING SCALE

1 = Strongly disagree   **2** = Disagree   **3** = Slightly disagree
4 = Slightly agree   **5** = Agree   **6** = Strongly agree

	Assessment	
	Pre-	Post-
When I approach a typical, routine problem		
1. I always define clearly and explicitly what the problem is.	____	____
2. I always generate more than one alternative solution to the problem.	____	____

3. I evaluate the alternative solutions based on both long- and short-term consequences.   ____ ____

4. I define the problem before solving it, thus avoiding imposing my predetermined solutions.   ____ ____

5. I keep problem-solving steps distinct, separating definitions, alternatives and solutions.   ____ ____

When faced with a complex or difficult problem that does not have a straightforward solution

6. I try to define the problem in several different ways.   ____ ____

7. I try to be flexible in the way I approach the problem, not relying on past concepts or practice.   ____ ____

8. I look for patterns or common elements in different aspects of the problem.   ____ ____

9. I try to unfreeze my thinking by asking lots of questions about the nature of the problem.   ____ ____

10. I try to apply both logic and intuition to the problem.   ____ ____

11. I frequently use metaphors or analogies to help me look more widely at a problem.   ____ ____

12. I strive to look at problems from different perspectives so as to generate multiple definitions.   ____ ____

13. I list the alternatives before evaluating any of them.   ____ ____

14. I often break the problem down into smaller components and analyse each one separately.   ____ ____

15. I strive to generate multiple creative solutions to problems.   ____ ____

When trying to foster more creativity and innovation among those with whom I work

16. I help others to work on their ideas outside the constraints of normal procedures.   ____ ____

17. I make sure there are divergent points of view represented in every problem-solving group.   ____ ____

18. I can produce wild ideas to help stimulate people to find new ways of approaching problems.   ____ ____

19. I try to acquire information from customers regarding their preferences and expectations.   ____ ____

20. I do involve outsiders – customers or recognised experts – in problem-solving discussions.   ____ ____

21. I acknowledge not only the ideas of people but also supporters, providers and implementers.   ____ ____

22. I encourage informed rule-breaking in pursuit of creative solutions.   ____ ____

SURVEY **3.2**

HOW CREATIVE ARE YOU?

The following questionnaire is based on the personality traits, attitudes, values, motivations and interests of known 'high creatives' and asks you to rate yourself against them. Be as frank as possible.

RATING SCALE

For each statement, write in the appropriate letter:
A = agree   **B** = undecided or do not know   **C** = disagree

The scoring key is at the end of the book (see Appendix 1).

1. I am usually certain that following the correct procedure will solve the problem.   ____

2. It is a waste of time to ask questions if I have no hope of obtaining answers.   ____

3. I concentrate harder than most people on whatever interests me.   ____

4. I feel that a logical step-by-step method is best for solving problems.   ____

5. In groups I occasionally voice opinions that seem to turn some people off.   ____

6. I am concerned about what others think of me.   ____

7. It is better to do what I believe is right than to try to win the approval of others.   ____

8. People who seem uncertain about things lose my respect.   ____

9. More than most, I need the things I take part in to be interesting and exciting.   ____

10. I know how to keep my inner impulses in check.   ____

11. I am able to stick with difficult problems over extended periods of time.   ____

12. On occasion I get overly enthusiastic.   ____

13. I often get my best ideas when doing nothing in particular.   ____

14. For solving problems I rely on hunches and the feeling of 'rightness' or 'wrongness'.   ____

15. When problem solving, I work faster when analysing the problem and slower when synthesising the information I have gathered.   ____

16. I sometimes enjoy breaking the rules and doing what I am not supposed to do.   ____

17. I like hobbies that involve collecting things.   ____

18. Daydreaming has provided the impetus for many of my better projects.   ____

19. I like people who are objective and rational.   ____

20. In choosing a different job for me, I would rather be a doctor than an explorer.   ____

21. I can get on better with people from the same social and business class.   ____

22. I have a high degree of aesthetic sensitivity.   ____

23. I am driven to achieve high status and power in life.   ____

24. I like people who are sure of their conclusions.   ____

25. Inspiration has nothing to do with the successful solution of problems.   ____

26. In an argument, my greatest pleasure would be for the person who disagrees with me to become a friend, even at the price of sacrificing my point of view.   ____

27. I am much more interested in having new ideas than in selling them to others.   ____

28. I would enjoy spending an entire day alone, just thinking.   ____

29. I tend to avoid situations in which I might feel inferior.   ____

30. In evaluating information, the source is more important to me than the content.   ____

31. I resent things being uncertain and unpredictable.   ____

32. I like people who follow the rule, 'business before pleasure'.   ____

33. Self-respect is much more important than the respect of others.   ____

34. I feel that people who strive for perfection are unwise.   ____

35. I prefer to work with others in a team effort rather than solo.   ____

35. I like work in which I must influence others.   ____

37. Many of my problems cannot be resolved in terms of a good or bad solution.   ____

38. It is important for me to have a place for everything and everything in its place.   ____

39. Writers who use strange and unusual words merely want to show off.   ____

Below is a list of terms that describe people. Highlight the 10 words that best characterise you.

alert	observant	self-confident	tactful	retiring
energetic	dedicated	factual	self-demanding	flexible
formal	unemotional	open-minded	cautious	efficient
curious	fashionable	well-liked	absent-minded	egotistical
persuasive	forward looking	involved	inhibited	poised
informal	modest	thorough	habit-bound	independent
stern	good-natured	impulsive	enthusiastic	acquisitive
practical	understanding	sociable	polished	helpful
realistic	determined	persevering	courageous	perceptive
restless	looking	dynamic	resourceful	predictable
organised	clear-thinking	original	innovative	quick

Source: Eugene Raudsepp (1981)

SURVEY **3.3**

INNOVATIVE ATTITUDE SCALE

Please indicate how far each of the following statements are true of either your actual behaviour or your intentions at work. Use the rating scale for your responses.

RATING SCALE

1 = Almost never true   **2** = Seldom true   **3** = N/A

4 = Often true   **5** = Almost always true

Use the scoring key in Appendix 1 to interpret your answers.

1. I discuss my progress and opportunities with my supervisor or boss. ____
2. I try new ideas and approaches to problems. ____
3. I take things or situations apart to find out how they work. ____
4. I welcome uncertainty and unusual circumstances related to my tasks. ____
5. I attempt to negotiate the conditions under which I work. ____
6. I can be counted on to find a new use for existing methods or equipment. ____
7. In my team, I will be the first, or nearly the first, to try out a new idea or method. ____
8. I like the opportunity to bring new information to my team from outside. ____
9. I demonstrate originality. ____
10. I will work on a problem that has caused others great difficulty. ____
11. I provide an important role in developing a new solution. ____
12. I will provide well-researched proposals of ideas to my work group. ____
13. I develop contacts with outside experts. ____
14. I will use influence to take on the parts of group projects I most enjoy. ____
15. I make time to pursue my own pet ideas or projects. ____
16. I set aside time and energies for the pursuit of risky ideas or projects. ____
17. I accept that rules may have to be broken to reach ideal solutions. ____
18. I speak out in group meetings. ____
19. I like working with others to solve complex problems. ____
20. I see myself as sometimes providing light relief to others. ____

Source: Ettlie and O'Keefe (1982)

Skill Learning

Problem solving, creativity and innovation

If there were no problems in organisations, there would be no need for managers, or putting it another way, no incompetent problem-solver succeeds as a manager.

Effective managers are able to solve problems both rationally and creatively, even though different skills are required. Thamia and Woods (1984), reviewing 146 problem-solving sessions in a R&D department of Unilever, found that problem-solving techniques were used throughout the development process, and that a range of techniques, both creative and rational, were applied with varying degrees of success. Of the projects tackled over a three-year period, 32 per cent were rational systems and 68 per cent were termed 'creative' systems. The success rate judged on an assessment by senior management some 10 years later was approximately 60 per cent for creative problem solving and about 80 per cent for rational systems. Geshka (1978), working with German industrial firms, gave figures for success of creative techniques of between 24 and 50 per cent.

Table 3.1 Stages in the innovation process and problem solving technique employed

Stage	No of sessions (total 146)	% of total sessions
Conception	42	29
Product/Process specification	12	8
Process engineer specification	19	13
Engineering/Production specification	32	22
Exploitation	12	18
Contingency planning	7	5
Clerical back-up	11	8
Completed commercial exploitation	11	8

Source: Thamia and Woods (1984)

Table 3.1 gives the split of the usage of techniques, both creative and rational, for the various stages of the development process.

In practice most managers begin the process of problem solving with rational systems and only move reluctantly towards the creative mode. (The Thamia and Woods data is obviously biased in its estimate of creative to rational problem solving since much of the rational problem solving occurred informally and is never recorded.) In spite of the reluctance on the part of many managers to think creatively, the ability to solve problems in the creative mode separates the sheep from the goats, career successes from career failures and achievers from derailed executives. It can also produce a dramatic impact on organisational effectiveness.

Therefore, the aim of this chapter is to harness the problem-solving skills of individuals. This process is not an isolated exercise but part of the effective manager's portfolio. We see training and skill development in this area as a very large contribution towards the development of a learning organisation. The advancement of specific techniques, of which there are many (Thamia and Woods recorded 15 distinct types in their study) will be left to more specialised texts (Twiss, 1980; Buzan, 1974; Rickards, 1974, 1988).

Steps in rational problem solving

Most people, including managers, don't like problems. Problems are time-consuming and stressful. In fact, most people try to get rid of problems as soon as they can. Their natural tendency is to select the first reasonable solution that comes to mind (March and Simon, 1958), but these are rarely the best solutions. In the West, as opposed to within the Pacific Basin, we often try to implement the marginally acceptable or satisfactory solution, as opposed to the optimal or ideal solution.

One of the objectives of the Bradford University MBA programme is to allow the delegates to explore cultural differences. Since the programme has delegates from all over the world, this is a unique opportunity for future managers in a global economy. Particular learning is when a multi-ethnic group engages in problem solving. On one occasion a Japanese student was reduced to total impotence in a group of two Latins and two Brits. In the feedback he explained what had happened. In his culture the solutions would have been fought out until an agreed compromise had been reached and then there would have been full commitment of all the team for implementation. The process of compromise might have taken a very long time. The Latins and Brits competed for their solution and the 'owner' of the 'winning' solution attempted to lead the group towards implementation. It was the implementation that took the long time and full commitment by all the members of the group was poor.

Some observers see the consensus mode of problem solving as a major factor in the growth of the Japanese economy. At the time of writing the success of the Japanese economy is in question.

A basis for all problem solving

The model shown in Figure 3.1 is due to David Kolb and has already been discussed in Chapter 1. Adapting the model to problem solving helps us to understand that problem solving can be divided into four phases and that these form a cycle. The phases should ideally be distinct and in sequence:

- Exploring and developing our motivation for solving the problem and that of the 'problem owner' – should that be different – asking WHY questions.

- Deciding WHAT needs to be done to satisfy the WHY issues.

- Seeking practical solutions to the specific WHAT issues – the HOW's.

- Looking at the consequences of the practical steps we have chosen (the HOW's) and reviewing our actions.

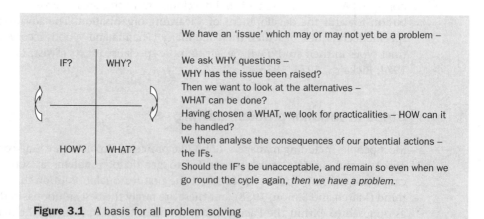

Figure 3.1 A basis for all problem solving

- If the consequences are acceptable, adopting the 'solution'; should they be unacceptable, returning to the WHY phase and finding new objectives and actions.

A management exercise we use to demonstrate the Kolb Cycle consists of asking a group to imagine that they are the Board of a subsidiary company. The Board receive a memo from head office instructing them to close the factory, sell the land as real estate and move the rump to another country with a very tight time scale. Ideally they should question the memo, to the extent of checking its factual content and then decide what needs to be done. They should then look at the practicalities of the proposals and only then look at the consequences.

Most groups, with or without a Chair, confuse all the stages and maintain no pattern. Thus the opening remark of one participant was to worry about his children's schooling after the move – a very assumptive consequence.

Kolb further points out that managers often prefer to approach problems from one or two of the phases, basically ignoring the others. Thus some managers will persist in reviewing the purpose and asking WHY questions well after the group has moved on to solutions and practicalities. More commonly managers will be bored by the analysis stages and want to get on with practicalities. Even more 'difficult' managers will, as in our example, assume everything and move on to consequences. The job of the Chair is to make sure that this does not happen:

If we do not know where we are going, we will finish up somewhere else.

A detailed model of rational problem solving – a modified Kepner Tregoe approach

The relatively informal and basically intuitive Kolb process may fail for three reasons. The first is that however many times we move through the cycle, the consequences of the actions we propose may not be acceptable. In this case we need to move to the creative processes we will describe later. The second reason is that the complexity of the issues is such that the informal approach gets bogged down. The information necessary for the decision making is not readily available or significant stakeholders cannot be brought together easily. The third and often related issue is that the matter is so important that nothing can be left to chance. We need a formalised approach that acts as a driving agenda.

The constructs behind the system are that individuals work within a personal 'area of concern'. Inside the 'area of concern' they are empowered to act, but that there is always an individual or group with a higher level 'area of concern'. Within our own 'area of concern' we must achieve the achievable. Things we feel are necessary to implement chosen solutions outside our own 'area of concern' need to be passed to this higher level.

The system we are proposing is due to Kepner and Tregoe (1965) and consists of an enlargement and formalisation of the basic model we have already discussed. Its formalisation does, in our opinion, fit the real world of complexity and politics, and is summarised and compared with the basic model.

Kolb phase	Step	Questions	Issues
WHY?	1. The problem as given		Problems as given are invariably 'wrong' containing implied solutions and misunderstandings.
WHAT?	2. Define the constraints	• What is our 'area of concern' in relation to the problem issue? • Who is the 'client' – who will decide whether we have a 'solution'? • What is our time scale and cost bracket? • What environment does our 'solution' face? • Who will implement the solution? • What are the 'legal' constraints?	• We define a 'cage' within which the potential solution or solutions will operate. • In looking at time and cost we often split potential solutions into short, medium and long term. • It can be argued that 'too much' problem analysis limits creativity – the analysis may be 'stored' to prevent this.
HOW?	3. Redefine the problem	• We need a consensus redefinition – recommended 200 words maximum. • If the problem 'splits' – short, medium and long term – take one at a time.	• Although a general consensus is desirable, agreement by the 'client' is essential. • The 'client' should be consulted at all times in this stage.
	4. Quantify the objectives – what MUST be achieved and what we would LIKE to achieve	• The objectives should be SMART: – **S**pecific in time, cost, quality, quantity – **M**easurable – **A**greed – **R**ealistic – **T**imed • The first step is to consider, and if necessary eliminate, the obvious. After this other perspectives need to be considered.	• In practice the client will probably have set the problem because he or she does not exactly understand it. • Often at this stage the problem 'vanishes' to the blindingly obvious. • **If the obvious should work – move to Stage 7.** • The 'stakeholders' very often have a solution that politically it has been impossible to table in acceptable form.

Kolb phase	Step	Questions	Issues
	5. Generate alternatives	• Collect alternatives without criticism and *within reason*, without reference to the constraints. • Take the stakeholders' views first. • Avoid any evaluation.	• Concurrent evaluation often means that the first reasonable solution 'wins'. • Evaluation often involves control issues.
IF?	6. Balance alternatives against the objectives	• Consider all the alternatives against the MUST achieve objectives. • A paper exercise where logic rules. • Distinguish between short- medium- and long-term objectives. • Alternatives meeting MUST objectives are 'traded' against the LIKE objectives.	• Alternatives failing the MUST test may have germs of ideas and be used to produce composite solutions. • This can be a lengthy process and often new or revised objectives 'appear'. • The process is often politically sensitive.
	7. Make a tentative decision	• Do not expect that any solution will 'work'. • Consult all the stakeholders. • Brief the 'Implementor' on the system and the checklists to be used.	• This stage is still relatively cheap – we need to make sure nobody can ever say – 'Well I could have told you, it went wrong last time.'
	8. Conduct a Potential Problem Analysis on the decision	• Consult ALL the stakeholders and relevant experience. • Seek out all potential problems and seek potential solutions. • Design contingency plans for potential problems outside our 'area of concern'. • Refer all likely contingencies to the client. • Accepting the review may mean changing the tentative decision.	
	9. Proceed and put contingency plan into action	• Plan in appropriate detail, resource and monitor.	• This is the expensive bit!

The total system looks and is, in its way, cumbersome. It is, however, common sense. We are suggesting that the process is always followed, each step being completed before the next is begun. Our only proviso is that the relative weight of the steps may vary and there are times when gambling on a quick decision is vital – however, this situation is MUCH rarer than we normally find argued.

> Thamia and Woods (1984) showed that an unfortunate history of failed projects had encouraged the use of the system – in fact the ruling from the Head of the Laboratory was that 'the system does not have to be followed but if the project fails and the system has not been followed then . . .'. The payoff was immediate, transparent and provided legitimacy for the other 'creativity tools' implemented at the same time.

Step 1 The problem as given

Problem issues are very often defined in terms of the symptoms and usually with implied solutions:

> Mary seems to have an attitude problem, she is always late – sort it out.
>
> The pallets in No 2 building are always falling over, see if you can get the packing more even.
>
> We are losing market share – see what the competitors are doing.

> Consultants were asked to look into labour turnover in an animal-testing unit in a large laboratory. The concern was that the percentage of people leaving far exceeded the laboratory average. Looking closer at the figures the consultants found that like was not being compared with like – labour turnover figures being used were for the whole laboratory whose average age was 37 with 15 per cent women in the population. Taking the animal handlers in isolation, the average age was 23 with 100 per cent women. Taking a similarly composed sample in other industries, the turnover was below average.

Step 2 Define the Constraints

Any potential solution has to operate with a cage – a cage of constraints. The cage has six walls – the client, cost, time, environment, staff and a strange concept we will call 'legal'. Let's take them one at a time using Mary's lateness as a vehicle. Who is the client, or putting it more simply, who has the problem? If Mary is the 'client' then we need to find out why she is late and solutions may range from buying her an alarm clock that works to social support. If the manager is the client then stopping Mary's lateness by any means, including sacking her, are potential solutions. However, in the real world – OUR MANAGER IS THE CLIENT. He or she operates in a higher level 'circle of concern'. This means that any proposed solution has to be approved implicitly or explicitly by him or her. He or she may be a control freak who watches every clock and every chart, a socially aware 'people person' or a professional in-between. Suppose he or she is the professional and in this case our proposed solutions need to fit the professional model or they will not be accepted.

Cost and time are our next constraints. Mary's lateness is costing £200 per incident in lost production, as the line cannot operate until she is in position. Mary is, however, a very skilled operative and replacing her would be costly – in time and cash. We do not want to lose her in the short or medium term.

The environment on the line is good. Years of good employee relationships have meant that everyone is positive and wants the company to succeed. Mary is a key worker and greatly liked by her co-workers. Her co-workers – the staff in our model – do not now have the skills to replace her.

Legally we could sack Mary since the plant is not unionised, but custom and practice – a very important issue in the constraint we have loosely called 'legal' – dictates that this would be unwise.

A map is of no use unless you know where you are. Solving a problem without understanding what it is you have to solve is worse than useless, but is unfortunately a common practice.

Step 3   Redefine the problem

Here we are looking at a 200 word maximum statement of what we see is the problem and we submit this to the client – our manager – for comment before we proceed.

In the long term the issue is that a single operative has skills which are not shared by any other employee. In the short term, the single operative – Mary Wellingborough – is arriving late on four or five mornings a month, costing up to £1,000 in lost production each month. In the immediate term the problem is to stop or significantly reduce this loss in production without alienating the rest of the work force, who are sympathetic to Mary. In the long term the issue is to avoid being in this position again.

Step 4   Quantify the objectives

In our experience the balancing of resources employed against potential gain is something we all need to consider.

> A number of engineers were asked to look at alternative feeding systems for fish farming. When the constraints were considered, the problem evaporated. It was necessary that one operator inspected each of the fish cages every day using a small boat. In addition, as safety regulations dictated that the operator needed a companion in case of trouble, it was fairly obvious that the companion might as well be feeding the fish as doing nothing.

If we go back to Mary – the problem is 'worth' £1,000 a month. However, the risk of alienating the line – and with possible industrial action by the others – is worth much more than this, about £60,000 a month. We will attempt the short-term solution.

The criteria against which the solutions we propose will be judged could be – and this has to be agreed with the client:

- We are talking about the short term.
- MUST be capable of implementation within 1 month – LIKE to achieve by next week.

- MUST not cost more that £1,000 a month – LIKE to be lost in 'management time'.
- MUST not disrupt the line or endanger industrial action.
- MUST not make a long-term solution – deskilling, succession training – more difficult.

These are strategic objectives that will not mean much to Mary. If we accept them we can chunk down the objectives to:

- How to get Mary in on time.
- How to get the line running if Mary is late.
- How to replace Mary.

What often happens is that we work on mixed objectives – in logical, and indeed creative, problem solving we need to hone in on one chosen objective at a time. Let us suppose we choose to 'get Mary in on time'.

Step 5   Generate alternatives

The generation of alternatives requires postponing the selection of one solution until several alternatives have been proposed. Deferring judgement, as Gordon (1961) would put it, is an essential step in any form of effective problem solving. Maier (1970) found that the quality of the final solution can be significantly enhanced by considering multiple alternatives. Judgement and evaluation, therefore, must be postponed so the first acceptable solution suggested isn't the one that is immediately selected. As Broadwell (1972, p. 121) noted:

> The problem with evaluating an alternative solution too early is that we may rule out some good ideas by just not getting around to thinking about them. We hit on an idea that sounds good and we go with it, thereby never even thinking of alternatives that may be better in the long run. As many alternatives as possible should be generated before evaluating any of them – poor alternatives often lead to good ones and without them quality solutions can often be missed.

With logical decision making the 'solutions' come from linear thinking; however, creative solutions can 'appear'. Creative solutions are invariably out of the mindset of at least some of the stakeholders and are subject to conceptual blocks that we will consider later in the chapter. Good alternative-generation should:

1. Work with the relevant stakeholders.
2. List all alternatives to be proposed before evaluation is allowed.
3. Allow as diverse a group as possible to contribute.
4. Create an atmosphere during the process which is positive. Angry or bitter people are unlikely to contribute much more than their discontent and may do actual harm by being given a platform.
5. Generate alternatives which cover both short- and long-term potential 'solutions' – the evaluation stage may well rule out ideas that do not meet the needs of the 'client', but the generation stage is not the right place to make such a judgement.

6. Create alternatives which are allowed to build upon one another – bad ideas may become good ideas if combined with, or modified by, other ideas.

7. Ensure that the agenda is adhered to and that alternatives are confined to potential solutions of the problem in hand. It is often interesting to go down new pathways, but this should be avoided if it does not relate to the current problem.

The issue is one of credibility. In our experience very few organisations, with the notable exception of advertising agencies, find the process of problem solving – and, in particular, problem solving involving people from all over and even outside the organisation – a natural activity. The presentation of half-baked, subversive or irrelevant ideas to managers not involved in the seductive process of idea generation can be a very dangerous activity, and can seriously damage people's career prospects.

Taking us back to Mary and the problem of getting her to work on time, the only relevant stakeholders are Mary and, if appropriate, a 'witness' to see fair play. Later we may choose to bring in her supervisor to consider possible solutions, but at present the group is very select. The first issue is to transfer the problem to Joe – to get her to understand the WHY of the issue:

- I have a problem in that your coming in late is delaying the start of the line; this cannot go on.
- Could we talk about why you have been so often late recently?

Then the WHAT:

- WHAT can WE do about it?

Unless we establish the problem as shared, there is no chance of Joe coming up with alternative solutions.

Step 6   *Balance alternatives against the objectives*

The evaluation and selection step involves careful weighing up of the advantages and disadvantages of the proposed alternatives before making a final selection. In selecting the best alternative, skilled problem solvers make sure that the alternatives are judged in terms of the extent to which:

- They meet the standards set for the 'solution' to the problem. Certain objectives are MUST while others are merely advantages.
- They fit within the organisational constraints (e.g., it is consistent with policies, norms and budget limitations).
- All the individuals involved will accept, and are happy to work with, the alternative suggested.
- Implementation of the alternative is likely.
- They will solve the problem without causing other unanticipated problems.

Care is taken not to short-circuit these considerations by choosing the most conspicuous alternative without considering others. March and Simon (1958, p. 141) point out:

> Most human decision-making, whether individual or organisational, is concerned with the discovery and selection of satisfactory alternatives; only in exceptional cases is it concerned with the discovery and selection of optimal alternatives. To optimise requires processes several orders of magnitude more complex than those required to satisfy. An example is the difference between searching a haystack to find the sharpest needle in it and searching the haystack to find a needle sharp enough to sew with.

Given the natural tendency to select the first satisfactory solution proposed, the evaluation and selection step must not be underrated.

1. The evaluation of alternatives should be systematic and rigorous. There are, however, exceptions:

> We were asked to consider how to promote a food product, which in this case was a factory-produced and very ordinary sausage. About 10 minutes into the discussion someone suggested that the sausages should be promoted along with the inevitable mustard to be found on the British sausage-eater's plate. The client, the brand manager for the sausage product, leapt to his feet and rang up a friend in Colman's Mustard and arranged a deal. The session finished in disarray but a placard promoting the sausage AND the mustard appeared on billboards within weeks.

If the client is satisfied, it is pointless to demand a structured approach to assessing ALL the ideas.

2. Alternatives should always be evaluated in terms of the goals of the organisation and the individuals involved. The implementation of ideas needs both the support of the organisation and of the key individuals concerned.

> We were asked to evaluate a concept for making quality envelopes for the domestic market in a continuous process from a single strip of paper, the standard method being 'old fashioned'. The idea was fine and it met the criteria for new ideas laid out by the organisation. However, nobody in the organisation was happy enough with the idea to put his or her career on the line to implement it. The idea was dropped.

3. Alternatives are evaluated in terms of their effects in the wider world – the 'legal' aspect of the constraints in Stage 2.

> The Shell Company in 1995 evaluated various alternatives for the disposal of a redundant oil rig in the Atlantic. Logically, disposal at sea was the obvious choice – provided one did not predict the way in which environmentalists could exploit the issue to bring publicity against industrial pollution. However, Greenpeace chose to fight the decision and won, so that a precedent of what they saw as bad practice was not established and the company had to back down from their 'logical' decision.

Step 7   Make a tentative decision

From Stage 6 we are likely to have an objective that stands out. Often it will be an amalgam of several ideas, thus Mary may be having trouble with one of her children and getting her to school cannot be left to the eldest. She may see that getting a neighbour to help is a possibility but that a little preparation the previous evening plus phoning in on difficult days could reduce the problem.

The tentative alternative chosen must be stated explicitly with the reasoning behind the decision, including the case for and against both the chosen route and the non-recommended alternatives. We now try to find fault with the tentative decision – with a group of the stakeholders where necessary. In Mary's case we would suggest that her line supervisor would compose the 'group'. We may decide that the tentative solution is worth further discussion, but if we were not satisfied we would return to select a different 'solution' or go back to the problem definition stage.

Step 8   Conduct a Potential Problem Analysis on the decision

Woods and Davies (1973) proposed a formal system between the assessment and implementation stages of structured problem solving. They suggested that a delegated team had a 'Circle of Concern' within which they were empowered to take all necessary actions for success. However, certain things were beyond the mandate of the team or individual and required higher authority. These they termed 'contingency actions'.

In the methodology they proposed, a 'Potential Problem Analysis' session would be conducted before the implementation stage (Stage 9) in which all likely snags would be considered and solutions proposed. Residual problems, the problems likely to involve contingency work, would be listed at this point and referred to the problem owner for him or her to review what should be done, and indeed whether a complete rethink would be necessary.

> In the 1970s, many food companies were considering alternative processes for making animal-protein substitutes from various plant products. One source of such protein was derived from various pulses. Unfortunately several pulses, in the uncooked or semi-cooked state, contained a toxin which inhibits the human digestive system. The detoxification of the pulse material needed to be at the boiling point of water to be effective.
>
> During a Potential Problem Analysis session with the team responsible for the implementation, it was pointed out that the factory designated for the production of the product was likely to be at a height well above sea level and that open cooking might not detoxify the beans. The contingency plan would be to cook the beans in pressure vessels. Due consideration of the cost of the implementation of such pressure cooking led to a complete re-evaluation and abandonment of the process.

Thamia and Woods (1984) found seven examples of such contingency planning work in their studies.

With Mary, the issues within our own 'Circle of Concern' include informing the necessary people of our arrangements. We need to make sure that Mary's phone call will be taken and acted up, agree what she needs to do in preparation the previous evening, making sure there is a supervisor available and, of course, monitoring and reviewing. However, we are establishing a precedent and this needs to be discussed with, in this case – the Personnel Department.

Stage 9   Proceed and put contingency plan into action

Implementation of any solution requires sensitivity to possible resistance from those who will be affected by it. Almost any change engenders some resistance. Therefore, the best problem solvers are careful to select a strategy that maximises the probability that the solution will be accepted and fully implemented. This may involve 'selling' the solution to others or involving others in the implementation of the solution. Tannenbaum and Schmidt (1958) and Vroom and Yetton (1973) provide guidelines for managers to determine which of these implementation behaviours is most appropriate in which circumstances. Generally speaking, participation by others in the implementation of a solution will increase its acceptance and decrease its resistance.

Effective implementation also requires some follow-up to check on implementation, prevent negative side-effects and ensure a solution of the problem. Follow-up not only helps to ensure effective implementation, but serves as a feedback function as well as providing information that can be used to improve future problem solving. Drucker (1974, p. 480) explained:

> A feedback has to be built into the decision to provide continuous testing of the expectations that underlie the decision, against actual events. Few decisions work out the way they are intended to. Even the best decision usually runs into snags, unexpected obstacles and all kinds of surprises. Even the most effective decision eventually becomes obsolete. Unless there is feedback from the results of the decision, it is unlikely to produce the desired results.

Effective implementation and follow-up should include some of the following attributes:

1. Implementation occurs at the right time and in the proper sequence.
2. The implementation process includes opportunities for feedback. We need to be able to communicate how well the selected solution works.
3. Implementation is supported by the whole 'team', all of which should have been involved wherever and whenever possible in the process.
4. A system for monitoring the implementation process is set up with short-, medium- and long-term goals clearly laid out.
5. Evaluation of success is based on problem-solution, not on side-benefits. Although the solution may provide some positive outcomes, unless it solves the problem being considered, it is unsuccessful.
6. Contingency planning.

Limitations of the rational problem-solving model

Most experienced problem solvers are familiar with these steps in rational problem solving, which are based on empirical research results and sound rationale (Kepner and Tregoe 1965; Maier, 1970; Huber, 1980; Elbing, 1978; Filley *et al.*, 1976). Unfortunately, managers do not always practise them: the demands of the job often pressure managers into circumventing some of these steps, thus problem solving suffers as a result. When these steps are followed, however, effective problem solving is markedly enhanced.

The research by Thamia and Woods records an incident where a senior manager in the multi-national they studied had been 'taught' the Kepner and Tregoe method on a course finishing on a Friday. On the next Monday he was in a senior management meeting where he proposed to use the technique to help to make a significant decision. He was told: 'I know you have been on a course, but we simply do not have time for all that clap trap – what does everyone think we should do?' On the other hand, simply learning about and practising the steps of problem definition, generating alternatives, evaluation and selection and implementation and follow up, does not guarantee success. There are two principle reasons for this.

Firstly, these problem-solving steps are useful mainly when the problems faced are straightforward, when alternatives are readily available, when relevant information is present, and when a clear standard exists against which to judge the correctness of a solution. Thompson and Tuden (1959) call problems with these characteristics 'computational problems', for which the main tasks are to gather information, generate alternatives and make an informed choice. The trouble is, many managerial problems are not of this type. Definitions, information, alternatives and standards are seldom unambiguous or readily available, so knowing the steps in problem solving and being able to follow them are not the same thing. Table 3.2 presents the internal and external constraints which make it difficult to follow any strict model.

A second reason why the rational problem-solving model is not always effective for managers concerns the nature of the problem itself. The problem may not be amenable to a systematic or rational analysis. In fact, for some problems, a rational problem-solving approach may not lead to an effective solution. Sufficient and accurate information may not be available, outcomes may not be predictable or the method of implementation may not be evident. In order to solve such problems, a new way of thinking may be required, multiple or conflicting definitions might be needed and alternatives never before considered may have to be generated; in short, creative problem solving must be used.

Impediments to creative problem solving

One of the ways we survive in an increasingly complex world is to create patterns, classifications, bundles of what we see, feel and hear around us. Once we have established a pattern we make generalities and assumptions about things within the pattern – 'People in organisations are inclined to . . .', 'He is German and we all know that Germans are good engineers . . .'. From our experience and 'learning' the classifications are convenient and help us survive without having to think about everything at every level. It is these very patterns, we will call them conceptual blocks, that we need to break down in creative problem solving, and the process makes us uncomfortable and vulnerable. The more we become experts or specialists, the more the patterns become unquestioned.

Table 3.2 Some constraints on the rational problem-solving model

Steps	Constraints
1. Define the problem	• There is seldom consensus as to the definition of the problem. • There is often uncertainty as to whose definition will be accepted. • Problems are usually defined in terms of the solutions already possessed.
2. Generate alternative solutions	• Solution alternatives are usually evaluated one at a time as they are proposed. • Usually, few of the possible alternatives are known. • The first acceptable solution is usually accepted. • Alternatives are based on what was successful in the past.
3. Evaluate and select an alternative	• Limited information about each alternative is usually available. • Search for information occurs close to home – in easily accessible places. • The type of information available is constrained by importance – primacy versus recency, extremity versus centrality, expected versus surprising, and correlation versus causation. • Gathering information on each alternative is costly. • The best alternative is not always known. • Satisfactory solutions, not optimal ones, are usually accepted. • Solutions are often selected by oversight or default. • Solutions are often implemented before the problem is defined.
4. Implement and follow up on the solution	• Acceptance by others of the solution is not always forthcoming. • Resistance to change is a universal phenomenon. • It is not always clear what part of the solution should be monitored or measured in follow-up. • Political and organisational processes must be managed in any implementation effort. • It may take a long time to implement a solution.

Place half-a-dozen bees and the same number of flies in a bottle, and lay it on its side, with its base to the window. The bees will persist, attempting to find a way through the glass of the base until they drop. The flies, moving at random, will soon find the neck of the bottle and escape. The bees' superior intelligence is the cause of their undoing. They appear to have learnt from past experience that the exit of EVERY prison is towards the brightest light, and they act accordingly. They persist on previous learning to their own destruction accepting that there is one right answer to escaping from confinement. In their persistence they ignore the new factor of the transparent barrier since they have no previous knowledge or experience of it and they do not have the adaptability to handle the new information. The less intelligent flies, with no such learning ability, ignore the call of the light and move at random until, suddenly, they are free. There is no one right answer because circumstances are always different.

We have a paradox which we need to understand when we develop creative problem solving as a skill. On the one hand, more education and experience may inhibit creative problem solving and reinforce conceptual blocks but expertise is necessary for evaluation and implementation. As bees, individuals may not find solutions because the problem requires less 'educated' or more seemingly playful approaches, so it is with people. As several researchers have found, training can significantly enhance creative problem-solving abilities and managerial effectiveness (Barron, 1963; Taylor and Barron, 1963; Torrance, 1965).

Creative thinking involves three stages:

1. The destruction of the set patterns in our thought.

2. An uncomfortable stage of insecurity while we establish new patterns.

3. The re-establishment of new patterns.

Allen (1974) defined conceptual blocks as 'mental obstacles that constrain the way the problem is defined and limit the number of alternative solutions thought to be relevant', but as we have said – we need them and therefore would advocate a temporary lifting.

Thus, for example, most of us do not think about the mechanisms involved in switching on an electric light every time we enter a room. If we are an electrician we may need to think about a fairly complex device connected by wires embedded in the plaster leading to a local distribution box, which is itself connected to . . . No, if we are to remain sane, we segment our recall and simply turn on the light. Yet all of this information is available and is held by your brain. What we have done is to group the complexities into patterns and set them aside, noticing only the deviations from the patterns when events lead us to question 'conventional wisdom'. The process of grouping and setting aside is the origin of our conceptual blocks.

Paradoxically a logical problem is an acceleration of the process of group and setting aside – we choose a pattern of actions and put other actions aside 'if needed'. Formal education, except for the very talented, is about accepting patterns so that further patterns can be learnt – so is the job experience that we all value. It has been estimated that most adults over 40 display less than 2 per cent of the creative problem-solving ability of a child under 5. Formal education is teaching about grouping information and how to present the grouping to the satisfaction of all-knowing examiners, and is based on 'right answers', analytic rules and thinking boundaries. Experience in a job teaches proper ways of doing things, specialised knowledge and rigid expectation of appropriate actions. Individuals lose the ability to experiment, improvise or take mental detours. Again, it is about grouping information to survive. John Gardner (1965, p. 21) identifies the paradox when he says:

> All too often we are giving our young people cut flowers when we should be teaching them to grow plants. We are stuffing their heads with the products of earlier innovation rather than teaching them to innovate. We think of the mind as a storehouse to be filled when we should be thinking of it as an instrument to be used.

Thus training in creative thinking is often a process of unlearning, and is more difficult for some people than others. It does, however, work. Parnes (1962), for example, found that training in thinking increased the number of good ideas produced in problem solving by 125 per cent. Bower (1965) recorded numerous examples of organisations that increased profitability and efficiency through training in the improvement of thinking skills. Increasingly organisations send their managers to creativity workshops in order to improve their creative-thinking abilities.

> Potters-Ballotini, an American-owned company operating in the UK, had two factories turning glass waste into beads – the size of the beads ranged from almost dust for glitter in Christmas Cards to quite large marbles used to de-burr stone and metals.
>
> The company's top six managers sat down together for a creative problem-solving session. No idea for a new use of the beads was rejected and some 100 ideas were collected. One idea – that of incorporating the beads into a reflective paint for road marking – won through and has provided the company with an obvious and visible success ever since.

Problems requiring a creative input

Some problems require creative rather than rational solutions. These are problems for which no acceptable alternative seems to be available, all reasonable solutions seem to be blocked or no obvious best answer is accessible. Handy (1994) tells the following story:

> I was travelling in Ireland and looking for a particular place in the Wicklow hills. I stopped to ask a local who gave me accurate directions involving going up a steep hill until I got to Dave's Bar: *'When you get to the bar, you have passed it.'*

DeBono (1971) gives a similar analogy of passing a turning and explains that creative thinking is like the reverse gear on a car. 'You do not need it all the time, but when you do, you better be able to use it.' Cyert and March (1963), and developed by Probst and Buchel (1997), discuss the concept of 'slack'. The time to be creative is not when you are against the wall but you have spare capacity.

Something happens that makes a rational approach ineffective – we find ourselves in a useless Dave's Bar or in a cul-de-sac – we need to move into a creative problem-solving mode and this can happen at all levels of the organisation. To illustrate creative problem solving we will use two examples – the invention of the microwave cooker for Raytheon, and Post-It Notes for 3M.

PERCY SPENCER AND THE MAGNETRON

During the Second World War, Sir John Randall and Harry Boot, working on improving radar for the British Admiralty, developed a device they called the Cavity Magnetron. Radar systems using the Cavity Magnetron allowed aeroplanes to 'see' the surface of the earth and the sea. Apart from improving the offensive nature of the bomber, the device made it possible to detect and destroy submarines on the surface at great distances and was significant in winning what was called the Battle of the Atlantic. The original development, one of the closest secrets of the Second World War, was completed for £200 on a laboratory bench, but when Sir John Cockcroft took it across the Atlantic in 1940, it was considered to be one of the most valuable cargoes ever to sail.

Raytheon was one of several US firms invited to produce magnetrons for the Second World War. The workings of a magnetron were not well understood, even by sophisticated physicists, and among the firms that made them few understood what made the device work. A magnetron was tested, in those early days, by holding a neon tube next to it. If the neon tube got bright enough, the magnetron tube passed the test. In the process of conducting the test, the hands of the scientist holding the neon tube got warm. It was this phenomenon that led to a major creative breakthrough that eventually transformed lifestyles throughout the world.

At the end of the war, the market for radar essentially dried up and most firms stopped producing magnetrons. In Raytheon, however, a scientist named Percy Spencer had been experimenting with magnetrons, trying to think of alternative uses for the devices. He was convinced that magnetrons could be used to cook food by using the heat produced in the neon tube. The problem was, Raytheon was in the defence business – cooking devices seemed odd and out of place. Spencer was convinced that Raytheon should continue to produce magnetrons, even though production costs were prohibitively high. But Raytheon had lost money on the devices, and now there was no available market for magnetrons. The consumer product Spencer had in mind did not fit within the bounds of Raytheon's business. As it turned out, Percy Spencer's solution to Raytheon's problem produced the microwave oven and a revolution in cooking methods.

SPENCE SILVER AND THE GLUE THAT DID NOT STICK

Spence Silver was assigned to work on a temporary project team within the 3M company searching for new adhesives. Silver obtained some material from AMD, Inc., which had potential for a new polymer-based adhesive. He described one of his experiments in this way: 'In the course of this exploration, I tried an experiment with one of the monomers in which I wanted to see what would happen if I put a lot of it into the reaction mixture. Before, we had used amounts that would correspond to conventional wisdom' (Nayak & Ketteringham, 1986). The result was a substance that failed all the conventional 3M tests for adhesives. It didn't stick. It preferred its own molecules to the molecules of any other substance. It was more cohesive than adhesive. It hung around without making a commitment – it was a 'now-it-works, now-it-doesn't' kind of glue.

For five years Silver went from department to department within the company trying to find someone interested in using his newly found substance in a product. Silver had found a solution; he just couldn't find a problem to solve with it. Predictably, 3M showed little interest. The company's mission was to make adhesives that adhered ever more tightly. The ultimate adhesive was one that formed an unbreakable bond, not one that formed a temporary bond. After four years the task force was disbanded and the team members assigned to other projects. But Silver was still convinced that his substance was good for something. He just didn't know what. As it turned out, Silver's solution has become the prototype for innovation in American firms and has spawned a half-billion dollars in annual revenues for 3M in a unique product called Post-It Notes.

The two case studies – the Magnetron and Post-It Notes – are examples of how solving a problem in a unique way can lead to phenomenal business success. Both examples show how conceptual blocks needed to be overcome.

Conceptual blocks

Table 3.3 summarises four types of conceptual blocks that inhibit creative problem solving. Each is discussed and illustrated below with problems or exercises. We encourage you to complete the exercises and solve the problems as you read the book because doing so will help you become aware of your own conceptual blocks. Later we shall discuss in more detail how you can overcome them.

Table 3.3 Conceptual blocks that inhibit creative problem solving

1. *Consistency*	
Vertical thinking	Defining a problem in only one way without considering alternative views.
One thinking language	Not using more than one language to define and assess the problem.
2. *Commitment*	
Stereotyping based on past experience	Present problems are seen only as the variations of past problems.
Ignoring commonalities	Failing to perceive commonalities among elements that initially appear to be different.
3. *Compression*	
Distinguishing figure from ground	Not filtering out irrelevant information or finding needed information.
Artificial constraints	Defining the boundaries of a problem too narrowly.
4. *Complacency*	
Non-inquisitiveness	Not asking questions.
Non-thinking	A bias towards activity in place of mental work.

Consistency

Consistency involves an individual becoming wedded to one way of looking at a problem or to one approach of defining, describing or solving it. Consistency is a valued attribute for most of us, most of the time. We like to appear at least moderately consistent in our approach to life, and consistency is often associated with maturity, honesty and even intelligence. We judge lack of consistency as untrustworthy, peculiar or erratic. Several prominent psychologists theorise, in fact, that a need for consistency is the primary motivator of human behaviour (Festinger, 1957; Heider, 1946; Newcomb, 1954). Many psychological studies have shown that once individuals take a stand or employ a particular approach to a problem, they are highly likely to pursue that same course without deviation in the future (see Cialdini, 1988, for multiple examples).

While consistency is a virtue when we are pursuing the correct course of action, it can be a fault when we are not and an alternative action would be better. Digging a different hole may well be better than digging the same hole deeper, faster or more cheaply. We can describe the block of consistency in terms of two ways of thinking – 'vertical' thinking and thinking confined to one 'language'. We will now explain these two terms.

Vertical thinking

The terms 'vertical thinking', and its converse, 'lateral thinking', were coined by Edward De Bono (1968). In vertical thinking, a problem is defined in a single way and that definition is then pursued without deviation until a solution is reached – no alternative definitions are considered. All information gathered and all alternatives generated are consistent with the original definition. In a search for oil, for example, vertical thinkers determine a spot for the hole and drill the hole deeper and deeper hoping to strike oil. Instead of drilling one hole deeper and deeper, lateral thinkers would drill a number of holes in different places in search of oil, or even drill somewhere else.

The vertical-thinking conceptual block arises from not being able to view the problem from multiple perspectives. Returning to our hole metaphor, we see that we are getting less and less advantage from the hole we have begun and stand aside to think that new holes, or even a tunnel, might be preferred. When faced with a problem, lateral thinkers generate alternative ways of viewing a problem and produce multiple definitions.

> Mechanical cod fish processing in Britain and Germany had been developed from the highly skilled craftsmanship of the fish filleter. The filleter had to prepare neat fillets to be attractive for sale from fishmongers' slabs. As more and more cod fish were sent directly to factories to be made into frozen shaped fish pieces, the craftsmanship of the filleter was mechanised and refined. Nobody asked: 'Why do we need perfect fillets when there is no fishmongers' slab to exhibit them?'
>
> Once the question had been asked, Nordsee in Germany and the Unilever company, Birds Eye, in the UK, came up with a range of new processes where the fish went directly into the process with no intermediate step of the perfect fillet.

What has happened is that the problem solver has changed the definition of the problem from 'How do you improve processing of fish fillets?' to 'How do you get whole fish in a form acceptable to a processing plant?'.

Plenty of examples exist of creative solutions that have occurred because an individual refused to get stuck with a single problem definition. Alexander Graham Bell was trying to devise a hearing aid when he shifted definitions and invented the phonograph. Colonel Sanders was trying to sell his recipe to restaurants when he shifted definitions and developed his Kentucky Fried Chicken business. Karl Jansky was studying telephone static when he shifted definitions, discovered radio waves from the Milky Way galaxy, and developed the science of radio astronomy.

In our first case study above, Percy Spencer shifted the definition of the problem from 'How do you save our military radar business at the end of the war?' to 'How do you find other applications for the magnetron?'. Other problem definitions followed, such as 'How do you make magnetrons cheaper?', 'How do you mass-produce magnetrons?', 'How do you convince someone besides the military to buy magnetrons?', 'How do you enter a consumer products market?', 'How do you make microwave ovens practical and safe?', and so on. Each new problem definition led to new ways of thinking about the problem, new alternative approaches, and eventually, to a new microwave oven industry. In the second case study, Spence Silver at 3M also needed to change problem definitions. He began with 'How can I get an adhesive that has a stronger bond?', but switched to 'How can I find an application for an adhesive that doesn't stick?'. Eventually, other problem definitions followed:

- 'How can we get this new glue to stick to one surface but not another (e.g., to note-paper but not normal paper)?'
- 'How can we replace staples, drawing pins and paper clips in the workplace?'
- 'How can we manufacture and package a product that uses non-adhesive glue?'
- 'How can we get anyone to pay $1.00 for a pad of scrap paper?'

And so on.

Shifting definitions is not easy, of course, because it is not normal behaviour. It requires that individuals deflect their tendencies towards constancy. Later we will discuss some hints and tools that can help overcome the constancy block while avoiding the negative consequences of being inconsistent.

A single thinking language

A second manifestation of the constancy block is the use of only one thinking language. Most people faced with a problem attempt to express it in words – spoken or written. The problem is that words almost always carry images with them.

Working with training groups in Unilever, Mike Woods and George Davies used to say that they were wishing to design a new garden 'truck' – a wheelbarrow. They would then ask the group members to describe what he or she saw when the word wheelbarrow was mentioned. Almost always, under questioning, the participant would be able to describe the wheelbarrow in detail; its colour, age, scars and even where it was – 'propped up against the wall of a garden shed'. The word 'wheelbarrow' produced a complete image, so any new design of the wheelbarrow needed to compete against that total image before it was accepted as a viable concept. Thus, if a new concept for a garden 'truck' was called a wheelbarrow and it would not park easily against a particular garden shed, it might well be rejected.

To confirm this, the groups were presented with a new concept 'wheelbarrow' and asked to write down the first comment that came into their heads. Eighty per cent of the comments were negative – comments related to the fact that the word 'wheelbarrow' conjured up the image of a very detailed status quo to be challenged by the concept.

Rational problem solving reinforces the use of words and the subsequent dangers. Some writers, in fact, have argued that thinking cannot even occur without words (Vygotsky, 1962). However, other thought languages are available, such as non-verbal or symbolic languages (e.g., mathematics), sensory imagery (e.g., smelling or tactile sensation), feelings and emotions (e.g., happiness, fear or anger), and visual imagery (e.g., mental pictures). The more languages available to problem solvers, the better and more creative will be their solutions. As Koestler (1967) puts it, '[Verbal] language can become a screen which stands between the thinker and reality. This is the reason that true creativity often starts where [verbal] language ends.' Percy Spencer at Raytheon is a prime example of a visual thinker:

> One day, while Spencer was lunching with Dr Ivan Getting and several other Raytheon scientists, a mathematical question arose. Several men, in a familiar reflex, pulled out their slide rules, but before any could complete the equation, Spencer gave the answer. Dr Getting was astonished. 'How did you do that?' he asked. Spencer replied that he had learnt cube roots and squares by using blocks as a boy. Since then he had retained the visualisation. (Scott, 1974, p. 287)

The microwave oven not only depended on Spencer's command of multiple thinking languages, but it would never have got off the ground without a critical incident that illustrates the power of visual thinking. By 1965, Raytheon was just about to give up on any consumer application of the magnetron when a meeting was held with George Foerstner, the president of the recently acquired Amana Refrigeration Company. In the meeting, costs, applications, manufacturing obstacles and so on were discussed. Foerstner galvanised the entire microwave oven effort with the following statement, as reported by a Raytheon vice president.

> George says, 'It's no problem. It's about the same size as an air conditioner. It weighs about the same. It should sell for the same. So we'll price it at $499.' Now you think that's silly, but you stop and think about it. Here's a man who really didn't understand the technologies. But there is about the same amount of copper involved, the same amount of steel as an air conditioner. And these are basic raw materials. It didn't make a lot of difference how you fitted them together to make them work. They're both boxes; they're both made out of sheet metal; and they both require some sort of trim. (Nayak and Ketteringham, 1986, p. 181)

In short sentences Foerstner had taken one of the most complicated military secrets of the Second World War and translated it into something no more complex than a room air conditioner. He had painted a picture of an application that no one else had been able to capture by describing a magnetron visually, as a familiar object, not as a set of calculations, formulas or blueprints.

A similar occurrence in the Post-It Note chronology also led to a breakthrough. Spence Silver had been trying for years to get someone in 3M to adopt his un-sticky glue. Art Fry, another scientist with 3M, had heard Silver's presentations before. One day while singing in Church, Fry was fumbling around with the slips of paper that marked the various hymns in his book. Suddenly, a visual image popped into his mind.

> 'I thought, gee! If I had a little adhesive on these bookmarks, that would be just the ticket. So I decided to check into that idea the next week at work. What I had in mind was Silver's adhesive. . . . I knew I had a much bigger discovery than that. I also now realised that the primary application for Silver's adhesive was not to put it on a fixed surface like the bulletin boards. That was a secondary application. The primary application concerned paper to paper. I realised that immediately.' (Nayak and Ketteringham, 1986, pp. 63–4)

Years of verbal descriptions had not led to any application for Silver's glue. Tactile thinking (handling the glue) had also failed. However, thinking about the product in visual terms, as applied to what Fry initially called 'a better bookmark', led to the breakthrough.

> This emphasis on using alternative thinking languages, especially visual thinking, is now becoming the new frontier in scientific research. With the advent of super-computers, scientists are more and more working with pictures and simulated images rather than with numerical data. 'Scientists who are using the new computer graphics say that by viewing images instead of numbers, a fundamental change in the way researchers think and work is occurring. People have a lot easier time getting an intuition from pictures than they do from numbers and tables of formulas. In most physics experiments, the answer used to be a number or a string of numbers. In the last few years the answer has increasingly become a picture.' (Markoff, 1988, p. D3)

To illustrate the differences among thinking languages, consider the following two simple problems.

1. Below is the Roman numeral 9. By adding only a single line, turn it into a 6. Look at page 623 to see how the problem is solved.

$$IX$$

2. Look at the configuration of seven match sticks in Figure 3.2 By moving only one matchstick, make the figure into a true equality (i.e., the value on one side equals the value on the other side).

Before looking up the answer on page 623, try to define the problems differently, and try to use different thinking languages. How many answers can you find?

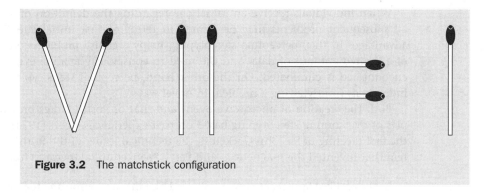

Figure 3.2 The matchstick configuration

Commitment

Commitment can also serve as a conceptual block to creative problem solving.

> Many local government-owned housing estates throughout Europe suffer from neglect and vandalism. A process whereby the houses are sold to the tenants is increasing – the political issues are not our concern. The concern is that many of the problems of disrepair vanish with ownership. Where previously the local government official was blamed for not repairing the gutter or painting the window and nothing was done, now with ownership the ladders appear and the paint pots are emptied. Commitment by ownership works.

A host of other studies have demonstrated the same phenomenon. However, commitment is not always a positive effect, it may well be its own conceptual block.

Stereotyping based on past experience – defending the status quo

March and Simon (1958) point out that a major obstacle to innovative problem solving is that individuals tend to define present problems in terms of problems they have faced in the past. Current problems are usually seen as variations on some past situation, so the alternatives proposed to solve the current problem are ones that have proved to be successful in the past. Both problem definition and proposed solution are therefore restricted by past experience. This restriction is referred to as 'perceptual stereotyping' (Allen, 1974). That is, certain preconceptions formed on the basis of past experience determine how an individual defines a situation. With perceptual stereotyping the new is compared with the established and dismissed accordingly.

> Working with a group developing new ready meals, we were testing various concepts including roast beef and Yorkshire pudding. The sample group showed a great divergence in acceptance of the concept, some members rejecting the concept completely. Further discussion with the people who were particularly dismissive found that these individuals had recently been in military service and 'roast beef and Yorkshire pudding' consisted of very thin over-cooked meat and biscuit-consistency Yorkshire pudding. The very words 'roast beef and Yorkshire pudding' conjured up a very unhappy experience in their lives and they reacted accordingly.

When individuals receive an initial cue regarding the definition of a problem, all subsequent problems may be framed in terms of that initial cue. There are advantages in this, perceptual stereotyping helps organise problems on the basis of a limited amount of data, and the need to consciously analyse every problem encountered is eliminated. On the other hand, perceptual stereotyping prevents individuals from viewing a problem in novel ways.

Both the creation of microwave ovens and that of Post-It Notes provide examples of overcoming stereotyping based on past experiences. Scott (1974) described the first meeting of Sir John Cockcroft, the technical leader of the British radar system that invented the magnetron, and Percy Spencer of Raytheon as follows:

> Cockcroft liked Spencer at once. He showed him the magnetron and the American regarded it thoughtfully. He asked questions – very intelligent ones – about how it was produced and the British scientist answered at length. Later Spencer wrote, 'The technique of making these tubes, as described to us, was awkward and impractical.' Awkward and impractical! Nobody else dared draw such a judgement about a product of undoubted scientific brilliance, produced and displayed by the leaders of British science.

Cockcroft saw the magnetron as university developed scientific equipment and had allowed its development as a war weapon to move linearly from this image of men and women in white coats supported by lab technicians. Spencer worked without this image and saw the magnetron as a commercial development issue – no white coats or subservient technicians.

Similarly, Spence Silver at 3M described his invention in terms of breaking stereotypes based on past experience.

> The key to the Post-It adhesive was doing the experiment. If I had sat down and factored it out beforehand, and thought about it, I wouldn't have done the experiment. If I had really seriously cracked the books and gone through the literature, I would have stopped. The literature was full of examples that said you can't do this. (Nayak and Ketteringham, 1986, p. 57)

This is not to say that one should avoid learning from past experience or that failing to learn the mistakes of history does not doom us to repeat them. Rather, it is to say that commitment to a course of action based on past experience can inhibit viewing problems in new ways, and it can even inhibit us from being able to solve some problems at all.

In Figure 3.3 there are four volumes of Shakespeare on the shelf. The pages of each volume are exactly two inches thick and the covers are each one-sixth of an inch thick. A bookworm started eating at page 1 of Volume I and ate straight through to the last page of Volume IV. What is the distance the worm covered? (The answer can be found in Appendix 1, page 624.) Solving this problem is relatively simple, but it requires that you overcome a stereotyping block to get the correct answer. (A clue – one of your authors finds the problem virtually impossible unless we can work with real books – we need to touch and try before we can come to an answer. However, we gave it to a 12-year-old on a rainy day on holiday and he came up with the correct answer within seconds.)

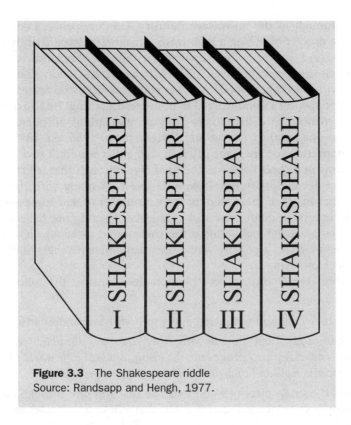

Figure 3.3 The Shakespeare riddle
Source: Randsapp and Hengh, 1977.

Ignoring commonalities

A second manifestation of the commitment block is the failure to identify similarities among seemingly disparate pieces of data. This is among the most commonly identified blocks to creativity. It means that a person becomes committed to a particular point of view, to the fact that elements are different, and becomes unable to make connections, identify themes or perceive commonalties.

The ability to find one definition or solution for two seemingly dissimilar problems is a characteristic of creative individuals (Dellas and Gaier, 1970; Steiner, 1978). The inability to do this can overload a problem solver by requiring that every problem encountered be solved individually. The discovery of penicillin by Sir Alexander Fleming resulted from his seeing a common theme among seemingly unrelated events. Fleming was working with some cultures of staphylococci that had accidentally become contaminated. The contamination, a growth of fungi and isolated clusters of dead staphylococci, led Fleming to see a relationship no one else had ever seen previously and thus to discover a wonder drug (Beveridge, 1960). The famous chemist Friedrich Kekule saw a relationship between his dream of a snake swallowing its own tail and the chemical structure of organic compounds. This creative insight led him to the discovery that organic compounds such as benzene have closed rings rather than open structures (Koestler, 1967).

For Percy Spencer at Raytheon, seeing a connection between the heat of a neon tube and the heat required for cooking food was the creative connection that led to his breakthrough in the microwave industry. One of Spencer's colleagues recalled: 'In the process of testing a bulb [with a magnetron] your hands got hot. I don't know when Percy really came up with the thought of microwave ovens, but he knew at that time – and that was 1942. He remarked frequently that this would be a good device for cooking food.' Another colleague described Spencer this way: 'The way Percy Spencer's mind worked is an interesting thing. He had a mind that allowed him to hold an extraordinary array of associations on phenomena and relate them to one another' (Nayak and Ketteringham, 1986, pp. 184, 205). Similarly, the connection Art Fry made between a glue that wouldn't stick tightly and marking hymns in a choir book was the final breakthrough that led to the development of the revolutionary Post-It Note business. Working with inventors we have found that many of them seem to carry a number of 'key solutions' in their minds, continuously searching for 'lock problems'. They do not tell others when the key fails to open the lock – this is the background of Tudor Rickards (1988) and his Puxxels. He sees a positive way of increasing inventiveness in deliberately listing the 'lock problems'.

To test your own ability to see commonalities, answer the following three questions:

1. What are some common terms that apply to both water and finance?

2. What is humorous about the following story? *Descartes, the philosopher, walked into a university class. Recognising him, the instructor asked if he would like to lecture. Descartes replied, 'I think not', and promptly disappeared.*

3. What does the single piece of wood look like that will pass through each hole in the transparent block in Figure 3.4, but that will touch all sides as it passes through?

Our answers are in Appendix 1, page 624.

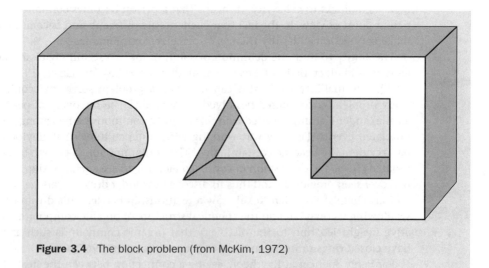

Figure 3.4 The block problem (from McKim, 1972)

Compression

Conceptual blocks also occur as a result of compression of ideas – looking too narrowly at a problem, screening out too much relevant data, or making assumptions that inhibit problem-solution, are common examples.

Artificial constraints

Sometimes people place boundaries around problems, or constrain their approach to them, in such a way that the problems become impossible to solve. Such constraints arise from hidden assumptions people make about problems they encounter. People assume that some problem definitions or alternative solutions are out of bounds – somehow cheating, and they ignore them. For an illustration of this conceptual block, look at Figure 3.5. Without lifting your pencil from the paper, draw four straight lines that pass through all nine dots. Complete the task before reading further.

By thinking of the figure as more constrained than it actually is, the problem becomes impossible to solve. To solve the problem we have to MOVE OUTSIDE THE SQUARE, which could be called 'cheating'! The assumption we make is that we have to 'join the dots' *without* moving outside the square. See Figure 3.6 for the basic solution.

Now 'cheat' some more – move further out on the assumptions that you have set for yourself when you saw the problem – join the dots with three lines and try it with one line. Can you determine how to put a single straight line through all nine dots without lifting your pencil from the paper? (Some rather exotic answers are given on page 624.)

Artificially constraining problems means simply that the problem-definition and the possible alternatives are limited more than the problem requires. Creative problem solving requires that individuals become adept at recognising their hidden assumptions and expanding the alternatives they consider – or, using the metaphor, MOVING OUTSIDE THE SQUARE.

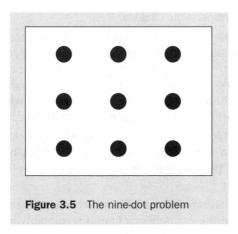

Figure 3.5 The nine-dot problem

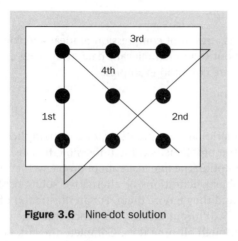

Figure 3.6 Nine-dot solution

A British-based textile company found itself faced with very strong opposition from the Far East and reduced sales. The large sales force was spurred on to work much harder and make more visits, but the situation only got worse and profitability fell still further. 'Moving outside the square' with the management team, the problem was was found to be that marginal sales to an increased number of customers was actually costing the company money. In the rush for sales at any price the sales staff were offering a diversity of products that made the manufacturing division operate at a loss. *The solution was not more visits but less.* Marginal customers were gently recommended to shop with competitors, and focused meetings with valued volume customers were set up.

Edward De Bono (1971) explains a technique for 'moving outside the square' and looking at the constraints that define a problem. He sees the constraints around a situation as being defined by five factors:

1. *The dominant idea*   This organises the approach to a problem and may be stated explicitly or merely implied. It may well be coached in language such as, 'we are a manufacturing company', 'we are responsible for the well-being of the neighbourhood and are responsible citizens'.

2. *Tethering factors*   'The dominant idea may be a powerful organisational idea, but the tethering factor may be a small, almost insignificant idea.' An example could be that the CEO is on the Board of Governors of a local school and is expected to award the prizes every year. Any change in policy towards local employment could well embarrass the relationship. We may well wish to consider the priorities of running a business against this 'tethering factor'.

3. *Polarising factors*   Polarising factors are constraints disguised as 'either, or'. An organisation could be either a manufacturer or an importer of finished goods. Polarising factors dismiss the possibility of the halfway house – for instance 'a part-finished goods assembler'.

4. *Boundaries*   Boundaries are the framework within which the problem is supposed to be considered. In the example of a fictitious company, we may think of these in terms of the position of the shareholders of the bank – 'we have to live within the constraints set by the bank', 'the shareholders have bought into a UK-based company'. The statement may be true but check it!

5. *Assumptions* Boundaries are the limits of the ideas and assumptions are the building blocks that created the boundaries. We assume that the bank is not open to negotiation and that the shareholders will not be open to reasoned argument.

Using a non-judgemental questioning of the five factors we can redesign the problem creatively and have a chance of reaching new solutions.

De Bono concludes that it is never possible to examine all the constraints, but that in setting them out to look for them logically, one becomes aware of the cage within which one is operating. Thus it is possible to consider whether this particular cage is relevant for the present time and place.

The Ford Motor Company EQUIP programme for training and developing engineers in Europe insists that assumptions are recorded and shared before meetings. The agenda of the meeting is circulated in advance and nothing is discussed before the sharing is completed. Thus, they might be discussing safety bags in small cars and the pooled assumptions might include:

- Too bulky for the current small cars range.
- European drivers would not want it.
- Difficult to make reliable at a price.

Any of the assumptions if not tabled BEFORE the discussion could well encourage the individual holding the assumption to act negatively or even sabotage the discussion. Tabled, they can be seen for what they are – assumptions capable of challenge.

Seeing the wood from the trees

Questioning constraints in the way that De Bono suggests will not always lead to solutions. Sometimes it is the lack of clear constraints that prevents clear thought. Problems almost never come clearly specified, so problem-solvers must determine what the real problem is. They must filter out inaccurate, misleading or irrelevant information in order to define the problem and to generate appropriate alternative solutions. The inability to separate the important from the unimportant – to appropriately compress problems – serves as a conceptual block because it exaggerates the complexity of the problem and inhibits a simple definition.

We expect the past to help us to predict the future – which may be true but is by no means always true.

You have tossed a coin three times and each time it has come down heads. What are the odds of it coming down heads on the fourth throw? The answer is 50:50, all other things being equal, but somehow we expect it to come down heads again.

Past history and past experience MAY help, but they are only one way to consider a new problem.

An example of using past history was given by a well-known weather forecaster when he was asked how he could improve the quality of his forecasts. He explained that if he said that the weather would be much the same as yesterday, his forecasts would be more accurate that those derived by detailed analysis.

The compression block – seeing the wood from the trees, and artificially constraining problems – were important factors in the microwave oven and the Post-It Note breakthroughs. George Foerstner's contribution to the development and manufacture of the microwave oven was directly a product of his ability to compress the problem – that is, to separate out all the irrelevant complexity that constrained others. Whereas the magnetron was a device so complicated that few people understood it, Foerstner focused on its basic raw materials, its size and its functionality. By comparing it to an air conditioner, he eliminated much of the complexity and mystery, and, as described by two analysts, 'he had seen what all the researchers had failed to see, and they knew he was right' (Nayak and Ketteringham, 1986, p. 181).

On the other hand, Spence Silver had to add complexity, to overcome compression, in order to find an application for his product. Because the glue had failed every traditional 3M test for adhesives, it was categorised as a useless configuration of chemicals. The potential for the product was artificially constrained by traditional assumptions about adhesives – more stickiness, stronger bonding – until Art Fry visualised some unconventional applications – a better bookmark, a bulletin board, a notepad, and, paradoxically, a replacement for 3M's main product, tape.

The issue of seeing the wood from the trees – refusing to accept the constraints implied by the question and the questioner – is an art and is the art practised by all good consultants.

Complacency

This occurs because of fear, ignorance, insecurity, or just plain mental laziness. Two especially prevalent examples of the complacency block are a lack of questioning and a bias against thinking.

Non-inquisitiveness

Sometimes the inability to solve problems results from a reticence to ask questions, to obtain information or to search for data. Individuals are often reluctant to admit that things are not clear or that they do not see the reason why particular assumptions are being made. We have a fear of looking stupid, naive or ignorant, and asking questions puts us at risk of exposing our ignorance. Others may also feel threatened by our questions and react with hostility or even ridicule. Comments such as 'If you had been here at the beginning of the project . . .', and 'Surely everyone knows that . . .', can be damaging remarks.

Creative problem solving is inherently risky because it potentially involves interpersonal conflict. In addition, it is also risky because it is fraught with mistakes. As Linus Pauling, the Nobel laureate, said, 'If you want to have a good idea, have a lot of ideas, because most of them will be bad ones.' Most of us are not rewarded for bad ideas. To illustrate, answer the following questions for yourself:

1. How many times in the last month have you tried something for which the probability of success was less than 50 per cent?

2. When was the last time you asked three 'why' questions in a row?

Children begin by asking WHY questions, but most are trained by the age of 10 to accept the status quo. The key to creativity is accepting the naivety of a child and building in the experience of an adult to provide the WHAT's and the HOW's.

> We were once asked to look at the future of food processing and chose to work with a small panel of 6- to 9-year-olds. The kids were all from middle-class families, most being concerned with the client company in some way. The first question we asked was – 'Does food go bad?' The answer was a resounding NO, but under pressure they admitted that milk occasionally 'went off' – 'and Daddy makes it into cream cheese, but Mummy throws it away when he is not looking'.
>
> We then went on to ask why we put things into tins – baked beans, for instance. 'Because if we didn't they would run all over the shelf', was the answer that came back. We persisted. 'Does meat go bad?', 'No', 'No never, we have some pigs behind our house running about and they don't go bad.'
>
> Very easy to laugh but the questions for us, after the children had left, were 'Why does meat on the hoof not go bad?' and 'Is life used as a method of preserving food anywhere in the world?' The answer to the last question is yes; many hot countries sell live animals in the market place for slaughter directly before preparation. The more adult question moves on to, 'What is different about life from death?' – a question we were not able to answer ourselves so we called in an expert enzymologist to help us. He explained that one way of looking at life and death is a battle fought by the enzymes of vitality and decay, with the decay processes winning once the brain ceases to referee the battle on the side of life. He explained that enzymes were used to 'tenderise' or accelerate the 'rotting' of meat by injection into live animals prior to slaughter and that there was no reason why they should not be used for the opposite purpose. We had a new line of research.

David Feldman (1988) lists more than 100 questions designed to shake complacency. For example:

- Why are people immune to their own body odour?
- Why are there twenty-one guns in a twenty-one-gun salute?
- What happens to the tread that wears off tyres?
- Why doesn't sugar spoil or get mouldy?
- Why doesn't a two-by-four measure two inches by four inches?
- Why doesn't postage-stamp glue have flavouring?
- Why is the telephone keypad arranged differently from that of a calculator?
- How do people who throw their hats in the air find them later?
- Why is Jack the nickname for John?
- How do they print 'M&M' on M&M sweets?

Tudor Rickards (1988) suggests that you should go about your work with a note-book and write down the things that annoy you, but about which you are too busy to do anything at the time. He suggests that you call them Puxxles. John Oakland (1994), working from the concept of Total Quality Management, calls these prob-lem items 'Snags' and advises managers to create a Snag list. The point of Puxxles and Snags is that by giving time and importance to the process of asking WHY we provide opportunities for innovation.

> In a session on Puxxles in the University of Miskolc in Hungary in 1993, a group run by Mike Woods came up with five 'problems' in the spectacles that many of us wear. Why do:
>
> • the screws holding the frames come out?
> • the lenses fall out?
> • the lenses get scratched?
> • long-sighted people always lose them?
> • they become a danger when they break?
>
> These problems were converted in statements beginning with the words 'How to . . .': 'How to stop the screws falling out.' 'How to avoid having any screws to fall out.' These reframed questions can be seen as an opportunity to develop a design that has hardly changed since the days of Samuel Pepys in the seventeenth century.

Most of us are a little too complacent to even ask such questions, let alone to find out the answers! We often stop being inquisitive as we get older because we learn that it is good to be intelligent and being intelligent is interpreted as already know-ing the answers (instead of asking good questions). Consequently, we learn less well at 35 than at 5; we take fewer risks; we avoid asking why; and we function in the world without trying to understand it. Creative problem solvers, on the other hand, are frequently engaged in inquisitive and experimental behaviour. Spence Silver at 3M described his attitude about the complacency block this way:

> 'People like myself get excited about looking for new properties in materials. I find that very satisfying, to perturb the structure slightly and just see what happens. I have a hard time talking people into doing that – people who are more highly trained. It's been my experience that people are reluctant just to try, to experiment – just to see what will happen.' (Nayak and Ketteringham, 1986, p. 58)

Bias against thinking

A second demonstration of the complacency block is in an inclination to avoid doing mental work. This block, like most of the others, is a mixture of cultural and personal bias. For example, assume that you passed by your assistant's office one day and noticed that she was leaning back in a chair, staring out the window. A half-hour later, as you passed by again, her position was the same. What would be your conclusion? Most of us would assume that no work was being done. We would assume that unless we saw action, our assistant was not being productive. However, she may well be THINKING.

When was the last time you heard someone say, 'I'm sorry. I can't go to the football (concert, dance, party or cinema) because I have to think?' or 'I'll do the dishes tonight. I know you need to catch up on your thinking?' The fact that these statements sound humorous illustrates the bias most people develop towards action rather than thought, or against putting their feet up, rocking back in their chair, looking off into space and engaging in solitary mental activity. This does not mean daydreaming or fantasising, but *thinking*.

There is a particular conceptual block in our culture against the kind of thinking that uses the right hemisphere of the brain. Left-hemisphere thinking, for most people, is concerned with logical, analytic, linear or sequential tasks. Thinking using the left hemisphere is apt to be organised planned and precise, for example, language and mathematics are left-hemisphere activities.

Right-hemisphere thinking, on the other hand, is concerned with intuition, synthesis, playfulness and qualitative judgement. It tends to be more spontaneous, imaginative and emotional than left-hemisphere thinking. The emphasis in most formal education is towards left-hemisphere thought development. Problem solving on the basis of reason, logic and utility is generally rewarded, while problem solving based on sentiment, intuition or pleasure is frequently considered tenuous and inferior.

A number of researchers have found that the most creative problem solvers are ambidextrous in their thinking; that is, they can use both left- and right-hemisphere thinking and easily switch from one to the other (Bruner, 1966; Hermann, 1981; Martindale, 1975). Creative ideas arise most frequently in the right hemisphere but must be processed and interpreted by the left, so creative problem solvers use both hemispheres equally well.

Try the exercise in Table 3.4, the idea of which came from von Oech (1986), and was developed by the authors of the work on Neuro Linguistic Programming

Table 3.4   Exercise in ambidextrous thinking

List 1	List 2	List 3	List 4
Decline	Sunset	Warmth	Explosion
Very	Cow	Sadness	Bell
Ambiguous	Red	Hugging	Piano
Resources	Brick	Burnt toast	Bugle
Term	Monkey	Daydream	Click
Conceptual	Castle	Handshake	Grunt
About	Pencil	Cut grass	Guitar
Appendix	Computer	Perfume	Rifle shot
Determine	Cheeseboard	Bonfire	Applause
Forget	Ship	Fur	Beethoven's 5th
Quantify	Tree	Slime	Referee's whistle
Survey	Rabbit	Toffee	Stamping feet

by Bandler and Grindler (1979). It illustrates this ambidextrous principle. There are four lists of words. Take a minute to memorise the first list. Then, on a piece of paper write down as many as you can remember. Now memorise the words in each of the other three lists, one at a time taking a minute for each, writing down as many as you can remember.

Most people will have a preferred list but few are most effective on the first list. The second list contains words that relate to visual perceptions, the third list relates to what Grindler and Bandler call 'kinesthetic' sensations, and the fourth list relates to the auditory senses. Your preference relates to the way in which you prefer to perceive your universe. Thus, some people visualise and 'see' things in context (List 2). Others need to 'feel' their way round a problem (List 3), while still others, those who remembered most from List 4, like to attach sounds to what they learn or remember.

All but the first list combine right-brain activity as well as left-brain activity. People can draw mental pictures, feel and sense or hear at the same time as attempting the cold process of intellectualisation. Fantasy is possible.

Allowing fantasy, the connection of the left and right brain, using visual, sensing and auditory communications allows us to remember more and, in the context of this book, to be more creative. We will discuss how we encourage fantasy later.

Review of conceptual blocks

So far we have suggested that certain conceptual blocks prevent individuals from solving problems creatively. These blocks, summarised in Table 3.3, narrow the scope of problem definition, limit the consideration of alternative solutions and constrain the selection of an optimal solution. Unfortunately, many of these conceptual blocks are unconscious, and it is only by being confronted with unsolvable problems because of conceptual blocks, that individuals become aware that they exist. We have attempted to make you aware of your own conceptual blocks by asking you to solve problems that require you to overcome these mental barriers. These conceptual blocks, of course, are not all bad; not all problems can be addressed by creative problem solving. But research has shown that individuals who have developed creative problem-solving skills are far more effective with problems that are complex and that require a search for alternative solutions, than others who are conceptually blocked (Dauw, 1976; Basadur, 1979; Guilford, 1962; Steiner, 1978).

In the next section we provide some techniques and tools that overcome these blocks and help improve creative problem-solving skills. In the last section we discuss how creativity and innovation can be fostered in others.

Conceptual blockbusting

Conceptual blocks cannot be overcome all at once because most blocks are a product of years of habit-forming thought processes. Overcoming them requires practice in thinking in different ways over a long period of time. You will not become a skilled creative problem solver, of course, just by reading this book. On the other hand, by becoming aware of your conceptual blocks and practising the following techniques, you can enhance your creative problem-solving skills.

Stages in creative thought

A first step in overcoming conceptual blocks is simply to recognise that creative problem solving is a skill that can be developed. Being a creative problem solver is not a quality that some people have and some don't. As Dauw (1976, p. 19) has noted:

> Research results [show] . . . that nurturing creativity is not a question of increasing one's ability to score high on an IQ test, but a matter of improving one's mental attitudes and habits and cultivating creative skills that have lain dormant since childhood.

Haefele (1962) reviewed the literature and found agreement that creative problem solving involves four stages: preparation, incubation, illumination and verification.

- The *preparation* stage includes gathering data, defining the problem, generating alternatives and consciously examining all available information.
- The *incubation* stage involves mostly unconscious mental activity in which the mind combines unrelated thoughts in the pursuit of a solution. Conscious effort is not involved.
- *Illumination*, the third stage, occurs when an insight is recognised and a creative solution is articulated.
- *Verification* is the final stage, which involves evaluating the creative solution relative to some standard of acceptability.

The primary difference between skilful creative problem solving and rational problem solving is in how the preparation stage is approached. Creative problem solvers are more flexible and fluent in data gathering, problem definition, alternative generation and examination of options. In fact, it is in this stage that training in creative problem solving can significantly improve effectiveness (Allen, 1974; Basadur, 1979; McKim, 1972) because the other three steps are not amenable to conscious mental work. We will therefore limit our discussion to improving functioning in this first stage.

Two types of techniques help the preparation stage. One type helps individuals to think about and define the problem more effectively; the other helps individuals to gather information and generate more alternative solutions to the problem.

One major difference between effective, creative problem solvers and other people is that creative problem solvers are less constrained. They allow themselves to be more flexible in the definitions they impose on problems and the number of solutions they identify. They develop a large repertoire of approaches to problem solving. In short, they do what Karl Weick (1979, p. 261) prescribes for unblocking decision making – they generate more conceptual options. As Interaction Associates (1971, p. 15) explained:

Flexibility in thinking is critical to good problem solving. A problem solver should be able to conceptually dance around the problem like a good boxer, jabbing and poking, without getting caught in one place or 'fixated'. At any given moment, a good problem solver should be able to apply a large number of strategies [for generating alternative definitions and solutions].

Moreover, a good problem solver is a person who has developed, through his understanding of strategies and experiences in problem solving, a sense of appropriateness of what is likely to be the most useful strategy at any particular time.

Anyone visiting a library or bookshop will find that the number of books claiming to enhance creative problem solving is enormous. Therefore, in the next section we present just a few tools and hints that we have found to be especially effective and relatively simple for executives and students of business to apply. Whereas some of them may seem a little game-like or playful, that is precisely what they are supposed to be – they are designed to unfreeze you and make you more like the child, asking WHY questions without fear of seeming naive.

Methods for improving problem definition

Problem definition is probably the most critical step in creative problem solving. Once a problem is defined appropriately, solutions often come easily. However, Campbell (1952), Medawar (1967) and Schumacher (1977) point out that individuals tend to define problems in terms with which they are familiar. Medawar (1967, Introduction) notes: 'Good scientists study the most important problems they think they can solve.' When a problem is faced that is strange or does not appear to have a solution (what Schumacher calls 'divergent problems'), the problem either remains undefined or is redefined in terms of something familiar. Unfortunately, new problems may not be the same as old problems, so relying on past definitions may lead to solving the wrong problem.

Birds Eye, part of the Unilever group in the UK, was considering a new product – pineapple fritters – based on fruit jelly. The pineapple jelly was cut into finger-shaped pieces and was to be battered ready for frying by the consumer. The initial pilot plant to make the product was developed from a redundant conveyor system that had been used to make fish fingers – a similarly SHAPED product produced by the company in vast quantities but made from hard frozen fish.

The modified fish finger equipment produced a sticky and ungovernable mess when used with the fruit jelly 'fingers'. Quite suddenly someone asked: 'Why do we expect fruit jelly slices to behave the same way as rigid fingers of fish?' Once asked, the answer was obvious. Once the conceptual block was broken the whole concept of making the fruit jelly product was reviewed and the final product was manufactured in a machine derived from the confectionery industry, not the technology of frozen fish.

Applying some hints for creative problem-definition can help individuals to see problems in alternative ways so their definitions are not so narrowly constrained. Three such hints for improving and expanding a definition are discussed below.

Make the strange familiar and the familiar strange

Synectics is a well-known technique for improving creative problem solving (Gordon, 1961). The goal of *Synectics* is to help you put something you don't know in terms of something you do know, and vice versa. By analysing what you know and applying it to what you don't know, new insights and perspectives can be developed.

It works like this. First you form a definition of a problem (make the strange familiar). Then you try to make that definition out-of-focus, distorted or transposed in some way (make the familiar strange). Use analogies and metaphors to create this distortion. Then you postpone the original definition of the problem while you analyse the analogy or metaphor. You impose the analysis on the original problem to see what new insights you can uncover.

For example, suppose you have defined a problem as low morale among members of your team. You may form an analogy or metaphor by answering questions such as the following about the problem:

- What does this remind me of?
- What does this make me feel like?
- What is this similar to?
- What isn't this similar to?

> In the days before the banning of CFCs a group was asked to consider 'How to avoid offensive odours in the John' – it was an American group who preferred the word 'John' to the more European WC.
>
> A member of the group suggested that holding down smells reminded him of smog, and they were caused by meteorological inversions. The problem was then, 'How to cause a meteorological inversion in a lavatory bowl'. The group member promptly left for his own laboratory and returned with a long graduated cylinder – added lemon oil and sprayed a neat CFC aerosol in at the top. The inversion of temperature stopped any odour of the lemon oil.
>
> The company sponsoring the 'session' – Glamorene of the States – launched the product named 'Before' within weeks of the concept, only to be stopped by Ozone Layer protection concerns.

Metaphors and analogies are immensely useful and often give us new insights. By analysing the metaphor or analogy, we identify attributes of the problem that were not evident before. Gordon (1961) provides a list of 'worlds' from which analogies can be drawn.

> The Trustee Saving Bank in the UK was concerned with the problem of direct mail going to customers who had already been refused the bank's credit facilities. Using the world of sport – football – the concept of 'own goals' appeared. Own goals are often scored by the most effective players in defence and are reduced by a continual dialogue between the goalkeeper and his players. The fruitful discussion that followed on what such a continual dialogue would look like in the bank led to a 'solution' to the problem.

The ideas of Gordon are not new. William Harvey used the pump analogy to the heart, which allowed him new insights into the body's circulation system. Niels Bohr compared the atom to the solar system and supplanted Rutherford's 'raisin pudding' model of matter. Creativity consultant Roger von Oech (1986) helped to turn around a struggling computer company by applying a restaurant analogy to the company's operations. By analysing the problems of a restaurant – 'safe' environment – the management of the computer company were able to highlight the problems of their own company by comparison. Major contributions in the field of organisational behaviour have occurred by applying analogies to other types of organisation, such as machines, cybernetic or open systems, force fields, clans and so on. Probably the most effective analogies (called parables) were used by Jesus to teach principles that otherwise were difficult for individuals to grasp, given their culture and heritage.

Some hints to keep in mind when constructing analogies are:

1. Include action or motion in the analogy (for example, driving a car, cooking a meal, attending a funeral).
2. Include things that can be visualised or pictured in the analogy (for example, stars, football games, crowded shopping malls).
3. Pick familiar events or situations (for example, families, kissing, bedtime).
4. Try to relate things that are not obviously similar (for example, saying an organisation is like a crowd is not nearly so rich a simile as saying an organisation is like a psychic prison or a poker game).

Synectics recommends four styles of analogy:

- *Personal*, where individuals try to identify themselves as the problem: 'If I were the problem, how would I feel, what would I like, what could satisfy me?'

  Technicians and scientists developing a machine to automate bacteriological testing – the Colworth 2000 – worked in the final stages of the design by 'becoming the machine'.

- *Direct*, where individuals apply facts, technology and common experience to the problem (e.g., Brunel solved the problem of underwater construction by watching a shipworm tunnelling into a tube). Often the analogies are from the living world and are then called bionic analogies.

  A design for a floor-cleaning mop was based on the way in which a cat's tongue works.

- *Symbolic*, where symbols or images are imposed on the problem (e.g., modelling the problem mathematically or diagramming the logic flow).

- *Fantasy*, where individuals ask the question: 'In my wildest dreams, how would I wish the problem to be resolved?' We might say, for example: 'I wish all employees could work with no supervision.'

Elaborate on the definition

There are a variety of ways to enlarge, alter or replace a problem definition once it has been specified. One way is to force yourself to generate at least two alternative

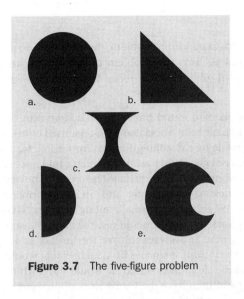

Figure 3.7   The five-figure problem

hypotheses for every problem definition. That is, specify at least two plausible definitions of the problem in addition to the one originally accepted. Think in plural terms rather than in singular terms. Instead of asking 'What is the problem?', 'What is the meaning of this?', 'What is the result?', ask questions like, 'What are the problems?', 'What are the meanings of this?', 'What are the results?'. As an example, look at Figure 3.7. Which shape is the odd-one out?

Most people select (b) because it is the only figure that is all straight lines, and they are, of course, correct. Others may pick (a) as it is the only figure with a continuous line and no points of discontinuity; they are also correct. The choice of (c) as the only figure with two straight and two curved lines; (d) as the only figure with one curved and one straight line, or (e) as the only figure that is non-symmetrical or partial, are ALL correct choices. The point is, there can often be more than one problem definition, more than one right answer and more than one perspective from which to view a problem.

Another way to elaborate definitions is to use a question checklist:

1. Is there anything else?

2. Is the reverse true?

3. Is there a more general problem?

4. Can it be stated differently?

5. Who sees it differently?

6. What past experience is this like?

As an exercise, take a minute now to think of a problem you are currently experiencing. Write it down so that it is formally specified. Now manipulate that definition by answering each of the six questions in the checklist. If you can't think of a problem, try the exercise with this one: 'I am not as effective as I would like to be.'

Reverse the definition

A third tool for improving and expanding problem definition is to reverse the definition of the problem – that is, turn the problem upside down, inside out or back to front. Reverse the way in which you think of the problem. For example, consider the following fable:

> Many years ago, a small businessman found himself with a large debt to a creditor. The creditor, rumoured to have been associated with organised crime, became adamant that repayment be made by a deadline that was impossible for the businessman to meet. Business was not good and the businessman could not even keep up the interest payments, let alone the loan principal. The creditor, however, had become attracted to the businessman's daughter and, in his conniving ways, decided he would rather have the girl than the small, failing business. The daughter, however, was repulsed by such a suggestion and resisted all his advances.
>
> The creditor was a gambling man and always enjoyed the thrill of a contest. He decided to propose a game to the businessman and his daughter that would decide her fate and that of the business. He indicated that he would put a white pebble and a black pebble into a bag and then have the young woman pick out a pebble. If she chose the black pebble, she would become his wife and the businessman's debt would be considered paid in full. If she chose the white pebble, she could stay with her father and the debt would be cancelled. If she refused to participate in the game, the entire balance would be made due by the end of the month.
>
> Reluctantly, the businessman agreed to the creditor's proposal. They met on the pebble-strewn path of a local park to conduct this game of chance. As they chatted, the creditor stooped down, picked up two pebbles and put them into a bag. The young woman, sharp-eyed with fright, noticed that the creditor had put two black pebbles in the bag. He held up the bag and asked the young woman to select the pebble that would decide her fate and that of her father's business.
>
> (Based upon De Bono, 1968)

Accepting that the story is a fable from a world before 'political correctness' had been invented, what would you advise the girl to do? A common approach is to maintain a constant definition of the problem and try to manipulate the circumstances. Most individuals suggest one of these alternatives:

1. The young woman should accuse the creditor of cheating. The negative consequence of this is that she risks antagonising the man and her father losing his business.

2. The young woman should try to change the rules of the contest. However, she should accept that the creditor is no fool and he is unlikely to make life more difficult for himself when he sees himself in a powerful position.

3. The young woman should try to cheat by picking up a white pebble from the ground. This is perfectly possible if the young woman is a practised conjuror but risky otherwise.

4. She should sacrifice herself and then try to get out of the marriage later.

All the suggestions maintain a single definition of the problem. Each assumes that the solution to the problem is associated with the pebble that the girl selects. If the problem is reversed, other answers normally not considered become evident. That is, the pebble remaining in the bag could also determine her fate:

> In the fable, the girl selects a pebble from the bag, but then quickly drops it to the ground on the pebble-strewn path. She exclaims, 'Oh, how clumsy of me. But never mind the one I chose will be obvious. All you have to do is look in the bag and see the colour of the one left.' By reversing the definition, she changed a situation with zero probability of success to a situation with 100 per cent probability of success.

This reversal is similar to what Rothenberg (1979) refers to as 'Janusian thinking'. Janus was the Roman god with two faces that looked in opposite directions. Janusian thinking means thinking contradictory thoughts at the same time – that is, conceiving two opposing ideas to be true concurrently. Rothenberg claimed, after studying 54 highly creative artists and scientists (e.g., Nobel Prize winners), that most major scientific breakthroughs and artistic masterpieces are products of Janusian thinking. Creative people who actively formulate antithetical ideas and then resolve them produce the most valuable contributions to the scientific and artistic worlds. Quantum leaps in knowledge often occur:

> An example is Einstein's account (1919, p. 1) of 'having the happiest thought of my life'. He developed the concept that, for an observer in free fall from the roof of a house, there exists during his fall, no gravitational field in his immediate vicinity. If the observer releases any objects, they will remain, relative to him, in a state of rest. 'The [falling] observer is therefore justified in considering his state as one of rest.' Einstein concluded, in other words, that two seemingly contradictory states could be present simultaneously: motion and rest. This realisation lead to the development of his revolutionary general theory of relativity.

> In another study, Rothenberg (1979) gave individuals a stimulus word and asked them to respond with the words that first came to mind. He found that highly creative students, Nobel scientists and prize-winning artists responded with antonyms significantly more often than did individuals with average creativity. Rothenberg argued, from these results, that creative people think in terms of opposites more often than do other people.

> For our purposes, the whole point is to reverse or contradict the currently accepted definition in order to expand the number of perspectives considered. For instance, a problem might be that morale is too high instead of (or in addition to) too low in our team, or that employees need less motivation instead of more motivation to increase productivity. Opposites and backward looks often enhance creativity.

> The techniques for improving creative problem definition are summarised below:

1. Make the strange familiar and the familiar strange.

2. Elaborate on the definition.

3. Reverse the definition.

Their purpose is not to help you generate alternative definitions just for the sake of alternatives, but to broaden your perspectives, to help you to overcome conceptual blocks and to produce more high-quality, relevant and 'simple' solutions.

Generate more alternatives

We began by pointing out that unskilled problem definition often contains an implied solution – how to stop Mary coming in late (March and Simon, 1958). This process reduces the scope of the problem solving unless we take time to redefine the initial problem. Guilford (1962) asserted that effective creative problem solvers were both fluent – able to produce a large number of ideas in a given length of time – and flexible – able to provide a diversity of ideas.

Brainstorming (Osborn, 1953) is perhaps the most widely used technique to promote both fluency and flexibility and operates under five rules:

1. Quantity and not quality.
2. Defer judgement.
3. Encourage wild ideas.

> The problem given to a team was to remove the bones from cooked chickens efficiently and quickly. The existing commercial equipment had been studied and an 'anatomical' report on chicken prepared. However, one jokey solution appeared – the chicken should be 'blown up' using an explosive charge placed in its body cavity: 'that would certainly take all the flesh off the bones'. The idea of blowing up the chicken, taken first as a joke, led to the use of rubber bags on stems inserted into the chickens and inflated so that the chickens could be held.

4. Build on ideas.

> In the chicken project, it was found that people who worked on taking the flesh off cooked chickens, found that they were slippery to handle. The rubber bag on a stem formed a sort of shoemaker's last that got over what proved to be the major problem. Logical processes allowed a creative and way-out solution to be implemented.

5. If a group is used – use as wide a range of experience as possible.

> A problem of handling frozen fish blocks at speed brought in 'experts' in guns ('How are bullets dispensed at speed?', paper ('How do photocopiers feed at speed?') and, quite accidentally, a player of arcade games. The solution that was adopted was similar to that used for a table ice hockey game where air reduced the friction of the puck.

Brainstorming techniques are best used in a group setting so individuals can stimulate ideas from each other. Maier (1967) showed that generating alternatives in a group setting produces more and better ideas than can be produced alone. The very quantity and rate of production of ideas – 100 ideas in a 30-minute session would be normal – means that people are unable to screen their own or other people's ideas to their own conceptual blocks.

In a brainstorming session one member of the group acts as a facilitator, recording the ideas – preferably numbered and on a flipchart. In no circumstances must the facilitator contribute to idea generation; his or her job is that of a scribe, a servant of the group who is allowed to clarify but not to modify.

A brainstorming session often works in spurts of creativity. In the first stage, fairly mundane ideas appear – often ideas that are already in the minds of the individuals in the group. There is often then a surge of ideas, building on the previous batch; the surge then stops but can be revived by the facilitator asking for votes on the 'worst idea' yet. By discussing what is positive on the bad idea a new surge of ideas often occurs.

The best way to get a feel for the power of brainstorming groups is to participate in one. Spend at least 20 minutes in a small group, brainstorming ideas.

> List as many uses as possible of a table-tennis ball. Give a token prize for the worst idea. As a variation you can table the worst idea and see if anyone can build on it so as to make it feasible and thus lose its status for the prize.

Examples of lists we have generated on training courses include: a bob for a fishing line, Christmas decoration, a toy for a cat, gear-lever knob, part of a molecular structure model, wind gauge when hung from a string, head of a puppet and a miniature football. Your list may well be much longer.

Sometimes brainstorming in a group is not possible or is too costly in terms of the number of people involved and the time required. Managers pursuing a hectic organisational life may feel that brainstorming is a waste of time and outside the organisational culture. This is a great pity, but even the process of individuals sitting together in relaxed circumstances jotting down ideas on a flipchart is better than nothing. Liam Hudson (1966) showed that even the most professed 'non-creatives' could produce quantities of ideas by being set the problem in rather manipulative terms. He asked his 'non-creatives' to pretend that they were brainstorming in the role of, say, the marketing manager who they regarded as a waste of time. His non-creatives produced some very sick ideas, but they were flexible and fecund.

Tony Buzan (1974) introduced the concept of 'mind mapping', a technique that has been developed considerably with the introduction of Total Quality Management systems. John Oakland (1994) cites a variation of brainstorming – the use of the cause and effect analysis. The technique was developed by Sumitomo Electric and is known as CEDAC – a cause and effect diagram with the addition of cards.

The concept of the cause and effect diagram is due to Ishikawa and provides a logical and acceptable way of structuring ideas from a brainstorming session devoted to solving a problem. Suppose we have a problem concerned with quality. The causes of the quality problem are grouped on the spines of a 'fishbone' classified as procedures, equipment and plant, materials, information and people. The effect side of the diagram is a quantified description of a problem with an agreed and quantified target. The cause side of the diagram uses two different coloured cards for writing FACTS and IDEAS. FACTS are placed on the left of the diagram and IDEAS on the right, each card being initialled by the individual owning it.

The cause and effect diagram systems have one considerable advantage over the brainstorming approaches from which they were built – they are seen to be practical and sensible. Many of the more esoteric systems, and in particular synectics, although very effective in practice, are difficult to justify in a hard-nosed environment.

Build on the current alternatives

One useful technique for building on the alternatives that comes from simple brain-storming is the technique of *subdivision*. This simply means dividing a problem into smaller parts. March and Simon (1958, p. 193) suggest that *subdivision* improves problem solving by increasing the speed with which alternatives can be generated and selected. They explain that:

> The mode of subdivision has an influence on the extent to which planning can proceed simultaneously on several aspects of the problem. The more detailed the factorisation of the problem, the more simultaneous activity is possible, the greater the speed of problem solving.

To see how subdivision helps to develop more alternatives and speeds the process of problem solving, go back to your list of ideas. Decide on the properties of the table tennis ball – weight, colour, texture, shape, porosity, strength, hardness chemical properties and conduction potential. This is one side of a matrix. The other side is a field of use – domestic, leisure, industrial, agricultural, transport, etc. Fit your existing ideas into the matrix and find new ideas for the empty squares:

- Shape/domestic – cut in half and used as a pastry cutter.
- Weight/agricultural – marking the surface of a liquid slurry tank.
- Chemical/property – a valve designed to fail when the gases overheat.
- Strength/transport – a collision damper.

The technique is also known as morphology and claims to have given rise to the Wankel engine. It is useful, when working for an industrial client, to use a matrix of the attributes and of the divisions of the organisation – industrial, domestic, medical, etc.

> Divide Figure 3.8 into exactly four pieces equal in size, shape and area. Try to do it in a minute or less. The problem is easy if you use subdivision. It is more difficult if you don't. One possible answer is given on page 625.

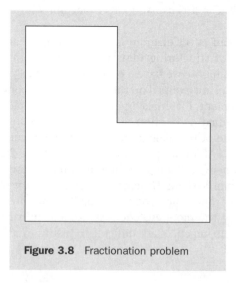

Figure 3.8 Fractionation problem

Combine unrelated attributes

A third technique focuses on helping problem solvers to expand alternatives by forcing the integration of seemingly unrelated elements. Dellas and Gaier (1970) have shown that an ability to see common relationships among disparate factors is a characteristic of creative people. A 'relational algorithm' was devised by Crovitz *et al.* (1970) to help us all share the process.

Suppose you are faced with the following problem: Customers are dissatisfied with our service. The two major elements in this problem are *customers* and *service*. They are connected by the phrase 'are dissatisfied with'. With the relational algorithm technique, the relational words in the problem statement are removed and replaced with other relational words to see if new ideas for alternative solutions can be identified. For example, consider the following connections where new relational words are used:

- Customers among service (e.g., customers interact with service personnel).
- Customers as service (e.g., customers deliver service to other customers).
- Customers and service (e.g., customers and service personnel work together).
- Customers for service (e.g., customer focus groups help improve our service).
- Service near customers (e.g., change the location of the service).
- Service before customers (e.g., prepare service before the customer arrives).
- Service through customers (e.g., use customers to provide additional service).
- Service when customers (e.g., provide timely service).

Looking at the strange connections and keeping an open mind, it is easy to become excited by the new ways of thinking they expose.

Hints for applying problem-solving techniques

Thamia and Woods (1984) found that a very large number of techniques were used during the three years of their study in one major organisation. The reasons for this were significant:

- A series of failures in innovation had been highlighted by a top management report: 'A major cause of failure had been the hardening of research effort on a limited range of solutions too early in projects.'

This had led to:

- The perceived need for creativity and the pressure for novel solutions came from the top management.
- Rational and creative problem solving were seen as activities in their own right with procedures for booking time spent in sessions employing the techniques.
- A core of two people was set up to provide 'hand-holding support' for groups and individuals requiring help in solving problems.

- Rarely was a 'pure' technique applied – only the key process of analysis, synthesis, collation and judgement was maintained and disciplines of brainstorming were imposed throughout.

We all have enormous creative potential, but the stresses and pressures of daily life, coupled with the inertia of conceptual habits, tend to submerge that potential. By following our hints, this potential can be unlocked.

1. Give yourself some relaxation time. The more intense your work, the more your need for complete breaks. Break out of your routine sometimes. This frees up your mind and gives room for new thoughts.

2. Find physical space where you can think. It should be a place where interruptions are eliminated, at least for a time. Reserve your best time for thinking and don't be made to feel guilty for not being 'active and doing something' – you are.

3. Talk to other people about ideas. Isolation produces far fewer ideas than does conversation. Make a list of people who stimulate you to think. Spend some time with them.

4. Ask other people for their ideas about your problems. Find out what others think about them. Don't be embarrassed to share your problems, but don't become dependent on others to solve them for you.

5. Read widely. Read at least one thing regularly that is outside your field of expertise. Keep track of new thoughts from your reading.

6. Protect yourself from idea-killers. Don't spend time with 'black hole people', people who absorb all of your energy and light but give nothing in return. Don't spend more time than you must on patent searches in your own area. Don't let yourself or others negatively evaluate your ideas too soon.

Figure 3.9 summarises the two problem-solving processes – rational and creative – and the factors you should consider when determining how to approach each type of problem.

- When you encounter a problem that is straightforward – that is, outcomes are predictable, sufficient information is available, and the way to achieve the end is clear – then the rational process is most appropriate.
- If the problem is not straightforward and, in particular, when rational processes have a history of failure – the creative problem-solving techniques are probably most appropriate.

Fostering innovation

The successful manager may or may not be creative but he or she must be able to unlock the creative potential of others. Fostering innovation and creativity among those with whom you work is at least as great a challenge as increasing your own creativity.

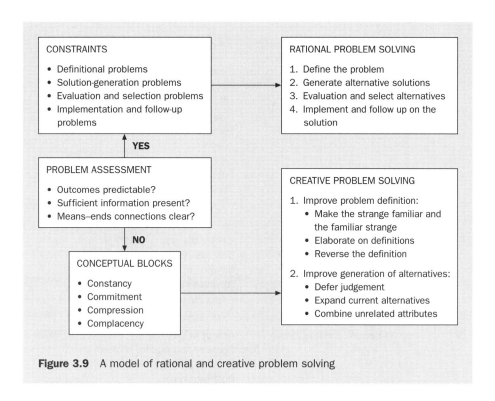

Figure 3.9   A model of rational and creative problem solving

Management principles for innovation

Neither Percy Spencer nor Spence Silver could have succeeded in their creative ideas had they not had managerial support, and an organisation that fostered innovation. The macro-organisational issues associated with innovation, e.g., organisation design, strategic orientation and human resource systems are covered well elsewhere (Galbraith, 1982; Kanter, 1983; McMillan, 1985; Tichy, 1983; Amabile, 1988). Here we will focus on the managerial level and what individual managers can do to foster **innovative thinking**. Table 3.5 presents the three management principles required.

Pull people apart – put people together

Percy Spencer's magnetron project was a consumer product hidden away from Raytheon's main-line business of missiles and other defence contract work. Spence Silver's new glue resulted when a polymer adhesive task force was separated from 3M's normal activities. Apple and IBM used task forces to develop products novel to them. Many new ideas come from individuals being given some time and resources and allowed to work apart from the normal activities of the organisation. 3M gives its staff 'skunk time' periods which are not formally accounted for and should be reserved for 'wild ideas' and 'personal projects' which just might work. Establishing nursery slopes, practice fields or sandlots is as good a way to develop

Table 3.5 Three principles for fostering innovative thinking

Principle	Examples
1. Pull people apart – put people together	Let individuals work alone as well as with teams and task forces Encourage minority reports and legitimise devil's advocate roles Encourage heterogeneous membership in teams Separate competing groups or subgroups Trust good people
2. Monitor and prod	Talk to customers Identify customer expectations both in advance and after the sale Hold people accountable Balance responsibility with authority Be interested Use a 'sharp' prod Never accept second best
3. Reward multiple roles	Accept and encourage the Idea Champion Sponsor and mentor Orchestrator and facilitator Rule breaker

new skills in business as it has proved to be in athletics. Because most businesses are designed to produce the 10,000th part correctly or to service the 10,000th customer efficiently, they do not function very well at producing a novel first part. That is why pulling people apart is often necessary to foster innovation and creativity:

> Data General divided their development effort for the new Eagle mini-computers into two competing groups on two separate sites. The 'high-status' site was beaten by the 'low-status' site.

However, in the real world of complexity, teams are almost always more productive than individuals. The lone inventor occurs but almost always in such an unplanned way as to make planning for it absurd. Teams do, however, need to be planned. Nemeth (1986) found that creativity increased markedly when minority influences were present in the team, for example, when devil's advocate roles were legitimised, a formal minority report was always included in final recommendations, and individuals assigned to work on a team had divergent backgrounds or views:

> Those exposed to minority views are stimulated to attend to more aspects of the situation, they think in more divergent ways and they are more likely to detect novel solutions or to come to new decisions. (Nemeth, 1986, p. 25)

Belbin, in his work with team role, showed that the presence of what he call a Plant in an otherwise dull group stimulated effective performance. Nemeth further found that positive benefits occur in groups even when the divergent or minority views are wrong. Similarly, Janis (1971) found that narrow-minded 'groupthink' was best overcome by establishing competing groups working on the same problem, participation in groups by outsiders, assigning a role of critical evaluator in the group, having groups made up of cross-functional participants, and so on. The most productive groups are those that are characterised by fluid roles, lots of interaction among members and flat power structures.

The point is that innovative thinking can be fostered when individuals are placed in teams and when they are at least temporarily separated from the normal pressures of organisational life. Those teams, however, are most effective at generating innovative ideas when they are characterised by attributes of minority influence, competition, heterogeneity and interaction. You can help foster innovation among people you manage, therefore, by letting people have their own space as well as putting people together in temporary teams.

Monitor and prod

Neither Percy Spencer nor Spence Silver were allowed to work on their projects with no accountability. Both men eventually had to report on the way they used their 'skunk time' and the freedom they were allowed was related to trust. They were, with some limits, allowed appropriate company materials and resources to work on them. We will discuss the concept of FRAME where individuals are given total freedom within absolute boundaries in our chapters on motivation and empowerment and delegation (Chapters 5 and 7).

Holding people accountable for outcomes, in fact, is an important motivator for improved performance. Data General made it clear to their two leaders for the Eagle project that their jobs were on the line.

> Two innovators in the entertainment industry captured this principle with these remarks: 'The ultimate inspiration is the deadline. That's when you have to do what needs to be done. The fact that twice a year the creative talent of this country is working until midnight to get something ready for a trade show is very good for the economy. Without this kind of pressure, things would turn to mashed potatoes.' (von Oech, 1986, p. 119)

In addition to accountability, innovative thinking is stimulated by what Gene Goodson at Johnson Controls called 'sharp-pointed prods':

> After taking over the automotive group at that company, Goodson found that he could stimulate creative problem solving by issuing certain mandates that demanded innovative thinking. One such mandate was: 'There will be no more forklift trucks allowed in any of our plants.' At first hearing, that mandate sounds absolutely outrageous. Think about it. You have a plant with tens of thousands of square feet of floor space. The loading docks are on one side of the building, and many tons of heavy metal raw materials are unloaded weekly and moved from the loading docks to workstations throughout the entire factory. The only way it

can be done is with forklifts. Eliminating forklift trucks would ruin the plant, right? Wrong. This sharp-pointed prod simply demanded that individuals working in the plant find ways to move the work stations closer to the raw materials, to move the unloading of the raw materials closer to the workstations or to change the size and amounts of material being unloaded. The innovations that resulted from eliminating forklifts saved the company millions of dollars in materials handling and wasted time, dramatically improved quality, productivity and efficiency, and made it possible for Johnson Controls to capture business from their Japanese competitors.

In our work as consultants we have found examples of managers who have heard of 'sharp-pointed prods' in some guise or other and applied them insensitively: *'Apply a prod and watch the eyes and keep watching the eyes. Always keep in mind why you are applying them and remember a prod that stays irritating can cause an infection.'*

One of the best methods for generating useful prods is to monitor customer preferences, expectations and judgements on a regular basis. Creative ideas often come directly or indirectly from customers. Everyone should be in regular contact with their own customers, internal and external, formally and informally, asking questions and monitoring performance.

We all have customers, whether we are students in college, members of a family, players on a rugby team, or whatever. Customers are simply those for whom we are trying to produce something or whom we serve. Students, for example, can count on their tutors, their fellow classmates and their potential employers as customers whom they serve. *A priori* and *post hoc* monitoring of their expectations and evaluations helps to foster new ideas and can be done by personal contact, follow-up calls, surveys, customer complaint cards and suggestion systems, whatever is appropriate.

Innovative thinking is best fostered by holding people accountable for having new ideas and by stimulating them with periodic prods:

> There is a story of a manager who delegated a subordinate to tackle a very difficult problem. The man wrote a report giving a solution. The manager rejected the report and said that the solution was not good enough. The man tried again, and again was rejected. Finally the man, close to resigning, handed in his third report. 'Good,' said his manager, 'I will read this report and we will take action on it.'

Reward multiple roles

The success of the sticky yellow notes at 3M is more than a story of the creativity of Spence Silver. In fact, without a number of people playing multiple roles, the glue would probably still be on a shelf somewhere. Instead, it provides a good illustration of the necessity of multiple roles in innovation and the importance of recognising and rewarding them. The four crucial roles in the innovative process are:

- The *champion* who owns and may have come up with the innovative problem solution.
- The *sponsor* or *mentor* who helps provide the resources, environment, and encouragement for the idea champion to work on the idea.

Several studies, notably Project SAPPHO developed by Andrew Robertson in his book *Lessons of Failure*, showed that the mentor had to be at the appropriate level in the organisation – not too lowly and not too senior. Lowly mentors did not have organisational 'clout' but too senior mentors were inclined to be too inaccessible for the informal contacts necessary to understand the gravity of problems and too involved in strategic success to accept failure.

- The *orchestrator* or *facilitator* who brings together cross-functional groups and necessary political support to facilitate implementation of the creative idea.

- The *rule breaker* who is able to go beyond organisational boundaries and barriers to ensure the success of the innovation.

Each of these roles is present in most important innovations in organisations, and they are illustrated by the Post-It Note case study below:

1. Spence Silver, by experimenting with chemical configurations that the academic literature indicated wouldn't work, invented a glue that wouldn't stick. He stuck with it, however, and spent years giving presentations to any audience at 3M that would listen, trying to pawn it off on some division that could find a practical application for it. The trouble was, no one else got stuck on it.

2. Henry Courtney and Roger Merrill developed a coating substance that allowed the glue to stick to one surface but not to others. This made it possible to produce a permanently temporary glue – that is, one that would peel off easily when pulled but would otherwise hang on for ever.

3. Art Fry found the problem that fitted Spence Silver's solution. He found application for the glue as a better 'bookmark' and as a note pad. The trouble was, no equipment existed at 3M to coat only a part of a piece of paper with the glue. Fry, therefore, carried 3M equipment and tools home to his own basement, where he designed and made his own machine to manufacture the forerunner of Post-It Notes. Because the working machine became too large to get out of his basement, he blasted a hole in the wall to get the equipment back to 3M. He then brought together engineers, designers, production managers and machinists to demonstrate the prototype machine and generate enthusiasm to make the product.

4. Geoffrey Nicholson and Joseph Ramsey began marketing the product inside 3M. They also submitted the product to the standard 3M market tests. The trouble was, the product failed miserably. No one wanted to pay $1.00 for a notepad. However, they broke 3M rules by personally visiting test market sites and giving away free samples. Only then did the consuming public become addicted to the product.

Spence Silver was both a rule breaker and an idea champion. Art Fry was also an idea champion, but more importantly he orchestrated the coming-together of the various groups needed to get the innovation off the ground. Henry Courtney and Roger Merrill helped to sponsor Silver's innovation by providing him with the coating substance that would allow his idea to work. Geoff Nicholson and

Joe Ramsey were both rule breakers and sponsors in their bid to get the product accepted by the public. In each case, not only did all these people play unique roles, but they did so with tremendous enthusiasm and zeal. They were both confident of their ideas and willing to put their time and resources on the line as advocates. They fostered support among a variety of constituencies both within their own areas of expertise as well as among outside groups. Most organisations are inclined to give in to those who are sure of themselves, persistent in their efforts and persuasiveness enough to make converts of others.

Not everyone can be an idea champion. But when managers also reward and recognise those who sponsor and orchestrate the ideas of others, innovative thinking increases in organisations. Teams form, supporters replace competitors and creativity thrives. Facilitating multiple role development is the job of the innovative manager. The converse is also true as the following example shows:

> A major multinational working from the UK was looking to diversify, and one idea that came forward was to use the Dolby sound system for a new generation of hearing aids. The idea, although exciting, had several 'issues' that needed to be settled before the project went forward.
>
> The senior manager in charge of the project asked one question: 'Who would like to run with the idea and to head a venture company to sell it?' Nobody wanted to stake their reputation on the idea so it was quietly killed in spite of the apparent general enthusiasm of the team.

SUMMARY

It is no accident that many of the techniques and studies described in this book date from the late 1970s and early 1980s. This was the period when the West began to stock-take and realise that it no longer had a monopoly of invention. The situation was highlighted in the UK by the Finneston Report (1980). Monty Finneston produced a well-argued case that not only had the UK declined as 'the workshop of the world', but that unless major effort was redirected into the engineering wealth-creation industries, the decline would accelerate. A key statistic was that whereas in the late 1970s UK, Sweden, France and the USA had between 1.3 per cent (France) and 1.7 per cent (UK) of the population as graduate engineers, Japan had 4.2 per cent (Germany was at 2.3 per cent.)

Engineering graduate numbers are obviously not the whole story, but the Finneston Report and the climate that commissioned it stirred activity in the West that has not faded. Innovation, and not just innovation in engineering, is the key to the survival of our economies. Innovation and problem solving, as treated in this book, are keystones to innovation.

We have shown that a well-developed model exists for solving problems. It consists of four separate and sequential stages: defining the problem; generating alternative solutions; evaluating and selecting a solution; implementing it and following it up. This model, however, is mainly useful for solving straightforward problems. Many problems faced by managers are not of this type and frequently they are called on to exercise creative problem-solving skills. That is, they must broaden their perspective of the problem and develop alternative solutions that are not immediately obvious.

We have also discussed and illustrated eight major conceptual blocks that inhibit most people's creative problem-solving abilities. Conceptual blocks are mental obstacles that artificially constrain problem definition and solution, and keep most people from being effective creative problem solvers. The four major conceptual blocks were summarised in Table 3.3 (page 180).

Overcoming these conceptual blocks is a matter of skill development and practice in thinking, not a matter of innate ability. Everyone can become a skilled creative problem solver with practice. Becoming aware of these thinking inhibitors helps individuals to overcome them. We also discussed three major principles for improving creative problem definition and three major principles for improving the creative generation of alternative solutions. Certain techniques were described that can help to implement these six principles.

We concluded by offering some hints about how to foster creativity and innovative thinking among other people. Becoming an effective problem solver yourself is important, but effective managers can also enhance this activity among their subordinates, peers and superiors.

Behavioural guidelines

1. Follow the four-step procedure outlined in Table 3.2 when solving straightforward problems. Keep the steps separate and do not take shortcuts.

2. When approaching a difficult problem, try to overcome your conceptual blocks by consciously doing the following mental activities:
   - Use lateral thinking in addition to vertical thinking.
   - Use several thought languages instead of just one.
   - Challenge stereotypes based on past experiences.
   - Identify underlying themes and commonalities in seemingly unrelated factors.
   - Ignore the superfluous and collect missing information when studying the problem.
   - Avoid artificially constraining problem boundaries.
   - Ignore reticence to be inquisitive.

3. When defining a problem, make the strange familiar and the familiar strange by using metaphor and analogy, first to focus and then to distort and refocus the definition.

4. Elaborate the problem definitions by developing at least two alternative and perhaps opposite definitions.

5. Reverse the problem definition by beginning with the end result and working backwards.

6. In generating potential solutions, defer judging any until the list is seen to be complete.

7. Use the four rules of brainstorming:
   - Do not evaluate.
   - Encourage wild ideas.
   - Encourage quantity.
   - Build on other people's ideas.

8. Expand the list of current alternative solutions by subdividing the problem along an attribute/usage matrix.

9. Increase the number of possible solutions by combining unrelated problem attributes.

10. Foster innovative thinking among those with whom you work by doing the following:

   • Find a 'safe place' to experiment and try out ideas.
   • Put people holding different perspectives in teams to work on problems.
   • Hold people accountable for innovation.
   • Use sharp-pointed prods to stimulate new thinking.
   • Recognise, reward, and encourage people in the roles of idea champion, sponsor, orchestrator and rule breaker.

Skill Analysis

CASE STUDY **3.1**

THE SONY WALKMAN

They had been disappointed at first, but it wasn't something that was going to keep them awake at nights. Mitsuro Ida and a group of electronics engineers in Sony Corporation's Tape Recorder Division in Tokyo had tried to redesign a small, portable tape recorder, called 'Pressman', so that it gave out stereophonic sounds. A year earlier, Ida and his group had been responsible for inventing the first Pressman, a wonderfully compact machine – ideal for use by journalists – which had sold very well.

But the sound in that tape machine was monaural. The next challenge for Sony's tape recorder engineers was to make a portable machine just as small, but with stereophonic sound. The very first stereo Pressman they made, in the last few months of 1978, didn't succeed. When Ida and his colleagues got the stereo circuits into the Pressman chassis (5.25 inches by 3.46 inches, and only 1.14 inches deep), they didn't have any space left to fit in the recording mechanism. They had made a stereophonic tape recorder that couldn't record anything. Ida regarded this as a good first try but a useless product. But he didn't throw it away. The stereo Pressman was a nice little machine. So the engineers found a few favourite music cassettes and played them while they worked.

After Ida and his fellow designers had turned their non-recording tape recorder into background music, they didn't entirely ignore it. They had frequent discussions about how to fit the stereo function and the recording mechanism into that overly small space. It was not an easy problem to solve, and because of that it was all the more fascinating and attractive to Ida and his group of inveterate problem solvers. Their focus on the problem of the stereo Pressman blinded them to the solution that was already in their hands, accepting that it was a solution to a different problem.

'And then one day,' said Takichi Tezuka, manager of product planning for the Tape Recorder Division, 'into our room came Mr Ibuka, our honorary chairman. He just popped into the room, saw us listening to this and thought it was very interesting.'

It is the province of honorary chairmen everywhere, because their status is almost invariably ceremonial, to potter about the plant looking in on this group and that group, nodding over the latest incomprehensible gadget. To this mundane task, Masaru Ibuka brought an undiminished intelligence and an active imagination. When he entered the Tape Recorder Division and saw Ida's incomplete tape recorder, he admired the quality of its stereophonic sound. He also remembered an entirely unrelated project going on elsewhere in the building, where an engineer named Yoshiyuki Kamon was working to develop lightweight portable headphones.

'What if you combined them?' asked Ibuka. 'At the very least,' he said, 'the headphones would use battery power much more efficiently than stereo speakers. Reduce power requirements and you can reduce battery consumption.' But another idea began to form in his mind. If you added the headphones, wouldn't you dramatically increase the quality of what the listener hears? Could you leave out the recorder entirely and make a successful product that just plays music? In the world of tape recorders, Ibuka's thought was heresy. He was mixing up functions. Headphones traditionally were supposed to extend the usefulness of tape recorders, not be essential to their success. This idea was so well established that if Ibuka had not made an association between a defective tape recorder design and the unfinished headphone design, Walkman may well have remained a little byway in musical history. Design groups within Sony tend to be very close-knit and remain focused on short-term task completion. Even when they weren't busy, there was no reason for tape recorder people ever to communicate with headphone people. They had nothing to do with each other. Tezuka, the man who later was described as the secretariat of the Walkman project, said, 'No one dreamed that a headphone would ever come in a package with a tape recorder. We're not very interested in what they do in the Headphone Division.'

But, even without this insularity, there was no guarantee that someone else at Sony would have made the connection that Ibuka made. To people today, the relationship between a cassette player and a set of headphones is self-evident. But to people at Sony, and at virtually every consumer electronics company, that connection was invisible in 1978.

Ibuka got a predictable response from the researchers in the electronics lab and from others in the Tape Recorder and Headphone divisions. They were painfully polite but non-committal. Ibuka might be right that the headphones would improve Pressman's efficiency, but nobody could guess how much of an improvement that would be. No one wanted to tell Ibuka that the idea of removing the speaker in favour of headphones was crazy. But it was! What if the owner of the device wanted to play back a tape so that more than one person could listen?

When Ibuka ventured further into illogic by suggesting a playback machine with no speaker and no recorder, he lost everybody. Who would want to buy such a thing? Who in Sony Corporation would support even ten minutes of development on such a hare-brained scheme?

In a way, they were right and Ibuka was wrong. This was an idea that violated most industries' well-established criteria for judging the natural increments of product development. It makes sense that a new product prototype should be better than the previous generation of product. Ida's non-recording prototype seemed worse. The idea had no support from the people who eventually would be responsible for funding its development, carrying out the research and trying to sell it to a consumer market. The idea should have been killed.

For Honorary Chairman Ibuka, the handwriting was on the wall. Even though he was a revered man at Sony, he had no authority to order such a project undertaken against the wishes of the division's leaders. It was clear that the only way to sell a bad idea to a group of cautious, reasonable businessmen was to find an ally. So, in his enthusiasm, he went straight to the office of his partner and friend, Akio Morita.

Source: Nayak and Ketteringham, (1986)

Discussion questions

1. What principles of rational problem solving and creative problem solving were used in this case?

2. How was innovative thinking fostered within Sony by top managers?

3. What roles were played by the various characters in the case that led to the success of the Walkman?

4. If you were a consultant to Sony, what would you advise to help foster this kind of innovation more frequently and more broadly throughout the company?

Skill Practice

EXERCISE **3.1**

APPLYING CONCEPTUAL BLOCKBUSTING

Creative problem solving is most applicable to problems that have no obvious solutions. Most problems people face can be solved relatively easily with a systematic analysis of alternatives. But other problems are ambiguous enough that obvious alternatives are not workable, and they require non-traditional approaches to find reasonable alternatives. This following assignment is one such problem. It is real, not fictitious, and it probably characterises your own college, university or public library. Apply the principles of creative problem solving in the book to suggest some realistic, cost-effective and creative solutions to this problem. Don't stop at the first solutions that come to mind, because there are no obvious right answers.

Assignment

Small groups should be formed to engage in the following problem-solving exercise. Each group should generate solutions to the case. The case is factual, not fictitious. Try to be as creative in your solutions as possible. The creativity of those solutions should be judged by an independent observer, and the best group's solution should be given recognition.

In defining and solving the problems, use the basic steps used in the Kepner and Tregoe system (*loc. cit.*), Table 3.2 and creative techniques to generate alternatives. Do not skip steps.

- Write down the problem.
- Consider the constraints and, in particular, determine who the client is. Make sure that all group members agree.
- Redefine the problem in not more than 200 words.
- Decide on the objectives that any potential solutions should satisfy.
- Propose some alternative solutions to the problem. Write these down and be prepared to report them to the larger group. All small groups should report their top three alternatives to the large group. The top three are the ones that most group members agree would produce the best solution to the problem.
- In your small group, generate at least five plausible alternative definitions of the problem. Use any of the techniques for expanding problem definition discussed in the text. Each problem statement should differ from the others in its definition, not just in its attributions or causes, of the problem.
- After the group has agreed on the wording of the five different statements, identify at least 10 new alternatives for solving the problems you identified. Your group should have identified some new alternatives, as well as more alternatives than you did initially.
- Report to the large group the three alternatives that your small group judges to be the most creative.

An observer should provide feedback on the extent to which each group member applied these principles effectively, using the Observer's Feedback Form found in the scoring key at the end of this book. Take one potential solution and decide what could go wrong, how this issue could be solved and whether you would need to review your recommendations.

The problem: The bleak future of knowledge

Libraries throughout the world are charged with the responsibility of preserving the accumulated wisdom of the past and gathering information in the present. They serve as sources of information and resources, alternate schools, and places of exploration and discovery. No one would question the value of libraries to societies and cultures throughout the world. The materials housed there are the very foundation of civilisation. But consider the following problems.

Hundreds of thousands of books are in such advanced states of decay that when they are touched they fall to powder. Whereas parchments seem to survive better when they are handled, and books printed before 1830 on rag paper stay flexible and tough, books printed since the mid-nineteenth century on wood-pulp paper are being steadily eaten away by natural acids. The new British Library has a backlog of 1.6 million urgent cases requiring treatment. At the newly constructed (but not yet opened) Bibliotheque Nationale in France, more than 600,000 books require treatment immediately. At the Library of Congress in the States, about 77,000 books out of the stock of 13 million enter the endangered category every year. Fairly soon, about 40 per cent of the books in the biggest research collections in America will be too fragile to handle. An example of the scale of the problem comes from the Library of Congress which estimates that it will take 25 years to work through the backlog of cases, even if the cost of $200 a volume can be met. The obvious solution of converting to CD ROM or microfiche is not only more costly but subject to its own form of 'decay' – no 'permanent' form is yet available.

Budgets are tight throughout the world and it is doubtful that book preservation will receive high funding priority in the near future.

Source: *The Economist*, 23 December 1989

Skill Application

ACTIVITY **3.1**

SUGGESTED FURTHER ASSIGNMENTS

1. Teach someone else to solve problems creatively and record your experiences in your diary.

2. Think of a problem that is important to you now and has no obvious solution. Use the principles and techniques discussed in the book and work out a satisfactory creative solution. Take your time and do not expect immediate results. Record any results in your diary.

3. Help to direct a group (your family, classmates, sports team) in a creative problem-solving exercise using the relevant techniques of the book. Issues could include arranging a social, raising funds, increasing membership or fixing a programme of activities. Record how it went in your diary.

4. Write a letter to a person in authority – MP, Managing Director, Senior Police Officer – about some difficult problem in his or her authority. Make the issue something about which you have both knowledge and concern and include within your letter possible solutions. Record how you arrived at these possible solutions as well as the solutions themselves.

ACTIVITY **3.2**

APPLICATION PLAN AND EVALUATION

This exercise is designed to help you apply your skill in a real life setting. There are two parts in the activity: Part 1 will help the preparation, and Part 2 will help you to evaluate and improve on the experience. Do not miss out the steps and be sure to complete each item.

Part 1: Plan

1. Write down the two or three aspects of a skill that is most important to you. This may be an area of weakness, an area you most want to improve or an area that is most salient to a problem that you face now. Identify the specific aspects of this skill that you want to apply.

2. Now identify the setting or the situation in which you wish to apply this skill. Establish a plan for the performance by actually writing down the situation. Who else is involved? When will you do it? Where will it be done?

3. Identify the specific behaviours you will engage to apply the skill. Put these behaviours into detailed actions.

4. How will you judge success?

Part 2: Evaluation

5. After you have completed your implementation, record the results. What happened? How successful were you? What was the effect on others?

6. How can you improve? What modifications would you make for next time?

7. Looking back on your experience, what have you learnt? What has been surprising? In what ways might the experience help you in the long term?

Further reading

Johnson, G. (1997) *Monkey business: why the way you manage is a million years out of date*. Aldershot: Gower.

Malone, S.A. (1997) *Mind skills for managers*. Aldershot: Gower.

Murdock, A. and Scutt, C.N. (1997) *Personal effectiveness*, 2nd edn. Oxford: Butterworth-Heinemann.

Pearce, S. and Cameron, S. (1997) *Against the grain: developing your own management ideas*. Oxford: Butterworth-Heinemann.

Interpersonal Skills

The second part of the book deals with interpersonal skills – how we work with other people. Chapter 4 takes the general issues of constructive communication while Chapters 5 and 6 discuss the skills required to motivate others and managing the inevitable conflicts that arise.

CHAPTER 4
Constructive Communication

- Communication for short- and long-term gain
- Avoiding dysfunctional communication
- The commandments of effective communication.

CHAPTER 5
Effective Motivation

- Looking at work performance
- Enhancing performance
- Improving the working environment.

CHAPTER 6
Constructive Conflict Management

- Constructive and dysfunctional conflict
- The sources of conflict
- Conflict management strategies
- The role of the mediator.

CHAPTER 4

Constructive Communication

SKILL DEVELOPMENT OUTLINE

Skill Pre-assessment surveys

- Communicating constructively
- Communication styles

Skill Learning material

- The importance of effective communication
- Focus on accuracy
- Constructive communication
- Coaching, counselling and consulting
- Setting objectives
- Defensive and patronising behaviours
- Summary
- Behavioural guidelines

Skills Analysis cases

- Find someone else
- Rejected plans

Skill Practice exercises

- Vulcan Computers
- Brown vs Thomas

Skill Application activities

- Suggested further assignments
- Application plan and evaluation

LEARNING OBJECTIVES

- To introduce the concept of choice in personal communication between immediate gain and long-term advantage.
- To develop techniques what we will call 'constructive communication' – communication between individuals where relationships are fostered and developed.

- An understanding of the processes that lead us to dysfunctional responses – aggressiveness and defensiveness.
- To understand where counselling and coaching are required.
- Develop the various roles in any conflict situation including that of the mediator.

INTRODUCTION

Not all communication is constructive or needs to be. Constructive communication is a two-way process – the speaker is also the listener and the listener can become the speaker. There is also a hidden agenda bringing in medium-term as well as immediate goals – it is preparing for the next communication, and the next. Non-constructive, directive communication has its place. There are times when the job to be done is so confining that there is no time, need or latitude for the communicator to accept feedback, worry about feelings or tomorrow. If a child is about to put its hand in a fire or a walker is about to fall down a hole, that is such a time. The crew of a sinking ship are unlikely to want the opportunity for discussion when the captain is ordering the lifeboats to be manned. However, directive communication can be totally ineffective.

> A long time ago Mike Woods, one of our authors, was in his pram, his mother was notified that the postman had been unable to deliver any post to their house 'due to their dangerous dog'. She duly attended an interview with a very pompous head postmaster who talked down to her explaining that the refusal by the postman to deliver mail, and run the risk of being bitten by the Woods' household pet, was entirely in the Woods' interest.
>
> 'If the postman is bitten, you may well have to pay significant damages.'
>
> He drooled on, not allowing Mrs Woods any comment. Finally, Mrs Woods had her chance. 'I agree with everything that you say, but there is just one thing that worries me. We don't have a dog.'

The story illustrates the breaking of virtually all of the 10 commandments of effective communication that we will develop in this chapter.

The spoken and sometimes written word is obviously one of the tools we use in communication, but we have seen previously that words in themselves conjure up images well beyond their literal meaning. Beyond words there lies a complexity of non-verbal signals and clues. Who we are or are perceived to be, how we dress, how we gesture in a myriad of complexities that, unless we understand them, stand between us and clear unequivocal communication.

(It may be useful, if the subject of human communication is new to you, to watch your favourite soap opera on TV. For the first half watch it as you would normally and for the second half, turn the sound off and watch only the gestures. The question is, how much did you miss when you could not hear the words? The answer may surprise you. Good television and good radio – and indeed quality face-to-face communication and e-mail or audio-only telephone 'conversations' – are different media.)

Skill Pre-assessment

SURVEY **4.1**

COMMUNICATING CONSTRUCTIVELY

Step 1 Before you read the material in this book, please respond to the following statements by writing a number from the rating scale below in the left-hand column (Pre-assessment). Your answers should reflect your attitudes and behaviour as they are now, not as you would like them to be. Be honest. The instrument is designed to help discover your level of competency in communicating constructively, so you can tailor your learning to your specific needs. The scoring key, which will help you to identify the areas of the book most important to you, is in Appendix 1.

Step 2 After you have completed the reading and the exercises in this book, and as many of the Skill Application assignments as possible, cover up your first set of answers. Then respond to the same statements again, this time in the right-hand column (Post-assessment). When you have completed the survey, check out your scores using the scoring key in Appendix 1. If your score remains low in specific skill areas, use the behavioural guidelines at the end of the Skill Learning section (page 260) to guide further practice.

RATING SCALE

1 = Strongly disagree   **2** = Disagree   **3** = Slightly disagree
4 = Slightly agree   **5** = Agree   **6** = Strongly agree

	Assessment	
	Pre-	Post-
There are times when all of us feel that others are not doing the things that we feel are correct in these situations, and when we feel it is necessary to do something:		
1. I understand clearly when it is appropriate to offer advice and direction to others and when it is not.	___	___
2. I help others recognise and define their own problems when I counsel them.	___	___
3. I am completely honest in the feedback that I give to others, even when it is negative.	___	___
4. I always give feedback that is focused on the problem and its solution, not on the characteristics of the person.	___	___
5. I always explain the reason for my giving negative feedback with an explanation of what I perceive as having been done wrongly.	___	___
6. When I correct someone's behaviour, our relationship is almost always strengthened.	___	___

7. I am descriptive in giving negative feedback to others. That is, I objectively describe the event, its consequences and my feelings about it. ____ ____

8. I always suggest some specific alternatives to those whose behaviour I am trying to correct. ____ ____

9. I make sure to reinforce other people's sense of self-worth and self-esteem in my communication with them. ____ ____

10. I convey genuine interest in the other person's point of view, even when I disagree with it. ____ ____

11. I don't talk down to those who have less power or less information than I do. ____ ____

12. I convey a sense of flexibility and openness to new information when presenting my point of view, even when I feel strongly about it. ____ ____

13. I strive to identify some area of agreement in a discussion with someone who has a different point of view. ____ ____

14. My feedback is always specific and to the point, rather than general or vague. ____ ____

15. I don't dominate conversations with others. ____ ____

16. I take responsibility for my statements and point of view by using, for example, 'I have decided' instead of acting as an agent and saying 'they have decided'. ____ ____

17. When discussing someone's concerns, I use responses that indicate understanding rather than advice. ____ ____

18. When asking questions of others in order to better understand their viewpoint, I generally ask WHAT questions instead of WHY questions. ____ ____

19. I hold regular, private, one-to-one meetings with people I work with and/or live with. ____ ____

20. I am clear about when I should coach someone and when I should provide counselling instead. ____ ____

SURVEY **4.2**

COMMUNICATION STYLES

In this questionnaire some managerial experience is assumed. If you do not have such experience, use your imagination.

The questionnaire is divided into two parts. In Part 1, four people complain about problems they face in their jobs. Following each complaint are five possible responses. Rank three of the responses you would be most likely to make in reverse order, with 3 being your first choice, 2 being your second choice and 1 being your third choice. Part 2 describes a particular situation. Several pairs of statements follow. Place a tick next to the one statement in each pair that you would be most likely to use in responding to the given situation. The scoring key for this questionnaire can be found in Appendix 1.

Part 1

1. *I've been in this job for six months and I hardly know anyone at all in the company. I just can't seem to make friends or be accepted by other people. Most people are extremely busy and don't take time to socialise. I feel isolated and excluded from what's going on.*

   a. Don't be concerned about not making friends so soon. Things will get better the longer you're with the company. _____

   b. When you first meet people, what do you say? Are you the one to be friendly first? _____

   c. Because company employees are so busy, probably no one has time to get close socially. You shouldn't expect too much. _____

   d. So you're feeling that people haven't accepted you in the company? _____

   e. It's not as serious as you may feel. When I first joined the company it took me more than six months to get settled in, I still don't know everyone. _____

2. *I can't stand my boss. He is the most autocratic, demanding person you can imagine. I've never worked around anyone who cared less for his employees than he does. His complete insensitivity and lack of humanity have made this place miserable.*

   a. You sound as if you're having difficulty dealing with rigid control and authority. _____

   b. I know how you feel because last year we had a woman in our department who would drive anybody round the bend. She was the ultimate domineering boss. _____

   c. You're going to have problems unless you work this out. I think you should go to him and tell him how you feel. _____

   d. You really are having a hard time adjusting to your boss, aren't you? _____

   e. Why is it you feel so strongly about him? _____

3. *What I want to know is, how was I passed over for Mac's job? I felt I was perfect for the job – I have the experience and the seniority – now you bring in someone from outside. Where do I go from here?*

   a. What was it that made you think the supervisor's job was yours, George? Are you aware of what it needed and what kind of person we were looking for? _____

   b. Don't be discouraged, George. Your work is good, and if you're patient I'm sure other chances will come along. I'll try to help you be ready next time. _____

   c. I think you have the wrong impression about this, George. The criteria were very clear for the job and we simply needed a fresh mind. _____

   d. In other words, George, you're puzzled about where you stand with the company. _____

   e. Are you interpreting this set-back as a challenge to your technical competence? _____

4. *Excuse me Paul, what's the idea of not approving my request for an update for our PC systems? We really need it. The ones we are using are not downward compatible with the systems in accounts and we have to do some jobs with paper and pencil. We are very busy as you know and this puts us back. Please don't come up with the tight resources argument – you know new equipment has been in the budget for at least two years.*

   a. You sound really upset about not getting your request approved, Susan. _____

   b. Why do you need a new system – surely when problem issues occur you can borrow a compatible machine? _____

c. You know Susan, several other departments have the same problem. A new system for you would get them all on my back and we don't have the time or money for training, let alone new systems. ____

d. I know you're upset, Susan. Believe me you have to be patient and leave it to me. I have changes in the pipeline. ____

e. I'm sorry, Susan, but it's true that resources are really tight. That's why we turned you down, so you're just going to have to make do. ____

Part 2

You are the manager of Carole Thompson, a 58-year-old supervisor with 21 years' service with the company. Carole retires in two years' time but her performance is sliding, she will not take on any extra work and the work she does do is often found to be lacking. Her attitude towards customers is often brusque and she shows a lack of sensitivity to her shop-floor staff. Her attitude to customers is particularly worrying since the company survives in this harsh world though its reputation for customer service.

Carole has done nothing that would merit a disciplinary interview, but you feel that unless her performance improves, it may lead to one. You are having your monthly one-on-one meeting with her in your office. Which of the statements in each pair is nearest to what you would say?

1. a. I've received complaints from some of your customers that you are not being sufficiently sympathetic to complaints and requests. ____
   b. You don't seem to be motivated to do a good job anymore, Carole. ____

2. a. I know that you've always done a good job, but there's just one small thing I want to raise with you about a customer complaint – probably not too serious. ____
   b. I have some concerns about several aspects of your performance on the job and I'd like to discuss them with you. ____

3. a. I've had one of your people seeing me about you criticising him in public and I am worried. I would like you to go to him direct and sort things out – then let me know what you have agreed. ____
   b. You know, of course, that you're wrong to have criticised your subordinate's work in public. That's a sure way to create antagonism and lower morale. ____

4. a. I would like to see the following changes in your performance: (1) . . . , (2) . . . and (3) . . . ____
   b. I have some ideas for helping you to improve; but first, what do you suggest? ____

5. a. I must tell you that I'm disappointed in your performance. ____
   b. Several of our employees seem to be unhappy with how you've been performing lately. ____

Skill Learning

The importance of effective communication

Effective communication is a key competence of management and its demonstration may range from giving effective orders to delivering formal speeches at dinners. The dominant skill required in all these activities is effective face-to-face, one-to-one communication. In a study of 88 organisations, both from the public and private sectors, Crocker (1978) found that, of 31 skills assessed, interpersonal constructive communication skills were rated as the most important. Thorton (1966) summarised a variety of survey results by stating, 'A manager's number-one problem can be summed up in one word: communication.' This is hardly surprising since some 80 per cent of all managers' time is spent on verbal communication.

In a study of major manufacturing organisations undergoing large-scale changes, Cameron (1988) asked two key questions:

1. What is your major problem in trying to get organisational changes implemented?

2. What is the key factor that explains your past success in effectively managing organisational change?

To both questions a large majority of managers gave the same answer – communication. Unfortunately most of us see ourselves as good communicators and that the problems are caused by other people. Haney (1979) reported on a survey of more than 8,000 people in universities, businesses, military units, government and hospitals, in which virtually everyone felt that he or she was communicating at least as well as, and in many cases better than, almost everyone else in the organisation. Most people readily admit that their organisation is fraught with faulty communication, but it is almost always other people who are responsible. Thus we are not ready to accept the necessity let alone the responsibility of improving our own skill level.

Focus on accuracy

Much of the writing on interpersonal communication focuses on the accuracy of the information being communicated, and emphasises that the communication skill which needs the greatest improvement is the ability to transmit clear, precise messages. Inaccurate communication can have humorous as well as serious results.

> A motorist in a veteran car was stopped by the police for a roadside check. Everything seemed fine. The officers decided to test the brakes.
>
> 'Right, we would like you to drive at about 30 mph in front of our police car and when you hear the sound of our horn, make an emergency stop. Give the brakes everything they have got – OK?'
>
> The driver did all that was asked of him but unfortunately at 30 mph the traffic began to pile up and one impatient driver of a sports car who was forced to overtake vented his anger by shaking his fist and sounding his horn. The old car, the brakes of which were in fact very good, stopped immediately and the police car banged straight into him.
>
> *Source*: A student legend of the 1950s used by
> Richard Gordon in his book, *Doctor in the House*.

A woman of 35 came in one day to tell me that she wanted a baby but had been told that she had a certain type of heart disease that, while it might not interfere with a normal life, would be dangerous if she ever had a baby. From her description, I thought at once of mitral stenosis. This condition is characterised by a rather distinctive rumbling murmur near the apex of the heart and especially by a peculiar vibration felt by the examining finger on the patient's chest. The vibration is known as the 'thrill' of mitral stenosis. When this woman had undressed and was lying on my table in her dressing gown, my stethoscope quickly found the heart sounds I had expected.

Dictating to my nurse, I described them carefully. I put my stethoscope aside and felt intently for the typical vibration which may be found in a small and variable area of the left chest. I closed my eyes for better concentration and felt long and carefully for the tremor. I did not find it, and with my hand still on the woman's bare breast, lifting it upward and out of the way, I finally turned to the nurse and said: 'No thrill.' The patient's eyes flashed, and with venom in her voice she said, 'Well, what a shame – may be just as well you didn't. That isn't what I came for.' My nurse almost choked, and my explanation still seems a nightmare of futile words. (Loomis, 1939)

Pizza Hut, in their point of sale advertisements. Include the words: 'Order by phone – if not collected in 20 minutes – £1 off.' Perhaps they meant: 'Order by phone – if not ready for collecting in 20 minutes we will charge you £1 less than our quoted prices.'

Attempts to improve the communications of an organisation often centre on improving the *mechanics*: networked phones, fax systems, e-mail, answering machines and desk publishing. Sophisticated information-based technology has made major strides in enhancing both the speed and accuracy of communication. There is a snag, however, about any mechanical information processing, and a statement Josiah Stamp made over 80 years ago illustrates this point:

The government is very keen on amassing statistics. They collect them, add them, raise them to the nth power, take the cube root and prepare wonderful diagrams. But you must never forget that every one of these figures comes in the first instance from the village watchman, who just puts down what he pleases.

Stamp might well have said 'garbage in garbage out'.

However, irrespective of the availability of sophisticated information technologies and systems, individuals still communicate much as they always did. They can be ineffectively abrasive, insensitive and plain misguided.

In my own office we used to abide by the rule of NEVER posting a rude letter to anyone the day of writing. Read it the next morning and then post it or bin it. E-mail has changed all that – e-mail allows instant misunderstanding that may take years to correct.

Group communications – team briefings, company newsletters, etc. – have also received much attention, but interpersonal aspects of communication have been largely ignored. People still become offended at one another, make insulting statements and communicate clumsily. The interpersonal aspects of communication involve the nature of the relationship between the communicators. The effect of who says what to whom, what is said, why it is said, and how it is said on the relationship between people has important implications for the effectiveness of the

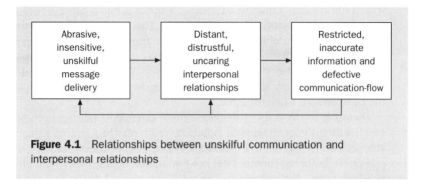

Figure 4.1   Relationships between unskilful communication and interpersonal relationships

communication, aside from the accuracy of the statement. The interaction between the message, the messenger and a backlog of suppositions and preconceptions about the messenger and his or her role – collectively called the *shadow* – is discussed by Woods and Whitehead (1993). Ineffective communication may lead individuals to dislike each other, be offended by each other, lose confidence in each other, refuse to listen to each other and disagree with each other. These interpersonal problems, in turn, generally lead to restricted communication flow, inaccurate messages and misinterpretations of meanings. Figure 4.1 summarises this process.

To illustrate, consider the following situation.

> Alan is in a team conceived to overcome a quality problem in the final assembly of video players. After Alan's carefully prepared presentation to the management meeting, John raises his hand. 'In my opinion, this is a naive approach to solving our quality problems. It's not as easy as Alan seems to realise. I don't think we should waste our time by pursuing his plan any further.'

John's opinion may be justified, but the manner in which he delivers the message will probably eliminate any hope of its being dealt with objectively. Instead, Alan will probably hear 'You're naïve' as 'You're stupid and incompetent'. Expectedly, Alan's response would be either defensive or hostile. Future communications between Alan and John would probably have been jeopardised and future communication between the two will probably be minimal. Issues of the quality improvement suggested will be marginalised.

Constructive communication

Communication is always about achieving a purpose. It is a process towards a task. At its simplest, we want a job done, so the communication needs to include WHY?, WHAT?, HOW? and IF?.

> Imagine we are visitors in a factory and we notice that a drum of material labelled as 'flammable' is leaking in front of the hut that we are to occupy to complete our report. We regard the situation as urgent and speak to a forklift truck driver who is passing.

WHY?   That drum is leaking and could cause a hazard.
WHAT? It is only the one drum – it should be moved to within a bund.
HOW?   Could you move it for me with your truck?
IF?   I will notify security of what is happening and your manager. OK?

Not much thought in our example of developing a sustained relationship with the forklift operator – just getting a dangerous situation resolved.

Constructive communication is about thinking about the individual and the future *as well as the task*. With constructive communication not only is a message delivered accurately, but the relationship between the two communicating parties is supported, even enhanced, by the interchange. The goal of constructive communication is not merely to be liked by other people or to be judged to be a nice person. It is not merely to produce social acceptance but has positive value in organisations. Researchers have found, for example, that organisations that encourage constructive communications enjoy higher productivity, faster problem solving, improved quality and reduced unproductive conflict, compared with groups and organisations where the communications style is less positive. Moreover, delivering world-class customer service is almost impossible without using constructive communication. Effective customer service requires constructive communication skills. Therefore, not only must managers be competent in using this kind of communication, but they must also help their subordinates to develop this competence.

Good employee relations are an essential for any effective organisation (Ouchi, 1981; Peters, 1987). Working with 40 major organisations in America, Hanson (1986) found that, over a five-year period, employee relations was by far the most significant factor in their success – more important than the four next most powerful variables (market share, capital availability, firm size and sales growth rate) combined. Techniques that foster good employee relations are not simply a 'feel good factor' that can be abandoned under pressure – they make sound business sense. There is, however, a strong proviso – some organisational cultures do not accept the concepts of constructive communication.

> A very simple test is recommended. Imagine your boss has asked you to prepare a detailed report on a particular part of your department's work to the Board. One of your subordinates has the skills, knowledge and aptitude for writing the report and you do not. He or she writes the report, which, on your restricted expertise, seems excellent. In your opinion would the organisation expect you to:
>
> (1) take the report and present it to the Board?
> (2) take your subordinate with you to the Board and endorse his or her presentation?
> (3) sit back while the report is presented?
> (4) allow the subordinate to present the report, your own presence being irrelevant?

If you feel that (1) or (2) would be 'the way things are done' in your organisation, you may find the whole idea of constructive communication a dangerous concept to pursue. The culture of such organisations is echoed by the phrase:

They are paid to do the job – what else do they want?

Coaching, counselling and consulting

Ross (1986) sees coaching, counselling and consulting as essential managerial activities and Hersey and Blanchard (1986) can be interpreted as seeing management of subordinates towards empowerment and delegation, as a sequence of steps using the activities in turn.

Step 1   We have individuals or groups who do not know what is required of them. The manager needs to be clear in explaining *why* the job needs to be done and *what* needs to be done – he or she is the only person who can impart this information and needs to TELL it to the others by setting clear objectives. The telling may be dressed up as selling but telling it remains – the manager is in authority.

The manager has high task concern and low individual concern. We need then to move progressively to Step 2.

Step 2   The task is clear but the means of doing it need to be clarified – the problem being that every one needs to be able to do the jobs allocated to them. This means *coaching* and the manager remains with a high task concern but now has a high concern for individuals. The penalty for the manager if he or she does not make sure that individuals can actually do, and feel confident in, their allocated jobs can be very severe.

> A chicken-processing plant in the north of England decided to move to the first phase of automation. The new equipment, as subsequent interviews showed, frightened a key supervisor, who saw as his skill as that of controlling 200 women working in quite stressed conditions. The managers, to whom the change was very elementary, dismissed the man's fear and gave him no training or coaching to face his new environment – 'he will soon get a hand on it or he can go'. The strike he organised subsequently closed the factory.

Step 3   When people know why they are doing the task, what their role is, and are competent and confident in it – the constructive manager allows them to detail how they do it. If this step is not reached the manager must continually *consult* his or her staff on 'the detail' and give *counselling* where the new roles do not 'fit' individuals in spite of the coaching. Without such consultation the task will drift. We will return to this point later when we discuss motivation, delegation and empowerment.

At this step the manager in consulting is less concerned with the task and remains with a high concern for individuals.

Step 4   As people take over the task, they begin to know more about how they will do it than the manager who, basically needs to trust them – the process of true *delegation* is happening. He or she must extend the role to outside communications and monitor the work that is done to ensure that it meets the standards and constraints that are laid down. The managerial job is now low in involvement with the task but needs maintain relationships.

The ineffective manager

The ineffective manager moves from TELLING to DELEGATING without passing through the two high relationship stages without using the principle skills of constructive feedback – coaching, counselling and consulting.

- The clarity of the progression is not always obvious in the real world. Coaching and counselling may be needed at any time in management – if only because employees lose motivation or the skills base towards the task changes. Thus, tasks do not *stay* delegated and the effective manager needs to able to act appropriately all the time.
- The progression from TELLING to DELEGATING is not inevitable. The manager may simply not have the time to coach, counsel and consult, the task may be unclear or the organisation may not ALLOW the manager to delegate.

Coaching, counselling and consulting are essential for the maintenance of relationships and are especially important for:

1. Facilitation – equipping the person for the job and finding training needs.
2. Dealing with inappropriate behaviour or attitudes.
3. Developing working procedures for the mutual benefit of the individual and all others concerned.
4. Appraising and rewarding good performance.
5. Correcting poor performance.
6. Developing standards and targets.

This chapter will discuss the first three roles and the final three will be covered in the chapter on motivation.

Setting objectives

The first question we always need to answer is: What are our objectives in each case?

If you do not know where you are going, you will certainly end up somewhere else.

As a manager, faulty human communication can have serious consequences.

Mary managed a floor of telephone salespeople in a major financial institution. One of her subordinates, Harry, was noted for leaving early and putting work onto other people. On the afternoon in question she was talking with her floor supervisor when she noticed that Harry was putting on his coat and leaving. Confirming on her watch that Harry should still be at his station she called out across the floor:

'Where are you going?'

'Out!'

Mary ran after Harry and narrowly missed hitting the door as Harry slammed it behind him. Mary's loss of face was never retrieved and she had to move jobs.

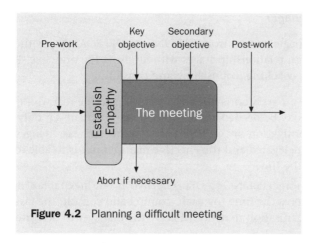

Figure 4.2 Planning a difficult meeting

The actual contact time for a potentially difficult meeting is a dangerous time and one for which a skilled manager plans. Figure 4.2 summarises the planning process.

Imagine that Mary had managed the encounter effectively. Firstly, the open office situation was NOT the time or the place for a difficult meeting. At the most, in hindsight she should have expressed non-verbal disapproval and left Harry's grand gesture unchallenged. Again, with hindsight, calling the supervisor over to her office, collecting 'records' and instructing that Harry should report directly to her in the morning would have been good. This was her pre-work.

Mary would see her key objective as establishing her authority over Harry. If Harry remained truculent, she would simply stop the meeting and take further action – action that Harry would not like. If Harry accepted her authority, Mary could go on to detail the office rules and close by setting up procedures to make sure that Harry observed them. There is one factor from our diagram that we have not mentioned: 'establish empathy'. We will discuss this later in our 10 Commandments of supporting communications. Summarising: in any potentially difficult meeting we need to plan and establish:

Pre-work   What do you need to do BEFORE the meeting?
Key objective   What do you HAVE to achieve at the meeting?
Second objective What would you LIKE to get from the meeting?
Post-work   What needs to be done AFTER the meeting?

As managers we need to defuse problem situations and at the same time develop relationships with our subordinates that will hold us in good stead for the next time.

Read the following case studies and consider your key objectives, visualising how you would achieve them:

Tim Nelson – Regional Sales

Your firm makes and sells components for the aerospace industry and Tim Nelson is a newly appointed regional sales manager, promoted from 'the ranks'. Tim reports directly to you and his sales results are consistently below those met by other regions. In addition to his poor performance, his monthly reports are almost always late. In honesty, you have allowed the situation to drift and have not devoted sufficient time to Tim's induction to his new and challenging job.

You make an appointment to meet him in his office to discuss the latest sales figures but he is out of his office. His assistant tells you that one of Tim's team leaders has complained of general slackness in the group – lateness and extended coffee breaks. At this moment Tim is giving the group a piece of his mind and reminding them of what is required of them in sales results. You wait for 15 minutes until he returns.

Betty Mason – MBA

Betty Mason came highly recommended when she joined your financial planning group some months ago. However, she seems to be trying to enhance her own reputation at the expense of others. You have heard increasing complaints lately that Betty is arrogant, self-promotional and openly critical of other group members' work. In your first conversation with her about her performance she denied that there was a problem. She said that, if anything, she was having a positive impact on the group by raising its standards. You arrange another meeting with Betty after the latest set of complaints from her colleagues.

Coaching and counselling issues

A wise manager thinks initially about coaching – checking whether people can *do* the tasks assigned, before he or she moves to counselling. Counselling – checking on the complexities surrounding motivation, attitudes and other 'soft' issues – is always more uncertain in its outcomes.

Returning to our case studies, Tim's manager has the overall objective of improving the unit's output. Tim, as far as his manager can see, is keen, highly motivated and personable. These are the reasons why he was promoted in the first place. The question is whether he has the tools or skills of his new trade – has he been trained in management skills or even company procedures, formal or informal? Does he know the importance and expected content and form of the monthly reports? Does he know company disciplinary procedures? These are about coaching. Using the Hersey and Blanchard model, we have a high task and a high relationship concern – the manager needs to maintain a strong concern for the task while helping the subordinate. Repeating ourselves, we would always recommend tackling the coaching issues first, and, should the problem remain, look at the more tortuous issues of motivation and attitudes. So we plan our meeting with Tim:

- *Pre-work*   What preparation has Tim had for promotion? Has he been on any training courses? Are there any special issues in his sales region? Are there any 'markers' that Tim is in serious trouble – excessive labour turnover for instance?

- *Key objective*   We believe he is a potentially good worker who needs help. We need to identify what help is needed.

- *Second objective*   To develop agreed procedures for training and information flow so that Tim can progress and develop.

- *Post-work*   Monitor that what has been agreed on for implementation.

Betty's manager has a completely different issue. Betty most certainly has the training and knowledge to perform satisfactorily but things are still going wrong. Even accepting Betty's qualifications, an aware manager would check out that she has the *correct* skills and understanding to perform the job – for our case study we will assume she has. This takes us to a counselling issue and we need to understand why 'things are going wrong', assuming nothing.

Counselling issues are about the person doing the task, their suitability, motivation and aptitudes. Belbin has a sound bite: 'We get our jobs for *what* we are and we get fired for *who* we are.' Counselling is about *who* we are.

The manager's starting point is his or her overall objective. Betty is presenting a serious challenge to the efficient running of the unit and this must be corrected. Should she not respond constructively, she will have to go. As a manager there is only a certain amount of quality time available, and although employee relations are a significant part of your job, they are rarely factors upon which YOU are judged. Betty, in the Hersey and Blanchard model, seems to have the task skills to do the job, but the way she is doing it is giving difficulty – the manager needs to keep a low concern for the task and a high concern for relationships.

The goal is to help Betty to recognise that a problem exists and that she is the only person who can solve it. Coaching applies to ability problems, and the manager's approach is: 'I can help you do this better.' Counselling applies to attitude problems, and the manager's approach is: 'I can help you to recognise that a problem exists. It gives me a problem because . . . and you have a problem because my problem needs to be resolved.'

- *Pre-work*   We would suspect the meeting could well become acrimonious so we need to prepare ourselves, perhaps reading the chapter on stress could help. We need to be clear on the organisation's disciplinary procedures and our own authority. We would also need, as in the Tim case study, to check on our facts for ourselves. Second-hand reports of a personal nature are often biased.

- *Key objective*   We must get Betty to recognise that *she* has a problem to handle. If she refuses to accept that there is any problem we should be prepared to close the meeting and reconsider our actions.

- *Second objective*   If Betty accepts a need for her to change, we agree some goals – for example, we could recommend the small-wins strategy discussed in the chapter on stress.

- *Post-work*   Monitoring the results of the agreed action, with the option of being flexible in our response if things do not go the way we want.

Many problems involve both coaching and counselling. Frequently managers have to give direction and advice (coaching), as well as help to facilitate understanding and willingness to change (counselling), but the two approaches must be kept apart.

'Right, we both agree that a few days in despatch will help you to understand some of the problems they have with order changes Tim. I'll see that that happens. You have to let me know how it goes. Now there is another issue, but let's have a coffee first.' Pause for refreshment and preferably some change of seating – possibly to an informal layout. 'Now, something else is giving me a problem. You know I am also responsible for expenses and recently some of your people have been using what at best could be called imagination. You simply have to get them under control.'

This works, but the reverse order undoes the good work. Suppose we have the following dialogue with Betty:

Thanks for helping me. Let's confirm what we have agreed. You do accept that the atmosphere in your group is less than useful and that some of it may be due to the way the others perceive you. I do not accept that is jealousy but the fact that you are more highly qualified than even some of the Board may be an issue and certainly you telling Harry just that was, in both our views, a mistake. I agree that I have not given you a detailed enough set of targets, and we will fix that. You will 'take it back a little' – your words, and maybe cut down the 'power dressing' – your words, again. I think 'being aware of the way others see you', my words, will help. OK? (*Pause for some movement to a more formal seating arrangement.*) Now there is just one more thing. I intend to send you on a basic finance course. I don't know what they taught you on that MBA but your book-keeping is appalling.'

Betty's response is likely to be explosive and in management speak, will move to defensiveness, aggression or a total resistance to change.

Summarising

Tim Nelson knows that a problem exists but he doesn't know how to resolve it. Coaching is needed, not problem recognition. Should you find yourself doing both coaching and counselling in the same interview, we suggest that you adopt some token way of underlining your changing role in the meeting. For instance, should the meeting with Tim go drastically wrong and he begins to attack you and the organisation, it may well be useful to stand up, go over to a window and sit down again in a different chair. People need to know whether they are talking to a coach, an expert, or a counsellor who may seem to be a friend but in this context is a potential threat.

If we accept that the purpose of constructive communication is to produce empowered subordinates, the strategy must be to relinquish as much control as possible to the subordinate.

The questions that remain, however, are: How do I effectively coach or counsel another person? What are the behavioural guidelines that help me perform effectively in this situation? Coaching and counselling both rely on the same set of key constructive communication principles.

Defensive and patronising behaviours

If the principles of constructive communication are not followed when coaching, counselling or consulting subordinates, two major problems result (Gibb, 1961; Sieburg, 1978) and are summarised in Table 4.1.

Table 4.1 Constructive communication helps to overcome defensive behaviour in others and patronising behaviour in ourselves

Defensive behaviour	Patronising behaviour
• One individual feels threatened or attacked as a result of the communication. • Self-protection becomes paramount. • Energy is spent on constructing a defence rather than on listening. • Aggression, anger, competitiveness, and/or avoidance are common reactions.	• One individual feels incompetent, unworthy or insignificant as a result of the communication. • Attempts to re-establish self-worth take precedence. • Energy is spent trying to portray self-importance rather than on listening. • Showing off, self-centred behaviour, withdrawal, and/or loss of motivation are common reactions.

Think of constructive communication as a process that occurs when people establish empathy – neither is superior nor inferior to the other as human beings and each respect the other's position. If either party feels that he or she is being placed in a situation where it is necessary to admit inferiority or indeed superiority to satisfy the other, constructive communication will be disrupted. The most obvious form of such positioning is direct persecution:

'You are inadequate in your job' or 'Your whole attitude is wrong', either of which 'demands' a response of 'Sorry'.

The recipient may say 'Sorry' backed with some mumbling that he or she is lucky to be alive on the planet and working for such a good boss, but is more likely to come back aggressively or defensively:

- 'If you were a better boss and gave me reasonably clear objectives.'
- 'Who are you to say that, you are always on the golf course when things happen.'
- 'I do my best with in a difficult situation. My spouse has been taken into hospital and . . .'

None of the three styles of response – craw eating, aggression or defensiveness – is useful. The recipient has turned inwards and is not listening to the intended message.

A less obvious way of tilting the level playing field of communication is patronising behaviour:

- 'It's quite a difficult problem Tim. Let me explain it in your language and give me feedback if I am going too fast.'
- 'Of course Betty, you are a new manager who will, when you have my experience, understand these things.'

Table 4.2 10 Commandments of constructive communication

1. Know where you are going – establish a key objective and plan.
2. Play the ball and not the player – your objective and style it must be related to the job and remain strictly professional.
3. Be prepared to be honest and dismiss any personal or hidden agenda.
4. Chose and appropriate time and place and be willing to postpone or move if necessary.
5. Find common ground and use this as a starting point for the communication.
6. Establish empathy – match the pace of your 'client', neither rushing nor delaying.
7. Be prepared to discuss the specific and never make global criticism.
8. Listen and never judge.
9. There must always be benefits for all parties – never play 'I win, you lose'.
10. Always remember that you can MAKE anyone do anything – ONCE.

Such a flawed attempt to communicate, what may well be a difficult problem, will get the recipients thinking – *Who does he think he is?* – rather than listening.

A version of patronising behaviour, which demands the opposite response, is flattery: 'This is your sort of area Betty with your MBA. You see I came up in the University of Life and don't know these things.' Betty or indeed any sensible recipient of flattery is so puzzled at what is the 'required' response as to be incapable of listening to the substance of the communication or indeed relating to the messenger for quite some time.

Accordingly we have 10 Commandments, or principles, of constructive communication (Table 4.2).

1. Know where you are going – classify your objectives and plan but, 'keep it simple'

The planning process was summarised in Figure 4.1. We would see the very act of thinking of a difficult communications 'event' in a logical way as being half way to making it successful, as Eisenhower, Supreme Commander Allied Forces Europe in the Second World War, is quoted as saying: 'Planning is everything, plans are nothing.' In the event, good management is about controlling chaos, and being prepared helps immeasurably. We have used the concept of 'Keeping it Simple' and perhaps we should have added – 'Keep it Modest'.

2. Play the ball and not the player – constructive communication is about problems and not personalities

Any communication that concentrates on the negative characteristics of the individual can be interpreted as saying that the person is inadequate. Since we can at least attempt to change what we do, but cannot begin to change what we are, there is nothing we can do about personally directed criticism. The relationship fails and the problems are not solved. Personal criticism is often used to try to persuade the other individual that 'this is how you should feel' or 'this is the kind of person you are': 'You are an incompetent manager, a lazy worker or an insensitive colleague.'

Most of us have learnt to accept ourselves as we are and when we are TOLD otherwise we devote our mental effort to defending, justifying or blaming. Any form of praise that is not tied into actual accomplishments or behaviour that we recognise will confuse us. The key is adding agreed and possible behavioural change to the communication. Always begin by describing the behaviour and how it effects you, the speaker:

> 'Betty, I have a department to keep happy and some things that I have observed you doing are not helpful. Firstly, the fact that you have been late on three occasions this week and that you are a manager, makes it impossible for me to tighten up on the others.'

Provided that you have your facts right, this is unarguable, but '*Betty, you are undisciplined*' is likely to start a row. Imputing motives to an individual is also 'playing the person and not the ball: '*I suppose you think that coming in when you want implies your seniority*' is equally dysfunctional. Remember the 'ball' you wish to play.

Our communication should also be linked to accepted standards or expectations rather than to personal opinions. Personal opinions are more likely to be interpreted as 'playing the person' and arouse defensiveness than statements where the behaviour is compared to an accepted standard. For example, the statement '*The way you dress is not appropriate*', is an expression of a personal opinion and will probably create resistance, especially if the listener does not feel that the communicator's opinions are any more legitimate than his or her own. On the other hand, 'Your dress is not in keeping with the company dress code', or 'Everyone is expected to wear a tie to work', may sound stuffy but have that have legitimacy. Provided that the standards to which the messenger refers are accepted by the recipient, we have constructive communication. It is possible, but still slightly dangerous, to express personal opinions or feelings about the behaviour or attitudes of others, as long as they are 'owned' – '*I feel unhappy about the way you dress in the office*'.

3. Be prepared to be honest and express personal feelings, dismissing any personal or hidden agenda

Rogers (1961), Dyer (1972) and others argue that the best interpersonal communications, and the best relationships, are based on congruence – that is, matching the communication, verbally and non-verbally, exactly to what the individual is thinking and feeling. Two kinds of incongruence are possible. One is a mismatch between what one is experiencing and what one is aware of. For example, an individual may not even be aware that he or she is experiencing anger towards another person or generating such anger, regardless of what an independent observer may feel. A second kind of incongruence, and the one more closely related to constructive communication, is a mismatch between what one feels and what one communicates, thus genuine compassion may come over as patronising behaviour.

Heather and Woods (1991), in their summary article on Neuro Linguistic Programming (NLP), describe an exercise where a volunteer from a training group is asked to think first of an individual he or she likes and then of an other individual he or she dislikes. In the process of 'fixing' the liked and disliked individuals the rest of the class observe the volunteer very carefully. The volunteer is then asked to choose at random one or other of the individuals and fix his or her thoughts on that individual. The observers have to 'guess' whether the individual now being concentrated upon is liked or disliked. The observers then have to give reasons for their choice.

A wide range of 'clues' are noted by the observers – twitching, tightening of the muscles about the mouth, crinkling about the eyes, foot movements. Using their observations, the analyses are very usually correct and almost always made with certainty.

The point of the exercise is that it is very difficult to hide one's feelings – others are continuously using a finely tuned 'computer' analysis of our smallest non-verbal signals, and believe in the analysis, whether it is consciously surfaced or not. We also believe our own judgement against what can be rising evidence. Put at its crudest – if we don't like people, it shows, however much we dress it up. For this reason alone it is better to be honest and straightforward in our communications. Genuine, honest statements are always better than artificial or dishonest statements. Managers who hold back their true feelings or opinions, or who don't express what is really on their minds, create the impression that a hidden agenda exists. Subordinates sense that there is something else which has not been said. Therefore, they trust the communicator less and focus on trying to work out what the hidden message is, not on listening or trying to improve. False impressions and miscommunication result.

Rogers (1961) suggests that congruence in communication lies at the heart of a general law of interpersonal relationships. The greater the congruence of experience and awareness with the communication, the more at ease we will be. The reverse is also true – a lack of congruence leads to distrust and a dysfunctional communication.

As we attempt to achieve congruence we must realise that the immediate surfacing of personal emotions may well be counterproductive. The time and place for anger or tears may not be on the shop floor in front of the night shift. We must always be aware of context. However, in general, where the communications issues are very difficult, error on the side of congruence – an indication of feelings in a controlled manner works, the emphasis is on the word controlled. Take, for example, an interview with a subordinate who is performing below his or her ability and displays a nonchalant attitude when given hints that the whole team is being affected. What could the superior say that would strengthen the relationship with the subordinate and still resolve the problem? How can one express honest feelings and opinions and still remain problem-focused, not person-focused? How can one be completely honest without offending another person? Does it matter that the other person is offended? Being aware of the issue is half the answer.

4. Choose an appropriate time and place and be willing to postpone or move if necessary

A very elementary aspect of congruence is 'choosing the right time and place' for a communication and abandoning the communication if the time and place become unsuitable.

> We were told of a case where an employee had just received a very worrying report from his doctor and was attempting to tell his manager that he had to take time off for an operation. The manager, who was under time pressures, heard but did not listen to the employee's concerns and continued with what was a very minor disciplinary matter. The relationship between the employee and the manager was permanently scarred and later the employee had no recollection of the focus of the 'minor disciplinary matter'. The manager remained unaware of the employee's issue – 'There is none so deaf as those that do not want to listen.' (English proverb).

There is a time and a place for everything and constructive communication needs to be part of the general flow and not something that stands out. The flow is not even when:

- The contributions are not balanced or relevant to the subject matter. This can happen when one person dominates and takes significantly more 'air time' than his or her contribution merits or constantly interrupts.

- There are extended pauses. When speakers pause for long periods in the middle of their speeches or when there are long pauses before responses, the communication becomes disjointed. Pauses do not necessarily equate to complete silences – umm's and aah's or repetitions can equally sabotage constructive communication.

- There are unilateral shifts in the topics being discussed. Sieburg (1969) found that more than 25 per cent of the statements made in small-group discussions failed to refer to or even acknowledge previous speakers or their statements.

Constructive communication requires discipline in all three areas.

It is perfectly possible to train individuals to improve their ability to maintain and not impede the flow of communications with others.

> We were working with a group who were becoming impatient with one of their members who boorishly dominated all the conversations, breaking all three of our principles. He consented to write down his statements before opening his mouth. He then, if he still wanted to speak, had to relate his interjection to what the previous person had said – proving it by a summary. The process was painful for him, but in a final statement he said that he had found, over the two days, that much of what he thought was vital was indeed being expressed by others. As an aside, the discipline at the workshop was relaxed during coffee breaks, where he talked incessantly.

Figure 4.3 illustrates that a continuum may exist for conjunctive statements.

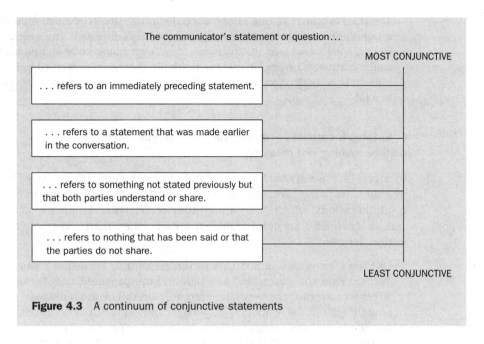

The communicator's statement or question...

MOST CONJUNCTIVE

. . . refers to an immediately preceding statement.

. . . refers to a statement that was made earlier in the conversation.

. . . refers to something not stated previously but that both parties understand or share.

. . . refers to nothing that has been said or that the parties do not share.

LEAST CONJUNCTIVE

Figure 4.3   A continuum of conjunctive statements

The principle whereby we move communications along a progression, building from previous statements and opinions, is important throughout a conversation, but vitally important when we begin a communication where no formal precedents have been established.

5. Establish common ground

Always check the basic facts before any form of professional communication. Is it the right person I have before me? Has the person been told anything in advance? Is he or she aware of what is going to be discussed? Think in terms of a lecturer meeting a class for the first time and beginning a new subject.

> 'My objective for today is to get you to be able to make a presentation with Power Point. Now we need to find out something about your needs. How many of you have already used Power Point? Good. Now, I imagine one or two of you may not be too certain of even using Windows – fine that's three of you. OK, but can I take it that all of you have actually used a PC? Fine. So let's bore the 'experts' by starting from using Windows, right at the beginning. When you switch the screen on . . .'

Without establishing common ground the communicator is wasting everyone's time. If Tim did not share his manager's unspoken desire to do well for himself and his firm, then the interview would be pointless. So it is with Betty, she needed to do better or lose her job and both she and her manager accept this. If Tim was into sabotage and Betty had a private income or had an exciting job offer from another company, then the manager's job would be much more difficult, if not impossible.

The chief executive of one of our associated universities circulated all staff with a beautifully crafted article about the University's finances. The article would certainly have answered the questions of his own ruling body and probably the bank. It answered none of the questions his staff were concerned with: What resources can I call upon next year? Where are the cuts going to be felt? Am I still in a job?

6. Establish empathy – match the pace of your 'client', neither rushing nor delaying

In Figure 4.1 we showed an overlapping area before the key objective which we called 'Empathy'. Empathy is a strange unquantifiable property in constructive communications, which cover a multitude of defects and allows a successful process. If individuals are comfortable with each other, then constructive communication 'happens'.

> Phil was a technician turned sales person responsible for selling a range of products to industrial customers. As a new and inexperienced sales person he was either accompanied or given 'safe' customers. On this occasion the 'safe' customer rang through to the regional sales manager and explained in no uncertain terms that *'If you send that young man to me again, you can forget my custom.'*
>
> The manager put Phil into a series of role plays with mock customers and watched the tapes. The first role play was excellent – the 'customer' was a busy buyer for a supermarket chain who had 'spared' Phil a few minutes. Phil got down to work immediately – the samples and the patter perfectly presented. Even watching it you became out of breath. In the second role play the buyer had his feet on the desk and was playing with a cup of coffee. Phil was offered a cup but declined. The buyer then asked Phil about the traffic but Phil was not to be drawn – out came the samples and on went the pressured patter. Discussing things afterwards Phil admitted that the 'safe' customer seemed to want to talk but that, it being the end of the day, Phil wanted to get home: *'I don't have time for all that social chit chat – it's a job.'*

The point of the story is that *'all that social chit chat'*, for someone who is relaxing after a hard day, is an indication of the pace the customer wants to conduct the interview. If the customer is standing up, answering telephone calls, breathing rapidly, talking in short bursts – then he or she is indicating that he or she wants to take the communication at a rapid pace. Reading the signals provided allows us to judge the pace at which we conduct the encounter. Heather and Woods (1991) regard the balancing of pace in communications as the first and most basic means of establishing empathy. Using the language of NLP they go further and explain how, by mirroring body postures and even styles of language, empathy can be further enhanced and the barriers to constructive communication further lowered.

7. Be specific and never global in any criticism

In general, the more specific a statement is, the more useful it is. For example, the statement, 'You're a poor time manager' is too general to be useful, whereas 'I am concerned that you appear to have spent an hour scheduling meetings today when that could have been done by your assistant' provides specific information that can serve as a basis for behavioural change. Specific statements avoid extremes and absolutes. Think about hearing these statements and see how you would feel:

- 'You never ask for my advice.'
- 'You have no consideration for others' feelings.'
- 'Your work is always inadequate.'
- 'Can't you ever come in on time?'

We suggest in all these cases that the obvious response is negative and is likely to block any future understanding – they are not a route to constructive communication.

Another poor route to communications failure is the 'either–or' statement:

- 'You either do what I say or I will be forced to get rid of you.'
- 'Do you want to do a good job or not?'

The uselessness of polarised statements lies in their denial of any alternatives, and possible responses are severely limited. About the only response to such statements is to contradict or deny it, and this simply leads to defensiveness and arguments. A statement in 1931 by Adolf Hitler illustrates the point: 'Everyone in Germany is a National Socialist – the few outside the party are either lunatics or idiots.' The non-global specific statement allows the smooth flow of the communication process to continue:

A: You made that decision yesterday without asking for my advice.
B: That is right, I did. Normally I do like to get your opinion, but on this occasion there wasn't time.

A: The tone of the memo you have just sent on the loss of the Smithson order will offend Finance unnecessarily.
B: Yes I regret that now. I unfortunately am inclined to put pen to paper without thinking out the consequences.

A: It's difficult to hear in this lecture room.
B: That may be true and perhaps we need to use a hotel for the next big presentation.

As these examples point out, the use of qualifier words such as 'normally', 'inclined', 'may' and 'perhaps' help to link the reply to a specific incident.

Specific statements may not be useful if they focus on things over which another person has no control. 'I hate it when it rains', for example, may relieve some personal frustration, but the referent of the statement is something about which little can be done. The communication is not very useful. Similarly, communicating the message (even implicitly) 'I don't like people of your background' or 'Your personality bothers me' only prove frustrating for the interacting individuals. Such statements are usually interpreted as personal attacks. Specific communication is useful to the extent that it focuses on an identifiable problem or behaviour about which something can be done (e.g., 'It bothers me that you checked up on me four times today').

8. Listen and never judge – communication is not a one-way street

Constructive communication is owned, not disowned. Taking responsibility for one's statements, acknowledging that the source of the ideas is oneself and not another person or group is owning communication. Using first-person words, such as 'I', 'me', 'mine', indicates owning communication. Disowning communication is suggested by use of third-person or first-person-plural words – 'We think', 'The Management Committee has decided' or 'They said'. In disowning the comments the communicator avoids taking responsibility for the message and conveys the message that he or she is aloof or uncaring for the receiver, or is not confident enough in the ideas expressed to take responsibility for them.

Glasser (1965) based his approach to therapy on the concept of responsibility for, or owning, communication and behaviour. According to Glasser, individuals are mentally healthy if they accept responsibility for their statements and behaviours. They are ill if they avoid taking responsibility. According to this theory, taking responsibility for one's communication builds self-confidence and a sense of self-worth in the communicator. It also builds confidence in the receiver of the communication by confirming that he or she is valued.

One result of disowning communication is that the listener is never sure whose point of view the message represents and is apt to misinterpret it: 'How can I respond if I don't know to whom I am responding?' Moreover, an implicit message associated with disowned communication is, 'I want to keep distance between you and me'. The speaker communicates as a representative rather than as a person, or as a message-conveyer rather than as an interested individual. Owning communication, on the other hand, indicates a willingness to invest oneself in the relationship and to act as a colleague or helper. The danger of owning the communication is that we can feel that we can become a judge. We forget that communication is a two-way street.

'Judge not or you will be judged' – our owned constructive communication must contain a description of the behaviour being discussed and not, at this point, be evaluative. Evaluative communication generally makes the other person feel under attack and respond defensively. If this does not matter and the actions demanded are immediate, evaluative communication is fine:

> 'Don't do that, you are not qualified to wire the machine safely – get an electrician and have it wired properly and get it cleared for safety.'

So the man about to be a danger to himself and anyone else who uses the equipment, has had his pride hurt. There may be an argument, bad feelings, exchanging blame and a weakening of the interpersonal relationship result, but nobody will get killed.

The tendency to evaluate others is strongest when the issue is charged with emotion or when a person feels threatened. When people have strong feelings about an issue or experience anxiety as a result of a situation, they have a tendency to make negative evaluations of others' behaviour. Sometimes they try to resolve their own feelings or reduce their own anxiety by placing a label on others: 'You are bad, and that implies I am good. Therefore, I feel better.' At other times they may have such

Table 4.3 Descriptive communication

Step 1
- Describe as objectively as possible the event, behaviour or circumstance.
- Avoid accusations.
- Present data or evidence, if needed.

Step 2
- Describe your own reactions to or feelings about the event, behaviour or circumstance.
- Describe the objective consequences that have resulted, or will likely result.
- Focus on the behaviour and on your own reaction, not on the other individual or his or her personal attributes.

Step 3
Suggest a more acceptable alternative.

strong feelings that they want to punish the other person for violating their expectations or standards.

The problem with this approach is that evaluative communication is likely to be self-perpetuating. Placing a label on another individual generally leads that person to respond by placing a label on you, which makes you defensive in return. The accuracy of the communication as well as the strength of the relationship deteriorates.

An alternative to evaluation is the use of descriptive communication. Because is it difficult to avoid evaluating other people without some alternative strategy, the use of descriptive communication helps to eliminate the tendency to evaluate or to perpetuate a defensive interaction. Descriptive communication involves three steps, as summarised in Table 4.3.

The first stage of descriptive communication is to describe, as objectively as possible, the event that occurred or the behaviour that needs to be modified. The description should contain the elements of the behaviour that can be related to accepted standards and are observable or observed. Subjective impressions or attributions to the motives of another person are not helpful in describing the event. The description 'You have finished fewer projects this month than anyone else in the unit' can be confirmed and relates strictly to the behaviour and to an objective standard, not to the motives or personal characteristics of the subordinate. Put as bluntly as in our example, the subordinate may still feel threatened, but over his or her job performance and not about him or her as a person. 'You are not up to the job' will produce quite different feelings. Describing a behaviour, as opposed to evaluating a behaviour, is relatively neutral.

The second stage is to focus on the reactions or consequences of the behaviour: 'I am unhappy that your performance will demotivate the whole team and will certainly reduce the group bonus.' By owning the feelings we reduce the chances of the person retreating into his or her shell, thinking only of defence and not of solving the problem.

Thirdly, we need to move on to a mutually acceptable 'solution'. It is important that the 'solution' is actionable. We have a paraplegic friend who at a job interview was told: *'You would have been ideal for this job except that you don't have legs.'* Brutality will get you nowhere.

The actionable solution can be presented on a scale of directness: 'This is what I want you to do' or 'I have a few ideas but would like to hear your ideas first', or preferably 'You see our problem. How do you think we should approach it?' The three approaches allow the person to save face (Goffman, 1955) and feel valued (Sieburg, 1978) by separating the individual from the behaviour. If self-esteem is preserved, the behaviour stands a good chance of being modified and the relationship with the boss improved. Our emphasis has moved from establishing who is right and who is wrong to a positive search for a solution. Blanchard and Johnson (1983), in their series of influential management monographs, suggest certain very firm guidelines for giving negative criticism:

- Warn the person involved before the meeting and have the meeting as soon as possible.
- Be specific about your criticism – detail the behaviour.
- Express your feelings in no uncertain terms – anger, sorrow, shame, disappointment.
- Allow your feelings to register with the other person.
- Outline what they have to do.
- Re-establish the relationship – it is the behaviour that is wrong not the person concerned.
- Close the meeting and the subject once and for all.

The whole interview should take less than one minute. Blanchard and Johnson regard this 'One Minute Manager' approach as suitable for most managerial communications, and certainly, with appropriate modifications, for giving praise.

Descriptive communication does require common ground to be established before it works. Thus if our subordinate does not share our objectives and values, or perhaps dislikes the rest of the team, then we will not have constructive communication and perhaps a row.

Effective managers never abandon the three steps. They simply switch the focus, chunking down or up to find common ground.

- 'I am surprised to hear that you do not think the work worth while. Obviously this needs to be discussed. Could we meet next week to go though your ideas?' (Chunking up)
- 'This is the first time I have heard the team bonus criticised. I would like to have your views. Could you give me a few points on paper for next week and we can discuss them?' (Chunking down)

McGregor (1960) would say that our assumption that most people are professionals who wish to do and be seen to do a good job as corresponding to Theory Y as opposed to Theory X. In Theory X employees are 'only doing it for the money, cannot be trusted and need a sharp stick to get them off their backsides'. It is our assumption that, given positive support, most people want to do better, to perform successfully and to be respected. To us, constructive communication is one aspect of that positive support.

It is important to keep in mind, however, that the steps of descriptive communication do not imply that one person should do all the changing. Constructive communication is not a one-way street and should break the stereotypical roles where management is about telling and subordinates are about complying.

'I have discussed what you said about the lack of direction in the unit with the Management Committee and we are forced to agree. What we propose is that we have a weekend off site and bring the whole team together. The Committee will attend on Sunday morning and listen. It's a real opportunity.'

We always have to be willing to move off our prepared agenda and listen. Looking back on Figure 4.1, this is what we showed as 'abort if necessary' – we stop in our tracks and listen, not necessarily only to our 'client'.

As Maier *et al.* (1973) stated: 'In any conversation, the person who talks the most is the one who learns the least about the other person. The good supervisor therefore must become a good listener.'

In a survey of personnel directors in 300 businesses and industries, conducted to determine the skills that are most important in becoming a manager, Crocker (1978) reported that effective listening was ranked highest. Despite its importance in managerial success, however, and despite the fact that most people spend at least 45 per cent of their communication time listening, most people have underdeveloped listening skills. Tests have shown, for example, that individuals are usually about 25 per cent effective in listening (Huseman *et al.*, 1976) – that is, they listen to and understand only about a quarter, on average, of what is being communicated. Even when asked to rate the extent to which they are skilled listeners, 85 per cent of all individuals rate themselves as average or worse. Only 5 per cent rate themselves as highly skilled (Steil, 1980). It is particularly unfortunate that listening skills are poorest when people interact with those closest to them, such as family members and colleagues.

When individuals are preoccupied with meeting their own needs (e.g., saving face, persuading someone else, winning a point, avoiding getting involved), when they have already made a judgement, or when they hold negative attitudes towards the communicator or the message, they can't listen effectively. Because a person listens at the rate of 500 words a minute but speaks at a normal rate of only 125 to 250 words a minute, the listener's mind can dwell on other things half the time. Therefore, being a good listener is neither easy nor automatic. It requires developing the ability to hear and understand the message sent by another person, while at the same time helping to strengthen the relationship between the interacting parties.

Rogers and Farson (1976) suggest that this kind of listening conveys the idea that 'I'm interested in you as a person, and I think what you feel is important. I respect your thoughts, and even if I don't agree with them, I know they are valid for you. I feel sure you have a contribution to make. I think you're worth listening to, and I want you to know that I'm the kind of person you can talk to.'

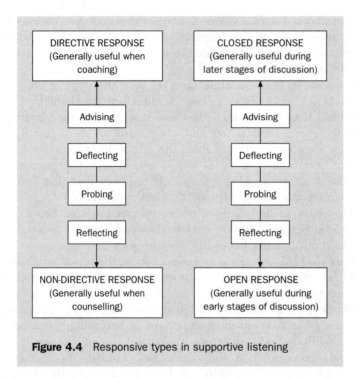

Figure 4.4 Responsive types in supportive listening

People do not know they are being listened to unless the listener makes some type of response; however, we would not suggest learning 'appropriate' responses, but we should be aware of our effect on others. Sophisticated non-verbal indicators of listening can include obscuring one's own mouth, nodding, echoing the end phrase of the other's sentence and a gaze which includes the mouth of the other person. Constructive listening is best learnt by watching competent managers at work.

We can, however, school ourselves in the verbal tools of response types. Figure 4.4 lists four major response types and arranges them on a continuum from most directive and closed to the most non-directive or open. Closed responses eliminate discussion of topics and provide direction to individuals. They represent methods by which the listener can control the topic of conversation. Open responses, on the other hand, allow the communicator, not the listener, to control the topic of conversation. Each of these response types has certain advantages and disadvantages, and none is appropriate at all times in all circumstances.

Most people get into the habit of relying heavily on one or two response types, and they use them regardless of the circumstances. Moreover, most people have been found to rely first and foremost on evaluative or judgemental responses (Rogers, 1961). That is, when they encounter another person's statements, most people tend to agree or disagree, pass judgement, or immediately form a personal opinion about the legitimacy or veracity of the statement. On average, only about 80 per cent of most people's responses have been found to be evaluative. Constructive listening, however, avoids evaluation and judgement as a first response. Instead, it relies on flexibility in response types and the appropriate match of responses to circumstances. Here are the four response types indicating active listening:

- Advising
- Deflecting
- Probing
- Reflecting

Advising

The advising response provides direction, evaluation, personal opinion or instruction. Advising responses place the 'listening manager' firmly in control. The advantages of an advising response are that it helps the communicator to understand something that may have been unclear before, it helps to identify a solution to a problem, and it can provide clarity about how the communicator should feel or act in the future. It is most appropriate when the listener has expertise that the communicator doesn't possess or when the communicator is in need of direction. This is a case where listening also does much of the talking and is not a difficult response for many people. The mouth takes over from the ears very quickly.

One problem with advising is that it can produce dependence. Individuals get used to having someone else generate the answers, directions or clarification. They are not permitted to work out the issues and the solutions for themselves. Rogers (1961) found that most people, even when they seem to be asking for advice, mainly desire understanding and acceptance, not advice. They want the listener to share in the communication, but not take charge of it. When we take on the role of adviser we concentrate more on the legitimacy of the advice or on the generation of alternatives and solutions than on simply listening attentively. We are often impatient and base our advice on our own experience rather than developing an understanding of the world of our 'client'. The final problem arises from the state of mind of the person asking for the advice. Quite often people ask for advice to demonstrate that the situation is impossible and that they have tried everything possible. They may want the adviser to admit his or her own incompetence, but more often they want their own inability shared. In either case the interview can close with a very sour note. Overall the disadvantages of advising are such that we would NOT recommend it as a first response.

> One concept that we find useful is that of seeing yourself as working with your ears – listening and not participating except to encourage and collate; working with your hands – showing others how to do things by example; and working with your mouth – advising. All need to be used appropriately. Sticking to one channel – ears, hands or mouth – all the time can be very ineffectual.

Responses that allow communicators to have control over the topics of conversation, that show understanding and acceptance, and that encourage self-reliance on the part of communicators have their place. In addition, the advice that is given should be connected to an accepted standard. 'You are expected to conform to the standards of dress on every day but Friday' or 'I am sorry but your behaviour is not acceptable'. An accepted standard means that communicators and listeners both acknowledge that the advice will lead to a desired outcome and that it is inherently good, right or appropriate. When this is impossible, the advice should be communicated as the listener's opinion or feeling, and as only one option (i.e., with flexibility), not as the only option. This permits communicators to accept or reject the advice without feeling that the adviser is being invalidated or rejected if the advice is not accepted.

Deflecting

A deflecting response switches the focus from the communicator's problem to one selected by the listener. It simply means that the listener changes the subject. Listeners may substitute their own experience for that of the communicator:

'Let me tell you something similar that happened to me.'

They may introduce an entirely new topic:

'That reminds me of [something else].'

The listener may think the current problem is unclear to the communicator and the use of examples or analogies will help. Or the listener may feel that the communicator needs to be reassured that others have experienced the same problem and that support and understanding are available.

Deflecting responses are most appropriate when a comparison or reassurance is needed. They can provide empathy and support by communicating the message:

'I can recognise what you are saying.'

They can also convey assurance:

'That's OK. These things happen.'

The disadvantages of deflecting responses, however, are that they can imply that the communicator's message is not important or that the experience of the listener is more significant than that of the communicator. It may produce competitiveness or feelings of being up-staged by the listener.

> In the earlier days of one of the authors, he was a caver on an international expedition. The expedition doctor had a simple way of avoiding any action whatsoever. Any complaint was greeted by the response: 'Yes that is terrible – I have exactly the same symptom.' The doctor was not well respected but the 'malingering' was negligible.

Deflecting responses are most effective when they are clearly connected to what the communicator just said, when the listener's response leads directly back to the communicator's concerns, and when the reason for the deflection is made clear. That is, deflecting can produce desirable outcomes in coaching and counselling if the communicator feels supported and understood, not invalidated, by the change in topic focus.

Probing

A probing response clarifies what has been said about a topic relevant to the interview. The intention makes clear what is being said and to progress the conversation towards a useful conclusion – it is neutral and implies no comment on what is being proposed. Probing questions help the listener adopt the communicator's frame of reference so that in coaching situations suggestions can be specific (not general) and in counselling situations statements can be descriptive (not evaluative).

Probing questions can sometimes have the unwelcome effect of switching the focus of attention from the communicator's statement to the reasons behind it. The question 'Why do you think that?' might force the communicator to justify a feeling or a perception rather than just report it and lose the direction of the remarks. Probing should be honest and not used to fog the communicator's presentation.

Two important points should be kept in mind to make probing more effective. One is that 'why' questions are seldom as effective as 'What' questions. 'Why' questions are inclined to lead to hostility of 'rabbit holes' where speculation overtakes real insights. For example, the question, 'Why do you feel that way?' can lead to statements such as 'Because my id is not sufficiently controlled by my ego' or 'Because my father was an alcoholic and my mother beat me – so what?' My professional problem is that production is down and in all honesty half-baked psychological analysis is not my job. 'What happened?' pushes us back to what earns both of us our daily bread.

A second hint is to tailor the probes to fit the situation. When the communicator's statement does not contain enough information or part of the message is not understood, check it out: 'Can you tell me more about that?' When the message is not clear or is ambiguous, clarify: 'What do you mean by that?' A repetition probe should be used when the communicator is avoiding a topic or hasn't answered a previous question: 'I am sorry but I still don't understand – where were you when the explosion occurred?' A reflective probe is most effective when the communicator is being encouraged to keep pursuing the same topic in greater depth.

Reflecting

A reflecting response mirrors the message that was heard, communicates understanding and encourages further development of the statement. Reflecting involves paraphrasing and clarifying the message and is not just a parrot-like mimicry of what has been said. It contributes to understanding and the acceptance of what is being said while allowing communicators to pursue topics of their choice. Rogers (1961), Benjamin (1969), Athos and Gabarro (1978) and others argue that this response should be used most of the time in coaching and counselling since it leads to the most clear communication and the most constructive relationships.

A potential disadvantage of reflective responses is that communicators can get the opposite impression to the one intended. That is, they can get the feeling that they are not being understood or listened to carefully. If they keep hearing reflections of what they just said, their response might begin to be:

'I just said that. Aren't you listening to me?'

A 'health warning' – Reflective responses can be perceived as a technique, as a superficial response lacking integrity.

9. There must be benefits for all parties – never play 'I win, you lose'

Constructive communication must never 'put people down'. Even descriptive communication can still be destructive. Barnlund (1968) observed:

> People do not take time, do not listen, do not try to understand, but interrupt, anticipate, criticise or disregard what is said; in their own remarks they are frequently vague, inconsistent, verbose, insincere or dogmatic. As a result, people often conclude conversations feeling more inadequate, more misunderstood and more alienated than when they started.

The key in our experience is to treat people as adults, unless you have very strong evidence that this is not so, and to act naturally.

> A personnel manager of a large company was well known as a dour Scot – he never joked and was known in the department as 'an ill wind that brings nobody any good'. He was, however, efficient and respected. He was sent on a course on constructive communication and returned with the objective of empowering the staff.
>
> One of his first gross failures was with a senior and highly effective, personal assistant to a colleague. He started the phone conversation by asking whether she wanted the good news or the bad news first. The bemused lady, who did not know about the training course, asked for the bad news and was told that she had sent a memo out with a typographical error. He then went on to the good news that was that she had been regraded and would receive a substantial pay increase. She only heard the bad news and was in tears to her manager because she thought she had been sacked.

Communication that is invalidating arouses negative feelings about self-worth, identity and relatedness to others. It denies the presence, uniqueness or importance of other individuals. Especially important are communications that invalidate people by conveying superiority, rigidity and indifference (Sieburg, 1978; Galbraith, 1975; Gibb, 1961). Communication that is based on assumptions of grade or seniority gives the impression that the communicator is informed while others are ignorant, adequate while others are inadequate, competent while others are incompetent, or powerful while others are impotent. It creates a barrier between the communicator and those to whom the message is sent.

Communication based on a feeling of superiority can take the form of put-downs, in which others are made to look bad so that the communicator looks good. Or it can take the form of 'one-upmanship', in which the communicator tries to elevate himself or herself in the esteem of others. We can, consciously or unconsciously put others down by various means:

1. We can use jargon, acronyms, or words in such a way as to exclude others or create barriers in communication. Doctors, lawyers, government employees and many other professionals are well known for their use of jargon or

acronyms to exclude others, or to elevate themselves rather than to clarify a message. Speaking a foreign language in the presence of people who don't understand it also creates the impression of superiority. In most circumstances, using words or language that a listener can't understand is simply bad manners.

2. We can be rigid and show that we do not listen. The communication is portrayed as absolute, unequivocal or unquestionable. No other opinion or point of view could possibly be considered. Individuals who communicate in dogmatic, 'know-it-all' ways often do so in order to minimise the contributions of others or to invalidate their perspectives. It is possible to communicate rigidity, however, in ways other than just being dogmatic. Rigidity is communicated, for example, by:

- never expressing agreement with anyone else, or when agreement is expressed expressing it in terms of 'they agree with me', not 'I agree with them'
- reinterpreting all other viewpoints to conform to one's own
- never saying, 'I don't know', but having an answer for everything
- not expressing openness to others' opinions or information
- using evaluative and invalidating statements, instead of communicating understanding and validation for others
- appearing unwilling to tolerate criticism or alternative points of view
- reducing complex issues to simplistic definitions
- using all-encompassing and over-generalised statements (that is, communicating the message that everything worth while that can be said about the subject has just been said)
- merging definitions of problems with solutions so that alternatives are not considered
- placing exclamation points after statements, creating the impression that the statement is final, complete or unqualified.

We can indicate our indifference by a variety of ways – silence, by making no verbal response, avoiding eye contact or any facial expression, by interrupting the other person frequently, or by doing unrelated activities. Indifference, however conveyed, indicates a lack of respect of the other and is hostile.

Sieburg (1978) discusses a further way in which we can 'put people down' – being impervious to arguments. We can show this by saying:

'You shouldn't feel that way' – who are you to know?
'You don't understand' – who has the duty to explain?
'Your opinion is uninformed' – who appointed me anyway?

In all these put downs we are expected to say sorry – perhaps for using the resources of the planet. Although most of us have non-OK days, hopefully most of us like feeling good about ourselves. People 'demanding' grovelling from their subordinates collect subordinates willing to grovel. This is not a good idea.

Invalidation is even more destructive in coaching and counselling than criticism or disagreement, because criticism and disagreement validate the other person by recognising that what was said or done is worthy of correction, response or at least notice (Jacobs, 1973). As William James (1965) stated, 'No more fiendish punishment could be devised, even were such a thing physically possible, than that one could be turned loose in a society and remain absolutely unnoticed by all the members thereof.'

> We abandoned an exercise to demonstrate this point when it proved too effective. In the exercise, five volunteers are assembled from a group of managers in a training course. The first in the group is praised for being him/herself – 'It's great to have a really positive person in a group – now sit down.' The second is praised for completing a trivial act well – clapping in tune. The third is given a further trivial task – clapping to the rhythm of a nursery rhyme – and is admonished for not being very good at the task. The fourth person is dismissed personally – 'Why you volunteered is beyond me; you are the sort of person who learns nothing from management courses.'
>
> When the four are seated, at various levels of discontent, the tutor resumed the session, leaving the fifth standing. After a few minutes a range of things may have happened. The ignored fifth person may have become hostile, crept back to his or her seat, or simply stayed looking awkward.
>
> We then debrief the five people. The one who was really hurt was not the one who was told off – the one who was ignored feels the worst. On one occasion, the man felt so bad about being left and ignored that we abandoned the use of the demonstration on all subsequent courses. He was HURT.

The obverse of invalidation communication helps people to feel recognised, understood, accepted and valued. Validating communication is not based on hierarchy and is flexible. It is also a two-way process.

Where coaches or counsellors are senior to those being counselled it is easy for subordinates to feel invalidated. They do have less organisational power and information than their manager. Constructive communicators, however, help subordinates to feel that they have a stake in identifying problems and resolving them 'together'. They treat subordinates as worth while, competent and insightful, and emphasise joint problem solving rather than project a superior position with a tacit acceptance that the roles are different and will stay that way. The point is that being a senior is a privilege with responsibilities and not some God-given right. There is, however, always a question of trust and confidentiality. Imagine the following situation.

> You are Harry's manager and are counselling him over lateness. Your key objective in the session is to stop lateness becoming endemic in your section and Harry becoming a role model for the others. Your secondary objective is to get Harry in work on time and, failing this, to begin disciplinary action. You have done your pre-work. During the interview, which you have explained to Harry is confidential and 'between equals', Harry admits that he is involved in serious crime – unrelated to his work with you. What do you do?

The manager's dilemma, which is based on an actual incident, is real and is based on a misconception. We glibly use the word counselling in a managerial context – working with individuals in a work situation so that the work may be performed more effectively – and think of counselling in a social services context. In the social service context the counsellor is, or should be independent and should be, or is, working purely in the interest of the client. They have points in common but diverge greatly in many situations.

1. The manager owes his or her loyalty to the organisation responsible for his or her wages. His or her loyalty to the 'client' is, in all but unusual cases, not part of the job. The social worker/counsellor has a divided loyalty to the organisation and to the 'client'. Few would argue that in all but extreme cases, the client comes first.

2. The manager's circle of concern is the job for which he or she is paid. Very clearly, if matters come to light that are not effecting the 'job' in any way, they are not the manager's concern. An example of the legal aspect of this is the case when an employee is *suspected* of a criminal activity such as theft, at work. The manager can suspend the employee on suspicion but is highly discouraged in investigating the 'crime'. His or her job is progressing the interests of the organisation and not becoming a policeman.

Returning to Harry, a manager is NEVER wise to say 'And I promise this will go no further'. If something is discovered during managerial counselling that is against the interests of the organisation, then the manager's duty is to pass on the information. Things are said in confidentiality and there can be confusion. Good managers maintain a level of professionalism that allows their subordinates to 'understand'. In situations such as the Harry issue they learnt to say such things as: *Listen Harry, this is not something that you should be telling me.*

Listening always means keeping an open mind and having genuine humility. As Bertrand Russell stated: 'One's certainty varies inversely with one's knowledge.' Disraeli noted that 'To be conscious that you are ignorant is a first great step towards knowledge.' We might say that only an expert is aware that there is more to learn.

A witness being sworn in at a trial, as reported by Haney (1979), put it beautifully:

Court Clerk: Do you swear to tell the truth, the whole truth, and nothing but the truth, so help you God?
Witness: Look, if I knew the truth, the whole truth, and nothing but the truth, I would be God!

10. Always remember that you can MAKE anyone do anything ONCE

Managerial power has some of the properties of potential energy – if you use it you lose it.

We were working with a major supermarket chain and one manager in particular, whose style was similar to that of Genghis Khan. Watching him move round the shelves was a revelation. There were sudden rumours that 'Ted was about' and people would become intensely busy. When he passed out of sight, everyone stopped working and gossiped. It was a very inefficient supermarket.

Pushing people unwillingly, however the communication is perfected, does not bring long-term success.

SUMMARY

Although the technical processes of communications in organisations have been greatly improved within and between organisations, the problems of interpersonal communications have hardly changed. A major reason for these problems is that the kind of communication used does not support a positive interpersonal relationship. Instead, it frequently engenders distrust, hostility, defensiveness, and feelings of incompetence and low self-esteem.

Most people have little trouble in giving good news – it is giving bad news that creates problems. Often when we intend to give actionable feedback, we simply generate hostility. Commenting on poor performance, saying 'no' to a proposal or request, resolving a difference of opinion between two subordinates, correcting problem behaviours, receiving criticism from others, or facing other negative interactions, are areas in which we can run into trouble. We often also fail in the key tasks of coaching and counselling subordinates. Handling these situations in a way that fosters interpersonal growth and a strengthening of relationships is one mark of an effective manager.

In this chapter we have pointed out that communication works best with greater clarity and understanding when the other person feels accepted, valued and supported. We pointed out that artificiality of any kind will be noticed and that the manager must always concentrate on the professional rather than the personal message. The principles we have discussed are important tools in helping to improve your communication competence.

Behavioural guidelines

The following behavioural guidelines will help you practise constructive communication:

1. Differentiate between coaching situations, where advice and direction are required, and counselling situations where the relative roles are much more equal, and understanding and consulting is needed.

2. Keep to the task or the problem – describe behaviours or events and not personalities.

3. Be honest – communicate using true feelings without acting them out in destructive ways.

4. Use descriptive, not evaluative statements: describe objectively what occurred; describe your reactions to the event and its objective consequences; and suggest an alternative that is acceptable to you.

5. Show that you value the other person and communicate that the relationship is important to you. Listen and be prepared to be flexible, revising your approach with what you hear. Encourage dialogue, identifying areas of

agreement or positive characteristics before working through areas of disagreement or negative factors.

6. Use specific statements rather than global statements. Allow yourself the use of words that do not reflect absolutes; practise being flexible. Focus on the things that can be controlled – 'You are too tall' is hardly a criticism that others can act upon.

7. Use statements that flow smoothly from what was said previously; don't dominate the conversation; don't cause long pauses; and acknowledge what was said before.

8. Own your statements: use personal words ('I') rather than impersonal words ('they').

9. Demonstrate constructive listening: use a variety of responses to others' statements depending on whether you are coaching or counselling someone else, but with a bias towards reflecting responses.

Skill Analysis

CASE STUDY **4.1**

FIND SOMEONE ELSE

Ron Davis, the relatively new general manager of the machine tooling group at Parker Manufacturing, was visiting one of the factories. He arranged a meeting with Mike Leonard, a plant manager who reported to him.

Ron: Mike, I've arranged this meeting with you because I've been reviewing performance data and I wanted to give you some feedback. I know we haven't talked face-to-face before, but I think it's time we review how you're doing. I'm afraid that some of the things I have to say are not very favourable.

Mike: Well, since you're the new boss, I'll just have to listen. I've had meetings like this before with new people who come onto my site and think they know what's going on.

Ron: Look, Mike, I want this to be a two-way interchange. I'm not here to read an edict to you, and I'm not here to tell you how to do your job. There are just some areas for improvement I want to review.

Mike: Fine. I've heard that before. But you called the meeting. Fire away.

Ron: Well, Mike, there are several things you need to hear. One is what I noticed during the site tour. I think you're too familiar with some of your female personnel. You know, one of them might take offence and get you involved in a sexual harassment charge.

Mike: Oh, come on. You haven't been around this factory before, and you don't know the informal, friendly relationships we have. The office staff and the women on the floor are flattered by a little attention now and then.

Ron: That may be so, but you need to be more careful. You may not be sensitive to what's really going on with them. And that raises another thing I noticed – the appearance of your shop floor. You know how important it is in Parker to have a neat and clean shop floor. As I walked through this morning, I noticed that it wasn't as orderly and neat as I would like to see it. Having things in disarray reflects poorly on you, Mike.

Mike: My site is as neat as any other in Parkers. You may have seen a few tools out of place because someone was just using them, but we take a lot of pride in our neatness. I don't see how you can say that things are in disarray. You've got no experience around here, so who are you to judge?

Ron: Well, I'm glad you're sensitive to the neatness issue. I just think you need to pay attention to it, that's all. But regarding neatness, I notice that you don't dress like a factory manager. I think you're creating a sub-standard impression by not wearing a tie, for example. Such casual dress can be used as an excuse for workers to come to work in really grubby attire. That may not be safe.

Mike: Look, I don't agree with making a big separation between the managers and the employees. By dressing like people out on the shop floor, I think we eliminate a lot of barriers. Besides, I don't have the money to buy clothes that might get oil on them every day. You seem to be nit-picking.

Ron: I don't want to nit-pick, Mike. But I do feel strongly about the issues I've mentioned. There are some other things, though, that need to get corrected. One is the appearance of the reports you send into head office. There are often mistakes, misspellings, and, I suspect, some wrong numbers. I wonder if you are paying attention to these reports. You seem to be reviewing them superficially.

Mike: If there is one thing we have too much of, it's reports. I could spend three-quarters of my time filling out report forms and generating data for some accountant in head office. We have reports coming out of our ears. Why don't you give us a chance to get our work done and eliminate all this paperwork?

Ron: You know as well as I do, Mike, that we need to carefully monitor our productivity, quality and costs. You just need to be more aware of your responsibility.

Mike: Fine. I'm not going to fight about that. It's a losing battle for me. No one on the top floor will ever reduce their demand for reports. But, listen, Ron, I also have one question for you.

Ron: What's that?

Mike: Why don't you go find somebody else to pick on? I need to get back to work.

Discussion questions

1. What principles of constructive communication and constructive listening are violated in this case?

2. How could the interaction have been changed to produce a better outcome?

3. Categorise each of the statements by naming the rule of constructive communication that is either illustrated or violated.

4. What should Ron do in his follow-up meeting with Mike?

CASE STUDY **4.2**

REJECTED PLANS

The following dialogue occurred between two employees in a large firm. The conversation illustrates several characteristics of constructive communication.

Helen: How did your meeting go with Mr Peters yesterday?

David: Not so well.

Helen: It looks as if you're pretty upset about it.

David: Yes, I am. It was a totally frustrating experience. Let's just say I would like to forget the whole thing.

Helen: Things can't have gone as well as you had hoped.

David: You can say that again. That man was impossible. I thought the plans I submitted were very clear and well thought out. Then he rejected the entire package.

Helen: You mean he didn't accept any of them?

David: Correct.

Helen: I've seen your work before, David. You've always done a first-rate job. I can't see why Mr Peters rejected your plans. What did he say about them?

David: He said they were unrealistic and too difficult to implement, and . . .

Helen: Really?

David: Yes, and then he said that I felt he was attacking me personally. But, on the other hand, I guess I was angry because I thought my plans were very good, and you know, I paid close attention to every detail in those plans.

Helen: I'm certain that you did.

David: It just annoys me.

Helen: I'm sure it does. I would be upset, too.

David: Peters must have something against me.

Helen: After all the effort you put into those plans, you still couldn't work out whether Mr Peters was rejecting you or your plans. Is that right?

David: Yes. How could you tell?

Helen: I can really understand your confusion and uncertainty when you felt Mr Peters' actions were unreasonable.

David: I just don't understand why he did what he did.

Helen: Right. If he said your plans were unrealistic, what does that mean? I mean, how can you deal with a rationale like that? It's just too general – meaningless, even. Did he mention anything specific? Did you ask him to point out some problems or explain the reasons for his rejection more clearly?

David: Good point, but I was so disappointed at the rejection that I just wasn't concentrating. You know what I mean?

Helen: Yes. It's such a demoralising experience. You have so much invested personally that you try to save what little self-respect is left.

David: That's right. I just wanted to get out of there before I said something I would be sorry for.

Helen: Yet, in the back of your mind, you probably thought that Mr Peters wouldn't risk the company's future just because he didn't like you personally. But then, well – the plans were good! It's hard to deal with that contradiction on the spot, isn't it?

David: Exactly. I knew I should have pushed him for more information, but I just stood there like a dummy. But, what can I do about it now? It's spilt milk.

Helen: I don't think it's a total loss, David. I mean, from what you have told me – what he said and what you said – I don't think a conclusion can be reached. Perhaps he doesn't understand the plans, or perhaps it was just his off day. Who knows, it could be a lot of things. What would you think about pinning Mr Peters down by asking for his objections, point by point? Do you think it would help to talk to him again?

David: Well, I would certainly know a lot more than I know now. As it is, I wouldn't know where to begin revising or modifying the plans. And you're right, I really don't know what Peters thinks about my work or me. Sometimes I just react and interpret with little or no evidence.

Helen: Perhaps another meeting would be a good thing, then.

David: Well, I suppose I'd better get off my high horse and arrange an appointment with him for next week. I am curious to find out what the problem is with the plans, or me. (*Pause*) Thanks Helen, for helping me sort this out.

Discussion questions

1. Categorise each statement in the case according to the communication characteristic or the type of response. For example, the first statement by David is obviously not congruent, but the second is much more so.

2. Which statements in the conversation were most helpful? Which do you think would produce defensiveness or close off the conversation?

3. What are the potential disadvantages of giving outright advice for solving David's problem? Why doesn't Helen just tell David what he ought to do? Is it incongruent to ask David what he thinks is the best solution?

Skill Practice

EXERCISE **4.1**

VULCAN COMPUTERS

The role of manager encompasses not only one-to-one coaching and counselling with an employee, but it also frequently entails helping other people to understand coaching and counselling principles for themselves. Sometimes it means refereeing interactions and, by example, helping other people to learn about the correct principles of constructive communication. This is part of the task in this exercise. In a group setting, coaching and counselling become more difficult because multiple messages, driven by multiple motives, all interact. Skilled constructive communicators, however, help each group member to feel supported and understood in the interaction, even though the solution to the issue is not always the one he or she would have preferred.

Assignment

In this exercise you should apply the principles of constructive communication. First, form into groups of four people. Next, read the case and assign the following roles in your group: Mike, Sheila, John and an observer. Assume that a meeting is being held with Mike, Sheila and John immediately after the end of the incidents in the following case. Play the roles you have been assigned and try to resolve the problems. The observer should provide feedback to the three players at the end of the exercise. (An Observer's Feedback Form, to assist the observer in providing feedback, can be found in the scoring key in Appendix 1, page 626).

Vulcan Computers is a medium-sized computer hardware manufacturer based in the south-east of England. The parts are part-made in Taiwan and finished and assembled in the English factory, which is also the company's research and engineering centre.

The process design group consists of eight male engineers and their supervisor, Mike Coombes. They have worked well together for a number of years, and good relationships have developed among all the members. When the workload began to increase, Mike recruited a new design engineer, Sheila Williams, who recently received a first-class honours degree in engineering at Durham University. Her first assignment is to join a project team which is working on Vulcan's computer notebook. The three other members of the team are John Smith (aged 38, 15 years with the company), Philip Jones (aged 40, 10 years with the company) and Kevin Robson (aged 32, 8 years with the company).

As a new Vulcan employee, Sheila is fired with enthusiasm. She finds the work challenging as it offers her the opportunity to apply much of the knowledge she has gained at University. Although she is friendly with the rest of the project team, Sheila doesn't socialise much with them at work and doesn't join them for their traditional Friday night get-together at the Red Lion.

Sheila takes her work seriously and she regularly works after hours. Because of her persistence, coupled with her more recent education, she regularly finishes her portion of the various project stages several days ahead of her colleagues. She finds this irritating as it means that she is constantly having to ask Mike Coombes for additional work to keep her busy until the rest of the team has caught up with her. Initially she offered to help John, Philip and Kevin with their assignments, but each time she was abruptly turned down.

About five months after Sheila had joined the design group, John asked to see Mike about a problem the group was having. Their conversation went as follows:

Mike: What's the problem, John?

John: Look Mike, I don't want to waste your time, but some of the other design engineers want me to discuss Sheila with you. She is irritating everyone with her know-it-all, pompous attitude. She's just not the kind of person we want to work with.

Mike: I can't understand that, John. She's an excellent worker, and her design work is always well done and usually flawless. She's doing everything the company wants her to do.

John: The company never asked her to disrupt the morale of the group or to tell us how to do our work. The animosity in our group could eventually result in lower-quality work from the whole unit.

Mike: I'll tell you what I'll do. Sheila has a meeting with me next week to discuss her six-month performance. I'll keep your thoughts in mind, but I can't promise an improvement in what you and the others believe is a pompous attitude.

John: Immediate improvement in her behaviour is not the problem, it's her coaching others when she has no right to. She publicly shows others what to do. You'd think she was lecturing an advanced class in design with all her high-powered, useless equations and formulas. If she keeps this up there's going to be some real trouble.

Mike could not ignore John's views. A week later he called Sheila into his office for her first six-month appraisal. Part of the conversation went as follows:

Mike: There is one other aspect I'd like to discuss with you. As I've explained there's no problem with your technical performance but there are some questions about your relationships with the other workers.

Sheila: I don't understand – what questions are you talking about?

Mike: Well, to be quite frank, certain members of the design group have complained about your apparent know-it-all-attitude and the manner in which you try to tell them how to do their jobs. You're going to have to be patient with them and not publicly call them out about their performance. This is a good group of engineers, and their work over the years has been more than acceptable. I don't want any problems that will cause the group to produce less effectively.

Sheila: Let me make a few comments. First of all, I have never publicly criticised their performance to them or to you. Initially, when I finished ahead of them, I offered to help them with their work but was bluntly told to mind my own business. I took the hint and concentrated only on my part of the work. What you don't understand is that after five months of working in this group I have come to the conclusion that these engineers are working as slowly as they possibly can – they're ripping off the company. They're setting a work pace much slower than they are capable of. They're more interested in the music from Sam's radio, the local soccer team and going to the Red Lion. I'm sorry, but this is just not the way I was brought up or trained. And finally, they've never looked on me as a qualified engineer, but as a woman who has broken their professional barrier.

Source: Revised from a case-study by Szilagyi and Wallace (1983)

EXERCISE **4.2**

BROWN VS THOMAS

Effective one-to-one coaching and counselling are skills that are required in many settings in life, not just in management. It is hard to imagine anyone who would not benefit from training in constructive communication. Because there are so many aspects of constructive communication, however, it is sometimes difficult to remember all of them. That is why practice with observation and feedback is so important. These attributes of constructive communication can become a natural part of your interaction approach as you conscientiously practise and receive feedback from a colleague.

Assignment

In the following exercise, one individual should study the role of Harriet Brown, another the role of Judy Thomas. To make the role play realistic, do not read each other's role descriptions. When you have finished reading, role play a meeting between Harriet Brown and Judy Thomas. A third person should serve as the observer. (An Observer's Feedback Form, to assist the observer in providing feedback, can be found in the scoring key in Appendix 1, page 626.)

Harriet Brown, Department Head

You are Harriet Brown, head of a bank's operations department. You have only been in the organisation for two years and have been quickly promoted. You enjoy working for this bank. It has a high reputation and is acknowledged for its commitment to management development and training programmes – the bank pays for all external courses. Each employee is given an opportunity for a personal management interview each month, and these sessions are usually extremely productive.

One of the department members, Judy Thomas, has been in this department for 19 years, 15 of them in the same job. She is reasonably good at what she does, and she is always punctual and efficient. She tends to get to work earlier than most employees in order to read the *Financial Times* and trade magazines. You can almost set your watch by the time Judy has her coffee breaks and by the time she phones her daughter every afternoon.

Your view is that although Judy is a good worker she lacks imagination and initiative. This has been indicated by her lack of merit increases over the last five years and by the fact that she has had the same job for 15 years. She's content to do just what is assigned, nothing more. Your predecessor must have given hints to Judy that she might be in line for a promotion, however, because Judy has raised this with you more than once. Because she has been in her job so long, she is at the top of her pay range, and without a promotion, she cannot receive a salary adjustment above the basic cost-of-living increase.

The one thing Judy does beyond the basic minimum job requirements is to help to train young people who come into the department. She is very patient and methodical with them, and she seems to take pride in helping them to learn. She has not been hesitant to point out this contribution to you. Unfortunately, this activity does not qualify Judy for a promotion, nor could she be transferred into the training and development department. Once you suggested that she take a few courses at the local college, paid for by the bank, but she simply said that she was too old to go back to school. You think that she might be intimidated because she didn't go to college.

As much as you would like to promote Judy, there just doesn't seem to be any way to do that in good conscience. You have tried putting additional work under her control, but she seems to be slowing down in her productivity rather than speeding up. The work needs to be done, and expanding her role just puts you behind schedule.

This impending interview is probably your best chance to talk openly with Judy about her performance and her potential. You certainly don't want to lose her as an employee, but there is not going to be a change in job assignment for a long time unless she changes her performance dramatically.

Judy Thomas, Department Member

You are a member of a bank's operations department. You have been with the bank for 19 years, 15 of them in the same job. You enjoy working for the bank because of its friendly atmosphere, and the job is fairly secure. However, lately you have become more dissatisfied as you've seen person after person come into the bank and get promoted ahead of you. Your own boss, Harriet Brown, is almost 20 years your junior. Another woman who joined the bank at the same time as you is now a senior manager at head office. You cannot understand why you've been neglected. You are efficient and accurate in your work, you have a near-perfect attendance record and you consider yourself to be a good employee. You have gone out of your way on many occasions to help to train and orient young people who are just joining the bank. Several of them have written letters later telling you how important your help was in getting them promoted. A lot of good that does you!

The only explanation you can think of is that there is a bias against you because you haven't been to college or university. On the other hand, others have moved up without a degree. You have not taken advantage of any college courses paid for by the bank. The last thing you want after a long day's work is another three hours in a lecture room. Anyway, you only see your family in the evenings, and you don't want to take time away from them. It doesn't take a college degree to do your job anyway.

Your monthly personal management interview is coming up with your department head, Harriet Brown, and you've decided that the time has come to get a few answers. Several things need explaining. Not only have you not been promoted, but you haven't even received a merit increase for five years. You're not getting any credit for the extra contributions you make with new employees, nor for your steady, reliable work. Could anyone blame you for being a little bitter?

Skill Application

ACTIVITY **4.1**

SUGGESTED FURTHER ASSIGNMENTS

1. Tape-record an interview with someone such as a co-worker, friend or spouse. Focus on the issues or challenges faced right now by that other person. Try to assume the role of coach or counsellor. Categorise your statements in the interview on the basis of the constructive communication principles in this book. (The Rejected Plans case (Case Study 4.2) provides an example of such an interview.)

2. Teach someone you know the concepts of constructive communication and constructive listening. Provide your own explanations and illustrations so that the person understands what you are talking about. Describe your experience in your work book.

3. Think of an interpersonal problem you share with someone, such as a flatmate, parent, friend or instructor. Discuss the problem with that person, using constructive communication. Write about the experience in as much detail as possible. Concentrate on the extent to which you and the other person used the eight principles of constructive communication. Record and describe areas in which you need to improve.

4. Write two mini case studies. One should recount an effective coaching or counselling situation. The other should recount an ineffective coaching or counselling situation. The cases should be based on a real event either in your own personal experience or in the experience of someone you know well. Use all the principles of constructive communication and listening in your cases.

ACTIVITY **4.2**

APPLICATION PLAN AND EVALUATION

Part 1: Plan

1. Write down the two or three aspects of this skill that are most important to you. These may be areas of weakness, areas you most want to improve or areas that are most salient to a problem you face currently. Identify the specific aspects of this skill that you want to apply.

2. Now identify the setting or the situation in which you will apply this skill. Establish a plan for performance by actually writing down the situation. Who else will be involved? When will you do it? Where will it be done?

3. Identify the specific behaviours you will engage in to apply this skill. Try it.

4. What are the indicators of successful performance? How will you know you have succeeded in being effective? What will indicate that you have performed competently?

Part 2: Evaluation

5. After you have completed your implementation, record the results. What happened? How successful were you? What was the effect on others?

6. How can you improve? What modifications can you make next time? What will you do differently in a similar situation in the future?

7. Looking back on your whole skill practice and application experience, what have you learned? What has been surprising? In what ways might this experience help you in the long term?

Further reading

Adair, J. (1997) *Effective communication.* London: Pan.

Baguley, P. (1994) *Effective communication for modern business.* London: McGraw-Hill.

Bishop, S. and Taylor, D. (1998) *44 activities for interpersonal skills training.* Aldershot: Gower.

Ludlow, R. and Panton, F. (1992) *The essence of effective communication.* London: Prentice Hall.

MacLennan, N. (1998) *Counselling for managers.* Aldershot: Gower.

Scholes, E. (ed.) (1997) *Gower handbook of internal communication.* Aldershot: Gower.

CHAPTER 5

Effective Motivation

SKILL DEVELOPMENT OUTLINE

Skill Pre-assessment surveys
- Motivating others
- Work performance assessment

Skill Learning material
- Increasing motivation and performance
- Diagnosing work performance problems
- Motivating others
- Enhancing an individual's ability
- Remedies for failing performance due to lack of ability
- Fostering a motivating work environment
- Elements of an integrated motivation policy
- Improving behaviours
- Internal job characteristics

- Equitable distribution of rewards
- Providing timely rewards and accurate feedback
- Summary
- Behavioural guidelines

Skill Analysis case studies
- Electro Logic

Skill Practice exercises
- Diagnosing work performance problems
- George's performance problems
- Reshaping unacceptable behaviours

Skill Application analysis
- Suggested further assignments
- Application plan and evaluation

LEARNING OBJECTIVES

To increase proficiency in:
- understanding performance problems in the workplace
- enhancing performance

- creating and maintaining a motivating environment

INTRODUCTION

John Syer, sports psychologist (1986), describes the most difficult problem a football manager has to face. It is when talented players are not giving of their best. As football is essentially a team game, it's not so easy to see when a talented player lets go of the ball a fraction too early to avoid a potentially damaging tackle or hesitates very, very slightly before tackling another player himself. In the language of the sports field, the player lacks motivation and it is the job of the captain, the support staff, the rest of the team and most of all the player himself, is to regain that motivation. Without the motivation of all the players, team spirit fails and the team loses. Football management is merely one area of management and its problems with motivation are universal.

> A large pilot plant to make smokeless fuel was operating in the British Midlands coal fields. In the process, air was forced into powdered coal by a massive fan. If the fan failed, the whole plant would be at risk. Just before the change-over to the night shift, the plant stopped. All the emergency procedures were initiated and the team managed a safe shut-down. At the end of the shut-down operation a shift operator who was due on the next shift appeared. He was very concerned and rather frightened. He had been passing the fan room on his way to sign in when he heard a rather strange noise. He was not normally allowed into the fan room but he went in all the same and heard the strange noise close up – he thought it was the main bearing of the main fan and he pressed the emergency button to stop the whole plant. In pressing the button he saved a very costly accident. He was not certain that he had done the right thing and was surprised to be thanked formally by the Plant Manager for his prompt action.

The process worker could well have ignored the noise, the fan would have seized up and the team, in the sporting analogy, would have failed. The fan was not the process worker's direct responsibility but he was motivated to act beyond his immediate area of work. Handy, in his book, *The Age of Unreason* (1993), sees a time when we will all have to accept what he calls the 'inverted doughnut' job description. Unlike a normal doughnut, the inside is solid (our core job) and the outside is the 'hole' (a fuzzy area of responsibilities). For many of us it is the fuzzy, outside area wherein our motivation lies. The core of the process worker's job was to attend the control room of the plant over a particular shift pattern and to watch a number of instruments. The fuzzy part of his job was concerned with the total function of his team. To work in this area, with the attendant risks, required his personal motivation, good and concerned communication from his manager and the support of the team. Communications, trust and support are the keys to motivation and are the basis of this chapter. We make no apology for what may be seen as a rather tough approach – management is, in most cases, about getting things done effectively, and we might say hesitatingly – at a profit. It's a tough world.

Skill Pre-assessment

SURVEY **5.1**

MOTIVATING OTHERS

Step 1   For each statement circle a number on the rating scale in the Pre-assessment column on the left. Your answers should reflect your attitudes and behaviour as they are now, not as you would like them to be. Be honest. When you have completed the survey, use the scoring key in Appendix 1 (page 627) to identify the skill areas discussed that are most important for you to master. The process of improving these skill areas should help you with your learning objectives.

Step 2   When you have completed the chapter and the Skill Application assignments, review your responses in the right-hand Post-assessment column using the scoring key in Appendix 1 to measure your progress. If your score remains low in specific skill areas, use the behavioural guidelines at the end of the Skill Learning section to guide your Application Planning.

RATING SCALE

1 = Strongly disagree   **2** = Disagree   **3** = Slightly disagree
4 = Slightly agree   **5** = Agree   **6** = Strongly agree

	Assessment	
	Pre-	Post-
Imagine that you are supervising the work of a subordinate		
1. If there is a problem of work being done badly or inefficiently the first thing I would do is to check whether the worker had the skills, knowledge and tools to do the job, then I would worry about motivation.	____	____
2. I would establish the standards I expect the subordinate to achieve.	____	____
3. If necessary I would offer to provide training and would not take over the job myself.	____	____
4. I would be straightforward in providing feedback of how he or she is doing and his or her chances of moving up in the organisation.	____	____
5. I always attempt to find ways of rewarding exceptional performances.	____	____
6. If it came to having to discipline the subordinate I would identify the problem, describe its consequences and explain how it should be corrected.	____	____
7. I try to make work both interesting and challenging.	____	____
8. I try to match the rewards to the person when the job is well done.	____	____
9. I make sure that the person feels fairly and equitably treated.	____	____
10. I make sure that the person gets timely feedback from those affected by task performance.	____	____

11. I attempt to find the reasons for poor performance before taking any remedial or disciplinary actions.   ____ ____

12. I always help the person to set targets that are challenging, specific and time-bound.   ____ ____

13. Only as a last resort do I attempt to move or fire anyone.   ____ ____

14. Whenever possible I make sure valued rewards are linked to high performance.   ____ ____

15. I am very tough when the effort is below what is required and I know what can be achieved.   ____ ____

16. I try to make work more interesting by moving people to other jobs and by modifying jobs so that there is variety.   ____ ____

17. I try to arrange for teamworking wherever possible.   ____ ____

18. I make sure that any judgements of performance are fair.   ____ ____

19. I reward success immediately.   ____ ____

20. I always determine if the person has the necessary resources and support to succeed in the task.   ____ ____

SURVEY **5.2**

WORK PERFORMANCE ASSESSMENT

Respond to the following statements, based on your current (or recent) work situation. Then turn to Appendix 1 (page 628) for the scoring key.

RATING SCALE

1 = Strongly disagree   **2** = Disagree   **3** = Neutral
4 = Agree   **5** = Strongly agree

Imagine that you are being supervised in a job

1. My supervisor and I agree on the quality of my performance.   1 2 3 4 5

2. I feel I have adequate training to perform my current job assignments.   1 2 3 4 5

3. I believe that my natural skills and abilities are matched very well with my job responsibilities.   1 2 3 4 5

4. I believe that I have adequate resources and supplies to do my job well.   1 2 3 4 5

5. I understand my boss's expectations and generally feel they are realistic.   1 2 3 4 5

6. I believe that rewards are distributed fairly, on the basis of performance.   1 2 3 4 5

7. The rewards and opportunities available to me if I perform well are attractive to me personally.   1 2 3 4 5

8. My supervisor says I am not performing as well as I should, but I disagree.   1 2 3 4 5

9. I could do a much better job if I had more training.   1 2 3 4 5

10. I believe that my job is too difficult for my ability level.   1   2   3   4   5

11. I believe that my job performance is hindered by a lack of resources.   1   2   3   4   5

12. I believe my boss's expectations are unclear and pretty unrealistic.   1   2   3   4   5

13. I believe my boss prefers favourites when allocating rewards.   1   2   3   4   5

14. I do not find the rewards and opportunities available to high performers very appealing.   1   2   3   4   5

Skill Learning

Increasing motivation and performance

> I can't understand why we have such bad luck with Directors of Engineering. Our first head of engineering was technically well qualified. He'd been a good designer for us before we promoted him. But he started drinking heavily, and he had to go. We replaced him with Harris who seemed so promising. They say he is doing well in his new job at the Beta Company. But they operate differently to us. Then we appointed Steve Spencer and he seemed to have all the qualifications we needed. And he certainly was a gentleman. But he never could get things done. Apparently he couldn't gain the respect of the design team. So, here we are, looking for another replacement. I'm beginning to wonder whether we'll ever find the right one.
>
> *Source*: Dalton *et al.* (1970)

This is how a well-developed case study, 'Higgins Equipment Company', closes. The comments of the company chairman reflect the frustration he had experienced in trying to staff a key post. He had filled the position three times with individuals of experience and high promise, but their performance was consistently disappointing. The case details several structural obstacles facing any occupant of the job:

- Several subunits in the engineering division perform production and marketing activities.

- The director is both the head of engineering and the director of a subunit called Engineering Services, which co-ordinates engineering and production activities.

- One of the department heads in engineering has informal direct access to the president.

A problem that was initially seen as one of motivation, turns out to be much more fundamental.

Diagnosing work-performance problems

Unfortunately, many managers share the bewilderment of the manager in the case study. His approach brings to mind the Chinese proverb: 'For every hundred men hacking away at the leaves of a diseased tree, only one man stoops to inspect the roots.' The purpose of this chapter is to examine the analytical and behavioural skills that are missing in the Higgins case. The first part of this chapter examines how to identify the underlying causes of performance problems. The second part presents a six-step process for creating a highly motivating work environment. We need a model to guide the inquiry process. Maier (1973) and Lawler (1973) have summarised the determinants of task performance as follows:

Performance = Ability, Motivation (Effort)
Ability   = Aptitude, Training, Resources
Motivation   = Desire, Commitment

According to these formulae, performance is the product of ability multiplied by motivation, and ability is the product of aptitude multiplied by training and resources. The fact that there is multiplication in these formulae suggests that all elements are essential. For example, workers who have 100 per cent of the motivation and 75 per cent of the ability required to perform a task can perform at an above-average rate. However, if these individuals have only 10 per cent of the ability required, no amount of motivation will enable them to perform satisfactorily.

Aptitude refers to the inherent skills and abilities a person brings to the job. These obviously involve physical and mental capabilities. But for a job where the people factors are paramount, they also include personality characteristics. Most of our inherent abilities can be enhanced by education and training. Indeed, much of what we call native ability in adults can be traced to previous experiences of developed skills, perhaps by informal contacts – modelling the social skills of parents or older siblings. Nevertheless, it is useful to consider training as a separate component of ability, since it represents an important mechanism for improving employee performance. When we are attempting to match people to jobs, in any selection process ability should be matched to the skill requirements of the job. If an applicant has minor deficiencies in skill aptitude but many other desirable characteristics, an intensive training programme can increase the applicant's qualifications to perform the job (Wanous, 1980).

The Barrett Performance Improvement Model – BARR-IMP ll (Barrett and Georgides, 1994) – lists six factors for individual work improvement: three work related and three personal.

- Work-related: abilities, motivation and role clarity
- Personal: work preference, personality and life goal planning.

Motivating others

Our definition of ability is broad. We are focusing on the ability to perform, rather than the ability of the performer. Frequently, highly capable and well-trained individuals are placed in situations that inhibit job performance. Specifically, they are not given the resources (technical, personnel, political) to perform assigned tasks effectively.

Motivation represents an employee's desire and commitment, and is recognised as effort. Some people want to complete a task but are easily distracted or discouraged. They have high desire but low commitment. Others continue with impressive persistence, but their work is uninspired. These people have high commitment but low desire.

The first question that must be asked by the manager of a poor performer is whether the problem stems from lack of ability or lack of motivation. Ask the question 'Can he or she do what is required?' before asking 'Does he or she WANT to do it?' There are four pieces of information that managers need in order to answer this question (Michener *et al.*, 1976):

1. The difficulty of the tasks assigned to the individual.

2. The known ability of the individual.

3. The extent to which the individual seems to be attempting to perform.

4. The degree to which the individual's performance improves with coaching.

Low ability is generally associated with very difficult tasks, overall low individual ability, evidence of strong effort and lack of improvement over time.

The answer to 'Is this an ability or motivational problem?' has far-reaching ramifications for manager/subordinate relations. Managers tend to become forceful if they believe that an individual is deliberately not doing what is requested and has no justifiable excuse. Managers justify their choice of action on the grounds that the subordinate has a poor attitude, is hostile to authority or lacks dedication (Kipnis, 1976).

Unfortunately, if the manager's assessment is incorrect and poor performance is related to ability rather than motivation, the response of increased pressure will make the problem worse. If poor performers feel that management is insensitive to their problems – that they lack resources, are inadequately trained or are forced into unrealistic time schedules – they may respond in a counter-productive manner to any tactics aimed at increasing their effort. They are likely to develop a motivational problem – their desire and commitment will decrease in response to management's insensitive, dictatorial behaviour. Seeing this response, management will feel that their original diagnosis is confirmed and they will proceed to use even stronger forms of influence to force compliance. The resulting vicious circle is extremely difficult to break and emphasises the dangers in faulty analysis of performance problems.

We will now examine the two components of performance in more detail. We will discuss manifestations of low ability and poor motivation, their cases and some proposed remedies. Overall, we will devote more time to motivation. While ability tends to remain stable over long periods of time, motivation fluctuates; therefore, it requires closer monitoring and frequent recharging.

Enhancing an individual's ability

Our problem-solving performance should be based on the principle of Occam's Razor: When you have eliminated all the obvious solutions from a problem, what remains, however unlikely, is the cause. In our case 'lack of ability' covers what we see as the obvious solution, and motivation, however unlikely, is only discussed when these have been eliminated.

Lack of relevant abilities to do a job effectively may come from several causes:

- The resources necessary for the job may not be available.
- Ability may have been improperly assessed during the selection process.
- The technical requirements of a job may have radically changed.
- The person who performed very well in one post may be promoted to a higher-level position that is too demanding (the so-called Peter Principle, where people are typically promoted to one grade above their level of competence).

The first cause – the lack of relevant resources – must be disposed of before we proceed with the others. This process may involve all the communication skills at our disposal. The skilled manager may note that 'lack of relevant resources' is really a criticism of him or her, and may well want to remove this as 'a wise career move'.

Having resolved the material problems, we need to look at the personal issues, and managers should be ready to look at the symptoms of failing personal performance. There are three danger signals which can be recognised in failing subordinates (Quick, 1977):

Taking refuge in a speciality   Managers or supervisors lose their ability to manage and retreat to their technical speciality. This often occurs in general managers who feel insecure addressing problems outside their area of expertise and experience. Anthony Jay, in *Management and Machiavelli* (1967), calls this type of manager a 'George I', who, after assuming the English throne, continued to be preoccupied with the affairs of his native Hanover in Germany.

Focusing on past performance   Another sign is measuring one's value to the organisation in terms of past performance or on the basis of former standards. Some cavalry commanders in the First World War relied on their outmoded military knowledge and, as a result, failed miserably in mechanised combat. This form of obsolescence is common in organisations that fail to shift their mission in response to changing market conditions.

Exaggerating aspects of the leadership role   Managers who have lost confidence in their ability tend to be very defensive. This often leads them to exaggerate one aspect of their managerial role. Such managers might delegate most of their responsibilities because they no longer feel competent or they may reduce their role to that of an administrator whose sole aim is to scrutinise every detail. Others become devil's advocates. Their negative approach doesn't stimulate creativity and indeed thwarts efforts towards any change.

Remedies for failing performance due to lack of ability

To begin with, once a manager has ascertained that lack of ability is the primary cause of poor performance, a performance review interview should be scheduled.

Five principal tools, which we will call the 5 Rs, are available for overcoming poor performance problems due to lack of ability:

- Refurbish
- Retrain
- Redeploy
- Reassign
- Release

We will discuss these in the order in which they should be considered by a manager.

Unless the manager has overwhelming evidence that the problem stems from low aptitude, it is wise to assume initially that it is due to a lack of resources or training. This gives the subordinate the benefit of the doubt and reduces the likely defensive reaction to an assessment of inadequate aptitude.

Refurbish   The refurbish option focuses on the support needs of the job, including personnel, budget and political clout. Asking, 'Do you have what you need to perform this job satisfactorily?' allows the subordinate to express his or her frustration over inadequate support. Managers should be cautioned that poorly performing subordinates typically blame external causes (Snyder *et al.*, 1978; Staw *et al.*, 1983). One should investigate the subordinate's complaints about lack of support in detail to determine their validity. But even if employees exaggerate their claims, starting your discussion of poor performance in this manner signals your willingness to help them to solve the problem from their perspective. The techniques and style of the discussions were detailed in Chapter 3, 'Effective Communication'.

Retrain   This is the next option to consider. The need for a continuous upgrading of skills is vital in rapidly changing work. Training programmes can take a variety of forms. For example, many firms are using computer technology more in education. This can involve interactive technical instruction and business games that simulate problems likely to be experienced by managers in the organisation. More traditional forms of training include subsidised external courses and in-house technical or management seminars. Some companies have experimented with company sabbaticals to release managers or technical specialists from the pressure of their work to enable them to concentrate on retraining. It is becoming more common for large organisations – the BBC, Allied Domecq – to sponsor their managers to take MBA programmes. General Motors in the UK, along with many other organisations, have established a learning facility in the Luton site open to all employees (and now the citizens of the area), where individuals can learn at their own pace subjects of their own choice. Retraining is becoming a continuous process and part of the new ideal: the 'Learning Organisation'.

Redeploy   If re-supplying and retraining are insufficient remedies for poor performance, the next step should be an attempt to redeploy. The employee maintains his or her position while the various components of the work are analysed. Once the job has been explored as a process it can be seen whether the particular employee can contribute to the accomplishment of the same task in some restructured form.

For example, an assistant may be brought in to handle many of the technical details of a first-line supervisor's position, allowing the supervisor more time to focus on people development or to develop a long-term plan to present to upper management.

Reassign   If a revised job description is unworkable or inadequate, the fourth alternative is to reassign the poor performer – to find new jobs more suited to the individual's capabilities. This may be, and often is, to a position of less responsibility or to one requiring less technical knowledge or interpersonal skills. For example, a medical specialist in a hospital who finds it increasingly difficult to keep abreast of new medical procedures but has demonstrated management skills might be shifted to a full-time administrative position.

Release   If retraining and creative re-definition of the task have not worked and there are no opportunities for reassignment in the organisation, releasing the employee from the organisation should be considered. This option may well be outside the immediate superior's responsibility and constrained by union agreements or company policies, but all too often chronic poor performers who could be released are not, because management chooses to side-step a potentially unpleasant task. Instead these individuals are put on the shelf, out of the mainstream of activities, where it is perceived that they cannot cause any problems. Even when this action is motivated by humanitarian concerns ('I don't think he could cope with being sacked'), it often produces the opposite effect to that desired. Actions taken to protect an unproductive employee from the embarrassment of dismissal just substitute it with the humiliation of being ignored. Obviously, dismissal is a drastic action that should not be taken lightly. However, the consequences for the unproductive individuals and their co-workers of allowing them to remain after everything else has been tried, should be weighed carefully. It is in the interest of both the company and those individuals that, if nothing else is possible, they are encouraged to do something new with their lives.

Fostering a motivating work environment

Once we have considered the above, we can move on to the issues of motivation. Effective managers devote considerable time in gauging and improving their subordinates' motivation. The tragedy of the Higgins case is the inability of the company chairman to diagnose the real reasons for the poor performance of the directors of engineering. He ignored the structural problems and attributed the repeated failures to inadequacies in those occupying the position. No matter how well qualified and highly motivated Steve Spencer's replacement, it is likely that he or she will also be judged as incompetent.

In a major contribution to management thinking, Douglas McGregor (1960) labelled a focus on the incompetence of workers as 'Theory X'. The basic assumption of Theory X is that people really do not want to work hard or assume responsibility. Accepting this assumption, the job of a manager is reduced to that of someone who coerces, intimidates, manipulates and supervises. McGregor provides an alternative set of assumptions, which he terms 'Theory Y'. In Theory Y employees want to do a good job and assume more responsibility. Management's

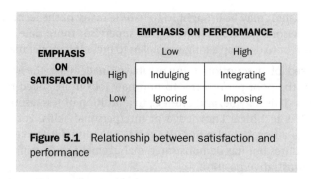

Figure 5.1 Relationship between satisfaction and performance

role is thus to enable workers to reach their potential by productively channelling their motivation to succeed. Unfortunately, McGregor believed most managers subscribe to Theory X assumptions about workers' motives.

The alleged prevalence of the Theory X view brings up an interesting series of questions about motivation:

- What is the purpose of teaching motivation skills to managers?
- Should managers learn these skills so that they can help employees to reach their potential?
- Are we teaching these skills to managers so that they can more effectively influence their employees' behaviour?

These questions naturally lead to a broader set of issues regarding employee/ management relations. Assuming that a manager feels responsible for maintaining a given level of productivity, is it also possible to be concerned about the needs and desires of employees? In other words, are concerns about employee morale and company productivity compatible, or are they mutually exclusive?

Contemporary research combined with training programmes (Greene, 1972; Levering *et al.*, 1984) support the position that concerns about morale and performance can co-exist. As shown in Figure 5.1, effective motivational programmes not only can, but must, focus on increasing both satisfaction and productivity.

A high emphasis on satisfaction with a low emphasis on performance represents an irresponsible view of the role of management. Managers have the job of making their organisations run effectively and measuring individual performance is part of that job. Managers who emphasise satisfaction to the exclusion of performance will be seen as nice people, but their management style undermines the respect of their subordinates. It is easy to imagine an organisational climate that is so focused to the goal of satisfaction that management becomes dominated by the needs of employees and the resulting club-like atmosphere hinders good performance.

A strong emphasis on performance to the exclusion of satisfaction is equally ineffective. This time instead of indulging, the manager is imposing. There is little concern for how employees feel about their jobs. The boss gives the orders and the employees must follow them. Employees who feel exploited are unhappy employees, and as Peter Herriot and Carole Pemberton (1995a/b) state, they have three strategies open to them:

- Get out
- Get safe
- Get even.

None of these is a satisfactory outcome for an organisation. While exploitation may increase productivity in the short run, its long-term effects generally decrease productivity through increased absenteeism, employee turnover and, in some cases, even sabotage and violence. We will discuss the work of Herriot and Pemberton with its implications to empowerment in the next chapter.

When managers emphasise neither satisfaction nor performance, they are ignoring their responsibilities. There is no real leadership, in the sense that employees are given neither priorities nor direction. Paralysed between what they consider to be mutually exclusive options of emphasising performance or satisfaction, managers choose neither. The resulting neglect, if allowed to continue, may ultimately lead to the failure of the unit for which the manager has responsibility.

An integrated approach emphasises performance and satisfaction in balance. Instead of accepting the conventional wisdom that says competing forces cancel each other out, enterprising managers capitalise on the tension between the combined elements and forge new approaches. However, this does not mean that both objectives can be fully satisfied every time. Some trade-offs occur naturally in certain situations – but, in the long run, both should be given equal consideration.

The integrated view of motivation proposes that while sustaining employee morale is important, it should not overshadow management's responsibility to hold people accountable for results. Managers should avoid the twin traps of working to engender high employee morale for its own sake or pushing for short-term results at the expense of long-term commitment. The best managers have productive people who are also satisfied with their work environment (Nadler and Lawler, 1977; Jordan, 1986).

This view of management is reflected in David Bradford and Allan Cohen's management guide, *Managing for Excellence* (1984, p. 21).

> Excellence requires budget and control systems, formalised ways to appraise, reward and promote long-range planning and forecasting systems, and division of labour and job descriptions. The dilemma for the manager, then, is not whether control needs to be exercised, but how to see that it is exercised without weakening the motivation of those with energy and enthusiasm.

Hersey and Blanchard (1982) contend that organisational success and performance are affected by the congruence between the objectives of the managers and those of their subordinates. They argue that the organisation can only accomplish its objectives if those of the managers and subordinates are supportive of each other and the organisation. As a result managers need to adjust their style to meet the needs of their subordinates. These needs are measured in terms of their psychological maturity. As maturity develops and subordinates are increasingly willing and able to accept greater responsibility, the manager's style changes from telling to selling to participating, and finally to delegation.

Table 5.1 Six elements of an integrative motivation programme

1. Establish moderately difficult goals that are understood and accepted.
   Ask: 'Do my people understand and accept what is required of them?'
2. Remove personal and organisational obstacles to performance.
   Ask: 'Do my people feel it is possible to achieve their objectives?'
3. Use rewards and discipline appropriately to prevent unacceptable behaviour and encourage exceptional performance.
   Ask: 'Do people accept the standards and that it is not acceptable to be a poor performer?'
4. Provide salient internal and external incentives.
   Ask: 'Do people feel the rewards used to encourage high performance are worth the effort?'
5. Distribute rewards equitably.
   Ask: 'Are work-related benefits distributed fairly?' or 'Are work-related rewards the correct way of rewarding individuals?'
6. Provide timely rewards and honest feedback on performance.
   Ask: 'Are the ways we reward effort useful and efficient?' Do people know where they stand in terms of current performance and long-term opportunities?'

Elements of an integrated motivation policy

The purpose of the remainder of this book is to lay out a step-by-step programme for creating an integrated, synergistic motivation policy grounded in the belief that employees can simultaneously be high performers and achieve personal satisfaction. Given that one of the critical management skills discussed in this book involves proper diagnosis of performance problems, each section will be introduced using the appropriate diagnostic question shown in Table 5.1.

The key assumptions underlying these six elements are:

1. Employees start out motivated. Therefore, a lack of motivation may be fostered by misunderstood or unrealistic expectations.
2. The role of management is to create a supportive, problem-solving work environment in which the necessary resources to perform a task are provided.
3. Rewards should encourage high personal performance, which is consistent with management objectives.
4. Motivation works best when it is based on self-management.
5. Individuals should be treated fairly.
6. Individuals deserve timely, honest feedback on work performance.

Goal setting

Managers should begin assessing the motivational climate of their work environment by asking: 'Do subordinates understand and accept my performance expectations?' The foundation of an effective motivation policy is proper goal setting (Locke and Latham, 1984; Miner, 1984). The importance of goal setting is so well recognised that it has been included in several formal management tools, such as *management by objectives* (MBO). MBO is, however, regarded by many people as only partially providing an answer, ignoring the basic human needs for recognition (Stewart and Joines, 1987, p. 72). Stewart and Joines argue that people need the recognition of others and that to recognise only failure is a profound mistake, leading to increased failure. People need to be recognised for themselves and what they do. Therefore, motivational goal setting has three critical components: the goal-setting process itself, goal characteristics and feedback – for the persona and the task, good or bad.

A common theme of this book is that: *The way you do things is very often as important as what you do.* This means that the process used to set goals must be understood and accepted if it is to be effective. Subordinates are more likely to own and accept the goals if they feel they were part of the generation process (Locke *et al.*, 1981). This is especially important if the work environment is unfavourable (Latham *et al.*, 1988). For example, a goal might be inconsistent with accepted practice, require new skills, or exacerbate poor management/employee relations. The key to goal acceptance is an overall management attitude of understanding and support (Latham and Locke, 1979). If this is not shown, then imposed goals or task assignments will probably be viewed as unwelcome demands – subordinates will question the premises underlying the goal or assignment and will comply only with reluctance.

The ideal is sometimes difficult to achieve – a manager is sometimes given goals by his or her superiors without due consultation, and has to pass them on without sufficient understanding or discussion. However, if people believe management is committed to involving them wherever possible, they will accept that there are times when things have to be done without question.

For example, a computer programming unit may not have any say about which application programs are assigned to the group or what priority is given to each incoming assignment. However, the manager can still involve unit members in deciding how much time to allocate to each assignment (*What is a realistic goal for completing this task?*) or who should receive which job assignment (*Which type of programmes would you find challenging?*).

In 1974, Volvo, the Swedish motor car manufacturer, opened a new and radically different car assembly plant in Kalmar. It cost 10 per cent more than a traditional factory to build, and the aim was to reduce the high labour turnover and absenteeism present in other Volvo plants.

Partially-built cars were transported on computer-controlled pods to work stations where groups of 15 to 20 workers (30 teams in the factory) performed a number of tasks, agreeing among themselves who would do what. The employees could rest in specially-designed rest areas whenever they wished, as long as certain agreed daily production targets were met. Workers enjoyed greater responsibility and jobs could be rotated.

Between 1977 and 1983 the production time per car fell by 40 per cent, the number of quality defects was reduced by 39 per cent and labour turnover was reduced from 25 per cent to 5 per cent. Volvo found that they needed fewer supervisors

Table 5.2 The concept of FRAME

	Explanation	Example – of a postal delivery worker (the information is NOT based on actual data but is intended for example only)
Few	Often the minutiae of a job is given. Goals should be confined to WHAT needs to be done, omit the HOW it is to be done and be as few in number as is reasonable. We are talking about STANDARD.	Deliver all the mail to the specified address or return it to the sorting office. Be available for work at 05.30 on regular days or notify the office in good time. Be honest.
Realistic	Miracles should not be called for; avoid such words as 'with no exceptions'. If the impossible is called for in any part of the goals it will become standard practice to allow ALL the goals to slip.	Obviously some mail will not be delivered or delivered to the wrong addresses perhaps because of mad dogs or snow. There must be an acceptable escape clause.
Agreed	Agreement means that the boss and the subordinate set up a dialogue – coaching and consultation as we discussed in the book – *Effective Communication*. The dialogue will weed out the impossible and establish commitment from the subordinate. Agreement is subject to constant feedback and review.	A new postal delivery worker will need to be coached to achieve the standard goals in the first place and every postperson is affected by external changes – population increase and decrease, new roads, etc.
Measured	The usual units are TIME and RESOURCES. This will be achieved at £s cost in three months. For example, milestone X MUST be achieved, but it would also be good (excellent performance is judged by achieving) if milestone Y could be achieved.	The corporate objectives would be something like: 98% of all first-class letters and packages delivered within 24 hours and 90% of all second-class mail within 2 days within the agreed budget. The postperson's objectives must be inside the corporate objectives and within his of her span of responsibility.
Explicit	We have often found catch-all goals in job definitions – e.g., 'and such other activities and duties as the management may require'. If things are part of standard duties they should be laid down.	What we have said must be clear and put in such a way that new postpersons can inherit it successfully.

and that production flexibility was much higher. As a result a number of similar techniques were applied in their other plants.

Sources: *Financial Times*, 19 April 1985; *Management Today*, June 1988

The Volvo experience had faults and was not continued in its original form – the systems being largely taken over by what we will call 'Japanese management practices'.

The introduction of Japanese management practices has had a marked effect on British industry as the research of White and Trevor (1983) has shown:

Japanese managers are well-regarded by their British subordinates because of their technical competence and their concern for high-quality work which was seen as reflecting upon workers and the reputation of the company. Being part of a competent and effective enterprise was what appeared to attract the British workers. So much so that the workers actually regarded with apprehension the eventual replacement of expatriate managers by the home-grown variety!

But the Japanese have had to adapt their approach to take account of the culture gap. For instance, Toyota UK's head of human resources, Brian Jackson, admitted that British employees ask five times as many questions as their Japanese counterparts. When they opened their plant in Derby in December 1992 they laid down in great detail a standard way of undertaking any procedure. Employees were expected to stick to them but were also encouraged to recommend improvements. Everything is geared to continuous improvement – what the Japanese call *Kaizen*.

At Toyota, employees, known as 'members', are divided into groups of about 25, headed by group leaders and subdivided into teams of around four or five with team leaders. Each group normally meets about two or three times a day: first thing in the morning, mid-morning and mid-afternoon, each time for five or ten minutes, to discuss problems and ideas. Anyone can pull a cord or push a button to call over their team leaders if there is a problem and the line will stop if it cannot be resolved in seconds. Toyota doesn't just pay lip service to ideas. For instance, in 1991 there were 40 suggestions from each Toyota employee in Japan and 90 per cent of them were adopted.

Shifting from process to content, research has shown that goal characteristics significantly affect the likelihood that the goal will be accomplished (Locke *et al.*, 1981). Effective goals are specific, consistent and appropriately challenging. Woods and Whitehead (1993) discussed the concept of FRAME and goal setting. The acronym FRAME stands for **F**ew, **R**ealistic, **A**greed, **M**easured and **E**xplicit (Table 5.2).

Specific goals reduce misunderstanding about what behaviours will be rewarded. Admonitions such as 'be dependable', 'work hard', 'take initiative', or 'do your best' are too general and impossible to measure, and therefore of limited motivational value.

The manager has to be very clear in making the FRAME and during the process of translating the organisational goals to the individual goals. Handy's discretional goals need even more development of the organisational goals. Only with a full understanding of what is happening can staff be motivated to enlarge their horizons towards the excellent performance.

American Express sees employee performance in three bands:

- Giving the customer what he or she wants and asks for – OK Bronze
- Giving the customer what he or she wants but has not asked for – Good Silver
- Giving the customer a service that he or she does not yet even know that he or she wanted – Excellent Gold

To provide an excellent or even a good service obviously needs a great deal of understanding of organisational objectives and capabilities.

Goals should also be consistent. An already hardworking general manager in a bank's regional office complains that she cannot increase both the number of reports she writes in a week and the amount of time she spends at branch offices, talking to employees and customers. Goals that are inconsistent in the sense that they are logically impossible to accomplish simultaneously, or incompatible in the sense that they both require so much effort that they cannot be accomplished at the same time, create frustration and alienation. When subordinates complain that goals are incompatible or inconsistent, managers should be flexible enough to reconsider their expectations.

One of the most important characteristics of goals is the perceived level of difficulty (Latham and Locke, 1979; Locke *et al.*, 1981). Simply stated, hard goals are more motivating than easy goals. One explanation for this is called *achievement motivation* (Atkinson and Raynor, 1974). A simple example of achievement motivation in action is the process of doing a crossword puzzle. The feeling of achievement in completing a full acrostic, as opposed to a simple tabloid word test is much greater. According to this perspective, workers size up new tasks in terms of (1) their chances for success and (2) the significance of the anticipated accomplishment.

Based only on perceived likelihood of success, one would predict that those who seek success would choose an easy task to perform, because the probability for success is the highest. However, most of us also take into account the significance of completing the task. To complete a goal that anyone can reach is not rewarding enough for highly motivated individuals. They need to feel that the accomplishment represents a meaningful achievement. Given their desire for success and achievement, it is clear that these workers will be most motivated by challenging but attainable goals.

The final component of an effective goal programme is feedback (Latham and Locke, 1979; Ivancevich and McMahon, 1982). Feedback provides opportunities for clarifying expectations, adjusting goal difficulty and gaining recognition. Therefore, it is important to provide benchmark opportunities for individuals to determine how they are doing. Reporting at milestones in the progress of projects is particularly critical when the time required to complete the total job or reach a goal is very long. Examples of milestone reporting would occur for an organisation writing a large computer program or raising a large sum of money for charity. In these cases feedback should be linked to accomplishing intermediate stages or completing specific components. The full use of the 'small wins' strategy was discussed in the Chapter 3, 'Effective Problem Solving'.

The discussion of goal setting has several important implications for managers.

- First, attention to the goal-setting process is important. Effective goals are both understood and accepted. Whether or not goals are imposed or self-generated, the process needs management support. One of the keys to self-motivation is self-determination. Therefore, in a situation where a goal (what) is predetermined, management would do well to encourage participation regarding the means (who, how, when).

- Second, the characteristics of goals matter a great deal. The purposes of setting goals are to increase motivation and direct activity. These objectives are most likely to be accomplished when the goals are specific, consistent and difficult.

- Third, individuals should receive frequent feedback on their progress. A key ingredient of an effective motivational programme is sustainability, and a key to sustain ability is feedback.

Helping subordinates achieve their objectives

One of the key ingredients of an effective goal-based programme is a supportive work environment. After goals have been set, the manager's focus should shift to facilitating a successful outcome and monitoring how individual goals fit into a whole. Therefore, the second diagnostic question is: *Do subordinates feel it is possible to achieve this goal?*

Help from management must come in many forms, including making sure that the worker has the required abilities for the job, providing the necessary training, securing needed resources, and encouraging co-operation and support from other work units. In other words, it is the manager's job to make the paths leading towards the targeted goals easier for the subordinate to travel. An enabling role will vary considerably across individuals, organisational settings and tasks. If subordinates believe that strong management support is needed, but don't receive the help required, then the manager will probably be regarded as being part of the employees' problem, rather than the source of solutions. By the same token, when management intervention is not needed or expected, managers who are constantly involved in the details of subordinates' job performance will be viewed as meddling and unwilling to trust. This view of management is incorporated in the views of House and Mitchell (1974).

The key question it addresses is 'How much help should a manager provide?' In response, the level of involvement should vary according to how much subordinates need to perform a specific task; how much they expect, in general; and how much support is available to them from other organisational sources.

The key task characteristics are structure and difficulty. A task that is highly structured (as reflected in the degree of built-in order and direction), and relatively easy to perform does not require extensive management direction. If managers offer too much advice, they will come across as controlling, bossy or nagging, since it is already clear to the subordinates what they should do. On the other hand, for an unstructured and difficult task, management's direction and strong involvement in problem-solving activities will be seen as constructive and satisfying.

The second factor that influences the appropriate degree of management involvement is the expectations of the subordinates. Three distinct characteristics influence expectations: desire for autonomy, experience and ability. Individuals who prize their autonomy and independence prefer managers with a highly participative, unobtrusive, leadership style because it gives them more latitude for controlling what they do. In contrast, people who prefer the assistance of others in making decisions, establishing priorities and solving problems welcome greater management involvement. However, a self-motivated workforce may well *evolve* its goals, and the manager's most difficult task is that of making sure that this evolution does not miss the overall goals of the organisation.

There is a direct connection between a worker's ability/experience level and the appropriate management style. Capable and experienced employees feel they need less assistance from their managers because they are adequately trained, know how to obtain the necessary resources and feel capable of handling political entanglements with their counterparts in other units. They appreciate managers who give them their head, but periodically check to see if further assistance is required. On the other hand, it is frustrating for relatively new employees or those with marginal skills, to feel that their manager has neither the time nor interest to listen to basic questions.

Jackson and Humble (1994) see middle managers as the key to the implementation of plans to satisfy customers and improve profitability. As more work becomes knowledge based requiring highly skilled workers, and as individuals understand that poor motivation is a lack of skilled leadership not a lack of desire within people, middle managers must become enablers, trainers, and coaches. Jackson and Humble see the factors influencing the change for the middle manager's role to include:

1. The information technology revolution.

2. The absence of a hierarchically based career path.

3. The need for greater creativity in organisations.

4. The increasing focus on values.

The concept of the manager out of control of the situation – the other side of the issue of subordinate autonomy – was brought to notice by the classical Hawthorne Studies (Roethlisberger and Dickson, 1939). In these studies a group of workers from the Hawthorne Works of the General Electric Company in the USA were found to be able to organise their own work, in spite of major management intervention and very strong control mechanisms.

> The General Electric managers, later with support of academics, decided to see how work performance could be influenced by such external factors as heating and lighting levels. The job of assembling railway break equipment had been analysed in detail using Work Study techniques. For the experiment, they used two rooms of assembly workers doing virtually identical jobs. One room was to act as control and was left untouched during the tests, while the other was subjected to the series of planned experiments on working conditions. The results baffled the researchers at the time and are still the subject of argument and discussion. Put very briefly, whatever they did to the experimental group, including restoring all the conditions to their original settings, production improved.

The initial conclusion was that the very act of recognising and showing an interest in workers was sufficient to improve productivity. The more contentious issue was understanding how it was possible for productivity to rise in an area where every movement in break assemble had literally been studied scientifically, noted and optimised. Further observation and discussion with the workers led to the conclusion that the work group itself had influenced the work study setting of rates to allow slack.

Workers appeared to be able to adjust production and the bonus rates as they wished. Phrases such as – *Marge is getting married and needs the money; It's coming up to Christmas and we ALL need the money; If we are seen to work anywhere near capacity, they will only change the norms and reduce the bonus rates* – appeared in the interviews. These remarks somehow did not fit the elitist views of management – people on the shop floor could think!

When the work was originally done the paradigm used by the people who have used the Hawthorne case study was of workers somehow beating the system and, surprisingly, being able to outsmart the managers.

We hope this book will challenge the elitist mindset. We see that an understanding that the workers at General Electric, as intelligent independent human beings, had asserted their rights to autonomy. With this assertion they had unleashed their creativity. By accepting the benefits of their autonomy we can begin to understand empowerment. We will move further along this route in the next chapter. Here we will look at the issue of empowerment, developing autonomy in individuals and groups, as a method of motivation.

James Gleick (1988) provides us with an elegant way of combining the concept of FRAME and motivation by empowerment. Willing workers given clear goals are the ONLY people who understand the minutiae of what is happening in their jobs. They, with the minimum of guidance, can make patterns of the inevitable local chaos of real working situations. Management beyond the minimum facilitation and monitoring reduce the creative dynamic or make useful order out of specific chaos.

Guest (1956) estimated that foremen perform between 237 and 1,073 separate transactions a day. There is no possibility that these can be scheduled or planned. Foremen are managing chaos and so are we all. The solution is to look at the processes in an organisation and to decide at what level WE are able to allow workers to be empowered – setting clear FRAMED goals and letting go of inessential regulations and controls. Semler (1993) talks about controlling the bottom line and not how long people spend in the washroom.

One of the important lessons from this discussion is that managers must tailor their management style to specific conditions. Although managers should, in general, focus on facilitating task accomplishment, their level of direct involvement should be calibrated to the nature of the work and the availability of organisational support, as well as the ability and experience of the individuals. This conclusion underscores how important it is that managers understand the needs and expectations of their subordinates.

Richard Branson is one of the most inspirational leaders in British industry and he describes his philosophy as 'Small is Beautiful', a quote from Schumacher, from his book of the same name.

In the early days we certainly could not have afforded a lavish corporate headquarters in central London. But now we don't have one as a matter of choice. It's not just that people prefer working in smaller units, but it helps to avoid some of the hazards of growth, and especially the tendency for managers to lose touch with the basics – and usually the customers and the staff. So when one of our companies gets beyond a certain size, we split it up into smaller units. Even though Virgin Records was, before we sold it to Thorn EMI, the sixth largest record company in the world, we managed through a series of semi-independent labels and subsidiaries in twenty countries. This 'keep it small' rule gives us the opportunity to pursue a policy of promoting from within the Group – a policy which clearly has a positive effect on morale. It means you can give more than the usual number of managers the challenge and excitement of running their own business. The kind of people I want running Virgin companies are those who would probably become millionaires if they weren't working for us. So if you can give them a stake in the company, they can become millionaires by working within Virgin.

Source: Cannon (1993)

Appropriate use of rewards and discipline

Once clear and achievable goals have been established and the means to achieve them understood and provided from the top, the next step in an effective motivational programme is to encourage goal accomplishment by linking performance to rewards and penalties. We need to be able to answer the question – Does the reward system recognise better than average performance? Our discussion of this important element of an effective motivational programme is based on two related principles:

1. In general, managers should link rewards to performance, rather than seniority.
2. Managers should be aware of the company objective transformed into their sub-objects and manage accordingly – acknowledging individuals, rewarding and reinforcing productive behaviour and penalising non-productive behaviour.

If rewards are not based on performance, then high performers are likely to feel they are receiving less than they deserve. Accepting that the most important individuals in any organisation are its high performers, systems to improve motivation in an organisation should be geared to keeping high performers happy. This observation has led some organisational consultants to use the performance ratings of individuals leaving an organisation as an index of the organisation's motivational climate. If the best people are leaving then a great deal is being said about the climate.

Some organisations are attempting to remove what they see as class barriers at work. There is pressure to reduce status distinctions by calling everyone 'associates', eliminating reserved parking spaces and removing titles from company visiting cards.

Charles Walls, a Public Relations and Marketing organisation in Leeds UK, found that job titles and distinctions were preferred by their customers. While going a long way to removing 'class' distinctions from their employees they allowed two sets of visiting cards to be used: internally Kate Brown, Charles Walls plc . . . and externally Mrs K. Brown, Head Media Consultant, Charles Walls plc . . .

Enforced egalitarianism may well remove the vital link between performance and rewards, and as a consequence find it difficult to attract and retain strong performers. Money rewards, however linked to performance, are not everything and some employees work for status – the key to the executive washroom is a big incentive for many of us.

In his book *Maverick* (1993) Ricardo Semler, CEO of the Brazilian company Semco, would not entirely subscribe to the views we have expressed. His company, making a range of white goods on licence, is certainly one of the most progressive and profitable organisations in the challenging financial climate of Brazil. Semler would claim to have a very highly motivated workforce by any standard, but provides, as a matter of policy, *no fringe benefits* in the way of 'social services' for his employees. Commercial success is always the objective.

Semco does call its employees Partners, Co-ordinators and Associates and the organisation decided, in 1989, to allow Partners and Co-ordinators to set their own pay. This did not go far enough for Paulo Pereira, ex-personnel manager and now Co-ordinator of Semco, who went even further. He proposed the concept of 'risk salary' – 'Each one of you now has the correct salary, according to your own estimate of your worth. I propose to pay you a little less, but in return will give you the possibility of earning more.'

Semler's view, that 'social' programmes that are unrelated to the company's core business are unnecessary, has led to much reappraisal in industry. The Social Clubs are being challenged and in their place we are finding more and more open learning services, day care and attractive share option programmes for all staff.

Semco is not alone in pioneering new motivational practices where commercial reality is coupled with empowerment and the concept of 'everybody wins'.

Zeneca, a company formed out of ICI to make speciality chemicals, working on the same concept as Semco, decided to remove all overtime payments. They set down a very simple principle: *Staff are only at work when they are needed. When they are at work they are effectively employed.*

Zeneca has annualised the expected hours for which each employee is paid and added a significant and agreed number of hours for good measure. When there is no work, the employees stay at home; when there is work, they are called in and are expected to do any job for which they are able and competent and can be done by them safely. With the potential merging of Astra and Zeneca it is interesting to see whether the process will continue. Rover, on the insistence of its owners, BMW, is beginning a form of annualising.

The strange by-product of the annualising observed by Zeneca is that the jobs that used to be done in overtime, have vanished. An example is plant-cleaning – the old practice was to do plant clean-ups during overtime and weekends; now the plant is kept clean and often no special cleaning shift is required. The same loss of a need for cleaning was noticed by British Gypsum operating the same principle.

Continental Can with 30 per cent of the total world production of cans, used a similar scheme and noted a similar 'remarkable' cure. The UK beer trade demanded a '15 per cent free beer offer' can which, obviously, is taller than the standard can. In production before the annualising of hours, the taller cans repeatedly fell over and had to be set up again by workers on overtime. Miraculously, with the new system, the cans did not fall over.

Such motivational programmes involve cultural change and cultural change does not occur without risk. Scott-Morgan (1994) estimates that only 17 per cent of re-engineering of work processes are truly satisfactory. Raissa Rossiter (1995) agrees with 8 per cent for a high-level of success and 37 per cent for accepting changes as satisfactory, when she looked at several hundred companies implementing changes in working practice in the UK. Chang (1995), discussing continuous improvement projects, gives the failure rate as 63 per cent.

Technological constraints sometimes make it difficult to link rewards and individual performance perfectly. For example, people working on a motor car assembly line, or chemists working on a group research project, have little control over their personal productivity.

> In a performance-related pay scheme, car assembly workers found they had a grudge. Their actual performance was damaged by a number of factors outside their control, including design defects, which stopped the line, and problems with the supply of spare parts.
>
> Another very large organisation stopped its productivity bonus scheme because of difficulties in currency transactions for its overseas operations.
>
> In both cases, in our opinion, the grudges were justified and should have been foreseen.

In these situations, rewards linked to the performance of the work group will foster group cohesion and collaboration and partially satisfy the individual member's concerns about fairness. When it is not possible to assess the performance of a work group, a performance bonus should be considered. While the merits and technical details of various group and organisational reward systems are beyond the scope of this book, the point is that managers should link valued rewards and good performance at the lowest possible level of aggregation (Lawler, 1971; Greene, 1972). A word of warning should, however, be expressed about general bonus payments: they may very soon be regarded as a right, and if withdrawn may become a significant *demotivator*.

A second word of warning is concerned with team bonus arrangements. In principle the team is given a task and rewarded accordingly. The individuals within the team *may* perceive this as unfair.

> Bradford Management Centre, as many other business schools, use group assignments as part of the learning process. The written and oral presentations of these assignments went towards the ultimate grading of individual students. The process was abandoned by many of the staff because of the interminable claims of

unfairness of the system: *I carried that man, he did nothing towards the project except in the final presentation and he gets the same marks as me!*

Team bonus systems need to fit the culture but are very often a real problem when highly competitive individuals are concerned.

Effects of managers' responses

An effective motivational programme goes beyond the design of the organisational reward system. Managers must also recognise that their daily interactions with subordinates can be important motivators. It is difficult for even highly sensitive and aware managers to fully understand the impact of their actions on the behaviour and attitudes of subordinates. Unfortunately, some managers don't even try to monitor these effects. The danger of this lack of awareness is that it may lead to managerial actions which actually reinforce undesirable behaviours in their subordinates. This has been called 'the folly of rewarding A while hoping for B' (Kerr, 1975). For example, a director of R&D with a low tolerance for conflict and uncertainty may unwittingly undermine the company's avowed objective of developing highly creative products by punishing work groups that do not exhibit unity or a clear, consistent set of priorities. Further, while avowing the virtue of risk, the manager may punish failure; while stressing creativity, he or she may kill the spirit of the idea champion. These actions will encourage a work group to avoid challenging projects, suppress debate and develop task into routines.

The do's and don'ts for encouraging subordinates to assume more initiative (shown in Table 5.3) demonstrate the power of managers' actions in shaping behaviour. Actions and reactions that might appear insignificant to the boss often have strong reinforcing or extinguishing effects on subordinates. Hence the truism, 'Managers get what they reward, not what they want', and its companion, 'People do what is inspected, not what is expected'. Indeed, the reinforcing potential of managers' reactions to subordinates' behaviours is so strong that it has been argued that 'the best way to change an individual's behaviour in a work setting is to change his or her manager's behaviour' (Thompson, 1978). Given the considerable leverage managers have over their subordinates' motivation to reach optimal performance, it is important that they learn how to effectively use rewards and punishment to consistently produce positive intended results.

The process of linking rewards and punishment with behaviours in such a manner that the behaviours are more or less likely to persist is called 'operand conditioning' by psychologists (Skinner, 1953; Nord, 1975). This approach uses a wide variety of motivational strategies that involve the presentation or withdrawal of positive or negative reinforcers, or the use of no reinforcement whatsoever. Although there are important theoretical and experimental differences in these strategies, such as between negative reinforcement and punishment, for the purposes of our discussion we will simply focus on three types of management responses to employee behaviour: no response (ignoring), negative response (disciplining) and positive response (rewarding).

The trickiest strategy to transfer from the psychologist's laboratory to the manager's work environment is no response. Technically, what psychologists refer to as

Table 5.3 Guidelines for fostering subordinates' initiative

Do	Don't
Ask, 'How are we going to do this? What can I contribute to this effort? How will we use this result?', thus implying your joint stake in the work and results.	Imply that the task is the employee's total responsibility, that they hang alone if they fail. Individual failure means organisation failure.
Use an interested, exploring manner, asking questions designed to bring out factual information.	Don't play the part of an interrogator, firing questions as rapidly as they can be answered. Also, avoid asking questions that require only 'yes' or 'no' replies.
Keep the analysis and evaluation as much in the employees' hands as possible by asking for their best judgement on various issues.	Don't react to their presentations on an emotional basis.
Do present facts about organisation needs, commitments, strategy, and so on, which permit them to improve and interest them in improving what they propose to do. Don't demand a change or improvement in a peremptory tone of voice or on what appears to be an arbitrary basis.	Don't redo their plans for them unless their repeated efforts show no improvement.
Ask them to investigate or analyse further if you feel that they have overlooked some points or over-emphasised others. Ask them to return with their plans after including these additional items.	Take their planning papers and cross out, change dates, or mark 'no good' next to certain activities.

Source: Kellogg (1979, p. 121)

extinction is defined as behaviour followed by no response whatsoever. However, in most managerial situations, people develop expectations about what is likely to follow their actions, based upon their past experience, office stories, etc. Consequently, what is intended as a non-response, or a neutral response, is generally interpreted as either a positive or negative response. For example, if a subordinate comes into your office complaining bitterly about a co-worker, and you attempt to discourage this type of behaviour by changing the subject or responding in a low, unresponsive monotone voice, the subordinate may view this as a form of rejection. If another subordinate sheepishly slips a report on your desk a week late, and you ignore his behaviour totally because you are busy with other business, he may be so relieved at not being reprimanded for his tardiness that he actually feels reinforced in failure.

These simple examples underscore an important point: any behaviour that is repeatedly exhibited in front of a boss is being rewarded, regardless of the boss's intention – *I don't want to encourage that type of behaviour, so I'm purposely ignoring it.* By definition, if behaviour persists, it is being reinforced. If an employee is chronically late or continually submits sloppy work, the manager must ask where the reinforcement for this behaviour is coming from – *What am I or others doing to reinforce this behaviour?* Consequently, while extinction plays an important role in the learning process if it is conducted in strictly controlled laboratory conditions, it is a less useful technique in organisational settings because the interpretation of a supposedly neutral response is impossible to control.

The disciplining approach basically involves responding negatively to an employee's behaviour with the intention of discouraging future occurrences. For example, if an employee is consistently late, a supervisor may reprimand him or her with the hope that this action will decrease the employee's tardiness. Nagging subordinates for their failure to obey safety regulations is another example. Yet problems occur with the disciplining approach to shaping behaviour when it is used excessively or inappropriately.

The rewarding approach consists of linking desired behaviours with outcomes the employee will value. Thus praise is given immediately when a trainee completes a report on time. If an executive takes the initiative to solve a thorny, time-consuming problem on his or her own, that person can be allowed to take time out after a business trip. The value of positive reinforcement, according to Tom Peters and Bob Waterman (1982), is that it keeps the management/subordinate dialogue focused on nudging good things onto the agenda, rather than ripping bad things off the agenda.

Disciplining and rewarding are both viable and useful techniques and each has its place in the effective manager's motivational repertoire. However, the techniques can produce quite different modifications of behaviour. Discipline should be used to begin the process of modifying unacceptable behaviours. However, once an individual's behaviour has reached an acceptable level, the process will cease to have a positive effect. It is very difficult to encourage employees to perform exceptional behaviours through nagging, threatening, or related forms of discipline. At a certain point subordinates fight against the criticism and don't improve their behaviour any further. Further improvement will only come through positive reinforcement when the employees have control over achieving what they want and, therefore, have the incentive to reach a level of exceptional performance. The same is true of rewarding behaviour. The positive reinforcement of desired behaviour has its downside in the avoidance of negative criticism – the manager needs to know when he or she should be firm.

The process of balance between discipline and rewards with unacceptable and acceptable behaviours, respectively, highlights two common misapplications of reinforcement principles. First, it helps us to understand better why top performers frequently get upset because they feel management is too soft on those people who are always messing things up. Feeling that it is good management practice to always be upbeat and optimistic, some managers try to ignore the seriousness of mistakes. They also try to temper the consequences by personally fixing errors, by encouraging high performers to be more tolerant and patient. Other managers feel so uncomfortable with confronting personal performance problems that they are willing to overlook all but the most flagrant mistakes.

Although there is a lot to be said for managers having a positive attitude and giving poor performers the benefit of the doubt, failure to reprimand and redirect is not effective over the long term. The work unit's morale is likely to suffer and, of course, the poor performer's behaviour is not improved.

Second, just as some managers find it unpleasant to issue reprimands for poor performance, other managers have difficulty praising exceptional performance. As a result, subordinates complain that 'nothing ever satisfies him'. This misapplication of the negative response, behaviour-shaping strategy is just as dysfunctional as the indiscriminate use of praise. These managers mistakenly believe that the best way to motivate people is by always keeping expectations a little higher than their subordinates' best performance and then chiding them for their imperfection. In the process, they run the risk of burning out their staff or inadvertently encouraging lower performance – *We'll get told off anyway, so why try so hard?* Furthermore, the irony is that they create a competitive, self-defeating situation in which the subordinates look forward to the boss making mistakes.

Unfortunately, many managers genuinely believe that this is the best way to manage – in all situations. They define their role as that of a sheepdog, circling the perimeter of the group, barking and nipping at the heels of those who begin to stray. Such managers establish a fairly broad range of acceptable behaviours and then limit their interactions with employees to restraining those who exceed the boundaries. This negative, desultory style of management creates a demoralising work environment and does not foster exceptional performance. Instead, workers are motivated to stay out of the boss's way and avoid doing anything unusual or untried. Innovation and involvement are extinguished, and mundane performance becomes not only acceptable but desirable.

> A laboratory managed by ex-scientists was a very happy place to work. People worked and lived together with very little to show between the levels of seniority. Positive reinforcement was the name of the game: 'That was a really good bit of work, perhaps a little late and over budget but . . . good all the same. A really good bit of work.'
>
> Appraisals were also self-congratulatory exercises until the company running the laboratory ran into trouble. Appraisals suddenly mattered and had to match the very patchy performance of the laboratory as a whole. Poor appraisal ratings meant that one's job was in jeopardy and the bad news had to be given by the managers who had *never* given anything but praise before. At the end of the appraisal process several employees had taken legal action against the company and it was suspected that the efficiency of the laboratory took about three months to recover.

Having looked at the consequences of misapplying rewards and discipline, we will now turn our attention to the proper use of behaviour-shaping techniques.

Improving behaviours

The mark of exceptional managers is fostering exceptional behaviour in their subordinates. They do this by making unacceptable behaviours acceptable and transforming the acceptable into exceptional. They are designed to avoid the harmful

Table 5.4 Guidelines for improving behaviours

Reprimand
1. Identify the specific inappropriate behaviour. Give examples. Indicate that the action must stop.
2. Point out the impact of the problem on the performance of others, on the unit's mission, etc.
3. Ask questions about causes and explore remedies.

Redirect
4. Describe the behaviours or standards you expect. Make sure the individual understands and agrees that these are reasonable.
5. Ask if the individual will comply.
6. Be appropriately supportive. For example, praise other aspects of their work, identify personal and group benefits of compliance; make sure there are no work-related problems standing in the way of meeting your expectations.

Reward
7. Identify rewards that are important and of value to the individual.
8. Link the attainment of desirable outcomes with incremental, continuous improvement.
9. Reward (including using praise) all improvements in performance in a timely and honest manner.

effects typically associated with the improper use of discipline discussed in the previous section (Hamner, 1974; Luthans and Kreitner, 1975; Maier, 1973) and they ensure the appropriate use of rewards (Latham *et al.*, 1981).

The nine steps for improving behaviours are shown in Table 5.4. These are organised into three broad initiatives: reprimand, redirect and reward. Steps 1–6 (reprimand and redirect) are used to extinguish unacceptable behaviours and replace them with acceptable ones. Steps 4–9 (redirect and reward) are used to transform acceptable behaviours into exceptional behaviours.

As shown in Table 5.4, an important principle to keep in mind regarding the use of reprimands is that the discipline should immediately follow the faulty behaviour and focus only on the specific problem. This is not an appropriate time to dredge up old concerns or make general, unsubstantiated accusations. The focus of the discussion should be on eliminating a problem behaviour, not on making the subordinate feel bad. This will reduce the hostility typically engendered by being reprimanded.

Secondly, an alternative behaviour should be suggested along with the discussion of what is seen to be wrong. It is important that persons being reprimanded understand how they can receive rewards in the future. This process of redirection reduces the despair that occurs when people feel they are likely to be punished no matter what they do.

If expected behaviours are not made clear, then individuals may stop the inappropriate behaviour but feel lost, not knowing how to improve. Keep in mind that the ultimate goal of any negative feedback should be to transform inappropriate behaviours into appropriate behaviours (in contrast to simply punishing a person for causing a problem or making the boss look bad). The lingering negative affects of a reprimand will wear off quickly if the manager is soon able to reward desirable behaviours. This goal can be achieved only if workers know how they can receive positive outcomes.

Experienced managers know it is just as difficult to transform acceptable behaviours into exceptional ones. Helping a mediocre subordinate catch the vision of moving up to a higher level of desire and commitment can be very challenging. This process begins at Step 4 (redirect) by first clearly describing the goal or target behaviour. The goal of skilled managers is to avoid having to administer any negative responses and especially to avoid trial-and-error learning among new subordinates. This is done by clearly laying out their expectations and collaboratively establishing work objectives, following the guidelines discussed in an earlier section on goal setting. In addition, it is a good idea to provide an experienced mentor, known for exceptional performance, as a sounding board and role model.

Providing salient rewards

Having established a link between performance and outcomes (via rewards and discipline) as part of an integrative motivational programme, it is now important to focus on the salience of various outcomes – here will only discuss rewards. Rewards are only effective if they are valued by the recipient. Our fourth diagnostic question, then is – *Do subordinates feel the rewards used to encourage high performance are worth the effort?*

One of the biggest mistakes made in implementing a basically sound and well-intentioned reward system is that managers wrongly assume that they understand their subordinates' preferences. The manager's lament – *What does Roger expect, anyway? I gave him a bonus, and he is still complaining to other members of the accounting department that I don't appreciate the hours he puts in* – says something about the manager's understanding of Roger. He might well have preferred a day off or the manager thanking him in public – both alternatives cost less to the company.

The old accepted view on composition of portfolios of salient rewards is that they somehow change with job grade (LeDue, Jr, 1980 and others). Alisdair Galloway (1990) working with a large UK sample, found that designing an ideal portfolio of salient rewards was a difficulty for many managers. His work is summarised in Table 5.5.

Predicting the rewards that will be most salient to their subordinates requires individual knowledge and not approximations based on organisational status. The very simple conclusion arising from Table 5.5 is that the average rankings are meaningless and the individual differences by far outweigh any collective considerations.

A flexible reward system helps managers to avoid the second common motivation mistake – projecting their preferences onto subordinates. Ineffective managers don't spend enough time with their workers to understand their personal needs and goals. In these circumstances, it is quite natural for managers to assume that their subordinates share their views regarding the attractiveness of various job outcomes. This judgement error is reflected in the case below:

Table 5.5 Ranking of salient rewards for management, monthly and hourly paid workers

Salient reward	Management		Monthly paid staff		Hourly paid staff	
	Average	S.D.	Average	S.D.	Average	S.D.
Wages/Salary	2.56	(2.84)	2.85	(4.87)	2.10	(3.96)
Job security	4.03	(4.42)	3.48	(7.17)	2.96	(5.42)
Job variety and interest	2.09	(3.28)	3.35	(5.84)	4.52	(5.45)
Freedom from supervision	5.78	(3.56)	5.73	(5.85)	6.69	(4.67)
Working conditions	6.34	(3.53)	5.37	(4.99)	3.67	(4.48)
Union org./activity	8.56	(2.00)	7.93	(5.23)	6.38	(6.06)
Promotion prospects	4.31	(3.46)	5.70	(7.94)	7.44	(5.99)
Control own work environment	4.34	(4.64)	5.10	(5.41)	6.10	(3.84)
Workmates	6.81	(3.19)	6.07	(5.43)	5.15	(3.98)

S.D. = standard deviation
Source: Galloway (1990)

A fashion garment manufacturer lost its most skilled machinist – the person who was able to structure a new style into a form where it could be costed for production. The obvious choice for a replacement was an outstanding member of the production team who was widely respected by her shift mates. The woman was duly promoted and given a significant rise in salary. She was also given a little workroom of her own where she could concentrate on her work without being bothered by the noise and bustle of the shop floor.

She handed in her notice in a matter of weeks – it was the noise and bustle that she liked – combined with being respected as the most skilled and experienced worker to turn to in time of trouble.

Unfortunately, this scenario is all too common. The practice of assuming similarity in preference across the workforce wouldn't be so detrimental if the population were relatively homogeneous.

A 30-year longitudinal study of employee values at AT&T in America indicates that this is clearly not the case. For example, when new employees were asked during the 1950s what their goals were, 52 per cent focused on moving quickly up the corporate ladder into senior, well-paid jobs. In contrast, this goal was foremost in the minds of only 29 per cent of the respondents surveyed in the 1970s. The second sample expressed less loyalty to the job and placed more emphasis on personal fulfilment. In the words of the survey's co-ordinator, Doug Bray, 'It's a whole new idea permeating society. People feel that no job is worth killing themselves for or devoting their lives to' (Colby, 1985).

Effective managers avoid problems by having frequent, personal and constructive discussions with their subordinates – a view covered at length in Chapter 2. The discussions should focus on career opportunities, life goals and personal priorities. Another technique used by managers is discussing with subordinates recent significant changes in the careers of common acquaintances. Subordinates' responses to changing circumstances affecting others (pay, personal time, travel requirements, etc.) often provide useful insights into their personal preferences.

Maslow's 'Hierarchy of Needs' suggests that they are a priority as well as a dynamic element in human needs. At the most basic level, individuals begin with physiological needs – the basic life-sustaining needs. Once these are satisfied they can consider personal security, and when these two needs are satisfied they proceed to the first of the social needs – belonging and relating to others. Once this simple belonging need is satisfied we move to the higher need for esteem, and finally to the need for personal growth – self-actualising, as Maslow called it. As individuals fulfil a specific need, they shift their focus to the next highest hierarchical level. Satisfied needs become dormant until a dramatic shift in circumstances rekindles them. For example, a middle-level executive who is fired during a hostile take-over may suddenly find that her interest in personal growth is overwhelmed by a pressing need for security. Other major events that may shift an individual's need priorities include a birth or death in the family, marriage or divorce, job transfer or job obsolescence, promotion or demotion. Effective managers are sensitive to shifts in their subordinates' needs and accommodate those shifts by implementing flexible organisational reward systems.

Internal job characteristics

All of the outcomes shown in Table 5.5, except for the single *Job variety and interest*, are called external motivators because someone else controls them – typically by the immediate supervisor. The supervisor can show appreciation for a job well done, offer job security, show personal loyalty to employees and provide good working conditions. It is a slightly different story for *interesting work*. Although managers control the components of a job, they have no direct control over whether a specific subordinate finds a job interesting. In other words, the outcomes associated with an interesting job come from internal motivators – factors inherent in the job itself, not from any particular actions of the manager.

Effective motivators understand that the person–job interface has a strong impact on how an employee performs the job. No matter how many externally controlled rewards managers use, if their subordinates find their jobs to be uninteresting and unfulfilling, performance will suffer. Attention to internal motivators is particularly critical in situations where managers have relatively little control over the organisational incentive system. In these cases it is often possible to compensate for lack of control over external factors by fine-tuning the person–job fit.

Job design is the process of matching job characteristics and workers' skills and interests. One popular job-design model proposes that particular job dimensions cause workers to experience specific psychological reactions, called 'states'. In turn, these psychological reactions produce specific personal and work outcomes. Figure 5.2 shows the relationship between the core job dimensions, the psycholo-

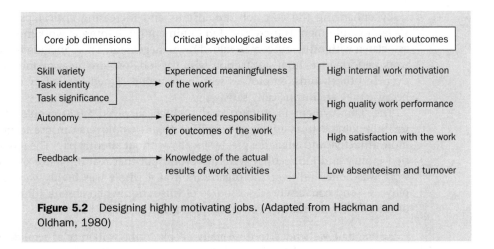

Figure 5.2 Designing highly motivating jobs. (Adapted from Hackman and Oldham, 1980)

gical states they produce, and the resulting personal and work outcomes (Hackman and Oldham, 1980). According to this model, intrinsically satisfying tasks are high on skill variety, task identity, task significance, autonomy and feedback.

The more variety in the skills a person can use in performing the work, the more the person perceives the task as being meaningful or worth while. Similarly, the more an individual can perform a complete job from beginning to end (task identity), and the more the work has a direct effect on the work or lives of other people (task significance), the more the employee will view the job as meaningful. On the other hand, when the work requires few skills, only part of a task is performed, and there seems to be little effect on others' jobs, experienced meaningfulness is low. The effect of such dull repetitive work on job performance will again depend on the individual.

> A legend has it that a major chocolate manufacturer gives IQ tests to all its job applicants for shop floor work. If the candidates pass the minimum standard – *they do not get the job*. The history was that the brighter applicants worked harder, quicker and better than their duller counterparts for a few weeks but their work rates then began to fall. Left in the job, they became troublemakers. It was noted also that several workers resisted any attempt to develop their jobs: 'It's a lousy job anyway – I do it for the money and I think about what I'm going to do when the whistle blows. I don't want to have to think.'

Autonomy can in itself enrich work and improve performance. As we have said before, the nearer a manager can achieve the role of monitor and facilitator the better. Autonomy can be increased by instituting flexible work schedules, decentralising decision making, or removing selected formalised controls such as the ringing of a bell to indicate the beginning and end of the work day.

Finally, the more feedback individuals receive about how well their jobs are being performed, the more knowledge of results they have. This permits workers to understand the benefits of the jobs they perform. This can be enhanced by increasing employees' direct contact with clients or by giving them feedback on how their jobs fit in and contribute to the overall operation of the organisation.

By enhancing the core job dimensions and increasing critical psychological stages, job fulfilment is increased. Job fulfilment (high internal work motivation) is associated with other outcomes valued by management. These include high-quality work performance, high satisfaction with the job, low absenteeism and high turnover. In other words, employees who have well-designed jobs enjoy doing them because they are intrinsically satisfying.

The 'Employment in Britain' study, which surveyed 5,000 people in the UK in 1992 pointed to relatively inexpensive means employers can use to make jobs more attractive and engender greater loyalty without altering pay. The report found that money and job security were important but that real influence over the way work was done and over the organisation as a whole was highly valued by employees – and conversely was a source of frustration when absent. John Stevens, a director of the Institute of Personnel Management in the UK, said:

> At one time we tended to treat many people in the workforce as semi-detached from the organisation. Competitive pressure, decentralisation and awareness of the need to develop skills, have merged what people want out of work and what employers want out of people.

This view is echoed by Hakan Astrom, COE of Sweden's Kabi pharmaceutical group. He says:

> Management is about getting the commitment and involvement of those around you. You get the best out of people if they have been involved in the decision-making process and understand why a decision has been taken.

Michael Hammer and James Champy in their book *Re-engineering the Corporation* (1993) developed five principles of job design:

1. *Combine tasks*. A combination of tasks is, by definition, a more challenging and complex work assignment. It requires workers to use a wider variety of skills, which makes the work seem more challenging and meaningful. For example, telephone directories at the former Indiana Bell Telephone company used to be compiled in 21 steps along an assembly line. Through job redesign, each worker was given the responsibility for compiling an entire directory.

2. *Form identifiable work units so that task identity and task significance may be increased*. Clerical work in a large insurance firm was handled by 80 employees organised by functional task. The tasks listed included opening letters, entering information into the computer, sending out statements. Work was assigned based on current workload by a supervisor over each functional area. To create higher levels of task identity and task significance, the firm reorganised the clerical staff into eight self-contained groups. Each group handled all business associated with specific clients.

3. *Face the customer* (Greenberg and Ornstein, 1984). A client relationship involves an ongoing personal relationship between an employee (the producer) and the customer, internal or external. We need to recognise the

value of this relationship, both for the motivation of the work teams and the organisation. At its highest level, for example, at GKN each customer group – Toyota, GM, BMW/Rover – has a specific GKN team attached. At much lower levels, Cottage Holidays, a holiday home lease business, identifies a particular telephone sales representative with each customer and this person acts as the name contact point.

4. *Grant more authority for making job-related decisions to those actually doing the jobs.* As supervisors delegate more authority and responsibility, their subordinates' perceived autonomy, accountability and task identity increase. Historically, workers on motor car assembly lines have had little decision-making authority. However, in conjunction with increased emphasis on quality, many plants now allow workers to adjust their equipment, reject faulty materials, and even shut down the line if a major problem is evident.

5. *Open feedback channels.* Workers need to know how well or how poorly they are performing their jobs if any kind of improvement is expected. It is imperative that they receive timely and consistent feedback which allows them to make appropriate adjustments in their behaviour to enable them to receive desired extrinsic and intrinsic rewards. The traditional approach to quality assurance is to 'inspect it in'. A separate quality assurance group is assigned to check the quality of the production team. The emerging trend is to give producers responsibility for checking their own work. If it doesn't meet quality standards, they immediately fix the defect. Following this procedure, workers receive immediate feedback on their performance. Although this management tool, like others, involves trade-offs, the record of job redesign interventions is impressive. Depending on the approach taken, firms typically report a substantial increase in productivity, work quality and worker satisfaction (reflected in lower rates of absenteeism). For example, General Electric realised a 50 per cent increase in product quality as a result of their job-redesign programme, while the absenteeism rate among data-processing operators at Traveller's Insurance decreased by 24 per cent (Kopelman, 1985).

In conclusion, this section on external and internal rewards contains two important lessons for managers:

- Make sure there are enough reward options available for subordinates so that they can personally select salient outcomes. The motivational potential of an effective goal-setting process and a supportive, obstacle-removing management style is dissipated if employees feel that high performance will not lead to personally attractive outcomes.

- Recognise that both external and internal outcomes are necessary ingredients of effective motivational programmes. In particular, ignoring internal outcomes can significantly undermine a manager's efforts to motivate. Most people want interesting and challenging work activities. Good wages and job security will do little to overcome the negative effects of individuals' feeling that their abilities are being under-utilised.

Equitable distribution of rewards

Once the appropriate rewards have been determined for each employee, the manager must then consider how to distribute the rewards (Greenberg, 1982). This brings us to concerns about equity. Any positive benefits of salient rewards will be negated if workers feel they are not receiving their fair share. (As in the previous section, we will focus only on rewards. However, the same basic principles also apply to the equitable use of discipline.)

Equity refers to workers' perceptions of the fairness of rewards. Evaluations of equity are based on a social comparison process in which workers individually compare what they are getting out of the work relationship (outcomes) with what they are putting into the work relationship (inputs). Outcomes include such items as pay, fringe benefits, increased responsibility and prestige, while inputs may include hours worked and work quality, as well as education and experience. The ratio of outcomes to inputs is then compared to corresponding ratios of other individuals judged to be an appropriate comparison group. The outcome of this comparison is the basis for beliefs about fairness.

If workers experience feelings of inequity, they will behaviourally or cognitively adjust their own, or fellow workers', inputs and/or outputs. In some cases, this may lead to a decrease in motivation and performance. For example, if employees believe that they are being underpaid, there are a number of options available to them. Cognitively, they may rationalise that they really are not working as hard as they thought they were; thus they reduce the perceived value of their own inputs. Alternatively, they might convince themselves that co-workers are actually working harder than they thought they were. Behaviourally, workers can request a pay rise (increase their outcomes), or they can decrease their inputs by leaving a few minutes early each day, decreasing their effort, deciding not to complete an optional training programme, or finding excuses not to accept difficult jobs.

Other obvious inequities may also be exposed. For example, the hourly rate of a worker may not be keeping up with recent skill upgrades or increased job responsibilities. The act of identifying and correcting legitimate inequities generates enormous commitment and loyalty. For example, a manager in the computer industry felt he had been unfairly passed over for promotion by a rival. Utilising the company's open-door policy, he took his case to a higher level in the firm. After a thorough investigation, the decision was reversed and the rival reprimanded. The individual's response was – *After that, I could never leave the company*.

The important thing to keep in mind about equity and fairness is that we are dealing with perceptions. Consequently, whether they are accurate or distorted, legitimate or ill-founded, until proven otherwise they are both accurate and legitimate in the mind of the perceiver. A basic principle of social psychology is: 'That which is perceived as being real is real in its consequences.' Therefore, effective managers should constantly perform a check on the 'real world' as perceived by their employees. Ask questions such as: *If you were asked to match yourself with one or two others in this department, who would you pick as most similar? What criteria for promotions, pay rises and so on do you feel management should be placing more/less emphasis on? Relative to others similar to you in this organisation, do you feel your job assignments, promotions and so on are appropriate? Why do you think Anne was recently promoted over John?*

Providing timely rewards and accurate feedback

Minimising the time lag between behaviours and feedback, and providing accurate feedback are our final topics in the integrated approach to motivation. The sixth diagnostic question is: *Are we getting the most out of our rewards by administering them on a timely basis, as part of the feedback process?*

We have emphasised that employees need to understand and accept perform-ance standards. They should feel that management is working hard to help them to reach their performance goals and they should feel that the internal and external rewards available are personally attractive. They should also believe that rewards and reprimands are being distributed fairly and should feel that these are being administered primarily on the basis of performance and not prejudice.

All these elements are necessary for an effective motivational programme, but they are not sufficient. Rewards, even highly valued ones, lose their motivating potential unless they are dispersed at the correct time. It is the timing of the rein-forcement that lets the employee know which behaviours are being encouraged. Giving a reward at the wrong time can inadvertently increase an undesirable behaviour. For example, giving a long overdue fully warranted rise to a subordinate during an interview in which she or he is complaining about the unfairness of the reward system, may reinforce complaining rather than good work performance. Moreover, failure to give a reward when a desired behaviour occurs will make it even more difficult to increase that behaviour in the future. If the owners of a new business have delayed the implementation of a promise to grant share options for the core start-up team as compensation for their low wages and 70- to 80-hour work-weeks, the willingness to sustain this pace on only promises and dreams may begin to wane.

The importance of timing becomes obvious when one considers that all the research findings supporting the value of operand conditioning as a motivational system assume that outcomes immediately follow behaviours. Imagine how little we would know about behaviour-shaping processes if, in the experiments with birds and rats described in psychology textbooks, the food pellets were dropped into the cage several minutes after the desired behaviour occurred.

Unfortunately, although timing is a critical aspect of reinforcement, it is frequently ignored in everyday management practice. The formal administrative apparatus of many organisations often delays for months the feedback on the con-sequences of employee performance. It is customary practice to restrict in-depth discussions of job performance to formally designated appraisal interviews, which generally only take place once every 6 or 12 months. This delay between perform-ance and feedback dilutes the effectiveness of any rewards or discipline dispensed as a result of the evaluation process.

In contrast, effective managers understand the importance of immediate, spon-taneous rewards. They use the formal performance evaluation process to discuss long-term trends in performance, solve problems inhibiting performance, and set performance goals. But they don't expect these infrequent, general discussions to provide much motivation. For this they rely on brief, frequent, highly salient performance feedback. For example, at least once a week they seek some opportunity to praise desirable work habits among their subordinates.

Peters and Waterman (1982) stress the importance of immediacy with a story of the Hewlett Packard Banana award.

> At Hewlett Packard, a technical advance was desperately needed for survival in the company's early days. Late one evening, a scientist rushed into the president's office with a working prototype. Dumbfounded at the elegance of the solution and bewildered as to how to reward it, the president bent forward in his chair. He rummaged through most of the drawers in his desk, found something, leaned over the desk to the scientist, and said, 'Here!' In his hand was a banana, the only reward he could immediately put his hands on. From that point on, the small gold banana pin has been the highest accolade for scientific achievement at Hewlett Packard.

Effective rewards are spontaneous rewards. Rewards that become rituals, especially those linked to formal performance appraisal systems, lose their immediacy. A prize awarded to almost anyone soon loses its appeal.

There is a second critical aspect – the consistency of giving rewards. Administering a reward every time behaviour occurs is called continuous reinforcement. Administering rewards on an intermittent basis (the same reward is always used but is not given every time it is warranted) is referred to as partial, or intermittent reinforcement. Neither approach is clearly superior; they both have drawbacks. Continuous reinforcement represents the fastest way to establish new behaviour. For example, if a boss consistently praises a subordinate for writing reports using the manager's preferred format, the subordinate will readily adopt that style in order to receive more and more rewards. However, if the boss suddenly takes an extended leave of absence, the learned behaviour may cease because the reinforcement pattern is broken. In contrast, while partial reinforcement results in very slow learning, it is very resistant to extinction. The persistence associated with gambling behaviour illustrates the addictive nature of a partial reinforcement schedule. Not knowing when the next pay-off may come preserves the myth that the jackpot is only one more try away.

This information about reinforcement timing derives from experimental research and has important implications for effective management.

- First, it is important to realise that continuous reinforcement systems are very rare in organisations unless they are mechanically built into the job, as in the case of the piece-rate pay plan. Seldom are individuals rewarded every time they make a good presentation or effectively handle a customer's complaint. When we recognise that most non-assembly-line work in an organisation is typically governed by a partial reinforcement schedule, we gain new insights into some of the more frustrating aspects of a manager's role. For example, it helps explain why new employees seem to take forever to catch on to how the boss wants things done. It also suggests why it is so difficult to extinguish outdated behaviours, particularly in older employees.

- Second, given how difficult it is for one manager consistently to reinforce the desired behaviours in a new employee (or an employee who is going through the reprimand, redirect, reward cycle), it is generally a good idea to use a team effort. By sharing your developmental objectives with other individuals who interact with the target employee, you increase the likelihood of the desired behaviours being reinforced during the critical early stages of improvement. For example, if a division head is trying to encourage a new member of staff to become more assertive, he or she might encourage other staff members to respond positively to the newcomer's halting efforts in meetings or private conversations.

Content and intent of the feedback

Before concluding this discussion of feedback, it is important to add a brief note about the message itself. The second part of the sixth diagnostic question related to feedback is: *Do subordinates know where they stand in terms of current performance and long-term opportunities?*

In addition to the timing of feedback, the content of the feedback and motivation guiding the feedback process can have a powerful impact on the target individual's willingness and ability to improve. If the content is inaccurate, improvement is frustratingly difficult. If the message is masked in subterfuge and obscured by mixed messages, the credibility of the entire motivational system is undermined.

Chapter 4, 'Constructive Communication', discusses the premise that it is much more difficult to deliver bad news than good news. That chapter contains a number of guidelines and principles for providing negative feedback in a non-threatening, constructive manner. Our purpose now is not to review that material, but only to stress the importance of being honest and open with subordinates regarding their current performance and future opportunities. The time-worn excuses

- *We don't want to run the risk of discouraging marginal performers*
- *We shouldn't tell people their future promotion opportunities are in jeopardy because upper management doesn't like their style*

generally constitute efforts to cloak managers' feelings of discomfort under the guise of doing what's best for the subordinate.

Reluctance to share unflattering or unhopeful feedback is usually an admission by managers that they are unwilling to spend sufficient time with the individuals receiving negative feedback to help them to understand it thoroughly, put it in perspective, consider options and explore possible remedies. It is simply easier to pass on an employee with a poor performance record or unrealistic expectations to the next supervisor than it is to confront the problem directly, provide honest and constructive feedback, and help the individual to respond appropriately. That is why many feel that supportive communication of negative performance information is the most difficult to master, and therefore the most highly prized management skill.

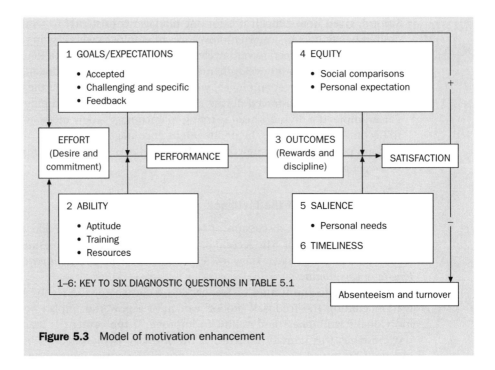

Figure 5.3 Model of motivation enhancement

SUMMARY

Our discussion of enhancing work performance has focused on specific analytical and behavioural management skills. We first introduced the fundamental distinction between ability and motivation. Several diagnostic questions for determining whether inadequate performance was due to insufficient ability were discussed. Also, a five-step process for handling ability problems (refurbish, retrain, redeploy, reassign and release) was outlined. Motivation was introduced by stressing the need for placing equal emphasis on concerns for satisfaction and performance. The remainder of the chapter focused on the second skill by presenting the six elements of an integrative approach to motivation.

Our discussions of ability and motivation are summarised in Figure 5.3.

This flowchart depiction of the factors influencing performance and satisfaction underscores the interdependence between the various components. Skilled managers incorporate all elements of this model into their motivational efforts rather than concentrate only on a favourite subset. There are no shortcuts to effective management. All elements of the motivation process must be included in a total, integrated programme for improving performance and satisfaction.

The flowchart begins with effort. Remember that motivation is manifested as work effort, and that effort consists of desire and commitment. Motivated employees have the desire to initiate a task and the commitment to do their best. Whether their motivation is sustained over time depends on the remaining elements of the model, which are organised into two major segments:

1. The effort → performance link

2. The outcomes → satisfaction link

These two crucial links in the motivational process can best be summarised as rhetorical questions pondered by individuals asked to work harder, change their work routine, or strive for a higher level of quality.

First, 'If I put in more effort, am I likely to be able to perform up to expectations?'

Second, 'Am I likely to find being a high performer personally rewarding?'

Beginning on the left side of the model, we see that the combination of ability and goals determines the extent to which effort is successfully transformed into performance. Individuals understand that their personal effort, by itself, is insufficient. In the discussion of the path–goal theory of leadership, the importance of fitting the right job to the right person, and providing the resources and training necessary to perform the job were emphasised. In addition, these factors must be combined with effective goal setting (understanding and accepting moderately difficult goals) if increased effort is to result in increased performance.

Proceeding to the outcomes → satisfaction segment of the model, the importance of reward salience and perceived equity stand out. The subjective value individuals attach to incentives for performance reflects their personal relevance or salience. Rewards with little personal value have low motivational potential. In addition, individuals must believe that the rewards offered are appropriate, not only for their personal performance level but also in comparison with the rewards received by 'similar' employees. These subjective factors combine with the timeliness and accuracy of feedback to determine the motivational potential of rewards.

Based upon the perceptions of their outcomes, workers will experience varying degrees of satisfaction or dissatisfaction. Satisfaction creates a positive feedback loop, increasing the individual's motivation, as manifested by increased effort. Dissatisfaction, on the other hand, results in decreased effort and, therefore, lower performance and rewards. If uncorrected, this pattern may ultimately result in absenteeism or high staff turnover.

Behavioural guidelines

This discussion has been organised around key diagnostic models and questions. These serve as the basis for enhancing the skills of (1) properly diagnosing performance problems; (2) initiating actions to enhance individuals' abilities and (3) strengthening the motivational aspects of the work environment.

The process for properly diagnosing the causes of poor work performance is summarised in the form of six diagnostic questions, shown in Table 5.1. (A 'decision tree' version of these questions is presented later in the Skill Practice section.) The behavioural guidelines governing this process is:

1. *Investigate work performance problems fully.*

- Separate ability from motivation problems.
- Agree on a programme for improving performance.
- Release a poor performer only as a last resort.

The key guidelines for enhancing ability and creating a highly motivating work environment are:

2. *Define an acceptable level of overall performance or specific behavioural objectives clearly.*

- Make sure the individual understands what is necessary to satisfy your expectations.
- If possible, formulate goals and expectations collaboratively.
- Make goals as difficult as possible.

3. *Help remove all obstacles to reaching the objective.*

- Make sure the individual has adequate technical resources, personnel and political support.
- If a lack of ability appears to be hindering performance, use the refurbish, retrain, redeploy, reassign or release series of remedies.

4. *Make rewards and discipline contingent on high performance or drawing nearer to the behavioural objective.*

- Examine the behavioural consequences of your 'non-responses'. (Ignoring a behaviour is rarely interpreted as a neutral response.)
- Consistently discipline individuals whose effort is below your expectations and their capabilities.

5. *When discipline is required, treat it as a learning experience for the individual.*

- Specifically identify the problem and explain how it should be corrected.
- Use the reprimand and redirect guidelines in Table 5.4.

6. *Transform acceptable into exceptional behaviours.*

- Reward each level of improvement.
- Use the redirect and reward guidelines in Table 5.4.

7. *Use reinforcing rewards that appeal to the individual.*

- Allow flexibility in individual selection of rewards.
- Provide both appealing external rewards as well as satisfying and rewarding work (intrinsic satisfaction).
- To maintain salience, do not overuse rewards.

8. *Check subordinates' perceptions regarding the equity of reward allocations periodically.*

- Correct wrong perceptions that serve as the basis for equity comparisons.

9. *Minimise the time lag between behaviours and feedback on performance, including the administration of rewards or reprimands. (Spontaneous feedback shapes behaviour best.)*

- Provide honest and accurate assessments of current performance and long-range opportunities.

Skill Analysis

CASE STUDY **5.1**

ELECTRO LOGIC

Electro Logic (EL) is a small R&D firm located in the Midlands (UK), near to a major university. Its primary mission is to perform basic research on, and the development

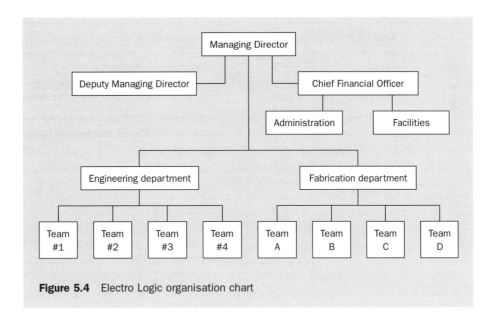

Figure 5.4 Electro Logic organisation chart

of, a new technology called Very Fast, Very Accurate (VFVA). Founded four years ago by David Morton, an electrical engineering professor who invented the technology, EL is primarily funded by government contracts, although it plans to market VFVA technology and devices to commercial organisations within the year. Figure 5.4 shows the management structure of EL.

The government is very interested in VFVA, as it will enhance radar technology, robotics, and a number of other important defence applications. EL recently received the largest small-business contract ever awarded by the government to research and develop this or any other technology. Phase I of the contract has just been completed and the government has also agreed to Phase II contracting.

The organisational chart of EL is shown in Figure 5.4. Current membership is 75 of which about 90 per cent are in engineering. Heads of staff are supposedly appointed according to their knowledge of VFVA technology and their ability to manage people. In practice, the managing director of EL hand-picks these people based on what some might call arbitrary guidelines – most of the staff leaders are David Morton's graduate students. There is no predetermined time frame for advancement up the hierarchy. Salary increases are, however, directly related to performance appraisal evaluations.

The technicians work directly with the engineers. These people generally have a university degree. They are trained on the job, although some have gone through a local college's programme on micro-technology fabrication. The technicians perform the mundane tasks of the engineering department: running tests, building circuit boards, manufacturing VFVA chips, and so on. Most are full-time employees, paid by the hour. The engineering titles and qualifications are shown in Table 5.6.

The administrative staff is composed of the staff head (a woman with an MBA from a major university), accountants, personnel director, graphic artists, purchasing agent, project controller, technical writers/editors and secretaries. Most of the

Table 5.6   Engineering titles and requirements

Title	Required qualification
Member of technical staff	HNC, Member or Associate of professional body
Senior member of technical staff	BSc (ENG) with two years industrial experience and membership of professional body
Research engineers	PhD or equivalent – membership of professional body and 7 years experience
Research scientist	PhD or 1st Hons BSc, appropriate research experience
Senior research scientist	DSc or relevant PhD Member or Fellow or professional body. Appropriate industrial and research experience

people on the administrative staff are women. All are hourly paid employees except the staff head, the personnel director and the project controller. The graphic artists and technical writers/editors are part-time employees. External contractors are used for maintenance and are controlled by the Facilities Department. EL is housed in three different buildings, and the primary responsibility of the facilities staff is to ensure that the facilities of each building are in good working order. Additionally, the facilities staff are often called upon to remodel parts of the buildings as staff numbers continue to grow. EL anticipates a major recruiting campaign. In particular, it is looking for more technicians and engineers. Before this recruiting campaign, however, the managing director of EL hired an outside consultant to assess employee needs as well as the morale and overall effectiveness of the firm. The consultant has been observing EL for about three weeks and has written up some notes of her impressions and observations of the company.

Consultant's notes from observations of Electro Logic

Facilities   EL is housed in three different buildings. Two are converted houses and one is an old school building. Senior managers and engineers are in the school; others are scattered between the houses.

Meetings   Weekly staff meetings in the main building are held to discuss objectives and to formulate and review milestone charts.

Social interaction   A core group of employees interact frequently on a social basis, e.g., sports teams, parties. The administration staff celebrate birthdays at work. The managing director occasionally attends.

Work allocation   Engineers request various tasks from the support staff – technicians and administrative unit personnel. There is obviously some discretion used by the staff in assigning priorities to the work requests, based on rapport and desirability of the work.

Turnover   The highest turnover is among administration personnel and technicians. Exit interviews with engineers indicate that they leave because of the company's crisis-management style, better opportunities for career advancement and security in larger organisations, and overall frustration with EL's pecking order. Engineers with the most responsibility and authority tend to leave.

Salaries and benefits   In general, wages at EL are marginal by national and local standards. A small group of scientists and engineers do make substantial salaries and have a very attractive benefits package, including share options. Salaries and benefits for new engineers tend to be linked to the perceived level of their expertise.

Offices and facilities   Only EL's managing director, deputy managing director, and chief financial officer have their own offices. Engineers are grouped together by project. There is very little privacy in these work areas and the noise from the shared printer is distracting. The head of administration shares a pod with the personnel director, facilities head and the project controller. One to three secretaries per building are located in or near the reception areas. The large building has an employee lounge with three vending machines. There is also a coffee and tea area. The smaller buildings have only a cold drinks machine in the reception area.

Consultant's interviews with employees

After making these observations, the consultant requested interviews with a cross-section of the staff in order to compile a company survey. Below are excerpts from these interviews.

Pat Donaldson, senior member of technical staff

Consultant: What is it about Electro Logic that gives you the most satisfaction?

Pat: I really enjoy the work. I've always liked to do research and working on VFVA is an incredible opportunity. Just getting to work with David Morton (EL's managing director and VFVA's inventor) again is exciting. I was his student about six years ago. He really likes to work closely with his people – perhaps sometimes too closely. There have been times when I could have done with a little less supervision.

Consultant: What is the least satisfying aspect of your work?

Pat: Probably the fact that I'm never quite sure that we'll be funded next month, given the defence budget problems and the tentativeness of our research. I've got a family to consider and this place is not the most financially stable. Perhaps it will change once we get more into commercial production.

Consultant: You've offered some general positives and negatives about Electro Logic. Can you be more specific about day-to-day dealings? What's good and bad about working here on a daily basis?

Pat: You're sure this isn't going to get back to anyone? OK? Well, in general I'm not satisfied with the fact that too often we end up changing horses midstream. In the past seven months, three of my engineers and four of my technicians have been pulled off my project onto projects with deadlines which were nearer than mine. Now I'm faced with a deadline and I'm supposed to be getting more staff – but I'll have to spend so much time briefing them that it might make more sense for me to just finish the project myself. On the other hand, David keeps telling me that we have to be concerned with EL's overall goals, not just our individual concerns – you know, we have to be 'team players' and 'good members of the family'. It's hard to remember that, though, when deadlines are bearing down and you know your neck is on the line, team player or not. But if you go along with this philosophy and don't complain, the higher-ups treat you well. Still, it seems to me there's got to be a better way to manage these projects.

Consultant: What are the positive aspects of your daily work?

Pat: The people are great to work with. I tend to be a social person and I really like playing in the darts team. I've got some good friends here which helps get my work orders filled quickly, if you know what I mean.

Bob Keegan, member of technical staff

Consultant: You said earlier that David Morton was your adviser for your Masters degree. So you've known him a long time.

Bob: Yes, that's right. I've known Professor Morton – David – for about eight years. I had him for a few undergraduate classes, then, of course, he was my adviser for my Masters programme, and now I've worked at EL for two years.

Consultant: It seems as if you enjoy working with David.

Bob: Oh, yes. But I really don't get to work directly with him any more. I'll see him at meetings but that's about it.

Consultant: So he's not your immediate supervisor?

Bob: No, but for the amount of time I spend with my supervisor, David might as well be. My boss and I meet perhaps once every three weeks for about an hour to see if all is well. And that's it. The rest of the time, I'm on my own. I used to talk to David when I had questions, but he's so busy these days that it's hard to see him – you need to make an appointment a few days in advance.

Consultant: Do you think your supervisor treats all his staff this way?

Bob: To be honest, I have heard some complaints. In fact, about six months ago the situation was so bad some other people and I had a meeting with him. He promised that he would be more available to us, and he was – for about a month. Then we got involved in a new proposal and he made himself scarce again. So nothing's really changed. We're finalising the proposal now and it's important that I see him to ask him questions. The last few drafts I've submitted to him, he's returned, rewritten in his own way and with no explanation of the changes. Sometimes I think he treats me like somebody who doesn't know anything, as if I had no training whatsoever. I realise his neck is on the line with this project, but it seems that he uses being busy to avoid talking to me.

Chris Chan, research scientist

Consultant: What kind of characteristics should a person have if he/she wants to work as a research scientist at Electro Logic?

Chris: Well, certainly technical knowledge is important – when I've interviewed recent graduates I insist they have got a good degree. But for experienced research scientists, technical knowledge shows up in their publication records, mostly. So I'll read their papers. I also think a research scientist has to be highly self-motivated, not look to others for praise. Particularly here. If you want someone to tell you you've done a good job, you'll be waiting a long time. It's not clear to me that research scientists really get the support we need from the rest of the staff here. Work orders are often lost or put off for one reason or another. Senior members seem to get more technicians than scientists do and they certainly get more attention from David. The rumour is that these people also get higher rises than the scientists; allegedly, this is to keep pay at an equitable rate – you know, they're supposedly more valuable to the company. Of course, everybody knows that most of the senior members are David's old graduate students, and so he takes care of them really well. One of the things that really galls me is that I need to keep up my publication record to maintain my career options, but publishing is frowned on here because it takes time away from your work. I've even been told that my work can't be published because of proprietary rights or that the defence department considers the information classified. However, if somebody important is working with me and needs the publication, then it's full steam ahead.

Consultant: You sound pretty disgruntled with your work.

Chris: It's not my work so much. I'm really very happy doing this work – it's cutting-edge, after all. The problem is that I'm never quite sure where the work is going. I do my part of a project, and unless I go out of my way to talk to other people I never find out the final results of the total project. That's just something you learn to live with around here – being part of a system that's not particularly open.

Margaret Conroy, assistant to the head of administration

Consultant: You've only been here a short time, is that correct?

Margaret: That's right – just a little over a year.

Consultant: Why did you take the job?

Margaret: Well, I was in my last term at university and was looking for a job, like most students. My fiancée at the time – now he's my husband – was already working for EL and found out that there was an opening. So I applied.

Consultant: Were you taking business studies at university?

Margaret: Oh, no. I was taking history.

Consultant: Do you like your job?

Margaret: It has a lot to offer. I get paid well for what I'm doing. And I'm learning a lot. I just wish the company would let me take some courses in administration, like accounting. The auditors ask some pretty tough questions. David says we should hire that expertise, but I'd still be responsible for supervising the people.

Consultant: Is there any particular aspect about your job that you really find satisfying?

Margaret: Well, let me see. I like the fact that I can do lots of different tasks so that things don't get so boring. I would hate to have to do the same thing, day in and day out. A lot of the time, I go to the library to do research on different things, and that's nice because it gets me out of the office.

Consultant: What don't you like about your job?

Margaret: Well, I often get the feeling that administration isn't taken seriously. You know, the engineers could get along without us quite nicely or so they seem to think. The whole structure of the departments shows that we're the catch-all department – if you don't fit anywhere else, they put you in here. Perhaps some of that is because our department is primarily women – in fact, I've been told that 95 per cent of all the female employees are in administration. Sometimes it's hard to work with the engineers because they treat you like you don't know anything – and they always want things to be done their way. Clearly, the engineers get the money and consideration and yet, well, we do contribute quite a lot to the whole team, as David would say. But words of praise just aren't as impressive as actions. We get our birthday parties, but that still seems to be a little patronising. We rarely get to see what's going on in the research area. I've asked a number of engineers some specific questions, and they just look at me with a blank stare and give me some really simplified answer. It seems to me if you want to build a team, like the boss says, you can't treat administration like a bad relation.

Gareth Roberts, technician

Consultant: I gather you've just been through your biannual performance appraisal. How did it go?

Gareth: Like I expected. No surprises.

Consultant: Do you find these appraisals useful?

Gareth: Yes. I get to find out what he thinks of my work.

Consultant: Is that all?

Gareth: Well, I suppose it's a nice opportunity to understand what my supervisor wants. Sometimes he's not so clear during the rest of the year. I suppose he's been given specific goals from higher-ups before he talks with me, so he's clear and then I'm clear.

Consultant: Do you like what you're doing?

Gareth: Of course. The best part is that I'm not at the main building, and so I don't have to put up with the 'important' people, you know? I've heard from other technicians that those people can be a real bore – trying to be nice, but really just being a nuisance. I mean, how can you get your work done when the managing director's looking over your shoulder all the time. On the other hand, if the MD knows your name, I suppose that's a good thing when it comes to rises and promotions. But my boss sticks up for his technicians – we get a fair deal from him.

Consultant: Do you think you'll be able to get ahead at Electro Logic?

Gareth: Get ahead? You mean become an engineer? No, and I really don't want to do that. Everyone here keeps pushing me to move up. I'm afraid to tell people how I really feel for fear they'll decide I don't fit into this high-tech environment. I like doing what I do and if the rises keep coming, I'll keep liking it. One of my daughters is starting college next year and I need the money to help her out. I get a lot of overtime, particularly when contract deadlines are near. I suppose the rush towards the end of contracts gives some people big headaches, but for me I don't mind. The work is pretty slow otherwise, and so at least I'm working all the time. But my family wishes my schedule was more predictable.

Consultant: Do you think you'll continue working for Electro Logic?

Gareth: I'm not sure I want to answer that. Let's just say that my ratings on the performance appraisal were good and I expect to see an improvement in my pay. I'll stay for that.

Chelsey Montgomery, technician

Consultant: In general, what are your feelings about the work you do for EL?

Chelsey: Well, I feel my work is quite good, but I also feel that I perform rather boring, tedious tasks. From what my supervisor says, the kinds of things I do are what electrical engineering students do in their last year in college. I gather their final project is to make a circuit board, and that's what I do, day in and day out.

Consultant: What is it that you would like to do?

Chelsey: Well, it would be nice to be able to offer some input into some of the designs of these boards. I know I don't have a PhD or anything, but I do have lots of experience. But because I'm a technician the engineers don't really feel I've got much to offer – even though I build the boards and can tell from the design which one will do what, the designer wants to do it. I also would like to supervise other technicians in my department. Some kind of advancement would be nice. As it is, lots of technicians ask me how to do things and of course I help, but then they get the credit. Around here, you have to have a piece of paper that says you're educated before they let you officially help other people.

Discussion questions

1. Using the behavioural guidelines and Figure 5.3 as diagnostic aids, what are the strengths and weaknesses of Electro Logic from a motivational perspective?

2. What are the high-priority action items you would include in a consulting report to David Morton, managing director of Electro Logic? Focus on specific actions that he could initiate that would better use the abilities of the staff and foster a more motivating work environment.

Skill Practice

DIAGNOSING WORK PERFORMANCE PROBLEMS

Proper diagnosis is a critical aspect of effective motivation management. Often managers become frustrated because they don't understand the causes of observed performance problems. They might experiment with various 'cures', but the inefficiency of this trial-and-error process often simply increases their frustration level. In addition, the accompanying misunderstanding adds extra strain to the manager–subordinate relationship. This generally makes the performance problem even more pronounced, which prompts the manager to resort to more drastic responses, and a vicious, downward spiral ensues.

The performance diagnosis model in Figure 5.5 offers a systematic way for managers and subordinates to collaboratively pinpoint the cause(s) of dissatisfaction and performance problems.

It assumes that employees will work hard and be good performers if the work environment encourages these actions. Consequently, rather than jumping to conclusions about poor performance stemming from deficiencies in personality traits or a bad attitude, this diagnostic process helps managers to focus their attention on improving the selection, job design, performance evaluation and reward allocation systems. In this manner, the specific steps necessary to accomplish work goals and management's expectations are examined to pinpoint why the worker's performance is falling short.

The manager and low-performing subordinate should follow the logical discovery process in the model, step by step. They should begin by examining the current perceptions of performance, as well as the understanding of performance expectations, and then proceed through the model until the performance problems have been identified. The model focuses on seven of these problems.

A. Perception problem *'Do you agree that your performance is below expectations?'* A perception problem suggests that the manager and subordinate have different views of the subordinate's current performance level. Unless this disagreement is resolved, it is futile to continue the diagnostic process. The entire problem-solving process is based on the premise that both parties recognise the existence of a problem and are interested in solving it. If agreement does not exist, the manager should focus on resolving the discrepancy in perceptions, including clarifying current expectations (Problem E).

B. Resources problem *'Do you have the resources necessary to do the job well?'* (Ability has three components, and these should be explored in the order shown in the model. This order reduces a subordinate's defensive reactions.) Poor performance may stem from a lack of resource support. Resources include material and personnel support as well as co-operation from interdependent work groups.

C. Training problem *'Is a lack of training interfering with your job performance?'* Individuals may be asked to perform tasks that exceed their current skill or knowledge

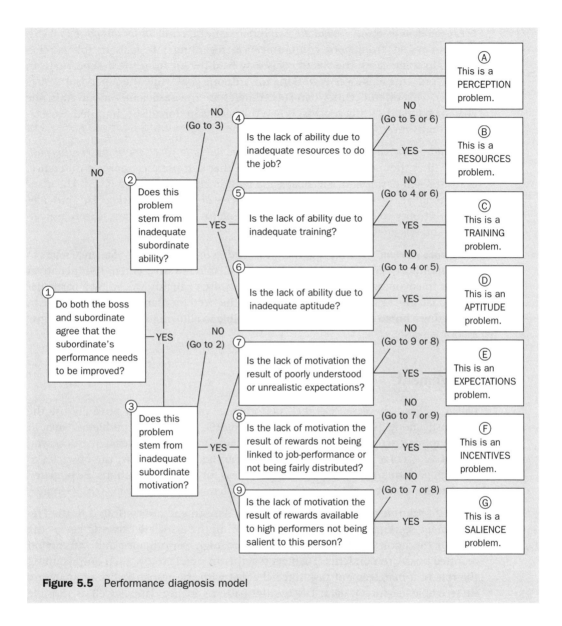

Figure 5.5 Performance diagnosis model

level. Typically this problem can be overcome through additional training or education.

D. Aptitude problem *'Do you feel this is the right job/blend of work assignments for you?'*
This is the most difficult of the three ability problems to resolve because it is the most basic. If the refurbish (providing additional resources) and retraining solutions have been explored without success, then more drastic measures may be required. These include redeploying the person's current job requirements, reassigning him to another position, or, finally, releasing him from the organisation.

E. Expectations problem *'What are your performance expectations for this position?'* This problem results from poor communication regarding job goals or job requirements. In some cases, the stated goals may be different from the desired goals. In other words, the employee is working towards one goal while the supervisor desires another. This often occurs when subordinates are not sufficiently involved in the goal- or standard-setting process. When this results in unrealistic, imposed expectations, motivation suffers.

F. Incentive problem *'Do you believe rewards are linked to your performance in this position?'* Either the individual does not believe that performance makes a difference, or insufficient performance feedback and reinforcement have been given. The manager should also ask, *Do you feel rewards are being distributed equitably?* This provides an opportunity to discuss subordinates' criteria for judging fairness. Often, unrealistic standards are being used.

G. Salience problem *'Are the performance incentives attractive to you?'* Salience refers to the importance an individual attaches to available rewards. Often, the incentives offered to encourage high performance simply aren't highly valued by a particular individual. The salience problem points out the need for managers to be creative in generating a broad range of rewards, and flexible in allowing subordinates to choose among rewards.

Assignment

Option 1 Read the case, 'George's performance problems', and privately use the diagnostic model (Figure 5.5) to pinpoint plausible performance problems. Next, in small groups discuss your individual assessments and list the specific questions you should ask George to identify accurately, from his point of view, the obstacles to his high performance. Finally, brainstorm ideas for plausible solutions. Be prepared to represent your group in role-playing a problem-solving interview with George.

Option 2 Administer the Work Performance Assessment survey (found in the Pre-assessment section) to several employees. Using the associated scoring key at the back of the book categorise the obstacles to high performance and satisfaction reported by the respondents. Then get together in small groups, each one assuming the role of a management task force charged with the responsibility of analysing these employee survey data. Discuss the patterns in the data as well as possible remedies for the problems, using the behavioural guidelines and motivational models in this book as guides. Be prepared to make a report on your analysis, and recommendations for specific changes.

EXERCISE **5.2**

GEORGE'S PERFORMANCE PROBLEMS

George joined your architectural firm two years ago as a draughtsman. He is 35 and has been a draftsman since leaving technical college. He is married and has four children. He has worked for four architectural firms in 12 years.

George came with mediocre recommendations from his previous employer, but you employed him because you needed help desperately. Your firm's workload has been extremely high due to a local construction boom. The result is that a lot of the practices that contribute to a supportive, well-managed work environment have tended to be overlooked. For instance, you can't remember the last time you conducted a formal performance review or did any career counselling. Furthermore, the tradition of closing the office early on Friday for a social hour was dropped long ago. Unfortunately, the tension in the office runs pretty high some days due to unbearable time pressures and the lack of adequate staff. Evening and weekend work have become the norm rather than the exception.

Overall, you have been pleasantly surprised by George's performance. Until recently he worked hard and consistently produced high-quality work. He frequently volunteered for special projects, made lots of suggestions for improving the work environment, and has demonstrated an in-depth practical knowledge of architecture and the construction business. However, during the past few months, he has definitely eased off. He doesn't seem as excited about his work, and several times you have found him daydreaming at his desk. In addition, he has got into several heated arguments with architects about the specifications and proper design procedures for recent projects.

After one of these disagreements, you overheard George complaining to his office partner, 'No one around here respects my opinion. I'm just a lowly draughtsman. I know as much as these trendy architects, but because I don't have the degree, they ignore my views, and I'm stuck doing the donkey work. Adding insult to injury, my wife has had to get a job to help support our family. I must be the lowest-paid person in this firm.'

When asked by a colleague about why he didn't take his degree in architecture, George responded, 'Do you have any idea how hard it is to put bread on the table, pay the mortgage, work overtime, be a reasonably good father and husband, plus go to evening classes? Come on, be realistic!'

EXERCISE **5.3**

RESHAPING UNACCEPTABLE BEHAVIOURS

One of the most challenging aspects of management is transforming inappropriate behaviours into appropriate behaviours. Managers commonly take insufficient action to transform negative actions into positive ones. Some of these insufficient responses include:

- assuming that ignoring the problem will make it go away
- praising positive aspects of an individual's performance in the hope that it will encourage him or her to re-channel unproductive energies
- discussing the problem in vague, general terms in a group meeting in the hope that the unproductive person will take a hint and change
- getting upset with the individual and demanding that he or she 'sort themselves out'.

Assume the role of Andrew Tate in the following case. After reading the case (do not read the role instructions for Ruth), be prepared to role play your discussion with Ruth in a small group. Obviously, one member of this group should play Ruth while the others assume the role of observers. Prior to the role play, the observers should familiarise themselves with the Observer's Feedback Form in the scoring key in Appendix 1. They should then proceed to complete this form during the role play so that the group can discuss the results after the role play has ended.

Ruth's lateness

Andrew Tate, manager

Ruth has been a member of your staff for only three months. You don't know much about her except that she is a single parent who has recently entered the work force after a difficult divorce. She is often 10 to 20 minutes late for work in the morning. You are the manager of a very hectic customer relations office for a utility company. The phones start ringing promptly at eight o'clock. When she is late for work, you have to answer her phone, and this interrupts your schedule. This morning you are particularly annoyed. She is 25 minutes late and the phones are ringing furiously. Because you have been forced to answer them, it will be difficult for you to complete an important assignment by the noon deadline. You are getting more annoyed by the minute.

While you are in the middle of a particularly unpleasant phone conversation with an irate customer, you look out of your window and see Ruth bounding up the steps to the building. You think to yourself, 'This is ridiculous, I've got to put a stop to her lateness. Maybe I should just threaten to sack her unless she sorts herself out.' Upon further reflection, you realise that would be impractical, especially during this period of retrenchment after the new wage demand was turned down. Given the rumours about a possible freeze on recruitment, you know it may be difficult to refill any vacancies.

Also, Ruth is actually a pretty good worker when she is there. She is conscientious and has a real knack with irate callers. Unfortunately, it has taken her much longer than expected to learn the computer program for retrieving information on customer accounts. She frequently has to put callers on hold while she asks for help. These interruptions have tended to increase an already tense relationship with the rest of the office staff. She has had some difficulty fitting in socially; the others are much younger and have worked together for several years. Ruth is the first new appointment in a long time, so the others aren't used to breaking someone in. Three of your staff have complained to you about Ruth's constant interruptions. They feel their productivity is going down as a result. She also seems to expect them to drop whatever they are doing every time she has a question. They had expected their workload to be lighter when a new person was hired, but now they are having second thoughts. (In the past you have had enough time to train new recruits, but your boss has had you tied up on a major project for almost a year.)

Ruth enters the office obviously flustered and dishevelled. She has 'I'm sorry' written all over her face. You motion for her to pick up the phone and then scribble a note on a notepad while you complete your call: 'See me in my office at 12.00 sharp!' It's time you got to the bottom of Ruth's disruptive influence on an otherwise smooth-flowing operation.

Ruth Call, staff member

What a morning! Your baby-sitter's Dad died during the night, and she called you from the railway station at 6.30 to say she would be away for three or four days. You tried three usually available backups before you finally found someone who could look after Katie, your 3-year-old. Then Sarah was really difficult over her breakfast. It's a miracle that Brian, your oldest, was able to pull himself out of bed after getting only five hours sleep. On top of soccer and drama, he's now joined the chess team and they had their first tournament last night. Why did it have to fall on the night before his final in physics? This morning you wished you had his knack for juggling so many activities. By the time you got the children sorted out, you were already 10 minutes behind time. Then there was this incredible accident on the motorway that slowed traffic to a crawl.

As you finally pull off the slip road, you notice you're almost 20 minutes late for work. 'My kingdom for a mobile phone!' you groan. 'Although by now I probably couldn't get an open line into the office, anyway.' As you desperately look for a parking space, you begin to panic. 'How am I going to explain this to Mr Tate? He'll be furious. I'm sure he's upset about my chronic lateness. On top of that, he's obviously disappointed with my lack of computer skills, and I'm sure the others complain about having to train a newcomer.' You're sure that one of the reasons you got the job was that you had completed a computer course at the local community college. Unfortunately, it didn't really prepare you for the incredibly complex computer program you use at work – it seems to defy every convention of logic.

'What am I going to tell him about my being late for work so often?' Unfortunately, there isn't an easy answer. 'Maybe it will get better as the children and I get used to this new routine. It's just very difficult to get the children to the bus stop and the baby-sitter, commute 20 minutes, and arrive precisely at 08.00. I wonder if he would allow me to come in at 8.30 and only take a half-hour for lunch? Staying late wouldn't work because they close down the computers at 5.00, unless there was some paperwork I could do for half an hour.'

And then what about the problems with the computer and the other women? 'Sooner or later he's going to get on to me about those things. Is it my fault that I don't think like a computer? Some people might be able to sit down and figure this program out in a couple of hours, but not me. So is that my fault or should someone be giving me more training? I wish the others weren't so cliquish and unwilling to help me out. I wonder why that's the case? It's like they're afraid I'll become as good as they are if they share their experience with me. I wish Mr Tate had more time to help me to learn the ropes, but he seems to always be in meetings.'

'Well, I'm probably going to catch it this morning. I've never been this late. Maybe I'll be back home full-time sooner than I expected.'

Skill Application

ACTIVITY **5.1**

SUGGESTED FURTHER ASSIGNMENTS

Assignment 1

Identify a situation in which you have some responsibility for another person whose performance is significantly below your expectation. Using the Work Performance Assessment Survey included in the Pre-assessment section, collect information on the individual's perceptions of the situation. Using the diagnostic model (decision tree) in that section, specifically identify the perceived performance problems. Compare these results with your own views of the situation. Conduct an interview with the individual and discuss the results, highlighting areas of disagreement. Based on this discussion, formulate a plan of action that both parties accept. If inadequate ability is a problem, follow the refurbish, retrain, redeploy, reassign and release remedial steps. If insufficient effort is a problem, use the steps for reprimanding, redirecting and rewarding discussed in this book. Implement this plan for a period of time and then report on the results.

Assignment 2

Focus on some aspect of your own work in which you feel performance is below your (or others') expectations. Using the Work Performance Assessment Survey, identify the specific obstacles to improved performance. Then formulate a plan for overcoming these obstacles, including getting commitments from others. Discuss your plan with individuals affected by it and arrive at a set of actions all parties accept. Implement the plan for a period of time and report on your results. How successful were you in making the changes? Did your performance improve as expected? Based on this experience, identify other aspects of your work that you could improve in a similar fashion.

Assignment 3

Identify four or five situations in which you are typically provoked to exhibit punishing behaviour. These might involve friends, family members or work associates. Examine these situations and identify one where punishment (discipline) is simply not working. Using the guidelines for reprimanding, redirecting and rewarding, design a specific plan for shaping the other person's behaviours so you can begin rewarding positive actions. Report on your results. Based on this experience, consider how you might be able to use this strategy in other similar situations.

Assignment 4

Using the six-step model for creating a motivating work environment (Table 5.1), design a specific plan for managing a new relationship (e.g., a new subordinate) or a new phase in an old relationship (e.g., friend, family member or subordinate about to begin work on a new project). Write down specific directions for yourself for implementing each of the six steps. Discuss your plan with this individual and ask for suggestions for improvement. Make sure your perceptions of the key aspects of the plan are consistent with his or hers. Implement your plan for a period of time and then report on the consequences. Based on this experience, identify changes that would be appropriate in similar settings.

ACTIVITY **5.2**

APPLICATION PLAN AND EVALUATION

The intent of this exercise is to help you to apply your skills in a real-life, out-of-class setting. Now that you have become familiar with the behavioural guidelines that form the basis of effective skill performance, you will most improve by trying out those guidelines in an everyday context. The trouble is, unlike a classroom activity in which feedback is immediate and others can assist you with their evaluations, this skill application activity is one you must accomplish and evaluate on your own. There are two parts to this activity. Part 1 helps to prepare you to apply the skill; Part 2 helps you to evaluate and improve on your experience. Be sure to actually write down answers to each item. Don't short-circuit the process by skipping steps.

Part 1: Plan

1. Write down the two or three aspects of this skill that are most important to you. These may be areas of weakness, areas you most want to improve, or areas that are most salient to a problem you currently face. Identify the specific aspects of this skill that you want to apply.

2. Now identify the setting or the situation in which you will apply this skill. Establish a plan for performance by actually writing down the situation. Who else will be involved? When will you do it? Where will it be done?

3. Identify the specific behaviours you will engage in to apply this skill. Put your skills into practice.

4. What are the indicators of successful performance? How will you know you have succeeded in being effective? What will indicate that you have performed competently?

Part 2: Evaluation

5. After you have completed your implementation, record the results. What happened? How successful were you? What was the effect on others?

6. How can you improve? What modifications can you make next time? What will you do differently in a similar situation in the future?

7. Looking back on your whole skill practice and application experience, what have you learned? What has been surprising? In what ways might this experience help you in the long term?

Further reading

Hale, R. and Whitlam, P. (1995) *Target setting and goal achievement*. London: Kogan Page.

Maitland, I. (1995) *Motivating people*. London: Institute of Personnel & Development.

Steers, R.M., Porter, L.W. and Bigley, G.A. (1996) *Motivation and leadership at work*, 6th edn. London: McGraw-Hill.

Vroom, V.H. and Deci, E.L. (eds) (1992) *Management and motivation*, 2nd edn. London: Penguin.

Constructive Conflict Management

SKILL DEVELOPMENT OUTLINE

Skill Pre-assessment surveys

- Managing interpersonal conflict
- Strategies for handling conflict

Skill Learning material

- Management conflict
- Personal beliefs that fog one's appropriate actions
- Interpersonal conflict
- Responses to conflict
- Negotiation strategies
- Selecting the appropriate approach
- Resolving confrontations using the collaborative approach
- Summary
- Behavioural guidelines

Skill Analysis case

- Health Provisions Limited

Skill Practice exercises

- Argyll Steakhouse
- Avocado Computers
- Phelan Ltd
- Where's my speech?
- Can Harry fit in?
- Meeting at Hartford Manufacturing Co.

Skill Application activities

- Suggested further assignments
- Application plan and evaluation

LEARNING OBJECTIVES

To enable individuals to:

- understand and recognise the sources of conflict – productive and dysfunctional
- select the most appropriate responses to conflict
- manage interpersonal confrontations in any of the roles – initiator, respondent or mediator

INTRODUCTION

If the word 'conflict' conjures up for you the image of two prize fighters battling it out to the death, this chapter may well come as a surprise.

> The Human Resource Director of a national charity asked us to work with his Executive Board. The Board consisted of six full-time directors and six lay members – the 'wise and the good'. The full-time directors worked well together but when the full Board of 12 met, lay and full-time members, nothing happened. The HRM Director put it very simply: 'We are all too nice. Nobody challenges anything, we discuss minutiae and skate round any discussion of principle. The lay members were called in to challenge principles. They don't even complain if the coffee is cold. When the full meeting is over, we send them packing and breathe a sign of relief, get on with our work and hope that the next month's full Board meeting gets cancelled.'

Without constructive conflict 'nothing happens', but there are limits:

> We were called to work with the Board of the UK subsidiary of a German manufacturer. The managing director's problem was dysfunctional conflict – also leading to nothing getting done. During our work with him – what trainers call 'team-building exercises' – we met the conflict head-on. The outsiders' impression was, in lay terms, that they hated each other. One director had left immediately before our work with them and another resigned during the team-building exercise itself. Later, but not much later, another director resigned and the CEO was faced with the problem, in this case welcome, of building a new team virtually from scratch.

This book is about the middle way – the situation where people are able to speak their minds, with due concern for others, and trust others to be honest with them and thus live and work more effectively.

Managing interpersonal conflict is about maintaining the middle way and is a major management skill that will bring together many of the skills discussed elsewhere in the book.

Skill Pre-assessment

SURVEY **6.1**

MANAGING INTERPERSONAL CONFLICT

Please complete the assessment as we explained at the beginning of Chapter 1.

RATING SCALE

1 = Strongly disagree **2** = Disagree **3** = Slightly disagree
4 = Slightly agree **5** = Agree **6** = Strongly agree

	Assessment	
	Pre-	Post-

On a personal level when I am working with others, and I feel that things are not going as they should be and I need to take a hand

1. I avoid making personal accusations and attributing self-serving motives to the other person. _____ _____

2. When stating my concerns, I present them as my problems. _____ _____

3. I describe the problem concisely in terms of the behaviour that occurred, its consequences, and my feelings about it. _____ _____

4. I specify my expectations and the standards that have not been achieved. _____ _____

5. I make a specific request, detailing a more acceptable option. _____ _____

6. I stay with my point of view until it is understood by the others. _____ _____

7. I encourage a dialogue by getting others to discuss their perspectives. _____ _____

8. When there are several concerns, I approach the issues one at a time, starting with the most straightforward and progressing to the more complex. _____ _____

When someone complains about something I've done

9. I look for our common areas of agreement. _____ _____

10. I show genuine concern and interest, even when I disagree. _____ _____

11. I avoid justifying my actions and becoming defensive. _____ _____

12. I seek additional information by asking questions that provide specific, descriptive information. _____ _____

13. I focus on one issue at a time. _____ _____

14. I find some aspects of the complaint with which I can agree. _____ _____

15. I ask the other person to suggest more acceptable behaviours. _____ _____

16. I strive to reach agreement on a remedial plan of action. _____ _____

When I find myself in the position of a mediator between two other people in dysfunctional conflict

17. I acknowledge that conflict exists and treat it as serious and important. _____ _____

18. I help create an agenda for the problem-solving meeting by identifying the issues to be discussed one at a time. _____ _____

19. I do not take sides but remain neutral. _____ _____

20. I help focus the discussion on the impact of the conflict on work performance. _____ _____

21. I keep the interaction focused on problems rather than on personalities. _____ _____

22. I make certain that neither party dominates the conversation. _____ _____

23. I help the parties generate multiple alternatives. _____ _____

24. I help the parties find areas on which they agree. _____ _____

SURVEY **6.2**

STRATEGIES FOR HANDLING CONFLICT

Indicate how often you use each of the following by circling the appropriate number. After you have completed the survey, use the scoring key in Appendix 1 at the end of the book to tabulate your results. Information on these five strategies is shown in Table 6.2 in the Skill Learning section.

RATING SCALE

1 = Never   **2** = Seldom   **3** = Sometimes   **4** = Usually   **5** = Always

1. I will stick with my position whatever.	1 2 3 4 5
2. I try to put the needs of others above mine.	1 2 3 4 5
3. I try to arrive at a compromise both parties can accept.	1 2 3 4 5
4. I try not to get involved in conflicts.	1 2 3 4 5
5. I strive to investigate issues, jointly and properly.	1 2 3 4 5
6. I try to find fault in the other person's position.	1 2 3 4 5
7. I strive to foster harmony.	1 2 3 4 5
8. I negotiate to get a portion of what I propose.	1 2 3 4 5
9. I avoid open discussions of controversial subjects.	1 2 3 4 5
10. I share information openly with others in resolving disagreements.	1 2 3 4 5
11. I enjoy winning an argument.	1 2 3 4 5
12. I go along with the suggestions of others.	1 2 3 4 5
13. I look for a middle ground to resolve disagreements.	1 2 3 4 5
14. I keep my true feelings to myself to avoid hard feelings.	1 2 3 4 5
15. I encourage the open sharing of concerns and issues.	1 2 3 4 5
16. I am reluctant to admit I am wrong.	1 2 3 4 5
17. I try to help others avoid losing face in a disagreement.	1 2 3 4 5
18. I stress the advantages of give and take.	1 2 3 4 5
19. I encourage others to take the lead in resolving controversy.	1 2 3 4 5
20. I state my position as only one point of view.	1 2 3 4 5

Skill Learning

Management conflict

Anthony Barnett (1998), discussing the world's biggest industrial merger to date – that of BP and Amoco – writes of a meeting between Brown and Fuller of BP and Amoco respectively:

This was the evening of the breakthrough (Saturday, 1 July 1998) – the carve up of key responsibilities of the top 22 executives. Messing with corporate egos is one of the thorniest problems in any merger and can scupper the best deals.

A less recent article in *Business Week* (1981) states that:

Some half to two-thirds of all company mergers fail. Why? One major reason is that key executives in the merging firms can't agree on their respective roles, status and 'perks'. Tensions are compounded by disagreements over which procedures to use and whose 'corporate culture' will dominate. The inability or lack of willingness to resolve these conflicts can unravel an otherwise attractive business marriage.

Paradoxically John Argenti (1976) claims that one of the leading causes of business failure among major companies is too much agreement among top management. They have similar training and experience, and this leads them to view conditions in the same way and to pursue similar goals. Boards of Directors failing to play an aggressive overview role compound this problem. They avoid conflict with the internal management team, who appear unified on key issues and very confident of their positions.

The Honda/ Rover/ BMW negotiations of 1994 showed issues of mishandling friendship as well as conflict that led to very personal 'pique'.

Mr Bernd Pischetsrieder, chairman of the BMW management board, is to meet Mr Nobuhiko Kawamoto, chief executive of Honda in Tokyo, next week in a first round of talks aimed at maintaining the alliance between the Japanese car maker and Rover.

BMW stunned Honda on Monday with its £800m take-over from British Aerospace of an 80 per cent stake in the UK car maker. Honda still holds the remaining 20 per cent of the equity in Rover and Land Rover vehicle operations. Mr Pischetsrieder is anxious to maintain Honda as a partner for Rover in vehicle production and development, at least in the medium term.

Honda and Rover have forged a close relationship in the past 14 years, and Mr Kawamoto was quick to express dismay at the entry of BMW as the majority owner of Rover. He said that the BMW take-over 'negated' the long-term efforts of Honda and Rover to establish a firm future for Rover as 'a British company with its own brand identity'.

Honda's resentment at the way that British Aerospace engineered the BMW take-over of Rover was also highlighted when Mr Andrew Jones, the company's UK plant manager, admitted the company was shocked by the deal.

Source: *Financial Times*, 2 February 1994

Constructive interpersonal conflict, correctly used, is an essential part of organisational life. Organisations in which there is little disagreement generally fail in competitive environments. Members are either so homogeneous that they are ill equipped to adapt to change, or so complacent that they see no need to change or improve. Conflict is the life-blood of vibrant, progressive, stimulating organisations. It sparks creativity, stimulates innovation and encourages personal improvement (Robbins, 1978; King, 1981; Thomas, 1977; Wanous and Youtz, 1986).

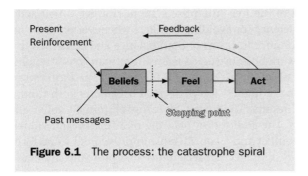

Figure 6.1 The process: the catastrophe spiral

This view is clearly in line with the management philosophy of Andrew Grove, President of INTEL:

> Many managers seem to think it is impossible to tackle anything or anyone head-on, even in business. By contrast, we at INTEL believe that it is the essence of corporate health to bring a problem out into the open as soon as possible, even if this entails a confrontation. Dealing with conflicts lies at the heart of managing any business. As a result, confrontation of issues about which there is disagreement can be avoided only at the manager's peril. Workplace politicking grows quietly in the dark, like mushrooms; neither can stand the light of day.
>
> *Source*: *Fortune*, 23 July 1984, p. 74

Appropriate conflict, neither too much nor too little, can be beneficial. Hambrick *et al.* (1998) in their collection of papers, *Navigating Change*, repeatedly allude to the importance of conflict in corporate governance – keeping companies on the road in the face of forceful individuals in authority. As these and other authors point out, conflict is a question of personal preference. Some people have a very low tolerance for disagreement while others seem to like to fly into the face of the tiger at the slightest provocation. The preference probably arises from family background, cultural values or personality characteristics, but is certainly reinforced by current experience.

Figure 6.1 illustrates the process. Past experience, confirmed by recent but perhaps irrelevant recent experiences, makes us believe that conflict is necessary or should be avoided. This is a knee jerk response NOT founded on a logical assessment of the detail of the present. We therefore feel either aggressive or passive, and act accordingly without review. If we act aggressively then others respond accordingly, and a new 'present' experience reinforces our decision to 'go for conflict' and a catastrophe spiral begins, ending dysfunctionally. Conversely, if 'knee jerk' turns into passivity, a spiral begins that results in our interests being crushed into the grass. The secret is to review our process before we feel either aggressive or passive and decide on appropriate action, which may or may not involve conflict.

While most writers would agree that some conflict is both inevitable and necessary in effective organisations, Abraham Maslow (1965) has observed a high degree of ambivalence regarding the value of conflict. Maslow notes that, intellectually, managers appreciate the value of conflict and competition. They agree it is a necessary ingredient of the free-enterprise system. However, their actions demonstrate a personal preference for avoiding conflicts whenever possible. Belbin (1981) emphasises the importance in teams of both balance and constructive conflict.

In Belbin's early work he constructed teams from managers attending a training programme on the basis of their IQs, and got the teams to perform competitive exercises. The teams with the highest IQs performed irregularly both from the point of view of conflict and results. The lowest IQ teams performed dully – little conflict and mediocre results. The addition or planting of a 'sparky' individual to the dull group caused both conflict and a considerable improvement in performance.

This tension between intellectual acceptance of a principle and emotional rejection of its enactment was more systematically studied in Boulding's (1964) classic study of decision making.

> Several groups of managers were formed to solve a complex problem. They were told a panel of experts would judge their performance in terms of the quantity and quality of solutions generated. The groups were identical in size and composition, with the exception that half of them included a 'mole'. Before the experiment began, the researcher instructed this person to play the role of 'devil's advocate'. This person was to challenge the group's conclusions, forcing the others to examine critically their assumptions and the logic of their arguments. At the end of the problem-solving period, the recommendations made by both sets of groups were compared. The groups with the devil's advocates had performed significantly better on the task. They had generated more alternatives and their proposals were judged as superior. After a short break, the groups were reassembled and told that they would be performing a similar task during the next session. However, before they began discussing the next problem, they were given permission to eliminate one member. In every group containing a 'mole', he or she was the one asked to leave. The fact that every high-performance group expelled their unique competitive advantage because that member made others feel uncomfortable demonstrates a widely shared reaction to conflict: 'I know it has positive outcomes for the performance of the organisation as a whole, but I don't like how it makes me feel personally.'

We believe that much of the ambivalence towards conflict stems from a lack of understanding of the causes of conflict, the variety of modes for managing it effectively, and from a lack of confidence in one's personal skills for handling the tense, emotionally charged environment typical of most interpersonal confrontations. It is natural for an untrained or inexperienced person to avoid threatening situations, and it is generally acknowledged that conflict represents the most severe test of a manager's interpersonal skills. The task of the effective manager, therefore, is to maintain an optimal level of conflict, while keeping conflicts focused on productive purposes (Robbins, 1974; Kelly, 1970; Thomas, 1976).

The balance requires that managers must be able to:

- recognise their own beliefs that may lead them to inappropriate action;
- diagnose the causes of conflict;
- decide upon their achievable objectives;
- settle upon a strategy to handle the conflict so that the objective is achieved (which normally will include making sure that the long-term relationships between the disputants is not damaged).

Personal beliefs that fog one's appropriate action

The concept is that the messages we have picked up from the past confuse us when we are attempting to handle current situations. Woods (1989) coined the name 'Mind Music' for these messages, his point being that the messages play in our heads when we 'think' we recognise a present situation that we can relate to something in our past experience. The confusion is enough to make us act inappropriately, and very often as others we respected from our past might have handled it. These messages we rationalise as our personal beliefs. Used appropriately, they are a bequest from the significant people of the past to guide us through our lives – used inappropriately, they lead us into the catastrophe spiral. Albert Ellis is quoted as saying that 99 per cent of the world's ills are founded in four beliefs:

- A cosmic order of things.
- A fundamental acceptance of hierarchy.
- Others.
- Self.

Cosmic order

The belief here is about absolute patterns, which at its strongest was described in *Einstein* by Stephen Hawking (1989). Einstein had the fundamental belief that 'God did not play dice' and that in his search for the laws of the universe he was looking at absolutes and not for probabilities. In Hawking's view, this delayed the advance of physics by many years. Cosmic beliefs lead us to think that in all our works, and we are somehow protected or somehow fated. Managers express this form of belief in phrases such as: 'It will be alright on the night' – blocking the need for detailed preparation; 'This sort of thing simply cannot happen' – blocking change; and 'It will never work' – blocking everything. With such messages in our heads we feel that conflict with the status quo is best avoided.

Hierarchy

The belief in hierarchy leads us to think that position determines the person. Thus, if people hold senior positions they are superior in *everything* and should not be challenged. It also leads us to think that there is an absolute man-made order. We hear managers with this belief system saying such things as '. . . they are bosses and they know best – they are on the shop floor and know nothing', and feeling in their hearts that '. . . there is small print under the small print of their contracts'. Conflicts with organisational structures should be avoided.

Others

The belief in others is a belief that because we behave in a particular way, others should have similar behaviour, beliefs and values. Those who do not behave in this way are somehow *wrong* as people. The Mind Music is concerned with messages such as: ' "Good" workers follow my example, believe in what I believe in and value what I value. Others should *understand* me and what I want done.'

> We were called into a medium-sized business which had been rescued by a management buy-out from a multinational. After about a year and half of success they had a walkout by the finance department. Listening to the story, we understood why. The directors owned the business and had got used to using 'midnight oil equity' – they all worked 80 plus hours a week and were proud of their success. As the emergency had faded the necessity for the long hours had faded, but the habit had remained.
>
> A junior member of the finance team had approached the finance director, who was drinking coffee, at 18.30 and asked whether it was OK for him to go home. He had recently become a father and wanted to bathe his son for the first time. The conversation went something like this:
>
> **A**: *Why cannot you have the same dedication to work as the other directors and me?*
> **B**: *It's not my problem that you are not organised. I have a home to go too.*
> **A**: *Look, if you want to stay home, you only have to say the word.*
>
> It got worse and the rest of the team supported the young man.

In the example, the finance director considered that others, her staff, should behave as she did. Her reactions to a reasonable request were dismissed because of the Mind Music in her head. She felt that the member of staff was somehow culpable because he did not conform to the same standards and values she had adopted and left unreviewed.

By following the Mind Music that others must behave in a proscribed way we inevitably fall into dysfunctional conflict.

Self

Beliefs in 'self' are concerned with reaching the targets set by people, probably well meaning, in the past. Parents and guardians set us objectives – *Do better than your father, pass exams, have a 'good' marriage, provide grandchildren*, etc. The snag is that having been given these objectives we believe that, to be a successful human being, we have to achieve them and not to achieve them is failure on the highest level – failure as a human being. Failures do not challenge assertively, and when they do challenge it is often at the wrong time or in the wrong place. Stewart and Joines (1987) describe a development of the Ellis codification which they term 'Drivers', and those wishing to pursue the area of beliefs are advised to look at their work.

Interpersonal conflict

The labelling of our workers and colleagues through our own belief systems does lead to serious interpersonal confrontations. We label others as 'trouble makers' or 'lazy' simply because they do not fit *our* patterns. Schmidt and Tannenbaum (1965) and Hines (1980) showed that unfortunate attitudes only account for a small percentage of organisational conflicts ('labelling'). We referred, in Chapter 4, to the

Table 6.1 Sources of conflict

Sources of conflict	Focus of conflict
Personal differences	Perceptions and expectations
Information deficiency	Misinformation and misrepresentation
Role incompatibility	Goals and responsibilities
Environmental stress	Resource scarcity and uncertainty

problems of constructive communication when we have a set image of those with whom we chose to communicate.

This proposition is supported by research on performance appraisals (Latham and Wexley, 1981). It has been shown that managers generally attribute poor performance to personal deficiencies in workers (e.g., laziness, lack of skill, lack of motivation). However, when workers are asked the causes of their poor perform-ance, they generally explain it in terms of problems in their environment (e.g., insufficient supplies, unco-operative co-workers). While some face-saving is obvi-ously involved here, the line of research suggests that managers need to guard against the reflexive tendency to assume that bad behaviours imply bad people. In fact, the aggressive or harsh behaviours sometimes observed in interpersonal con-frontations often reflect the frustrations of people who have good intentions but are unskilled in handling intense, emotional experiences.

On this basis we would propose four explanations for interpersonal conflict in Table 6.1, and not include 'attitudes' in these four. Our four categorisations are:

• Personal differences
• Information deficiency
• Role incompatibility
• Environmental stress.

Personal differences

Individuals bring different attitudes to their roles in organisations. Their values and needs have been shaped by different socialisation processes, depending on their cultural and family traditions, level of education, breadth of experience, etc. As a result, their interpretations of events, and their expectations about relationships with others in the organisation, will vary considerably. Conflicts stemming from incompatible personal values and needs are some of the most difficult to resolve. They often become highly emotional and take on moral overtones. A disagree-ment about who is factually correct easily turns into a bitter argument over who is morally *right*.

The following situation occurred in a major American company between a 63-year-old white executive vice-president and a 35-year-old black member of the corporate legal department who had been very active in the civil-rights movement during the 1960s. They disagreed vehemently over whether the company should accept a very attractive offer from the South African government to build a manufacturing facility. The vice-president felt the company had a responsibility to its stockholders to pursue every legal opportunity to increase profits. In contrast, the lawyer felt that collaborating with the South African government was tantamount to condoning apartheid.

Information deficiency

Conflicts can arise from deficiencies in the organisation's information system. An important message may not be received, a boss's instructions may be misinterpreted, or decision makers may arrive at different conclusions because they used different databases. A conflict based on misinformation or misunderstanding tends to be factual, in the sense that clarifying previous messages or obtaining additional information generally resolves the dispute. This might entail rewording the boss's instructions, reconciling contradictory sources of data, or redistributing copies of misplaced messages. This type of conflict is very common in organisations, but it is also easy to resolve. Because value systems are not being challenged, these confrontations tend to be less emotional. Once the breakdown in the information system is repaired, the disputants are generally able to resolve their disagreement with a minimum of resentment.

Role incompatibility

The complexity inherent in most organisations tends to produce conflict between members whose tasks are interdependent, but whose roles are incompatible. This type of conflict is exemplified by the classic goal conflicts between line and staff, production and sales, marketing and research and development (R&D). Each unit has different responsibilities in the organisation and, as a result, each places different priorities on organisational goals (e.g., customer satisfaction, product quality, production efficiency, compliance with European Union directives). It is also typical of firms whose multiple product lines compete for scarce resources.

> In the early days at Apple Computer, the Apple II division accounted for a large part of the company's revenue. It viewed the newly-created Macintosh division as an unwise speculative venture. The natural rivalry was made worse when a champion of Macintosh referred to the Apple II team as 'the dull and boring product division'. Since this type of conflict stems from the fundamental incompatibility of the job responsibilities of the disputants, it can often be resolved only through the mediation of a common superior.
>
> *Source*: Summarised from Sculley and Byrne (1989)

Conflicts arising from role incompatibility interact with personal differences and the way individuals seek power and influence. Personal differences may well lie dormant until individuals are forced to work together with unclear organisational boundaries. Members may also perceive that their assigned roles are incompatible because they are operating from different bases of information. They communicate with different sets of people, are tied into different reporting systems and receive instructions from different bosses.

Environmental stress

Conflicts stemming from personal differences and role incompatibilities are greatly exacerbated by a stressful environment. For example, when an organisation is forced to operate on an austere budget, its members are more likely to become embroiled in disputes over territorial claims and resource requests. Scarcity tends to lower trust, increase awareness of sexual, racial and class differences and reduce participation in decision making. These are ideal conditions for incubating interpersonal conflict (Cameron and Whetten, 1987).

> When a large bank announced major staff reductions, the threat to employees' security was severe that it disrupted long-term, close working relationships. Even friendships were not immune to the effects of the stress induced by the enforced changes. Long-standing golf partnerships and car pools were disbanded because the tension among members was so high.

A second environmental condition that fosters conflict is uncertainty. When individuals find it difficult to predict what is going to happen to them from month to month, they become very anxious and prone to conflict. This type of conflict, arising from frustration, often stems from rapid, repeated change. If the way jobs are allocated, management philosophy, accounting procedures and lines of authority are changed frequently, members find it difficult to cope with the resulting stress. Sharp, bitter conflicts can easily erupt over seemingly trivial problems. This type of conflict is generally very intense, but dissipates quickly once a change becomes a routine and individuals' stress levels are lowered.

> When a major pet-food manufacturer announced that one-third of its managers would have to support a new third shift, the feared disruption of personal and family routines prompted many managers to consider resigning. In addition, the uncertainty of who was going to be required to work at night was so great that posturing and infighting disrupted even routine management work.

The issues often come to the fore when management decides that change is needed. Marks and Spencer has been a paragon of the well-managed store group and in the 1980s was judged by its own management as risking smugness. They decided, as an experiment, to introduce a group of highly motivated and brilliant young graduates to 'stir things up'. The outsiders were given a vague brief and appointed to various stores throughout the country.

> A fairly typical story was of a newcomer who set up an in-store promotion to sell some slow-moving goods. He found, after he had invested a great deal of time and effort in providing point-of-sale publicity, that the whole concept was against Marks and Spencer's philosophy and was 'asked' to stop.

The newcomers went two ways – they either left or they became so completely enveloped in the 'M&S' culture as to be barriers to change in themselves.

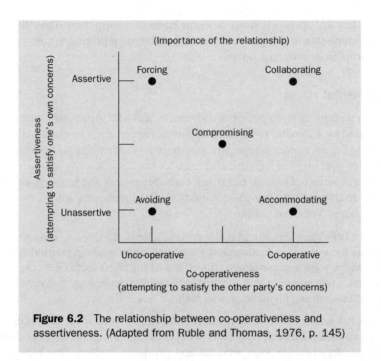

Figure 6.2 The relationship between co-operativeness and assertiveness. (Adapted from Ruble and Thomas, 1976, p. 145)

Responses to conflict

Now that we have examined the typical causes of conflict, we will discuss common responses. Figure 6.2 shows that conflict falls into five categories

- Forcing
- Accommodating
- Avoiding
- Compromising
- Collaborating

(Filley, 1975, 1978; Robbins, 1974). Each category can be organised along two dimensions, as shown in the figure. The five approaches to conflict reflect different degrees of co-operation and assertiveness. The co-operation dimension reflects the importance of the between-individual's relationship, whereas the assertiveness dimension reflects individuals' attempts to satisfy their own concerns.

The forcing response (assertive, unco-operative)

The forcing response involves an attempt to satisfy one's own needs at the expense of the other person's. This can be done by using formal authority, physical threats, manipulation, or simply by ignoring the claims of the other party. The blatant use of the authority of one's office: 'I'm the boss, so we'll do it my way', or manipulation 'I think you will find that to get on here you will need to do it my way', is a reflection of egoistic leadership style. Manipulative leaders often appear to be democratic by proposing that conflicting proposals be referred to a committee for further investigation. However, they make sure that the composition of the committee reflects their interests and preferences, so that what appears to be a selection based on merit is actually an authoritarian act. A related ploy used by some managers is to ignore a proposal that threatens their personal interests. If the originator enquires about the receipt of his or her memo, the manager pleads ignorance, blames the new secretary, and then suggests that the proposal be redrafted. After several of these encounters, subordinates generally get the message that the boss isn't interested in their ideas. The repeated use of the forcing approach is that it breeds hostility and resentment. While observers may intellectually admire authoritarian or manipulative leaders because they appear to accomplish a great deal, these management styles generally produce a backlash in the long run as people become unwilling to absorb the emotional cost. We discussed this point in the last of the 10 Commandments of Effective Communication.

The accommodating approach (co-operative, unassertive)

The accommodating approach is the obverse of the forcing approach, in that we may satisfy the other party while missing on our own concerns. As James Thurber said: 'One might as well fall flat on one's face as lean too far backwards.' An example of the accommodating approach would be a board of directors neglecting their responsibilities in favour of accommodating the wishes of their employees – a strategy which generally results in a lose–lose situation. The problem of a habitual use of the accommodating approach is that friendly relationships are temporarily preserved at the expense of tackling real issues.

During the early 1980s the boom in R&D expenditure was halted and subjected to critical appraisal in many organisations. Prior to this, R&D managers were typically R&D scientists and engineers who had been promoted, sometimes simply because of seniority. In one laboratory such appointment procedures had been accepted for years and management was entirely by accommodation. Unfortunately when belts had to be tightened and disciplines had to be imposed there was no history or any other approach to accommodation. Management had to say 'no' to requests but staff had never heard 'no' before and simply did not accept it. The subsequent dysfunctional conflicts incapacitated the laboratory for some three months.

The avoiding response (unco-operative, unassertive)

Avoidance neglects the interests of both parties by side-stepping the conflict or postponing a solution. The avoiding response is often the response of managers who are emotionally ill-prepared to cope with the stress associated with confrontations. It might also reflect recognition that a relationship is not strong enough to absorb the fall-out of an intense conflict. The repeated use of this approach causes considerable frustration for others because issues never seem to get resolved, tough problems are avoided because of their high potential for conflict, and the subordinates engaging in conflict are reprimanded for undermining the harmony of the work group. Sensing a leadership vacuum, people from all directions rush to fill it, creating considerable confusion and animosity in the process.

The compromising response

The compromising response is the intermediate between assertiveness and co-operation. A compromise is an attempt to obtain partial satisfaction for both parties, in the sense that both receive the proverbial 'half a loaf'. Both parties are asked to make sacrifices to obtain a common gain. While this approach has considerable practical appeal to managers, its indiscriminate use is counter-productive. If subordinates are continually told to 'split the difference', they may conclude that their managers are more interested in resolving disputes than in solving problems. This creates a climate of expediency that encourages game playing, such as asking for twice as much as you need.

We see a common mistake in management as trying to appear fair to both parties by compromising on competing corporate policies and practices – from Green issues to redundancy. When decisions are made on the basis of 'spreading the pain' rather than on the basis of merit, then harmony takes priority over value. Ironically, actions taken in the name of 'keeping peace' often end up being so illogical and impractical that the final showdown is often unyieldingly bitter. On a national scale it is the subject of bitter civil wars – on the corporate scale these are not unknown.

Collaboration (co-operative, assertive)

The collaborative approach is attempts to fully address the concerns of everyone and is often called the 'problem-solving' approach. The approach is objective as opposed to process driven, and it attempts to bring conflicts to conclusions that are satisfactory to both parties rather than to find fault or assign blame. In this way both parties can feel that they have 'won', and indeed this is the only win–win strategy. The avoiding mode results in a lose–lose outcome and the compromising, accommodating and forcing modes all represent win–lose outcomes. We will show later that the collaboration approach is not appropriate for all situations, but when appropriate, it is the most satisfactory. Constructive communication can be maintained without losing control of the situation, it encourages individuals to focus their disputes on problems and issues rather than on personalities, and it encourages empowerment.

A comparison of the five conflict management approaches is shown in Table 6.2.

Negotiation strategies

Savage *et al.* (1989) and Smith (1987) have drawn attention to the similarity of conflict management and negotiation practice. We find that negotiation strategies are commonly divided into two types: integrative and distributive. The negotiators

Table 6.2 A comparison of five conflict-management approaches

Approach	Objective	Your posture	Supporting rationale	Likely outcome
1. Forcing	Get your way.	'I know what's right. Don't question my judgement or authority.'	It is better to risk causing a few hard feelings than to abandon the issue.	You feel vindicated, but the other party feels defeated and possibly humiliated.
2. Avoiding	Avoid having to deal with conflict.	'I'm neutral on that issue. Let me think about it. That's someone else's problem.'	Disagreements are inherently bad because they create tension.	Interpersonal problems don't get resolved, causing long-term frustration manifested in a variety of ways.
3. Compromising	Reach an agreement quickly.	'Let's search for a solution we can both live with so we can get on with our work.'	Prolonged conflicts distract people from their work and cause bitter feelings.	Participants go for the expedient, rather than effective, solutions.
4. Accommodating	Don't upset the other person.	'How can I help you feel good about this? My position isn't so important that it is worth risking bad feelings between us.'	Maintaining harmonious relationships should be our top priority.	The other person is likely to take advantage.
5. Collaborating	Solve the problem together.	'This is my position, what is yours? I'm committed to finding the best possible solution. What do the facts suggest?'	Each position is important though not necessarily equally valid. Emphasis should be placed on the quality of the outcome and the fairness of the decision-making process.	The problem is most likely to be resolved. Also, both parties are committed to the solution and satisfied that they have been treated fairly.

Table 6.3 Comparison between negotiation and conflict-management strategies

Negotiation strategies	Distributive	Integrative
Conflict-management strategies	Compromising	Collaborating
	Forcing	
	Accommodating	
	Avoiding	

using a distributive strategy start on the basis of a 'fixed size cake' whereas those using an integrative approach look for ways of expanding 'the cake' by collaboration. The distributive negotiators adopt an adversarial stance, assuming that for someone to gain, someone has to lose. The integrators, by adopting a 'problem-solving' approach, attempt to obtain a 'win–win' outcome. They are interested in finding the best solution rather than forcing a choice (Fisher and Brown, 1988; Bazerman, 1986; Pruitt, 1983).

Table 6.3 shows that four of the five conflict management strategies involve one or both parties sacrificing something in order to resolve the conflict. Compromising, forcing, accommodating and avoiding are distributive solutions. Compromise occurs when both parties make sacrifices in order to find common ground. Compromisers are generally more interested in finding an expedient solution than they are in finding an integrative solution. Forcing and accommodating demand that one party gives up its position in order for the conflict to be resolved. When parties to a conflict avoid resolution, they do so because they assume that the costs of resolving the conflict are so high that they are better off not even attempting resolution. The 'fixed cake' still exists, but the individuals involved view attempts to divide it as threatening, and so they avoid decisions regarding the allocation process altogether.

In Chapter 3 we explained that the adversarial strategies seem ingrained in western culture as opposed to that in Japan. Many people approach conflicts from the construct of W.C. Field's 'never give a sucker an even break' and actually use conflict to prove virility, with little thought of the short-term let alone the long-term consequences. We see effective negotiators as gladiators in spite of the growing evidence that 'macho' negotiation is generally ineffective and frequently counterproductive. There are times when each of the forms of conflict management are effective, but generally the integrative approach is recommended. Northcraft and Neale (1990) laid down a plan for effective integrative negotiation and these closely parallel the system shown in Table 3.2 of our chapter on effective problem solving, and the rules under which it operates are similar to those described in the chapter on constructive communication.

1. *Establish mutually agreed objectives – common goals.* In order to foster a climate of collaboration, both parties need to focus on what they have in common. Focusing on their shared goals – increased productivity, lower costs, reduced design time or improved relations between departments – allows everyone to

see that there can be a solution. Sometimes chunking up or down on the initial goal best sets the goals:

- *We want an improved remuneration package.*
- *UP – Basically we both want this company to survive. Right, let's start from there.*
- *How do we get more cash to distribute?*
- *DOWN – Right, let's get down to detail . . .*

2. *Play the ball and not the person.* We do, however, have to agree on a mutually acceptable ball first. Then we can see the other party as the advocate of a point of view, rather than as a rival – 'I find that an unreasonable request' rather than 'You are an unreasonable person.'

3. *Focus on interests, not positions.* Positions are demands the negotiator makes. Interests are the reasons behind the demands. Experience shows that it is easier to establish agreement on interests, given that they tend to be broader and multi-faceted. Recalling the discussion on creative problem solving, this step involves redefining and broadening the problem to make it more tractable. An integrative comment would be: 'Help me to understand where you are coming from.'

4. *Look for creative options.* Although it is true that some negotiations may necessarily be distributive, it is a mistake for negotiators to automatically adopt a win–lose posture. There are often alternatives that are valued by one party and cost the other party very little.

   > Amex were designing a flatter organisation and reducing the number of grades from 15 to 5. Obviously this meant, in a very status conscious staff, some sadness. The creative solution was to split the five grades into classes – Gold, Silver and Bronze. The integrative negotiator would say something like: *Now that we better understand each other's concerns and needs, let's brainstorm ways of satisfying both of us without adding significantly to overheads.*

5. *Use objective criteria.* No matter how much we attempt to be integrative, there are bound to be some incompatible interests. Rather than seizing on these as opportunities for testing wills, it is far more productive to determine what makes most sense. This shift in thinking from 'getting what I want' to deciding 'what makes most sense' fosters an open, reasonable attitude. It encourages parties to avoid over-confidence or over-commitment to their initial position.

6. *Define success in terms of gains, not losses.* If a manager seeks a 10 per cent salary rise and receives only 6 per cent, that outcome can be viewed as either a 6 per cent improvement or as a 40 per cent shortfall. The first interpretation focuses on gains, the second on losses – in this case, unrealised expectations. The outcome is the same, but the manager's satisfaction with it varies substantially. It is important to recognise that our satisfaction with an outcome is affected by the standards we use to judge it. Recognising this, the integrative negotiator sets reasonable standards by which to judge the value of proposed solutions. The integrative approach to assessing proposals is: *Does this outcome constitute a meaningful improvement in current conditions?*

What happens if you are trying to collaborate and the other party is using combative, high-pressure negotiation tactics? Should you simply persist, hoping the other party will eventually follow suit, while at the same time risking the other party taking advantage of your non-combative posture? Or should you risk the possibility that you will eventually become so frustrated that you'll join the fraças?

In essence, the guidelines suggest shifting the focus of the discussion from 'content' to 'process'. By presenting your frustration, you are able to draw attention to the unsatisfactory negotiation process. In the course of a conversation of this type, the other party's underlying reasons for using a particular negotiation style often surface. We find time pressures, lack of trust, or unrealistic expectations and working on these we can build a more collaborative mode of interaction – 'How can we work together to resolve our concerns about how we work together so that we can both get something out of this?'

Selecting the appropriate approach

The presentation of alternative approaches inevitably leads to the question, 'Which of the five is best?', and for this we have no answer. The collaborative approach is probably the safest, but all the approaches can be appropriate, given the 'players' and the situation. However, we have preferred styles based on the value we place on conflict and our personality profile – we have a choice of three according to Cummings *et al.* (1971) and Porter (1973). The language they use might be criticised as jargon, but the concept is sound.

* *Altruistic-nurturing* personalities seek gratification through promoting harmony with others and enhancing their welfare, with little concern for being rewarded in return. This personality type is characterised by trust, optimism, idealism and loyalty.

* *Assertive-directing* personalities seek gratification through self-assertion and directing the activities of others with a clear sense of having earned rewards. Individuals with this personality characteristic tend to be self-confident, enterprising and persuasive.

* *Analytic-autonomising* personalities seek gratification through the achievement of self-sufficiency, self-reliance and logical orderliness. This personality type is cautious, practical, methodical and principled.

When altruistic-nurturing individuals encounter conflict, they tend to press for harmony by accommodating the demands of the other party. In contrast, the assertive-directing personality tends to challenge the opposition by using the forcing approach. The analysing-autonomising personality becomes very cautious when encountering conflict. Initially an attempt is made to rationally resolve the problem. However, if the conflict becomes very intense, this individual will withdraw and break contact.

While there appears to be a strong link between dominant personality characteristics and preferred modes of handling conflict, research on leadership styles has demonstrated that the most effective managers use a variety of styles (Schriesheim

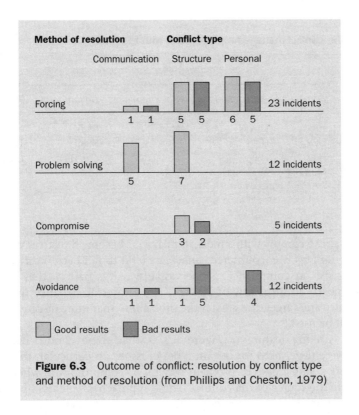

Figure 6.3 Outcome of conflict: resolution by conflict type and method of resolution (from Phillips and Cheston, 1979)

and Von Glinow, 1977), tailoring their response to the demands of the situation. This general principle has been borne out in research on conflict-management.

In one study, 25 executives were asked to describe two conflict situations – one with bad results and one with good (Phillips and Cheston, 1979). These incidents were then categorised in terms of the conflict-management approach used. As shown in Figure 6.3, there were 23 incidents of forcing, 12 incidents of problem solving, 5 incidents of compromise and 12 incidents of avoidance. Admittedly, this was a very small sample of managers, but the fact that there were almost twice as many incidents of forcing as problem solving, and nearly five times as many as compromising, is noteworthy. It is also interesting that the executives indicated that forcing and compromising were equally as likely to produce good as bad results, whereas problem solving was always linked with positive outcomes, and avoidance generally led to negative results.

It is striking that, despite the fact that forcing was as likely to produce bad as good results, it was by far the most commonly used conflict-management mode. Since this approach is clearly not superior in terms of results, one wonders why these senior executives reported a propensity for using it.

A likely answer is expediency. Evidence for this supposition is provided by a study of the preferred influence strategies of over 300 managers in three countries (Kipnis and Schmidt, 1983). The study reports that when subordinates refuse or

Table 6.4   Matching the conflict-management approach with the situation

Situational considerations	Conflict-management approach				
	Forcing	Accommodating	Compromising	Collaborating	Avoiding
Issue importance	High	Low	Med	High	Low
Relationship importance	Low	High	Med	High	Low
Relative power	High	Low	Equal-High	Low-High	Equal-High
Time constraints	Med-High	Med-High	Low	Low	Med-High

appear reluctant to comply with a request, managers become directive. When resistance in subordinates is encountered, managers tend to fall back on their superior power and insist on compliance. So pervasive was this pattern that Kipnis and Schmidt proposed an 'Iron Law of Power': 'The greater discrepancy in power between influence and target, the greater the probability that more directive influence strategies will be used.'

A second striking feature of Figure 6.3 is that some conflict-management approaches were never used for certain types of issues. In particular, the managers did not report a single case of problem solving or compromising when personal problems were the source of the conflict. These approaches were used primarily for managing conflicts involving incompatible goals and conflicting reward systems between departments. Two conclusions can be drawn from this study:

1. No one approach is most effective for managing every type of conflict.

2. Managers are more effective in dealing with conflicts if they feel comfortable using a variety of approaches.

If these conclusions are correct, to progress we need to look at where each of the techniques are most effective. Only then can we fit the style to the situation. The situational factors are summarised in Table 6.4.

The **forcing** approach is most appropriate when a conflict of values or perspectives is involved and it is necessary to defend the 'correct' position; when hierarchical control must be maintained and when being respected is more important than being liked, or when time pressures are over-riding. An example of such a situation might be when a subordinate needs to follow safety procedures.

The **accommodating** approach is most appropriate when keeping good working relationships outweighs all other considerations. Such a situation can happen anywhere, but is more common where the power does or could rest with the other party – a client, a colleague from another unit or a powerful boss. Time is also a consideration. Accommodation becomes especially appropriate when the issues are not vital to your interests and the problem must be resolved quickly.

Compromise is most appropriate when the issue is only moderately important, there are no obvious or simple solutions, and both parties have a strong interest in different facets of the problem. Time must not be a pressure. A classic case where compromise is essential would be a negotiation to avoid an industrial conflict. Experience shows that compromises are most appropriate when both parties have equal power and wish to maintain good long-term relationship. When either of these is not the case the issue may be one of damage limitation and not of conflict management.

The **collaborating** approach is most appropriate when the issues are critical, maintaining an ongoing supportive relationship between peers is important, and time constraints are not pressing. Although collaboration can be effective where there is a discrepancy of real or perceived power between the groups or individuals, it is most often employed when peers are involved. Here collaboration is more appropriate than either forcing or accommodation.

The **avoidance** approach is most appropriate when one's stake in an issue is not high and there is no strong interpersonal reason for getting involved, regardless of whether the conflict involves a superior, subordinate or peer. Severe time constraints can bring in avoidance by default, however much one might prefer to use compromise and collaboration.

Resolving confrontations using the collaborative approach

Part of the skill of effective conflict management is choosing an appropriate approach based on a thoughtful assessment of the situation. Characteristics of unsuccessful conflict managers are their habitual reliance on one or two strategies regardless of changing circumstances. For these managers the preferred strategies rarely include collaboration.

The study by Kipnis and Schmidt (1983), discussed earlier, found that although most managers appeared to support the collaborative approach in principle, they often took a directive approach under pressure. The reason for this may be that the collaborative approach to conflict management is the most difficult to implement successfully, requiring much more skill than the other systems. It is, for example, a fairly simple matter for managers to either give in or impose their will, but resolving differences in a truly collaborative manner is a very complicated and taxing process. Thus unskilled or highly pressured managers often take the path of least resistance and opt for more comfortable and familiar ground. Another explanation for the retreat from the collaborative approach may involve the issues of Mind Music we mentioned earlier. If we have a fundamental belief in hierarchy, then if the person of 'lower status' continues to wriggle when we are being 'reasonable', we listen to the messages in our head telling us that that person SHOULD respect our authority and and we should move over to asserting that authority.

The collaborative approach needs enhanced skills and practice.

While the general negotiation strategies and conflict management are similar in concept, they diverge when we deal with specific cases. This is probably because the nature of the issues is generally different. There are obvious overlaps, but negotiations tend to focus on substantive issues – the responsibility for the distribution of a new product – while interpersonal conflicts are more likely to be triggered by issues rooted in emotion, such as career failures, expenses or even sexual harassment. Because of this, interpersonal conflicts do not often lend themselves easily to collaborative solutions, even when collaboration is likely to be the most effective approach. To treat confrontations, often involving complaints and criticisms, we need a step-by-step approach similar to that covered in our chapter on problem solving. There are four stages:

1. Problem identification
2. Solution generation
3. Action plan formulation and agreement
4. Implementation and follow-up.

In real conflicts the first two stages – **problem identification** and **alternative generation** – are the most critical steps as well as the most difficult to manage effectively, in spite of being the only ones that can be controlled. If you get them wrong, everything goes wrong. When you initiate a complaint, you can control how you state it and whether you request a change in behaviour, but you cannot control whether the other party agrees to change or, having agreed, actually undertakes a follow-up. This is where we are subjected to our own Mind Music. We will, therefore, focus primarily on phases one and two during our skill training. Also in the early phases of a confrontation, the parties concerned often come from completely different spaces. And thus we need to look at the roles of each participant individually.

Virtually every confrontation involves two principal participants whom we shall term the **initiator** and the **respondent** – the individual with the issue and the person required to handle it. For example, a subordinate might complain about not being given a fair share of the opportunities to work overtime (the initiator); or the head of production (the initiator) might complain to the head of sales (the respondent) about frequent changes in order specifications.

Such a confrontation represents a greater challenge for respondents because they basically have responsibility for transforming a complaint into a problem-solving discussion. The transformation requires considerable patience and self-confidence, particularly when the initiator is unskilled. In such circumstances the unskilled initiator will generally begin the discussion by blaming the respondent for the problem, and should the respondent also be unskilled he or she will adopt a defensive position and probably look for an opportunity to come back aggressively.

If these lose–lose dynamics persist, a third party, whom we shall term the **mediator**, is needed to cool down the initiator and the respondent, to re-establish constructive communication and help the parties reconcile their differences. The presence of a mediator takes some of the pressure off the respondent because an impartial referee provides assistance in moving the confrontation through the problem-solving phases.

Below, we present guidelines for each of three roles – initiator, respondent and mediator – guidelines which those in the other two roles do not follow.

The initiator

Maintain personal ownership of the problem

It is important to recognise that your emotions and feelings are your problem and not the other person's. The first step in addressing this concern is acknowledging accountability for your feelings. Suppose someone enters your office with a smelly cigar without asking if it is all right to smoke. The fact that your office is going to stink for the rest of the day may infuriate you, but the odour does not present a problem for your smoking guest. One way to determine ownership of a problem is to identify whose needs are not being met. In this case, your need for a clean working environment is not being met, so the smelly office is your problem. Own your problem and, should it be wise to do so, explain your problem to the smoker. If the smoker happens to be your senior and is well known for his or her inability to take the mildest criticism, then we may decide that tolerating a smelly office and holding one's peace is the wisest action. Always remember the old riddle:

'*What do you call a mad terrorist with a gun?*'
'*Sir.*'

The advantage of acknowledging ownership of a problem when registering a complaint is that it reduces defensiveness (Adler, 1977). In order for you to get a problem solved, the respondent must not feel threatened by your initial statement of the problem. By beginning the conversation with a request that the respondent help solve your problem, you immediately establish a problem-solving atmosphere. For example, you might say, 'Mary, have you a few minutes? I have a problem I need to discuss with you.'

Describe your problem

The key is to reduce your concern to a few words, describing what has happened, the consequences and your feelings. A useful model for remembering how to state your problem effectively has been prescribed by Gordon (1970): 'I have a problem. When you do X, Y results, and I feel Z.' While we don't suggest using set formulas, we find that knowing they exist allows us confidence to build our own.

1. Describe the specific **behaviours** (X) that present a problem for you. This will help you to avoid what may be an automatic response to your feeling upset and avoid being evaluative: 'Your behaviour is bad' leads to trouble, but if we are specific the 'accused' has an opportunity to take actions other than defence. Your subordinate may have missed an important deadline – tell that person, detailing the circumstances. Another department may have missed giving you relevant information – tell them, explaining the information you needed.

2. Outline the specific, **observable consequences** (Y) of what you have detailed. Simply telling others that their actions are causing you problems

is often sufficient stimulus for change. In fast-paced work environments, people generally become insensitive to the impact of their actions. They don't intend to cause offence but become so busy meeting deadlines associated with 'getting the product out the door' that they don't notice subtle negative feedback from others. When this occurs, bringing to the attention of others the consequences of their behaviours will often prompt them to change.

Unfortunately, sometimes problems can't be resolved this simply. At times offenders are aware of the negative consequences of their behaviours and yet persist in them. In such cases, this approach is still useful in stimulating a rational discussion because it is non-threatening. Possibly the respondents' behaviours are constrained by the expectations of their boss or by the fact that the department is currently understaffed. Respondents may not be able to change these constraints, but this approach will encourage them to discuss them with you so that you can work on the problem together.

3. Describe the **feelings** (Z) you experience as a result of the problem. It is important that the respondent understands that his or her behaviour is not just inconvenient but is important to YOU. You need to explain how it is affecting you personally by engendering feelings of frustration, anger and insecurity. Explain how these feelings are interfering with what you see as your job. The named behaviour is – making it more difficult for you to concentrate, to satisfy customer demands, to be supportive of your boss, to work up to the 100 per cent you know is necessary.

Use the three-step model as a guide rather than as a formula, and do not use the same words every time. For example, it would get pretty monotonous if everyone in a work group initiated a discussion about an interpersonal issue with the words 'I have a problem'. Examples in Adler (1977) illustrate the process:

'I have to tell you that I get upset [feelings] when you make jokes about my bad memory in front of other people [behaviour]. In fact, I get so angry that I find myself bringing up your faults to get even [consequences].'

'I have a problem. When you say you'll be here for our date at six and don't show up until after seven [behaviour], the dinner gets ruined, we're late for the show we planned to see [consequences], and I feel hurt because it seems like I'm just not that important to you [feelings].'

'The employees want to let management know that we've been having a hard time lately with the short notice you've been giving when you need us to work overtime [behaviour]. That probably explains some of the grumbling and lack of co-operation you've mentioned [consequences]. Anyhow, we wanted to make it clear that this policy has really got a lot of the workers feeling pretty resentful [feeling].'

In presenting your problem, avoid the pitfalls of making accusations, drawing inferences about motivations or intentions, or attributing the respondent's undesirable behaviour to personal inadequacies. Statements such as 'You are always interrupting me', 'You haven't been fair to me since the day I disagreed with you in the board meeting', or 'You never have time to listen to our problems and suggestions because you manage your time so poorly', are good at starting rows but less effective for initiating rational problem solving.

Another key to reducing defensiveness is to delay proposing a solution until both parties agree on the nature of the problem. When you become so upset with someone's behaviour that you feel it is necessary to initiate a complaint, it is often because the person has not met the criteria you have laid down for that individual. For example, you might feel that your subordinate has failed to complete a project on time. Consequently, you might begin the interview by assuming that the subordinate was aware of your time scale. If he or she is not aware of that time scale and was working to another set of priorities, we will have a potentially dysfunctional conflict. Check on common ground: 'Were you aware that the whole project has to be completed by next week and that we are waiting on your parts before we complete?' Establish common ground first. If the respondent was unaware of the deadlines or the importance of his or her contribution, then you are the one who has slipped up. In this case any recriminations will lead at best to defensiveness.

Besides creating defensiveness, the principal disadvantage to initiating problem solving with a suggested remedy without establishing common ground, is that it doesn't work. Before completing the problem-articulation phase, you have immediately jumped to the solution-generation phase, based on the assumption that you know all the reasons for, and constraints on, the other person's behaviour.

Persist until understood

There are times when the other person will not clearly receive or acknowledge even the most effectively expressed message. Suppose, for instance, that you share the following problem with a co-worker (Adler, 1977):

> 'I've been bothered by something lately and I would like to discuss it with you. To be honest, I'm uncomfortable [feeling] when you use so much bad language [behaviour]. I don't mind an occasional "damn" or "hell", but the f-word is difficult for me to accept. Lately I've found myself avoiding you [consequences], and that's no good either, so I wanted to let you know how I feel.'

When you share your feelings in this non-evaluative way, it is likely that the other person will understand your position and possibly try to change behaviour to suit your needs. On the other hand, there are a number of less satisfying responses that could be made to your comment:

- Defending, rationalising and counter-attacking: *'Listen, these days everyone talks that way. And besides, you've got your faults, too, you know!'*

- Failing to understand how serious the problem is to you: *'Yes, I suppose I do swear a lot. I'll have to work on that some day.'*

- Totally misunderstanding: *'Listen, if you're still angry about my forgetting to tell you about that meeting the other day, you can be sure that I'm really sorry. I won't do it again.'*

- Showing discomfort and seeking to change the subject: *'Speaking of avoiding, have you seen Chris lately? I wonder if anything is wrong with him?'*

When we receive an unsolicited response it is quite likely that our Mind Music will be triggered, and to return to constructive communication we need to buy time. Think of your mind as a computer and the Mind Music as a series of unstructured programmes that take up our available RAM. When such an event happens, we need to switch off and reboot. So it is with us when the Mind Music appears, such thoughts as – *I'm his boss, he ought to agree. Look I'm being reasonable and nice, he ought to respond* – trigger us back to being directive. We have to buy time to restore our constructive communication processes.

The ideal response to buy us thinking time is the same for all these responses – acknowledge what the respondent says and return to your own bottom line, as often as is required. Thus, in the response that indicates misunderstanding: *The issue of the meeting is not the point. What is the point is that your use of the f-word is not acceptable.*

The respondent may continue to wriggle and change approach: *Everyone uses the occasional four-letter word,* but the reply is the same: *Other people's behaviour is not the point, your use of the f-word is not acceptable.*

To avoid introducing new concerns or shifting from a descriptive to an evaluative mode, keep in mind the 'X, Y, Z' formula for feedback. Persistence is most effective when it consists of 'variations on a theme', rather than 'variation in themes'. Woods (1989) describes the methodology as a combination of two techniques – Broken Record and Fielding. With Broken Record we define our bottom line, 'using the f-word is unacceptable', and repeat it calmly, whatever the other person says, until he or she hears our determination. We do not have to answer questions or defend our position.

Broken Record alone will win us no friends and is not part of constructive communication, so we add a second technique – Fielding. With Fielding we acknowledge what the other person says and accept that he or she has a right to that opinion, using some of his or her own words. We then return to the Broken Record theme.

The process continues until the respondent acknowledges our position.

Encourage two-way discussion

It is important that you establish a climate for rational problem solving by inviting the other person to express opinions and ask questions. Often there is a very simple explanation for another's behaviour, perhaps a radically different view of the problem. The sooner this information is introduced into the conversation, the sooner the issue is likely to be resolved. As a rule of thumb, the longer the opening statement of the initiator, the longer it will take the two parties to work through their problem. The reason for this is that the more lengthy the statement of the problem, the more likely it is to encourage a defensive reaction. The longer we talk, the more worked-up we get, and the more likely we are to violate the principles of constructive communication. Long statements can be seen as threatening and encourage a rebuttal or counter-attack. People simply turn off, and a collaborative approach is usually discarded in favour of the accommodation or forcing strategies, depending on the circumstances. When this occurs, it is unlikely that the actors will be able to reach a mutually satisfactory solution to their problem without third-party intervention. Keep it simple and keep it short. Only make one point and make sure that it is the best point. Here again we return to negotiation strategy – do not produce a range of arguments, the respondent will simply dispose of the weakest and ignore the strongest. Start and continue with your bottom line, only moving on when you know you have been heard. If and when the two-way communication occurs – listen.

Manage the agenda: approach multiple or complex problems incrementally

Your opening statement should only contain one point. This should be the essential point that must be resolved or your meeting is a failure. Thus swearing may only be one issue that is causing you concern – the respondent's dress may cause you lesser concern and the time he or she spends in the doorway smoking might also be a subject of discussion. Leave them and focus on what is, for you, the most important issue. The other issues may be taken up later, but not until he or she has accepted your primary issue as being important.

Focus on commonalities as the basis for requesting a change

Once the problem is clearly understood, the discussion should shift to the solution-generation phase of the problem-solving process. Most of us share some goals (personal and organisational), believe in many of the same fundamental principles of management, and operate under similar constraints. The most straightforward approach to changing another's offensive behaviour is making a request. The legitimacy of a request will be enhanced if it is linked to common interests. These might include shared values such as treating co-workers fairly and following through on commitments, or shared constraints such as getting reports in on time and operating within budgetary restrictions. This approach is particularly effective when the parties have had difficulty getting along in the past. In these situations, pointing out how a change in the respondent's behaviour would positively affect your shared fate will reduce defensiveness:

> 'Jane, we are not talking about a big deal. You are the most influential member of the accounts department and simply by abiding by the Flexi-Time rules, you will allow us to keep the system that has advantages for all of us.'

The respondent

Now we shall examine the problem-identification phase from the viewpoint of the person who is supposedly the source of the problem – the respondent, or 'the accused'. In a work setting, this could be a manager who is making unrealistic demands, a new employee who has ignored safety regulations or a co-worker who is claiming credit for your ideas. The overall strategy is to listen before responding. The tactics for doing this are shown in the following guidelines.

Establish a climate for joint problem solving

When a person complains to you, you should not treat that complaint lightly. While this sounds self-evident, it is often difficult to focus your attention on someone else's problems when you are in the middle of writing an important project report or concerned about preparing for a meeting scheduled to begin in a few minutes. Also it is often wise to come prepared for a difficult meeting, and preparation may well necessitate your buying time. Therefore, unless the other person's emotional condition means that you need to take immediate action, it is usually fine to agree a time for another meeting after you have understood the issue to be discussed.

In most cases, the initiator will be expecting you to set the tone for the meeting. The tones to be avoided are over-reaction or defensiveness. Even if you disagree with the complaint and feel it has no foundation, you need to respond empathetically to the initiator's statement of the problem. The initiator MAY not have expressed the criticism correctly.

Most of us have had experience in not satisfying our bosses in the presentation of a written report. What frequently happens is that when we present a report, the grammar and even the spelling are criticised, but we would be unwise to leave it there. In experience many people find it easier to criticise the detail rather than explain their real complaint – i.e., that the report is inadequate in some much more radical way. It is the job of the respondent to tease out the 'real' criticism without dismissing the detailed complaints.

Learning from criticism is best done by conveying an attitude of interest and receptivity through your posture, tone of voice and facial expressions. One of the most difficult aspects of establishing the proper climate for your discussion is responding appropriately to the emotions of the initiator. Sometimes you may need to let a person blow off steam before trying to address the substance of a specific complaint. In some cases the therapeutic effect of being able to express negative emotions to the boss will be enough to satisfy a subordinate. This occurs frequently in high-pressure jobs where tempers flare easily as a result of the intense stress.

However, an emotional outburst can be very detrimental to problem solving. If an employee begins verbally attacking you or someone else, and it is apparent that the individual is more interested in getting even than in solving an interpersonal problem, you may need to interrupt and interject some ground rules for collaborative problem solving. By explaining calmly to the other person that you are willing to discuss a genuine problem but that you will not tolerate personal attacks or making scape-goats, you can quickly determine the true intentions of the initiator. In most instances he or she will apologise, emulate your emotional tone and begin formulating a useful statement of the problem.

Learning from criticism

Mike Woods (1989) calls the most effect techniques for learning from criticism Appropriate Assertion and Constructive Enquiry. Appropriate Assertion is designed to take the sting and negative emotion from a criticism by assertively affirming that you either agree or disagree with the comments:

'You are late with the training programme'

'That is correct, the training programme has been delayed'

– and then stop. If, however, the programme has not been delayed:

'That is completely untrue – the training programme is on schedule'

– and then stop.

The clarity and the uncompromising nature of the response disarms most people who have the intention of (persecuting) you. Once you have 'disarmed' the initiator you can move on to the next phase of learning from the criticism. The process of 'disarming' certainly includes removing the emotional element from the criticism. An adage that may be of use is: 'It is no use pouring the cold water of logic onto the hot coals of emotion.'

Learning from criticism involves rational problem solving on the part of the initiator and the respondent. Untrained initiators will typically present complaints that are both very general and highly evaluative. They will make generalisations from a few specific incidents about your motives and your personal strengths and weaknesses. If you are going to transform a personal complaint into a joint problem, you must redirect the conversation from general and evaluative accusations to descriptions of specific behaviours.

To do this, ask for details about specific actions that are forming the basis for the evaluation. You might find it useful to phrase your questions so that they reflect the 'X, Y, Z' model described previously: 'Can you give me a specific example of my behaviour that concerns you?', 'When I did that, what were the specific consequences for your work?', 'How did you feel when that happened?' When a complaint is both serious and complex, it is especially critical for you to understand it completely. In these situations, check your level of understanding by summarising the initiator's main points and asking if your summary is correct. Mike Woods, in the jargon of assertiveness training, calls this Constructive Enquiry.

Sometimes it is useful to ask for additional complaints: 'Are there any other problems in our relationship you'd like to discuss?' If the initiator is just in a griping mood, this is not a good time to probe further; you don't want to encourage this type of behaviour. But if the person is seriously concerned about improving your relationship, your discussion to this point has been helpful and you suspect that the initiator is holding back and not talking about the really serious issues, you should probe deeper. Often people begin by complaining about a minor problem to 'test the water'. If you lose your temper, the conversation finishes and the really critical issues aren't discussed. However, if you are responsive to a frank discussion about problems, the more serious issues are likely to surface.

Agree with some aspect of the complaint

Appropriate Assertion involves a clear acceptance or denial of the truth of criticism, unfortunately things are seldom black and white. There is an element of truth in many harsh criticisms, but this is difficult to accept. Acceptance may well fuel the complaining behaviour, so we need a further formula. In practice, this step is probably the best test of whether the respondent is committed to using the collaborative approach to conflict management rather than the avoiding, forcing or accommodating approaches. People who use the forcing mode will grit their teeth while listening to the initiator, just waiting to find a flaw they can use to launch a counter-attack. Or they will simply respond, 'I'm sorry, but that's just the way I am. You'll simply have to get used to it.' Accommodators will apologise profusely and ask for forgiveness. People who avoid conflicts will acknowledge and agree with the initiator's concerns, but only in a superficial manner because their only concern is how to end the awkward conversation as quickly as possible.

In contrast, collaborators will demonstrate their concerns for both co-operation and assertiveness by looking for points in the initiator's presentation with which they can genuinely agree. Even in the most blatantly malicious and hostile verbal assault (which may be more a reflection of the initiator's insecurity than evidence of your inadequacies), there is generally a grain of truth.

> A few years ago a junior member in a business school who was being reviewed for promotion received a very unfair appraisal from one of his senior colleagues. Since the junior member knew that the critic was going through a personal crisis, he could have dismissed this criticism as irrelevant and insignificant. However, one particular phrase, 'You are stuck on a narrow line of research', kept coming back to his mind. There was something there that couldn't be ignored. As a result of turning what was otherwise a very vindictive remark into something personally useful, he accepted the partial truth of the remark and acted accordingly, changing his career path. Furthermore, by publicly giving the senior colleague credit for the suggestion, he substantially strengthened the interpersonal relationship.

There are a number of ways you can agree with part of a message without accepting it in full (Adler, 1977). You can find an element of truth and accept it: '*I accept that I may be seen to be pursuing a narrow line of research and I thank you for bringing it to my attention.*' (Accepting that this person may observe my behaviour in a certain way but NOT accepting that this was my intention or indeed that the remark is true.)

We may then move on and request further information and guidance: '*As I was unaware of the potential problem, perhaps you could help me by suggesting how I could be seen to broaden my approach.*'

Again, do not be stuck in a formal set of words: '*Well, I can see how you would think that. I have known people who have deliberately shirked their responsibilities.*' Or, you can agree with the person's feelings: '*It is obvious that our earlier discussion greatly upset you.*'

You are not agreeing with the initiator's conclusions or evaluations but accepting that the initiator has a right to his or her views. You will be seen to be listening, attempting to understand and foster a problem solving, rather than argumentative, discussion and this in itself will assist in developing a supportive environment. Generally, initiators prepare for a complaint session by mentally cataloguing all the evidence supporting their point of view. Once the discussion begins, they introduce as much evidence as necessary to make their argument convincing; that is, they keep arguing until you agree. The more evidence that is introduced, the broader the argument becomes and the more difficult it is to begin investigating solutions.

Ask for suggestions of acceptable alternatives

Once you are certain that you fully understand the initiator's complaint, proceed with the next aspect of constructive enquiry – look for possible solutions with the initiator. Mutual problem solving is an important transition in the discussion. Attention moves from negative historical aspects to positive and future concerns. It also tells the initiator that you are concerned with his or her opinions – a key element in the joint problem-solving process. Some managers listen patiently to a subordinate's complaint, express appreciation for the feedback, say they will rectify the problem, and then close the discussion. This leaves the initiator guessing about the outcome of the meeting. Will you take the complaint seriously? Will you really change? If so, will the change resolve the problem? It is important to eliminate this ambiguity by agreeing on a plan of action. If the problem is particularly serious or complex, it is useful to write down specific agreements, including assignments and deadlines, as well as providing for a follow-up meeting to check progress.

The mediator

Frequently it is necessary for a third party to intervene in a dispute (Walton, 1969). While this may occur for a variety of reasons, we will assume in this discussion that the mediator has been invited to help the initiator and respondent resolve their differences. We will further assume that the mediator is senior and concerned with both the initiator and the respondent, though this assumption is not necessary to discuss the process.

> A hair stylist in a beauty salon complained to the manager about the way the receptionist was favouring other beauticians who had been there longer. This allegation violated the manager's policy of allocating walk-in business strictly on the basis of beautician availability. The manager investigated the complaint and discovered considerable animosity between these two employees. The stylist felt the receptionist was keeping sloppy records, while the receptionist blamed the stylist for forgetting to hand in her slip when she finished with a customer. The problems between these two appeared serious enough to the participants and broad enough in scope that the manager called both parties into her office to help them resolve their differences.

Ten guidelines, due to William Morris and Marshall Sashkin (1976), which are intended to help mediators avoid the common pitfalls associated with this role, are presented in Table 6.5.

It is vital that the mediator takes the problems between conflicting parties seriously. If they feel they have a serious problem, the mediator should not belittle its significance. Remarks such as *'I'm surprised that two intelligent people like you*

Table 6.5 Ten ways to FAIL as a mediator

1. After you have listened to the argument for a short time, begin to non-verbally communicate your discomfort with the discussion (e.g., sit back, begin to fidget).
2. Take sides and communicate your agreement with **one** of the parties (e.g., through facial expressions, posture, chair position, reinforcing comments).
3. Say that you shouldn't be talking about this kind of thing at work or where others can overhear.
4. Discourage the expression of emotion. Suggest that the discussion would be better held later after both parties have cooled off.
5. Suggest that both parties are wrong. Point out the problems with both points of view.
6. Suggest part-way through the discussion that possibly you aren't the person who should be helping solve this problem.
7. See if you can get both parties to attack you.
8. Minimise the seriousness of the problem.
9. Change the subject (e.g., ask for advice to help you solve one of your problems).
10. Express displeasure that the two parties are experiencing conflict (e.g., imply that it might undermine the solidarity of the work group).

Source: Adapted from Morris and Sashkin (1976)

have not been able to work out your disagreement. We have more important things to do here than get all worked up over such petty issues', will make both parties defensive and interfere with any serious problem-solving efforts. While you might wish that your subordinates could have worked out their disagreement without bothering you, this is not the time to lecture them on self-reliance or inducing guilt that 'they are being emotional'.

One early decision a mediator has to make is whether to convene a joint problem-solving session or to first meet with the parties separately. The diagnostic questions shown in Table 6.6 should help you to weigh up the advantages and disadvantages of each approach.

The overall methodology for the mediator

What is the current position of the disputants?

- Are they both aware a problem exists?
- Do they agree on the definition of the problem?
- Are they equally motivated to work on solving the problem?

The nearer the answer YES is to all three of the questions, the more likely are things to be resolved. If the answer to any of the three questions is NO, then the mediator should work towards some agreement through one-on-one meetings before bringing the disputants together.

CONSTRUCTIVE CONFLICT MANAGEMENT

Table 6.6   Choosing a format for mediating conflicts

Factors	Hold joint meeting	Hold separate meetings
Awareness and motivation		
• Both parties are aware of the problem	Yes	No
• They are equally motivated to resolve the problem	Yes	No
• They accept your legitimacy as a mediator	Yes	No
Nature of the relationship		
• The parties hold equal status	Yes	No
• They work together regularly	Yes	No
• They have a good overall relationship	Yes	No
Nature of the problem		
• This is an isolated (not a recurring) problem	Yes	No
• The complaint is substantive in nature and easily verified	Yes	No
• The parties agree on the root causes of the problem	Yes	No
• The parties share common values and work priorities	Yes	No

What is the current relationship between the disputants?

• Does their work require them to interact frequently?

• Is a good working relationship critical for their individual job performance?

• What has their relationship been like in the past?

• What is the difference in their formal status in the organisation?

As we discussed earlier, joint problem-solving sessions are most productive between individuals of equal status who are required to work together regularly. This does not mean that joint meetings should not be held between a supervisor and a subordinate, only that greater care needs to be taken in preparing for such a meeting. Specifically, if a department head becomes involved in a dispute between a worker and a supervisor, the department head should make sure that the worker does not feel that this meeting will serve as an excuse for two managers to gang up on a subordinate.

Separate fact-finding meetings with the disputants before a joint meeting are particularly useful when the parties have a history of recurring disputes, especially if these disputes should have been resolved without a mediator. Such a history often suggests a lack of conflict management or problem-solving skills on the part of the disputants, or it might stem from a broader set of issues that are beyond their control. In these situations, individual coaching sessions before a joint meeting will increase your understanding of the root causes and improve the individuals' abilities to resolve their differences. Following up these private meetings with a joint problem-solving session, in which the mediator coaches the disputants through the process for resolving their conflicts, can be a positive learning experience.

What is the nature of the problem?

Is the complaint substantive in nature and easily verifiable? If the problem stems from conflicting role responsibilities and the actions of both parties in question are common knowledge, then a joint problem-solving session can begin on a common information and experimental basis. In contrast, if the complaint stems from differences in managerial style, values, personality characteristics, etc., bringing the parties together immediately following a complaint may seriously undermine the problem-solving process. Complaints that are likely to be interpreted as threats to the self-image of one or both parties (Who am I?, What do I stand for?) warrant considerable individual discussion before a joint meeting is called. To avoid individuals feeling as though they are being ambushed in a meeting, you should discuss serious personal complaints with them ahead of time, in private.

In seeking out the perspective of both parties, maintain a neutral posture regarding the disputants, if not the issues. Effective mediation requires impartiality. If a mediator shows strong personal bias in favour of one party in a joint problem-solving session, the other party may simply get up and walk out. However, this type of personal bias is more likely to creep out in private conversations with the disputants. Statements like, 'I can't believe he really did that!' and 'Everyone seems to be having trouble working with Andrew these days', imply that the mediator is taking sides, and any attempt to appear impartial in a joint meeting will seem like mere window dressing to appease the other party. No matter how well intentioned or justified these comments might be, they destroy the credibility of the mediator in the long run. In contrast, the effective mediator respects both parties' points of view and makes sure that both perspectives are expressed adequately.

Occasionally, it is not possible to be impartial on the issues. One person may have violated company policy, engaged in unethical competition with a colleague or broken a personal agreement. In these cases the challenge of the mediator is to separate the offence from the offender. If a person is clearly in the wrong, the inappropriate behaviour needs to be corrected, but in such a way that the individual doesn't feel his or her image and working relationships have been permanently marred. This can be done most effectively when correction occurs in private.

Manage the discussion to ensure fairness

Keep the discussion confined to the issues in hand and do not allow them to stray on to criticism of personalities. The mediator must maintain the role of the problem solver and not the referee. This is not to say that strong emotional statements don't have their place. People often associate effective problem solving with a calm, highly rational discussion of the issues and associate a personality attack with a highly emotional outburst. However, it is important not to confuse affect and effect. Placid, cerebral discussions often don't solve problems, and impassioned statements don't have to be insulting. The critical point about conflict management is that it should be centred on the issues and the consequences of continued conflict on performance. Even when behaviour offensive to one of the parties obviously stems from a personality quirk, the discussion of the problem should be limited to the behaviour. As we stated earlier, attributions about motives or generalisations about specific events or personal proclivities distract participants from the problem solving process. It is important that the mediator establishes and maintains these ground rules.

It is also important for a mediator to ensure that neither party dominates the discussion. A relatively even balance in the level of inputs improves the quality of the final outcome. It also increases the likelihood that both parties will accept the final decision, because there is a high correlation between feelings about the problem-solving process and attitudes about the final solution. If one party tends to dominate a discussion, the mediator can help balance the exchange by asking the less talkative individual direct questions: 'Now that we have heard Bill's view of that incident, how do you see it?', 'That's an important point, Malcolm, so let's make sure Brian agrees. How do you feel, Brian?'

Facilitate exploration of solutions rather than judge responsibility for the problem

When the parties must work closely, and have a history of chronic interpersonal problems, it is often more important to teach problem-solving skills than to resolve a specific dispute. This is done best when the mediator adopts the posture of facilitator. The role of judge is to render a verdict regarding a problem in the past, not to teach people how to solve their problems in the future. While some disputes obviously involve right and wrong actions, most interpersonal problems stem from differences in perspective. In these situations it is important that the mediator avoids being seduced into delivering a verdict by comments like, 'Well, you're the boss, tell us which one of us is right', or more subtly, 'I wonder if I did what was right?' The problem with a mediator's assuming the role of judge is that it sets in motion processes that are antithetical to effective interpersonal – problem solving. The parties focus on persuading the mediator of their innocence and the other party's guilt rather than striving to improve their working relationship with the assistance of the mediator. The disputants work to establish facts about what happened in the past rather than to reach an agreement about what ought to happen in the future. Consequently, a key aspect of effective mediation is helping the disputants to explore multiple alternatives in a non-judgemental manner.

Explore options by focusing on interests, not positions

Conflict resolution is often hampered by the perception that where there are incompatible positions there are irreconcilable differences. As noted in the negotiation section, mediation of such conflicts can best be accomplished by examining the interests (goals and concerns) behind the positions. It is these interests that form the driving force behind the positions, and it is these interests that are ultimately what people want satisfied.

It is the job of the mediator to discover where interests meet and where they conflict. Interests tend not to be stated, often because they are unclear to the participants. In order to flesh out each party's interests, ask 'Why' questions: 'Why have they taken this position?', 'Why does this matter to them?' Understand that there is probably no single, or simple, answer to these questions. For example, each side may represent a number of constituents, each with a special interest.

After each side has articulated its underlying interests, help the parties identify areas of agreement and reconcilability. It is common for participants in an intense conflict to feel that they are on opposite sides of all issues – that they have little in common. Helping them recognise that there are areas of agreement and reconcilability often represents a major turning point in resolving long-standing feuds.

Make sure that all parties fully understand and support the agreed solution and that follow-up procedures have been established

Before concluding this discussion of conflict-management principles, it is important to briefly mention the last two phases of the problem-solving process: agreement on an action plan and follow-up. These will be discussed within the context of the mediator's role, but they are equally applicable to the other roles.

A common mistake of ineffective mediators is terminating the discussion prematurely. They feel that once the problem has been solved in principle, the disputants can be left to work out the details on their own. Or, they assume that because one of the parties has recommended a solution that appears very reasonable and workable, the second disputant will be willing to implement it. It is very important that when serving as a mediator you insist on a specific plan of action that both parties are willing to implement. If you suspect any hesitancy on the part of either disputant, this needs to be explored explicitly: 'Susan, I sense that you are somewhat less enthusiastic than Jane about this plan. Is there something that bothers you?' When you are confident that both parties support the plan, you should check to make sure that they are aware of their respective responsibilities and then propose a mechanism for monitoring progress. You might schedule another formal meeting, or you might pop into the offices of the individuals to get a progress report.

SUMMARY

In western culture conflict brings out a number of negative constructs and we place a high value on getting along with people – *good managers do not make waves*. For this reason many people feel uncomfortable in conflict situations. Conflict correctly handled can be highly productive and this chapter has attempted to show how this correct handling can be achieved. A summary model of conflict management is shown in Figure 6.4.

There are basically five approaches to handling conflict:

- Forcing
- Accommodating

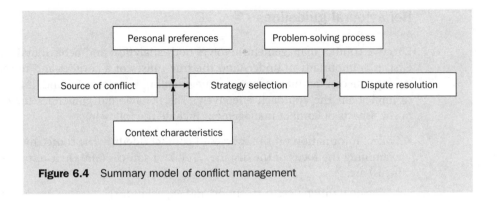

Figure 6.4 Summary model of conflict management

- Avoiding
- Compromising
- Collaborating

The model contains three phases: diagnosing the sources of conflict, selecting the appropriate conflict management strategy and using specific problem-solving techniques to resolve interpersonal disputes effectively. The first two phases comprise the diagnostic and analytical aspects of conflict management. We need to understand the causes of the conflict and hence how to respond. The third phase focuses on the behavioural component of conflict management. We have argued that conflict plays an important role in effective organisations. The operational component of this model focuses on successful resolution of specific disputes and not on eliminating, or preventing, all conflict.

Conflict can be produced by a variety of circumstances: irreconcilable personal differences, discrepancies in information, role incompatibilities and environmentally induced stress. These causes, and the resulting conflicts, differ in both frequency and intensity. For example, information-based conflicts occur frequently but are easily resolved because the disputants have low personal stakes in the outcome. In contrast, conflicts grounded in differences of perceptions and expectations are generally very intense and difficult to diffuse.

There is no best way to handle all conflicts. Instead, in choosing a response mode, managers should consider the quality and duration of the ongoing relationship between the actors, the nature and seriousness of their problem, as well as their personal preferences. Successful strategies need to be set into the context of the overall situation and the overall attitudes, philosophy and personality of the implementers.

The collaborative approach, like the integrative negotiation strategy, generally produces the highest-quality solutions and has the least detrimental effect on relationships. When it is used effectively, all parties tend to be satisfied with the outcome. The impositions of authority, withdrawal, splitting the difference or giving in, are easy options. The recommended option – the problem-solving collaborative approach – requires real skills, which are the basis of our behavioural guidelines.

Behavioural guidelines

Effective conflict management involves both analytical and behavioural elements. First, it is important to understand the true causes of a conflict and to select the appropriate conflict-management, or negotiation, approach. Second, it is necessary to implement the approach effectively. The behavioural guidelines for the diagnostic aspects of conflict management include the following:

- Collect information on the sources of conflict. Identify the source by examining the focus of the dispute. The four sources (and their respective focus) are:
  1. Personal differences (perception and expectations)
  2. Information deficiency (misinformation and misinterpretation)
  3. Role incompatibility (goals and responsibilities)
  4. Environmental stress (resource scarcity and uncertainty).
- Use the collaborative approach for managing conflict, including integrative negotiation tactics, unless specific conditions dictate the use of an alternative approach.
- Use the forcing approach only when: the issue is extremely important to you; a close, ongoing relationship is not necessary; you have much more power than the other person; there is a high sense of urgency.
- Use the accommodating approach only when: the issue is not important to you; a close, ongoing relationship is critical; you have no other option (low power); time is not a factor.
- Use the compromising approach only when the issue is very complex and of moderate importance to both parties (and the parties feel strongly about different aspects of the issues); the relationship is of moderate importance; the parties have relatively equal power; time constraints are low.
- Use the avoiding approach only when: the issue is not important to you; the relationship is not critical; your relative power is equal to high; time is not a factor.

The behavioural guidelines for effectively implementing the collaborative (problem-solving) approach to conflict management are summarised below. These are organised according to three roles. Guidelines for the problem-identification and solution-generation phases of the problem-solving process are specified for each role. Guidelines for the action plan and follow-up phases are the same for all three roles.

The first party: the initiator

Problem identification

1. Describe your problem briefly and clearly in terms of behaviours, consequences and feelings. ('When you do X, Y happens and I feel Z.')

- Maintain personal ownership of the problem.
- Use a specific incident to illustrate the expectations or standards violated.
- Stick to the facts, avoid drawing evaluative conclusions and attributing motives to the respondent.

2. Persist until understood and encourage two-way discussion.
   - Restate your concerns or give additional examples.
   - Avoid introducing additional issues or letting your frustration sour your emotional tone.
   - Invite the respondent to ask questions and express another perspective.

3. Manage the agenda carefully.
   - Approach multiple problems incrementally – proceeding from simple to complex, easy to hard, concrete to abstract.
   - Conversely, don't become fixated on one issue. If you reach an impasse, expand the discussion to increase the likelihood of an integrative outcome.

Solution generation

4. Make a request.
   - Focus on those things you have in common (principles, goals, constraints) as the basis for recommending preferred alternatives.

The second party: the respondent or 'accused'

Problem identification

1. Establish a climate for joint problem solving.
   - Show genuine concern and interest; respond empathetically, even if you disagree with the complaint.
   - Respond appropriately to the initiator's emotions; if necessary, allow the person to 'let off steam' before addressing the complaint.

2. Seek additional information about the problem.
   - Ask questions that channel the initiator's statements from general to specific and from evaluative to descriptive.

3. Agree with some aspect of the complaint.
   - Signal your willingness to consider making changes by agreeing with facts, perceptions, feelings or principles.

Solution generation

4. Ask for recommendations.
   - To avoid debating the merits of a single suggestion, brainstorm multiple alternatives.

The mediator

Problem identification

1. Acknowledge that a conflict exists.
   - Select the most appropriate setting (one-to-one conference vs group meeting) for coaching and fact-finding.
   - Propose a problem-solving approach for resolving the dispute.

2. Maintain a neutral posture.
   - Assume the role of facilitator, not judge. Do not belittle the problem or berate the disputants for their inability to resolve their differences.
   - Be impartial towards the disputants and the issues (as long as policy has not been violated). If correction is necessary, do it in private.

3. Manage the discussion to ensure fairness.
   - Focus discussion on the conflict impact on performance and the detrimental effect of a continued conflict.
   - Keep the discussion issue-oriented, not personality-oriented.
   - Do not allow one party to dominate the discussion; ask directed questions to maintain a balance.

Solution generation

4. Explore options by focusing on the interests behind stated positions.
   - Explore the 'whys' behind disputants' arguments/claims.
   - Help disputants see commonalities among their goals, values and principles.
   - Use commonalities to generate multiple alternatives.
   - Maintain a non-judgemental manner.

Action plan and follow-up for all roles

1. Ensure that all parties support the agreed plan.
   - Verify understanding of, and commitment to, specific actions.

2. Establish a mechanism for follow-up.
   - Create benchmarks for measuring progress and ensuring accountability.
   - Encourage flexibility in adjusting the plan to meet emerging circumstances.

Skill Analysis

CASE STUDY **6.1**

HEALTH PROVISIONS LIMITED

Health Provisions Limited (HPL) provided one of the first private health-care schemes to the British market. The founders had all worked in the National Health

Service in some capacity and retained a conservative philosophy to the business, putting patient care very high on their list of priorities. Their main business was providing employee cover for blue-chip companies, and they kept out of the more competitive direct-consumer-marketing approach of the growing number of rivals. Until very recently they felt secure and in a good position to handle further changes in the economic and political environment.

Carolyn Richardson was one of the founders of HPL and is highly respected in the profession. The other partners, comfortable with Carolyn's conservative, yet flexible nature, elected her to the position of the first managing director. After that, Carolyn became known as 'the great equaliser'. She worked hard to make sure that all the partners were included in decisions and that strong relations were maintained. Her management philosophy was built on the concept of trust and loyalty – loyalty to the organisation, loyalty to its members, loyalty to friends and, most of all, loyalty to the clients.

As the total market grew, various overseas-funded health-care groups began to encroach on HPL's client base and its growth increasingly failed to keep pace with those of its rivals. As a result, Carolyn has reluctantly begun to consider the merits of more aggressive promotion and moving into direct selling.

One evening Carolyn talked about her concern with her bridge partner and life-long friend, Susan Ross, who owned a private hospital developed in conjunction with HPL. Everyone respected Susan for her knowledge, work rate and uncanny ability to predict trends. Susan knew what to do and when to do it, and her present preoccupation was modifying her hospital group for long-term mental-health patients.

When Susan heard Carolyn's concerns and need for an aggressive approach, she suggested to her friend that what HPL needed was some fresh blood, someone who could infuse enthusiasm into the organisation. She suggested a friend, Mark Western, who had worked in health-care in Canada and 'was good at sorting things out – if a bit abrasive'.

Carolyn suggested the idea of employing Mark at the next staff meeting, but it was met with caution and scepticism. 'Yes, he's had a brilliant career on paper,' said one senior partner, 'but he's never stayed in one place long enough to really finish what he has started. Look at his CV. During the past seven years, he's been with four different organisations.'

'That's true,' said Carolyn, 'but his references are really good. In fact, he's been described as a rising star, aggressive and productive. He's just what we need to help us explore new opportunities.' Throughout the discussion, Carolyn defended Mark's record and pointed to his impressive performance. She deflected concerns about his reputation by saying that he had been recommended by a loyal and trusted friend. Eventually, the other partners agreed, albeit reluctantly, to recruit Mark. When Carolyn offered Mark the job, he was promised the freedom to work out his own ideas.

Mark worked hard, regaining corporate clients and developing telephone-selling techniques for smaller companies and individuals. He set HLP on the road to recovery and was liked by many of the junior staff as a breath of fresh air. He was open to new ideas and was exciting to work with. His abrasive manner confused and annoyed the other partners who thought Mark was attempting to move things too quickly. It was not uncommon for sharp disagreements to erupt in staff meetings but Carolyn tried to smooth ruffled feathers and maintain a productive atmosphere.

Mark seemed oblivious to all the turmoil he was causing. He was optimistic about potential growth opportunities. His main idea was similar to Susan Ross's – he thought that the group should go into long-term care of the mentally ill. The generous government grants now available should be used. His attitude was that – 'If we don't, the others will steal a march on us and we will be stuck doing what we do now for ever with smaller and smaller margins.'

Months passed and dissension among the managers grew. Mark's frustration over the lack of support among the senior partners began to undermine the day-to-day operations of HPL. He began to criticise his detractors in discussions with younger HPL employees. In addition, he moved staff away from the core business into his own, and as yet unproven, scheme.

Amid a rapidly spreading undercurrent of tension, one of the founding partners, Neville Watson, approached Carolyn one day: 'Carolyn, I speak for most of the senior staff when I say we are very troubled by Mark's approach. We've expressed ourselves well enough for Mark to understand, but his actions defy everything we've said. He's a catastrophe just waiting to happen.'

'You are right, Neville,' replied Carolyn. 'I'm troubled, too. We have an opportunity to attract new business with some of Mark's new ideas. And the younger staff love working on his projects. But he has stirred up a lot of turmoil'.

Neville agreed. 'The real issue is that HPL is no longer presenting a unified image. Mark is wilfully defying the stated objectives of our organisation. And some of our oldest clients don't like that. There is real concern for the sort of patients Mark's ideas will produce. They just won't mix with our existing people.'

'That's true, Neville. However, some of the clients think he is a breath of fresh air, and he does have a reputation for being right.'

'Come on, Carolyn. You and I both know that we must not risk our reputation and our core business in this way. Mark must be made to understand that or go. I'm sorry, I don't like speaking this way but the other partners agree.'

Carolyn realised that she faced the most difficult challenge of her career. She felt a strong personal investment in helping Mark to succeed, having personally recruited him and been his ally in the early days. Carolyn was also haunted by her promise to Mark that he would have the freedom and flexibility to perform as he pleased. However, this flexibility had clearly caused problems.

Reluctantly, Carolyn called Mark in for a meeting, hoping to find some basis for compromise.

Carolyn: I gather you know the kinds of concerns the senior partners have expressed regarding your approach.

Mark: I suppose you've talked with Neville. Well, we did have a small disagreement earlier this week.

Carolyn: The way Neville tells it, you're moving staff about without any form of discussion and the core business is suffering – he has tried to discuss it with you and you simply ignored him and went ahead. He is a senior partner and he calls it dangerous insubordination.

Mark: Well, it's just like Watson to see progressive change as an attempt to take away his power.

Carolyn: It's not quite that simple, Mark. When we founded HPL, we all agreed that a conservative stance was best. And right now, with the economic indicators looking soft, many experts agree that it may still be the best alternative.

Mark: Carolyn, what are you going to rely on – predictions or performance? Old views need to be challenged and ultimately discarded. How else are we going to progress and keep up with our competitors?

Carolyn: I agree we need to change, Mark, but gradually. Your ideas are good, but you have to have patience. You also have to take the people that matter with you. It's the way you try and do things. You make people defensive.

Mark: You're telling me. And at this rate, it doesn't make much difference which direction we're heading.

Carolyn: Come on, Mark, you are making things very difficult for yourself and me. They do have a point in saying that the presence of long-term mental patients will antagonise our existing clients. The sums sound fine, but you have to convince everyone – work with them and not against them – you could be wrong. The way ahead is likely to be a compromise and, the way we are going now, compromise seems a million miles off.

Mark's emotions betray his impatience with the pace of the organisation and he becomes agitated.

Mark: I've admired your enthusiasm and I value your advice but I honestly think you're kidding yourself. You seem to think you can get things done without ruffling a few feathers. Are you interested in appearance or substance? If you want appearance, then hire a good PR person. If you want substance, then back me up.

Carolyn: Mark, it simply isn't that easy. I'm not HPL, I'm simply its caretaker. You know we make decisions around here by consensus; that's the backbone of this organisation. To move ahead, the confidence of the others has to be won, especially that of the partners. Frankly your attitude is one of the main problems.

Mark: You promised me flexibility and autonomy. I'm not getting that any more, Carolyn. All I'm getting is grief.

Carolyn: That may be true. But your whole approach . . .

Mark: Oh, yes, I thought you would get onto that. The sports car, the bachelor lifestyle, the messy office. But, again, that's appearance, Carolyn, not substance. Performance is what counts. That's what got me this far. You know I could walk out of here and sell my ideas to any other group – and for more money.

Carolyn: Wow, slow down.

Mark: Do you honestly believe this can be salvaged? I don't think so. Maybe it's time for me to move on. Isn't that why you called me in here anyway?

Carolyn, feeling uncomfortable, breaks eye contact and shifts her gaze to the London skyline. After a long pause, she continues, still gazing out of the window.

Carolyn: I don't know, Mark. I feel I've failed. My grand experiment in change has polarised the office; we've a war out there. On one hand, you really have done a good job here. HPL will no doubt lose a good part of its customer base if you leave. You have created a good atmosphere in your department – with customers and staff. If you go we will lose all that, and the chance to change.

Mark: It's just like you Carolyn to take this problem personally. You take everything personally. Even when I beat you at squash. Your heart's in the right place but you just can't ever seem to go for the jugular. You know and I know that HPL needs change. But it doesn't appear to be ready for it yet. And I'm certainly not willing to move slowly.

Carolyn: Yes. Perhaps. It's just hard to give up . . . [long pause]. OK, forget it.

Mark: Fine.

Discussion questions

1. What are the sources of conflict in this case?

2. What approaches to conflict management are used by the people in this situation? How effective was each approach?

3. Based on the behavioural guidelines for the collaborative approach, how could Carolyn have managed this conflict more effectively?

Skill Practice

Not all conflicts are alike, therefore they should not all be managed in exactly the same way. Effective managers are not only able to assess the true cause(s) of conflict, but they are also able to match the type of conflict with the appropriate management strategy. For each of the following brief scenarios, select the most appropriate conflict-management strategy. Refer to Table 6.4 (page 350) to help you to match situational factors with the strategies:

- Forcing
- Accommodating
- Compromising
- Collaborating
- Avoiding.

EXERCISE **6.1**

ARGYLL STEAKHOUSE

You have decided to take your family out to the local steak house, Argyll Steakhouse, for dinner to celebrate your son's birthday. You are a single parent, so getting home from work in time to prepare a nice dinner is very difficult. On entering the restaurant, you ask the waiter to seat you in the non-smoking section because your daughter, Sheila, is allergic to tobacco smoke. On your way to your seat, you notice that the restaurant seems crowded for a Monday night.

After you and your children are seated and have placed your orders, your conversation turns to the family plans for the approaching Christmas holidays. Suddenly you notice that your daughter is sneezing and her eyes are beginning to water. You look around and see a lively group of businessmen seated at the table behind you, all of whom are smoking. Your impression is that they are celebrating a special occasion. Looking back at Sheila, you realise that something has got to be done quickly. You ask your son to take Sheila outside while you go and find the waiter.

Selection

1. The salient situational factors are:_____

2. The most appropriate conflict-management strategy is:_____

Please refer to the scoring key in Appendix 1 for an example of how this particular scenario could be tabled.

EXERCISE **6.2**

AVOCADO COMPUTERS

Your name is Bran Greenway. When the head of Avocado Computers ran into production problems with its new automated production line, you were lured from Western Computers – a competitor. It meant a significant increase in pay and the opportunity to manage a state-of-the-art production plant. What's more, there were very few other female production managers in the region. You've been in the post for a year, and it's been exciting to see your staff start working together as a team to solve problems, improve quality and finally get the plant up to capacity. In general, Robert, the owner, has also been a plus. He is energetic, fair and a proven industry leader. You feel fortunate to be in a coveted position, in a 'star' firm, in a growth industry.

However, there is one distraction that annoys you. Robert has an obsession with cleanliness, order and appearance. He wants all the robots painted the same colour, the components within the computer laid out perfectly on a grid, the workers wearing clean overalls and the floor 'clean enough to eat off'. You are worried by this compulsion. 'It might impress potential clients when they tour the production facility, but is it all that important? After all, who's ever going to look at the inside of their computer? Why should customers care about the colour of the robot that built their computers? And who, for heaven's sake, would ever want to have a picnic in a factory?'

Today is your first yearly performance appraisal interview with Robert. In preparation for the meeting, he has sent you a memo outlining 'Areas of strength' and 'Areas of concern'. You look with pride at the number of items listed in the first column. It's obvious that Robert likes your work. But you are a bit annoyed at the single item of concern: 'Needs to maintain a cleaner facility, including employee appearance'. You mull this 'demerit' over in your mind, wrestling with how to respond in your interview.

Selection

1. The salient situational factors are: _____
2. The most appropriate conflict-management strategy is: _____

EXERCISE **6.3**

PHELAN LTD

You are Philip Jameson, the head of sales for an office products firm, Phelan Ltd. Your sales personnel sell primarily to small businesses in Scotland. Phelan's performance is about average for this rapidly growing market. The firms new president, James Owen, is putting a lot of pressure on you to increase sales. You feel that a major obstacle is the firm's policy on extending credit. Celia, the head of the credit office, insists that all new customers fill out an extensive credit application. Credit risks must be low; credit terms and collection procedures are tough. You can appreciate her point of view, but you feel it is unrealistic. Your competitors already are much more lenient in their credit examinations, they extend credit to higher risks, their credit terms are more favourable, and they are less aggressive in collecting overdue payments. Your sales personnel frequently complain that they aren't playing on a 'level playing field' with their competitors. When you brought this concern to James, he said he wanted you and Celia to work things out. His instructions didn't give many clues to his priorities on this matter. You realise the need to increase sales, but the small business failure rate is alarming, so you want to be careful that you don't make bad credit decisions.

You decide it's time to have a serious discussion with Celia. A lot is at stake.

Selection

1. The salient situational factors are: _____
2. The most appropriate conflict-management strategy is: _____

Exercises in resolving interpersonal disputes

The heart of conflict – management is resolving intense, emotionally charged confrontations. We have extensively discussed guidelines for utilising the collaborative (problem-solving) approach to conflict management in these situations. Assuming that the collaborative approach is appropriate for a particular situation, an initiator, a respondent or a mediator can use the general guidelines.

The following three situations involve interpersonal conflict and disagreement. The instructions at the beginning of each exercise will explain the situation. The wording of the assignment refers to work in large or medium-sized groups.

EXERCISE **6.4**

WHERE'S MY SPEECH?

- Divide the main group into subgroups of three.
- Choose two members who will take the roles of Janet as the initiator and Sarah as the respondent – making sure that each does not read the other's brief. The third member of the group acts initially as an observer working the Observer's Feedback Form to be found in Appendix 1.
- Run the role play for not more than 15 minutes and at the end allow the observer to give feedback for a similar time.

If the role play has not reached a satisfactory resolution:

- Continue the role play from the point previously reached, using the observer as mediator.
- Discuss what has happened using the Observer's Feedback Form.
- Discuss where in Beacon Lights organisation a mediator might be found and the consequences of failing to find one in time.
- Present to the whole group: (1) What went well in your role plays. (2) What went badly. (3) The key learning points for you.

Brief for Janet, director of personnel, Beacon Lights

You have been director of personnel for Beacon Lights for 10 years. Just when you thought you had everything under control, disaster struck. You have just heard that a former employee is suing the company for unfair dismissal, the sales director was forced to resign last month because of the company's poor performance, and your secretary just died of a heart attack.

You have been asked to give a speech at a seminar on a new productivity programme your company has pioneered, and you are looking forward to getting away from the office for a few days to catch your breath. You dictated your speech to your new secretary, Sarah, a couple of days ago so that she would have plenty of time to get it typed and reproduced.

This morning you have come into the office to proof-read and rehearse your speech before catching the midday train, and you are shocked to find a sick note from your secretary. You rush over to her desk and frantically begin searching for your speech notes. You find them mixed up with some material for the quarterly report that should have been completed two weeks ago, a stack of overdue correspondence and two days' unopened post. As you dial your secretary's home phone number, you realise that you are perspiring heavily and your face is flushed. This is the biggest disaster you can remember happening in years.

Brief for Sarah, secretary

You hear the phone ring, and it is all you can do to get out of bed and limp into the kitchen to answer it. You feel dreadful. Last night, you slipped on your son's skateboard in the drive and sprained your knee. You can hardly move today and the pain is excruciating. You are also reluctant to answer the phone because you know it is probably your boss, Janet, who will be moaning about your work rate. You realise you deserve some of the blame, but it isn't all your fault. Since you began working for Janet a month ago, you have asked several times for a thorough job description. You find you don't really understand either Janet's priorities or your specific responsibilities. You are replacing a woman who died suddenly after working for Janet for 10 years. You have found working with Janet extremely frustrating. She has been too busy to train you properly and she assumes that you know as much about the job as your predecessor. This is particularly a problem since you haven't worked as a secretary for three years and you feel that your skills are a bit rusty.

Janet's speech is a good example of the difficulties you have experienced. She gave you the notes a couple of days ago and said it was urgent, but that was on top of a quarterly report that was already overdue, a backlog of correspondence, filing and more. You have never compiled a report like this before, and every time you asked Janet a question she said she'd discuss it with you later and promptly ran off to another meeting. When you requested that you be given additional help to catch up on the overdue work, Janet said the company couldn't afford it because of poor sales. This annoyed you because you know you are being paid far less than your predecessor. You knew Janet faced some urgent deadlines, so you had planned to return to the office last night to type her speech and try to complete the report, but two hours in the waiting room at the hospital put an end to that plan. You tried calling Janet to explain the problem only to find out that her home number is ex-directory.

You sit down, prop up your leg and wince with pain as you pick up the phone.

EXERCISE **6.5**

CAN HARRY FIT IN?

- Divide the main group into subgroups of three.
- Choose two members who will take the roles of Harry as the initiator and Margaret as the respondent – making sure that each does not read the other's

brief. The third member of the group acts initially as an observer working the Observer's Feedback Form to be found in Appendix 1.

- Run the role play for not more than 15 minutes and then allow the observer to give feedback for a similar time.

If the role play has not reached a satisfactory resolution:

- Continue the role play from the point previously reached, using the observer as mediator.
- Discuss what has happened using the Observer's Feedback Form.
- Discuss where in the auditing team a mediator could be found and the consequences of not finding such a person.
- Present to the whole group: (1) What went well in your role plays. (2) What went badly. (3) The key learning points for you.

Brief for Margaret, office manager

You are the manager of an auditing team sent to Bangkok, Thailand, to represent a major international accounting firm with headquarters in Zurich, Switzerland. You and Harry, one of your auditors, were sent to Bangkok. Harry is seven years older than you and has been with the firm five years longer. Your relationship has become strained since you were recently appointed office manager. You feel you were given the post because you have established an excellent working relationship with the Thai staff as well as a broad range of international clients. But Harry has told other members of the staff that your promotion simply reflects the firm's heavy emphasis on 'Yes' people. He has tried to isolate you from the all-male accounting staff by focusing discussions on to sports, local night-spots, etc.

You are sitting in your office reading some complicated new reporting procedures which have just arrived from head office. Your concentration is suddenly interrupted by a loud knock on your door. Without waiting for an invitation to enter, Harry bursts into your office. He is obviously very upset, and you already know why he is in such a nasty mood. You recently posted the audit assignments for next month, and you scheduled Harry for a job you knew he wouldn't like. Harry is one of your senior auditors and the company norm is that choice assignments go with seniority. This particular job will require him to spend two weeks away from Bangkok in a remote town, working with a company with notoriously messy records.

Unfortunately, you have had to assign several of these less desirable audits to Harry recently because you are short of personnel. But that's not the only reason. You have received a number of complaints from the junior staff (all Thais) that Harry treats them in a condescending manner. They feel he is always looking for an opportunity to boss them around, as if he were their supervisor instead of an experienced, supportive mentor. As a result, your whole operation works more smoothly when you can send Harry out of town on a solo project for several days. It keeps him from coming into your office and telling you how to do your job, and the morale of the rest of the auditing staff is significantly higher. Harry slams the door and proceeds to express his anger over this assignment.

Brief for Harry, senior auditor

You are really fed up! Margaret is deliberately trying to undermine your status in the office. She knows that the company tradition is that senior auditors get the better jobs. And this isn't the first time this has happened. Since her promotion she has tried to keep you out of the office as much as possible. It's as if she doesn't want her rival for leadership of the office around. When you were asked to go to Bangkok, you assumed that you would be made the office manager because of your seniority in the firm. You are certain that the decision to pick Margaret is yet another indication of positive discrimination against white males.

In staff meetings, Margaret has talked about the need to be sensitive to the feelings of the office staff as well as the clients in this multi-cultural setting. She's got a nerve to be preaching about sensitivity! 'What about my feelings, for heaven's sake?' you wonder. This is nothing more than a straightforward power play. She is probably feeling insecure about being the only female accountant in the office and being promoted over someone with more experience. 'Sending me out of town,' you decide, 'is a clear case of out of sight, out of mind.'

Well, it's not going to happen that easily. You are not going to roll over and let her treat you unfairly. It's time for a showdown. If she doesn't agree to change this assignment and apologise for the way she's been treating you, you're going to register a formal complaint with her boss in Zurich. You are prepared to submit your resignation if the situation doesn't improve.

EXERCISE **6.6**

MEETING AT HARTFORD MANUFACTURING CO.

- Divide into subgroups of five.
- Choose one observer and four people to play the main characters – Peter Smith, Richard Hootten, Barbara Price and Christopher Jones. The person playing the role of Peter Smith, and nobody else, should read the letters shown as Exhibits 6.1, 6.2 and 6.3 – although he may choose to share them during the meeting. No characters should read other people's roles.
- The observer should watch the meeting using the Observer's Feedback Form found in Appendix 1.
- Run the role play for not more than 30 minutes and allow the observer to give feedback using the Observer's Feedback Form for a similar time.

If the role play has not reached a satisfactory resolution:

- Continue the role play from the point previously reached, using the observer as mediator.
- Discuss what has happened and present to the whole group: (1) What went well. (2) What went badly. (3) Key learning points.

```
                                                              T.J. WRIGHT
                                                              Chartered Accountants
                                                              Chorley Road
                                                              Birmingham
10 February 1999
Mr Peter Smith
Managing Director
Hartford Manufacturing Company
Chorley Industrial Estate
Birmingham


Dear Mr Smith


As you requested last month, we have now completed our audit of Hartford Manufacturing
Company. We find accounting procedures and fiscal control to be very satisfactory. A more
detailed report of these matters is attached. However, we did discover during our perusal of
company records that the production department has consistently incurred cost overruns during
the past two quarters. Cost per unit of production is approximately 5 per cent over budget. While
this is not a serious problem given the financial solvency of your company, we thought it wise to
bring it to your attention.


Yours sincerely


Trevor J Wright
```

Exhibit 6.1

The company

Hartford Manufacturing Company is the largest subsidiary of Riding Industries. Since its formation in 1918, Hartford Manufacturing has become an industrial leader in the UK. Its sales currently average approximately £25 million a year, with an annual growth of approximately six per cent. There are over 850 employees in production, sales and marketing, accounting, engineering and management.

Peter Smith has been managing director for two years and is well respected by his subordinates. He has the reputation of being firm but fair. Peter's training in college was in engineering, so he is technically minded, and he frequently likes to walk around the production area to see for himself how things are going. He has also been known to roll up his sleeves and help work on a problem on the shop floor. He is not opposed to rubbing shoulders with even the lowest-level employees. On the other hand, he tries to run a tight company. He holds high expectations for performance, especially from those in managerial positions.

Richard Hooton is the director of production at Hartford Manufacturing. He has been with the company since he was 19. He has worked himself up through the ranks and now at the age of 54 he is the oldest manager. Hooton has his own ideas of how things should be run in production and he is reluctant to tolerate any intervention from anyone, even Peter Smith. Because he has been with the company so

---

BAILDON INDUSTRIES
New Hall Way
Bradford
West Yorkshire

Mr Peter Smith   8 February 1999
Managing Director
Hartford Manufacturing Company
Chorley Industrial Estate
Birmingham

Dear Mr Smith

We have been purchasing your products since 1975 and we have been very satisfied with our relations with your sales personnel.

Unfortunately this is no longer the case. Your sales representative for the Bradford area, Sam Sneddon, has looked like and smelled like he was under the influence of alcohol on the last three occasions he has appeared on our premises. Not only that, but our last order was mistakenly recorded, so we received the wrong quantity of products.

I'm sure you don't make it a practice to put your company's reputation in the hands of someone like Sam Sneddon, so I suggest you get someone else to cover this area. We cannot tolerate, and I am sure that other companies in the Bradford area cannot tolerate, this kind of relationship to continue. While we judge your products to be excellent, we will be forced to find other sources if some action is not taken.

Yours sincerely

David Stokoe
Purchasing Manager

Exhibit 6.2

---

long, he feels he knows it better than anyone else, and he believes he has had a hand in making it the success that it is. His main goal is to keep production running smoothly and efficiently.

Barbara Price is the director of sales and marketing. She joined the company about 18 months ago after completing her MBA at Keele. She previously held the position of assistant manager of marketing at Riding Industries. Price is a very conscientious employee and is anxious to make a name for herself. Her major objective, which she has never hesitated to make public, is to be a general manager one day. Sales at Hartford Manufacturing have increased in the past year to near-record levels under her guidance.

Christopher Jones is the regional sales manager for the Yorkshire region. He reports directly to Barbara Price. The Yorkshire region represents the largest market for Hartford Manufacturing, and Jones is considered to be the most competent salesperson in the company. He has built personal relationships with several major clients in his region, and it appears that some sales occur as much because of Christopher Jones as because of the products of Hartford Manufacturing. Jones has been with the company 12 years, all of them in sales.

HARTFORD MANUFACTURING COMPANY
CHORLEY INDUSTRIAL ESTATE
BIRMINGHAM
A subsidiary of Riding Industries

Memorandum
TO: Peter Smith, Managing Director
FROM: Barbara Price, Sales and Marketing Director
DATE: 11 February 1999

Mr Smith:
   In response to your concerns, we have instituted several incentive programmes among our sales force to increase sales during these traditionally slow months. We have set up competition among regions with the sales people in the top region being recognised in the company newsletter and presented with engraved plaques. We have introduced a 'holiday in America' award for the top salesperson in the company and we have instituted cash bonuses for any salesperson who gets a new customer order. However, these incentives have now been operating for a month and sales haven't increased at all. In fact, in two regions they have decreased by an average of 5 per cent.
   What do you suggest now? We have promised that these incentives will continue to run for the rest of this quarter, but they seem to be doing no good. Not only that, but we cannot afford to provide the incentives within our current budget, and unless sales increase, we will be in the red. **Regretfully, I recommend dropping the programme.**

Exhibit 6.3

This is Friday afternoon and tomorrow Peter Smith leaves for Copenhagen to attend an important meeting with potential overseas investors. He will be gone for two weeks. Before he leaves, there are several items in his in-tray that must receive attention. He calls a meeting with Richard Hooton and Barbara Price in his office. Just before the meeting begins, Christopher Jones calls and asks if he may join the meeting for a few minutes since he is at head office and has something important to discuss. It involves both Peter Smith and Richard Hooton. Smith gives permission for him to join the meeting as there may not be another chance to meet Jones before the trip. The meeting convenes with Smith, Hooton, Price and Jones all in the room.

Brief for Peter Smith, managing director

Three letters arrived today and you judge them to be sufficiently important to require your attention before you leave on your trip (see Exhibits 6.1, 6.2, and 6.3). Each letter represents a problem that requires immediate action, and you need commitments from key staff members to resolve these problems. You are concerned about this meeting, because these individuals don't work as well together as you'd like.

For example, Richard Hooton tends to be very difficult to pin down. He always seems suspicious of the motives of others and has a reputation for not making tough decisions. You sometimes wonder how a person could become the head of production in a major manufacturing firm by avoiding controversial issues and blaming others for the results.

In contrast, Barbara Price is very straightforward. You always know exactly where she stands. The problem is that sometimes she doesn't take enough time to study a problem before making a decision. She tends to be impulsive and anxious to make a decision, whether it's the right one or not. Her general approach to resolving disagreements between departments is to seek expedient compromises. You are particularly disturbed by her approach to the sales-incentive problem. You felt strongly that something needed to be done to increase sales during the winter months. You reluctantly agreed to the incentive programme because you didn't want to dampen her initiative. But you aren't convinced this is the right answer, because frankly, you're not sure what the real problem is, yet!

Christopher Jones is an aggressive sales manager. He is hard driving and sometimes ruffles the feathers of other members of staff with his uncompromising 'black-and-white' style. He is also fiercely loyal to his sales staff, so you're certain that he'll take the complaint about Sam Sneddon personally.

In contrast to the styles of your colleagues, you have tried to utilise an integrative approach to problem solving, focusing on the facts, treating everyone's input equally, and keeping conversations about controversial topics problem-focused. One of your goals since taking over this position two years ago is to foster a team approach within your staff.

(Note: *For more information about how you might approach the issues raised by Exhibits 6.1, 6.2 and 6.3 in your staff meeting, review the collaborating approach in Table 6.2 as well as the mediator's behavioural guidelines at the end of the Skill Learning section.*)

Brief to Richard Hooton, director of production

The backbone of Hartford Manufacturing is production. You have watched the company grow from a small, struggling factory to a thriving business, built on outstanding production processes. Your own reputation among those who know manufacturing is a good one, and you are confident that you have been a major factor in the success of Hartford Manufacturing. You have turned down several job offers over the years because you feel loyal to the company, but sometimes the younger employees don't seem to afford you the respect that you think you deserve.

The only time you have major problems in production is when the young know-it-alls fresh from college have come in and tried to change things. With their scientific management concepts and fuzzy-headed human relations training, they have more often made a mess of things. The best production methods have been practised for years in the company, and you have yet to see anyone who could improve on your system.

On the other hand, you have respect for Peter Smith as the managing director. He has lots of experience and the right kind of training, and he is also involved in the production side of the organisation. He has often given you good advice but he usually lets you do what you feel is best and he rarely dictates specific methods for doing things.

Your general approach to problems is to avoid controversy. You feel uncomfortable when production is made the scapegoat for problems in the company. Just because this is a manufacturing business, it seems as if everyone tries to pin the blame for problems on the production department. You've felt for years that the firm was getting away from what it does best – mass-producing a few standard products. Instead, the trend has been for marketing and sales to push for more and more products, shorter lead times, and greater customisation capability. These actions have increased costs and caused incredible production delays as well as higher reject rates.

(*Note: During the impending meeting, you should adopt the avoidance approach shown in Table 6.2. Defend your territory, place blame on others, defer taking a stand and avoid taking responsibility for making a controversial decision.*)

Brief for Barbara Price, director of sales and marketing

You are anxious to impress Peter Smith because you have your eye on a position in the parent company, Riding Industries, that is opening up at the end of the year. It would mean a promotion for you. A positive recommendation from Peter Smith would carry a lot of weight in the selection process. Given that both Hartford Manufacturing and Riding Industries are largely male dominated, you are pleased with your career progress so far, and you are hoping to keep it up.

One current concern is the suggestion of Peter Smith some time ago that you look into the problem of slow sales during the winter months. You implemented an incentive plan that was highly recommended by an industry analyst at a recent trade conference. It consists of three separate incentive programmes:

1. Competition among regions in which the salesperson in the top region would have his or her picture in the company newsletter and receive engraved plaques.

2. A holiday in America for the top salesperson in the company.

3. Cash bonuses for salespeople who obtained new customer orders.

The trouble is, these incentives haven't worked. Not only have sales not increased for the company as a whole, but two of the regions are down by an average of 5 per cent. You have told the salesforce that the incentives will continue in this quarter, but if sales don't improve your budget will be in the red. There is no budget for the prizes, since you expected the increased sales to more than offset the cost of the incentives. Obviously this was a bad idea that is not working, and it should be dropped immediately. You are a bit embarrassed about this aborted project. But it is better to cut your losses and try something else rather than support an obvious loser.

In general, you are very confident and self-assured. You feel that the best way to get work done is through negotiation and compromise. What's important is making a decision quickly and efficiently. Maybe everyone doesn't get exactly what they want, but at least they can get on with their work. There are no absolutes in this business, but you feel that the management process is being bogged down with 'paralysis by analysis'. You are impatient over delays caused by intensive studies and investigations of detail. You agree with Peter Smith: action is the hallmark of successful managers.

(*Note*: *During this meeting, use the compromise approach shown in Table 6.2. Do whatever is necessary to help the group make a quick decision to enable you to get on with the pressing demands of your work.*)

Brief for Christopher Jones, regional sales manager

You don't go to company headquarters very often because your customer contacts take up most of your time. You regularly work 50 to 60 hours a week and you are proud of the job you do. You also feel a special obligation to your customers to provide them with the best product available in the most timely fashion. This sense of obligation comes not only from your commitment to the company but also from your personal relationships with many of the customers.

Recently, you have been receiving more and more complaints about late deliveries. The time lag between ordering and delivery is increasing, and some customers have been greatly inconvenienced by the delays. You have sent a formal enquiry to production to find out what the problem is. They replied that they are producing as efficiently as possible and they see nothing wrong with past practices. The assistant to Richard Hooton even suggested that this was just another example of the salesforce's unrealistic expectations.

Not only will sales be negatively affected if these delays continue, but your reputation with your customers will be damaged. You have promised them that the problem will be quickly solved and that products will begin arriving on time. Since Richard Hooton is such a rigid person, however, you are almost certain that it will do no good to talk to him. His subordinate probably got his negative attitude from Hooton.

In general, Hooton is a 1960s production worker who is being pulled by the rest of the firm into the new age of the 1990s. Competition is different, technology is different and management is different. You need shorter lead times, a wider range of products and the capacity to do some customised work. Admittedly, this makes production's work harder, but other firms are providing these services with the use of just-in-time management processes, robots, etc. But Hooton is reluctant to change.

Instead of getting down to the real problems, head office, in their typical high-handed fashion, announced an incentives plan. This implies that the problem is in the field, not the factory. It made some of your people angry to think they were being pressed to increase their efforts when they weren't receiving the back-up support they required. They liked the prizes, but the way the plan was presented made them feel as if they weren't working hard enough. This isn't the first time you have questioned the judgement of Barbara, your boss. She certainly is intelligent and hard-working, but she doesn't seem very interested in what's going on out in the field. Furthermore, she doesn't seem very receptive to 'bad news' about sales and customer complaints.

(*Note*: *During this meeting, use the forcing approach to conflict management and negotiations shown in Table 6.2. However, don't overplay your part – you are the senior regional sales manager and if Barbara continues to move up quickly in the organisation, you may be in line for her position.*)

Skill Application

ACTIVITY **6.1**

SUGGESTED FURTHER ASSIGNMENTS

Assignment 1

Select a specific conflict with which you are very familiar. Using the framework for identifying the sources of a conflict, discussed in this book, analyse this situation carefully. It might be useful to compare your perceptions of the situation with those of informed observers. What type of conflict is this? Why did it occur? Why is it continuing? Next, using the guidelines for selecting an appropriate conflict-management strategy, identify the general approach that would be most appropriate for this situation. Consider both the personal preferences of the parties involved and the relevant situational factors. Is this the approach that the parties have been using? If not, attempt to introduce a different perspective into the relationship and explain why you feel it would be more productive. If the parties have been using this approach, discuss with them why it has not been successful thus far. Share information on specific behavioural guidelines (or negotiation tactics) that might increase the effectiveness of their efforts.

Assignment 2

Identify a situation where another individual is doing something that needs to be corrected. Using the respondent's guidelines for collaborative problem solving, construct a plan for discussing your concerns with this person. Include specific language designed to assertively state your case without causing a defensive reaction. Role play this interaction with a friend and incorporate any suggestions for improvement. Make your presentation to the individual and report on your results. What was the reaction? Were you successful in balancing assertiveness with support and responsibility? Based on this experience, identify other situations that you feel need to be changed and follow a similar procedure.

Assignment 3

Act as a mediator between two individuals or groups. Using the guidelines for implementing the collaborative approach to mediation, outline a plan of action prior to your intervention. Consider whether initial private meetings are appropriate. Report on the situation and your plan. How did you feel? What specific actions worked well? What was the outcome? What should you have done differently? Based on this experience, revise your plan for use in related situations.

Assignment 4

Identify a difficult situation involving negotiations. This might involve transactions at work, at home or in the community. Review the guidelines for integrative bargaining and identify the specific tactics you plan to use. Write down specific questions and responses to likely initiatives from the other party. In particular, anticipate how you might handle the possibility of the other party's utilising a distributive negotiation strategy. Schedule a negotiation meeting with the party involved and implement your plan. Following the session, debrief the experience with a co-worker or friend. What did you learn? How successful were you? What would you do differently? Based on this experience, modify your plan and prepare to implement it in related situations.

ACTIVITY **6.2**

APPLICATION PLAN AND EVALUATION

The objective of this exercise is to help you apply your skills in a real-life setting. Now that you have become familiar with the behavioural guidelines that form the basis of effective skill performance, you will improve the most by trying out those guidelines in an everyday context. The trouble is, unlike a classroom activity in which feedback is immediate and others can assist you with their evaluations, this skill application activity is one you must accomplish and evaluate on your own. There are two parts to this activity. Part 1 helps to prepare you to apply the skill. Part 2 helps you to evaluate and improve on your experience. Be sure to actually write down answers to each item. Don't short-circuit the process by skipping steps.

Part 1: Plan

1. Write down the two or three aspects of this skill that are most important to you. These may be areas of weakness, areas you most want to improve or areas that are most salient to a problem you face currently. Identify the specific aspects of this skill that you want to apply.

2. Now identify the setting or situation in which you will apply this skill. Establish a plan for performance by actually writing down the situation. Who else will be involved? When will you do it? Where will it be done?

3. What specific behaviours will you engage in to apply this skill? Practise them.

4. What are the indicators of successful performance? How will you know you have succeeded in being effective? What will indicate that you have performed competently?

Part 2: Evaluation

5. After you have completed your implementation, record the results. What happened? How successful were you? What was the effect on others?

6. How can you improve? What modifications can you make next time? What will you do differently in a similar situation in the future?

7. Looking back on your whole skill practice and application experience, what have you learned? What has been surprising? In what ways might this experience help you in the long term?

Further reading

Arnold, J.D. (1993) *When the sparks fly: resolving conflicts in your organization.* London: McGraw-Hill.

Eunson, B. (1998) *Dealing with conflict.* Chichester: Wiley.

Fritchie, R. and Leary, M. (1998) *Resolving conflicts in organizations: a practical guide for managers.* London: Lemos & Crane.

Hiltrop, J.M. and Udall, S. (1995) *The essence of negotiation.* London: Prentice Hall.

PART 3

People Management

This part of the book deals with the actual skills used by managers in their daily work – empowerment, delegation and leadership.

CHAPTER 7

Effective Empowerment and Delegation

SKILL DEVELOPMENT OUTLINE

Skill Pre-assessment surveys

- Effective empowerment and delegation
- Personal empowerment assessment

Skill Learning material

- Empowerment and delegation
- What is empowerment?
- Historical roots of empowerment
- Inhibitors to empowerment
- Dimensions of empowerment
- Developing empowerment
- Principles of empowered delegation
- Summary
- Behavioural guidelines

Skill Analysis cases

- Minding the store
- Changing the portfolio

Skill Practice exercises

- British Airways
- Satisfy the customer

Skill Application analysis

- Suggested further assignments
- Application plan and evaluation

LEARNING OBJECTIVES

The purpose of this chapter is to allow the reader to understand:

- the principles of empowerment at work
- the limitations of empowerment
- how to delegate effectively
- how to share power with others for mutual gain

INTRODUCTION

The world of the manager has changed significantly since the 1980s. When re-organisation was discussed in the 1980s it was the manager who was doing the reorganising and the blue collar and clerical staff who were reorganised. Maslow earlier talked about 'self-actualisation' as a 'Holy Grail that allowed the individual – manager – to achieve a personal fulfilment through work'.

Somehow the 1990s have been different. Charles Handy, from his questioning and optimistic book, *The Age of Unreason* (1993), has moved to his still question-ing, but profoundly depressing, *The Empty Raincoat* (1994) where he questions whether the professionalism demanded of us, in the new world, is where we want to be going. Herriot and Pemberton (1995) go even further and discuss what they see as a betrayal of contract by organisations that, at its worst, leads to industrial sabotage.

The New World, for good or evil, is about professionalism and the new gurus headed by Hamner of the 'inverted doughnut'. It is about increased efficiency and its output is codified by Handy who sees half the workforce working to three times the effect and gaining twice the rewards they had previously. The key word for the facilitation is 'empowerment' and the morality or indeed prudence of such a pro-cess is a very hot political issue in current management thinking. Hamner quotes an example from IBM where the same workforce were 'empowered' to produce 100 times the work output. These were the days of easy pickings.

The case for a move from a disempowered workforce is given by the General Motors poem, quoted by Peters and Waterman (1982):

Are these men and women,
Workers of the World?
or is this an outgrown nursery
with children – goosing, slapping, boys
giggling, snotty girls?
What is it about the entrance way,
these gates to the plant?
Is it the guards, the showing of your badge – the smell?
is there some invisible eye that pierces you through and
transforms your being? Some aura
or ether, that brain and spirit washes you
and commands, 'For eight hours
you shall be different.'
What is it that instantaneously makes
a child out of a man?
Moments before he was a father, a husband,
an owner of property, a voter, a lover, an adult.
When he spoke at least some listened.
Salesmen courted his favour. Insurance men appealed to his family responsibility

and by chance the church sought his help . . .
But that was before he shuffled past the guard,
climbed the steps, hung up his coat and
took his place on the line.

Empowerment can couple the enormous potential of mankind by not allowing
individuals to hang up their brains as they hang up their coats:

You are empowered to make the best and most beautiful grommets in the world.
I don't want to make grommets – I want to make dreams.
You're fired.

It is also unfortunate, as Herriot and Pemberton have pointed out, that empowerment is almost always coupled with words such as downsizing and restructuring –
crude euphemisms for sacking people.

Our treatment of empowerment will be optimistic and we will hold the cynics
at bay, at least until the next edition. It will also draw heavily on other elements in
the book:

- Empowerment and delegation, although initially stressful, are a powerful way
  of diminishing personal stress.
- 'Constructive communication' is essential throughout the empowerment
  process.
- 'Creative problem solving' is empowering in itself and has to be delegated.
- Empowered managers will conflict with their bosses and question the very
  roots of their organisations – this conflict needs to be managed. The manager
  seeking to empower his or her staff must not see themselves as resolving
  conflicts. This is not the job of the empowering manager – he or she must,
  however, be available as a mediator. He or she must also maintain the role of
  a monitor, holding the empowered individuals and teams on course. Ken
  Durham, ex-Chairman of Unilever, on meeting new recruits, used to explain
  his policy on empowerment: 'If you have dispute with your boss that you
  two cannot resolve – come to see me. Explain the issues, and one of you
  will leave this room without a job.' It was perhaps surprising that very few
  disputes were left unresolved and, of the remainder, very few were referred
  back to him.
- Finally, and not least, empowerment calls for great skills of leadership and, in
  particular, the leadership of teams. This will be the subject of Chapter 8.

We see the current world becoming more and more demanding of managers and
a mastery of the skills of empowerment are fundamental for survival, let alone
growth. A survey according to the Industrial Society's best practice report (1995) found
that the trend towards empowerment was growing.

Skill Pre-assessment

SURVEY **7.1**

EFFECTIVE EMPOWERMENT AND DELEGATION

Step 1 For each statement circle a number on the rating scale in the Pre-assessment column. Your answers should reflect your attitudes and behaviour as they are now, not as you would like them to be. Be honest. When you have completed the survey, use the scoring key in Appendix 1 to identify the skill areas discussed that are most important for you to master. The process of improving these skill areas should help you with your learning objectives.

Step 2 When you have completed the chapter and the Skill Application assignments, review your responses in the Post-assessment column, using the scoring key in Appendix 1 to measure your progress. If your score remains low in specific skill areas, use the behavioural guidelines at the end of the Skill Learning section of the chapter to guide your Application Planning.

RATING SCALE

1 = Strongly disagree   **2** = Disagree   **3** = Slightly disagree
4 = Slightly agree   **5** = Agree   **6** = Strongly agree

	Assessment	
	Pre-	Post-

In situations where I have an opportunity to empower others:

1. I help people develop personal mastery of their work by involving them first in less complex tasks, and then in more difficult tasks. _____ _____

2. I value people by recognising and praising their successes however small. _____ _____

3. I try to demonstrate successful task accomplishment. _____ _____

4. I point out other successful people who can serve as role models. _____ _____

5. I frequently praise, encourage and express approval of other people. _____ _____

6. I provide regular feedback and needed support. _____ _____

7. I try to foster friendships and informal interaction. _____ _____

8. I highlight the important impact that a person's work will have. _____ _____

9. I try to provide all the information that people need to accomplish their tasks. _____ _____

10. I pass along relevant information to people as I become informed myself. _____ _____

11. I ensure that people have the necessary resources – equipment, space and time – to succeed. _____ _____

12. If I do not have resources to hand, I help others obtain what they need. _____ _____

13. I help people become involved in teams in order to increase their participation. _____ _____

14. I let teams make decisions and implement their own recommendations. ____ ____

15. I foster confidence by being fair and equitable in my decisions. ____ ____

16. I show a personal concern for everyone with whom I have dealings. ____ ____

When I find I can delegate work to others:

17. I specify clearly the results I desire. ____ ____

18. I specify clearly the level of initiative I want from others (e.g., do part of the task and then report, do the whole task and then report, etc.). ____ ____

19. I consult with subordinates on when and how work will be done. ____ ____

20. I make certain that the amount of authority and responsibility are in balance when I delegate work. ____ ____

21. I work within existing organisational structures when delegating assignments and never by-pass someone without informing him or her. ____ ____

22. I identify constraints and limitations people face, but also provide support. ____ ____

23. I maintain accountability for results, not for methods used. ____ ____

24. I delegate consistently – not just when I'm overloaded. ____ ____

25. I avoid upward delegation by asking people to recommend solutions, rather than merely asking for advice or answers when a problem is encountered. ____ ____

26. I make clear the consequences of success and failure. ____ ____

SURVEY **7.2**

PERSONAL EMPOWERMENT ASSESSMENT

Step 1   This instrument helps identify the extent to which you are empowered in your own work. You should respond to the items based on your own job or on the work you do as a student. The items listed below describe different orientations people can have with respect to their work roles. Use the following scale to indicate the extent to which you believe each is true of you using the Pre-assessment column. Then use the scoring key in Appendix 1 to determine the extent to which you are empowered.

Step 2   As in the previous questionnaire, after you have completed the reading and exercises in the book, cover up your first set of answers and respond to the same statements again, this time using the Post-assessment column. If your score remains low, use the behavioural guidelines at the end of the Skill Learning section to direct you towards areas where further work is needed.

RATING SCALE

1 = Very strongly disagree   **2** = Strongly disagree   **3** = Disagree
4 = Neutral   **5** = Agree   **6** = Strongly agree
7 = Very strongly agree

	Assessment	
	Pre-	Post-
1. The work that I do is very important to me.	____	____
2. I am confident about my ability to do my work.	____	____
3. I have significant autonomy in determining how I do my work.	____	____
4. I have a large impact on what happens in my work group.	____	____
5. I trust my co-workers to be completely honest with me.	____	____
6. My work is important to me personally.	____	____
7. My work is well within the scope of my abilities.	____	____
8. I can decide how to go about doing my own work.	____	____
9. I have a great deal of control over what is done in my work group.	____	____
10. I trust my colleagues to share important information with me.	____	____
11. I care about what I do in my work.	____	____
12. I am confident about my capabilities to perform my work.	____	____
13. I have considerable opportunity for independence and freedom in how I do my work.	____	____
14. I have significant influence over what happens in my department.	____	____
15. I trust my co-workers to keep the promises they make.	____	____
16. The work I do is meaningful to me.	____	____
17. I have mastered the skills necessary to do my work.	____	____
18. I have a chance to use personal initiative when carrying out my work.	____	____
19. My opinion counts in departmental decision making.	____	____
20. I believe that my colleagues care about me and how I am.	____	____

Skill Learning

Empowerment and delegation

Books on management skills often concentrate on helping managers to control the behaviour of other people. They focus on how managers can increase the performance of subordinates, engender conformity, or motivate to achieve set objectives.

In the previous chapter we discussed the implications of what is known as the Hawthorne Experiment. In the studies carried out at the Hawthorne Works of General Electric in the 1930s managers appeared to be surprised that a workforce, within a high level of control systems, was able to determine its own work patterns. Our contention is that all workers, whatever the measure of imposed control, at some level, determine their own work patterns and this – if harnessed effectively – is good for them, and the organisation.

It is a case of perspective. If we see people determining their work patterns we can see it either as a threat, and therefore increase our control, or as an opportunity. In this book we see it as an opportunity and discuss the skills necessary to grasp that opportunity. In the introduction we included the General Motors Poem where it is accepted that workers are capable and competent in their own private lives, and act in a way that meets all our criteria of empowerment; but somehow when they enter the factory door they have to be controlled. Before the 'hanging of the coat' and the simultaneous 'hanging up of the individuality' the organisation has already 'trusted' the worker. Imagine the worker leaving for work. The starting time for duty is set, but the means of getting to the fixed point by the appointed time is normally left to the worker. The myriad of minor decisions that have to be made cannot be usefully proscribed – how to react to children who are slow getting up, to cars that fail to start, to bad weather, to minor ailments and injuries. These not only can be left for the individual to handle, but it would be madness to do otherwise. The manager's job is only to facilitate where necessary and monitor success and failure. In the jargon of this book, workers are empowered at this level because any intervention is accepted as dysfunctional. Empowerment at this stage is accepted, if not remarked upon.

We can ask a further question – What is important; getting to work at a proscribed time or doing the job effectively? Once we ask this question and all the related questions, we are beginning to discuss empowerment and the coincident factor of trust in a meaningful way.

With any job, at some level of activity, tight ruling is impossible. We are arguing in this book that the supreme management skill lies in (1) finding the *highest* level of activity that workers can be left to handle in the chaos of the working environment, and (2) defining a new role of management – the role of facilitator, mentor/guide, monitor and provider of direction.

James Gleick (1988), in *Chaos*, developed a metaphor in which he sees us operating as free running ball bearings trapped in a bowl. Within the bowl we use all our native skills to produce order – to establish equilibrium. Using the metaphor, the manager's job is to provide depth to the bowl (i.e., a clear definition of task and purpose), energy to keep moving in the bowl (i.e., resources) and to guard us from spilling out of the bowl.

> Mike Woods, using the metaphor in lectures, demonstrated the concept using a real metal bowl representing the work situation and a ball bearing representing the individuals or teams within. Passing round the bowl, scratched by the movement of myriad's of ball bearing movements seeking their own equilibrium, the students notice that from any viewpoint, the scratches seem to have an unique focus. So it is, for us, when we are empowered. We feel we are the focus of the activity and this makes us feel good – empowered and motivated.

The empowering manager can leave the demeaning jobs of timing how long people spend in the washroom or how they travel to work, and concentrate on the important issues of cash flow, contributions, product, process and service development. Issues around providing for customers, developing the business and ensuring that all the stakeholders receive just rewards are the real jobs of managers. Close supervision of peripherals not only degrades the role of the manager and the individuality of the worker but is also downright unproductive. The Hawthorne Experiment told us that in the 1930s.

Managers who empower people or teams remove controls, constraints and boundaries, and facilitate work – providing resources, stimulating, motivating, steering and most of all creating a world of mutual, but realistic trust. Rather than being a 'push' strategy, in which managers induce employees to respond in desirable ways through incentives and influence techniques, empowerment is a 'pull' strategy. Empowerment focuses on ways that managers can design a working practice to energise and provide a positive atmosphere of encouragement. In such an atmosphere, people accomplish tasks because they want to and not because they are offered a carrot on a stick.

> Sumantra Ghoshal (1996), Professor of Strategic Leadership at London Business School, says that management is all about making things happen that otherwise would not, about making ordinary people produce extraordinary results. Ghoshal argues that it is archaic for the modern corporation to rely on top managers to be the designers of the strategy. In an environment where the fast-changing knowledge and expertise required to make such decisions are usually found on the front lines, this assumption is untenable. Senior managers of today's large enterprises must move beyond strategy, structure and systems to a framework built on purpose, process and people.

Empowering others, however, can lead to dilemmas. On the one hand, evidence shows that empowered employees are more productive, more satisfied and innovative, and that they create higher-quality products and services than non-empowered employees (Sashkin, 1982, 1984; Kanter, 1983; Greenberger and Stasser, 1991; Spreitzer, 1992). Organisations are more effective when an empowered workforce exists (Conger and Kanungo, 1988; Gecas, 1989; Thomas and Velthouse, 1990). On the other hand, empowerment means giving up control and letting others make decisions, set goals, accomplish results and receive rewards. The manager moves from the captain's cabin to the helmsman's platform – the manager has to learn to steer, a less high profile role. It means that other people probably will get credit for success. Managers with high needs for power and control (see McClelland, 1975) face a challenge when they are expected to sacrifice their needs for someone else's gain. They may ask themselves: 'Why should others get all the prizes when I am in charge? Why should I allow others to exercise power, and even facilitate their acquiring more power, when I naturally want to receive the rewards and recognition myself?'

Ricardo Semler, in his book *Maverick* and the BBC TV documentary of the same name, describes what is certainly the most widely publicised example of the empowerment of a whole workforce. In his Brazilian company Semco every authority and responsibility was vested at the lowest possible level in an already very flat organisation. There is, however, a very telling quotation:

> Fernando, the last of our Attilas, was the first key manager to be expelled by the new Semco. He was very smart and very capable, but unequivocally autocratic. (Semler, 1993)

Not every manager can or wishes to take the challenge. The second dilemma is concerned with the definition of control, or perhaps monitoring and control. We will extend our discussion of the new roles of leadership and management in Chapter 8.

Empowered teams within workforces may well reach their objectives but the manager, aware of a broader picture, needs to make sure that the objective is and remains within the general strategy of the organisation. The manager's understanding of the 'general strategy of the organisation' is a major step to him or her being empowered – managers without appropriate empowerment cannot empower their staff.

In our explanation of an empowering manager we have used the word 'steering' and we must not forget that steering will always need judgement and, on occasion, tough decisions should 'the boat not respond to the tiller'. This issue will be illustrated by the British Airways case study at the end of the chapter.

Although empowering others is neither easy nor natural (we are not born knowing how to do it), it need not actually require a great amount of self-sacrifice. A person doesn't need to sacrifice desired rewards, recognition or effectiveness in order to be a skilful empowering manager. On the contrary, through real empowerment, managers actually multiply their own effectiveness and need to broaden their sphere of understanding. They and their organisations become more effective than they could have been otherwise. Nevertheless, for most managers, empowerment is a skill that must be developed and practised, because despite the high visibility of the concept of empowerment in popular literature, its actual practice is all too rare in modern management. McClelland (1975) gives an example of how it can be done, and some of the difficulties. The attitude survey at the end of the article indicates that there is still a long way to go.

> While chairmen pronounce their latest vision for their company, more often than not in the bowels of the organisation their instructions are being interpreted, subverted or merely ignored. Alex Krauer, chairman of Ciba, the Swiss chemicals and drugs group, should know. For two years senior managers at the company, which last week reported post-tax profits up 19 per cent, have been struggling to implement a 'cultural revolution'. The revolution's aim is to make the organisation more flexible and responsive by giving its shop-floor employees more responsibility. The scheme, called Vision 2000, is, in current management jargon, all about empowerment.
>
> Krauer explains: 'Everything depends on implementation; this mustn't just be a declaration of intent. We must actively involve every employee in the process. The danger is that we create a level of expectation and then nothing happens.'
>
> The implementation of Ciba's vision has not run smoothly as Heini Lippuner, chief operating officer, admits: 'We do not have a uniform adoption of the leadership style we would like. The causes for the different degrees of implementation are multiple. Partly it depends on the attitudes of the individuals at the top of Ciba's 14 divisions.'
>
> Italy is touted as one of the examples where empowerment has worked. Sergio Giuliani, corporate head of Ciba Italy, says the Italian management during the early 1980s was authoritarian, hierarchical and bureaucratic. 'By definition a successful company becomes complacent and conservative,' he says. Since then, layers of

management have been ripped out and a start made in devolving decision making down the organisation.

But in Basle, at Ciba's headquarters, Lippuner claims that a risk-averse bureaucratic culture still exists: 'There is a passion in Basle for avoiding mistakes. That makes empowerment difficult because personal initiative brings the possibility of making errors. The Swiss character cherishes its traditional ways.'

The company has moved the headquarters of three of its divisions out of Basle in an effort to escape the deadening hand. A fourth, the eyecare division, Ciba-Vision, is relocating to Georgia later this year. At Ciba's pigment division headquarters in Paisley, Scotland, Jean-Luc Schwitzguebal, managing director, says moving divisional headquarters out of Basle is vital: 'Our performance is now our responsibility. We can't blame anyone else. We can't bitch that we are doing everything right, but Basle is screwing it up.'

Krauer identifies a further key component for successful implementation: 'The critical area is middle management. If it stops there, then the whole exercise is wasted. Some fully support the changes, while others are afraid. Others refuse to delegate because they believe that by doing so they lose power.' Lippuner explains further: 'I meet young people on the shop-floor who tell me they like the vision, they believe we are sincere about empowerment. But they complain that there has been no real change. To put it pointedly, it looks as though we have a layer of clay that prevents anything going either way – up or down. That layer is middle management.'

The resistance to change is sometimes unconscious, says Giuliani. 'There is often an unspoken contract between boss and employee. They play a game.'

Ciba is putting immense effort into explaining the programme. As Krauer says: 'If you don't understand and don't believe, you won't take on the vision.'

Senior management plans to crack the layer of clay by creating pressure from both above and below, and through education. Questionnaires about superiors' leadership behaviour were sent to the 20,000 employees in Switzerland. The aim, says Krauer, was to set up a level of expectation from employees and use that expectation to force middle managers into dialogue. Krauer believes that 90 per cent of managers are capable of adopting the vision: *'A few, and I hope only a few, will not want to co-operate and they had better look for a job outside Ciba. There is too much at stake for people in key positions not to be part of the process.'*

Lippuner says he does not want to paint too black a picture. There have been changes in small units away from Basle where leaders have been particularly dynamic and deployed private initiative. Jim McDonald says he is at the bottom of Ciba. A team leader at Paisley – a plant cited by Lippuner as a success – McDonald says the vision has filtered its way down. Colin McKay, the boss of his plant, is delighted. He explains how maintenance problems have been resolved by giving workers responsibility. Attitude surveys at Paisley suggest that nearly 70 per cent of employees are proud to work for Ciba. 'That includes people who spend most of their day shovelling chemicals. They are surprisingly good figures,' says Schwitzguebal who claims Paisley was the only classical pigment producer making money in western Europe last year.

McDonald agrees that management is now far more effective, allowing the possibility of avoiding problems before they happen. But in spite of Paisley's model status, he argues that there are still difficulties. Team leaders wanted to meet to

Table 7.1   Ciba: attitude survey

Over all of Ciba	Strongly agree	Agree	Unsure	Disagree	Strongly disagree
I feel my boss recognises my work's importance	11.1	32.2	16.3	21.3	19.1
I need more training to do my job	17.5	21.6	12.9	29.7	16.5
I feel very much left on my own	15.4	20.3	17.6	30.3	16.5
I enjoy the challenge of my job	23.6	44.8	12.5	10.6	8.5
I feel proud to work for Ciba	22.9	46.4	20.2	5.0	5.6
I can't wait to leave and find a better job	9.3	13.3	14.4	27.0	36.0

discuss similar issues, but the middle management initially blocked their meetings. 'We should meet one another – we have plenty to talk about,' he says. In the end, permission was given. Elsewhere, employees are also enthusiastic about the changes. At Ciba's epoxy-resin plant in Duxford, Cambridgeshire, Lionel Webb, customer service centre manager, describes proudly how his department was restructured after employees were polled about the business's problems.

Ciba managers admit that the success of the Italian and Paisley businesses cannot be put down just to the vision. For various reasons, the cultural change started earlier still has a long way to go. As Lippuner says: 'I have no illusions about inertia – I've worked in this organisation for 35 years. But that does not mean we will capitulate.'

Source: *Financial Times*, London, 5 April 1993

A attitude survey taken in 1993, and before Ciba's latest acquisitions, is shown in Table 7.1. Tarek Hosni (1998), working from the UAE, benchmarked his own company, SmithKline Beecham, against Emirates Airlines – a company based in Dubai and accepted as a leader in the empowerment of staff. His main finding was a lack of clarity in employees understanding of the term empowerment – 35 per cent of his sample, albeit small, believed there was no difference between empowerment and delegation. However, most managers saw the role of a manager in an empowered organisation as being facilitator, coach, supporter and controller. We do, however, from experience backed by Hosni's survey, need to consider our terms. What is empowerment and how does it differ from delegation?

What is empowerment?

First let us look at your own empowerment in your own organisation.

Imagine your boss has asked you to prepare a detailed report on a particular part of your department's work to the Board. One of your subordinates has the skills, knowledge and aptitude for writing the report and you do not. He or she writes the report, which, on your restricted expertise, seems excellent. In your opinion would the organisation expect you to:

(1) take the report and present it to the Board?
(2) take your subordinate with you to the Board and endorse his or her presentation?
(3) sit back while the report is presented?
(4) allow the subordinate to present the report, your own presence being irrelevant?

We now need to look at the reasons for your choice. If you have chosen (1) or (2) it may be that you feel your subordinate, for some logical reason, should not be exposed. It is more likely, however, that you are yourself insecure. You have not been empowered by the culture of the organisation and its custodians. If you feel that (1) or (2) would be 'the way things are done' in your organisation, and you may find the whole concept of empowerment a dangerous concept to pursue.

One of the most well-researched findings in organisation and management science over the last four decades has shown that when environments are predictable and stable, organisations can function as routine, controlled, mechanistic units. Under such conditions, workers can be expected to follow rules and procedures and to engage in standardised, formalised behaviour. Managers can maintain control and issue top-down mandates regarding the strategy and direction to be pursued by the organisation. This is not the way most businesses are today. Emery and Trist (1965) described four stages of organisational climate.

- **Placid** – an environment where companies can 'graze'. There is plenty for every player.

- **Clustered** – where smaller companies are joining together to form 'empires'.

- **Reactive** – where organisations are looking to optimise their position against others in what is seen to be a relatively static and stable market place.

- **Turbulent** – where very little can be predicted and the rule is 'decide where you want to be and go for it'.

The modern jargon attached to our present way includes such words as 'hyper-turbulence', 'complexity', 'speed', 'competition', 'chaotic', 'revolutionary change', suggesting that, for most of our world, we are in Emery and Triss's fourth turbulent state. Under such conditions, prescriptions for organisational and management effectiveness call for a flexible, autonomous, entrepreneurial workforce (Peters, 1992; Drucker, 1988) rather than one which relies on management for direction and control. Less centralised decision making, less top-down direction, and less autocratic leadership are all prescribed as prerequisites for high-performing modern organisations.

When environments are unstable and unpredictable – when they change a lot or change in unpredictable ways – organisations must be more flexible and organic. Workers are expected to be adaptable and self-managing. Managers must involve others in decision making, and facilitate broad participation and accountability (Eisenhart and Galunic, 1993; Lawrence and Lorsch, 1967). The flexibility of the workers must match the flexibility of the environment (Ashby, 1956).

A water authority ran a management development program over a period of $2\frac{1}{2}$ years. The purpose of the program was to move the management style away from a directing and controlling paradigm towards a supportive and trust-based paradigm. A significant requirement of the program, as specified by senior management, was the empowerment of middle management. However, the implications of this were not fully appreciated by senior management until late in the program when issues of control came back into prominence. Eventually, the program was curtailed and middle managers were consequently disillusioned rather than empowered.

Quoted from Hopfl and Dawes (1995)

Our own research has discovered, however, that instead of becoming adaptable, flexible, autonomous and self-managing, individuals in rapidly changing, complex environments tend to react in the opposite way. Both managers and employees tend to become less flexible, less adaptable, less autonomous, less self-managing, more stable, more rigid and more defensive when they face turbulence and change (Cameron *et al.*, 1987b). When they face decline, turbulence, a reducing labour force and change, they stick to the 'devil that we know' attitude.

The devil that we know

The tendency to prefer the 'devil that we know' in response to change was dubbed 'threat-rigidity' by Staw *et al.* (1981). At the very point when people need to be proactive in facing change, they tend towards the exactly opposite behaviour. They become conservative and defensive, relying more than ever on old habits and past behaviours. In reaction to a perceived threat, they do that which they know how to do best, or that which has worked best in the past. Despite new circumstances in which old behaviours may not be effective, there is an escalating commitment to habitual behaviour. People seek fewer options, look for information that confirms their previous biases, and become more narrow-minded in their perspectives. In addition, less communication occurs among workers. When individuals in organisations are divulging information, they become vulnerable by putting their personal expertise or untested ideas at risk. This sense of vulnerability magnifies the feeling of uncertainty brought about by changing conditions. In such circumstances, people are less likely to become contributing team members and to try out new, innovative ideas. Fear and conflict increase, while trust, morale and productivity decrease. The reactionary mode is typical of most interactions, as loyalty and commitment to the organisation become eroded. The tendency in such circumstances is for most important decisions to be made at the top of the organisational hierarchy, because managers at the top feel an increasing need to be in control and to be closer to decisions. On the other hand, people at lower organisational levels become hesitant to make decisions without getting approval from a superior.

If people become more dependent on top managers in uncertain times rather than more independent, how can we ever foster effective performance? How can we ever expect a workforce in a changing environment to develop the prescribed characteristics for effectiveness – that is, to be adaptable, flexible, autonomous and self-managing?

The answer to these questions is to use empowerment. If managers are empowered and are skilled at empowering their subordinates, the inertia that drives organisations towards a dysfunctional 'devil that we know' attitude is counteracted. Workers become more effective, even in the face of trying times. Empowerment is a key to unlocking the potential of a successful workforce in a modern era of chaotic change and escalating competitive conditions.

But what is empowerment? What does it mean to be an empowered worker? What is the set of management skills associated with empowerment?

To empower means to enable; it means to help people develop a sense of self-worth; it means to overcome causes of powerlessness or helplessness; it means to energise people to take action; it means to mobilise intrinsic excitement factors in work. It is more than merely giving power to someone. Power does allow us to get things done, but empowerment involves not only the capacity to accomplish a task, but also includes a way of defining oneself. Empowered people not only possess the wherewithal to accomplish something, they also think of themselves differently than they did before they were empowered.

Antoinette O'Connell (1995), writes about effective organisations. Her view is that the key to success is to continually energise its people around emerging business themes. When organisations fail to recognise the themes, or to empower its people to use their potential to utilise these themes to advantage, the organisation is doomed to insignificance or failure. She sees technology alone leading to mediocrity at best unless the human dimension is developed at the same time. The more people are self-actualised by their work, the more they are empowered to contribute to the organisation's success. 'Top executives need to take a fresh look at the responsibilities of management, the path to productivity, and training. Managers need more than the classic planning, organising, leading, and controlling skills. Those will never be obsolete, but managers need to effectively integrate technological invention as a resource. They also need greater depth in communication and integration skills.'

Historical roots of empowerment

The word empowerment has been in vogue in the 1980s and 1990s, yet as a concept it is by no means new. The concept of empowerment has been referred to in many books and articles in the last few years, and it has become popular to use the term to refer to everything from team building to decentralised structures. In fact, the word has been so over-used that its precise meaning may have become obscured. It may be helpful, therefore, to provide a brief background of the roots of empowerment. This should help to avoid confusing empowerment with other related management behaviours. Empowerment has roots in the disciplines of psychology, sociology and theology, dating back decades – even centuries.

The concept of 'mastery motivation' emphasises the way people strive for competence in dealing with their world. Similar concepts introduced several decades ago include:

- 'Effectance motivation', an intrinsic motivation to make things happen (White, 1959).
- 'Psychological reactance', which refers to seeking freedom from constraints (Brehm, 1966).
- 'Competence motivation', a striving to encounter and master challenges (Harter, 1978).
- 'Personal causation', a drive to experience free agency (DeCharms, 1979).

These 'variations on a theme' are similar to the notion of empowerment discussed in this book – i.e., the inclination of people to experience self-control, self-worth and liberation.

In sociology, notions of empowerment have been fundamental to most 'rights' movements – e.g., Civil Rights, Women's Rights, Gay Rights (see Solomon, 1976; Bookman and Morgan, 1988) – in which people campaign for freedom and control of their own circumstances. Moreover, much of the writing attacking problems through social change has centred fundamentally on the empowerment of groups of people (Marx, 1844; Alinski, 1971). That is, people seek social change in order to increase their access to an empowered condition.

In theology, debates about free will versus determinism, self-will versus submissiveness, predestination versus faith and works, and humanism versus positivism have been hotly debated for centuries. At their root, they are all variations on a theme of empowerment versus helplessness. The more recent literature on 'liberation theology' (Friere and Faundez, 1989) emphasises the empowerment of individuals to take charge of their own destinies, rather than relying on the dictates of an all-controlling, supernatural force. This does not mean that people who believe in a Supreme Being cannot feel empowered; rather, it implies that they can couple a sense of self-mastery and self-determination with their faith in a higher power.

Empowerment, then, is not a new concept. It has appeared in various forms throughout modern management literature. In the 1950s, for example, management literature was filled with prescriptions that managers should be friendly to employees – the human relations school. In the 1960s, it was proscribed that managers should be sensitive to the needs and motivations of people by a process of sensitivity training. By the 1970s it was fashionable to tell managers to ask employees for help with employee involvement schemes. In the 1980s teams and quality circles were fashionable. As Byham (1991) points out – the word is now empowerment. But despite the continuing emphasis on various versions of employee involvement and empowerment, the ability to empower employees is still not common in most managers' repertoire of skills. Empowerment is more rarely seen than prescribed. Woods (1997a) describes it as the 'new Holy Grail'.

Inhibitors to empowerment

In his book on managerial empowerment, Peter Block (1987) noted that empowerment is very difficult to accomplish:

Many, increasingly aware of the price we pay for too many controls, have had the belief that if some of these controls were removed, a tremendous amount of positive energy in service of the organisation would be released. While in many cases this has happened, too often our attempts at giving people more responsibility have been unwelcome and have met with persistent reluctance. Many managers have tried repeatedly to open the door of participation to their people, only to find them reluctant to walk through it.

Block studied managers who were offered total responsibility for their work areas. About 20 per cent of the managers took the responsibility and ran with it, about 50 per cent of the managers cautiously tested the sincerity of the offer and then over a period of six months began to make their own decisions. The frustrating part of the effort was that the other 30 per cent absolutely refused to take the reins. They clutched tightly to their dependency and continued to complain that top management did not really mean it, that they were not given enough people or resources to do their jobs properly, and that the unique characteristics of their particular location made efforts at participative management unreasonable.

As Block noted, many managers and employees are reluctant to accept empowerment, but they are even more reluctant to **offer** empowerment. One reason for this is the personal attitudes of managers. Several management surveys, for example, have examined the reasons managers have for not being willing to empower their employees (Newman and Warren, 1977; Preston and Zimmerer, 1978; Byham, 1991). These reasons can be organised into three broad categories, as follows.

1. **Attitudes, beliefs and assumptions about subordinates.** Managers who avoid empowering others often believe their subordinates are not competent enough to accomplish the work. They assume that workers are not interested in taking on more responsibility, are already overloaded and are unable to accept more responsibility, and would require too much time to train. They may even believe that workers should not be involved in tasks or responsibilities typically performed by the boss. They feel that the problem of non-empowerment lies with the employees, not with themselves. The rationale is: 'I'm willing to empower my people, but they just won't accept the responsibility.' They adopt the Theory X stance we discussed in the previous chapter. We met one manager who famously said to us – *'I keep on telling my people they are empowered, but they don't believe me.'*

2. **Personal insecurities.** Some managers fear they will lose the recognition and rewards associated with successful task-accomplishment if they empower others. They are unwilling to share their expertise or 'trade secrets' for fear of losing power or position. They have an intolerance for ambiguity which leads them to feel that they personally must know all the details about projects assigned to them. They prefer working on tasks by themselves rather than getting others involved, or they are unwilling to absorb the costs associated with subordinates making mistakes. The rationale is: 'I'm willing to empower people, but when I do, they either mess things up or try to grab all the glory.'

3. **Need for control.** Non-empowering managers often have a great need to be in charge and to direct and govern what is going on. They presume that an

ι and goals from the boss and a slackening of controls
ustration and failure on the part of employees. They
he top is mandatory. Moreover, they often see short-
lived, disappointing results from pep talks, work teams, suggestion systems,
job-enrichment programmes and other 'fix-it' activities (i.e., 'We tried that,
and it didn't work'). The rationale is: 'I'm willing to empower people, but they
require clear directions and a clear set of guidelines; otherwise, the lack of
co-ordination leads to confusion.'

The rationale associated with each of these inhibitors may be partially true,
but they nevertheless inhibit managers from achieving the success associated with
skilful empowerment. Even if managers demonstrate the willingness and courage to empower others, success still requires skilful implementation. Incompetent
empowerment can undermine rather than enhance the effectiveness of an organisation and its employees. Incompetent empowerment, such as giving employees
freedom without clear directions or resources, has been found to lead to psychological casualties among individuals. Alloy *et al.* (1984) records increased depression,
and Averill (1973) heightened stress. Decreased performance and job satisfaction was
recorded by Greenberger *et al.* (1989) and a lowered alertness and even increased
mortality by Langer and Rodin (1976). Ineffective empowerment cannot be blamed
for everything, but these symptoms were noted when empowerment programmes
were ineffective and unskilful. For example, when managers associated empowerment with behaviours such as 'simply letting go', refusing to clarify expectations,
abdicating responsibility, having an absence of ground-rules, or giving inflexible or
inconsistent directions – none of which is consistent with skilful empowerment –
the results were not only unsuccessful, but even harmful. Because of the negative
psychological and physiological consequences for workers resulting from non-
empowerment or from incompetent empowerment, Sashkin (1984) labelled skilful
empowerment 'an ethical imperative' for managers.

Dimensions of empowerment

In one of the best empirical studies of empowerment to date, Spreitzer (1992)
identified four dimensions of empowerment. We have added two dimensions to her
model, based on the research of Mishra (1992), and in this section we shall explain
these six key dimensions. In order for managers to empower others successfully,
they must engender these six qualities in those they intend to empower. Skilful
empowerment means producing a sense of:

- Self-esteem
- Self-efficacy
- Self-determination
- Personal control
- Meaning
- Trust in other people

When managers are able to foster these six attributes in others, they have succeeded in empowering others. We suggested earlier that empowered people could not only accomplish tasks, but that they also think differently about themselves.

Self-esteem

If we value ourselves then we are able to value what we do.

Many of the management practices of the past have led to the concept of a number – a work unit, a cipher. Our bookshops have shelves devoted to books advocating assertive behaviour – behaviour based on the concept of self-esteem and valuing the rights of others. We discuss some of the techniques in our chapter on constructive communication and refer the reader to Gael Lindfield (1989), Anne Dickson (1982) and Mike Woods (1989).

> A British Coal smokeless fuel plant in the Midlands of the UK was giving considerable trouble in the commissioning period. The plant, because of its very nature was dirty and there had been several serious accidents. Morale was very low. The management team was working unhealthily long hours and had allowed themselves to 'go native' – matching the griminess of the plant with their own appearance. A top manager made a surprise visit to the plant and met the team. His very clear instructions were to clean the plant up, repaint the main office and most of all get out and get washed. New overalls were acquired and razors applied. At a good dinner he told the team how much he depended on them and how important their work was. Although the project failed, as indeed did most projects concerned with the dying market for domestic coal, the team made the plant work.

Self-efficacy

When people are empowered, they have a sense of self-efficacy – the feeling that they possess the capability and competence to perform a task successfully. Empowered people not only feel competent, they feel confident that they can perform adequately. They feel a sense of personal mastery, and believe they can learn and grow to meet new challenges (see Bennis and Nanus, 1985; Conger and Kanungo, 1988; Bandura, 1989; Gecas, 1989; Zimmerman, 1990). Some writers believe that this is the most important element in empowerment because having a sense of self-efficacy determines whether people will try and persist in attempting to accomplish a difficult task.

> The strength of people's conviction in their own effectiveness is likely to affect whether they would even try to cope with given situations. They get involved in activities and behave assuredly when they judge themselves capable of handling situations that would otherwise be intimidating . . . Efficacy expectations determine how much effort people will expend and how long they will persist in the face of obstacles and adverse experiences. (Bandura, 1977b)

Much research has been done on the consequences of self-efficacy and its opposite, powerlessness, especially in relation to physical and psychological health.

For example, self-efficacy has been found to be a significant factor in overcoming phobias and anxieties (Bandura, 1986), alcohol and drug abuse (Seeman and Anderson, 1983), eating disorders (Schneider and Agras, 1985), smoking addiction (DiClemente, 1985) and depression (Seligman, 1975). It has also been associated with an increasing tolerance for pain (Neufeld and Thomas, 1977). People who have developed a strong feeling of self-efficacy more resilient, in mind and body, are hence more likely to cope with illness or injury and job disruptions (Schwalbe and Gecas, 1988; Gecas, *et al.*, 1988). Bandura (1977b) suggested that personal beliefs are necessary for people to feel a sense of self-efficacy. They believe:

1. that they have the ability to perform a task;
2. that they are capable of putting in the necessary effort;
3. that no outside obstacles will prevent them from accomplishing the task.

People feel empowered when they develop a sense of self-efficacy by having a basic level of competence and capability, a willingness to put in effort to accomplish a task, and the absence of overwhelming inhibitors to success.

Self-determination

Empowered people also have a sense of self-determination. Whereas self-efficacy refers to a sense of competence, self-determination refers to feelings of having a choice. 'To be self-determining means to experience a sense of choice in initiating and regulating one's own actions' (Deci *et al.*, 1989). People feel self-determined when they can voluntarily and intentionally involve themselves in tasks, rather than being forced or prohibited from involvement. Their actions are a consequence of personal freedom and autonomy. Empowered individuals have a sense of responsibility for, and ownership of, their activities (Rappaport *et al.*, 1984; Rose and Black, 1985; Staples, 1990; Zimmerman, 1990). They see themselves as proactive self-starters. They are able to take initiative on their own accord, make independent decisions and try out new ideas (Conger and Kanungo, 1988; Thomas and Velthouse, 1990; Vogt and Murrell, 1990). Rather than feeling that their actions are predetermined, externally controlled or inevitable, they experience themselves as the locus of control. Research shows that a strong sense of self-determination is associated with:

* less alienation in the work environment (Seeman and Anderson, 1983)
* more work satisfaction (Organ and Greene, 1974)
* higher levels of work performance (Anderson *et al.*, 1977)
* more entrepreneurial and innovative activity (Hammer and Vardi, 1981)
* high levels of job involvement (Runyon, 1973)
* less job strain (Gennill and Heisler, 1972).

In medical research, recovery from severe illness has been found to be associated with having the patient 'reject the traditional passive role and insist on being an active participant in his own therapy' (Gecas, 1989). People who are helped to feel that they can have personal impact on what happens to them, even with regard to the effects of disease, are more likely to experience positive outcomes than those who lack this feeling.

Self-determination is associated most directly with having choices about the methods used to accomplish a task, the amount of effort to be expended, the pace of the work and the time frame in which it is to be accomplished. Empowered individuals have a feeling of ownership for tasks because they can determine how they are accomplished, when they are accomplished and how soon they are completed. Having a choice is the critical component of self-determination.

Personal control

Empowered people have a sense of personal control over what they do. They believe that they can make a difference by influencing the environment in which they work, the method of working or the work itself. Personal control is 'an individual's beliefs at a given point in time in his or her ability to effect a change in a desired direction' (Greenberger and Stasser, 1991). It is the conviction that through one's own actions, a person can influence what happens. Personal control, then, refers to a perception of impact.

Empowered individuals do not believe that obstacles in the external environment control their actions. Rather, they believe that those obstacles can be controlled. They are proactive and not reactive to the world around them (see Rothbaum *et al.*, 1982; Rappaport, *et al.*, 1984; Zimmerman and Rappaport, 1988; Greenberger and Stasser, 1991; Thomas and Velthouse, 1990).

> Newton and Wilkinson (1995) made a study of a comprehensive management development programme within the public health sector at Ashworth Hospital (UK). It was concluded that 'there must be a pre-specified set of strategic linked outcomes. Programmes that do not result in managers feeling empowered will be criticised for not impacting positively on the organisation.'

Having a sense of personal control is related to, but distinct from, having power and influence. Power and influence are associated with such things as an individual's position, appearance, skill and visibility. Usually, obtaining power is desirable in order to influence or control the behaviour of others. On the other hand, personal control is focused internally, and the emphasis is on controlling one's own life, space and results. Control of self, more than control of others, is the objective. Research on personal control suggests that people are intrinsically motivated to seek personal control (White, 1959). They fight to maintain a sense of control over themselves and their situations. Prisoners of war, for example, have been known to refuse to eat certain food, to walk in a certain place or develop secret communication codes, in order to maintain a sense of personal control. A certain amount of personal control is necessary for people to maintain psychological and physical well being. When people lose their personal control, we usually label them 'insane' or 'psychopathic'.

Even small losses of personal control can be harmful, both physically and emotionally. For example, loss of control has been found to lead to depression, stress, anxiety, low morale, loss of productivity, burnout, learned helplessness and even increased death rates (see Langer, 1983; Greenberger and Stasser, 1991). The major predictor of suicide is also the sense of loss of personal control. Having a sense of personal control, then, is necessary for health as well as for empowerment. On the other hand, even the most empowered people are not able to control everything that happens to them. No one is in complete control of his or her life. But empowerment helps people to increase the number of personal outcomes that they can control. Often, this is as much a matter of identifying areas in which personal control is possible as it is of manipulating or changing the external environment to increase control.

Meaning

Empowered people have a sense of meaning. They value the purpose or goals of the activity in which they are engaged. Their own ideals and standards are perceived as consistent with what they are doing. The activity 'counts' in their own value system. Empowered individuals believe in and care about what they produce. They invest psychic or spiritual energy in the activity, and they feel a sense of personal significance in their involvement. They experience personal involvement and personal integrity as a result of engaging in the activity (Rappaport *et al.*, 1984; Bennis and Nanus, 1985; Block, 1987; Conger and Kanungo, 1988; Manz and Sims, 1989). Meaningfulness, then, refers to a perception of value.

Activities infused with meaning create a sense of purpose, passion or mission for people. They provide a source of energy and enthusiasm, rather than draining energy and enthusiasm from people. Merely getting paid, or helping an organisation to earn money, or just doing a job, does not create a sense of meaning for most people. Handy (1994), in his book *The Empty Raincoat*, regrets that unfortunately he has met many people who are 'empty shells' because they seem to exist entirely for the job. Handy is expressing the hope that we can be something better than mere 'empty raincoats' and instead become associated with something more fundamental, personal, value-laden and, most importantly, more worthy of a human being. It is better perhaps to hope that many people do need to be associated with something more fundamental, personal and more value-laden – i.e. with something more human.

Acquiring personal benefit does not guarantee meaning. For example, service to others may bring no quantifiable personal reward but may be far more meaningful than work that produces a hefty pay-cheque. Involvement in activities without meaning, on the other hand, creates dissonance and annoyance, and produces a sense of disengagement from the work. People become bored or exhausted. Other incentives – such as rules, supervision or extra pay – are required to get people to invest in the work. Unfortunately, these extra incentives are costly to organisations and represent below-the-line expenses that constrain organisational efficiency and effectiveness. It costs companies a lot of money to require work that has little or no meaning to its workers. Self-estrangement results from lack of meaning; vigour and stimulation result from meaningful work (see Hackman and Oldham, 1980; Alday and Brief, 1979; Kahn, 1990; Thomas and Velthouse, 1990).

Research into the personal meaning of jobs has found that when individuals engage in work which they feel is meaningful, they have greater commitment and register greater energy and persistence. Workers feel more excitement and passion for meaningful work; and it gives them a greater sense of personal significance and self-worth. Individuals empowered with a sense of meaning have also been found to be more innovative, upwardly influential, and personally effective than those with low-meaning scores (Kanter, 1968; Bramucci, 1977; Nielson, 1986; Deci and Ryan, 1987; Vogt and Murrell, 1990; Spreitzer, 1992).

Trust

Empowered people have a sense of trust. They are confident that they will be treated fairly and equitably. They have an assurance that when they are in subordinate situations, those in power will not take advantage of them. They believe, with due care, that principles of justice will guide the behaviour of those who control resources. This is not through naivety, but a belief that this is a better way. Even though trust implies being in a position of vulnerability (Zand, 1972), empowered individuals have faith that no harm will come to them (Deutsch, 1973; Luhmann, 1979; Barber, 1983; Mishra, 1992). When they are at the mercy of someone else's decisions, empowered individuals believe that they will not deliberately be injured. Trust, then, refers to a sense of security. Research has found that trusting individuals are more apt to replace superficiality and façades with directness and intimacy; they are more apt to be open, honest and congruent rather than deceptive or shallow. They are more search-oriented and self-determining, more self-assured and willing to learn. They have a larger capacity for interdependent relationships, and they display a greater degree of co-operation and risk-taking in groups than do those with low trust. Trusting people are more willing to try to get along with others and to be a contributing part of a team. They are also more self-disclosing, more honest in their own communication, and more able to listen carefully to others. They have less resistance to change and are better able to cope with unexpected traumas than are those with low levels of trust. Individuals who trust others are more likely to be trustworthy themselves and to maintain high personal ethical standards (see Gibb and Gibb, 1969; Golembiewski and McConkie, 1975; Mishra, 1992).

Because 'trusting environments allow individuals to unfold and flourish' (Golembiewski and McConkie, 1975), empowerment is closely tied to a sense of trust. A feeling that the behaviour of others is consistent and reliable, that information can be held in confidence and that promises will be kept, are all a part of developing a sense of empowerment in people. Trusting others allows people to act in a confident and straightforward manner, without wasting energy on self-protection, trying to uncover hidden agendas, or playing politics. In brief, a sense of trust empowers people to feel secure.

A major issue is concerned with the sense of betrayal that is fostered when a workforce is 'empowered' and then finds that the empowerment is a sham. Herriot and Pemberton (1995a/b), as mentioned before, describe the dysfunctional behaviour in terms of:

- Get out
- Get safe
- Get even.

They quote examples where the empowerment process had led the workforce to feel that their trust had been betrayed. The most able individuals left the organisation while the rest either dug in, taking an extremely conservative approach, or acted as a cancer in the organisation, stopping little short of sabotage. Herriot and Pemberton advocate the linking of empowerment programmes with new formal contracts covering the new working conditions and practices.

Conclusion

In summary we find that working within the five dimensions of empowerment produces both personal and organisational advantage. Helping people feel a certain way about themselves and their work also helps them to be more effective in the behaviours they display. Some authors have gone so far as to claim that helping others develop this feeling of empowerment is at the very root of managerial effectiveness. Without it, they claim, neither managers nor organisations can be successful in the long term (Kanter, 1983; Bennis and Nanus, 1985; Block, 1987; Conger, 1989). As a psychological state, however, empowerment is never under the complete control of a manager. It is possible for individuals to refuse to feel empowered. However, a sense of empowerment can be influenced significantly by the conditions in which people find themselves. For that reason, the next section of this book discusses specific actions that managers can take to empower others.

Developing empowerment

We cannot overemphasise the issue of competence and the importance of training. Everything we are about to say is pure waffle if people do not have the ability to do the jobs they are called upon to perform. We will discuss the sequence Tell–Coach–Consult–Delegate in the final chapter. In the meantime let us work from the point where the basic skills are available – the job can be done, but we feel that it can be done better and have chosen the route of empowerment to 'do it better'.

Empowerment as a 'tool' is most effective when individuals or teams feel threatened or their jobs are unclear, overly controlled, coercive or isolating. In particular when they feel:

- inappropriately dependent or inadequate
- stifled in their ability to do what they would like to do
- uncertain about how to behave
- that some negative consequence is likely
- unrewarded and unappreciated.

Ironically, most large organisations engender these kinds of feelings in people, because, as Block (1987) noted, bureaucracy encourages dependency and submission. Rules, routines and traditions define what can be done, thus stifling and supplanting initiative and discretion. In such circumstances, the formal organisation, not the individual, is the recipient of empowerment. Therefore, in large organisations, empowerment is especially needed but difficult to achieve.

But empowerment is also important outside vast bureaucracies. For example, studies demonstrate the positive effects of empowerment on child development, learning in school, coping with personal stress and changing personal habits (see Ozer and Bandura, 1990).

Despite the applicability of empowerment in many different contexts, our discussion focuses on ways in which managers can empower their employees in organisations. We focus on empowerment mainly as a skill needed by managers, even though other people such as parents, teachers, coaches, tutors and friends can also benefit by developing the skills of empowerment.

Research by Kanter (1983), Bandura (1986), Hackman and Oldham (1980) and others has produced at least eight specific prescriptions for fostering empowerment, i.e., producing a sense of competence, choice, impact, value and security. These include:

- Fostering personal mastery
- Modelling
- Providing support
- Creating personal enthusiasm
- Providing information
- Providing resources
- Organising teams
- Creating confidence.

We will discuss each of these factors in turn and, as we do so, the reader will find some overlap with other parts of this book. We make no apology for this.

Fostering personal mastery

Bandura (1986) found that the single most important thing a manager can do to empower other people is to help them experience personal mastery over some challenge or problem. By successfully accomplishing a task, defeating an opponent or resolving a problem, people develop a sense of mastery. Personal mastery can be fostered by providing people with the opportunity to accomplish successively more difficult tasks, which eventually lead to the accomplishment of desirable goals. The key is to start with easy tasks, then progress by small steps to more difficult tasks until the person experiences a sense of mastery over an entire complex of problems.

Managers can help workers to feel more and more empowered by helping them to develop an awareness that they can succeed. One way to do this is by breaking apart large tasks and giving workers only one part at a time. The manager watches for small successes achieved by workers and then highlights and celebrates them. Jobs can be expanded incrementally so that tasks become broader and more complex as workers master their basic elements. We discussed this in the chapter on motivation under the acronym of FRAME.

Working in this way employees are given more problem-solving responsibility as they succeed in resolving more rudimentary difficulties. Managers can also provide opportunities for employees to direct or lead others in a project, task force or committee. Individuals are given opportunities to succeed in small ways, even though an overall challenge may be formidable (Weick, 1979). Small wins can occur when large problems are divided up into limited units which can be attacked individually. Small wins may seem insignificant by themselves, but they generate a sense of movement, progress and success. When small wins are recognised and celebrated by managers, momentum is generated that leads people to feel empowered and capable.

Lee Iacocca used this strategy to turn around a failing Chrysler Corporation in the early 1980s. An analysis of his speeches to the top management team at Chrysler over a period of five years reveals that even though Chrysler was losing money, costs were too high and quality was a major problem, Iacocca continued to celebrate small successes. For example, he regularly announced that a certain amount of money had been saved, a particular improvement had been produced, or a compliment had been received from a Wall Street analyst – even though the firm was losing a billion dollars a year. A great deal of emphasis was placed on succeeding at small things, all of which were aimed at eventually toppling the much larger challenge of company survival. In this case, continual small wins led to a big achievement.

Modelling

A second way to empower people is to model or demonstrate the correct behaviour they are to perform. According to Bandura (1977b), observing someone else succeed at challenging activities provides a forceful impetus for others to believe that they, too, can succeed. It helps people presume that a task is 'do-able', that a job is within their capabilities and that success is possible.

The manager may also serve as the role model by demonstrating desired behaviours. On the other hand, it may not be possible for a manager to model desired behaviours personally for every single employee he wants to empower. The manager may not see an employee often enough to show that person how to accomplish his or her work, or the manager may not have time for frequent demonstrations of success. As an alternative, however, managers may be able to draw their employees' attention to other people who have been successful in similar circumstances. They might make it possible for employees to associate with senior or other visible people who could serve as role models, and they could provide opportunities for workers to be coached by these successful people. They can provide employees with mentors who can discuss their own past experiences that were similar to those of the employee. In other words, empowering people involves making available to them examples of past success. This is consistent with the learning model upon which this book is based. The Skill Analysis step of the learning model exemplifies appropriate and inappropriate behaviour engaged in by others. It provides a model of people who have succeeded in accomplishing the desired skill. This modelling function helps to foster a sense of empowerment in individuals who are trying to develop and improve management skills by showing ways in which such skills can be demonstrated successfully.

Think of what happens when a barrier is broken. In track and field athletics, for example, once John Thomas broke the seven-foot high jump barrier and Roger Bannister broke the four-minute mile, a host of other athletes quickly exceeded that standard. But before the first person broke those barriers, they were considered for many years as insurmountable. It took someone to demonstrate that the standard could be exceeded in order for others to experience the empowerment necessary to replicate the accomplishment themselves.

Providing support

A third technique for helping others to experience empowerment is providing them with social and emotional support. If people are to feel empowered, managers should praise them, encourage them, express approval of them, back them and reassure them. Kanter (1983) and Bandura (1986) each found that a crucial part of empowerment is having responsive and supportive managers. Managers seeking to empower their subordinates should find ways to praise their performance regularly. They can write letters or notes to workers, to members of their unit, or even to their family indicating that the employee's good work has been noticed. They can provide feedback to workers about their abilities and competencies. They can arrange for opportunities where workers can receive social support from others by becoming part of a team or social unit. They can express confidence in employees by supervising them less closely, or by allowing longer intervals between the reporting of results. Managers can hold regular ceremonies where recognition is provided for employees' achievements. It may simply be a matter of listening to employees and trying to understand their feelings and points of view.

Managers can empower others, then, by engendering a feeling that they are accepted, that they are a valued asset, and that they are an integral part of the overall mission or objective of the organisation. This support can be provided either by the manager himself or by co-workers.

Cameron *et al.* (1991) described a variety of support activities undertaken by a highly effective manager who was forced to lay off workers due to a cost-reduction exercise by the holding company. The cost-reduction exercise forced layoffs and understandably caused trust to be undermined, scepticism to rise and a sense of powerlessness to escalate among employees. Because the announcement came down from the parent company, workers felt that they had lost the ability to control their own destinies. In short, they felt un-empowered.

The manager held personal meetings with each remaining employee to reaffirm his or her value to the organisation. People were told in a straightforward manner that they were considered to be valuable human resources, not human liabilities. A special 'Build with Pride' week was held in which outsiders – the press, government officials, family members, school classes – were invited to tour the site, and exhibitions allowed individuals to demonstrate special achievements and skills. An impromptu barbecue was held one lunch hour to recognise and celebrate the exceptional efforts of one group of employees. People were assured that counselling, training and assistance would be provided when job assignments changed or positions were merged as a result of the cost-cutting exercise, which was explained in detail. In general, this notable manager attempted to re-empower his workforce by providing social and emotional support in a variety of ways. He helped to provide the assistance people needed to cope with the uncertainty resulting from this uncontrollable event. Predictably, both organisational and individual performance results did not deteriorate. Instead, contrary to the general rule, performance actually improved.

Creating personal enthusiasm

Creating personal enthusiasm means replacing negative emotions such as fear, anxiety or irritability with positive emotions such as excitement and anticipation. To empower people, managers help to make the work environment fun and attractive. They make certain that the purpose behind the work is clear. Bandura (1977b) found that the absence of personal enthusiasm (he calls it positive emotional arousal) makes it difficult, if not impossible, for individuals to feel empowered.

Managers need to be very clear about the vision and mission of their organisations. Empowerment without vision leads to chaos. Managers must have a clear picture of what employees are empowered to do and where they are going. This vision and mission must be linked, not only to a desirable future, but also to personal values. Workers must see how their everyday tasks are associated with their basic beliefs. Employees can get more excited about working for the betterment of humankind, for the improvement of the quality of people's lives, and for personal growth and development, than they can for a 10 per cent return to institutional investors. This is not to say that revenue for shareholders is unimportant, but it may well be difficult for many people to get enthusiastic about. Managers can also increase workers' sense of empowerment by holding periodic social gatherings to foster friendships among co-workers. In their official communications, they can occasionally include a joke or light-hearted message to relieve tension. They can use superlatives in providing feedback or describing successes (e.g., say 'terrific' instead of 'good'; 'fantastic' instead of 'acceptable'). They can make sure that employees are clear about how their work will affect the company's customers. Managers can schedule regular events where employees can hear compelling motivational messages. They can help identify external threats or challenges that need to be met. The successful creation of enthusiasm is often associated with athletic teams. Syer and Connolly (1984) in their book, *Sporting Body, Sporting Mind*, explain techniques for 'warming up' sports people which are very similar in principle to those already discussed here for managers. Chuck Coonradt (1985) observed that 'people are willing to pay for the privilege of working harder than they will work when they are paid'. That is, individuals will actually pay money in order to work at a more demanding level than the level at which they work when they are receiving a salary. The following is an example of this:

> The frozen foods industry involves people working in refrigerated warehouses in sub-zero temperatures, with both management and the unions attempting to make conditions more bearable. Companies are required to provide insulated clothing and boots, to make hot drinks easily available and to allow ten-minute breaks every hour. In these conditions recruitment is difficult. However, the very same people will dream of a winter holiday in the snow resorts of Austria or Switzerland. They will buy the most expensive equipment, paid for by themselves, and, once there, they will 'work' very hard with none of the hot-drink vending machines on the slopes or the ten-minute breaks every hour.
>
> (Adapted from Coonradt, 1985)

People actually end up working harder, in worse conditions – and paying for the privilege – than when they are at work getting paid. Why is this so? Why does recreation produce such energy, commitment and sense of empowerment?

Part of the explanation relates to the personal enthusiasm that is a characteristic of many sports. For example, all recreation has a clear goal (e.g., winning, exceeding a personal best). Without a clearly defined goal, no one gets excited. That goal is always pitted against a standard that people care about (e.g., winning the European Cup, wearing a yellow jersey in the Tour de France, scoring a century against the West Indies). In recreation, the score-keeping and feedback systems are objective, self-administered and continuous. In cricket, for example, everyone knows that if a ball is hit beyond the boundary, it counts as six runs. There is an umpire to make sure that the rules are obeyed and anyone can check on the score at any time. The scoring and feedback systems are one logical explanation of why people enjoy watching sports and athletic events. In recreation, the out-of-bounds is clearly identified. People are aware of the consequence of kicking a soccer ball over the touchline, of dropping the ball in rugby, or of stepping over the end of the take-off board in the long jump. They are all out-of-bounds, and everyone knows that out-of-bounds behaviour stops action.

A second explanation is that the sporting situation has tight boundaries – clear in time as well as objective.

Empowerment does not only consist of making pretty speeches but also of restructuring tasks so that they are FRAMED – with clear and explicit boundaries, measurable results and agreed objectives. However, if the principles of empowerment are not to divide a workforce, they must be applied throughout the workforce. Empowering the R&D staff while ignoring the shop floor is a recipe for disaster, only mitigated by dividing sites.

Providing information

Kanter (1983) identified information as one of the most crucial 'power tools' available to managers. Acquiring information, particularly information that is viewed as central or strategic in an organisation, can be used to build a power base and to make oneself indispensable and influential in that organisation. On the other hand, when managers provide their people with more information instead of keeping it to themselves, those people gain a sense of empowerment and are more likely to work productively, successfully and in harmony with the wishes of the manager. The manager actually enhances his or her power base by involving others in the pursuit of desirable outcomes. With more information, people tend to experience more self-determination, personal control and trust. The resulting sense of empowerment enhances the probability that they will not resist the manager, defend against his or her power, or work at protecting themselves. Rather, they are likely to collaborate with the empowering manager.

Therefore, a manager who wishes to increase an employee's sense of empowerment will make sure that the employee is given all task-relevant information needed to carry out an assignment. The manager will make available, on an ongoing basis, pertinent technical information and data collected by others as it crosses his desk. Managers will keep workers informed about what is happening in other areas of the organisation that might have an impact on what the worker is doing. Managers will keep employees informed of policy making meetings and senior-level discussions related to their area of responsibility. Workers can be given access to sources closest to the information they need – e.g., senior level people in the organisation, customers or the market research staff. Historical or 'context' information can be shared in order to give the worker as broad a background as possible. Managers should make certain that employees have information about the effects of their own behaviour on others and the organisation's goals.

Of course it is possible to overload people with information and to create anxiety and confusion with too much data. But our experience has been that most people suffer from too little information instead of too much. Furthermore, if the operative term 'relevant information' is applied in this context, overload is less likely to occur. Spreitzer (1992) found, for example, that people who received relevant information about costs, customers and strategy felt significantly more empowered than those who did not. Block (1987) argued:

> Sharing as much information as possible is the opposite of the military notion that only those who 'need to know' should be informed. Our goal is to let people know our plans, ideas and changes as soon as possible. If we are trying to create the mindset that everyone is responsible for the success of this business, then our people need complete information.

Further confirmation of the importance of providing information to enhance empowerment comes from our own research (Cameron et al., 1993). In one study, for example, we interviewed chief executives of large, well-known companies every six months to assess the organisational changes and strategies being used to cope with declining revenues. In one firm, little progress was being made in improving the financial outlook. The executive was very careful to share information on financial, productivity, cost and climate indicators in the company only with his senior management team. No one else in the firm had access to that information. However, a change of top executive led to a dramatic change in the information-sharing policy. The new executive began to provide information to every single employee in the firm who wished it. No item of data was treated as the sole possession of senior management. The sweepers had the same access as the vice-presidents. The resulting empowerment experienced by employees led to dramatic results. Employee-initiated improvements increased dramatically, morale and commitment surged, and the resulting financial turnaround made the top executive look like a genius. He attributed his success to his willingness to empower employees by sharing the information they needed to improve.

Providing resources

In addition to providing information, empowerment is also fostered by providing people with other kinds of resources that help them to accomplish their tasks. In this sense, managers who empower others act more like defenders in a soccer team than strikers. They are less directors and commanders than they are resource providers (holding the ball in defence and releasing it to their own mid-field players) and obstacle eliminators (stopping the opposing forward line). One of the primary missions of empowering managers, then, is to help others to accomplish their objectives.

Managers attempting to enhance employees' empowerment by providing them with needed resources will make certain that workers receive adequate and ongoing training and development experiences. Sufficient technical and administrative support will be provided to ensure success. Managers will provide employees with space, time or equipment that may not be readily available otherwise. They will make sure that workers have access to communication and/or interpersonal networks that will make their jobs easier. Workers can also be given discretion to spend money on, or commit resources to, activities that they think are important.

It is not realistic, of course, to assume that everyone can have everything he or she desires. Very few successful organisations have excess resources to be distributed at will. On the other hand, the most important resources that empowering managers can provide are those that help people to achieve control over their own work and lives – ones that foster a sense of self-efficacy and self-determination. When individuals feel that they have what they need to be successful, and that they have the freedom to pursue what they want to accomplish, performance is significantly higher than when these types of resources are not available (Spreitzer, 1992).

One of the best examples of using resources to empower comes from Carl Sewell (1990), one of the most successful car salesmen in the United States, who described his approach to empowerment through providing resources:

> Not many people get to see our service repair shop – our insurance company wants to keep traffic there to a minimum – but those who do always comment on its cleanliness. And, in fact, it's immaculate. Why? Because – while customers rarely see it, our technicians do. They live and work there every day. Where would you like to spend your day – in a place that's dirty or in one that's spotless? But it's more than just aesthetics. If we make the technicians' work environment more professional, more pleasant and more efficient, and if we provide them with the very best equipment and tools, we're going to be able to hire the best technicians. . . . All this gives them another reason for working for us instead of our competition.

One reason that Carl Sewell has been successful is that he provides each individual with everything needed to accomplish desired goals. This is true whether Sewell is dealing with mechanics or top salespeople, and whether his company is selling Rovers and BMWs or Hyundais and Fords. And it is not only 'need to have' resources that Sewell provides, but also some 'nice to have' resources. The watchword is: 'Resources lead to empowerment.'

Organising teams

There is nothing inherently empowering about being a member of a team. What is empowering is if that team is given the opportunity to share information among its members, make its own decisions, generate and select solutions to important problems, and either implement their solutions personally or present them to those who can implement them. Participating on a problem-solving team or a task force is empowering to the degree that people get a chance to do things they couldn't do by themselves. Not only is it easier to participate in, and influence the decisions of a small team (as opposed to an entire department), but also the subsequent influence of the team can be far greater than the influence of a single individual. A sense of empowerment, therefore, comes from participating in the coalition itself.

In addition to the participation advantages of teamwork, empowerment is also associated with three particular characteristics of teams – autonomy, influence and responsibility. Each of these attributes operates at individual and team levels. Empowerment of individuals and the effectiveness of teams are most probable when:

- individuals have the ability to maintain autonomy over the roles they perform in the team
- the team maintains autonomy over its own functioning and direction
- individuals can influence others in the team itself, and the team can influence outside agents
- individuals take responsibility for their own success
- the team takes responsibility for its own success.

When teams are formed, they fulfil the empowerment function if they are given a certain amount of autonomy for their own functioning, influence over their own outcomes and responsibility for their own success. Individuals will reap the advantages of participating in an empowered team just because they are members. But they will experience even greater amounts of empowerment if they are able to maintain autonomy in the team, influence with other team members and responsibility for their own success in the team. A manager who wishes to increase an employee's sense of empowerment through teams, therefore, might consider asking the person to join a team that will tackle an important problem that the organisation faces. The manager can spend time training and coaching the worker on how to perform various roles in the team to facilitate its success (e.g., task roles and facilitating roles). The worker should be assigned to a team in which his speciality or expertise is not the same as that of other team members, so that each person can bring value and insight to the others. The team can be empowered, not only by solving the problem, but also by being allowed to help to implement the solution. Avoid assigning a superior to lead the team; instead, assign a facilitator who can ensure that all team members participate and reach consensus. Organise cross-functional teams that will permit workers to get acquainted with others they don't know throughout the organisation and to acquire information that will assist them in accomplishing their jobs. Base part of the appraisal and reward system on successful team membership rather than solely on individual task-specific behaviour. Lawler (1992) identified three types of teams that managers can use to foster a sense of empowerment: suggestion teams, job-involvement teams and high-involvement teams.

- **Suggestion teams** are formed mainly to generate ideas for improvement. Interaction with team members helps to generate more ideas than any person would have had alone.

- **Job-involvement teams** include self-managing work teams organised to accomplish tasks. Work is co-ordinated among all members of the team, and team members take responsibility to teach one another their own jobs.

- **High-involvement teams** are organised to affect an entire organisation. They function like semi-independent businesses, and are rewarded on the basis of how well they provide needed products or services to customers.

Deborah Kezsbom (1994), in an article on project management in team-based organisations, discusses the changing role of leadership. Managers can select among the three different types of teams, or from all three types, in order to help individuals to increase their sense of empowerment through team membership.

Creating confidence

The final technique for engendering empowerment is to create a sense of confidence among workers in the trustworthiness of the manager. Rather than being on-guard and suspicious of being mistreated, workers are secure in their feeling that the manager and the organisation are honourable. This confidence helps to drive out uncertainty, insecurity and ambiguity in the relationships between employees and the manager. Employees don't feel a need to be defensive or cautious.

There are at least two reasons why individuals feel more empowered as they develop greater confidence in their manager. For one thing, the wasteful, unproductive behaviours associated with mistrust and suspicion are avoided. When people distrust one another, they don't listen, they don't communicate clearly, they don't try hard and they don't collaborate. On the other hand, when trust exists, individuals are free to experiment, to learn and to contribute without fear of retribution.

Secondly, individuals who are admirable and honourable always create positive energy for others and make them feel more capable. Not without reason do universities trumpet the number of Nobel Prize winners on their faculties, the publications of their staff, the number of outstanding faculty members in their business schools and the notable achievements of their best students. Although other members of the university may have nothing to do with the achievements being publicised, they gain an enhanced self-image and sense of empowerment because they are affiliated to the same organisation. For the same reasons, creating confidence in a manager helps employees to develop a sense of empowerment. In creating such a sense of confidence and trustworthiness, five factors are especially important:

- **Reliability**   Managers who wish their employees to develop confidence in them need to exhibit reliability. Their behaviour must be consistent, dependable and stable. Their action must be congruent with their words and attitudes.

- **Fairness**   Good managers also need to be fair and not take wrongful advantage of anyone. They are equitable in their actions. Workers are clear about the criteria used by the manager in making judgements, and how the manager applies those criteria. Managers must make clear the standards by which workers will be judged, and ensure that those standards are applied in an unbiased way.

- **Caring**   Managers must show a sense of personal concern for workers, and help each one feel that he or she is important. Managers must validate the points of view of their workers, and avoid denigrating them as individuals. When correction is needed, caring managers focus on the mistake or the behaviour, not on the worker's personal characteristics.

- **Openness**   Confidence-building managers are open in their relationships. No harmful secrets exist, and relevant information is shared openly and honestly with employees. This does not mean that a manager cannot keep confidences, but it does mean that workers should not have to worry about hidden agendas that could negatively affect them, because their managers are straightforward and honest.

- **Competence**   Workers need to be made aware of their manager's competence. Employees need to be assured that their manager has the necessary ability and knowledge to perform tasks and to solve problems. Without flaunting their expertise, skilful managers inspire a feeling on the part of employees that their confidence in the expertise and proficiency of their leader is not misplaced.

The power of creating confidence in employees is illustrated by several chief executives who were interviewed regarding their keys to successful organisational change. Each executive had managed a reduction of staffing levels or redesign of his organisation, and was attempting to maintain a healthy, productive workforce in the midst of turmoil. The key role of trust and confidence in management is hard to miss (see Cameron *et al.*, 1993; Mishra, 1992).

> 'If they don't believe what I'm telling them, if they think it's all rubbish designed to confuse, don't expect them to go out there and work a little harder. They won't work differently or better. They're not going to be receptive to change unless they understand and trust that the things we're talking about are true. I think trust is the biggest single issue.'

'I had a boss who used to say, "What you do speaks so much louder than what you say." I've always kept that in the back of my mind. I believe that. People watch very closely what you do. You cannot underestimate that, you are on trial all the time.'

'What's most important in my organisation is this: being truthful. Tell them what it is – right or wrong or different. Tell them the truth.'

'My people are all 150 per cent dedicated to helping one another. Because nobody can do it alone, they need each other badly. But here comes the openness and trust. You have to talk about those things. I don't think you can go in and accomplish things without talking about what the barriers are going to be in trying to make a change or set a new direction.'

Successful managers create confidence in themselves among their employees. They are authentic, honourable and trustworthy.

Review of empowerment principles

The actions we have suggested to increase empowerment are not all relevant in every circumstance or with every person, of course, but developing the skill of empowerment is at least partly dependent on knowing the alternatives that are available. Our list is not comprehensive; other activities may be equally effective in empowering people. But the eight prescriptions and the suggestions associated with each of them represent actions that you will want to practise as you try to improve your competence in the skill of empowerment. The Skill Practice section of this book provides an opportunity for you to do so.

Research has found that those who are empowered are most inclined to empower others. For that reason, we included a Pre-assessment instrument at the beginning of this chapter that assesses the extent to which you experience empowerment in your own work. Your scores on the instrument entitled Personal Empowerment Assessment (Survey 7.2) should indicate how much your own work is empowering for you in terms of self-efficacy, self-determination, personal control, meaning and trust. Knowing what provides a sense of empowerment for you can be helpful as you consider ways in which you, in turn, can empower others. The other instrument that you completed in the Skill Pre-assessment section – Effective Empowerment and Delegation (Survey 7.1 – identifies the extent to which you behave in ways that empower people with whom you work and the extent to which you delegate work effectively. This is our next topic.

Principles of empowered delegation

Empowerment is most needed when other people must become involved to accomplish the task. Obviously, if a person is doing a task alone, knowing how to empower others is largely irrelevant. On the other hand, it is impossible for a manager to perform all the work needed to carry out an organisation's mission, so work and the responsibility to carry it out must be delegated to others. All managers, therefore, are required to empower their employees if they are to accomplish the tasks of the organisation. Without delegation and the empowerment that must accompany it, no organisation and no manager can succeed in the long term. Delegation involves the assignment of work to other people, and it is an activity inherently associated with all managerial positions. In this section, we discuss the nature of delegation as well as ways in which delegation can be most effectively empowered. Delegation normally refers to the assignment of a task: it is work-focused. Empowerment, on the other hand, is focused on individuals' feelings: it relates to the way people think about themselves. We have previously discussed ways in which managers can affect people's sense of being empowered. We shall now discuss ways in which managers can get work accomplished effectively through **empowered delegation**.

Most of us would claim to delegate; however delegation is often badly performed. How often have we been in the sequence – TELL, DELEGATE, BLAME? One of the grand masters of management, Lester Urwick (1944), claimed that the 'lack of courage to delegate properly, and of knowledge of how to do it, is one of the most general causes of failure in organisations'. Moreover, as pointed out by Leana (1987), researchers have paid little attention to delegation, and less is known about the relationships between delegation and management effectiveness than about many other common management skills (Locke and Schweiger, 1979).

Advantages of empowered delegation

Learning to delegate effectively is, as we have said, an essential skill. It obviously helps managers to accomplish more work than they could accomplish otherwise, and free up time for what may be more strategically important activities. However, if delegation occurs only when managers are overloaded, those receiving the delegated tasks may feel resentful and sense that they are being treated only as objects to meet the managers' ends. Such delegation will lead to disenchantment among subordinates, and perhaps peers. Empowered delegation allows everybody to gain – a win–win situation.

Empowered delegation can help to develop the capabilities and knowledge of subordinates so that their effectiveness is increased. As such, it can be a technique to encourage personal mastery. Delegation can also be used to demonstrate trust and confidence in the person receiving the assignment. Mishra (1992) and Gambetta (1988) summarised research showing that individuals who felt trusted by their managers were significantly more effective than those who didn't feel trusted. Empowered delegation can be used to enhance the commitment of individuals receiving work. Beginning with the classic study of participation by Coch and French (1948), research has consistently demonstrated a positive relationship between having an opportunity to participate in work and subsequent satisfaction, productivity, commitment, acceptance of change, and desire for more work. Empowered delegation can also be used to improve the quality of decision making by bringing to bear more information, closer to the source of the problem, than the manager has alone. Delegating tasks to those who have direct access to relevant information can enhance efficiency (i.e., require less time and fewer resources) as well as effectiveness (i.e., result in a better decision). Finally, empowered delegation can increase the co-ordination and integration of work by funnelling information and final accountability through a single source. Empowering managers, in other words, can ensure that no cross-purposes occur in delegation and that different tasks are not producing contradictory effects. Competently administered, empowered delegation can produce all five dimensions of empowerment – a sense of competence, choice, impact, value and security.

Ineffective delegation however, can not only inhibit empowerment but also subvert the ability to get work accomplished at all. For example, instead of freeing up time, ineffective delegation may require even more time to supervise, evaluate, correct and arbitrate disagreements among employees. Employees may find themselves spending a longer time to accomplish a task because of lack of know-how, experience or information. Stress levels and interpersonal conflict may increase when tasks, accountability or expectations are unclear. Managers may find themselves out of touch with what is really going on with employees, may lose control, and may find goals being pursued that are incompatible with the rest of the organisation. Chaos rather than co-ordination can result. Subordinates may also begin to expect that they should be involved in all decisions and that any decision made by the manager alone is autocratic and unfair.

In the next section, we identify ways in which the positive outcomes of delegation can be cultivated and the potential negative outcomes of poor delegation can be avoided. Of necessity, empowerment and delegation must be linked to the accomplishment of work. We will present guidelines for deciding when to delegate, to whom to delegate, and finally, how to delegate.

Deciding when to delegate

Empowered delegation involves deciding, first of all, when to delegate tasks to others and when to perform them oneself. When should subordinates be assigned to design and perform work or make decisions? To determine when delegation is most appropriate, managers should ask five basic questions (Vroom and Yetton, 1973; Vroom and Jago, 1974). Studies have shown that when delegation occurred based on these criteria, successful results were almost four times more likely than when these criteria were not followed or considered. These criteria are equally applicable whether assigned work is to be delegated to a team or to a single subordinate.

1. *Do subordinates have the necessary (or superior) information or expertise?* In many cases, subordinates may actually be better qualified than their managers to make decisions and perform tasks because they are more familiar with customer preferences, hidden costs, work processes, etc., due to being closer to actual day-to-day operations.

2. *Is the commitment of subordinates critical to successful implementation?* Participation in the decision-making process increases commitment to the final decision. When employees have some latitude in performing a task (i.e., what work they do, and how and when they do it), they generally must be involved in the decision-making process to ensure their co-operation. Whereas

participation usually will increase the time required to make a decision, it will substantially decrease the time required to implement it.

3. *Will subordinates' capabilities be expanded by this assignment?* Delegation can quickly get a bad name in a work team if it is viewed as a mechanism used by the boss to get rid of undesirable tasks. Therefore, delegation should be consistent (not just when overloads occur). It should reflect an overall management philosophy emphasising employee development. Enhancing the abilities and interests of subordinates should be a central motive in delegating tasks.

4. *Do subordinates share with management and each other common values and perspectives?* If subordinates do not share a similar point of view with one another and with their manager, unacceptable solutions, inappropriate means, and outright errors may be perpetuated. In turn, this produces a need for closer supervision and frequent monitoring. Articulating a clear mission and objective for subordinates is crucial. In particular, managers must be clear about why the work is to be done. Coonradt (1985) found that important people are always told why, but less important people are merely told what, how or when. Telling subordinates why the work is meaningful creates a common perspective.

5. *Is there sufficient time to do an effective job of delegating?* It takes time to save time. To avoid misunderstanding, managers must spend sufficient time explaining the task and discussing acceptable procedures and options. Time must be available for adequate training, for questions and answers, and for opportunities to check on progress.

Empowered delegation depends on a positive answer to each of the above criteria. If any of these conditions is not present when delegation is being considered, the probability is greater that it will not be effective. More time will be required, lower quality will result, more frustration will be experienced and less empowerment will occur. However, a negative answer to any of the above questions does not necessarily mean that effective delegation is forever precluded, because managers can change situations so that subordinates get more information, develop common perspectives, have adequate time to receive delegation, etc.

Deciding to whom to delegate

Having decided to delegate a task, managers must then decide whether to involve only a single individual or a team of subordinates. If the decision is made to form a team, it is also important to decide how much authority to give the members of the team. For example, managers should decide if the team will only investigate the problem and explore alternatives, or if they will make the final decision. Managers must also decide whether or not they will participate in the team's deliberations. Figure 7.1 presents an analytical framework for helping managers decide who should receive delegated tasks – individuals or teams – and whether the manager should be an active participant in a team if it is formed.

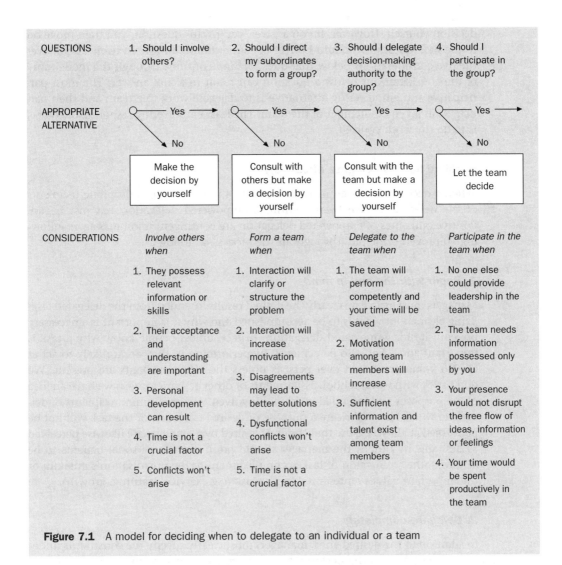

Figure 7.1 A model for deciding when to delegate to an individual or a team

Figure 7.1 is constructed as a 'tree diagram' which allows a manager to ask questions and, as a result of the answer to each question, move along a path until a final alternative is selected (Huber 1980, Vroom and Jago, 1974). It works in the following way.

If you are a manager determining whether to involve others in accomplishing a task or making a decision, you should look over the considerations below the question, 'Should I involve others in the task or the decision?' If you decide that subordinates do not possess relevant information or skills, that their acceptance is not important, that no personal development can occur for members of the team, that time is tight, or that conflicts will arise among subordinates, you should answer 'no' to this question. The tree then prescribes that you perform the task or make the decision yourself. However, if you answer 'yes' to this question, you then move on to the next question: 'Should I direct my subordinates to form a team?' Look over the five considerations below that question and continue through the model. Any of the considerations below a question can result in a 'no' answer. The most participative and empowering alternative is to delegate work to a team and then participate as an equal member of the team. The least empowering response, of course, is to do the work yourself.

Deciding how to delegate effectively

When a decision has been made to delegate a task, and the appropriate recipients of the delegation have been identified, empowered delegation has just begun. Positive outcomes of empowered delegation are contingent upon managers following 10 proven principles throughout the process, as follows.

1. Begin with the end in mind

Managers must articulate clearly the desired results intended from the delegated task. Being clear about what is to be accomplished and why it is important is a necessary prerequisite for empowered delegation. In fact, unless people know why a task is important and what is to be achieved by performing it, they are unlikely to act at all. No voluntary action ever persists unless these two elements are present. We don't stick with work, school, assignments or other activities unless we have an idea of the purposes and intended outcomes involved. At a minimum, recipients of delegation will infer or fabricate a purpose or desired outcome, or the task will not be performed at all. To ensure that the ends desired by a manager are likewise perceived as desirable by others, the manager should point out the personal benefits to be achieved, the connection of task-accomplishment to the organisation's mission, or the important values represented by the task (e.g., service, learning, growth).

2. Delegate completely

In addition to the desired ends, managers must clearly specify the constraints under which the tasks will be performed. Every organisation has rules and procedures, resource constraints or boundaries that limit the kind of action that can be taken. These should be made clear at the time the task is delegated. In particular, managers must be clear about deadlines and the time-frame for reporting back. When should the task be completed, who should receive the report and to whom is accountability being assigned? No empowerment can occur without knowing what these boundaries are. Managers also must specify precisely the *level of initiative* expected. No other oversight in the delegation process causes more confusion than the failure to delineate clearly expectations regarding the level of initiative expected or permitted. At least five levels of initiative are possible, each of which may vary in terms of the amount of empowerment available to subordinates. These initiative levels differ in terms of the amount of control permitted over the timing and content of the delegated task:

a. **Wait to be told what to do**   Take action only after specific directions are given. This is the least empowering form of delegation because it permits no initiative on the part of the subordinate. There is no control over timing, i.e., when the task is to be accomplished; or content, i.e., what is to be done.

b. **Ask what to do**   Some discretion is provided to subordinates in that they have some control over the timing of the task, but not its content. Subordinates may formulate ideas for approaching the task, but because no action can be taken until the manager gives approval, empowerment is highly constrained.

c. **Recommend, then take action**   This alternative is more empowering because subordinates are given some freedom over both the timing and the content of the delegated task. However, at least three different types of recommendations are possible, each with a different level of empowerment, as follows:

   • the subordinates simply gather information, present it to the manager, and let him decide what needs to be done;
   • the subordinates determine alternative courses of action for each part of the task, leaving the manager to choose the course to be followed;
   • the subordinates outline a course of action for accomplishing the entire task and have the whole package approved at once.

Progressively more empowerment is associated with each of the following two re-commendation types.

d. **Act, then report results immediately**   Subordinates are given the freedom to act on their own initiative, but they are required to report to the manager immediately upon completion to ensure that their actions are correct and compatible with other organisational work. Subordinates may be permitted to perform only one part of a task at a time, reporting the results of each individual step. Or, they may be given the discretion to perform the entire task, reporting only when the final result has been accomplished. The latter alternative, of course, is the most empowering, but may not be possible unless the necessary ability, information experience, or maturity is present in the subordinates.

e. **Initiate action and report only routinely**   Subordinates are given complete control over timing and content of the tasks assigned. Reporting occurs only in a routine fashion to maintain co-ordination. With sufficient ability, information, experience and maturity among subordinates, this level of initiative is not only the most empowering, but is also the most likely to produce high satisfaction and motivation among subordinates (Hackman and Oldham, 1980).

The important point for managers to remember is that they must be very clear about which of these levels of initiative they expect of their subordinates.

3. Allow participation in the delegation of assignments

Subordinates are more likely to accept delegated tasks willingly, perform them competently, and experience empowerment when they help to decide what tasks are to be delegated to them and when. Often, it is not possible to give subordinates complete choice about such matters, but providing opportunities to decide when tasks will be completed, how accountability will be determined, when work will begin, or what methods and resources will be used in task-accomplishment increases empowerment. Such participation should not be manipulative, that is, opportunities for participation should not be provided merely to convince subordinates of decisions already made. Rather, managers should promote participation when task requirements allow it and when acceptance and personal development can result.

Bernard (1938) formulated an 'acceptance theory of authority' in which he proposed that people will accept and fulfil assignments only if four conditions are met. Subordinates must:

1. Understand what they are being asked to do.
2. Perceive that the assignment is consistent with the purpose of the organisation.
3. Believe that the assignment is compatible with their own interests.
4. Be able to perform the assignment.

Bernard's theory underscores the importance of two-way communication during the delegation process. Not only should subordinates be encouraged to ask questions and seek information regarding delegated assignments, but they should also feel free to express ideas about the parameters of the work to be delegated. Expecting subordinates to seek answers to questions, or providing guidance on every aspect of the delegated assignment can perpetuate over-dependence if the manager answers every detailed question or provides continual advice. On the other hand, managers who remain available for consultation and idea interchange, foster two-way communication and encourage a climate of openness and sharing, make the delegation process empowering.

4. Establish parity between authority and responsibility

The oldest and most general rule of thumb in delegation is to match the amount of responsibility given with the amount of authority provided. It is common for managers to assign responsibility for work to subordinates without furnishing a corresponding amount of discretion to make decisions and authority to implement those decisions. If subordinates are to be successful, they must have as much authority as they need to accomplish the tasks assigned to them. An important part of developing a sense of self-determination and a sense of personal control – both critical dimensions of empowerment – is ensuring this match. Of course, managers also must take care not to delegate more authority than responsibility, thereby giving subordinates more authority, discretion, resources or information than they can use. Such a mismatch leads to lack of accountability, potential abuses of power and confusion on the part of subordinates. For example, without the necessary responsibility, providing a child with a loaded gun or a £20 note in a sweet shop, could result in actions that would not lead to desirable outcomes.

Although managers cannot delegate ultimate accountability for delegated tasks, they can delegate prime accountability. This means that 'the buck stops', eventually, at the manager's desk. Final blame for failure cannot be given away. This is ultimate accountability. On the other hand, managers can delegate prime accountability, which means that subordinates can be given responsibility for producing desired short-term results. Their accountability is to the manager who delegated to them. Giving subordinates prime accountability is an important part of empowered delegation.

5. Work within the organisational structure

Another general rule of empowered delegation is to delegate to the lowest organisational level at which a job can be done. The people who are closest to the actual work being performed or the decision being made should be involved. They are usually the ones with the largest, most accurate fund of information. By definition, this increases efficiency (lower labour and information collection costs) and it frequently increases effectiveness (better understanding of problems). Whereas managers have a broader overall view of problems, the detailed knowledge needed to accomplish many tasks is most likely to reside with those who are lower in the organisational hierarchy. In delegating a task down more than one level in an organisation, it is important that the organisational chain of command be followed. In other words, delegation must occur through subordinates, not around them. If a senior manager circumvents the formal hierarchy, bypassing a manager to communicate directly with that manager's subordinate, the manager becomes unempowered. The subordinate now becomes accountable to the senior manager, not the manager with direct responsibility for the subordinate. The entire accountability system is destroyed. Therefore, following the chain of command by involving those at affected levels of the hierarchy in delegation is important for empowered delegation.

All individuals affected by a decision must be informed that it has been delegated. This applies to cross-functional co-ordination as well as hierarchical co-ordination. If a subordinate has been delegated responsibility, others who may need the information, who may influence the results, or who may implement the recommendations must be notified of the delegation. If delegation occurs but no one knows, authority is essentially nullified.

6. Provide adequate support for delegated tasks

When authority is delegated to subordinates, managers must provide as much support to them as possible. As discussed above, this involves making public announcements and presenting clearly stated expectations. It also involves continuously providing relevant information and resources to help subordinates to accomplish tasks. Reports, recent clippings, customer data, articles and even random thoughts that pertain to the delegated task should be passed on as they become available. This support not only aids task-accomplishment but also communicates interest and concern for subordinates. Managers should help subordinates to learn where to acquire needed resources, since the manager cannot be the sole source of all the support that subordinates will need.

Agreeing on the limits of resource use is also important. Since unlimited access to resources is never possible, managers must be clear about the limit beyond which no further resources can be used. Formulating a budget or establishing a set of specifications is a common way to specify limits. Another form of support that managers can provide is to bestow credit – but not blame – publicly. Public blame, however justified, embarrasses and creates defensiveness. It also gives the impression that the manager is trying to pass the blame and get rid of final accountability – guaranteeing that your people will be less willing to initiate action on their own in the future. Correcting mistakes, criticising work and providing negative feedback on task-performance of subordinates should be done in private, where the probability of problem solving and training can be discussed.

7. Focus accountability on results

Once tasks are delegated and authority is provided, managers generally should avoid closely monitoring the way in which subordinates accomplish tasks. Excessive supervision of methods destroys the five dimensions of empowerment: self-efficacy, self-determination, personal control, meaningfulness and trust. Successful accomplishment of a task, after all, is the primary goal of delegation, rather than use of the manager's preferred procedures. To be sure, harmful or unethical means for accomplishing tasks cannot be tolerated, nor can methods be used that obstruct other employees or subvert organisational rules. But, for the most part, managers should focus their attention primarily on results achieved by subordinates, rather than on the techniques used to achieve those results.

In order to maintain accountability, there must be agreement on acceptable levels of performance. Managers must specify clearly the level of performance that is expected, those items that constitute unacceptable performance, and the requirements associated with the result. Without such clearly understood specifications, it becomes difficult for managers not to worry about means as well as ends. By allowing subordinates to exercise initiative regarding how to tackle a task, their sense of empowerment is enhanced, as are innovation and originality.

8. Delegate consistently

Managers should delegate before it becomes necessary to do so. Sometimes, when managers have time to do work themselves, they do just that – even though that work could and should be delegated. Two problems result. First, delegation becomes simply a method for relieving the manager's workload and stress. A primary reason for delegation – empowering subordinates – is forgotten. Employees begin to feel that they are merely 'pressure valves' for managers – useful only for reducing stress – rather than valued team members.

Secondly, when delegation occurs only under pressure, there is no time for training, providing needed information or engaging in two-way discussions. Clarity of task-assignments may be impaired. Workers' mistakes and failures increase, and managers are tempted to perform tasks alone in order to ensure quality. When managers delay delegating until they are overloaded, they create pressure on themselves to perform delegatable tasks personally, thereby increasing their own overload.

Another key to consistent delegation is for managers to delegate both pleasant and unpleasant tasks. Sometimes managers keep for themselves the tasks they like to perform and pass less desirable work along to subordinates. It is easy to see the detrimental consequences this has on morale, motivation and performance. When individuals feel that they are being used only to perform 'dirty work', success completion of delegated tasks is less likely. On the other hand, managers must not be afraid to share difficult or unpleasant tasks with subordinates. Playing the role of martyr by refusing to involve others in disagreeable tasks or drudgery creates unrealistic expectations for employees and isolates managers. Consistency of delegation, then, means that managers delegate tasks continuously, not just when overworked, and that they delegate both pleasant and unpleasant tasks.

9. Avoid upward delegation

Although it is very important for subordinates to participate in the delegation process in order to become empowered, managers must conscientiously resist all so-called 'upward delegation', in which subordinates seek to shift responsibility for delegated tasks back onto the shoulders of the superior who did the initial delegating. Managers who fail to forestall upward delegation will find their time being used to do subordinates' work rather than their own.

Suppose a worker comes to a manager after delegation has occurred and says, 'We have a problem. This job just isn't turning out very well. What do you suggest I do?' If the manager replies, 'I'm not sure. Let me think about it and I'll get back to you,' the original delegated task has now been shifted from the employee back to the manager. Note that the manager has promised to report to the employee, i.e., to maintain prime accountability, and the employee is now in a position to follow up on the manager's commitment, i.e., supervising the manager. Thus, the subordinate has become the manager and the manager the subordinate.

Managers, in the hope of being helpful to, and supportive of their subordinates, often get caught in the trap of upward delegation. One way to avoid upward delegation is to insist that workers always take the initiative for developing their own solutions. Instead of promising the subordinate a report on the manager's deliberations, a more appropriate response would have been, 'What do you recommend?' or 'What alternatives do you think we should consider?'. Rather than sharing problems and asking for advice, subordinates should be required to share proposed solutions or to ask permission to implement them. Managers should refuse to solve delegated tasks. That is why specifying the expected level of initiative (see rule 2 above) is so important. Not only does this avoid upward delegation, but it also helps managers to train employees to become competent problem solvers and to avoid working on tasks for which someone else has prime accountability.

Yielding to upward delegation does not empower subordinates, but makes them more dependent.

10. Clarify consequences

Subordinates should be made aware of the consequences of the tasks being delegated to them. They are more likely to accept delegation and be motivated to take initiative if it is clear what the rewards for success will be, what the opportunities might be, what the impact on the ultimate customer or the organisation's mission can be, and so on. In particular, managers should help employees to understand the connection between successful performance and financial rewards, opportunities for advancement, learning and developmental opportunities, informal recognition, etc. Most specifically delegated assignments do not result in a direct payoff from the formal reward system. They are usually rewarded by something as 'small' as a pat on the back or a congratulatory mention in a staff meeting. They might even merit a financial bonus or incentive. Whatever the reward, the delegation is enhanced.

Clarifying consequences can also help to ensure an understanding that delegation not only implies task accomplishment, but also an enhancement of interpersonal relationships. Relationships with others in the organisation, in the team, or with the manager individually should be strengthened as a result of task-accomplishment. Accomplishing assignments while damaging or destroying relationships creates more long-term costs than any organisation can bear. Therefore, a desirable consequence of any delegation experience is the enhancement of interpersonal relationships and a strengthening of the organisation.

Review of delegation principles

The 10 principles summarising how to delegate, preceded by the five criteria for determining when to delegate, and the four questions for identifying to whom to delegate, provide guidelines for ensuring not only that subordinates will experience a sense of empowerment, but also that other positive consequences will result. In particular, research results clearly show that empowered delegation leads to the following consequences:

1. Delegated tasks are readily accepted by subordinates.

2. Delegated tasks are successfully completed.

3. Morale and motivation remain high.

4. Workers' problem-solving abilities are increased.

5. Managers have more discretionary time.

6. Interpersonal relationships are strengthened.

7. Organisational co-ordination and efficiency are enhanced.

SUMMARY

Empowerment means helping to develop in others a sense of self-worth, self-efficacy, self-determinism, personal control, meaning and trust. The current business environment is not particularly compatible with the principles of managerial empowerment. Because of the turbulent, complex, competitive circumstances that many organisations face, managers frequently experience a tendency to be less, rather than more, empowering. When managers feel threatened, they become rigid and seek more control over their employees, not less. However, without empowered employees, organisations cannot succeed in the long run. Learning how to be a competent empowering manager is therefore a critical skill for individuals who probably will face a predilection not to practise empowerment.

Eight prescriptions that managers can use to empower others were discussed. We also offered a series of principles and criteria for ensuring empowered delegation, which results in better acceptance of delegated tasks by subordinates, enhanced motivation and morale, improved co-ordination and efficiency, better development of subordinates, increased discretionary time, strengthened relationships and successful task-performance. Producing a sense of empowerment in others and delegating in a way that empowers subordinates also produces desirable outcomes for organisations as well as employees. Empowered employees are more productive, psychologically and physically healthy, proactive and innovative, persistent in work, trustworthy, interpersonally effective, intrinsically motivated, and have higher morale and commitment than employees who are not empowered.

Behavioural guidelines

As you practise empowering others and carry out empowered delegating, you will want to use the following guidelines as cues to ensure empowerment in others.

1. *Foster personal mastery experiences for others by:*
   - Breaking apart large tasks and helping the person do one part at a time.
   - Involving people in simple tasks before difficult tasks.
   - Highlighting and celebrating small wins that others accomplish.
   - Incrementally expanding the job responsibilities of others.
   - Giving increasingly more responsibility to others to solve problems.

2. *Successfully model the behaviours you want others to achieve by:*
   - Demonstrating successful task-accomplishment.
   - Pointing out other people who have succeeded at the same task.
   - Facilitating interaction with other people who can serve as role models.
   - Finding a coach or tutor for the person.
   - Establishing a mentor relationship with the person.

3. *Provide needed support to other people by:*
   - Praising, encouraging, expressing approval for, and reassuring others when they perform well.
   - Writing letters or notes of praise to employees, as well as to their family members and co-workers, in recognition of noteworthy accomplishments.
   - Providing regular feedback to people.
   - Fostering informal social activities in order to build cohesion among people.

- Supervising less closely and providing more time between reports on results.
- Holding formal and informal recognition ceremonies.

4. *Arouse positive emotions among others by:*

- Fostering activities to encourage formation of friendships.
- Periodically sending light-hearted messages to people to keep the climate fun and interesting.
- Using superlatives in giving positive feedback.
- Highlighting compatibility between important personal values held by your employees and the organisation's goals.
- Clarifying the impact of outcomes on ultimate customers.
- Fostering attributes of recreation in work by making goals clear, instituting effective score-keeping and feedback systems, and specifying out-of-bounds behaviour.

5. *Provide information needed by others to accomplish their work by:*

- Providing all information relating to the accomplishment of a task.
- Continuously providing technical information and objective data that may come to you from time to time.
- Passing along relevant cross-unit and cross-functional information to which others may not have access.
- Providing access to information or to people with senior responsibility in the organisation.
- Providing access to first-hand rather than second-hand information.
- Clarifying the effects of employees' actions on customers.

6. *Provide resources needed for others to accomplish their work by:*

- Providing training and development experiences or information about where they can be obtained.
- Providing technical and administrative support or information about where they can be obtained.
- Providing needed time, space, equipment or information about where they can be obtained.
- Ensuring access to relevant information networks.
- Providing discretion to others to commit resources that will help accomplish ultimate objectives.

7. *Involve others in teams and task forces by:*

- Assigning a team an important task or problem.
- Letting a team not only solve a problem but implement the solution as well.
- Assigning facilitators instead of leaders to the team, in order to foster equal participation and involvement.
- Fostering information-sharing and learning among team members.
- Basing reward systems at least partly on effective team membership, not just on individual performance.
- Helping team members teach and develop one another.

8. *Create confidence among others by:*
- Being reliable and consistent in your behaviour towards others.
- Being fair and equitable in all your decisions and judgements.
- Exhibiting caring and personal concern for others.
- Being open and honest in your communications.
- Exhibiting competence and expertise with regard to objectives to be achieved.

The achievement of effective delegation

9. *Determine when to delegate work to others by addressing the following six key criteria:*
- Do subordinates have the information or expertise necessary to perform a task? Are they closer to the relevant information than you are?
- Is the commitment of subordinates critical to successful implementation?
- Can subordinates subvert task accomplishment?
- Will subordinates' capabilities be expanded by this assignment? Will it help others to develop themselves?
- Do subordinates share a set of common values and perspectives? Are there likely to be conflicting points of view?
- Does sufficient time exist to do an effective job of delegating? Can adequate information and training be provided?

10. *Determine to whom work should be delegated:*
- Decide whether you should do the task yourself.
- Consult with individual subordinates.
- Consult with a team of subordinates, or
- Participate as an equal member of a team of subordinates by analysing the characteristics of the subordinates – using the decision tree (Figure 7.1).

11. *To delegate work effectively, follow these 10 rules of thumb:*
- Begin with the end in mind; specify desired results.
- Delegate completely; identify the level of initiative to be taken by subordinates.
- Allow participation, especially regarding how and when tasks will be accomplished.
- Match levels of authority with levels of responsibility; maintain balance.
- Work within the structure; when delegating work at lower levels, delegate through subordinates, not around them.
- Provide support for tasks being delegated; identify resource limitations.
- Maintain accountability for results; avoid overly close monitoring of methods.
- Delegate consistently; do not delegate merely because you are overloaded.
- Avoid upward delegation; ask subordinates to recommend solutions rather than asking for assistance or advice.
- Clarify consequences; identify important effects of successful task-accomplishment.

Skill Analysis

CASE STUDY **7.1**

MINDING THE STORE

On 1 January, Claire Cummings was formally named branch manager of a regional super store. On her first day, her boss, Ken Harris, said: 'Claire, I'm putting you in charge of this store. Your job will be to run it so that it becomes one of the best stores in the group. I have a lot of faith in you, so don't let me down.'

One of the first things Claire did was to take on an administrative assistant to handle stock levels. Because this was such an important part of the job, she agreed to pay her assistant slightly more than some of the others. She felt that having an administrative assistant would free her to handle marketing, sales and personnel matters – areas which, she felt, were crucial if the store was to be a success. Within the week, however, she received a call from Harris: 'Claire, I heard that you have taken on an administrator. Do you think this is a good idea? Besides, I hear you are paying him over the odds. That could be bad for morale, don't you think? I wish you had cleared this with me before you made the move. It sets a bad precedent for the other stores, and it makes me look like I don't know what is going on in the branches.'

Three weeks later, Claire appeared on local radio to discuss new trends in fashion. She had worked hard to make contact with the hosts of the show, and she felt that public exposure like this would increase the visibility of her store. Although the interview lasted only 10 minutes, she was pleased with her performance and with the chance to get public exposure.

Later that night, at home, she received another phone call from Harris: 'Don't you know the policy of the group? Any radio or TV appearances have to be cleared through Head Office. We like to have you showing initiative but it is normally better to leave that sort of thing to the PR people. It's too bad that you didn't tell me first – the whole thing is a trifle embarrassing.'

Just before Easter, Claire was approached in the store by one of the sales clerks. A customer had asked for credit on approximately £1,000 worth of china as a gift for his wife. He had been a customer of the store for several years and Claire had seen him on several occasions, but store rules indicated that no credit could be given more than £500 for any reason. She told the customer that she was not authorised to agree the full sum but would check it out with Head Office and see if special arrangements could be made.

Later in the day, an irate Harris called again: 'What in the world are you thinking about, Claire? Today we had a customer come into the main store and say that you wouldn't make a sale to him because the charge was too much. Do you know how long he has been a customer of ours? And do you know how much he spends in the store every year? I certainly hope we have not lost him as a customer because of your blunder. This makes me very upset. You've just got to learn to use your head.'

Claire thought about the conversation for several days and finally decided that she needed to see Ken Harris. She called his secretary to arrange an appointment for the following day.

Discussion questions

1. What rules-of-thumb of empowerment were violated by Ken Harris? By Claire Cummings?
2. What rules-of-thumb of delegation were violated by Ken Harris? By Claire Cummings?
3. What should Claire Cummings and Ken Harris discuss in their meeting? Identify specific agenda items that should be raised.
4. What are the questions that Claire should ask Ken to help her to acquire the necessary elements of empowerment? What questions should Ken ask Claire in order to be better able to ensure her success?
5. If you were an outside consultant attending the meeting, what advice would you give Ken? What advice would you give Claire?

CASE STUDY **7.2**

CHANGING THE PORTFOLIO

You are head of a staff unit reporting to the finance director. He has asked you to provide a report on the firm's current portfolio, including recommendations for changes in the selection criteria currently employed. Doubts have been raised about the efficiency of the existing system given the current market conditions, and there is considerable dissatisfaction with prevailing rates of return. You plan to write the report, but at the moment you are perplexed about the approach to take. Your own speciality is the bond market and it is clear to you that detailed knowledge of the equity market, which you lack, would greatly enhance the value of the report. Fortunately, four members of your staff are specialists in different segments of the equity market. Together, they possess a vast amount of knowledge about the intricacies of investment. However, they seldom agree on the best way to achieve anything when it comes to investment philosophy and strategy.

You have six weeks before the report is due. You have already begun to familiarise yourself with the firm's current portfolio and have been provided by management with a specific set of constraints that any portfolio must satisfy. Your immediate problem is to come up with some alternatives to the firm's present practices and to select the most promising for detailed analysis in your report.

Discussion questions

1. Should this decision be made by you alone? Why, or why not?

2. If you answered the question 'Should I involve others?' affirmatively, which of the alternatives in Figure 7.1 should be used in making a decision? Justify your choice.

3. What are the most important considerations in deciding whom to involve in this task?

4. If others are to become involved, how much empowerment should they have? What would you do specifically to achieve the appropriate level of empowerment?

Skill Practice

EXERCISE **7.1**

BRITISH AIRWAYS

At the beginning of the 1980s British Airways (BA) was in trouble. The growing de-regulation of international air traffic meant that air fares were no longer fixed and the resulting price war hit BA hard. At the same time it was beset by internal problems. The merger of British Overseas Airways Corporation (BOAC) and British European Airways (BEA) had left the airline overstaffed, it had a bureaucratic style of management, there were damaging industrial disputes and its customer service was poor. By 1981–82 it was losing money rapidly.

That was when Margaret Thatcher's government decided to cut its losses and privatise the airline. In order to sell BA shares on the stock market it was necessary to make BA profitable. Lord King, a senior British industrialist, was appointed chairman and he embarked on a survival plan. Staff numbers were cut from 60,000 to 38,000 by a combination of voluntary severance and natural wastage. Unprofitable routes were abandoned. Surplus assets, particularly aircraft, were sold off and within two years BA was back in profit.

But to ensure long-term success there had to be a fundamental shift in the way BA did business. The airline had to change from being operationally driven to being market led. Shortly after he was appointed chief executive in February 1983, Colin Marshall described the organisation as one that '. . . didn't really understand the word profit, that was fearful of moving into the private sector, that was quite demoralised'.

The appointment of Marshall represented a significant departure from BA culture. An outsider to BA, Marshall had a marketing background that was quite different from many of his predecessors, many of whom were retired senior Royal Air Force officers.

It was Marshall who decided, shortly after his arrival, that BA's strategy should be to become 'the World's Favourite Airline'. Without question, critical ingredients in the success of the overall change were Marshall's vision, the clarity of his understanding that BA's culture needed to be changed in order to carry out that vision, and his strong leadership of that change effort.

Marshall's direct style of management energised the 'unfreezing' stage of the change process. His senior managers were given specific goals and he cut through the traditional 'management by committee' approach. Training had been a casualty of the early 1980s, a trend which Marshall quickly reversed. He saw the need to 'create some motivational vehicle with the employees so that we had a better prospect of raising their morale and in turn seeing better customer service flow'. Extensive market research had revealed a gulf between customer and staff expectations of the delivery of service. This set the direction for the first of the company-wide, culture-change interventions under the campaign banner of: 'Putting the Customer First – if we don't someone else will.'

An ambitious corporate event, 'Putting People First' (PPF), was launched in November 1983. It focused on the idea that 'if you feel OK about yourself you are more likely to feel OK about dealing with other people'. The target was the airline's 12,000 customer-contact staff, but this was soon extended to include support staff, highlighting the concept of 'internal' and 'external' customers. One hundred and fifty staff from every level took part – baggage-handlers mixing with Concorde pilots, engineers with marketing managers.

Aimed at helping line workers and managers understand the service nature of the airline industry, it was intended to challenge the prevailing wisdom about how things were to be done at BA. But PPF also signalled to the workforce the attitude and intentions of BA's management. It represented a considerable investment of time and money, not least by the chief executive and his directors, one of whom appeared to round off every event with a talk about their vision for the airline in the future. A key element of PPF was that staff also became actively involved in developing ideas for improving customer service. Customer First Teams, using the techniques of quality circles, were formed in many departments. Task forces continue to be used to solve emerging problems, such as those resulting from the acquisition of British Caledonian Airlines.

Nick Georgiades' appointment as human resource (HR) director in September 1984 signalled a new role for the Personnel Department. The change of name represented a more fundamental shift in the way the function was to operate to support the change process. All HR professionals went on an intensive programme which focused on consultancy skills in the context of organisational change. Administrative procedures hitherto associated with the personnel role were handed over to line management to free up human resources to act as change agents within the organisation.

The 1,400 managers themselves needed to adapt their style in this brave new world and a week-long residential programme 'Managing People First' (MPF) was launched in 1985. This advocated a more open, visible and dynamic management style. The key themes were:

- Urgency (emanating from leaders not events)
- Vision (having the image of the cathedral while mixing the cement)
- Motivation (expect the best, catch someone doing it right)

- Trust (giving confidence to the individual to act alone, and spirit to the group to act together)
- Taking responsibility (i.e., 'I am in charge of my own behaviour').

MPF represented one element of a change strategy which became known as 'The Three Legged Stool' – without one leg the stool would collapse. The other two legs were a performance appraisal system and a performance-related pay system for all managers. These schemes were created to emphasise customer service and subordinate development.

While PPF and MPF focused on the individual, a third major corporate event was launched in November 1985 which emphasised the benefits of collaborative working. The programme, 'A Day in the Life', gave staff a better understanding of what the major departments did and helped break down the barriers which exist in large organisations. A key element of the programme was the appearance again of either the chief executive or one of the directors to show top-level commitment.

A number of internal BA structures and systems were changed. By introducing a new bonus scheme, for example, Georgiades demonstrated management's commitment to sharing the financial gains of BA's success. The opening of Terminal 4 at Heathrow Airport provided a more functional work environment for staff. The purchase of Chartridge House as a permanent BA training centre permitted an increase in the integration of staff training and the new user-friendly management information system (MIS) to get the information they needed to do their jobs in a timely fashion. During the refreezing phase, the continued involvement and commitment of BA's top management ensured that the changes became fixed in the system. People who clearly exemplified the new BA values were much more likely to be promoted, especially at higher management levels.

Attention was also paid to BA's symbols – new, improved uniforms; refurbished aircraft; and a new corporate coat of arms with the motto 'We fly to serve'. A unique development was the creation of teams for consistent cabin-crew staffing, rather than the ad-hoc process typically used.

'To Be the Best' was launched in 1987, against the background of growing competition, and focused on the competitive threats facing the airline and the importance of achieving and sustaining excellence in service delivery.

BA's culture had been transformed from what BA managers described as 'bureaucratic and militaristic' to one that is 'service-oriented and market-driven'.

This cultural upheaval wasn't without its problems. For instance, many managers had trouble reconciling having to show care and concern for their people with delivering profit and productivity improvements with fewer resources. The success of this radical change process was put to the test when BA's next crisis came in February 1991. BA was forced to lose some 4,500 staff and stand down a further 2,000 to weather the economic and political storms created by recession and the Gulf War. This twin threat had the potential to destroy much of the commitment and loyalty built up during the 1980s.

The external pressures driving the cut-backs were understood as being beyond the control the BA's management. The subsequent decision to allow strong American competition into Heathrow with no *quid pro quo* for British carriers in the

US domestic market served to rally staff around the company. Over the previous year the airline had become increasingly concerned about its uncompetitive cost base and had commissioned McKinsey's to advise on a process for carrying out a company-wide overhead value analysis to identify and implement wide-scale cost savings. This was the third time the airline had had to resort to redundancy measures to tackle over-manning. On the positive side, this meant that BA had the experience of managing the redundancy process. But the announcement was also likely to invoke memories of the 1983 reorganisation which was still referred to as the 'Night of the Long Knives'.

Past experience also influenced the way the severance scheme was to be used this time. As previously, it was to be voluntary, but it was now targeted at specific jobs and work groups, rather than a free-for-all, which resulted in the airline losing some of its talented and highly marketable individuals.

A key decision which influenced the reactions of the majority of the workforce who were not personally affected by the cuts was to transform BA's recruitment centre into an outplacement service. This was inspired by one of the basic customer-service principles: namely, the way you handle an individual passenger will be observed by all those passengers in the immediate vicinity and will affect their view of the company as a whole.

The Advice and Support Centre signalled the extent of BA's concern for its people in tough times. BA were seen to be offering both practical and emotional support to redundant staff. The fact that the service was available to people for up to six months after they had officially left BA was another sign of the company's level of commitment. BA's sensitivity in this redundancy exercise, far from representing a betrayal of corporate values, actually reinforced them more strongly. This is what makes the sad saga of the 'dirty tricks' campaign against Virgin Airlines so mystifying. It appears that some of BA's staff became over-zealous and penetrated the customer data of their BA's rival, Virgin Airlines. They were accused of using this data to pressurise Virgin customers to switch to BA. This débâcle has cost the corporation millions of pounds in compensation to date, and also been a public relations disaster. So much so that it has threatened to undo all the good work of Lord King and Marshall.

The fact that such dirty tricks were allowed to flourish during this period puts a question mark over the calibre of senior management in key areas of operations. But another more disturbing element is that BA may have become so inward-looking during this time of transition that they underestimated the threat which Richard Branson's airline posed. It also resulted in Lord King's departure from the helm on a particularly sour note. The fact that this sad episode blotted an otherwise exemplary book in BA's history is one thing, but what is perhaps more worrying for the long term is the admission by a senior BA executive that they underestimated Richard Branson 'because he did not wear a suit'. This suggests that the change process within BA still has a long way to go.

It may be that BA's biggest problem now is not so much to manage further change but to manage the change that has already occurred. The people of BA have achieved significant change and success; now they must maintain what has been achieved. They still had to concentrate on continuing to be adaptable to changes in their external environment, e.g., the further deregulation of Europe. They also had to continue their search for partnerships in the United States and their future response to Richard Branson and Virgin Airlines. Managing momentum may be more difficult than managing change.

Discussion questions

1. Why did King and Marshall undertake a major exercise in empowerment?

2. What did they actually do to make the 'teams' within the organisation work as empowered teams?

3. How was the empowerment exercise conducted and was it successful?

4. What went wrong – as managers; what process of empowerment did they ignore?

EXERCISE **7.2**

SATISFY THE CUSTOMER

This exercise is designed for subgroups of 10 people. Thus, in a class/group of 30 people there will be three subgroups. Each subgroup will be divided into three teams which together represent one advertising organisation.

The top team consists of two people, the middle team consists of three people, and the bottom team consists of five people. Each team has its own responsibilities, described below. You will be assigned to one of the three teams on a random basis.

The object of this exercise is to satisfy the customer. You should try, therefore, not only to deliver what is expected, but to actually exceed customer expectations. The customer is a distributor of new, cutting-edge products that have not yet become established in the marketplace. Your advertising organisation has been requested to create as many creative and exciting television commercials as you can for each product in this portfolio. The customer wants to choose among several different options for each product, so you need to generate an array of choices. At the end of the exercise, only one advertising organisation will be selected. The products in the customer's portfolio are:

- A new kind of soft drink that contains fruit juice.
- A new kind of baby food formulation with extra vitamins.
- A new video game based on the principles of chess.
- A new hand-held photocopying machine.
- A new light bulb that lasts twice as long as regular bulbs.
- A new kind of shampoo for grey hair that adds 'body'.

Your task is to create, in written form, as many television commercials as you can for each product. You will be given 25 minutes. Your ideas will be evaluated by the customer, based on innovativeness, excitement, perceived effectiveness and cost. Your costs are associated with script writing, filming, actors and location. The use of well-known personalities, lots of people, and exotic locations increases your costs.

Members of the top team have the following responsibilities:

- Task-assignments for organisation members
- Organisation design
- Reward and recognition system
- Control over production resources (paper, pens, Post-It notes)
- Determination of whether the product is of sufficient quality to be shown to the customer.

Members of the middle team have the following responsibilities:

- Supervising the work of the bottom team
- Evaluating quality
- Serving as liaisons between the top and bottom teams
- Carrying out assignments from the top team
- Determining whether the commercials are high, moderate or low cost
- Passing products to the top team.

Members of the bottom team have the following responsibilities:

- Generating ideas for commercials
- Outlining the scripts
- Passing products to the middle team.

At the end of the exercise, each organisation will be given three minutes to describe its products. Presentations, therefore, must be brief and to the point. The 'customer' will be other members of the class who will rate the product portfolio. Individuals may not evaluate their own organisation's products.

Each class member or 'customer' will complete, for each organisation, a Customer Scoring Sheet from the scoring key in Appendix 1. The scoring sheets will determine which organisation receives the highest point total. The organisation which obtains the highest score will be hired.

Discussion questions

1. What principles of empowerment were most successful in this organisation?

2. What tendencies exist to maintain power differentials among teams?

3. What kinds of resistance to co-operation and teamwork did you experience?

4. What methods of organising work were most effective?

5. How effective was the delegation?

6. How could empowerment have been improved? What advice would you give others?

Skill Application

ACTIVITY **7.1**

SUGGESTED FURTHER ASSIGNMENTS

1. Teach someone else (a fellow student, a colleague, your boss) how to empower others and delegate effectively. Use your own examples and illustrations.

2. Interview a manager about his or her empowerment practices. Try to determine what is especially effective, what doesn't work, what appears to be condescending and what motivates people to perform. Identify the extent to which the manager knows and uses the principles discussed in the Skill Learning section.

3. Think of a situation you now face with which you would like some help. It may be a task you want to accomplish, a tough decision you need to make or a team you want to form. Make sure you think of something that requires the involvement of other people. Write down specific things you can do to empower other people to help you. How can you help them do what they want to do, and at the same time have them do what you want them to do?

4. Arrange a meeting with a manager who is not very good at empowerment. As a student who has learned about and practised empowerment and delegation, share what you have learned and offer suggestions which could help this manager improve.

ACTIVITY **7.2**

APPLICATION PLAN AND EVALUATION

The intent of this exercise is to help you apply your skills in a real-life, out-of-class setting. Now that you have become familiar with the behavioural guidelines that form the basis of effective skill-performance, you will improve most by trying out those guidelines in an everyday context. Unlike a classroom activity, in which feedback is immediate and others can assist you with their evaluations, this skill application activity is one you must accomplish and evaluate on your own. There are two parts to this activity. Part 1 helps to prepare you to apply the skill. Part 2 helps you to evaluate and improve on your experience. Be sure to write down answers to each item. Don't short-circuit the process by skipping steps.

Part 1: Plan

1. Write down the two or three aspects of this skill that are most important to you. These may be areas of weakness, areas you most want to improve, or areas that are most salient to a problem you face currently. Identify the specific aspects of this skill that you want to apply.

2. Now identify the setting or the situation in which you will apply this skill. Establish a plan for performance by actually writing down a description of the situation. Who else will be involved? When will you do it? Where will it be done?

3. What behaviours will you show while you test the skills?

4. What are the indicators of successful performance? How will you know you have been effective? What will indicate that you have performed competently?

Part 2: Evaluation

5. After you have completed your implementation, record the results. What happened? How successful were you? What was the effect on others?

6. How can you improve? What modifications can you make next time? What will you do differently in a similar situation in the future?

7. Looking back on your whole skill practice and application experience, what have you learned? What has been surprising? In what ways might this experience help you in the long term?

Further reading

Foy, N. (1994) *Empowering people at work*. Aldershot: Gower.

Johnson, R. and Redmond, D. (1998) *The art of empowerment*. Pitman.

Kinlaw, D. (1995) *The practice of empowerment*. Aldershot: Gower.

Mumford, A. (1998) *How managers can develop managers*. Aldershot: Gower.

Wilson, T. (1996) *The empowerment manual*. Aldershot: Gower.

Teams, Leaders and Managers

LEARNING OBJECTIVES

To allow individuals to:

- understand how the work of the manager and leader is changing and why

- understand the present emphasis on team working

- understand how teams develop and to work with this process effectively

- choose an appropriate form of leadership for the spectrum of working situations

---

INTRODUCTION

This last chapter involves the application of all the skills we have discussed in the previous chapters. Managing and leading real people and real teams is an unforgiving process and one where we can very rarely say – 'Sorry about that, I'll come in again and start all over.' One can almost say that it is a case of doing so much right that you are forgiven for rare and inevitable lapses of judgement. With this in mind we could summarise our whole book by saying that it is about 'showing how to engage the brain before putting the mouth into gear', and this is never more true than in the final chapter.

In the 'good old days' of management, if they ever existed, there was a general acceptance of certain truths, divine and man-made order, and the wise manager slipped into this flow and made it work for him or her. From where I am sitting, this general acceptance of certain truths can no longer be assumed and the manager or leader survives, and hopefully prospers, on his or her own merits. How and when the change happened is not the concern of this book – it probably has happened in history but was not chronicled in a way to help us directly. It pays to see the threats as challenges leading to opportunities. However, one of your authors is always mindful of the Chinese Curse: 'May you live in interesting times.' If this is true, then we are all well cursed.

Skill Pre-assessment

SURVEY **8.1**

TEAM DEVELOPMENT BEHAVIOUR

Step 1 Before you read the material in this chapter, please respond to the following statements by writing a number, from the rating scale, in the column headed Pre-assessment. Your answers should reflect your attitudes and behaviour as they are now, not as you would like them to be. Be honest. This instrument is designed to help you to discover your level of competence in building effective teams so that you can tailor your learning to your specific needs. When you have completed the survey, use the scoring key in Appendix 1 to identify the skill areas discussed in this chapter that are most important for you to master.

Step 2 After you have completed the reading and exercises in this chapter and, ideally, as many of the Skill Application assignments as you can, cover up your first set of answers. Then respond to the same statements again, this time in the Post-assessment column. When you have completed the survey, use the scoring key in Appendix 1 to measure your progress. If your score remains low in specific skill areas, use the behavioural guidelines at the end of the Skill Learning section to guide further learning.

RATING SCALE

1 = Strongly disagree   **2** = Slightly disagree   **3** = Agree
4 = Slightly Agree   **5** = Agree   **6** = Strongly agree

	Assessment	
	Pre-	Post-
When attempting to build and lead an effective team:		
1. I know the stages teams go through as they develop.	____	____
2. When a team first forms, I make certain that all team members are introduced to one another.	____	____
3. When the team first comes together, I provide direction, answer team members' questions, and clarify goals, expectations, and outline working procedures.	____	____
4. I help team members to establish a mutual foundation of trust.		
5. I ensure that standards of excellence – not mediocrity or mere acceptability – characterise the team's work.	____	____
6. I provide quality feedback for team members' performance.	____	____
7. I encourage team members to balance individual autonomy with interdependence.	____	____
8. I help team members to become at least as committed to the success of the team as to their own personal success.	____	____
9. I help members to learn to play roles that assist the team in accomplishing its tasks as well as building strong interpersonal relationships.	____	____
10. I express a clear, exciting, passionate vision of what the team can achieve.	____	____
11. I help team members to become committed to the team vision.	____	____
12. I encourage a philosophy in the team where individual success is the success of the entire team.	____	____
13. I help the team to avoid 'group think' or making the group's survival more important than accomplishing its goal.	____	____
14. I use formal procedures to help the group to become faster, more efficient, and more productive, and to prevent errors.	____	____
15. I encourage team members to represent the team's vision, goals, and accomplishments outside the team.	____	____
16. I understand, use and develop the team's core competence.	____	____

17. I encourage the team to achieve dramatic breakthrough innovations as well as small continuous improvements. ____ ____

18. I help the team to work towards preventing mistakes, not just correcting them later. ____ ____

When preparing for and conducting team meetings:

19. I make certain that the purpose of a meeting is clear. ____ ____

20. I ensure that the proper number and mix of people are invited to attend. ____ ____

21. I prepare an agenda for every meeting. ____ ____

22. I distribute the meeting agenda in advance, follow up after the meeting with action minutes, and make sure that the agreed actions are completed. ____ ____

23. I have a clear idea of the stages an effective meeting should pass through, from start to finish. ____ ____

24. I manage difficult team members effectively through supportive communication, collaborative conflict management, and empowerment. ____ ____

SURVEY **8.2**

DIAGNOSING THE NEED FOR TEAM DEVELOPMENT

Teamwork has been found to have a dramatic effect on organisational performance. Some managers have credited teams with helping them to achieve incredible results. On the other hand, teams do not work all the time in all organisations. Therefore, managers must decide when teams should be organised. To determine the extent to which teams should be built in your organisation, complete the following survey.

Think of an organisation you know well and answer the questions with that organisation in mind. Circle the number on the right that you consider to be most appropriate.

RATING SCALE

1 = No evidence   **2** = Very little evidence   **3** = Some evidence
4 = A fair amount of evidence   **5** = Lots of evidence

---

1. Production or output has declined or is lower than desired.   **1 2 3 4 5**

2. Complaints, grievances, or low morale are present or increasing.   **1 2 3 4 5**

3. Conflicts or hostility between members is present or increasing.   **1 2 3 4 5**

4. Some people are confused about assignments, or their relationships with other people.   **1 2 3 4 5**

5. There is a lack of clear goals and lack of commitment to those that there are.   **1 2 3 4 5**

6. We see apathy or lack of interest and involvement by members.   **1 2 3 4 5**

7. There is insufficient innovation, risk taking, imagination, or initiative.   **1 2 3 4 5**

8. Ineffective and inefficient meetings are common.   **1 2 3 4 5**

9. Working relationships across levels and units are unsatisfactory.   **1 2 3 4 5**

10. Lack of co-ordination among functions is apparent.   **1 2 3 4 5**

11. Communications are poor; people do not listen, information is not shared and people are afraid to speak up.   **1 2 3 4 5**

12. There is a lack of trust between group and hierarchical leaders.   **1 2 3 4 5**

13. Decisions are made that some members do not understand, or do not agree with.   **1 2 3 4 5**

14. People feel that good work is not rewarded or that rewards are unfairly administered.   **1 2 3 4 5**

15. People are not encouraged to work together for the good of the organisation.   **1 2 3 4 5**

16. Customers and suppliers are not part of organisational decision making.   **1 2 3 4 5**

17. People work too slowly and there is too much redundancy in the work being done.   **1 2 3 4 5**

18. Issues and challenges that require the input of more than one person are being faced.   **1 2 3 4 5**

19. People must co-ordinate their activities in order for the work to be accomplished.   **1 2 3 4 5**

20. Difficult challenges that no single person can resolve or diagnose are being faced.   **1 2 3 4 5**

Source: Adapted from Dyer (1987)

SURVEY **8.3**

360° FEEDBACK QUESTIONNAIRE

This instrument is designed to let you see how others see you and how their view may differ from your own. We suggest that you photocopy the form and hand it out to between 5 and 8 people who work with you – members of your team, a boss or tutor and subordinates, where relevant. Complete Column 1 on your own form and ask each of your colleagues to complete column 2. Collect the forms and summarise the information on a blank form. Allow your 'observers' the option of remaining anonymous.

Look at the 'Areas for improvement' column and, in particular, where your own views differ from those of others. **Do Not** repeat the exercise immediately. Make your action plans, wait at least six months before repeating the exercise and, if possible, take different observers.

	Positive attribute (1)	Areas for improvement (2)	Not relevant (3)	No opinion (4)

Instructing and controlling

- Gives clear instructions
- Sets clear standards and challenging targets
- Listens to feedback
- Respected
- Loyal and reliable

Coaching

- Understanding and watchful
- Coaches skilfully
- Accepts the limits of his/her expertise

Consulting

- Builds a climate of trust
- Is willing to share views
- Makes time and is available
- Seeks and actions feedback
- Willing to learn

Delegating

- Values different approaches
- Plays to the strengths of others
- Delegates unselfishly
- Praises success appropriately
- Energises and motivates
- Matches authority with responsibility
- Delegates cleanly

Monitoring

- Remains appropriately in control
- Accepts appropriate responsibility
- Is respected up, across and below
- Maintains declared standards
- Vigilant but not smothering

	Positive attribute (1)	Areas for improvement (2)	Not relevant (3)	No opinion (4)

Communicating

- Good relations up, across and below
- Maintains links with other groups
- Is effective in 1 : 1 communication
- Is effective in group communication
- Runs effective meetings

Facilitating

- Encourages teamwork
- Anticipates the resource demands
- Able to stand in when necessary
- Loyal and dependable

Leadership

- Transmits sense of vision
- Maintains strategic direction
- Able to accept feedback and act flexibly
- Challenging
- Can enable others
- Models good attitudes and behaviours
- Tough in the face of opposition

Skill Learning

Developing teams and teamwork

Near the home of one of our authors, scores of Canada geese spend the winter. They fly over the house to the natural pond nearby almost every morning. What is distinctive about these flights is that the geese always fly in a V pattern. The reason for this pattern is that the flapping wings of the geese in front create an up draft for the geese that follow. This V pattern increases the range of the geese collectively by 71 per cent compared to flying alone. On long flights, after the lead goose has flown at the front of the V for some time, it drops back to take a place in the V where the flying is easier. Another goose then takes over the lead position, where the flying is most strenuous. If a goose begins to fly out of formation, it is not long before it returns to the V because of the resistance it experiences when not supported by the other geese's wing flapping.

Another noticeable feature of these geese is the loud honking that occurs when they fly. Canada geese never fly quietly, and one can always tell when they are in the air because of the noise. There is a reason for the honking; it occurs among geese in the rear of the formation in order to encourage the lead goose. The leader doesn't honk – just those who are supporting and urging it on.

If a goose becomes ill, or falls out of formation, two geese break ranks and follow the wounded or ill goose to the ground. There they remain, nurturing their companion, until it is either well enough to return to the flock or dies.

This remarkable phenomenon serves as an apt metaphor for our chapter on teamwork and leadership. The lessons garnered from the flying V formation help to highlight important attributes of effective teams and skilful teamwork. For example:

- Effective teams have interdependent members. Like geese, the productivity and efficiency of an entire unit is determined by the co-ordinated, interactive efforts of all its members.
- Effective teams help members to work together more efficiently.
- Like geese, effective teams outperform even the best individual's performance.
- Effective teams function so well that they create their own magnetism.
- Like geese, team members desire to affiliate with a team because of the advantages they receive from membership.
- Effective teams do not always have the same leader. Like geese, leadership responsibility often rotates and is shared broadly in skilfully controlled teams.
- In effective teams, members care for and nurture one another.
- No member is devalued or unappreciated.
- Each member is treated as an integral part of the team.
- In effective teams, members cheer for and bolster the leader, and vice versa.
- Mutual encouragement is given and received by each member.
- In effective teams, there is a high level of trust among members.
- Members are interested in others' success as well as their own.

Because any metaphor can be carried to extremes, we don't wish to over-emphasise the similarities between Canada geese and work teams. But several points, which are the focus of this chapter, are among the important attributes of teams. Learning how to foster effective team processes, team roles, leadership, and positive relationships among team members are among the most important team-building skills discussed in this chapter. Our intent is to help you to improve your skill in managing teams, both as a leader and as a team member.

There are two sets of words of warning: one concerned with individuals and the other concerned with the process of moving towards teamworking in itself.

All this talk about teams and team membership is not good news for all of us, but there is a hope. Not all of us enjoy working in teams and indeed need to have a group around us to be effective. Look back at your FIRO-B scores in the first chapter and consider your *inclusion* needs. Those of you with very low scores in the Wanted Inclusion box – less than 3, say – really prefer to work alone. There is hope, however. Forget the geese and think of a football team. To belong to a team and to work for a team does not mean you have to work AS a team. In a football team the mid-field players and the defenders must work as a team – a sub-team of the whole. However, the goalkeeper and the strikers are individuals in most of the teams at least one of your authors watches at great cost. The goalkeeper and the strikers have a special licence to be individuals – their record is for everyone to see in the record books. So it is for us. If we choose to work as specialists in a team, we had better be good specialists and not expect the special care of the injured team player. When we look at the new organisational structures proposed by Handy (1993) and Semler (1993), among others you will see that the team members who do not like being team players are well considered. Handy calls these portfolio people.

Our second consideration is concerned with the rush towards teamworking. Unfortunately the majority of restructurings fail. Rossiter (1995), working on a sample of small and medium-sized businesses in the north of the UK, confirmed the generally discussed 70 per cent failure rate. Moving towards teamworking is one process in restructuring. Although restructuring and the management of change are not the subject of this book, the discussion is relevant. In our opinion, borne out by Probst and Buchel (1997), there are two fundamental reasons for the failure of restructuring: the first is an insistence towards inappropriate teamworking and the second is timing.

We leave the restructuring until it's too late. Organisations with slack, undertaking change before they have fire-fighting problems, have a better chance of success. Handy (1994) uses the metaphor of Davy's Bar. He asks directions to a particular farm in Wicklow and is told how to find Davy's Bar. He is then told that when you have got to the Bar, you have passed the turning for the farm. Many organisations, in Handy's metaphor, are actually drinking in the Bar before they think they need to restructure. Reflect on the management arrogance we discussed in the interpretation of the Hawthorne Experiment. Managers still, in our observation as consultants, discount the wisdom of the shop floor. They bring teamworking as a 'new idea', ignoring the teams that already exist.

> AE Goetz, a major manufacturer of motor components, decided on teamworking. The issue was that these were 'new teams'. The workers already considered that they worked in teams – in a structure not dissimilar to those of the Hawthorne factory. There was considerable resentment over what was seen as the imposition of 'synthetic' teams.
>
> The Royal Mail move to teamwork has also been handicapped by a lack of understand of existing delivery teams.

In the beginning

Whether one is a manager, a subordinate, a student, or a homemaker, it is almost impossible to avoid being a member of a team. Teams are everywhere and therefore our discussions will centre on, but not be confined to, the workplace.

Biologists and anthropologists would claim that teamwork in human nature was greatly encouraged by the necessity of hunting on the savannah (Johnston, 1997). However, more mundanely the *Wall Street Journal* reports the first work team ever formed in organisation was established in Filene's department store in Boston in 1898. This innovation was slow to catch on, however, because the Industrial Revolution emphasised work processes and production techniques predicated on individualised tasks and specialised roles. Mass production focused the principles of scientific management and the 'one-person/one-job' philosophy. Frederick Taylor (1911), was the guru of such a philosophy. Bernard Burnes (1996) in his admirable book Managing Change quotes Taylor as he explains one of the roots of scientific management:

> The managers assume . . . the burden of gathering together all the traditional knowledge which has in the past been possessed by the workmen and then of classifying and reducing this knowledge to rules, laws and formula . . .

Taylor (1911) again lays down his principles by writing: 'All possible brainpower should be removed from the shop (floor) and centred in the planning (department).'

Taylor, who is widely accredited with the development of our mass production based society, feared, along with his contemporaries, organised labour and teams, which represented a local manifestation of workers wanting to determine how they performed tasks, were regarded as the enemy. The reader may like to look back at the original interpretation of the Hawthorne Experiment in our chapter on Motivation to see how this view lasted.

> The empire that became the Anglo-Dutch combine Unilever, was initially dependent of whale oil for its staples – margarine and soap. Initially whaling was regarded a highly skilled trade controlled by teams of highly prized and highly paid Norwegians, but William Hesketh Lever – later Lord Leverhulme – was unhappy with this arrangement and set about deskilling the process using locally recruited landlubbers from the area near his factories in Merseyside.

This was only one example. An inevitable consequence of scientific management was the encouragement of hierarchical or 'military model' organisations. In this chapter we will use the alternative title – the command and control organisation. In these organisations, everyone, except the mythical top, has someone to detail his or her job for them.

The death of the command and control organisation

In the world of the military

In the 1914–18 war much of French and British tactics were determined by the principle that people could not be trusted and provided the stereotype military model of organisations which had hardly changed from Roman days. However, the German Army was already questioning the system:

> In the final German attack in France for World War 1, Hauptmann Geyer virtually invented the concept of shock troops. His men were given a direction of attack and 'were told to move as fast and as deep as they could into the British lines without regard to what was happening on the flanks'. They were allowed in fact,

for what was probably the most disciplined army in the world, to become a self-directed team. They were given careful briefing but were allowed to decide for themselves how their orders were carried out. Successful fighting men had been doing this since the beginning of recorded time, but now they were fully equipped and trained to do so. (From Middlebrook, 1983)

Again in warfare:

Major John Howard commanded D Company of the Oxfordshire and Buckinghamshire Light Infantry to capture a key bridge in the first operation of the battle for Normandy on June 6th 1944 using the same 'loose–tight' command approach of Geyer.

He had to capture the bridge at Benouville and 'hold until relieved'. The army recognised that detailed instructions were impossible and that only empowered and highly trained troops could deal with the inevitable chaos of battle.

When the operation was successfully completed the 'team' or what was left of them, was broken up and sent to standard regiments. Elite forces are probably best as temporary arrangements. (From Ambrose, 1985)

More recently, pressure from the enquiry over a major aircrash in Tenerife led to an 'official' change in management style in the world's airways. A loaded KLM Boeing 747 collided with an American 747 on the runway. At the enquiry the voice recorder on the KLM machine revealed that the co-pilot had attempted to get the very experienced and authoritarian pilot to reverse his intention to take off in spite of not having full clearance. The pilot appeared to have ignored the warning and the crash, at the time of writing, was the most costly ever recorded, directly related to 'management style'. After the crash, airlines adopted a more teamworking approach and the authoritarian managerial style was actively discouraged. As one senior member of cabin crew said – 'It used to be just coffee and whitener. Now they actually tell you what is happening and why.'

The pressures for the rethinking of the military, strictly hierarchical, command and control organisation were a general acceptance of the reality of war. Generals, however well briefed, cannot know exactly what happens when a battle begins – things happen too quickly and the smoke and noise make monitoring from anyone other than those involved impossible. Inspirational leadership, clear briefing, careful training, detailed consultation and relevant equipment are the best that authority can provide. The people on the ground *have* to be left to get on with it. The choice against a strict command structure and for a measure of empowerment has become more imperative as battlefield skills become more specific and the necessity for rapid response, more demanding.

In the later 1980s Mike Angus, then chairman of Unilever, made a speech where he chided his fellow industrialists for maintaining the military model in their organisations, when it had been abandoned by the military for decades. Pressures on industry exactly parallel those that led to a review of the command and control model by the very organisations who created it.

The military metaphor we have chosen stands.

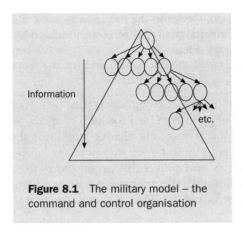

Figure 8.1 The military model – the command and control organisation

The new world of commerce, public service and industry

The traditional hierarchical organisation as laid down by Taylor and his supporters was top down – orders came as successive waves through a layered structure (Figure 8.1). Leadership came from the top and managers were there to see that orders were carried out. The number of employees largely determined the number of layers in an organisation. An arbitrary rule set the number of subordinates that could reasonably report to one manager as being five, so the number of layers was set accordingly. The overall philosophy of the system was that 'people could not be trusted' – extreme Theory X as we discussed in the chapter on motivation. It was also supported by a number of assumptions.

Omniscience of the top

First and foremost, since orders come from the top, we have to assume that the 'top' either knows everything necessary to run the business or can find out in time to make 'good' decisions and 'good' orders.

> There are stories about William Hesketh Lever when he was in total control of the vast soap works of his own building in Port Sunlight, Merseyside. Every day he would arrive on his horse, dismount and be met by his first line management. They would hurry like a cloud behind him waiting for him to stop at 'their' area of responsibility and be issued with their orders for the day: make more Lifebuoy, close line 2 . . .

More recently we were visiting a plastics reclaimer – a factory making millions of plastic refuse bags from low-grade polythene.

> The chairman and owner was explaining to us how he was empowering his staff and now left all the day-to-day running of the factory to his son and some very responsible divisional managers he had just hired. At this point, one of the new responsible managers knocked at the walnut door and was allowed in. The chairman was presented with a black polythene disposal bag: 'It doesn't seem right to me. Should I close the line?'

The chairman excused himself, blew into the bag so as to make it a balloon, tied its neck, placed it on his imperial chair, jumped up and landed hard on the bag. It deflated feebly. 'Yes, close the line.'

The 'empowered' manager bowed slightly, turned and left the room. He presumably closed the line.

The world of most organisations is more complicated than two types of soap for a new marketplace or one line of polythene bags for local councils. Such 'simple' environments are rare and in most parts of our chaotic world it is absolutely impossible for the 'top' to know everything he (or she) needs to know. The job of manager is to understand, analyse and convert his or her orders to the subset of orders required by direct subordinates so that they can in turn pass them down. The job is not only impossible – it is counter-productive in our changing world.

Chinese Whispers

The childhood game of Chinese Whispers, often played in the adult parties of our youth when nobody had anything else to do, involves passing a message along a line of people allowing no feedback. After four or five people, the message becomes hopelessly distorted.

> There is a legend, again of war, where a divisional commander sent the message down the line through a series of runners: 'Send reinforcements, I'm going to advance.' The message received at headquarters was: 'Send three and four pence, I'm going to a dance.'

The currency, well before decimalisation, let alone the EU, tells the age of the joke. Hunter (1957) details more scientific evidence of the Chinese Whisper phenomenon in descriptions of the Bartlett experiments in 1932. All but the simplest messages distort as they are passed 'down the line'. To pass messages down the line the context, made relevant to each recipient, needs to be understood and feedback is essential: *Sorry, do you actually mean . . . ?*

Feedback and the 'specialist'

We assume that true feedback is not necessary. Local feedback for reaffirming the accuracy of messages can occur in the command and control organisation but it seldom is more than local – the 'old man' rarely hears it from anyone other than his immediate deputies.

However, there has emerged a strange individual in the organisation who has specialised knowledge. He or she is the expert.

> The first that one of your authors saw the effect was when he was working for British Coal in the 1960s. The organisation was attempting to develop a number of open fire products and one promising alternative was the very rapid heating of coal dust in a device looking like a vast Dyson vacuum cleaner. The device was in a very early state of development and the scientist in charge, Stuart Troughton, was pressured to take on a 100-fold scale up. He refused, saying that the state of knowledge would not justify the risk. He was right.

In our organisations we now have people who *know*. They are computer specialists who *know* that particular systems are not stable enough to be allowed into the hands of customers, and marketing specialists who *know* that the sampling procedures *possible* in the time given will be biased. Senior management and strategic thinkers had better hear local experts and the command and control organisation has no way of hearing them since **the communication channels are down from the top, rarely two-way and never down up**. In the language of the book, command and control organisations do not support constructive communications.

People do what they are told

Maybe they did, in the years gone by or, in restricted places in the world, they may still do. Maybe leaders and managers supported by power, unemployment and a rigid social order can expect blind obedience, but now it is safer to assume no such thing. Our example of the scientist Stuart Troughton indicates that often it is just as well that people question instructions in a world of complexity. However the command and control organisation assumes that they do obey and, if they fail to obey, simply applies more pressure – including the summary courts martial.

> Working in countries outside Europe, and in particular Asia and the Middle East, the transition from the command and control assumptions is accelerating but by no means as complete as it is in Europe.
>
> One personnel manager for a company in Dubai, UAE, explained that the problems we have just discussed simply did not happen with the workforce at his command. *If they fail me in any way, their work permits are revoked and without work permits, they are deported.*

Organisational responses to the death of the command and control organisation

Coulson-Thomas and Coe (1991) conducted a survey for the then British Institute of Management (BIM) on the ways in which companies and organisations could better face the changing world (see Table 8.1). The survey showed that 86 per cent of the sample, taken from the membership of the BIM, regarded teamworking as a response to the changing world. In addition, the next two responses – flatter and more responsive organisations – can also be related to teamworking. This and other surveys indicated a fundamental questioning of current organisations and the leadership/management styles they had followed since the beginning of the Industrial Revolution.

The movement towards teams is not only concerned explicitly but also implicitly in all but the last factor. We will discuss teams specifically in the next sections of the chapter. Here we will discuss what companies actually do and how this further emphasises the team approach. To help us continue, Table 8.2 list some of the concepts that managers apply to the teamworking approach.

- **Teamworking**, and in particular the cross-functional team. Here individuals from a range of disciplines are taken, on a permanent or temporary basis, from

Table 8.1 Coulson-Thomas's survey of BIM membership

British Institute of Management survey – what respondents felt needed to be done to face the new business environment	Percentage regarding this factor as 'very important'
More work should be undertaken in teams	86
Creating a slimmer and flatter organisation	81
Creating a more responsive organisation	79
Procedures and permanency should give way to flexible and temporary arrangements	79
Functions should become more interdependent	76
Organisations should become more interdependent	67

Table 8.2 Essential associated concepts

- A **self-directed team** in which a group handles its own work structuring.
- A policy of **single customer contact**: organising teams around projects focused to the customer.
- **Multiskilling**: reducing the number of 'crafts' employed in an activity by deskilling and training within a working team.
- **Problem categorising**: accepting that many issues can be handled within a team and that only a few require specialist action.
- **Categorising decisions**: accepting the principle that decisions should be made at the lowest point – by working teams if possible.
- **'Annualising' or 'stacking'** working hours: accepting that when people are not required they are not around, but that they are available when needed. Work is done where, when and by whom it is appropriate.

the silos of their functional departments – finance, marketing, etc. – and formed into project or customer-based teams. The results have been mixed in that few organisations have appreciated the cultural changes involved. Where such projects have worked – Kodak and Rover, for example – the response has been very positive. The problems seem to arise when strong teams are developed with loyalties to themselves and particular customers, but the appraisal and reward systems continue to be supported by the function units – i.e., people are still rewarded for applying their professional skills and not for their personal contribution to team effort. We recognise the accountant, the chemist and the production specialist, but seldom the 'team player'.

- **Multiskilling** has followed in the wake of deskilling and the dying out of the apprentice system. Again the cultural changes needed to accept such changes have often been underestimated.

- **Problem and decision categorising**, although obvious in concept, involve a major training initiative on the part of the organisation. The current jargon states that the organisation needs to transform itself into a learning organisation – everyone, on a continuous basis, needs to extend his or her understanding of the skills necessary to perform the whole job. Handy (1997) discussed this as the Law of Subsidiarity – A higher-order body should not assume responsibilities that could and should be exercised by a lower-order body. He goes on to say that taking over another's responsibilities is wrong because it ultimately deskills them.

- **Annualising hours** – accepting that there is such a thing as a working year – is perhaps the most contentious of the new mechanisms.

We discussed some of these issues on the chapter on motivation. Correctly introduced they do motivate staff but, in the case of the changes, took Zeneca 18 months of hard bargaining.

Downsizing and flatter organisations

With the tactical techniques, real attempts have been made to turn organisations away from the hierarchies so suited to the command and control organisation. We will discuss two such concepts. The Shamrock Organisation of Charles Handy (1993) and the Three-Ring Circus of Ricardo Semler (1993).

In the shamrock organisation (Figure 8.2) we have three categories:

1. Core personnel who maintain the strategy and core activities of the organisation.

2. Contracted staff who perform the core activities of the organisation.

3. Out-sourcing – contracted outside organisations to perform 'support' activities, such as canteen, maintenance, training, wage rose, etc.

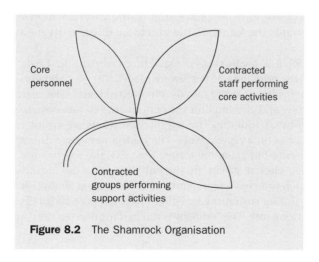

Core
personnel

Contracted
staff performing
core activities

Contracted
groups performing
support activities

Figure 8.2 The Shamrock Organisation

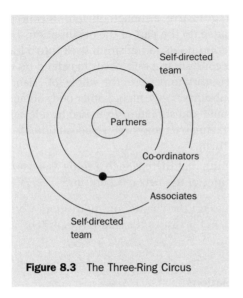

Figure 8.3 The Three-Ring Circus

In the 'Three-Ring Circus' organisation (Figure 8.3) we have reduced the hierarchy to three layers and Semler found it convenient to draw these layers in a circular representation:

1. Partners who are responsible for the direction of the company.
2. Co-ordinators (often called team leaders) who are responsible for steering teams of associates working on specific projects – usually identified around a customer.
3. Associates who, in self-directed teams, perform the actual project work of the organisation.

Very few companies have fully adopted either of the two new models, but many have taken steps towards the leaner, flatter and more directed organisation:

Charles Walls (1997), a medium-sized marketing company in Leeds, UK, has adopted many of the principles of the Semler model. The co-ordinators are however called 'coaches' who assist the various self-directed teams. The coaches retain their functional roles and also monitor the performance of the teams using internal and customer-based auditing. The self-directed teams are customer focused and elect their leaders on a regular basis. The leaders have no authority beyond their personal presence but guide the teams. The CEO, the coaches and the team members with their elected leaders are the only 'layers' in the organisation. For internal purposes job titles beyond the three layers have been abolished. (They are retained or developed for customer convenience, as the CEO puts it.) Pay is tightly related to team performance. The company is still in transition but the current news is favourable.

The growth of team culture

It is important for the reader not to see the historical description of the development of teams as an inevitable evolution. There has been a general progression, but,
as we will detail later, the stage of development needs to fit the organisation and its
environment. From the 1898 experiments of Filene's department store in Boston,
there was a gap in the development of recognised and formalised teamworking,
although it obviously occurred naturally in millions of small organisations. In the
1920s, small-scale efforts were made to form **problem-solving** teams in some
companies. These teams consisted of 5 to 12 workers who met for an hour or two
each week to discuss ways to make improvements or solve problems in their
company. By the time the 1987 General Accounting Office (GAO) study was conducted, 70 per cent of 476 large companies surveyed had installed these types
of teams (although less than half the workforce actually participated in the teams).
The widely publicised Japanese **quality circles** of the 1970s and 1980s present a
variation on this type of team. Problem-solving teams have no power to implement
decisions or changes; they simply meet to discuss issues and make recommendations to upper management.

In the early and middle 1980s special-purpose teams emerged in which members help to redesign work processes, introduce new technology, resolve labour and
management differences, link with suppliers or customers, or co-ordinate across
functional boundaries. These teams have power to take action and initiate changes
in organisations as a result of delegated assignments from the top. They not only
recommend, but also implement. Such teams are currently spreading in many industries, mainly among lower-level employees and especially in firms faced with the
need to improve efficiency, competitiveness, and responsiveness. Poza and Markus
(1980) demonstrated that a team approach to restructuring resulting in a lower head
count, reduced absentee levels, reduced turnover and increased productivity in an
automotive plant in Kentucky. Japanese transplants have been particularly effective in their use of teamworking – Wickens (1987) and Susman (1990) record the
details for the UK and US respectively.

Table 8.3 list some 'early adopters' of teamworking principles among US companies.

Teams and teamwork are much more typical of manufacturing firms than of
service firms, since relatively few service organisations have established work teams
as yet (Hoerr, 1989).

The 1990s have witnessed the emergence of a new form of work team, **self-
managing** teams. This type of team is still relatively rare and represents the most
advanced form of teamwork. Self-managing teams plan and schedule their own
work processes, hire and train team members, praise and reward their team's performance, and manage their own leadership. Team members learn all the tasks
necessary for a particular process, product or service, and members rotate from job
to job. Each team member can substitute for another member in case of absence
or special demand. As summarised in Table 8.4, self-managing teams maintain
all the responsibilities within the team that are normally spread across multiple

Table 8.3 Early examples of US companies using teamworking principles

Company	When started
Boeing	1987
Caterpillar	1986
Champion International	1985
Cummins Engine	1973
Digital Equipment	1982
Ford	1982
General Electric	1985
General Motors	1975
LTV Steel	1985
Procter and Gamble	1962
A.O. Smith	1987
Tektronix	1983

Source: *Business Week*, 'The payoff from teamwork,' July 10, 1989, p. 58

Table 8.4 The claimed advantages of self-managed teams

Self-managed teams:
- plan, control, and improve their own work processes
- share leadership and management functions
- set their own goals
- inspect their own work
- create their own schedules
- review their own performance
- prepare their own budgets
- co-ordinate with other units
- order their own supplies
- Manage their own inventories
- negotiate and contract with suppliers
- acquire training when needed
- hire their own replacements
- discipline their own members
- take responsibility for rewarding and recognising members
- are led by coaching and facilitating rather than controlling and directing
- reward based on team not individual performance
- rely on fewer management layers and fewer functions to accomplish work
- encourage individual member initiative and accountability
- **require a special type of leadership if they are not to become a danger to the organisation**

hierarchical levels and functions. In contrast to problem-solving or special-purpose teams, members of self-managing teams work together on an ongoing basis, not just as a temporary assignment. By 1991, surveys of more than 500 organisations by two consulting firms, Wyatt and DDI, found that about 27 per cent of organisations had begun using self-directed work teams (Moskal, 1991; Wellins *et al.*, 1991). A 1993 survey of 1,293 US organisations by the American Society for Quality Control (ASQC) and the Gallup Organisation found that over 80 per cent of respondents reported some form of teamwork activity, mainly problem-solving teams. Typically, two or more teams were found per company, but almost all teams were of recent origin, the median life span being only five years. Two-thirds of full-time employees indicated that they participate in teams, and 84 per cent participate in more than one team (ASQC, 1993).

The advantages of teams

Teams have captured the attention of modern managers because of increasing amounts of data that show improvements in productivity, quality, and morale when teams are utilised. For example, a noted management consultant, Tom Peters (1987, p. 306) claimed:

> Are there any limits to the use of teams? Can we find places or circumstances where a team structure doesn't make sense? Answer: No, as far as I can determine. That's unequivocal, and meant to be. Some situations may seem to lend themselves more to team-based management than others. Nonetheless, I observe that the power of the team is so great that it is often wise to violate apparent common sense and force a team structure on almost anything.

We would not entirely agree.

Many companies have attributed their improvements in performance directly to the institution of teams in the workplace (Wellins *et al.*, 1991). For example, by using teams:

- Shenandoah Life Insurance Company in Roanoke, Virginia, saved $200,000 annually because of reduced staffing needs, while increasing its volume 33 per cent.
- Westinghouse Furniture Systems increased productivity 74 per cent in three years.
- AAL increased productivity by 20 per cent, cut personnel by 10 per cent, and handled 10 per cent more transactions.
- Federal Express cut service errors by 13 per cent.
- Carrier reduced unit turnaround time from two weeks to two days.
- Volvo's Kalmar facility reduced defects by 90 per cent.
- General Electric's Salisbury, North Carolina, plant increased productivity by 250 per cent compared to other GE plants producing the same product.
- Corning cellular ceramics plant decreased defect rates from 1,800 parts per million to 9 parts per million.

- AT&T's Richmond operator service increased service quality by 12 per cent.
- Dana Corporation's Minneapolis valve plant trimmed customer lead time from six months to six weeks.
- General Mills plants using teams are 40 per cent more productive than plants operating without teams.

Other more scientific and systematic studies of the impact of teams have found equally impressive results. Literally thousands of studies have been conducted on groups and teams and their impact on various performance outcomes. One of the first and most well-known studies ever conducted on teams was undertaken by Coch and French (1948) in the Harwood Company, a manufacturer of men's shirts, shorts, and pyjamas. Faced with the necessity of responding to competitors' lower prices, Harwood decided to speed up the line and make other process changes. Workers had responded badly, however, to previous changes in the production process, and they resisted the threat of further changes. To implement these planned changes, Harwood management used three different types of strategies.

- One group of employees received an explanation of the new standards to be imposed, the proposed changes in the production process to be implemented, and why the changes were needed. A question–answer period followed the explanation.
- A second group of employees was presented the problem, asked to discuss it and reach agreement on solutions, and then elect representatives to generate the new standards and procedures.
- In a third group, every member was asked to discuss and become involved in establishing and implementing the new standards and procedures. All members participated fully as a team.

The results of this comparison were dramatic. Despite having their jobs simplified, members of the first group showed almost no improvement in productivity; hostility towards management escalated; and, within 40 days, 17 per cent of the employees had left the company. Members of the second group regained their previous levels of productivity within 14 days and improved slightly thereafter. Morale remained high and no employee left the company. Members of the third group, on the other hand, who fully participated as a team, regained earlier productivity levels by the second day and improved 14 per cent over that level within the month. Morale remained high, and no one left the company.

Other classic studies of coal miners, pet food manufacturers, and auto workers revealed similar advantages of teams (e.g., Trist, 1969; Walton, 1965). More recently, one of the most comprehensive surveys ever conducted on employee involvement in teams was carried out among the Fortune 1000 companies by Lawler *et al.* (1992). They found that employee involvement in teams had a strong positive relationship with several dimensions of organisational and worker effectiveness. Table 8.5 shows the percentage of organisations reporting improvement and positive impact as a result of team involvement. In general, Lawler and his colleagues found that among firms that were actively using teams, both organisational and individual

Table 8.5 The impact of improvement teams on organisations and workers

Performance criteria	Percentage Indicating improvement	Percentage Indicating positive impact
Changed management style to more participatory	78	
Improved organisational processes and procedures	75	
Improved management decision making	69	
Increased employee trust in management	66	
Improved implementation of technology	60	
Elimination of layers of management supervision	50	
Improved safety and health	48	
Improved union–management relations	47	
Quality of products and services		70
Customer service		67
Worker satisfaction		66
Employee quality of work life		63
Productivity		61
Competitiveness		50
Profitability		45
Absenteeism		23
Turnover	22	

effectiveness were above average and improving in virtually all categories of performance. In firms without teams or in which teams were infrequently used, effectiveness was average or low in all categories.

In studies of self-directed teams, Near and Weckler (1990) found that individuals
in self-directed teams scored significantly higher than individuals in traditional
work structures on innovation, information sharing, employee involvement, and
task significance. Macy *et al.* (1990) reported that the use of self-directed teams
correlated highly with increases in organisational effectiveness, heightened productivity, and reduced defects. Wellins *et al.* (1991) reported that two-thirds of companies that implemented self-directed work teams could run their companies with
fewer managers, and in 95 per cent of the cases a reduced number of managers was
reported to be beneficial to company performance. The results of other well-known
studies have produced similar outcomes (Ancona and Caldwell, 1992; Hackman,
1990; Gladstein, 1984). Many of the reasons for these positive outcomes of teams
have been known for years.

Maier (1967), for example, in a classic description of the conditions under which
teams are more effective than individuals acting alone, and vice versa, pointed out
that teams:

- Produce a greater number of ideas and pieces of information than individuals acting alone, so decision making and problem solving are more informed and are of higher quality.

- Improve understanding and acceptance among individuals involved in problem solving and decision making due to team members' participation in the process.

- Have higher motivation and performance levels than individuals acting alone because of the effects of 'social facilitation', that is, people are more energised and active when they are around other people.

- Offset personal biases and blind spots that inhibit effective problem analysis and implementation but that are not noticed by single individuals.

- Are more likely to entertain novel alternatives and to take innovative action than individuals acting alone.

- Teams are usually more fun to work with.

On the other hand, teams are not a panacea for everything that ails organisations, nor do they represent a magic potion that managers can use to accomplish their objectives. Just getting people together and calling them a team by no means makes them a team. A leading expert on teams, Richard Hackman (1993), pointed out that mistakes are common in team building and team management.

- Rewarding and recognising individuals instead of the team.
- Not maintaining stability of membership over time.
- Not providing teams with autonomy.
- Not fostering interdependence among team members.
- Using the team to make all decisions instead of having individuals make decisions when appropriate.
- Failing to orient all team members.
- Having too many members on the team.
- Not providing appropriate structure for the team.
- Not providing the team with needed resources.

Choosing, placing and maintaining teams are the jobs of the new leaders and managers.

There are, however, many situations where teamworking is not appropriate – for example, simple, routine, or highly formalised work (e.g., stuffing Pimentos into olives) is not well suited for teams. Verespei (Iggo) observed:

All too often corporate chieftains read the success stories and ordain their companies to adopt work teams – NOW. Work teams don't always work and may even be the wrong solution to the situation in question.

Teams, in other words, can be very powerful tools for managers in producing organisational success, but they are by no means a 'sure thing'. Survey 8.2, 'Diagnosing the need for team development', helps to identify the extent to which teams will help an organisation to improve its performance.

Teams can take too long to make decisions; they may drive out effective action with 'group think'; and they can create confusion and frustration for their members. Many people have been members of an inefficient committee, or a team dominated by one member, or have had to take responsibility for the output of a team that compromised on excellence in order to get agreement from everyone – 'to attempt to please everyone is to please nobody'.

If team failure is common, then, how can success in teams be assured? How can managers ensure the effectiveness of the teams in which they are involved? What should one learn to become a skilful team leader and team member?

However, team working is a real challenge that will not go away for management, and understanding the mechanisms of teams and their formation is a vital management skill.

Stages of the development of teams

Teams and groups

> Observations on my reading history, in Library, May Nineteen, Seventeen Hundred Thirty-one:
> - That the great affairs of this world, the wars, revolutions, etc., are carried on and effected by parties.
> - That the view of these parties is their present general interest, or what they take to be such.
> - That the different views of these different parties occasion all confusion.
> - That while a party is carrying on a general design, each man has his particular private interest in view.
> - That as soon as a party has gained its general point, each member becomes intent upon his particular interest; which, thwarting others, breaks that party into divisions, and occasions more confusion.
>
> *Source*: Benjamin Franklin as quoted by Eric Berne (1963)

Franklin, in 1731, was echoing a fundamental truth that is now being accepted by organisations – to achieve anything effectively you need a team with a clear purpose. Without that purpose, or when that purpose is achieved, individual issues and the issues of individuals will destroy the team – if you let it happen.

Woods (1989) sees the first job of a team manager as keeping the team in touch with the purpose.

> 'Keeping the team in touch with the purpose' will include supplying the facilities, the controls and the direction the team needs to fulfil that purpose – a great deal of work. Should, however, the purpose be weak or unclear the manager needs to be able to take firmer control of the individuals and the group – the management style will have to move away from Consensus and Consultation and adopt a more directive approach.

Secondly the manager needs to understand the relevant needs of individuals in the group. We are not asking the manager to become a universal social worker but to consider and put priority onto what is relevant regardless of his or her prejudice or personal beliefs and values.

> In the final Scott expedition to Antarctica it was relevant that Evans was undernourished and had lost essential strength. Evans was a larger man than the others and needed more than basic rations to survive. Scott felt that he should not allow for any special pleading and with what we would now call machismo, probably contributed to Evans' death and the failure of the whole expedition. (Woods, 1989)

The skilful manager listens to individuals and reserves the time to understand what may be relevant.

Thirdly, the manager needs to understand the needs of the group in relation to its purpose, the facilities and the individuals within it. These are 'old fashioned' management skills but understanding the needs of the group is by no means an obvious task. We have used the word group and not team – the difference between a 'team' and a 'group' is crucial.

A team is a group of people dedicated towards a goal – a purpose. Every team is a group but only the rare group is a team.

Stages of team development

Wanous *et al.* (1984) classified the stages of team development from various authors. Their work is summarised in Table 8.6. The Tuckman sequence for team formation – Forming, Storming Norming, Performing and Adjourning – will be used as our primary model. Other common names for the stages, such as Forming, Developing, Consolidating and Mature, will be mentioned as will be the Schutz's Firo-B needs of Inclusion, Control and Affection mentioned in the first chapter.

The purpose of working

People at work are motivated in two ways:

1. *The task.* Issues concerned with the quality of the work in hand.
2. *The process.* The satisfaction of the human needs to relate to the rest of the human race.

Table 8.6 Five models of team development

Schutz (1958)	Model/Faris (1958) Four-stage developmental model	Whittaker (1970) Integrative model	Hill and Gruner (1973) Three-stage developmental model	Tuckman (1965) Integrative model

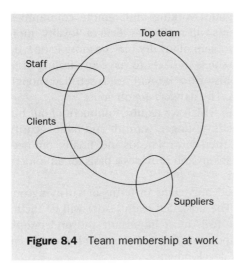

Figure 8.4 Team membership at work

We differ in the balance of our concerns for the process and the task. Some extreme individuals are motivated almost by the task alone. Others, equally extreme, are almost unconcerned with the task, and are happy provided that their human needs are satisfied. Most of us lie between these two extremes – being concerned with both human contact and with the nature of the task with which we are engaged.

Our concern to relate to other human beings can be split into three components:

1. The need for inclusion: the gregarious instinct in mankind – the need to join and to belong. (Woods 1989)

2. The need for control: the wish to know one's position in relationship to others – role and control.

3. The need for affection: the wish to relate and be accepted by others on an individual basis, the need to pair and share.

If you look back to your Firo-B scores you will see the balance of your needs. However, your 'people needs' are provided by the multitude of 'teams' in your life – home, leisure and work. Remaining at work, you may belong to teams of your own staff, your clients, your suppliers and be a junior member of the 'top team' of your bosses (see Figure 8.4).

The issue for management is that individuals – and managers are just as much a part of this 'activity' as anyone – balance our contributions to provide our chosen quantity and quality of the satisfaction of our people needs.

United Agricultural Merchants were concerned about the quality of advice given by their salespersons to farmers. The advice 'looked' as if it was to the advantage of the farmer and not of the company. Looking at the pattern of communications in their workforce they found that the company contact provided virtually no people needs for their staff. The salespersons were on the road meeting the farmers on a professional and semi-social basis. This was where the people needs were being satisfied and this was where the 'loyalty' of the staff lay.

The new trends towards home working and remote communications from laptops to head office by modems will make this issue of 'loyalty' more acute. For the home-based manager the problem of loyalty may be most acute when he or she relates to the 'top team'. He or she is unlikely to have any feeling of belonging to the 'top team' and may get all his or her human needs satisfied though colleagues or his or her subordinate teams. The dangers are obvious.

There is a logic in the order in which we require fulfilment of our human needs. Assuming that our material needs – hunger, warmth and basic security – are met, our inclusion needs come next, then control needs and, finally, our needs for affection. The same order is true for teams and provides a basis for an understanding for the stages of team development.

Unless we are skilled, we lead our teams in terms of satisfying our own level and balance of human needs. The unskilled team leader will be inclined to over-emphasise the needs he or she feels most important and underemphasise those he or she finds personally unimportant. This imbalance of leadership emphasis will have an adverse effect on team development.

The process of team development

The process of movement from group to team is in stages:

> Suppose you are invited to a social occasion – say a barbecue – and you only know the host, everyone else is a stranger. One can imagine questioning why you had been invited and feeling quite uncomfortable in spite of obvious helpful introductions by the host. There is a 'situation vacant' serving drinks and you jump at it. You have acquired a purpose and a role. As the party matures you find someone who has a mutual interest and settle down in a corner to discuss military history, the European Union, cars . . . Just as you are settled, it's time to go and you exchange cards with your new found friend, promising to 'give you a call'.

This is the forming stage where individual inclusion needs are satisfied. Our quotation from Ben Franklin drew attention to the fact that a team needs to have a purpose to distinguish it from a group. The sooner the group hears of that purpose, clearly and understandably, the better. Without that purpose or when that purpose is achieved, individual issues and the issues of individuals will destroy the team. A manager, however, at any given time needs to balance the needs of the task, the team and the individual. Adair used a Venn diagram to illustrate this point and this is shown in Figure 8.5. We need to remind ourselves continually that a team is a group of people dedicated to a goal – a purpose. Every team is a group but only rarely is a group a team.

The process of movement from group to team takes place in stages:

1. Stage 1 – the forming stage – where the inclusion, joining and belonging needs are being settled by a group of people potentially coming to work as a team.

2. Stage 2 – the developing team – where the issues of control are being settled. The issues of control may lead to dissent and hence Tuckman's nomenclature – the storming stage.

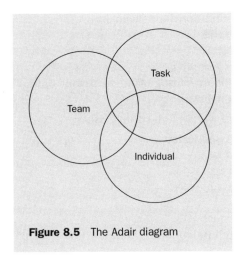

Figure 8.5 The Adair diagram

3. Stage 3 – the consolidating team – where individual relationships and norms are being established, hence Tuckman's norming stage.

4. Stage 4 – the mature or self-actualised team.

5. Stage 5 – the mourning stage where the team is disbanded.

Ideally we are looking at a smooth progression to a mature team (Figure 8.6). 'A fly on the wall' could recognise each of the stages of team development.

The eye of a fly on the wall

A 'fly on the wall' – an unbiased observer – would notice:

1. Stage 1 – the undeveloped and forming team working on fulfilling the inclusion needs of individuals.

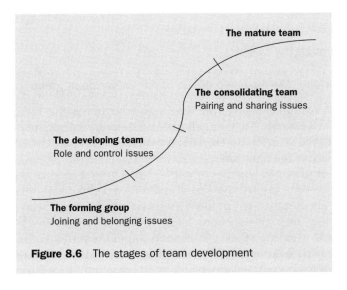

Figure 8.6 The stages of team development

- grumbling on immediate conditions, intellectualism
- swift 'dashes' to complete tasks
- one-sided definitions of position
- temporary and stereotyped groupings
- suspicion and a great deal of attributing blame to anyone or anything
- total reliance on them or the boss.

2. Stage 2 – the developing team working on control issues:

- defensiveness, competition and jealousy
- challenges to structure and task
- experimental hostility and aggression
- ambivalence to the appointed leader
- 'stag fights' and 'try ons'
- intense brittle links and cliques
- tantrums or impatience from individuals who know that their skills already match the task.

This stage may well justify its name – the storming stage.

3. Stage 3 – the consolidating or norming team working on affection issues. (Woods, 1989, calls these Pairing and Sharing issues):

- potential alienation with other teams
- blossoming of personal relationships
- re-definition of physical boundaries
- lack of formal leadership control
- some uniformity of habits or dress.

4. Stage 4 – the mature team – all the needs of the team have been satisfied and the properties of a self-directed team. The reader might like to refer to Table 8.4 or the metaphor of the geese. The fly would notice pragmatic harmony.

5. Stage 5 – the mourning team – the task has been accomplished or has been lost and the members are departing. The fly would notice sadness, regret and delaying.

Managing through the stages

Stage 1: Providing the inclusion needs of an undeveloped group

When we have a group of people who have been brought together for the first time they have many concerns. They will all have the basic insecurities of not knowing exactly why they have been chosen, what is required of them and whether they are in the right place at the right time.

The leader or manager, whether or not he or she is in a command and control organisation, needs to resolve those insecurities by assuming authority and *telling* people. He or she needs to tell people about who is present and who is expected. The initial process may consist of providing name tags, places to settle in, instructions of where to get a cup of tea, guided tours round the site and introductions to key people. Only then do we need to detail what is required of the group as a whole. He or she needs to concentrate on the task, its purpose and its content (Figure 8.7).

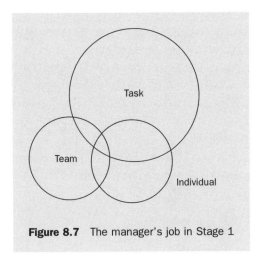

Figure 8.7 The manager's job in Stage 1

Those with high inclusion needs will be most concerned that this stage is correctly structured and will be unhappy until it is. Late comers need to be brought up to speed and introduced appropriately to the forming group.

The group and its members will stay in this undeveloped stage indefinitely if:

- the task remains unclear
- there is genuine or perceived insecurity of group membership
- the management decision-making style remains directive or authoritarian and the group depends on external decisions for its purpose and patterns to be decided – which would be quite normal in a command and control management structure.

The group will return to the undeveloped stage should any of these factors return – the task changes, redundancy threatens or people leave or join. A manager working in an authoritarian management structure or with a task that is changing uncontrollably, may well choose to keep the team in the undeveloped joining and belonging stage. The reason behind this may be that he or she is unable to provide a clear purpose to the group or because he or she wants to remain in complete control – his or her role and control needs are high.

Stage 2: Providing the role and control needs of a developing team

Once the inclusion needs of the individuals in the group are satisfied we can progress to the next set of needs. We have established a form of definition of the task, understand why we are included and now we need to establish, with clarity, the official and unofficial roles of everyone in the forming team. The formal leadership is probably accepted but the informal pecking orders are not. Consultation is possible but it is always consultation marred by suspicion : 'I'm not certain why the boss is asking her, she only graduated last year . . .' The leader/manager needs to concentrate on developing the team (Figure 8.8).

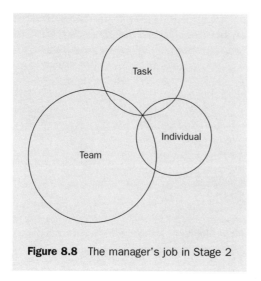

Figure 8.8 The manager's job in Stage 2

'No individual is more important than the team.'

Source: Bill Shankly as manager of Liverpool Football Club in their great days

The group may stay in this rather uncomfortable developing stage if:

- the management chooses to keep competition among the group – a high-pressure sales team.

    We were working with a company concerned with high-pressure selling to the trade. The country was divided into what seemed arbitrary divisions – all controlled by a very authoritarian marketing manager. At the sales conference it was quite obvious that a team spirit was emerging and one of the regions, with a strong emergent team, had won the 'golden rose' for sales two years running. The marketing manager chose to use the conference to announce a redistribution of the regions. As he told us: 'We don't want them getting too cocky, do we?'

- the roles demanded by functions do not fit the preferred way individuals wish to work – the hierarchy does not fit the functions necessary

- individuals in the group will not accept the principles behind the task

- individuals will not accept the values being imposed on them by the forming team – the politics or the Politics

- the management decision-making style within the organisation remains predominantly authoritarian and there is no history of consultative or consensus management.

    This reason can lead to some very dangerous decisions. Michael Edwards in his book *Back from the Brink* (1984) describes the near collapse of British Leyland – later to become the Rover wing of BMW. When he took over the company in 1977 the workforce had become alienated from the management. In our model, management saw no reason to provide for any inclusion needs and indeed was hostile to any movement towards team working. Management was entirely authoritarian. However, a union leader known as (Red Robbo) Robinson was able to provide group membership needs and, with this, generated a great measure of loyalty from the workforce. The consequences of this were a series of intractable industrial disputes. Edwards had to 'include' the workforce into the company processes before he was able to regain loyalty and respect from the workforce.

• the task is not clear or not ready to be defined – sometimes we need to keep a group of workers in reserve, in a 'lay-by', while other things are sorted out, and this is often thinly disguised as a training programme.

Stage 3: Providing for the human need for individual contacts – the affection or pairing and sharing needs of a consolidating team

People are working out their working relationships – norming as it has been called. Often the norming involves dressing the same.

The Charles Walls Group, a company we have mentioned previously, set up two teams with parallel functions. One team was becoming successful and the other was floundering. The 'consolidating' team had adopted a uniform style of dress for both the male and the female members – casual, decorous and in pastel colours. The other team, trapped in the developing stage and control issues, dressed competitively.

The outsider may see the consolidating team as a real team. The individuals in the consolidating team no longer need to jockey for position and are valued as members of something that can be given a discreet title – be it the 'boffins' or 'accounts'. People are in the process of finding out who they like to work with and who they can trust on an intimate level.

Obviously 'uniforms' and various forms of equipment standardisation are used on one level to encourage team development. On a more subtle level, the leader/manager needs to provide support – training, coaching and counselling – for individuals (Figure 8.9).

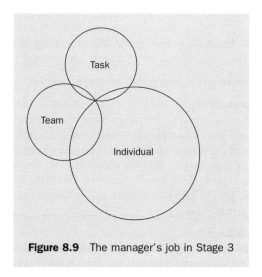

Figure 8.9 The manager's job in Stage 3

The process of moving from the second stage of the role and control battles to the pairing and sharing stage will most probably have involved some individuals deciding that they are not wanted or that they do not accept the roles on which the success of the team depends. In this case they will choose their moment and leave. Otherwise, the leader needs to recognise that some individuals may not like the standards laid down by the team in the previous stage – their values may not fit, and these individuals may also be encouraged to leave.

A team remaining too long in the pairing and sharing stage may well become smug. The consolidating team may never complete its progress to a mature team if:

- the group is allowed to modify the task to suit its members' preferred way of working
- management has 'forgotten' the importance of monitoring the team's processes
- the fit of personality is 'too good', and there is no 'sand in the oyster to produce the pearl'
- the team membership is static
- the management decision-making style has become the consensus as of right.

Stage 4: Establishing a mature team

The mature team is a team which takes personal and collective liability for its actions:

> I am sorry but Pat is out of the office at the moment. I can see from her notes that she would want you to buy the steelwork at that price for delivery but I cannot give you complete authority. Put in a provisional order and I will get Pat to ring back. Yes, I'm Henry Patterson, Patterson with two t's.

The manager now has to manage appropriately – bringing his or her weight for the task, the team and the individual; it is complex, is not to the taste of many who undertake it, and will be the subject of much of the rest of this chapter.

Stage 5: Allowing the team to break – managing the mourning stage

The Yorkshire clue to managing the disbandment of the team is in the word 'wake'. We have many examples from our experience and have chosen two:

Case study 1: Team in failure

Birds Eye had decided to develop a high technology route to making frozen fish portions. The technology was too advanced and the team failed. The failure was spectacular but there was no criticism of the team – it was a mature team with everything that that meant to the organisation and the individuals concerned. When everything possible had been done, the senior management of Birds Eye decided to close the project. A spectacular party was held and every stakeholder was invited. Taxis took the participants home.

Case study 2: Team in change

We were asked to advise on a very strange change. SELA, a major European manufacturer of industrial fasteners, had decided that its warehousing arrangements did

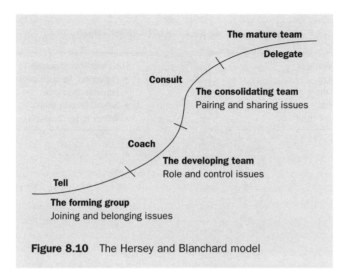

Figure 8.10 The Hersey and Blanchard model

not meet its new significance in the market. The warehouse team was mature but was unhappy and insecure about the new automated warehouse being built along-side their building which was more than 60 years old. The old warehouse had worn pine-wood trolleys and sorting pigeon holes – the new warehouse was metal and computer controlled. Nobody from the old team was to be redundant.

Our advice was to have a wake. There was a party in the new warehouse and during the party the bulldozers crashed through the old building. An old pine-wood trolley was to be presented to the assembly.

Even we were surprised that members of the 'old team' spent their weekend working with the demolition team, unpaid, to speed the work of destruction – and to rescue mementoes.

The leader/manager's job is to support the team. The mature team will survive if the task and the membership have evolved together, the management adopts a flexible and appropriate style of decision making and outside factors allow it.

The diagrams we have seen until now are from Adair. The Hersey and Blanchard (1969) model sees things in a slightly different way (Figure 8.10).

Styles of management

David Kolb, standing on the shoulders of many giants, including Jung, developed his Learning Cycle. We discussed this in some detail in the first chapter. Readers should refer back to their own responses to the Learning Style Indicator in the Survey material of Chapter 1.

The Learning preferences have been related to preferred management styles (Woods, 1989 and Figure 8.11). The reader will be able, by weighting the four quadrants, to look at the likely way he or she functions as a manager.

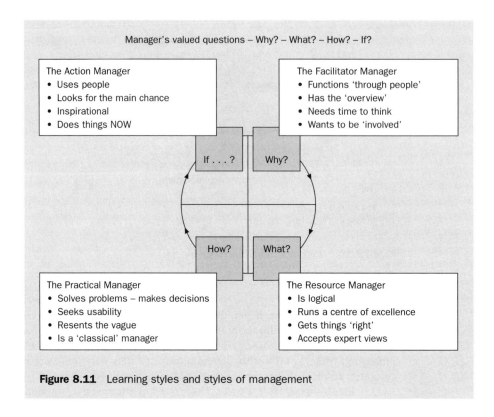

Figure 8.11 Learning styles and styles of management

The facilitator manager

This person works through his or her staff, bringing them on as individuals. They are slow to decide and inclined to need all sides of a question before deciding. They see management as a privilege and not a right – it could be said that they are not natural managers.

> Unilever Foods Research had one facilitator manager who had reached senior status, and many regarded him as a minor genius. His human management skills were such that he was given no line authority. However, the whole operations research, commanded by a resource manager, was at his disposal when he had an idea that needed study or development. He was one of the few people we have ever met who was universally liked and respected.

The resource manager

This person considers the staff to be very much as other resources necessary for the task. This does not mean to say he or she does not value them, but the valuation is in terms of professional competence. He or she works by facts, and on the advice of experts. He or she can well treat staff as a group that needs to be protected.

> One of the author's University computer department was commanded by a resource manager. The computer group was on a floor slightly below ground level

and underneath the library. Ideally suited for main frame working, the place resembled a temple and its staff acolytes. It was not suited for the casual world encouraged by the universal ownership of PC's.

The practical manager

This manager is in the 'classical' mode and is not at home in a command and control organisation. He or she is interested in the skills of the staff in relationship to the tasks they have to accomplish. The practical manager likes systems, order and competence.

> When Hicksons Chemicals decided to introduce teamworking, they found that the majority of their managers were practical managers and, in the opinion of the consultants, unsuited for the new world of empowerment. This presented a major problem in recruitment, retraining, refitting, redeployment and release.

The action manager

This person is only interested in results. People are a means to an end and are judged entirely on how they achieve. He or she is often an inspirational leader, and transformational, as we will discuss later. An action manager has a clear vision but may, in the urgency and enthusiasm of the moment, forget to pass it on effectively to 'slower' colleagues.

The manager in the new organisations needs to be flexible and not rooted in one style.

Leadership in the new organisations

Warren Bennis (1997) is quoted as saying: 'Has my thinking changed? Not really. I would say what has changed is the kind of leadership that is now going to be required in organisations. It's a different form of leadership. The Lone Ranger is clearly dead.'

Over many years we have been asking students to provide a list of the people they regard as leaders. The lists are unsurprisingly the same, wherever we are; many are associated with war (Churchill, Zukov, Guderian, Haig, Joan of Arc, Foch) or with religions (Christ, Ghandi, Mohammed) or with world events (Thatcher, Nightingale, Ben Grunion) or of great evil (Hitler, Manson) or great good (Mother Theresa). Very few will be ordinary people doing a job.

Because, until recently, leadership is not associated in general with ordinary people, teaching leadership has been regarded with suspicion outside military academies or top management seminars. We are now recognising that, without leadership at all levels, our world will simply drift into anarchy. However, perhaps more importantly for this chapter, some forms of leadership can be taught. Peter Topping (1997) emphasises this point. He sees that we have gone well past the crude 'great man' theory of leadership and cites three critical factors of leadership in the present world:

1. Personal characteristics

2. The unique demands of situations

3. Actual behaviour.

Topping goes further and lists the basic ingredients of the new leadership:

- Understanding of one's self and self confidence.
- The ability to trust others, credibility and steadiness.
- The ability to foster teamwork and collaboration.
- Strong interpersonal communications skills.
- Openness to new ideas and innovation.
- Decisiveness tempered by solid analysis and problem solving.
- An awareness of relevant situational and environmental factors.
- An understanding of human behaviour in an organisational context.
- A desire to coach and teach so that others may grow.

These are the very skills that we hope to have covered in this book.

Sources of power

Imagine the scene of a Captain in command of a small warship given the task of protecting his convoy of ships from submarine attack. He is given the location of the submarine – directly underneath a number of sailors swimming towards his ship and expecting rescue. With very little hesitation he orders the attack and incidentally causes the death of all the swimming sailors. The scene is described graphically in Monsarrat's book *The Cruel Sea* (1951). What were the sources of power that gave the Captain 'permission' to make such a hard decision and be certain that it would be obeyed? Leaders without followers are not leaders. The 'sources of power' that allowed the acceptance of such a command include:

- **Experience/expertise.** At the commissioning of the corvette – a very simple ship – the Captain, his Number 1 and the Chief Engineer would know every nut and bolt of the ship. As in the novel, when the Captain was promoted to command a frigate – a much larger and technologically advanced ship – his expertise became less relevant but his experience had grown and his rank was increased to compensate.
- **Hierarchy.** The Captain has rank invested in him through the Admiralty. Later he calls a group of junior officers to order by simply patting his sleeve.
- **Charisma/credibility.** Rank, experience, expertise mean nothing if people simply do not accept your right to lead.
- **Dedication/role model.** Working harder, longer and to more purpose is expected of some leadership styles, but not all.
- **The team and followers.** The skills of the team and the presence of people willing to follow are essential to leadership 'power'. Maintaining the team is the first priority of a leader.

- **Patronage and influence.** Visible support of 'the boss', in this case the Admiral, is an essential of leadership power.
- **Clarity of purpose.** The Captain had clear written orders: 'Destroy enemy submarines and guard the convoy.' Picking up survivors was not his primary and explicitly stated concern.

Any leader needs some of these sources of power, the balance changing with time. Thus as the Captain becomes out of touch with expertise he is given more hierarchical authority – promotion.

> Andrew S. Groves, the CEO of Intel who stepped down in March 1997, saw his changing power base very clearly. His solo expertise became replaced by the ability to judge the advice and feeling he obtained by walking the plants and laboratories and judging the respect his various specialists received from their peers.

One of Topping's criteria for leadership concerned understanding the situation and the environment. The concepts of situational leadership are widely taught.

Situational leadership

Vroom and Yetton (1973) classified the decision-making styles and showed that the choice of style was entirely situational. The styles are shown in Table 8.7.

The coding of the Vroom and Yetton classification is possibly of the most elitist type, and to save the reader trouble: A stands for Authoritarian, C stands for Consultative and G for Group. The '1' is for individual and '11' for more than one. Thus C11 stands for where the manager consults more than one person at a time.

The reader might like to try a test. Forget the warship and imagine that you need to get your fellow students or workers to read the whole of our current book. This time we would like you to work on your fellow students using each of the Vroom and Yetton styles.

A1. In the A1 style you may choose to use a bald 'telling' statement: 'You will all read the book', or you may choose to soften the blow by some 'selling'. the idea: 'You will all benefit from reading the book and improve your management skills to such an extent as to guarantee promotion (or pass the exam)'

Equally, and still in A1, you could delegate the message giving to some unfortunate: 'Get them to read the book.'

A11. In A11 we need to collect information before the instruction: 'Will everyone be in the office on Thursday? Fine, now get them together and . . .'

C1. C1 allows the subordinate some knowledge of what is to come: 'I am very keen on them all reading the book. What sort of resistance are we likely to get if I tell them on Thursday? I need to make up my mind on how to proceed.'

Table 8.7 The Vroom and Yetton classification of management decision-making styles

---

Authoritarian styles

A1. The individual manager solves the problem or makes the decision using the information available to him or her at the time.

A11. The individual manager collects the relevant information from subordinates and then decides on a solution or makes the decision. The manager may or may not choose to tell the subordinates about the nature of the problem while he or she is collecting the information. The subordinates act as a data source and not in any way as decision makers.

Consultative styles

C1. The manager shares the problem with relevant subordinates individually, without getting them together in a group but telling them that he or she will make a considered decision which may or may not reflect individual advice.

C11. The manager shares the problem with relevant subordinates in a group, explaining that the decision may or may not reflect the suggestions and views collected.

Delegated or group styles

(G1*The manager acts as non-directive counsellor to individual subordinates getting them to work out a solution to a problem which is personal to them).

G11. The manager shares problems with subordinates in a group, giving them formal permission to develop alternatives and hopefully reach consensus on what is to be done. Using G11 the manager may or may not take on the role of Chairperson at the meeting or meetings of the group but makes it clear that he or she will accept and implement any decision or solution that has the support of the whole group.

C11. The C11 strategy could involve many of the same words as the C1 but the words would of course be addressed to a meeting of the group. The whole group would have to share their views and the views be heard in public by us before we make up our minds.

G11. In G11 you would then define the importance you give a problem and its resolution. Exactly how the group responds to the criticism, and respond it must, is not something you are going to tell them. However, if the group does come up with a legitimate, possible and agreed strategy to reduce future management mistakes, you will abide by and implement the recommendations. How much further you 'assist' in the groups decision-making process depends very much on individual styles.

Managers who are perceived as democratic may well be able to sit in for the group discussions and attempt to push their own points of view on a 'one person one vote' basis. Most managers will not be able to do this and would find that they always possessed at least 1.5 votes at the meeting. In G11 style most of us would be advised to say something like: 'I must say again that I will abide by the decision and I'm going to leave you to it. Let me know when you have decided.' The serious mistake for any manager is to indicate a G11 and then not accept the G11 recommendations of the group. A group is often flattered by being allowed a G11 process and can be helped by the process to form a team. However, a team will hit back if the manager 'betrays' it by reverting to control, i.e., A or C styles.

Often we take the gut response to decision making without checking logically whether we have a choice and whether our gut reaction is the best way. The key to effective management is clarity – if you are in A1, NEVER give the idea that you are consulting. If you are in C11, indicate that you are consulting and do not give the impression of G11. If C1/C11 or G11 does not work or cannot be completed in time and you have to move to A1/A11, explain carefully beforehand. A move from A1/A11 to G11 is virtually impossible.

Each decision-making style has short-, medium- and long-term consequences. Thus the authoritarian style might, for our example, get the job done but it is hardly a tool of constructive communication. The consultative styles still retain authority but will assist a group towards team development. The group style may well assist a feeling of team, but may not give the 'appointed' leader the control he or she needs.

The point we are making is that we all possess flexibility in our decision-making style and that pausing to look at the consequences of our choice is worth while. The Appendix contains a number of case studies for discussion (see pp. 635–7). In all the case studies certain issues have recurred in defining the situation surrounding the choice of management decision-making styles.

Factors in situational leadership

Vroom and Yetton found that the choice of decision-making style depends on a number of factors. In making each decision we have to ask ourselves a number of questions (see Table 8.8).

Vroom and Yetton prepared an algorithm (Woods, 1989) whereby the style of decision making could be arrived at automatically by asking the questions in sequence. G11 is always difficult with large groups and the accepted wisdom is that G11 without help, does not work when more than seven are involved. However, 'with help' much larger numbers can be involved.

> Lada Cars – an importer of cars from the Eastern Bloc – asked us to run a G11 meeting for all middle managers. The venue of the meeting was chosen at an isolated hotel over a weekend and the meeting started with the managing director giving very stark news of the balance sheet. In the last year the company had lost half its business and was in serious trouble. A survival plan was needed. The MD then announced that he was leaving and would return on Sunday afternoon to endorse the plan developed by the group of his managers, and he left. We ran a brainstorming session for ideas and, at 200, we stopped and separated the ideas into the company functions – marketing, manufacture, distribution, accounts, etc. At the hour, on the hour, each of the groups reported to plenary and went away again to refine their ideas. When the MD returned the managers had come up with a

Table 8.8 Questions for decision makers

A. **The quality of the decision.** Do we have to get someone else's approval? Is the decision to be audited by some external authority or is the demand that we make a decision, any decision, almost regardless of its nature, and that decision will be upheld? Examples of decisions with a quality requirement would involve time, money, resources, legal implications and less easily defined factors concerned with image, precedent and correctness.

B. **Information.** Do you, as the decision maker, have enough data or expertise to decide unaided?

C. **Logical structure.** Do you, as the manager, either by experience or analysis, understand what needs to be done and what data need to be collected for a high-quality decision? Do you know how to collect the alternatives and the rules that govern their selection?

D. **Acceptance.** Do we, as the decision makers, need the commitment of others to get the decision implemented? Do others care strongly enough about the result of the decision to block or sabotage certain courses of action if they do not agree? Would monitoring of certain decisions be a problem?

   The issue occurs where others have to execute the decision using initiative, judgement, supervision is minimal and overt or covert resistance could block effective implementation.

E. **Power.** Do we have the power or the inclination to use power to enforce the decision? Power is like potential energy – power used is power lost. If you have to use raw power regularly then your power will soon become exhausted.

F. **Shared goals.** Do your subordinates share the same goals as you, the decision maker? Are their objectives, as your objectives, thinking of the organisation or group as a whole, the same as those who are affected by the decision?

G. **Conflict within the group.** Even with shared goals, certain potential solutions may be liable to cause conflict within the group.

H. **Time.** Time limits push us towards more authoritarian styles.

drastic reorganisation, well beyond the scope of anything he could have suggested without consent.

New models of management

Overall the new models of management are a challenge to the classical approaches of management put forward by Taylor, the Galbraiths, Fayol and Weber from the late nineteenth and early twentieth century and often unquestioned to the very recent past. (Burnes, 1992). The responses call for a new form of management and leadership. The issue we have to face is the role of the middle manager, or, as he or she often is now, the co-ordinator of a group moving towards the perceived ideal of a self-directed team. With the concepts of the self-directed team comes the word with almost magical significance – empowerment.

Stages of empowerment

Leadership in the new organisations has been saddled with a whole range of accepted wisdom linked with words such as 'total empowerment' and the 'self-directed team'. In our opinion both 'total empowerment' and the 'self-directed team' (Woods, 1997b) are Holy Grails whose attainment could well be a false objective.

> 'You are now empowered to make grommets.'
> 'I don't want to make grommets, I want to make dreams.'
> *'You are fired!'*

'You are fired!' has been heard many times in so called 'empowered' organisations. We have even heard:

> 'I keep telling them they are empowered, but they don't listen.'

Repeating what we have already discussed in our chapter on empowerment and motivation, we see empowerment in much less idealistic terms. Charles Handy would see personal empowerment as being allowed to understand WHY a job has to be done, agreeing WHAT has to be done but being allowed to develop the HOWs for oneself – with understanding and agreement by one's manager. We would say:

> *Empowerment is working within a set of rules to achieve an agreed objective.*

However, even in these simplistic and practical terms, the whole concept of empowerment brings stresses to managers – it's not the job that many managers signed up for.

Stages of organisational development towards total empowerment

Many of the attempts to move towards an empowered workforce flounder because they require too much of both organisations and existing managers. They are a 'bridge too far'. Table 8.9 illustrates the stages of maturity of organisations (Woods, 1997b).

Organisations are not homogeneous: some areas may be fully empowered while others may retain completely hierarchical control. Very often there is a hierarchical split of empowerment – thus the top team may well be fully empowered, as indeed may parts of the shop floor, whereas those at a sticky level of first line supervision may see themselves as at the beginning of the dialogue stage of development.

The stage of development is entirely situational. There is no universally desired level and, if there were, this would certainly NOT be the level of universal involvement or empowerment.

ND Marsden, a Japanese subsidiary making precision cooling equipment for the motor industry based in West Yorkshire, is proud of its advanced industrial relations. On our scale it is at the dialogue stage of development – in our opinion, entirely appropriate for the industry in which it thrives.

Table 8.9 Stages of organisational maturity

Stage	Organisational behaviour	Maintenance leadership behaviour	Progressive leadership behaviour
1. Awareness of the need to change	Military style culture. Training for tasks. Teams based on function, skill or 'task forces'	Top down. Procedures and manuals. A1 and A11 expected	Employee surveys. 'Tea and toilets' staff committees. Staff newsletters
2. Basic involvement	'Tea and toilets' staff committees. Staff newsletters – notice boards. 'Need to know' basis	Formal feedback on suggestions. Upward questioning allowed. C1 styles accepted	Active use of consultative committees – top team involvement
3. Established dialogue	Time for consultation – changes publicised. Customer relationship training. Consultants. Quality Circles WITHIN the hierarchy are tested. Formally analysed data – 'bench-marking' – available	Control of pace and direction of change. Appraisal systems involve real feedback. A1, A11, C1 accepted and C11 beginning	TQM discussions. Cross-departmental discussions. Departmental managers encouraged to consult
4. Participation	Matrix management in some areas. Team training starts. Information available to representatives on demand	Team working encouraged, and reassessment of managers' roles. G11 is accepted in very restricted areas	Decisions are delegated with responsibility as appropriate
5. Consultation	The teams are allowed to function with reduced supervision. The atmosphere is one of listening and hearing. Company information available on request	The symphony conductor model (see later) adopted. Setting up BPR systems. Everything and everyone is open to question. Management decision making is entirely situational	Development of open structures and a learning organisation (Senge, 1991) approach
6. Involvement or total empowerment	Self-Directed teams are the norm in the organisation. The encouragement of the learning organisation where everyone is expected and facilitated to develop his or her own skills to an appropriate level. On demand training	The football manager (see later) approach is encouraged where teams and individuals are empowered to manage their own chaos. The managers and leaders establish direction and monitor progress, arbitrate between teams and the organisation, maintain resources and provide an atmosphere of learning	Maintain the vision

Progression or regression of an organisation in the stages of development is an exercise in change management and must come from the top. In the opinion of the author **attempting to move more that one step at a time** is a delicate and often unwise exercise in change management. This is why we see impatience to reach a perceived ideal of total empowerment as being 'a bridge too far'.

A simple procedure for all management

Whatever stage of development is required, managers and leaders need to follow the same routine as discussed by Hersey and Blanchard (1969). Management is about the efficient deployment of resources, one of which is people. Managers need to define objectives, plan and then move into the soft world of people management:

- **Tell** people why things are required and **WHAT** needs doing.
- **Coach** them so that people are competent to do the job.
- **Consult** to the relevant level so that people understand what they are doing AND that they are doing it in a way that still meets your needs.
- **Delegate** given authority matched to the level of responsibility.
- **Monitor** and review what is being done – if necessary repeating the cycle of *tell, coach, consult and delegate* again.
- **Communicate** the work of the team to the 'outside'.

There is a question of balance between the **task**, the **individual** and the **team** (see Figure 8.5). The balance of task-centred activity is most intense at the beginning of any project, being added to successively by the development of the team and then the individuals. The successful manager or leader maintains the balance.

There are four dimensions of the management of people:

1. The **individual** – the more experienced and motivated he or she is, the easier it is to move to delegation.
2. The **team** – teams will move, unless prevented, to their own level of empowerment.
3. The **organisation** – overall the balance of managerial energy changes with the stage of development towards empowerment of the organisation.
4. The **manager** – the balance of control and empowerment of teams and individuals for which one has responsibility will be changed. The way in which the balance may change may well not satisfy the manager. Thus a manager brought up and comfortable in a command and control organisation where telling and monitoring are the human resource management demands of the job, may well be totally unsuited for more empowered organisations where delegation and communication may be the key elements.

We have attempted to summarise how the balance of energy between the various human resource elements of a manager's job relates to the stage of development of the organisation in Figure 8.12.

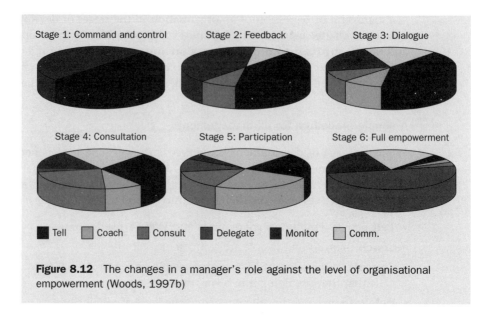

| Tell | Coach | Consult | Delegate | Monitor | Comm. |

Figure 8.12 The changes in a manager's role against the level of organisational empowerment (Woods, 1997b)

Looking at the balance and the way it changes, it is easy to see the pressures on managers when organisations decide to 'empower their staff'.

Stage 1 The command and control organisations where leadership is largely devoted to telling and monitoring.

Stage 2 Where suggestion schemes have begun – telling and monitoring predominate but consulting and communication are becoming important.

Stage 3 Where meaningful dialogue is allowed and coaching and consulting become significant, although telling and monitoring are still strong.

Stage 4 Active participation where consultation in the decision-making process is beginning to be encouraged and delegation without responsibility is also beginning.

Stage 5 True consultation where coaching and communication have become most important and telling and monitoring are falling against rise in delegation – the cross-functional teams have their own controls.

Stage 6 Involvement where the self-directed teams, that are now the norm of the organisation, are left to manage their own chaos and management is largely about monitoring and communicating.

Problems from the top

Question: What are the three most import factors in managing a change in an organisation?

Answer: 1. Top management commitment
       2. Top management commitment
       3. Top management commitment

However, a movement towards a fully empowered organisation means progressive loss of power for the top team, and it would be unusual for all the top team to enjoy this loss of power.

> A company whose chief executive was driving the organisation towards total empowerment found that, 18 months along the journey, the Board was still split. Conceptually there was full endorsement by everyone but two directors remained with a lack of commitment on a personal level. This lack of commitment was repeatedly demonstrated as they continued to exercise their 'right' not to follow the rules that had been negotiated with all the staff (in G11). The staff, initially suspicious of the move to empowerment were now enthusiastic but the confused messages from the Board were putting the company itself in danger, until some key resignations were accepted!
>
> *A chicken may well be involved in supplying the eggs in a plate of eggs and bacon, but the pig is actually committed.*
>
> Attributed to Martina Navratilova – tennis star.

A second factor may well come from the chief executive, or at least a senior member of the top team. Driving through an organisational development requires real leadership and often a very directive style of decision making. Here lies the paradox – we call it the Claudius Paradox (Woods, 1997b). The objective of establishing Rome as a republic was *second* on Emperor Claudius's list of priorities throughout his reign, which ended when his wife poisoned him. The first priorities, jostling for pole position, were always more urgent. So it is with many managers who sincerely believe in change but also value their own survival in the present.

Managing chaos: a theory of empowerment

Imagine a scene from the daily life or your most junior and most inexperienced worker.

> Every working day he or she has to get up, prepare for work and get there. The cycle is accepted and assumed, unless the worker arrives late or is incapable of work for some reason. He or she is *delegated* the task of getting into work and allowed to manage his or her own chaos – the milk not arriving, the cat being sick, children unwilling to go to school, the car failing to start. . . . He or she is delegated – with the associated authority and responsibility – to manage this individual chaos because it would be ridiculous to do otherwise.

We are arguing that at some level it is obvious that individuals and teams **must** be left to organise their own chaos, and that the level that it is beneficial to do so is related to the stage of empowerment of the organisation or the sub-organisation being considered. We would refer the reader to the chapter on empowerment and the work surrounding the Hawthorne experiment.

The duties of the manager or leader of these new teams are, first, to decide on the 'rules' that the teams need to follow to fit into the stage of maturity of the organisation.

Self-directed teams

These can be formed at any stage of organisational maturity but the cage within which they operate will be different. The cage will be defined by the clarity of the task definition and the reporting period. Thus a self-directed team in a command and control organisation will have a firm objective and reporting procedures, a clear start and end date. For this reason alone self-directed teams in command and control organisations are given names such as 'ephemeral teams', 'project groups', 'task forces', etc. They are necessary, but not always found, in all organisations in recognition that the chaos of the new and unexpected is best dealt with by well-briefed, motivated and trained people on the ground. The two military examples (Hauptmann Geyer and Major Howard) were quoted previously.

Quality circles would be a more contemporary commercial example. As an organisation matures, the 'rules' can be relaxed because people can be trusted more and people are in sympathy with and understand more of the environment within which they operate.

The further strategic task is to determine the size and position for groups or teams to best handle their own chaos within their own circle of concern. Thus, for instance, in a hospital the teams may be best arranged in what remained as hierarchical levels. Often the decision was in fact a confirmation of what was known already – thus nurse teams had always IN PRACTICE organised the chaos on the ward level, the consultants at the next level, and the politicos of administration worked in their own way at the next level. In manufacturing the choice may still be in hierarchical levels but preferably at a level of responsibility and distinguished by their customer base. These are the customer-focused teams.

The manager/leader has three tasks once the self-directed team has been established:

1. *Focusing and maintaining focus for the team.* In order to allow any form of self-direction in teams the manager has to know his or her vision and transmit it in suitable form to the teams. Without this clarity and understanding of the goal and vision, the new teams cannot function independently within their circle of concern. This vision of purpose must be maintained. As Covey says: *Understand and then communicate that understanding.*

2. *Resourcing the team.* The team is essentially getting on with the task and must not be diverted to forage for supplies – be they people or materials.

3. *Maintaining the team within the total environment.* The manager or leader is responsible as spokesperson between teams and towards the organisation as a whole. The manager or leader is also responsible for fitting the team into the 'big picture'.

Monitoring results, focusing, resourcing and maintenance are the jobs for a new person – the facilitator manager for the vision and focus, the resource manager and the practical manager, all bound up in one person. This is not an easy task for the manager who values the role of controller.

New management and leadership models

The military role and control organisation saw its managers as officers in a chain of command. In the new organisations we need new models and we find two models are appropriate:

- The football manager
- The symphony orchestra conductor.

The football manager may, for very special reasons, act in a dual role of player/manager, but more normally he or she is not allowed on the pitch once the whistle has blown. All the work has to be done BEFORE the players go on the pitch and once the game has begun even slight interference can be penalised by the referee. He or she has levels of responsibility for wider 'teams', including all the support staff and the Board.

The football manager would seem to have three roles:

- Determining the tactics that meet the strategy of the Board.
- Making sure that the team have the tools to perform.
- Support and liaison with the outside world – the fans, the press, the Board, etc.

The symphony orchestra conductor has a similar function *but* is actually 'on the pitch' and remains in control. The conductor model is more comfortable for many organisations.

A manager who has grown up in a military style, command and control organisation will require a great deal of relearning before it is possible to think of his or her job in these three roles. Sometimes that type of relearning may well be seen to be impossible.

Managers and leaders

Field Marshall Bill Slim is quoted by Colin Sharman (1997) when he distinguished between managers and leaders in 1970. As a great military leader who became Governor General of Australia, he is likely to have met both.

> The leader and those who follow him represent one of the oldest and most effective of human relationships . . . Leadership is of the spirit, compounded of personality and vision; its practice is an art. Management is of the mind, more a matter of accounts calculation, of statistics, of methods, timetables and routine: its practice is a science. Managers are necessary, leaders are essential. A good system will produce efficient managers, but more than that is needed. We must find managers who are not only skilled organisers, but are also inspired and inspiring leaders.

This is the origin of what we call the *leager* – a strange hybrid between a manager and a leader, able to function as either when appropriate. However, before we get to that point we need to look at how others have distinguished the two roles.

Managers and leaders are often seen as quite distinct beings:

- Leaders chose the road for managers to drive on.
- Managers get people to do things – leaders get people to do the right things.
- Managers get people to do things – leaders get people to want to do them.
- Managers get people to do the same better – leaders get people to do better things.

A more sophisticated view is that leadership and management are on a continuum of thought. Think like a leader and you are on the way to becoming a leader. Think like a manager, and you are a manager.

- Managers think in terms of danger, strategy, rivals, authority, standardisation, policy, management by objectives, control, consistency, stability, reorganisation, systems, logic, hierarchy, scepticism, science, duty, performance, dependence, conserving.
- Leaders think in terms of opportunity, culture, partnership, customers, influence, unity, example, management by walking about, example, empowerment, commitment, crisis, rethinking, insight, proactivity, lateral thinking, equality, optimism, art, dreams, potential. To the leader these are not 'management speak' but realities, at least for a moment in time.

This leads us to certain generalities about leaders and leadership.

- **Leaders are dangerous.** The Captain Kirk's of Star Fleets rule but the Mr Spocks pick up the pieces. However, most of us are capable of thinking as leaders *and* managers when the situation calls. We may, for instance, be leaders of our team and managers for our top team – it's a safer way of working!
- **Leadership is situationally dependent.** J.M. Barrie in his play *The Admirable Crichton*, describes how a butler and his upper-class family are castaways on a desert island. Here he has the necessary aptitudes and skills to make him the natural leader. After rescue he returns to the subservient role of butler. A factual example in British twentieth-century history would be the cases of Chamberlain and Churchill. Both were leaders for their own day and not for any other. Leadership can demonstrate itself at any level of an organisation and is not in any way related to formally recognised hierarchical position.
- **Leaders need followers.** Your leadership style, at the right time and place, is a very personal affair, but in all cases is a culmination of previous circumstances. Leadership is above all about human resource skills, skills that may be developed by watching those you admire and modelling their behaviour. All of this means, as Charles Handy (1997) points out, that leaders must be given the time and space to prove themselves – 'leaders are grown and not made'.

The currency of transactional leadership

Perhaps the most contentious issue in military organisations is the way potential leaders are **made** to think as managers by the control of patronage and of credibil-

---

Table 8.10   The currencies of transactional leaders

There are four currencies for the manager wishing to work as a transactional leader:

- **Economic** – buying service by providing goods or money.
- **Political** – protection or patronage.
- **Psychological** – a shoulder to cry on.
- **Customised empowerment** – rewarding desired behaviour with gaining empowerment.

---

ity. These two factors are outside the control of the individual. In a strictly command and control organisation very few managers are able to hire, fire or materially reward their own staff. Patronage is limited to participation in the appraisal system and the occasional award of medals. Credibility exists in such organisations by the security of status. If I do not 'get on with my boss' I will be seen to be unable to support my subordinates.

The four currencies available for the transactional leader

Table 8.10 summarises the four processes – we term them currencies – by which managers acting in the transactional mode achieve power and status with their 'followers'.

Economic   Physical rewards are often difficult for an individual manager hoping to lead and develop followers. The use of economic currency may be quite subtle – the 'blind eye' to expenses, the conference, redistribution of workload to enable overtime, various allowances. They are ways of 'buying' loyalty, however hidden.

Political   Political patronage relies on the individual 'belonging to the club'. When a manager uses this currency he or she makes an implicit or explicit contract with a follower of support. The non-verbal 'hand on the shoulder' in public or immediate access to hierarchical superiors for problem solving, often grants it. Patronage is an acceptance of a hierarchy and may easily be withdrawn should one fail to meet the requirements of the 'club'.

> In January 1994 Tim Yeo resigned as a Minister in the UK Conservative government of the time. As a politician a Minister needs to be able to lead. Yeo was Environment Minister in a political party concerned with what amounted to a crusade for 'family values'. He was unfortunate enough to have been widely publicised for having an illegitimate child. The reality of the child and its unmarried mother did not make him resign – he was finally forced to resign from office, in our opinion, because his patronage base, the constituency that elected him, withdrew support.

Psychological   Time has a high currency for the transactional manager. Giving time and concern develops 'followers'. Following the models proposed in our chapter on constructive communication is a very good start to 'banking' psychological currency.

Customised empowerment The concept is that many people work for 'space'. We suggest that the rules governing any job conform to a FRAME – a concept we discussed in the chapter on motivation. On this basis we can define empowerment as working within rules without the concept of obedience. The transaction is about allowing more scope for the individual as a reward for 'followship'.

Without being empowered ourselves we are relegated to the role of a manager. Transactions, honoured by both parties, are the currency of the transactional leader. Obligations make the world go round for the transactional leader. Your ability to function as a transactional leader depends on:

- your ability to promise and to deliver – promising to deliver and failing will reduce your personal power base
- your own status and 'membership of the club', which can be removed at any time
- your own empowerment
- your personal and interpersonal skills.

You have to be 'allowed' by others to honour your obligations.

Transformational leadership

Andrew Korac-Kakabadse and Nada Korac-Kakabadse (1997), in their recent review of Best Practice in the Australian Public Service, bring together many of the arguments we have covered. They also distinguish between transactional and transformational leaders – a distinction that has attracted considerable debate. The emerging argument holds that 'most leaders are good managers, but good managers are not necessarily good leaders' (Warburton, 1993). The world beyond the 1990s will not belong to managers, but to passionate, driven leaders who are innovative path-finders able to empower others to lead (Fairholm, 1991; Leavett, 1987; Manz and Sims, 1990; Warburton, 1993). They continue to argue that managers use transactions to maintain the balance of operations and are process- or means-oriented (Burns, 1978) – what Warburton (1993) calls 'caretakers of the status quo' and Bennis (1984) thinks of as 'replicability with a focus on control and accountability'. In contrast, transformational leaders – according to Bennis (1984), Bennis and Nanus (1985), Burns (1978), Peters and Waterman (1982) and Zaleznik (1977) – are creatively devoted to ends and not means. They think globally and seek to break moulds to create and achieve their visions (Bradford and Cohen, 1984; Henry, 1991; McAller, 1991; Selznick, 1957). Summarising, we may say that transformational leaders provide a new sense of direction. **They are change agents.**

The 'pure' manager with no pretensions of leadership is one end of the spectrum and the 'pure' transformational leader is the other. The transactional leader encroaches on both their territories. They provide vision, mobilise commitment, model and institutionalise the change they facilitate.

Providing a vision

The transformational leader, driving with personal charisma or bringing others with him or her by inspirational means has clarity of purpose that can be called vision.

- Questioning of the status quo
- A discussion of alternatives
- A presentation of an ideal.

Mobilising commitment

- Changing personal objectives into group objectives – 'all for one and one for all'
- Stimulation, drive and emotional appeal.

Modelling

- Bringing in example, symbolism and meaning with the message
- The consistency that inspires trust.

Institutionalising change

- Making the new into the norm
- Becoming the subject of legend.

The role of the Court Jester

Transformational leadership in organisations is always controversial. Unlike the transactional leader, who can be turned on or off by the patronage he or she gets from those around, and in particular 'management', the transformational leader has vision. The wrong vision for the time and place, or the right vision for too long, is dangerous for the survival of the organisation. An example would be Margaret Thatcher whose vision (in the opinion of one author) transformed a society but then became stale and dangerous. Leaders need to be able to listen to their followers and two classes of followers in particular: the Vizier and the Court Jester.

The Vizier is the loyal and able administrator who refines the vision to practical terms. Dreams cost money, detractors usually accompany followers, things take time. It is the job of the Vizier to provide substance to the vision.

The Court Jester has a quite different function. He or she, in a position without authority, tells the truth in a way that the transformational leader can hear, and process.

> Margaret Thatcher appears not to have had a Court Jester or, if she had, she did not listen. The issue was Poll Tax – a system where all citizens were taxed equally, regardless of wealth or status. For good or bad the opposition to the Tax had become united and deafening. Court Jesters, while accepting the vision of their

leaders, need to 'hear' the noise and inform their chiefs in an unchallenging way, when the noise becomes patterned (Dixon, 1994). Then the great leader changes course. Margaret did not change course and was deposed.

Churchill had a great Vizier and Court Jester rolled into one man – Auchinleck. One of Churchill's great visions was concerned with avoiding the battles of attrition that he had witnessed during the Great War. He saw the planned invasion of the French coast in 1944 as having the potential of draining so much life and asked Auchinleck to devise another plan – an invasion of Hitler's Europe through Portugal. The Auk, as he was known, did not cross the great man, which he knew would have made him more adamant and cause his own dismissal. What he did was prepare the plan in such a way as to emphasise 'impracticability' and also present a 'bill' for how much work had been involved and how working on it had damaged the grand plan for the invasion of Normandy. Churchill, a great leader, thanked the Auk and forgot the plan to invade in the South.

Really great transformational leaders:

- are in the right place at the right time
- have the strength to cultivate empowered supporters
- have the ability to stick to the vision but the flexibility to move.

All leaders need to balance:

- the needs of the task, individuals and the team
- his or her own personal needs with that of the organisation.

Work to a strategy in which you know where you want to go – or, if you prefer, have a vision. In addition:

- Plan to achieve their objective or vision using the best information available.
- Develop the resources, including the 'followers' necessary for success.
- Set up procedures for monitoring the 'advance signs' of whether the projects are on the right or wrong course.
- Remain dedicated to the objective but retain flexibility on tactics.
- If the 'signs' begin to form a cluster – review everything. Remember that your vision is rooted in a particular set of circumstances and these may have changed.
- Take care of yourself and your followers.
- Know when to quit.

A model for leadership and the learning organisation

A significant change in the role of the new leader/manager occurs when we discuss the largest change currently considered in organisations – developing the learning organisation. In a learning organisation, contrary to the irony of Scott Adams (1996) who sees all these changes as fads designed to get more work for less money,

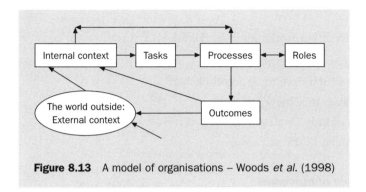

Figure 8.13 A model of organisations – Woods *et al.* (1998)

we do have a chance of facing the new world proactively. Understanding the learning organisation allows us to model management behaviour.

We will side-step the innumerable definitions of learning organisations, such as:

> Organisational learning is the process by which the organisation's knowledge and value base changes, leading to improved problem-solving ability and capacity for action. (Probst and Buchel 1997)

We will also side-step the arguments as to whether organisational learning is greater or less than the sum of the learning of groups and individuals. We are looking for a definition and a model that can be used – such niceties may only confuse. Our definition is:

> *A learning organisation has a structure and ethos that allow it and its parts – groups and individuals – to learn and adapt productively from its and others' errors and successes.*

This is the definition of an organic structure, but we see the later organisational models of Argyris and Schone (1981) as closed systems. Working models need to describe the open systems within which the new managers need to operate.

Herriot and Pemberton (1995a) proposed a further model which was modified by Woods *et al.* (1998) to provide a background to our considerations of the way we all – managers, leaders and followers – behave (Figure 8.13).

The concept behind the model is that management is about making things happen. The skills that assist us towards competencies are about making our organisations successful – however that is determined. We agree with Herriot and Pemberton in that outcomes are not merely as simple as Shea and Guzzo (1987) state:

> We believe that real world, real time group effectiveness is what matters, and it boils down to the production of designated products or the delivery of contracted services, per specification.

We see outcomes as the products, tangible or intangible, of our endeavours, functional or dysfunctional. They are what we can measure and by measuring, learn. Thus as we will see in our case study of the hospital ward, a potential risk to a member of staff is as much an outcome worthy of learning from, as a new grommet.

The model

The elements of our working model (Figure 8.13) are:

- The internal and external context
- The tasks which have to be accomplished
- The processes to achieve the tasks
- The roles of individuals and groups within these processes
- The outcomes of the processes

The principle of outcomes

The processes alone can produce **measurable** outcomes. Although other workers see **roles** and **tasks** as producing **outcomes**, we argue that this is not so. A 'role' is an abstract entity and a 'task' is merely a wish until performed – these are starting points. Thus, for instance, Belbin (1981) sees nine roles in his ideal team. We can describe one of his roles as a **Shaper** – the ideal 'tough' manager – but without the shaper in a 'context' and with a 'task' he or she does nothing. The word 'shaper' is at best a descriptor of 'how' a particular person might go about the process of a given task in a team context. Understanding the role tells us nothing about the only thing we can measure – the outcome of the task itself.

So it is with tasks. Tasks have to be performed – in our language, become **processes**, before they can produce measurable outcomes. It is outcomes alone that can be monitored and learnt from. Our model thus differs profoundly from that of Herriot and Pemberton who saw outcomes arising from the context, the tasks and the roles, in addition to the processes.

External and internal context

The **external context** is outside the immediate control of the organisation, and is the gate to the **total** environment – the world. We assume that no individual or organisation is a free agent – the external context defines the cage within which we exist and in which our behaviours are shaped. The external context comprises a world of competitors, legislators, cultures, suppliers, Unions, etc. The world is less easily defined but includes the environment.

The **internal context** is the assumptions, boundaries, tethering factors, stated or otherwise that act as our starting point for structuring the work of an organisation. They are the items we learnt to challenge in our chapter on effective problem solving.

From the internal context, tasks can be listed, new tasks arising from perceived changes and old or revised tasks to deal with what is known.

Tasks

Tasks are the response to the question of 'What needs to be done?' within the existing or changing internal context. Thus, if an organisation finds itself under increasing competitor pressure in its external context, this reflects directly on the internal context. Changed internal contexts may well demand a revision of the tasks required – money may well be seen to be tight and the tasks set of the individuals and teams within the organisation will be defensive. Another internal context could well produce an aggressive strategy reflected in tasks designed to produce new products and processes.

Processes

Processes are the practical response to accomplishing the tasks set through the internal context; however, they may well influence the internal context itself.

> Birds Eye in the 1970s was an extremely successful manufacturer of Frozen Foods for the UK market. Its domination of the market and the growth of the total market allowed it to expand some 20 per cent in its twenty-first year of operation. In the twenty-first year the market became mature. New product launches failed to meet the targets set. From experience of mature products, competitors became strong and the distributors grew in influence. From a 20 per cent growth, the growth was marginal one year later.

Prior to the downturn of Bird's Eye's business, tasks were related to producing and distributing quantity in what was virtually a seller's market – the processes reflected this. After the downturn, processes moved to cost efficiency and improved customer service.

Roles

The roles individuals and teams choose depend on the tasks they are asked to perform. Inversely, the roles individuals and teams are able or willing to adopt will feed directly back to the tasks.

> We were asked to advise on the reorganisation of two departments into one single department on a single site. The company, a family based concern, was struggling. Working with the teams concerned it was immediately apparent that strong leadership was required. Unfortunately the chief executive had a very inflexible consultative style and lacked the confidence to actually give firm orders.

In our model the tasks required for the company to survive involved the senior management adopting the role of a firm leadership, something of which they proved incapable. As they also refused to take on a strong manager to replace the CEO, the company had another reason to move towards complete collapse.

The dynamic of the model

We would affirm that learning and change are not events but a process. A learning organisation and its parts work within the inner circle of our model, recognising changes in its internal environment though monitoring the outcomes of its processes while observing the external context and working proactively with it

(Woods, 1998). We would doubt that the Zen Buddhist concept of moving towards Nivana by a series of deaths and rebirths, apply to the organisations of which we have experience; however, our observations lead us to be more modest in our claims. Most organisations at best survive by continuous and often painful change, a very few prosper. Managed discontinuous change, and learning by it, is often quoted as having about a 25 per cent chance of success (Rossiter, 1995). This does not mean that managed discontinuous change is by nature a 'bad thing' but that the response to change in the external context may be too late. Once again we return to the metaphor of Davy's Bar. Using the metaphor, many organisations are drinking in Davy's Bar and it is too late to go back that critical half-mile to refocus their business.

Our first point is that we need to accept change as a process that allows us the opportunity of learning, and that the skill of managing it lies in acting *before* we are pushed and *before* our options are reduced (Probst and Buchel, 1997). The time for organising for discontinuous change is when we have slack, and not when we are against the wall!

Using our model we see that learning – adaptation of an organisation or any sub-set of the organisation – can be triggered at any point.

A training organisation was 'lucky' enough to recruit a pedantic and assertive accountant. In her **role** she was able to release the 'creative' staff from routine admin-istration and get on with developing programmes that delighted their customers. The internal and the external contexts moved in a favourable way for the com-pany. When she was 'head hunted' the innovative processes had to alter and the outcomes became dysfunctional, leading to an unfocused internal context and, very soon, the external context became hostile.

Our second point is that the learning organisation does not have the limitations of the command and control organisation in that change is instigated from the top. Learning organisations learn through the actions of individuals (Walsh and Ungson, 1991).

Who, then, is responsible for the attainment of goals? EVERY member of the company is responsible. Our success depends on everyone acting responsibly. To enable all members to work responsibly and to attain their common goals together and in harmony, all those in leadership must act responsibly. This is our view of responsibility in action and in leadership (Schmidt, 1991):

• The internal context can be limited to a desk or be a view from Gaia herself.

A manager of GKN was responsible for facilitating two teams from her desk. The one team was in Wolverhampton in the industrial Midlands of the UK and the other is Westland Helicopters in Somerset. Westland Helicopters is a high technology subsidiary of GKN but Yeovil is an area based in agricultural culture. The internal contexts are totally different – difference not implying criticism. To manage the two teams requires an understanding of the internal contexts. At its crudest, an ex-farmer will do a good job in his or her good time, an ex-factory worker will do as he or she is told. Manage the two internal contexts in the same way and you will fail.

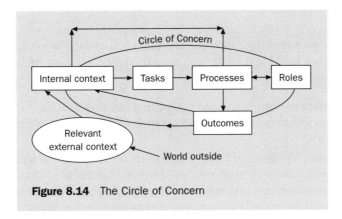

Figure 8.14   The Circle of Concern

Managing and leading within the model

What within our model is the role of the manager? We see the manager as working proactively within the Circle of Concern (see Figure 8.14). His or her job (Woods, 1997b) as a manager/leader is to:

• Convert the internal context into tasks.
• Communicate the 'what needs to be done' – the tasks – so that his or her staff can develop the processes to accomplish the tasks. Along with developing the HOW issues the manager needs to coach his or her staff so that we are not blocked by inability.
• Consult so that the HOWs meet the organisational objectives.
• Monitor the outcomes from the processes so that adjustments can be made, learn from them and, if relevant, communicate the learning and the changes to the organisation or subsets of the organisation.

Some of the outcomes will potentially develop the internal context favourably, others will be perceived as dysfunctional. We need to 'accentuate the positive and eliminate the negative' as with Kurt Lewin's process of force field analysis (1951). Looking at the roles, we see confusion. Drucker saw the role of a manager to follow the paths drawn up by the leader. No such distinction now occurs. The new manager needs to draw the path and develop processes for his or her staff to follow and understand the vision of the whole. We have therefore concocted the new role of **leager**. Leagers both lead and implement.

Richard Pascale, quoted in an AMA report (1996), states:

> Management is the exercise of authority and influence to achieve levels of performance consistent with demonstrated levels.
>
> Leadership is making happen what wouldn't happen anyway, and this is always working on the edge.

SUMMARY

The model, in its simplicity, allows individuals and groups to understand their role in a changing world and learn from the experience. We have brought forward several key concepts:

- The open nature of change and the subsequent learning process – we have presented a model that sees change and learning as a continuous process rather than an event.
- The concept of an individual Circle of Concern – within our model there are tasks, processes, roles and outcomes, all of which contribute to changing our internal context and, perhaps in a small way and maybe in a large way, affect our external environment. However, within the grand order of things, our Circle of Concern is only a subset of the whole.

  Managing effectively within our Circle of Concern involves us changing our role. The old distinction between managers and leaders, and indeed the subdivision of leadership into transactional and transformational, is no longer valid. New managers need to adopt roles primarily of visionary guide, monitor and facilitator. For this we have coined the word 'leager'.

Skill Analysis

CASE STUDY **8.1**

CHARITY MISSION STATEMENT

A charity had been established for over 100 years by a group of Methodists to provide homes for impoverished children in the northern industrial cities of the UK. A new chief executive – Joan Brown – decided to review the Mission Statement of the charity against the new world.

The old Mission Statement, found in some literature dating back over 70 years, was:

> *To provide healthy and protective homes for the homeless children of the new industrial cities and thereby lead them into the Christian fellowship.*

Her new Mission Statement was:

> *To support underprivileged parents, regardless of race, class or creed towards being able to provide a constructive life for themselves and their children.*

She now found herself in an impossible situation. The previous friendly atmosphere of the charity had vanished and people were in open and dysfunctional conflict. Work was not being done.

Discussion questions

1. What would you see as the changes that had forced a rethink of the original Mission Statement?

2. How would you expect the internal context of the team to be affected?

3. What new tasks and roles would you see the team members adopting – or indeed *not* adopting?

4. What forms of dysfunctional behaviour would you expect from the 'team'?

5. What would be the reasons for this dysfunctional behaviour?

6. What would you advise?

CASE STUDY **8.2**

HARRY GREENWAYS

Harry Greenways is a successful Leeds, West Yorkshire-based service organisation. They handle a range of services for clients ranging from arranging advertising campaigns to advising on public relations.

In 1995 the CEO – Harry Greenway, the founder and long concerned with the expansion of the organisation – was influenced to change the processes from a departmentalised system to teamworking. Using the Semler model (Semler, 1988) his new organisation consisted of a top team termed 'coaches' who were responsible for strategy and assisting the 'associates' arranged in two teams to perform the work of the organisation. A further team provided support – gardening to reception.

The new processes impacted on the roles of the associates immediately. As the Processes were based on self-directed teams, some individuals found that their role as team leader was no longer required and the consensus systems were not to their liking. After some stress, they left.

The processes led to customer-focused teams where individual responsibility to clients became collective. This was not liked by some clients and the external context of the organisation changed – clients were unhappy, reflecting on the internal context, which became more demanding. The internal context was also fundamentally altered by the 'consensus' processing of the teams. The movement of servicing teams rather than individuals was deeply resented by certain members of the organisation – as tasks altered in nature, the change in the processes became irreversible with further changes in the roles of staff and further discontent and departures.

The CEO who had implemented the change – by, it must be said, a rather authoritarian move – felt the major change in role when the changes he had imposed became organisational learning, and he moved towards a leager and not a dictator. This is the issue we have previously termed the Claudian Paradox after the Roman Emperor who always had establishing a republic as **second** on his agenda. Claudius found, as do many managers, the issues of maintaining a company pushing into number one slot ahead of their intellectual wish to empower their employees. The very people who are needed to vision and propel a change programme find it hard to delegate realistically when the changes have been learnt and implemented.

Discussion questions

1. Would you see the external context leading directly to the changes Harry Greenway decided upon for the internal context?

2. In hindsight, what could Harry have done to improve the likelihood of success for his changes?

3. Considering the duties of a manager, what could have been done to make sure that employees and customers were happy with the changes? Whose responsibility should this have been?

CASE STUDY **8.3**

THE HOSPITAL WARD

A nursing sister was accompanying the registrar on his tour round her trauma ward. At the end of the tour she attempted to explain a difficulty she was having with a patient. As she saw it, the patient was a danger to the safety of the ward and in particular the safety of her staff and the patients – her internal context.

The patient, a woman, had been admitted two days previously drunk and with a moderately serious injury from a fall. Initially passive she had become increasingly violent and threatening to her staff, the auxiliaries and other patients. The first major problem had come when a trainee nurse noticed that the patient had smuggled alcohol in her locker, and mentioned it to the patient who threw a full bedpan at her. The climax had come when the patient made a well-directed and co-ordinated attack on the team physiotherapist.

The sister wanted the patient taken to a secure unit. The registrar simply ignored the sister and went on with his review of the surgical condition of the patients. Finally the sister – in front of the final section of her ward – blocked the passage of the registrar and his party and insisted that she be heard. Her case had become slightly modified – the action of the patient was endangering the recovery of HIS patients as they recovered from surgery. The registrar took action and the problem patient was moved.

CASE STUDY **8.4**

BRUDDERSFORD

Bruddersford is an engineering company making a range of products and operating under the umbrella of a conglomerate. The whole Bruddersford company is moving into dire financial straits. Looking at the whole company, the external context had become more competitive, with unfavourable exchange rates and competitors reorganising and outsourcing. Cash flow problems and low moral dominated the internal context of the company and the response was to downsize and reduce costs. The processes for this were put in hand and unfortunately the output was further and deeper cash flow problems. The 'cash cow' of the company continued to be pressured by exchange rates and the potential star – a new product range, now starved of development cash – floundered. If the internal context continued to deteriorate for long, the bailiffs would dominate the external context.

The company was already in divisions and we decided to look at the internal context of each in turn – for the sake of this case study, the Cash Cow Division and the Potential Star Division.

The Cash Cow Division had a very small number of key industrial customers who were becoming increasingly cost conscious and demanding. Bruddersford was supplying a whole range of services to these customers, some of which had to be outsourced. Increasingly it was becoming a factoring operation with equipment idle and working at a loss when real costs were taken into account. The profits from the Potential Star Division were subsidising the operation. However, it was the foundation of Bruddersford's world and seen as its key business and provider of essential cash flow.

The Potential Star Division provided a unique product to an expanding range of industrial customers. Because of its uniqueness, price was not the main concern but staying ahead of the competition was. The Division made profits but was cash hungry. Its managers were also not in the 'Bruddersford Old Boy Network'. They were brash newcomers. The internal context of the Potential Star Division has very little in common with the Cash Cow Division.

Discussion questions

1. What would you propose?
2. What problems would you predict for your proposals?

Ancillary case studies

In subgroups consider the following three case studies: the Car Parking Problem, the R&D Laboratory reorganisation and the Production Manager's Problem. The objective is NOT to make the decision but to decide which of the Vroom and Yetton 'styles' is most fitted to solve the problem. Use Tables 8.8 and 8.9 to decide your views.

Share your individual views and reach a consensus decision. While you come to a consensus consider the criteria you and your colleagues have used in the discussion.

CASE STUDY **8.5**

THE CAR PARKING PROBLEM

You are the new manager entrusted with setting up a small office with five subordinates – all of whom are of equal status. (Various ancillary workers supply functions such as cleaning, but these are not the concern of the exercise.)

The office has been created out of two terraced houses backing onto a small cobbled street with jobbing garages and similar small businesses using the access. There are two obvious parking spaces in front of the houses and a Public Car Park is readily accessible at about 400 metres with standard charges. All your staff have cars and use them to get to work. They are all recognised users of cars and claim normal company mileage rates.

You need to arrange for car parking at the office.

CASE STUDY **8.6**

THE R&D LABORATORY REORGANISATION

You are head of a R&D laboratory in the basic research department of a multinational. The programme of research in the laboratories has been arranged by your predecessor to all aspects of research – from 'blue skies' to service work. In your view the 'blue skies' work has evolved so that its commercial exploitation within the capability of the company is highly unlikely.

The skills of the 'blue skies' team are likely to be exactly what the company needs for some scientifically boring but commercially exciting projects that are appearing from the service work. The 'pure' research team are coherent and have a high morale. Their work is highly respected in the academic community and you are concerned that to get them to change goals to a less 'interesting' area, as indeed you must, will affect both their morale and their productivity.

The operating division requiring a shift in resources needs your laboratory's commitment within two weeks. The team could work on 'blue skies' projects as well as the strictly applied work but the effort of all of the team, even if only on a part-time basis, is necessary for success, so total commitment is necessary from all members of the team. The choice of the actual 'pure' research projects still to be pursued in the new environment is also completely open and you do not have the expert skills to decide the priorities.

Get it settled.

CASE STUDY **8.7**

THE PRODUCTION MANAGER'S PROBLEM

You are the production manager of an electronics company. An investment programme has not succeeded in reducing costs – quality has fallen and key workers continue to leave. To the limit of your knowledge in the industry as it is now, the systems you have installed are not defective but you do suspect that the working procedures that the robotics equipment has demanded, are not ideal. This view is not shared by your immediate subordinates, or indeed by the shop floor. Training and the confusion on bonus payments has led to poor morale and, hence, avoidable mistakes.

The situation has now come to a head and your divisional director is asking for a response by 12.00 to the quantifiable loss in productivity in the last six months. The director has confidence in you and will accept your views.

He needs concrete plans from your division to present to his Board meeting at 13.30.

The case studies are discussed in Appendix 1.

Skill Application

EXERCISE **8.1**

SUGGESTED FURTHER ASSIGNMENTS

1. List all the teams with which you are currently involved – home, leisure, work, college, etc. Classify these teams in terms of satisfying your human needs for inclusion, control and affection. Is the balance satisfactory? Is any imbalance likely to give you conflict? What can you do to avoid potential imbalance?

2. What is the stage of development of each of the teams? How do you recognise this? Is this stage of development appropriate?

3. List the managers and leaders that you respect in your world. What features do they have in common? How could you model your behaviour on these?

EXERCISE **8.2**

APPLICATION PLAN

Refer back to the 360° Feedback Questionnaire at the beginning of the chapter. The objective is to make you more effective in your chosen path. Taking not more than three items:

- What new or improved behaviours do you wish to adopt?
- What specifically do you need to do to take on these new or revised behaviours?
- What specific results would you expect from these changes in behaviour?
- How would you monitor these changes? (Remember the 'small wins' strategy.)
- With whom would it be useful to share your plans?
- Do you need additional support?
- What would be the adverse consequences of your behavioural change?
- If you still intend to go ahead – how do you celebrate success?

Further reading

Adair, J. and Thomas, N. (1998) *The John Adair handbook of management and leadership.* London: Thorogood.

Belbin, R.M. (1996) *Team roles at work.* Oxford: Butterworth-Heinemann.

Bennis, W.G. (1998) *On becoming a leader.* London: Arrow.

Hardingham, A. (1995) *Working in teams.* London: Institute of Personnel & Development.

Katzenbach, J.R. and Smith, D.K. (1994) *The wisdom of teams: creating the high performance organization.* Boston: Harvard Business School Press.

Kelly, G. (1998) *Team leadership.* Aldershot: Gower.

Wright, P. (1996) *Managerial leadership.* London: Routledge.

PART 4

Specific Communication Skills

SUPPLEMENT A
Conducting Meetings

- Planning
- Conducting
- Participating

SUPPLEMENT B
Making Oral Presentations

- Formulating strategy and structure
- Utilising an enhancing style
- Answering questions and challenges

SUPPLEMENT C
Interviewing

- Conducting general interviews
- Conducting specific purpose interviews

Conducting Meetings

SKILL DEVELOPMENT OUTLINE

Skill Learning material

- Principles for managing meetings
- The four P's – steps in planning and conducting meetings
- Suggestions for group members
- Summary and behavioural guidelines

Skill Practice exercises

- Staff meeting at Thames Pump and Value
- Conducting a task force meeting
- Jim Lewis
- Group dynamics evaluation

LEARNING OBJECTIVES

To increase proficiency in

- conducting effective meetings
- participating effectively in meetings

Skill Learning

Principles for managing meetings

Few aspects of management have been criticised more than the group meeting. Managers complain that they are frequently forced to sit through boring presentations, waste time discussing a decision the boss should have made alone, or interrupt important tasks to attend a meeting, the purpose of which is ill-defined and the duration of which seems interminable. Committee meetings and their decisions have become the focus of office jokes.

It is unfortunate that this management tool has been so broadly maligned. Properly managed group meetings can improve the quality of decision making and increase the efficient use of a manager's time. Managers generally agree that the problem is not so much committees in management as it is the management of committees.

The purpose of this supplement is to look at common pitfalls in poorly managed groups and discuss techniques for avoiding them. We will focus specifically on the effective management of group meetings rather than on the effective supervision of ongoing work groups. The basic skills required to manage work teams – delegation, motivation, supportive communication and conflict management – have been discussed earlier. Although these specific techniques were generally targeted at one-to-one interactions, they also provide the general skill base required for effectively managing ongoing work groups.

When we speak of group decision making in this supplement, we are referring not to decisions made in a group, but to decisions made by a group. Similarly, the terms 'group process', 'group structure' and 'group leader' refer to the process, structure and leadership of a specific group meeting. The material in this chapter is relevant to almost any type of meeting, whether it's called to inform participants, to obtain their opinions, or to solve a problem. We will assume that the participants have an ongoing working relationship, that they understand the purpose of the meeting, and that the meeting has been called by someone who will have presiding authority.

This type of task-related group meeting occupies a large portion of the typical manager's work week. A recent study showed that the number of meetings and conferences in industry had nearly doubled during the previous decade and that their cost had nearly tripled. Some sources suggest that most businesses spend 7 to 15 per cent of their personnel budgets on meetings. This is easy to believe when one realises that a one-hour meeting with eight members whose salaries average £30,000 is costing the organisation approximately £250. Additionally, research shows that the amount of time an individual manager spends in meetings increases with that manager's organisational level. Middle-level managers may spend as much as 30 per cent of their time in meetings, while top management spends closer to 50 per cent (Seibold, 1979). In light of the increasing costs of meetings as the salaries of participants rise, these figures are quite significant. They underscore the importance of good meeting-management skills. Since managers spend so much time in meetings, their success is to a large extent determined by how effectively those meetings are managed. While ineffective stress- or time-management skills impede the productivity of a single manager, and inadequate delegation skills create frustration for three or four subordinates, poor meeting-management skills affect the performance of everyone in attendance. As one frustrated senior executive grumbled, 'To waste your own time is unfortunate, but to waste the time of others is unforgivable.'

To avoid this outcome, managers should follow the 4 P's – the four steps for managing an effective meeting – shown in Figure A.1. These are sequential steps in the planning and implementation of a meeting. Obviously, the quality of planning influences the effectiveness of implementation.

1. Specify the purpose of the meeting. The manager's objectives 'drive' the rest of the model.

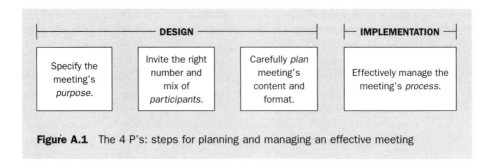

Figure A.1   The 4 P's: steps for planning and managing an effective meeting

2. Invite the right number and mix of participants. Based on the purpose, invite individuals with the appropriate knowledge and orientation.

3. Carefully plan the meeting's content and format. The meeting agenda should reflect the purpose of the meeting and the participants who will attend.

4. Effectively manage the process of the meeting. The quality of the group dynamics to a large extent reflects the quality of the meeting's design. However, the meeting chair needs to be prepared to handle unforeseen problems in group dynamics that may emerge as the meeting progresses.

Guidelines for implementing these four components of the planning and implementation process will be given in the following sections.

The 4 P's – steps in planning and conducting meetings

Step 1   Purpose

Before announcing a meeting, managers should ask themselves two questions:

- 'What is my communication, or decision-making, objective?'
- 'Is a meeting the most appropriate means for accomplishing this purpose?'

A meeting can be invaluable when its purpose is clear and its need legitimate, but it can also be a hindrance to a productive work environment if it is held at inappropriate times or for inappropriate reasons. 3M's Audio Visual Division cites three legitimate reasons for a manager to convene a group meeting:

1. To discuss complex problems that require extensive information-sharing.

2. To build commitment among group members.

3. To disseminate information and conduct training.

It also gives five reasons for *not* calling a meeting:

1. When the information could be conveyed in a phone call or in a memo.

2. When you are not prepared.

3. When all of the key people cannot attend.

4. When the cost of the meeting is out of proportion to what it will accomplish.

5. When there is no advantage to holding the meeting, even if it is regularly scheduled.

1. Discussing complex issues

Often, a group leader cannot make an effective decision about an important issue or define and solve a problem without consulting or meeting others. In Chapter 2, we indicated that a manager who lacks the expertise or data to make a well-informed decision should identify who has the necessary information and how it can best be obtained. If the information required is factual (e.g., last year's budget for project X), a phone call or memo is better than a meeting. However, if the manager is not sure who has the information, or if several people have bits and pieces of the data, a meeting is possibly justified.

Groups are also superior to individuals in performing complex tasks that require a division of labour (Jewell and Reitz, 1981). When several types of specialised knowledge are required to solve a problem, a well-organised group will out-perform isolated individuals. Well-managed groups also outperform individuals at tasks requiring the learning of ideas or the retention of information because groups tend to learn faster than individuals (Filley, 1970). Not only do groups have a larger pool of knowledge and experience to draw from, but they are also able to recognise and correct individual members' errors.

2. Building commitment

Solidifying members' commitment to a chosen course of action is especially important when the decision requires that group members change their work activities or when their reward structure is altered. Research has repeatedly demonstrated that subordinates are more likely to go along with a decision when they are involved in its formulation (Shaw, 1976). The greater the potential impact of a decision on group members, the more important it is to involve them in the decision-making process.

Another important factor concerns what group meetings mean to the individual participants. It has been observed that staff meetings have a high personal value for participants (3M Meeting Management Team, 1987). They value the involvement and participation that the meeting allows as well as the information and contacts that come from colleagues. Through this interaction, commitment to the group itself is strengthened. This is most likely to occur when the atmosphere of a meeting is congenial and supportive.

3. Disseminating information

Information-sharing is often more efficiently handled in a group meeting than one-to-one. For example, in work groups performing tasks that are highly interdependent (e.g., scheduling the production of customised orders), periodic staff meetings facilitate co-ordination. Also, a manager can be assured that the same information is reaching relevant people in the same way at the same time. Feedback is an important element within these meetings because the group has an opportunity to share its reactions with the manager and to provide input for further improvements. Also, regular work meetings are useful for groups operating in rapidly changing environments, since they enable the supervisor to disseminate up-to-date information regarding changes in work priorities, emerging crises, etc. Daily briefings in police departments serve this function. The following example from a large retail operation demonstrates the value of meetings.

> Since fewer teenagers were willing to work for the minimum wage, the store was having difficulty keeping sales staff but more people were required for the Christmas season. A meeting was called to develop a solution; all departments were included that had information to contribute or could be affected by any decisions made. Included were individuals from personnel and accounting as well as floor managers and buyers. All had a stake in the issue, whether it was in recruiting and training the new employees, determining their wages, or managing and scheduling them on the sales floor. Finally the meeting decided to increase hourly wages and allow flexible schedules. These changes resulted in a 50 per cent increase in applications and a 75 per cent reduction in turnover.

Step 2 Participants

It is apparent from this discussion that group meetings can facilitate solving complex problems, build commitment and foster communication. But they can also hinder effective performance and lower morale if either too many or too few people are involved or if the mix of participants is inappropriate. Therefore, the second planning question that should be asked by meeting organisers is, 'Given my purpose, what is the appropriate size and composition of the group?'

Group size

A common planning error is inviting too many people. Thinking that it is important to obtain input from as many people as possible, the leader draws up a large, diverse list of participants. The result is a superficial discussion of the issues, since the pressure to hear from everyone precludes an in-depth debate. In addition, more points of view will probably be aired than can be considered. Also, if the group is too large, some members will simply say nothing. As a rule, the larger the group, the lower will be the percentage of participants actively involved in the discussion (Hackman and Vidmar, 1970).

It is also possible to invite too few participants. If a group is too small, the potential for problem solving is reduced. Small groups have such limited personal resources that members can become easily discouraged in a problem-solving task. This is especially true when the group task requires technical knowledge that none of the members possess.

The appropriate size of the group is dependent on the purpose of the meeting. The optimal size can vary from less than five to an unlimited number of attendees (3M Meeting Management Team, 1987). For example, for the purpose of decision making or problem solving, a maximum of five members is recommended. In a group this size, members feel they have the resources to collectively attack a problem, while at the same time their unique contributions are still highly visible. Committee meetings are most effective with a maximum of seven members; any more will slow down work significantly. For problem-identification meetings (e.g., brainstorming sessions), a maximum number of ten is recommended. Interactive seminars and training sessions should include no more than 15 members, while informational meetings can accommodate as many as 30. For formal presentations, the size of the room is the only limiting factor.

Characteristics of members

Membership composition also plays an important role in group dynamics. Apart from the obvious need to assemble a group containing the skills and knowledge required to address the business of the meeting, three other characteristics of group composition are critical:

* Homogeneity vs heterogeneity
* Competition vs co-operation
* Task vs process

A **homogeneous group** is composed of members with similar backgrounds, personalities, knowledge and values. As one might expect, there is less likelihood of conflict during a homogeneous group's discussions, but these placid dynamics tend to produce mundane, unimaginative outcomes. In contrast, heterogeneous groups have great difficulty building strong interpersonal relationships, but they allow members to take greater risks and to be more critical of others' ideas. Overall, it appears that heterogeneous groups are better for addressing novel, complex tasks, providing group members can cope with a high degree of conflict (Shaw, 1976).

Despite its inherent disadvantages, some leaders prefer a small, homogeneous decision-making group. They select an intimate group of advisors who are supportive, loyal, and unlikely to produce any surprises. Such a 'kitchen cabinet' possesses a certain seductive appeal since it allows the manager to avoid the inefficient and conflict-laden decision-making process inherent in larger, more diverse groups. The problem here is that the probability of the group's making a serious mistake is substantially increased. Indeed, as discussed in the Chapter 7, an expert in corporate bankruptcy in the United States has argued that this type of group decision-making process at the senior executive level is a leading cause of business failure (Argenti, 1976).

The empirical results of research on the effect of **competitive vs co-operative** attitudes on the quality of group problem solving are compelling. Studies have consistently shown that groups whose members are working towards a common goal perform more effectively and produce higher levels of member satisfaction than groups whose members are striving to fulfil individual needs or pursuing competing goals (Terborg, *et al.*, 1976). Co-operative groups enjoy more effective interpersonal communication, more complete division of labour, higher levels of involvement and better task performance. The Ford Motor Company now trains its engineers on the EQUIP programme, to share their assumptions *before* the meeting begins, to achieve such understanding.

These first two dimensions are often linked. Homogeneous groups tend to be more co-operative, while heterogeneous groups are generally more competitive. For example, a budget meeting of representatives from five departments is less likely to be co-operative than one containing five members from the same department. Although not all heterogeneous groups are more competitive, they certainly place a greater burden on group leaders' conflict management skills. The challenge is to preserve the creative spark present in lively, often heated, discussions while at the same time preventing members from advancing personal interests. One way to achieve this is by identifying a broad goal that all members can identify with, such as getting the budget in on time or improving co-ordination between departments. The effective chair uses such goals to encourage co-operation.

Research on group dynamics has shown that effective groups contain some members who are highly **task-oriented** and others who are concerned about maintaining the quality of the group's **process** (Lord, 1977). Task-oriented members have little patience with small talk and joking around. They are only concerned with the work in hand and focus on outcomes, not worrying too much about other members' feelings and attitudes. Meetings that are dominated by task-oriented members tend to operate very efficiently, but at the expense of member satisfaction. In contrast, participants who are primarily concerned about maintaining *esprit de corps* in the group err in favour of encouraging everyone to participate, even if some have little to contribute. They are concerned primarily with members' affective assessments of the group process. They can be heard saying things like: 'That's an excellent idea', 'Let's allow John to finish stating his opinion before we interrupt', 'I'm interested in hearing what Mary has to say about this problem', and 'I think we have made a lot of progress on this matter'. Although certain types of meetings lend themselves to one orientation or the other, it is generally a good idea to ensure that both task and process orientations are represented in group meetings. Balance, as we have discussed elsewhere, is the issue.

Step 3   Plan

Often the justification for a meeting is clear – for instance, there is a problem with the re-work in Process Room Number 1 – and the appropriate individuals are present, but the group still seems to flounder, wandering aimlessly and unable to reach a consensus. Such meetings commonly begin with the boss saying, 'We've got a problem that I think we all need to sit down and discuss.' The chair erroneously assumes that because the need to meet is apparent to the participants, the meeting will be successful. As a result, he or she prepares for the meeting casually and overlooks critical factors. People come to the meeting without a clear understanding of the specific objectives. They are not informed of their specific role in the decision-making process or of how the decision will be made. They have not been asked to think about the problem ahead of time, so they waste time discussing ill-conceived suggestions. If the leader does not discuss the problem with his or her superiors before the meeting, the group may spend a lot of time trying to estimate how far top management will allow them to proceed on their own. These common pitfalls suggest the third planning question – what preparation is required to ensure effective group performance during the meeting?

A poorly organised meeting does not always reflect a casual attitude towards meeting preparation. Inexperienced chairs may work hard at developing meeting objectives, agendas and so on, but make some ill-advised decisions that create a disorganised meeting. For example, they may try to cram too much into a single meeting, scheduling too many presentations, handing out too many documents, or trying to cover too much business. As a result, members cannot adequately discuss the topics and often leave the meeting with little sense of accomplishment: 'We covered a lot of business, but didn't complete anything.'

Several specific planning tips can greatly improve the quality of a meeting:

- **The 'hygiene factors'** – the necessary arrangements for the meeting room, visual aids and equipment. Checking whether any of the participants need formal approval for attending

- **Timing** – the best time to meet and agreement on how long the meeting will last

In determining when and how long, the following factors should be considered: At what time of day are participants at their best? When are we least likely to be interrupted? Will the necessary people be available to attend? Have the participants had sufficient time to prepare for the meeting? How much time will be needed to cover the proposed agenda?

Agenda

A complete agenda must be prepared and, if possible, be distributed before the meeting. A sample agenda to be used in the Skill Development exercise is included in Appendix 1 on page 638. In addition to identifying the major points of business, the agenda should specify who will be in attendance, as well as the scheduled beginning and ending times. If a member is to make a report, the item on the agenda could be circled as a helpful reminder. If a business item requires advance preparation (e.g., reviewing background documents), this should also be noted and the necessary reading materials listed or included.

Pre-meeting discussion

Besides taking care of these planning details, the meeting chair may want to discuss specific agenda items with key members prior to the meeting. If a subordinate is making an important presentation, the chair might offer to critique a dress rehearsal. When a controversial policy is on the agenda, it is advisable to discuss the matter before the meeting with key opinion leaders. This polling of sentiment is useful for gauging how much time should be set aside for discussing an issue and how it should be presented to the group. In addition, if the chair can obtain the support of key group members before the meeting, it is less likely that a controversial issue will dominate the group discussion to the point that insufficient time is left to discuss other agenda items.

One of the most important decisions that needs to be made before a meeting is seldom explicitly considered by managers. Several decision-making formats can be used in a group meeting, but almost all management meetings use only one format. Available formats include:

- Ordinary group discussion
- Brainstorming
- Nominal group technique (NGT)

Each format has advantages and disadvantages; none of them is inherently superior. Consequently, the selection of a decision-making process should be linked to the specific objectives of the meeting (Murnighan, 1981).

Ordinary group discussion

This format is by far the most common. In a sense it serves as the default option; unless a deliberate decision is made to use one of the other formats, it is adopted. Basically, the chair states a problem and then encourages open, free-flowing discussion. When a consensus has been reached, the chair shifts to a new topic and the procedure is repeated.

Experience has shown that because this type of meeting is so unstructured, this decision-making format is most vulnerable to the process pitfalls discussed in detail in the next section. Group members are easily swayed by social pressure, a discussion can drag on far beyond its utility, overpowering personalities can easily dominate the meeting, and few alternative solutions are likely be generated. On the other hand, because it is so unstructured, it tends to enhance *esprit de corps* among group members. Participants are able to interject humour, joke with one another, and in other ways build strong social ties. Due to its lack of structure, the success of the ordinary group format usually depends on the skill of the group leader.

Brainstorming

This is a well-known process for generating ideas. People are brought together and asked to think of all the ways a problem could be solved. To conduct a successful brainstorming session, a few simple rules need to be followed:

1. People should be encouraged to generate as many diverse ideas as possible. The best way to come up with the 'right' idea is to have lots of ideas.

2. A premium should be placed on proposing unusual alternatives. In particular, ideas that are at variance with current practice or philosophy should be encouraged.

3. Members should be advised to 'piggyback' on each other's ideas ('Jill's suggestion has made me think about another alternative').

4. Members should not criticise the ideas as they are proposed.
Evaluation should take place after all the ideas have been generated.

The reason that the last rule is so important is this: group members often compete to see who can be the first to point out why a proposal won't work. A typical response is, 'That's a good idea, but it is inappropriate for this situation.' As a result, the idea generation process is stifled. People are reluctant to make suggestions that are unusual for fear of being ridiculed or labelled naive. When an overtly critical climate is allowed to develop during a brainstorming session, members begin to censure their own ideas before they are even expressed. They think 'John argued that Mary's idea wasn't feasible, and my idea is similar to hers, so I suppose there is no need to mention it.'

Brainstorming sessions are generally very enjoyable. Participants appreciate being asked for their input and leave the meeting with a strong sense of accomplishment. However, research has shown that brainstorming groups do not generate as many alternatives as one might expect. It is difficult for members not to violate this format's rules, and as a result, meetings often shift towards the ordinary group format (Bouchard, 1971).

The nominal group technique (NGT)

This was developed by Andre Delbecq and his colleagues at the University of Wisconsin (Delbecq *et al.*, 1976) to overcome the problems inherent in these discussion formats. In general, the NGT can be thought of as a highly structured form of brainstorming, involving four stages:

1. After a problem has been stated, group members are asked to write down as many alternative solutions as they can.
2. The chair asks members to report their ideas in round-robin fashion while a scribe records them on a flip-chart or blackboard.
3. A brief discussion is held, primarily to clarify any ambiguously stated or recorded items.
4. Members are asked to vote for the alternatives they prefer. This can be done in a variety of ways. For example, each member might be given 10 points to divide among all the items, or each might cast one to three votes. If an obvious winner emerges, the task has been completed. If not, the vote can be discussed and a second vote taken. This process is repeated until a consensus emerges.

The advantages and disadvantages of these decision-making approaches are summarised in Table A.1. On the left-hand side are criteria for judging the effectiveness of a group meeting.

The choice of the most appropriate group decision-making technique depends on the nature of the business to be conducted, the participants to be included, the objectives of the group leader, time and financial constraints and group morale. While no approach is clearly superior in all cases, the table highlights the choice that a manager has other than the 'default option' of the group meeting. For example, if

Table A.1 Comparison of group decision-making formats

Criteria	Ordinary	Brainstorming	Nominal
Number of ideas	Low	Moderate	High
Quality of ideas	Low	Moderate	High
Social pressure	High	Low	Moderate
Time/money costs	Moderate	Low	Low
Task orientation	Low	High	High
Potential for inter-personal conflict	High	Low	Moderate
Feelings of accomplishment	High to low	High	High
Commitment to solution	Hign	N/A*	Moderate
Development of 'we' feeling	High	High	Moderate

* N/A = not applicable.
Source: Murnighan (1981)

the objective is to generate ideas for solving a persistent safety problem, the group meeting is the worst possible option.

Group leaders need to be clear in their objectives and choose the decision-making process that is most appropriate for each area to be covered. A frequent cause of unproductive group meetings is the failure of the chair to complete this part of the planning process.

Step 4   Process

Once a meeting begins, chairs quickly learn that there is more to a good performance than conscientious preparation. Managing the fluid, actual dynamics during meetings is probably the most challenging aspect of the leader's role. Therefore, the fourth diagnostic question is, 'Are the group dynamics in this meeting helping us reach our objectives?'

Group dynamics guidelines

A seven-step process for managing effective meetings can ensure that meeting plans are not derailed by the emerging problems of ambiguity, turmoil and lack of control (Huber, 1980).

1. At the beginning of a meeting, review current progress

For instance if the purpose of the meeting is to evaluate four cost-cutting alternatives generated at the end of the previous meeting, the chair could begin by briefly reviewing each proposal and summarising the pros and cons expressed previously. This type of introduction serves two purposes. First, it highlights the group's previous successes. Second, it ensures that members understand the objectives of the current meeting. Once this common agreement has been established, the chair can refer back to it periodically during the meeting to maintain the focus of the discussion. For example, frequent statements like, 'Now that we have successfully evaluated the first two alternatives, let's move on to number three', will help sustain the interest and motivation of group members.

Earlier we stressed the importance of preparing agendas for all meetings. The confirmation of an opening position statement and an extensive agenda increases the chances that the group will 'stay on course'. Members understand the purpose of the meeting and their own expected contribution. Timeliness as well as time are settled – this way the leader has made the job of controlling the meeting much easier. Of course, flexibility within the agenda is often necessary or desirable. But it is much easier to loosen up an agenda that it is to bring order to an out-of-control situation.

2. Help group members feel comfortable with one another

This is especially critical if the meeting is likely to produce emotional confrontations, the group is large, or several members have been recently added. Table A.3 lists suggestions for helping people who have not previously worked together. Participants are generally reticent if they aren't sure where other members are 'coming from' in terms of background, expertise, status and their stake in the issues on the agenda. Huber (1980) suggests the following tactics for helping group members get to know each other:

- Before the first meeting, send each member a brief biographical sketch of the other members, perhaps in conjunction with a description of the group's assignment, schedule of meetings, etc.

- Before the first meeting, provide an opportunity for the members to socialise, such as a coffee break.

- At the first meeting, introduce each member or have the members introduce themselves. (Generally the chair's introductions are more informative, as the members may be too modest to say much about themselves.)

- During long meetings, provide breaks during which members can resume the social conversations they have had to set aside while they focused on the group task.

3. Establish ground rules

The tendency in most meetings is to begin solving the first problem on the agenda before agreeing on the proper methodology. The impulse of group members is to immediately focus on the task. The initial discussion typically focuses on questions such as, 'What do we need to decide today?' or 'What is the nature of the problem?' When groups fail to devote some time initially to specifying process ground rules, they invariably take longer to accomplish tasks.

Given the strong 'action orientation' in business, this may seem counter-intuitive, since it appears that time spent discussing anything but the task at hand is wasted. However, research has shown that process issues will be discussed at some point in most meetings, and the sooner they surface, the less time is required to deal with them adequately (Hackman and Morris, 1975). When they are discussed at the beginning, questions about what the structure of the meeting should be, how much time should be spent discussing an item before voting on it, whether alternatives should be selected by majority vote or unanimous agreement etc. can be dealt with explicitly and efficiently. In contrast, when a group jumps right into discussing the business of the meeting, process issues tend to surface in a haphazard fashion and often with considerable emotion: 'Why are we spending so much time discussing this item?' or 'Why don't we just hurry up and vote on the issue and move on?'

4. As early as possible in a meeting, get a report from each member who has been preassigned a task

This action reinforces the principle of accountability and provides public recognition for the presenter. It also reduces the apprehension of a presenter. It is very demoralising to stay up late the night before a big meeting polishing a presentation and then find that the presentation has been postponed or, worse, forgotten. If an emergency requires that new business takes priority, scheduled presenters should be informed when the meeting's agenda is being prepared. If that is not feasible, the scheduling conflict should be resolved at the beginning of the meeting. Otherwise, while other business is being conducted, the presenters will be thinking about what they are going to say or worrying that too little time is being left for them to cover their material, and they will not be useful contributors.

5. Use appropriate tools – handouts, summary sheets, flipcharts, overhead projectors, video, slides, etc., to sustain the flow of the meeting

It is often difficult, especially in long, complex meetings, for participants to concentrate on detail. It is easy to lose interest because of information overload. A useful way to sustain interest and help members process information effectively is to use displays. For example, during a brainstorming meeting, suggestions should be listed on a blackboard or flipchart. Technical presentations should include handouts for overhead transparencies. Contingency arguments can be illustrated effectively by means of a decision-tree diagram on a blackboard. Discussions about the advantages and disadvantages of a proposal or the rank ordering of work objectives also tend to flow better when a scribe is recording the group's suggestions on a flipchart.

6. Manage the discussion to achieve equitable participation

Group task performance and member satisfaction tend to be highest when the rate of participation of individuals in a meeting corresponds to their information and knowledge. In poorly managed meetings, some members, whether due to habit, personality, desire for status, or genuine interest, participate at a rate beyond their ability to actually make a contribution.

To prevent certain individuals from dominating a meeting, the chair should 'invoke the norm of fairness'. By stressing the merits of a fair discussion, the chair is able to foster broad participation without appearing to personally take sides or criticise the behaviour of participants. This is accomplished by the use of guiding comments. For example, the leader might suggest to a member that it is time for others to contribute by saying, 'Jill, you have done a good job expressing your views on this matter. In all fairness, we should encourage others to have their say.'

An equitable distribution should be maintained not only between individuals but also between points of view. To prevent supporters of one side of an argument from dominating the meeting, the chair could interject, 'Now that we have heard arguments for the proposal, it seems appropriate that we hear from those who are opposed to it.' Particularly in large meetings, these comments may be insufficient to draw all the members into a discussion. In this case the chair should formally invite non-contributors to participate: 'Julian, we haven't heard from you yet. What are your feelings on this proposal?' If these guiding comments are not sufficient to ensure broad and equitable participation, the chair should consider a more structured form of discussion, such as the nominal group technique.

Additional tips for promoting group discussion are:

- Ask open-ended questions rather than questions that can be answered with a 'yes' or a 'no'.
- Ask questions using the language of the participants.
- Encourage participants to link their personal experiences to the discussion of a topic.
- Use examples from your own experience to clarify your point.
- Make eye-contact with those who are talking, and summarise their points when they conclude.
- Ask group members for reactions to others' points.
- When appropriate, involve other group members in answering a question addressed to you.
- Keep in mind that effective leaders facilitate, rather than dominate, the group process.

7. Close the meeting by summarising what has been accomplished and reviewing assignments

One of the critical functions of the leader is to ensure a sense of accomplishment after a meeting. This will motivate participants to perform assignments made during the meeting and make them feel positive about attending the next meeting. This is especially important at the end of a meeting in which progress was not obvious. If the meeting dealt primarily with examining alternatives or exchanging views, members may not recognise how constructive this process was. The chair can make this more apparent by pointing out how the discussion fits into the overall plan for accomplishing a task. It may be useful to review the stated purpose or agenda items for the meeting and indicate the progress made on each topic.

Before the group breaks up, it is also important to review and clarify assignments for the next meeting. For example, the chair might say, 'Mary, as I understand it, you are going to examine a copy of last year's budget and prepare a report for our next meeting.' Once the leader has found that there is agreement on the nature of the task, he or she should sample members' feelings about what they have agreed to do and check that they are ready able and willing to do it. This can be done in a number of ways. For example, the leader might ask, 'Will you need any help in getting those materials out of the archives?' or, 'Is that assignment feasible before the next meeting?'

Finally, the chair should review plans for the next meeting, when appropriate. Just as it is important at the beginning to place the meeting in an historical context, it is useful to end the meeting by building links to future activities. If the group's recommendations must be approved at a higher level, the chair should state plans for getting that approval and reporting back to the group. If the meeting has focused on a component of an ongoing task, it is important to point out what will be considered next. If a follow-up meeting is not regularly scheduled, plans for the next meeting should be finalised before members leave. Attending to these details at the end of a meeting facilitates a smooth, productive work environment between meetings.

Avoiding some pitfalls in group dynamics

The seven steps enable chairpersons to effectively manage most group dynamics. However, here are several special group-process problems that chairs should be aware of:

1. **'Groupthink'** drives out critical judgement.
2. **'Social loafing'** reduces members' contributions.
3. **'Group shift'** distorts individual members' positions.
4. **'Personal agendas'** subvert group goals.

Groupthink

A widely documented pitfall in group decision making is that the pressure to reach a consensus interferes with critical thinking. The reluctance of members to express views contrary to the prevailing sentiment of the group is especially acute when high-status members or formal leaders dominate the discussion. Research into group problem solving has shown that groups tend to select the first solution that receives favourable support from opinion leaders in the group, even when solutions that are technically better are introduced subsequently (Maier, 1967). When this occurs, a basic irony of group decision making occurs. This is illustrated in the following, frequently observed, scenario.

> Not wanting to make a serious judgement error, a leader convenes a meeting of trusted advisers. In the process of discussing the issue, he or she expresses a strong

Table A.2 Symptoms of groupthink

Symptom	Explanation
Illusion of invulnerability	Members feel assured that the group's past success will continue.
Shared stereotypes	Members dismiss contradictory information by discrediting its source ('lawyers are needlessly conservative').
Rationalisation	Members rationalise away threats to an emerging consensus.
Illusion of morality	Members believe that they, as moral individuals, are not likely to make bad decisions.
Self-censorship	Members keep silent about misgivings and try to minimise their doubts.
Direct pressure	Sanctions are imposed on members who explore deviant viewpoints.
Mind-guarding	Members protect the group from being exposed to disturbing ideas.
Illusion of unanimity	Members conclude that the group has reached a consensus because the most vocal members are in agreement.

Source: Janis (1972)

preference for one option. Others, wanting to appear supportive, present arguments justifying the decision. One or two members tentatively suggest alternatives, but they are strongly overruled by the majority. The decision is carried out with great conviction but with disastrous consequences. So while the leader brought together a group to help guard against making a bad decision, because of the strong pressure to conform during the group meeting, the leader actually became more vulnerable to making an error. Without the social support provided by the group, the leader would probably have been more cautious in implementing the personally preferred solution.

Research into the characteristics of an effective meeting chair has produced what appears at first to be a paradoxical model (Maier, 1967; Prince, 1969; Huber, 1980). Previously, we noted that poor meetings can result from leaders' providing too little structure for the discussion. These leaders assume a passive role either because they are unsure of their skills or because they assume the group will perform better if it is given a free rein. On the other hand, the research on groupthink argues that when a chair expresses strong opinions during a group discussion, members are less likely to think critically or creatively, and bad decisions often result. So it appears that whether a chair adopts a strong or a weak leadership role, the group suffers.

This apparent contradiction is resolved when we examine the leader's involvement in the structure in the context of the particular issues of the meeting (Janis, 1972; Jewell and Reitz, 1981). When the purpose of the meeting is to stimulate critical thinking, effective leaders take an active role in structuring the discussion but refrain from expressing strong opinions during the discussion. They work hard at facilitating the discussion but abstain from actively determining its direction. This conclusion is supported by a classic study of 72 management committees (Berkowitz, 1953), which found that a high degree of sharing of the leadership role was negatively related to member satisfaction and group performance. Groups worked most effectively when they had a 'takecharge' leader who provided a well-defined structure for their activities.

The following are additional remedies for the perils of groupthink consistent with the emphasis on the leader's responsibility to provide structure. These actions show how the group leader can use structure and group norms to increase, rather than impede, critical thinking during meetings.

1. Leaders should assign the role of critical evaluator to every group member.
2. Leaders should not state their preferences at the beginning of a meeting.
3. Assign subgroups to independently develop proposals.
4. Periodically have outside experts review the group's deliberations. Invite them to sit in on some meetings.
5. During important deliberations, assign one member of the group to play the role of devil's advocate.
6. After formulating a tentative proposal, hold a second-chance meeting. Invite all members to express any residual doubts.

Source: Janis (1972)

Social loafing

A related pitfall of group performance was first identified by a French agricultural engineer who observed that when three people pulled together on a rope they could only achieve two-and-one-half times the individual rate. This tendency, called social loafing, has been widely documented in all forms of group activity. In general, researchers have found that the larger the group size the less the effort of the individual members (Latane *et al.*, 1979). The explanations put forward to explain this problem include:

1. Equity of effort ('No one else is working up to their potential so why should I?').
2. Loss of personal accountability ('I'm an insignificant part of the crowd, so who cares?').
3. Motivational loss due to sharing of rewards ('Why should I work harder than the others when everyone will get the same reward anyway?').
4. Co-ordination loss as more people perform the task ('Does anyone know what's going on?').

Recent research findings (Jackson and Harkins, 1985) provide group leaders with clues for ways in which they can counteract the social loafing tendency. First, they can make sure group members understand that their assigned task is important. If necessary, they can bring in a senior manager to make this point. Second, they should hold some members of the group personally responsible for certain aspects of the task. Effective group leaders make sure all members are involved in meaningful tasks. Third, leaders should express positive expectations that everyone in the group will be working hard. In this regard, it is useful to recall the observation of a seasoned management veteran, quoted in Chapter 5: 'We get about what we expect.'

Group shift

During intensive group discussions, individuals commonly shift their personal views either towards more conservative or more risky directions, depending on their initial positions. That is, as a result of group discussion, members tend to adopt a more extreme position than they held before the meeting. If they are either more reckless or conservative than others in the group, they tend to become more so as the discussion progresses (McGrath and Kravitz, 1982).

Although both conservative and risk-taking polarisation effects can emerge from group discussions, the tendency seems to be greater in the direction of willingness to take greater risks. Thus group leaders need to be aware that at the end of a discussion, members will likely be more willing to accept a riskier alternative than they were at the beginning of the meeting and this can have serious implications, especially in groups formulating organisational strategies. In conducting post-mortem examinations on business failures, researchers have noted that several of these firms pursued extremely risky courses. In retrospect, individual decision makers have difficulty understanding how they could have 'let it happen'. They had found themselves swept along with group sentiment favouring reckless alternatives, ignoring early warning signals, and putting their faith in unrealistic forecasts (Argenti, 1976).

Several explanations for this group phenomenon have been offered (Clark, 1971). One possibility is that discussion creates familiarisation among members; as they become more comfortable with one another, they become more daring. Another is that our society places a high value on taking risks, and a group discussion motivates members to show they are as willing as their peers to take risks. The most likely explanation is similar to one of the underlying causes of social loafing – the diffusion of responsibility. Group discussions free any single member from feeling accountable for the group's final decision. Therefore, they are more willing to take greater risk because, if the decision fails, no individual will be held wholly responsible.

Group leaders aware of this tendency can draw upon a variety of alternative antidotes to aggressively counteract it, as follows.

1. Formally poll individuals prior to meetings in which critical issues will be discussed, especially those where a risky shift might court disaster. This gives the leader a baseline to work from.

2. Assign someone the role of process observer to monitor signs of an emerging shift. For particularly critical issues, the observer might administer private-opinion surveys during the discussion. With the leader's support, an observer should interject feedback regarding discussion-induced trends. The leader should then shift the focus of the discussion from content (debating the merits of the issue) to process (examining the merits of the debate).

3. Use a structured decision-making process, such as NGT, that limits discussion. Obviously, this option sacrifices the richness and sharpness of a free-flowing exchange, so it should be used only when a minimal value-added contribution to the quality of a decision is expected from the group discussion. A typical example would be a meeting in which the purpose is to formalise a decision rather than to debate alternatives.

4. Assign two groups to prepare position papers on the issue, advocating the pros and cons, or conservative and risky positions. Then have them argue their positions before the decision makers. In lawyer-like fashion, their task would be to demonstrate the merits of their position and search for flaws in their opponent's arguments. This 'dialectical inquiry' form of policy debate is used widely in corporations, such as Eastman Kodak, to prevent faulty group decisions (Mitroff and Emshoff, 1979).

Personal agendas

Individuals bring a great deal of 'personal baggage' with them to meetings. In poorly managed meetings, outspoken individuals can divert the discussion from shared purposes to personal concerns. For example, in an organisation that is having considerable financial difficulties, it is common for a problem-solving meeting to turn into a gripe session. Instead of concentrating on coming up with ideas for saving money, group members debate the merits of top management's ability to cope with the crisis.

A related dysfunctional group dynamic is the process of jockeying for position of status in the group (Jewell and Reitz, 1981). A group that meets frequently becomes a miniature organisation. It is quite natural in this microcosm for a division of labour and a status hierarchy to emerge. This by itself is not dysfunctional, but when members become preoccupied with personal concerns (e.g., 'How can I enhance my status in this group?'), they tend to lose interest in conducting the business of the meeting. In these cases, problem-solving meetings degenerate into speech-making sessions in which members attempt to score points against one another. The meeting turns into a staged polemical debate in which antagonists strive to win arguments rather than solve problems. The effort to enhance one's personal status in the group as a powerful orator or tenacious debater subverts the problem-solving objective of the group.

Tips for handling various forms of disruptive actions are shown in Table A.3. A common theme runs through these guidelines: maintain control of the meeting but don't use your role as chair to embarrass or intimidate group members. The way you handle problem group members sets the tone for the group discussion.

Table A.3   Suggestions for handling disruptive and inappropriate behaviours

Type	Behaviour or words used	Suggested response
Hostile	'It'll never work.' 'That's a typical engineering viewpoint.'	'How do others here feel about this?' 'You may be right, but let's review the facts and evidence.' 'It seems we have a different perspective on the details, but we agree on the principle.'
Know-it-all	'I have worked on this project more than anyone else in his room . . . or I have a PhD in Economics, and . . .'	'Let's review the facts.' (Avoid theory or speculation.) 'Another noted authority on this subject has said . . .'
Loudmouth	Constantly blurts out ideas or questions. Tries to dominate the meeting.	Interrupt: 'Can you summarise your main point/question for us?' or 'I appreciate your comments, but we should also hear from others' or 'Interesting point. Help us understand how it relates to our subject.'
Interrupter	Starts talking before others are finished.	'Wait a minute, Jim, let's let Jane finish what she was saying.'
Interpreter	'What John is really trying to say is . . . , John would respond to that question by saying . . .'	'Let's let John speak for himself. Go ahead, John, finish what you were saying.' 'John, how would you respond?' 'John, do you think Jim correctly understood what you said?'
Gossiper	'Isn't there a regulation that you can't . . .' 'I thought I heard the V.P. of Finance say . . .'	'Can anyone here verify this?' (Assuming no response.) 'Let's not take the time of the group until we can verify the accuracy of this information.'
Whisperer	Irritating side conversation going on between two people.	Hints: 1. Walk up close to the guilty parties and make eye contact. 2. Stop talking and establish dead silence. 3. Politely ask the whisperers to wait until the meeting is over to finish their conversation.
Silent distracter	Reads newspapers, rolls their eyes, shakes their head, fidgets.	Hints: Ask them questions to determine their level of interest, support and expertise. Try to build an alliance by drawing them into the discussion. If that doesn't work, discuss your concerns with them during a break.

Table A.3   (Cont'd)

Type	Behaviour or words used	Suggested response
Busy-busy	Ducks in and out of the meeting repeatedly, taking messages, dealing with crises.	Hints: Schedule the presentation away from the office. Check with common offenders before the meeting to ask if the planned time is OK for minimum interruptions.
Latecomer	Comes late and interrupts the meeting.	Hints: Announce an odd time (8.46) for the meeting to emphasise the necessity for promptness. Make it inconvenient for latecomers to find a seat, and stop talking until they do. Establish a 'latecomer's kitty' for refreshments.
Early leaver	Announces, with regrets, that they must leave for another important activity.	Hints: Before starting, announce the ending time and ask if anyone has a scheduling conflict.

Source: Adapted from Peoples (1988)

Therefore, instead of attacking or becoming defensive, you should practice the skills of supportive communication and collaborative conflict management in these situations. In short, discuss your concerns in an open, direct, problem-oriented and supportive manner.

Suggestions for group members

Throughout this discussion of effective meeting management, we have focused on the role of the leader. This role is key to the success of any group activity. However, participants also bear responsibility for their group's performance. Indeed, it can be argued that strong group members have strong leaders. This statement has a dual meaning: leaders are only as strong as their followers; strong followers eventually become leaders. Either way, it is important for non-leaders attending meetings to appreciate the impact of their contribution, both in shaping the short-term outcomes of meetings and in affecting their long-term career opportunities.

The following are hints for contributing to the effectiveness of meetings, for nonleaders.

1. **Decide whether you really need to attend the meeting.** Don't attend merely because you have been invited. If you have doubts about whether the meeting's agenda applies to you, discuss with the leader why he or she feels your presence is important.

2. **Prepare.** Acquaint yourself with the agenda, and prepare any reports or information which will facilitate others' understanding of the issues. Come prepared with questions that will help you understand the issues.

3. **Be on time.** Stragglers not only waste the time of other participants by delaying the meeting or by requiring summaries of what has happened, but they also hinder effective team-building and hurt morale.

4. **Ask for clarification on points that are unclear or ambiguous.** Most of the time, you will find that others in the room have the same questions but were too timid to speak out.

5. **When giving information, be precise and to the point.** Don't bore everyone with anecdotes and details that add little to your point.

6. **Listen.** Keep eye contact with whoever is speaking, and try to ascertain the underlying ideas behind the comments. Be sensitive to the effect of your non-verbal behaviour on speakers, such as slouching, doodling or reading.

7. **Be supportive of other group members.** Following the guidelines on supportive communication, acknowledge and build on the comments of others. (For example, 'as Jane was saying . . .')

8. **Assure equitable participation.** Take the lead in involving others so that everyone's talents are used. This is especially important if you know that critical information from particular points of view is not being included in the discussion. This can be rectified by encouraging those who rarely participate. (For example, 'Jim, your unit worked on something like this last year. What was your experience like?')

9. **Make disagreements principle-based.** If it is necessary to disagree with, or challenge, the comments of others, follow the guidelines for collaborative conflict management. For example, base your comments on commonly held principles or values. (For example, 'That's an interesting idea, Bill, but how does it square with the president's emphasis on cost cutting?')

10. **Act and react in a way which will enhance group performance.** In other words, leave your personal agendas at the door and work towards the goals of the group.

Summary and behavioural guidelines

Meetings are a pervasive part of organisational life, especially for managers. Few important initiatives are forged without extensive and intensive group efforts. However, meetings are one of the most maligned aspects of organisational membership. To avoid poorly managed meetings, consider the 4-P's approach.

1. **Purpose.** Use meetings to accomplish the following purposes:
   - A complex problem needs to be resolved using the expertise of several people.
   - Group members' commitment to a decision or to each other needs to be enhanced.
   - Information needs to be shared simultaneously among several people.

2. **Participants.** Make decisions regarding who and how many to invite on the following bases:

- The size of the group should be compatible with the task (for interactive groups, five to seven participants tends to work best).
- A balance between individuals with strong task orientations and others with strong group-process orientations should be sought.
- Individuals should share some common goals or values.
- All relevant experience and knowledge need to be represented.
- The group's composition should reflect the goals of the meeting (homogeneity encourages solidarity and commitment; heterogeneity fosters creativity and innovation).

3. **Plan.** In preparing for the meeting, be sure to do the following:

- Provide for adequate physical space, audio-visual equipment and so on.
- Establish priorities by sequencing agenda items and allotting time limits to each item.
- Prepare and distribute an agenda before, or at the beginning of, the meeting.
- Choose the most appropriate decision-making format structure for each item (ordinary group discussion, brainstorming or nominal group technique).

4. **Process.** In managing the group dynamics of the meeting:

- Present the overall purpose of the meeting, specify the target time length, and highlight specific tasks.
- Establish process ground rules, such as how decisions will be made.
- Allow members to become acquainted (if necessary) and make them feel comfortable.
- Get a report from each member with a pre-assigned task, preferably early in the meeting.
- When critical thinking is important, avoid 'groupthink' by playing a strong role in structuring the discussion but refraining from expressing strong personal opinions; also, assign the role of critical evaluator to group members.
- Sustain the flow of the meeting by using information displays.
- Encourage the group not to stray from assigned tasks.
- Manage the discussion to achieve equitable participation.
- Discourage the premature evaluation of ideas.
- Prevent 'social loafing' by assigning specific responsibilities and stressing the importance of group tasks.
- Counteract the natural tendency for groups to make risky decisions by polling members prior to the meeting so that discussion-induced trends can be detected; also, consider using either the NGT, or the dialectical inquiry, format.
- Deal with disruptive members by using supportive communication and collaborative conflict management skills.
- Conclude the meeting by summarising what was accomplished, reviewing assignments, and making preparations for subsequent meetings, if necessary.

5. **Foster constructive group dynamics** as a participant by doing the following:

   - Take time to prepare for the meeting, and gain a clear understanding of the purposes of the meeting.
   - Respect other group members by arriving on time and leaving personal agendas at the door.
   - Listen to other group members, be supportive of them, and clarify and build upon points made by others.
   - Encourage participation by all members.

Skill Practice

Exercises in planning and conducting meetings

Conducting effective meetings is one of the most challenging aspects of day-to-day management. A great deal of time can either be saved or wasted in meetings. The following exercises are designed to help you develop this important management skill.

EXERCISE **A.1**

STAFF MEETING AT THAMES PUMP & VALVE

In this exercise you should assume the role of Richard or Rebecca West, the new plant manager at TP&V. Review the memos in the TP&V (exercise on pages 19–26) and identify several agenda items for a staff meeting. Assume you have already met once with your staff, following your return form Cologne, so introductions and discussion of your general management philosophy have already been taken care of. The purpose of the meeting you are planning now is to conduct actual business.

Based on your understanding of the conditions within the plant, plan a working staff meeting. Following the behavioural guidelines presented earlier, plan the agenda for the meeting, using the form in Appendix 1, page 638. You need to decide when the meeting should be held, who should attend, how long it should last, the type of decision-making process you plan to use for each item, in what order business will be conducted, what assignments need to be made before the meeting, guidelines for formal presentations (if appropriate), and so forth. Use the in-basket materials in the TP&V exercise as the basis for planning this meeting.

Next, on the form in Appendix 1, page 638, identify any interpersonal problems you are likely to encounter during the meeting, based on your knowledge of the personalities of your staff and the potential for conflict among them. Using this assessment, prepare contingency plans for handling potential problems in order to minimise the chances that emerging, disruptive group dynamics will undermine your planned objectives.

After you have completed your plans, one student/colleague will be selected to actually conduct this meeting in class; others will act as staff members. Prior to the meeting, the assigned Mr/Ms West should take 15 minutes to distribute the meeting agenda, arrange the physical setting, and assign seating by placing a name plate at each position. While these arrangements are being made, the assigned staff should prepare for the meeting by reviewing both the agenda and the TP&V case to refresh their memories of the issues related to their roles in the company. When the arrangements for the meeting have been made, Mr/Ms West will invite the staff to take their places and call the meeting to order.

Following the meeting, a discussion of what transpired should be conducted between the participants and assigned observers, using the Observer's Feedback Form in Appendix 1, page 637, as a guide.

EXERCISE **A.2**

CONDUCTING A TASK FORCE MEETING

Identify a group you are working in that has been given a specific task, for example, a class study group, a student organisation, or a project committee at work. If the committee has a formal chair, ask that person if you could conduct one of the group's meetings.

Based on your understanding of the current status of work activities within this group, plan the next meeting. Following the behavioural guidelines presented earlier, plan the agenda for the meeting, using the form in Appendix 1, page 638. You need to decide when the meeting should be held, who should attend, how long it should last, the type of decision-making process you plan to use for each item, in what order business will be conducted, what assignments need to be made before the meeting, the guidelines for formal presentations (if appropriate) etc.

Next, on the form in Appendix 1, page 638, identify any interpersonal problems you are likely to encounter during the meeting, based on your knowledge of the personalities of the members and the potential for conflict among them. Using this assessment, prepare contingency plans for handling potential problems in order to minimise the chances that emerging, disruptive group dynamics will undermine your planned objectives.

After you have completed your plans, send out your agenda to members prior to the meeting. Also before the meeting, you should arrive early to arrange the physical setting, make sure any equipment needs have been met, and that refreshments, if appropriate, are available. Following the meeting, ask the participants to give you feedback on your role as chair. This can be done either orally, immediately following the meeting, or by using the Observer's Feedback Form in Appendix 1, page 637. Finally, write down the highlights of your experience to share with class members.

EXERCISE **A.3**

JIM LEWIS

There are six roles described in this exercise. After reading the case, fill out the 'personal preference' part of the worksheet in Appendix 1, page 639. Do this from the perspective of your assigned role.

When the worksheet has been completed, the supervisor should act as chair of the committee and begin the discussion. The group's assignment is to reach consensus on the rank-ordered options (from this list). Group members should stay in character during the discussion. For example, they should not compare their lists and use a statistical process to generate their rank-order. Observers should be assigned to give the group feedback on their performance, using the Observer's Feedback Form in Appendix 1, page 637, as a guide. The Group Diagnostic Questions in the next exercise can also be used to analyse the group's dynamics.

The case

Jim has a grim personal background. He is the third child in an underprivileged inner-city family of seven. He has not seen his parents for several years. He recalls that his father used to come home drunk and beat up family members; everyone ran when his father came staggering home.

His mother, according to Jim, wasn't much better. She was irritable and unhappy, and she always predicted that Jim would come to no good. Yet she worked, when her health allowed, to keep the family in food and clothing. She frequently decried the fact that she was not able to be the kind of mother she would like to be.

Jim left school in the fifth form. He had great difficulty conforming to the school routine – misbehaving often, playing truant frequently, and getting into fights with schoolmates. On several occasions he was picked up by the police and, along with members of his group, questioned during investigations into cases of both petty theft and burglary. The police regarded him as a 'high-potential troublemaker'.

The *guardian ad litem* ('juvenile probation officer') of the court saw in Jim some good qualities that no one else seemed to sense. This man, Mr O'Brien, took it on himself to act as a father figure to Jim. He had several long conversations with him and he managed to penetrate to some degree Jim's defensive shell. He represented to Jim the first semblance of personal, caring influence in his life. Through Mr O'Brien's efforts, Jim returned to school and completed his GCSEs. Afterwards, Mr O'Brien helped him obtain his first job.

Now 22 years old, Jim is a stockroom clerk at Cavendish Pharmaceutical Laboratory. On the whole, his performance has been acceptable, but there have been glaring exceptions. One involved a clear act of insubordination, though the issue was fairly unimportant. On another occasion, Jim was accused by a co-worker, on circumstantial grounds, of destroying some expensive equipment. Though the investigation is still open, it appears that the destruction was accidental. He also appears to have lost an extremely important requisition (although he claims never to have seen it). In addition, his laid-back attitude and wisecracking ways tend to irritate his co-workers. It is also important to note that Jim is not an attractive young man. He is rather weak and sickly, his appearance is dishevelled. Researchers in the lab have commented that his appearance doesn't fit in with the company's image. Others have wondered aloud (half jokingly, half seriously) whether he is taking drugs.

Jim's supervisor is fairly new to management and is not sure how to handle this situation. He sees merit in giving Jim the benefit of the doubt and helping him out, but he wonders whether it is worth the 'hassle'. Seeking advice, the supervisor organises a committee of individuals close to the situation. These include the supervisor (who has expressed frustration about the effects of Jim's performance and reputation on the morale of the work group), a seasoned manger (who has a reputation for being evenhanded), a union representative (who tends to view most acts of employee discipline as an infringement on employee rights), a member of the personnel department (who is concerned about following proper company procedures), and the company's equal opportunities representative (who is concerned that managers at Cavendish do not fully understand the handicap workers like Jim bring with them to the workplace – hence the need to give them special assistance and direction).

Exercise in Effective Participation

EXERCISE **A.4**

GROUP DYNAMICS EVALUATION

It is common knowledge in management circles that performance tends to improve when it is measured and reported. Feedback provides the stimulus for ongoing development. This principle holds for group, as well as individual, performance. It is especially appropriate for groups (e.g., task committees) that meet on a regular basis and have specific performance responsibilities. The group's output is typically monitored by an outside party (often a higher-level manager), who looks for clear, visible results, asking such questions as, 'Did they solve the problem?', 'Did their proposal work?', 'How long did it take them to make a decision?' and 'Did they stay within their budget?'

However, this type of evaluation does not take into account that the quality of a group's process affects the quality of what it produces. Frankly, outside evaluators are typically not interested in the why's or how's behind a process. Their concentration on results ignores the efficiency of the internal decision-making process, the distribution of work among members, or the role of leadership. Therefore, if the processes that affect the group's visible performance as well as members' commitment and satisfaction are going to be improved through evaluation and feedback, group members must take the initiative.

This is best done by setting aside time at the end of a meeting to discuss what happened and what was the effect on both performance and the way people felt. The following series of diagnostic questions will be a useful guide for focusing this discussion. During the discussion, individuals should solicit feedback from other members regarding their contribution to effective group dynamics.

Assignment

Identify a group of which you are a member that meets regularly. Get permission from other members to discuss the questions on this diagnostic tool. Allow about an hour for a good discussion. Distribute the questions prior to your discussion and ask other members to reflect on the group's internal dynamics. Lead the group discussion and write a summary of the outcome. Include in your report specific changes that could improve future group meetings, using the behavioural guidelines at the end of the Skill Learning section as a reference.

Group meeting evaluation questions

Communications

1. Who responded to whom?
2. Who interrupted? Was the same person interrupted consistently?
3. Were there identifiable communication clusters? Why, or why not?
4. Did some members say little? If so, why? Was level of participation ever discussed?
5. Were efforts made to involve everyone?
6. Did those with the most relevant information, expertise or experience do most of the talking?

Decision making

1. Did the group decide how to decide?
2. How were decisions made?
3. What criteria were used to establish agreement? Majority vote? Consensus? No opposition interpreted as agreement?
4. What was done if people disagreed?
5. How effective was your decision-making process?
6. Does every member feel his or her input into the decision-making process was valued by the group, or were the comments of some members frequently discounted? If so, was this issue ever discussed?

Leadership

1. What type of power structure did the group operate under? One definite leader? Leadership functions shared by all members? Power struggles within the group? No leadership supplied by anyone?
2. How does each member feel about the leadership structure used? Would an alternative have been more effective?
3. Did the chair provide an adequate structure for the discussion?
4. Was the discussion governed by the norms of equity?
5. Was the chair's contribution to the content of the discussion overbearing?

Awareness of feelings

1. How did members in general react to the group meetings? Were they hostile (towards whom or what?), enthusiastic, apathetic?

2. Did members openly discuss their feelings towards each other and their role in the group?

3. How do group members feel now about their participation in this group?

Task behaviour

1. Who was the most influential in keeping the group task-oriented? How?

2. Did some members carry the burden and do most of the work, or was the load distributed evenly?

3. If some members were not contributing their fair share, was this ever discussed? If so, what was the outcome? If not, why?

4. Did the group evaluate its method of accomplishing a task during or after the project? If so, what changes were made?

5. How effective was your group in performing assigned tasks? What improvements could have been made?

Making Oral Presentations

SKILL DEVELOPMENT OUTLINE

Skill Learning material

- Making oral presentations
- Summary and behavioural guidelines

Skill Practice exercises

- Speaking as a Leader
- Quality circles at Bradfield Foods
- A look at some of the evidence for quality circles

LEARNING OBJECTIVES

To increase proficiency in

- making effective oral presentations
- effectively answering questions and challenges

Skill Learning

Making oral presentations

John Thompson, the founder of Apex Communications, died two weeks ago from a heart attack. Suddenly, Trevor Billinge, previously in charge of long-distance services, was thrust into the role of managing director. Though he had anticipated assuming this position sometime in the future, the tragic death of his former mentor required him to take on the senior position much sooner than he expected.

Trevor faces a formidable task. The company is in the middle of a major upheaval taking it out of the state-owned sector into a market-driven and customer-oriented private company. Results to date have been quite impressive but many of this year's goals have not been met. Trevor intends to lead the firm down the same course set by John Thompson for the time being, but he wants to ensure that the company goals are achieved in future. He is also eager to establish his own credibility; he wants to make his employees and other stakeholders understand and appreciate his personal commitment and management style.

In the first few days on the job, Trevor had several opportunities to communicate his philosophy and expectations through a number of speeches. Immediately following the announcement of his appointment he gave a speech to all the headquarters management personnel in which he outlined some of his ideas for moving the company forward. In a separate meeting that same day, he spoke to the engineering staff of the Research and Development Centre, introducing a new project and encouraging them to move ahead at full speed to develop a technology with great promise for the future of the company.

Then Trevor began a tour of company facilities in other cities. He gave short impromptu talks to groups of company salesmen gathered at field sales offices, reminding them of the importance of customer service in all areas of the company. The message to them all was 'quality service . . . practise excellence in all your work, do things right the first time.'

On the train to yet another meeting, this time at the northern headquarters, he looked over Apex's latest financial reports. Quarterly figures were unexpectedly down and some costs had risen dramatically. Trevor was concerned. When he arrived for his scheduled meeting with the region's top managers he adjusted the agenda to reflect these new developments. He called on all the northern staff to do whatever they could to reduce company costs.

Following this meeting, Trevor was asked to put in an appearance at the opening ceremony of a new showcase facility nearby, where he spoke to all those people who had played a role in building the new state-of-the-art switching centre that employs the newest in sophisticated technologies and puts the company ahead in traffic handling. Trevor congratulated them on a job well done.

Later that afternoon his work became less pleasant. When this new facility becomes fully operational, two existing out-dated facilities will be closed. Though no formal announcement has been made, many existing employees fear, quite correctly, that there will be some redundancies. Trevor chose to speak to the employees of both sites – the first in the works canteen and the second in a large assembly hall. His objective was to calm fears and, if possible, to hold on to the more talented employees.

The talk at the first site was successful but at the other site, less so. The second site was based in a deprived inner city area, and Trevor knew that closing this facility would affect the whole community, even if all employees are retained and transferred to the new site. Trevor's advisers have told him that he should expect a good deal of hostility to his address from these workers and his advisers were correct. That night in the assembly hall they asked him some extremely difficult questions and challenged much of the information he presented to support the company's plan (Linowes, 1989).

Trevor Billinge experienced a challenging introduction to his new position as head of Apex. During the first 14 days he gave as many talks, covering a broad range of subjects and addressing a wide variety of audiences. In most of those talks, Trevor was not simply presenting facts, as one customarily does when presenting a report. Instead, he was conveying support, pointing out a new direction, generating enthusiasm, communicating a sense of caring, building goodwill, and underscoring the value of teamwork. Some talks were polite, ceremonial events; others were hostile confrontations. Some covered familiar material; others stretched his ability to quickly absorb large briefing documents.

This speaking schedule would challenge even veteran public speakers. For most individuals it would appear impossible or very stressful. We have maintained throughout this book that effective personal performance is the result of skill, knowledge and practice. This is especially the case with public speaking. The key to overcoming uneasiness when making oral presentations is guided practice, but practice guided by the correct principles. The following section outlines these principles. Because managers need to be prepared to make presentations in a variety of situations, we have included material in this section that applies in a variety of contexts (Barrett, 1977; Mambert, 1976; Peoples, 1988; Sanford and Yeager, 1963; Wilcox, 1967).

There are four steps to making effective presentations. These are sequential, in the sense that each step builds on, or incorporates, the output from the preceding steps. The first two steps involve preparation, the second two focus on the presentation itself:

1. Formulate a strategy for the specific audience. This is the conceptual design phase in which you develop a general plan.

2. Develop a flexible, flowing structure. Broad strategy is translated into specific content.

3. Combine prepared material with an enhancing, not distracting, presentation style. After all that preparation, it is important to remember that how you present is as important as what you present.

4. Supplement the presentation with confident, informed responses to questions and challenges. Your performance in a spontaneous, free-flowing discussion should be as impressive as your prepared formal remarks.

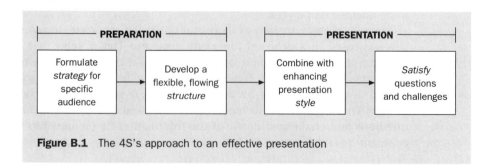

Figure B.1 The 4S's approach to an effective presentation

Strategy

Understand your purpose and role

Before plunging into the details of collecting information, writing notes, etc., you should first clarify your objective. Is your purpose to motivate, inform, persuade, or teach? Each of these purposes suggests a different approach. If you are trying to encourage better performance in a demoralised work unit, your content and presentation style will be radically different than if your goal is to teach an accountancy group the implications of recent changes in the tax law.

Similarly, you should clarify what role you will be performing during the presentation. Will you be acting as a coach, advocate, teacher, devil's advocate, watch dog, or messenger? Each of these roles dictates a different approach in both content and style and determines whether you should adopt a neutral, supportive or antagonistic approach to the topic. Also, it influences the audience's attitude towards your presentation. Thus it is very important during the preparation phase to ensure that you and your audience agree on both your purpose and your role. If you come prepared to play the role of an impassioned advocate when the audience is expecting a neutral messenger, your presentation is likely to engender confusion, frustration and hostility.

Tailor your message to a specific audience

One of the 'Ten Deadly Sins' characterising ineffective presentations is 'Use a presentation designed for one audience for a different audience.' Here is the complete list:

1. Show up late and/or apologise for lack of time to prepare adequately.
2. Bore the audience with details of who you are, the history of your department, and where it fits into the company's organisation chart.
3. Do not explain why the subject is relevant to this audience.
4. Use the presentation designed for another audience for this audience.
5. Tell the audience more than they want to know.
6. Turn the lights out and show slides or transparencies while reading a script.
7. Read verbatim every word on every visual.
8. Do not rehearse – play it by ear.
9. Do not treat audience as peers – act either condescending or intimidated.
10. Overdo jokes, gimmicks and teasers, thus undermining your credibility as a presenter and trivialising your message.

Source: Adapted from Peoples (1988)

Accomplished public speakers, like Trevor Billinge, understand that there is no such thing as a context-free presentation. The success of a talk depends on the audience's understanding and receptiveness. It is, therefore, impossible to write a generic presentation explaining a new work procedure that will be equally well received by all the work groups, managers at all levels in the organisation, union officials or suppliers.

The key to developing an audience-specific message is to understand their knowledge of the topic, and to empathise with them so that you will know what they expect from you, your presentation and your message. For instance, if the audience could well think that they know more about the topic than you do and could be hostile to your interference, you might arrange to have one-to-one discussions with key informal leaders prior to your formal presentation. You should probably also bring selected members into the presentation. For example, 'Given your experience with this set of customers, how do you think we should implement this new strategy?'

The old adage, 'I don't care how much you know until I know how much you care', has special significance for preparing a presentation. Members of an audience are more likely to support a presenter's position if they feel she or he has done sufficient homework to understand their fears, dreams, etc. Basically, members of an audience want to be treated as individuals, even though they are part of a group. Effective presenters find ways to personalise their message for the various members of subgroups in the audience by establishing some common areas of agreement. Abraham Lincoln observed, 'My way of opening and winning an argument is first to find a common ground of agreement.'

When the boss of Apex made a presentation to a division advocating the adoption of a new product line, he followed that advice, appealing to the chief accountant on the basis of cost efficiency, to the head of production by emphasising the small amount of re-tooling required, and to the general manager on the basis of increased profits and enhanced image. Speaking to the audience's point of view requires using their language. A speaker before a group of naval personnel who repeatedly refers to 'ropes' and 'boats' as opposed to 'lines' and 'ships' is automatically an outsider with little hope of having influence.

Structure

Begin with a statement of intent, the expected benefits, the structure you intend to follow, and ground rules within which you are working

In general, effective preparation is reflected in an introduction that convinces the audience that your presentation will be specific, practical, relevant and interesting. Examine the topic from their perspective and proceed to show how your topic will help them solve relevant, pressing problems, reach important personal or group goals, sustain core values or satisfy critical needs. This approach will help you avoid another of the 'Ten deadly sins' of ineffective presentations: 'Do not explain why the subject has any value to the audience.'

It is also important to give your audience a 'road map' – a general outline of your talk. This helps allay the natural concerns of the audience and the chair during long presentations. Consider handing out an outline of your presentation or projecting the outline onto a screen not used for other visual aids. The second option allows you to control how much of the outline the audience can see. Your audience also needs to understand your ground rules – where, when and whether you expect questions or comment. Do you want people to break in at any time with their questions or hold them to the end? Avoid needless confusion and misunderstanding by stating your preference before beginning your talk.

Organise the body of the presentation logically

One of the most common complaints about poor presentations is that they are hard to follow. They appear to start nowhere in particular and proceed randomly in all directions. To increase audience comprehension, organise your thoughts in a logical sequence. As shown in Table B.1, this can take various forms: the most obvious are either inductive or deductive arguments. An inductive presentation starts with several examples or a set of data and then uses them to construct arguments to support a proposal. A deductive approach begins by outlining a set of general principles, values or beliefs and then proceeds to show how the proposed programme has been logically derived. Whichever approach you use, be sure to avoid the eight common logical fallacies shown in Table B.2. One serious logical flaw can undermine the credibility of your entire argument.

Table B.1 Presentation Outline

Introduction
- What? (Overview of presentation. If outline is complex, use visual aids)
- Why? (Purpose of presentation – why subject is important to this audience)
- How? (Format to be used, including how questions will be handled. Address the 'how long?' question if the presentation is lengthy or the group is on a tight schedule.)
- Who? (If more than one person is involved or responsible for developing the presentation)

Body (alternative formats)
- Rhetorical questions and answers (why, what, when, where, how)
- Logical progression (steps A, B, C)
- Time series (beginning to end)
- Compare and contrast (old vs new, wrong vs right, current vs proposed, ours vs theirs)
- Problems and solutions (consequences and benefits)
- Simple to complex (use knowledge building blocks)
- Deductive reasoning (from basic principles or shared values to specific recommendations)
- Inductive reasoning (from specific cases to broad conclusions)

Conclusion
- Review and highlight (key points, recommendations, benefits)
- Draw conclusions (Where are we? What's the next step?)

Table B.2 Eight common logical fallacies

1. *Hasty generalisations* (jumping to conclusions). *Example:* 'Because the Conservatives have been elected, we can expect a more balanced budget and, therefore, less government demand for credit. This will result in lower interest rates for the next four years.'

2. *Coincidence of events* (X followed Y, therefore, X was caused by Y). *Example:* 'Our decrease in productivity last year was the result of our poorly negotiated union agreement.'

3. *No relationship* (a connection of unconnectable events). *Example:* 'Apex Chemical doubled its sales last year, so it must be well managed.'

4. *Insufficient relationship* (false analogy). *Example:* 'Because Liverpool and Cardiff both have important harbours, they must have similar labour problems on the docks.'

5. *Either–or proposal* (offering only two solutions when others are possible). *Example:* 'Either we increase our price or we accept our current financial problems.'

6. *Begging the question* (false or dubious assumption). *Example:* 'We all know that a recession is inevitable, so let's begin planning now for the inevitable layoffs.'

7. *Personalising the argument* (referring to irrelevant personal characteristics). *Example:* 'I urge you not to vote for Bill Ash as a school governor. Just look at how he has raised his own children.'

8. *Arguing in a circle* (using a point to prove itself). *Example:* 'Dr Hansen, who has lectured far and wide on robotics, is well known in his field because he talks to many groups.'

Source: Adapted from Barrett (1977)

The logical flow of your arguments will also be enhanced if they proceed from the simple to the complex, from the familiar to the unfamiliar, from accepted practice to its replacement. In general, you should order your thoughts using continua like time, direction, causal process, problem-solving sequence, complexity, space or familiarity. A related technique is to organise your material as a series of answers to typical questions. This allows the presenter to establish a rapport with the audience by demonstrating an understanding of their perspective. It also might be used to organise a segment of a long talk, focusing, for example, on the implementation plan.

Logical ordering not only improves audience comprehension, it also allows you to build a compelling case for your plan. Irrespective of which organising framework is used, it is important to build a case supporting a proposal that does not rest solely on the presumed 'inherent merits of the plan'. One of the most common mistakes of inexperienced presenters is assuming that the audience will share their appreciation of the merits of a proposal. Members of a task force who have studied a problem for several months should not expect that the rest of the management team will accept their recommendation at face value. As stated earlier, the key to gaining audience support is showing how a proposal will fulfil a common objective, give expression to a salient value, or resolve a perplexing problem.

It is particularly difficult for an audience to follow the flow of a very long presentation. To facilitate comprehension, it is a good idea to use internal transitions and summaries at the end of major sections (e.g., 'Now that we have discussed the four key elements of this plan, we will explore the pros and cons of adopting it').

When appropriate, plan ways to encourage audience participation

Consider the desired level of audience involvement. If you prefer, or if the audience expects, a high degree of involvement in your presentation, it is a good idea to organise your material using a series of leading questions to introduce or summarise sections. You can use them not only to check comprehension but also to brainstorm solutions to a difficult problem, to explore ways to overcoming implementation obstacles, or to demonstrate and build support for a point of view.

You should not, however, rely exclusively on 'planned participation'. If two-way communication is engaged in only on cue, your efforts will appear manipulative and ill-conceived.

> Harold Wilson as Leader of the Labour Party, had a style of public speechmaking that relied on hecklers. He would use rude and untimely interjections from the audience to achieve his empathy with the rest of the audience and, some suspected, to determine the content and structure. As Prime Minister, on many occasions, the hecklers were more subdued and he had to change his style.

Although it is important to plan some key questions, look for opportunities for spontaneous interaction. For example, ask volunteers from the audience to demonstrate a technique, involve a resident expert in a highly technical discussion, or encourage dialogue between audience members on particularly controversial issues. Table B.3 contains several suggestions for using questions effectively during a presentation.

Maintain credibility: discuss the pros and cons

Audiences tend to distrust biased presentations. If the speaker obviously has much to gain from the acceptance of a plan, the audience tends to adopt a 'checks and balances' role by looking for counter-arguments and potential negative consequences. The more extreme the presenter's bias, the more deliberate the audience's counterbalancing tendency. This obviously makes it difficult to reach consensus. To avoid this polarisation phenomenon in presentations intended to persuade the audience to adopt a plan of action, you should discuss both the advantages and disadvantages of the plan.

A technique commonly used to persuade a sceptical audience is called 'sandwiching'. This involves three steps:

Table B.3 Suggestions for effective use of questions

Format of questions
1. Avoid rhetorical questions. Ask thought-provokers which your audience is able to answer.
2. Ask some open-ended questions, with no right or wrong answers. Use questions to encourage sharing experiences, feelings, opinions, etc.
3. Put 'you' elements into questions. Make them relevant to the respondent's personal experience.
4. Prepare key questions prior to the presentation. It is difficult to think of good questions on your feet. If extensive discussion is desired, organise the presentation around a series of leading questions.

Use of questions
1. Ask 'friendly' questions. Don't use questions to embarrass or badger. Avoid known 'sore spots.' Some very effective speakers use the technique of asking 'five **yes** questions' at the beginning to establish empathy – 'I hope you are all able to hear me', 'Do we have enough seats for everyone?' etc.
2. Make the interchange a mutually satisfying experience. Give respondents time to think and phrase their answer. If they get stuck, help them by summarising and then asking if anyone else has something to add.
3. When you ask a specific question, limit the answer to the information wanted. Don't let the respondent wander or attempt to take control of the presentation. A polite, 'Thank you, that's what I was looking for', can get you back on track.
4. If extensive audience discussion is desired, avoid isolated one-to-one dialogues with specific individuals. (You ask question 1, person A answers; you ask question 2, person B answers, etc.) Instead, encourage audience members to respond to and ask questions of each other.

Source: Adapted from Mambert (1976)

1. You emphasise the advantages of the plan.
2. You assess the risks or concerns associated with adoption in a realistic way.
3. You reinforce the benefits by showing how they outweigh the costs, demonstrate how risks can be minimised with proposed safeguards, or show how resistance to change can be overcome.

Conclude on a high note; include an overall summary and proposed actions or options

The most important parts of a presentation are the first and last few minutes. You establish an initial impression in your introduction that colours the rest of the presentation, and the impression created during the conclusion influences the audience's overall, long-term evaluation of your performance. Since these are the most important segments of your presentation, they warrant the most preparation.

In particular, many public-speaking experts suggest that you should 'begin with the end in mind'. That is, you should write your conclusion first. This allows you to organise the rest of your material so that it flows naturally into your conclusion.

Effective conclusions can take a variety of forms. For example, you might emphasise legitimacy by highlighting several authoritative quotes; emphasise the 'I'm here to help' theme; predict conditions in the future – with and without your plan; underscore the utility of your proposal by emphasising its impact on the bottom line; use an emotional appeal to increase commitment and loyalty.

The conclusion of a lengthy presentation should also review and summarise the main points. (A visual outline enables you to do this efficiently.) It should also highlight what actions need to be taken following the presentation. ('Now that this plan has been explained in detail and voted on by the committee, the logical next step is to communicate our intentions to the sales division.')

Incorporate visual aids effectively

If by itself a picture is worth a thousand words, then a picture properly integrated with an oral presentation is worth ten thousand words. However, not all pictures have equal impact. Effective visual aids are used for emphasis and to increase audience comprehension and interest, not as cue cards for the presenter (see the 'Ten deadly sins', page 551). With that purpose in mind, remember too that the form of the visual aid should not impede its function. It should be simple, clear and visible to your entire audience. Avoid showing a long list of key points in your presentation. Break a list of items into subsections, so that no major heading has more than three or four items under it. In fact, you might prefer to organise lists of items into meaningful categories: Advantages and Disadvantages; What to do? Why? Who? When?; Old Way and New Way; Problem, Cause and Solution.

In summary, the purpose of a visual aid is to augment your presentation, not replace it or distract from it. Additional suggestions for effective visual aids are shown in Table B.4.

Practise your presentation and prepare for contingencies

The mark of effective presenters is the appearance of effortlessness. They have such command of their material it appears they are ad libbing. But don't be fooled by appearances. Hours of practice have preceded the actual performance.

After you have carefully considered your role, the purpose of your presentation, and the expectation of the audience, it is a good idea to write an idea draft. The purpose of this step is not to focus on specific wording, but on the key points. These can be written down on cards and then arranged in a logical order. Next comes a word-for-word script. This is especially important for inexperienced presenters or for presentations covering unfamiliar material. This step forces you to focus on the important details that are the trademark of polished presentations. These include: questions for stimulating audience participation (when appropriate); transition statements and internal summaries; phrases or quotes that improve audience com-

---

Table B.4 Pointers for using visual aids effectively

Purpose
1. Both the quality and number of visual aids should enhance, not distract from, your message.
2. Display or distribute an outline to help the audience follow long, or group, presentations.
3. Use variety to increase interest. Remember the value of pictures, graphs, symbols, and best of all, objects.

Appearance
1. Never use a black-and-white transparency of a typewritten page. Do it in colour. Use at least two, but not more than three colours.
2. Ask yourself: Can the audience quickly and easily grasp what they see?

Format – text
1. Make one and only one key point per visual (unless audience is very familiar with the subject).
2. Organise material into natural categories: before and after, problem and solution, advantage and disadvantage, beginning to end.
3. Include no more than three or four points under one heading.
4. Don't use whole sentences or paragraphs. Use bulleted words or short phrases only, except for quotes.

Format – graphics
1. No more than three curves on a graph.
2. Don't use a page full of numbers. Translate complex numbers into pie charts or bar graphs.
3. Use diagrams or models to present complex concepts. Use multiple versions, illustrating different stages or parts. Start simply and add complexity.

Source: Adapted from Peoples (1988)

---

prehension of key points and the logical flow of ideas. This step also helps you avoid the presentation pitfalls of internal contradictions, logical fallacies, and inappropriate emphasis.

In critical situations it is a good idea to memorise this written script and rehearse it several times. In no circumstances should the written script be used during the actual presentation. To avoid being tempted to read your material, take only a set of 'cheat sheets' with you to the podium. These should contain an outline of key points, quotations, facts and figures, and questions. In addition, it is a good idea to add marginal notations that remind you when to use the chalkboard, hold up an exhibit, turn the flipchart, pause for questions and so on. Also, add timing cues for long presentations.

An important part of rehearsing is preparing for unexpected contingencies. What will you do if a bulb or the data projector fails, people can't see your key visual aid, your audience is obviously more familiar with the material than you expected, or some troublemakers start challenging your assumptions? To help you prepare for these possibilities, it is a good idea to rehearse your presentation under simulated conditions in terms of room size, type of audience, time of day and length of presentation. This experience will help you anticipate difficult questions, problems and situations. It will also help you develop a flexible format, allowing you to adjust both your pace and approach according to audience reactions. In general it is a good idea to prepare several different methods of presenting key points; then you'll be prepared to select the approach that suits the mood of the audience. You can avoid content-driven presentations that force the audience to hear every item in the outline and view every overhead in the briefcase. Effective presenters build in periods of 'dialogue time' (typically initiated by a question) as a way of gauging audience comprehension, interest and attitude.

But how should you respond if something totally unexpected happens? What if the deafening roar of an overhead plane drowns out your voice? What if the microphone goes dead, a window blows open, or the room becomes extremely hot? A good rule of thumb is to respond the same way you would if you were in the audience. Take off your jacket if it is too hot, close the window, raise your voice, or pause during a momentary disruption. In addition, if the disruption is particularly obtrusive, you can relieve some of the tension in a hot or noisy room with a humorous comment that acknowledges how you and the audience are feeling.

Style

Convey controlled enthusiasm for your subject

A survey asked 1,200 people to identify the characteristics of effective presentations (Peoples, 1988). The results contained adjectives such as flexible, co-operative, audience empathy, pleasant and interesting. What was striking about these results is that only the last item on the list of 12 outstanding characteristics was specifically related to the content of the presentation. This suggests that the preceding discussion of effective format, while necessary, is not sufficient to guarantee your success. Put another way, a rambling, poorly organised presentation will surely produce an overall negative evaluation. On the other hand, a well-organised, highly logical, and easy-to-follow presentation that is poorly delivered will also be viewed negatively. This study points out an extremely important point about successful presenters. They understand that communication is partly intellectual and partly emotional. Therefore, they ensure that their presentations are both intellectually sound and emotionally satisfying.

Years of research on student evaluations of classroom teaching performance have consistently shown that enthusiasm is the hallmark of a good teacher. Students will forgive other deficiencies if the teacher obviously loves the subject and is genuinely interested in conveying that appreciation to the students. The same holds true for presenters. Unfortunately, most are not intense enough. If you are dull, the audience will also be dull. If you are alive, alert, intense and enthusiastic, your audience will be compelled to listen. Your posture, tone of voice, and facial expressions are all critical indicators of your attitude. Whenever possible, speak standing; do not lean on a podium or against a wall. If you must sit down, avoid a casual, low-key style; sit erect, lean forward, and use gestures to convey an attitude of earnestness. Remember, your audience will mirror your attitude.

Although enthusiasm is important, it must be controlled. Do not confuse enthusiasm with loudness. Remember, your audience listens most intently when you whisper. A good rule of thumb is to use vigorous but conversational tones of voice and inflections. Avoid 'orating' or 'bellowing' at the audience, but make sure you can be easily heard and that your tone is sufficiently strong and emphatic to convey meaning effectively. In general, your tone of voice and facial expressions should be used to convey a range of emotions: concern, anticipation, excitement, dismay, etc.

Provide variety and relief, and emphasise novelty and uniqueness

Another key to maintaining audience attention is variety. Alternate moving and standing still, speaking and listening, doing and thinking. Intersperse your lecture with chalkboard use, demonstration, audience participation and audio visuals so that no single activity occupies a large portion of the presentation. Also, add some spice to your presentation by including war stories, testimonials, analogies and demonstrations.

If variety is the key to maintaining interest, novelty and uniqueness are the keys to increasing impact. The presentation that will be remembered the longest invariably contains an unpredictable twist. Instead of a lecture on how to do strategic planning, the audience actually completes a plan for their respective work units. Instead of a graph showing an alarming increase in the number of customer complaints, a disgruntled customer is brought to the meeting.

Humour is a challenging aspect of presentations that deserves special attention. Used appropriately, it is an effective source of variety and novelty. Especially during a long presentation, the interjection of humour can ease the tension of intense concentration. However, humour must always play a subordinate role, and it must be in good taste. If you are uncertain about how the audience will react to a joke or if you feel uncomfortable with your ability to tell a humorous story, you can rely on spontaneous, unplanned incidents during the presentation to provide comic relief. You can seize the opportunity to exaggerate or understate a point, respond in a witty manner to a question, or link a point to a common local complaint, such as poor lunchroom food or cramped office space. However, it is important to avoid getting a laugh at the expense of a member of the audience.

Use physical space and body movement to enhance your message

It is important to remember that presentations are movies, not snapshots. If you are working from a stage, arrange it so that you can use physical movement. If you need a microphone, use a portable one wherever possible so that you can move freely *Always* practise with the microphone before 'going live'. Physical movement can be used to punctuate important points, signal a transition, build rapport with a person who asks a question, heighten the interest of particular segments of the audience, and help your audience stay alert by refocusing their attention. It also gives you a feeling of being in command of the situation. Of course, annoying mannerisms such as pacing back and forth or bouncing around the platform should be avoided – we would recommend making a video of your presentations and watching them in solitude as a way of avoiding such mannerisms.

There are other aspects of physical space that impact on the quality of your presentation. If possible you should arrange the stage area and seating in the room to remove distractions. If you are speaking in a large room, arrange the audience so that they are not disturbed by late arrivals. Also try to group participants so there is little space between them. Eliminate unnecessary or distracting materials from the podium, such as unused equipment, signs and displays. Keep your visual aids covered until actually in use, and keep the chalkboard clean. Have cleaning materials at hand. Never walk across areas illuminated by projectors. Turn them off before you cross.

It is also important to position yourself so as to enhance rapport with the audience. Do not get so close to individuals in front that they feel threatened, or so far removed from the rear of your audience that they feel detached. Also, try to position yourself roughly in the middle of your audience, from left to right, and to have the front of the audience on either side far enough back that you can comfortably maintain eye contact. If possible, it is desirable before your presentation to sit down in the far corners of the room to feel the psychological distance your audience will be experiencing. With this in mind, you can deliberately alter your presentation style to build rapport with members of the audience seated in undesirable locations.

Eye contact is your primary tool for establishing audience involvement. If handled properly, it makes listeners feel they are involved in a one-to-one, semi-private discussion with you. It also allows you to gauge their attentiveness to your message. Breaking of eye contact suggests individuals are getting tired, bored or overwhelmed. Experienced presenters avoid the common mistakes of reading notes or visual aids and looking over the audience's heads or at their feet. Effective eye contact involves looking directly at members of the audience, one at a time, on a random, rotating basis. Generally, the smaller the group, the longer each occasion of eye contact should last. Normally, however, three to five seconds is about the right length of time.

Use gestures sparingly and naturally

Gestures should appear spontaneous and natural so that they enhance rather than distract from your message. When you concentrate on your message, not your movements, and put your whole body and personality into conveying it, the appropriate gestures will come naturally. Be careful not to step out of character. Use gestures merely to accentuate your normal mode of expression. For example, a normally conservative person should not try to become artificially effervescent during a presentation. There is no single, right form of expression, only appropriate ones – those suited to your personality, the subject matter and the context. It is particularly important to fit your actions to your audience. Large, dramatic gestures that would be appropriate in a banquet hall would be overpowering in a small committee meeting. Also, the number and type of gestures you use should vary, depending on whether you are simply making a report or presenting an appeal for support.

Although what is appropriate is relative to the situation, there are some gestures that are always wrong. Inexperienced presenters betray their nervousness through irrelevant and annoying mannerisms such as jingling change in a pocket, toying with notes, shifting from one foot to the other, or adjusting spectacles. In fact, any movement repeated too often creates a distraction. To avoid repeating the same gesture over and over, practise using a variety of body movements to illustrate, describe, enumerate, add emphasis or direct attention. For variety, some gestures should involve the entire upper body, not just the dominant hand. When hand movements are used they should be flowing and complete. Gestures should also be long enough in duration to register with the audience, just as visual aids need to appear long enough for comprehension.

Additional hints: questions and challenges

Be prepared for queries

Questions and challenges are most difficult to handle when they catch you off guard and you may come over as arrogant or ineffectual. Therefore, the key to formulating effective responses is preparation. Ask colleagues to critique your material, discuss their questions and objections with experts, collect supporting documentation or evidence, and practise your responses. Despite your best efforts, someone may manage to catch you off guard. But in general, an apologising presenter is a poorly prepared presenter.

When challenged, be candid and firm but avoid over-responding

A question may only interest a minority in the audience and by answering it, you may lose the majority. If you permit an audience to annoy or intimidate you or to make you feel you are being indulged or patronised, you lose control of the situation. If you do not take negative reactions personally, you will be less likely to permit this to happen. A look of disbelief or disapproval from a member in the front row should be registered but never taken to heart. If you ask a rhetorical question and get a predictably dull reaction, adjust to it and continue.

Respond to objections in a positive manner. By linking objections to positive features of your proposal, you maintain an optimistic climate in your discussion. For example, 'While it is true that the initial start-up costs will be high, we project a faster than normal rate of return.'

When questions are asked, don't try to fool your audience. When you are unsure of your facts, be candid, but offer to follow up with the questioner later. However, don't avoid being unequivocal. People respect an unequivocal message even if they don't agree with it. Don't be afraid to take a stand, 'to tell it like it is'. Hedging weakens your credibility and the impact of your entire presentation.

Answer questions as succinctly as possible. Long, complex answers are generally not required and tend to discourage further interaction. Complex answers only raise more questions, and rambling answers suggest an inability to think concisely or to handle a give-and-take situation.

Maintain control of the meeting

Questioners tend to take the offensive, placing presenters on the defensive. A good presenter never stays in a defensive position for long and avoids it altogether if possible. If you do not wish to engage in an interchange at that time, you have every right to explain that the answer will be covered later or to offer to discuss the matter after the presentation. You have an objective, and you should decide what is most relevant for its accomplishment. Allowing your audience to dictate the pace or direction of your presentation places you in a position of weakness that undermines your credibility. Although you should certainly be sensitive to feedback and flexible enough to respond to legitimate concerns, you should alter your plans only if the majority of your audience will view it as a responsible shift rather than a placating response to a minority voice.

Experienced presenters soon learn that people don't always ask questions just because they want information. Audience members may ask questions to get attention from you or the group or to sabotage your position if they resent your knowing more than they do or perceive your ideas as a threat. Being sensitive to a person's true motive for asking a question enables you to respond appropriately.

Suggestions for handling disruptive and inappropriate behaviours are shown in Table A.3, page 537, in the Conducting Meetings supplement. In addition to these suggestions for specific cases, several broad guidelines for handling argumentative questions are shown in Table B.5.

Table B.5 Guidelines for answering argumentative questions

General approach
1. Never argue in public. In the eyes of the audience, both parties lose.
2. Be firm and assertive but never defensive or aggressive.
3. Treat your audience as equals. Don't talk up or down to them.

Specific techniques
1. Listen attentively. Repeat the question if it is very long or if others did not hear it. This gives you time to think, shows interest, and makes sure you have understood the question.
2. Answer hostile questions with questions, drawing out your interrogator and regaining the offensive.
3. Broaden the discussion. Don't get trapped into an argument with one person. Involve others to determine if this is an isolated concern.
4. Return to your plans as soon as possible. Defer extensive discussions until the end of your presentation. Express willingness to discuss specialised or detailed issues after your presentation.

Summary and behavioural guidelines

A key aspect of management is communication, and formal presentations are an essential communication tool. Therefore, effective managers must be able to make informative and inspiring speeches. This is not welcome news for people who share the widespread fear of public speaking. We have argued that the way to reduce this natural fear is through guided practice.

This supplement has outlined a number of guidelines based on a 4 S's model:

1. Formulate a strategy for a specific audience.

2. Develop a flexible, flowing structure.

3. Combine with an enhancing, not distracting, presentation style.

4. Supplement with confident, informed responses to questions and challenges.

This material is summarised in the following behavioural guidelines.

Strategy

1. Tailor your message to your audience.
   - Understand their needs, desires, knowledge level and attitude towards your topic.
   - Make sure your approach is consistent with your role.
   - Be concrete, specific, practical and relevant.

2. Develop a logically compelling case for your plan.
   - Demonstrate how it will resolve a pressing problem, advance a salient value, or help reach a common goal.
   - Avoid the eight logical fallacies.

Structure

3. Organise your presentation in a logical sequence.
   - Begin by placing your topic in context.
   - State your objective.
   - Move from familiar to unfamiliar, simple to complex, old to new, before to after.
   - Use internal summaries and transitions.
   - Conclude with a general overview and a specific proposal (or list of options).

4. Use visual aids to enhance your message.
   - Keep graphs, charts and other visuals simple.
   - Use variety to keep your audience's attention.
   - Don't let the mechanics of the presentation interfere with your message.

5. Prepare for contingencies.

- Adjust your pace and language to audience interest and comprehension.
- Anticipate comprehension difficulties, and prepare for unforeseen problems with equipment.

Style

6. Present your material with controlled enthusiasm.

- Project high levels of intensity and interest without shouting or preaching.
- Radiate confidence while maintaining willingness to make reasonable changes.

7. Discuss the pros and cons of your proposal realistically.

- Begin by explaining its advantages.
- Then present a realistic assessment of its risks or challenges.
- Conclude by reinforcing its benefits or proposing remedies for problems.

8. Use natural and spontaneous body movements and facial expressions.

- Use your body as well as the physical space to enhance your message.
- Avoid distracting mannerisms.
- Maintain eye contact with members of the audience rather than speaking to the room in general.

9. Provide variety and relief.

- Alternate between speech and action, lecture and discussion.
- Use spontaneous humour wisely.

Questions and challenges

10. Anticipate questions and thoroughly prepare responses.

- Rehearse answers to difficult questions.
- If necessary, offer to obtain additional information and follow up with answers.

11. Use questions to strengthen your main arguments.

- Answer questions candidly but positively.
- Link objections to attractive features of your proposal.

12. Maintain control of the meeting.

- Be firm and assertive without being aggressive or defensive.
- Don't let interruptions disrupt your composure.
- Avoid circumstances that require an apology.

Skill Practice

Exercises in Making Effective Oral Presentations

EXERCISE **B.1**

SPEAKING AS A LEADER

As illustrated in the opening case about Trevor Billinge at Apex Communications, one of the major challenges facing leaders is the requirement to deliver a wide range of presentations. Effective communicators must be skilled at both informing and inspiring. They must be able to hold their own with hostile audiences as well as impress content experts and instil confidence in novices. They must be skilled at building consensus, pointing out a new direction, and explaining a complex topic. This exercise (developed by Richard Linowes) gives you an opportunity to practise speaking on a variety of leadership topics.

Assignment

To practise playing this important leadership role, prepare a talk on one of the following topics:

1. *Taking charge of an established group.* The speaker is a manager now newly assigned to a group that has worked together under other managers for some time.

2. *Announcing a new project.* The speaker is announcing a new undertaking to members of his/her department and is calling on all to rally behind the effort.

3. *Calling for better customer service.* The speaker is motivating all employees to be as attentive and responsive to the customer as possible.

4. *Calling for excellence and high-quality work.* The speaker is motivating all employees to perform their jobs with a commitment to meeting the highest possible standards.

5. *Announcing the need for cost reductions.* The speaker is requesting that everyone look for ways to cut expenditure and immediately begin to slash spending.

6. *Commending a job well done.* The speaker is extolling a group of people who have worked very hard for an extended period to produce outstanding results.

7. *Calming a frightened group of people.* The speaker is trying to restore calm and give confidence to those who feel panic in the face of distressing business developments.

8. *Addressing a challenging opposition.* The speaker is presenting some heartfelt belief to a critical, even hostile, audience.

9. *Mediating between opposing parties.* The speaker is serving as judge, or arbiter, between two groups who are bitterly opposed on a key issue.

10. *Taking responsibility for error.* The speaker is a spokesperson for an institution whose actions have produced an unfortunate result that affects the audience.

11. *Reprimanding unacceptable behaviour.* The speaker is taking to task certain individuals who have failed to perform up to required levels.

12. *Petitioning for special allowances.* The speaker is presenting the case for an institution seeking certain rights that must be authorised by some external body.

Your speech should last from three to five minutes unless you are otherwise instructed. Create a context for your talk by assuming a management role in a familiar organisation. Before beginning your talk, explain the details of the context to your audience (either orally or in a written summary). Explain your organisational position concisely, the makeup of the audience, and their expectations of your presentation. The specific content of your talk is less important than how well it is prepared and how persuasively it is delivered. Be prepared to respond to questions and challenges.

In preparing your presentation, review the behavioural guidelines at the end of the Skill Learning section. The checklist in this exercise may also be of use. After your talk is completed, you will receive feedback based on the criteria shown in the Observer's Feedback Form in Appendix 1, page 641.

Checklist for developing effective presentations

1. What is my objective and my role?

2. What is the context of my presentation? (Size of audience and room, location and time of day, what precedes and follows.)

3. How will I close the presentation?

4. How will I open the presentation?

5. How will I organise the body of the presentation?

6. How will I get their attention?

7. How will I keep their interest?

8. What questions will I ask?

9. What visual aids will I use?

10. How will I tailor the presentation to this audience?

11. What questions will they be likely to ask?

12. What notes do I need?

EXERCISE **B.2**

QUALITY CIRCLES AT BRADFIELD FOODS

One important innovation in group decision making has been the introduction of quality circles (QCs). This technique has been described by senior Japanese industrialists as being critical to their manufacturing success. Ironically, an American, Edward Deming, first brought the concept of 'statistical quality control' to the Japanese in the early post-World War II years. The Japanese combined these ideas with the assumption that the person who performs a job is the one who best knows how to identify and correct its problems. As a result, the Japanese, with Deming's help, developed the QC. A QC is a group of people (usually about ten) who meet periodically to discuss and develop solutions to problems related to quality, productivity, or product cost.

The Japanese have also introduced QCs into the UK. One example is described in Kazuo Murata's book *How To Make Japanese Methods Work In The West* (Gower, 1991). A Japanese firm, Yuasa, set up a battery manufacturing subsidiary in Ebbw Vale and soon established itself as a market leader. Its success was due to its ability to set quality targets which were at least as good as the parent company based in Japan, and against which benchmarks could be set.

Quality circles were an integral part of this process but the British approach was slightly different to that of the Japanese. Murata says: 'Japanese people volunteer for QCs because they do not want to be isolated. In the UK, people come up with improvement ideas because they want to: it's a game to play.'

The purpose of this exercise is to give you an opportunity to make a presentation on this important topic.

Assignment

You are the Director of Personnel at Bradfield Foods, a leading manufacturer of breakfast cereal. Productivity has been sagging industry-wide and your organisation is starting to see its effect on profitability. In response, you have been asked by the board of directors to make a 20-minute presentation on QCs. The board knows that QCs have been adopted in several factories by your leading competitor, and it would like your recommendation as to whether Bradfield Foods should follow suit. They have read about QCs in the popular press but they don't know any more about the subject. Using the following reference material, prepare a presentation on QCs. Explain the QC structure and process and the advantages/disadvantages of QCs. The final section of the presentation should include a recommendation regarding their adoption at your plants. Be prepared to respond to questions and challenges.

In preparing your presentation, refer to the behavioural guidelines for effective presentations at the end of the Skill Learning section and the checklist in the preceding exercise. At the conclusion of your presentation you will receive feedback based on the Observer's Feedback Form in Appendix 1, page 641.

Source: Dubrin (1985)

A Look at some of the evidence for quality circles

Quality circles, on balance, appear to be making a positive contribution to product quality, profits, morale, and even improved employee attendance. The widespread attention QCs have received in recent years has led logically to their evaluation by both business-people and researchers. Here we will rely on several types of evaluation methods, sampling first the positive evidence, then the negative.

Favourable outcomes with QCs

Honeywell, a high-technology electronics firm, has become a pioneer in the application of QCs in North America. It currently operates several hundred QCs in the US. Typically about six assembly workers are brought together every two weeks by a supervisor or team leader. 'We feel that this type of participatory management programme not only increases productivity,' says Joseph Riordan, director of Honeywell Corporate Productivity Services, 'but it also upgrades the quality of work life for employees. Line workers feel that they are more a part of the action. As a result, we find that the quality of work improves and absenteeism is reduced. With this kind of involvement, we have, in many cases, been able to increase the capacity of a line without the addition of tooling or extra shifts.'

Honeywell used the QC method to manage the problem of winning a renewable bid for a government contract. 'Here was a situation,' Riordan relates, 'where we had already cut our rejects down, where all of the learning had effectively gone out of the process.' The problem was assigned to the QC representing that particular work area. 'They came up with a suggestion for further automating the process that enabled us to improve our competitive position by about 20 per cent and win the contract.'

In an attempt to determine the appropriateness of QCs to North American firms, a team of researchers set up a one-year field experiment at a metal fabricating facility of an electronics firm.

Eleven QCs, averaging nine production employees each, were established. Performance was measured by a computerised monitoring system created from the company's existing employee performance reporting system. Both quantity and quality measurements were taken. Employee attitudes were also assessed, using the Motivating Potential Score (MPS) of the Hackman-Oldham Job Diagnostic Survey.

The major result of the circle programme was its positive impact on reject rate, as shown in the top half of Figure B.2. Reject rates per capita for QC participants dropped by one-third to one-half of the former rates by the time the programme had run three months. The reject rates for the control group surprisingly increased during the same period.

An explanation offered by the researchers for these results is that circle members tackled the issues of internal communication as a top priority item. For example, one of the initial projects implemented by the QCs was improving training manuals and procedures, including translating materials into a worker's native language if the worker desired. Careful attention to better training in fundamentals prevented many errors.

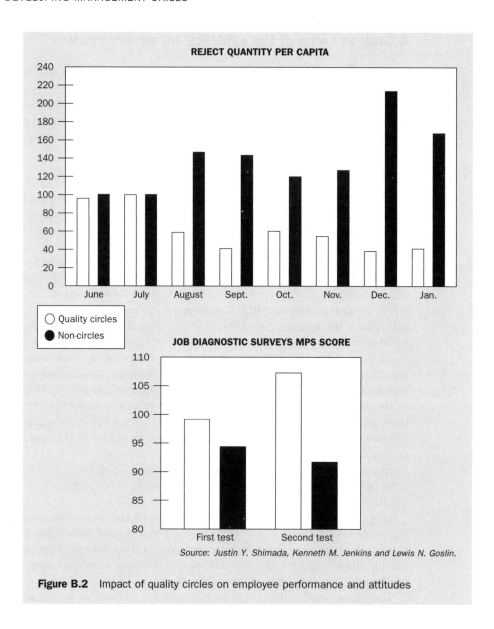

Figure B.2 Impact of quality circles on employee performance and attitudes

Circle members also made fewer errors. In addition the defective parts the circle members did make tended to be less expensive to scrap or rework into usable parts. The explanation given for these results is that circle training instructs employees in how to prioritise problems on the basis of 'dollar impact' on the company. The cost savings generated by the lower reject rate represented a 300 per cent return on the cost of investment in the programme.

The impact of QCs on participants' level of work satisfaction was equally impressive. Results shown in Figure B.2 indicate the Motivating Potential Score (MPS) for the circle participants increased, while the control group showed a decrease. No other changes were present in the work environment that would affect the experimental group differently from the control group. The researchers concluded that the improvement in employee job attitudes could be attributed to the circle training programme and the problem-solving activity. The job characteristic most influenced by the quality activity was skill variety – the extent to which the job requires a variety of different skills.

Negative outcomes of quality circles

Despite these successes, many negative results have been reported. A review of the results of the first surge of QC activity in the United States revealed that as many as 75 per cent of initially successful programmes were no longer in operation after a few years. Even Lockhead, one of the American pioneers in this method, had decreased its involvement with QCs. Robert Cole, a recognised authority on the Japanese workforce, made these pessimistic remarks:

> That fact is that the circles do not work very well in many Japanese companies. Even in those plants recognised as having the best operating programmes, management knows that perhaps only one-third of the circles are working well, with another third borderline, and one-third simply making no contribution at all. For all of the rhetoric of voluntarism, in a number of companies the workers clearly perceive circle activity as coercive. Japanese companies face a continuing struggle to revitalise circle activity to ensure that it does not degenerate into ritualistic behaviour.

A study of QCs in 29 companies conducted by Matthew Goodfellow found only eight of them to be cost-effective in terms of gains in productivity. Management consultant Woodruff Imberman investigated the 21 unsuccessful QC efforts and found four major causes of failure. Firstly, in many firms the employees intensely disliked management. Their antagonism carried over into the QCs which some employees perceived to be a management ploy to reduce overtime and trim down the workforce by increasing productivity. Secondly, most organisations did a poor job of selling the QCs. Instead of conducting individual discussions with employees, they relied on flipcharts, booklets, and formal management presentations. The workers were left wondering, 'What's in it for me?'

Thirdly, the supervisors chosen to lead the circles received some training in human relations and group dynamics, but they felt that little of this information satisfied the specific needs of their own departments. And fourthly, most of the 21 firms regarded the QC programmes as merely a way of improving the efficiency of production techniques. They did not realise that QCs cannot succeed unless top management is willing to shift its philosophy towards emphasising good relations among employees and between management and workforce. This last point hints at the importance of establishing the conditions that allow a quality circle programme to succeed.

Key elements of a successful programme

Quality circle programmes show some variation from company to company, whether these companies are engaged in manufacturing or service. They may differ in how frequently they meet, how much authority is granted to the team leader or supervisor, whether they use a group facilitator in addition to a supervisor, and how much co-ordination there is with the existing quality control department. Based on the judgements of several observers, the successful programmes have certain elements in common, as follows:

- *Quality circles work best in firms where good employee–management relations already exist.* QCs are not likely to succeed in organisations suffering from acrimonious union–management conflict or high levels of distrust between employees and management.

- *Top management is committed to the programme.* Without commitment from top management, the initiation of a QC programme is inadvisable. Instead the director of the circle project should first prepare reports on other companies where QCs have been successful and present them to top management.

- *Circle leaders use a participative leadership style.* Laurie Fitzgerald, a QC consultant, advocates the 'leader as a worker for the members' concept. When the circle leader takes on a highly authoritarian role, the members are usually unresponsive.

- *The right people and the right area are selected.* For QCs to be effective, the programme manager has to be enthusiastic, persistent and hard-working. The facilitator or team leader must be energetic and co-operative. Another important step in getting the programme off the ground is to select an area of the company where one can expect co-operation and enthusiasm from participants.

- *Programme goals are stated explicitly.* Objectives should be made clear in order to avoid confusion or unreasonable expectations from the circle programme. Among the goals of QC programmes are improving product quality, increasing productivity, improving communications between workers and supervisors, decreasing product costs, improving the quality of work life, and preparing people for future supervisory assignments.

- *The programme is well publicised throughout the firm.* Once the programme is started, information about it should be disseminated widely throughout the company. Better communication results in less resistance and fewer negative rumours about the programme. The content of the communication should be open and positive.

- *The programme starts slow and grows slowly.* A gradual introduction of the programme helps expose people to new concepts and helps reduce doubts about its intention and potential merit.

- *The QC programme is customised to meet the needs of the firm.* A subtle source of failure in some QC programmes is the use of a canned set of procedures that don't fit local circumstances. A QC participant whose work is data processing may have difficulty with the translation of a case from the aerospace industry. A workable compromise is to use standard training as a framework and build on it with the unique problems of the firm in question.

- *Quality circles are used as a method of employee development.* A key purpose of these circles is to foster personal development of the participating workers. If managers intend to install a QC as a tool for their own selfish gain, they would do better not to begin.

- *Management is willing to grant recognition for ideas originating in the circles.* If management attempts to manipulate the circle volunteers or take credit from improvements away from them, it is most likely that the programme will backfire. More will be lost than gained.

- *Membership is voluntary.* As with job enrichment and all forms of participative management, employee preference is an influential factor. Employees who desire to contribute their ideas will generally perform better than employees who are arbitrarily assigned to a QC.

- *Achievements of quality circles are recognised as results of group, not individual, effort.* Recognising them as such decreases competitiveness and increases co-operation and interdependence within the group or department. QCs, not individual employees, receive credit for innovations and suggestions for improvement.

- *Ample training is provided.* Programme volunteers generally need some training in conference techniques or group dynamics. As a minimum, the circle leader will need skills in group-participation methods. Otherwise, he or she will wind up lecturing about topics such as quality improvement and productivity improvement. Leaders and participants will also need training in the use of whatever statistical and problem-solving methods are to be used. The following are major problem-solving techniques and their purposes.

1. Brainstorming is used to identify all problems, even those beyond the control of the circle members.
2. A check-sheet is used to log problems within the circle's sphere of influence within a certain time frame.
3. A Pareto chart graphically illustrates check-sheet data to identify the most serious problems, that is, the 20 per cent of the problems that cause 80 per cent of the major mistakes.
4. A cause-and-effect diagram graphically illustrates the cause of a particular problem.
5. Histograms or bar charts are graphed to show the frequency and magnitude of specific problems.
6. Scatter diagrams or 'measle charts' identify major defect locations, which show up as dense dot clusters on the pictures of products.
7. Graph-and-control charts monitor a production process and are compared with production samples.
8. Stratification, generally accomplished by inspecting the same products from different production areas, randomises the sampling process.

- *Creativity is encouraged.* As illustrated above, brainstorming sessions fit naturally into the quality-circle method and philosophy. Maintaining an attitude of 'anything goes' is particularly important, even if rough ideas must be refined later. If half-processed ideas are shot down by the leader or other members, idea generation will quickly be extinguished.

- *Projects are related to members' actual job responsibilities.* QCs are not arenas for amateur speculation about other people's work. People make suggestions about improving the quality of work for which they are already responsible. However, they should be willing to incorporate, for example, information from suppliers and customers.

The arguments for and against quality circles

A major argument for QCs is that they represent a low-cost, efficient vehicle for unleashing the creative potential of employees. In the process, highly desirable ends are achieved, such as improvements in the quality of both products and work life. QCs, in fact, are considered part of the quality of work life movement.

Another favourable feature of these circles is that they are perceived positively by all-management, workers, unions and stockholders. A firm contemplating implementing such a programme thus runs no risk of either internal or external opposition. (It is conceivable, however, that opposition will be forthcoming if management fails to act on QC suggestions.)

Quality circles contribute to organisational effectiveness in another important way. They have emerged as a useful method of developing present and future managers. Recently, a major computing manufacturing firm established a QC programme. After the programme had been operating for two years, the director of training observed that the supervisors who were QC leaders were significantly more self-confident, knowledgeable and poised than other supervisors who were attending the regular training programme. The director believed that the supervisors' involvement in the QC training programs and activities had been the major contributor to this difference.

One major criticism of QCs is that many of them are not cost-effective. Furthermore, even more pessimistic is the criticism that the reported successes of QCs may be attributable to factors other than the actual QC programme. One explanation is that the attention paid to employees by management may be the force behind the gains in productivity and morale (the well-known Hawthorne effect). Another possible explanation of the success of QC programmes is that the gains are due to improved group dynamics and problem-solving techniques. Therefore, an entire QC programme need not be conducted just to achieve these gains.

QCs may prove to be breeding grounds for friction and role confusion between the quality control department and the groups themselves. Unless management carefully defines the relationship of QCs *vis-à-vis* the quality control department, much duplication of effort (and therefore waste of resources) will be inevitable.

Exclusive reliance upon volunteers for the circles may result in the loss of potentially valuable ideas. Many non-assertive people may shy away from participation in the circles, despite having valid ideas for product improvement.

Some employees who volunteer to join QCs may be doing so for the wrong reasons. The circle may develop the reputation of being a good way to get away from the line for a while and enjoy a coffee break. (To counter such an abuse of the QC programme, QC group members might monitor the quality of input from their own group members.)

Guidelines for action

An early strategic step in implementing a QC is to clarify relationships between the circle and the formal quality control department. Otherwise, the quality control department may perceive the circle as a redundancy or threat. One effective arrangement is for the QC to complement the quality control department; the QC department thus does not become subject to the loss of authority.

Membership in the circle should be voluntary and on a rotating basis. In many instances a team member will soon run out of fresh ideas for quality improvement. Rotating membership will result in a wider range of ideas. Experience suggests that group size should be limited to nine.

QCs should be implemented on a pilot basis. As the circle produces results and wins the acceptance of managers and employees alike, it can be expanded as the demand for its output increases.

Do not emphasise quick financial returns or productivity increases from the output of QCs. The programme should be seen as a long-range project that will raise the quality consciousness of the organisation. (Nevertheless, as noted in the report from Honeywell, immediate positive results are often forthcoming.)

Management must make good use of many of the suggestions forthcoming from the QC, yet still define the limits of the power and authority of the circle. On the one hand, if none of the circle's suggestions is adopted, the circle will lose its effectiveness as an agent for change. Circle members will become discouraged because of their lack of clout. On the other hand, if the circle has too much power and authority, it will be seen as a governing body for technical change. In the latter circumstances, it is also possible that people will use the circle for political purposes. An individual who wants to get a technical modification authorised may try to influence a member of the QC to suggest that modification during a circle meeting.

Training in group dynamics and methods of participative management will be particularly helpful. It may also prove helpful at the outset to appoint a group facilitator (an internal or external consultant) who can help the group run more smoothly.

Interviewing

SKILL DEVELOPMENT OUTLINE

Skill Learning material

- Planning and conducting interviews
- Specific types of organisational interviews
- Summary and behavioural guidelines

Skill Practice exercises

- Evaluating the new employee-orientation programme
- Appraisal interview with Chris Jacobs
- Selection interview at Smith Farley Insurance

LEARNING OBJECTIVES

To increase proficiency in conducting

- general interviews
- information-gathering interviews

- selection interviews
- appraisal interviews

Skill Learning

Planning and conducting interviews

After conversations, interviews are probably the most frequent form of communication in organisations (Sincoff and Goyer, 1984). We have interviews for selection, information gathering, performance reviewing, counselling, disciplining and coaching.

Interviews are so common that they are often taken for granted. People view interviews as simply conversations during which information is gathered. While interviews are very similar to conversations, there are important differences. Specifically, an interview is a specialised form of communication conducted for a specific task-related purpose (Lopez, 1975; Downs *et al.*, 1980). Indeed, one reason why some managers perform poorly as interviewers is that they treat this 'purposeful communication' too casually, as though it were merely a conversation. As a result of poor planning and lack of attention to managing the interview process, they fail to accomplish their purpose and often alienate the interviewee in the process.

These outcomes are illustrated in the following counselling interview between John Owen, director of management services, and Ken Irwin, a management consultant on his staff (DuBrin, 1981).

John: Ken, I have arranged this meeting because I want to talk about certain aspects of your work. And my comments are not all that favourable.

Ken: Since you have formal authority over me, I suppose I don't have much choice. Go ahead.

John: I'm not a judge reading a verdict to you. I want your input.

Ken: But you called the meeting; go ahead with your complaints. Particularly any with foundation. I remember once when we were having lunch you told me that you didn't like the fact that I wore a brown suit with a blue shirt. I would put that in the category of unfounded.

John: I'm glad you brought up appearance. I think you present a sub-standard impression to clients. A consultant is supposed to look sharp, particularly at the rates we charge clients. You often give the impression that you cannot afford good clothing. Your trousers are baggy. Your ties are unfashionable and often food-stained.

Ken: The firm may charge those high rates, but the money I receive does not allow me to buy fancy clothes. Besides, I have very little interest in trying to dazzle clients with my clothes. I have heard no complaints from them.

John: Nevertheless, I think that your appearance should be more businesslike. Now, let's talk about another concern. A routine audit of your expense account shows a practice that I think is improper. You charged one client for a Thursday night dinner for three consecutive weeks, yet your airline ticket receipt shows that you returned home at three in the afternoon each week. That kind of behaviour is unprofessional. How do you explain your charges for these phantom dinners?

Ken: The flight ticket may say 3pm, but with our unpredictable weather, the flight could very well be delayed. If I eat at the airport, then my wife won't have to run the risk of preparing a dinner for me that goes to waste. Food is very expensive.

John: But how can you eat dinner at 3pm at the airport?

Ken: I consider any meal after one in the afternoon to be dinner.

John: Well, OK. Next I want to comment on your reports to clients. They are much more careless than they should be. I know that you are capable of more meticulous work. I saw an article you prepared for publication that was fist-rate and professional. Yet on one report you mis-spelled the name of the client company. That's unacceptable.

Ken: A good secretary should have spotted that mistake. Besides, I never claimed that I was able to write perfect reports. There are only so many hours in the working day to spend on writing up reports.

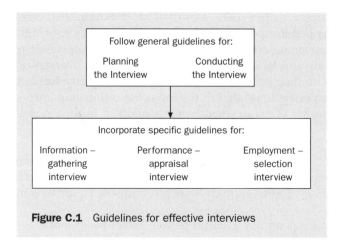

Figure C.1 Guidelines for effective interviews

Effective interviews don't just happen. Like other purposeful communication activities, interviews must be properly planned and executed. To help you become an effective interviewer, this supplement presents a series of guidelines, organised according to the scheme shown in Figure C.1. First, we will present broad guidelines for planning and conducting interviews in general. These establish a foundation of general principles, many of which build on more extensive discussions in Chapters 4, 5 and 6. These guidelines are divided into two steps: planning the interview and conducting the interview. Following this discussion, more specific guidelines will be presented for conducting specialised interviews with limited purposes: gathering information, selecting new employees and reviewing subordinate performance.

Planning the interview

Establish the purpose and agenda

As with any planned communication, you need to define clearly your purpose for holding the interview. In an interview, as in an oral presentation, you need to ask yourself what you want to accomplish. Do you want to gather information? Persuade? Counsel? Evaluate? You also need to consider the relationship you want to develop with the other participant. Consider you interviewee and how your performance will affect the relationship that already exists. This is similar to the process of adapting your message to your audience in an oral presentation, but somewhat easier since there is only one member in your interview 'audience'.

Once you have determined your purpose, develop an agenda. Consider what kinds of information you need to obtain with respect to your purpose. Based on this, list the topics that need to be covered in the interview. While these topics do not have to be listed in any particular order, you may want to decide which topics have priority.

Create good questions that encourage information sharing

Questions arise out of your purpose and agenda and are the means by which you obtain information in an interview. Any interviewer can ask questions; only well-prepared interviewers can ask effective questions which will elicit the information they need. Make sure that the questions are worded clearly and that they ask for the information you want. Adapting to your interviewee is critical. Phrase your questions in language the interviewee can understand and in ways that will enhance your relationship with that person.

Different types of questions can be used for different effects. Open questions, such as 'How are you feeling today?' or 'How has the new regulation affected department morale?' elicit general information. **Open questions** are used when you want to let the interviewee talk without restriction. They allow interviewees freedom to discuss how they feel, what their priorities are, and how much they know about a topic. Open questions are useful for developing rapport in the interview because they involve the interviewee in the interaction. Of course, remembering the answers to open questions is a problem, particularly if the interviewee talks on and on. Open questions are also time-consuming, and using them too often makes it difficult for the interviewer to control the interview. However, if you are looking for broad, general information, you should ask open questions.

If, on the other hand, you need specific information, you should ask **closed questions**. Closed questions, such as 'Where were you last employed?' or 'Would you rather work on Project A or Project Z?' restrict the possible answers an interviewee can give. They are best used when you have limited time and need very specific information or want to clarify a point made in an answer to an open question. Table C.1 shows when you should use open or closed questions.

As you plan your questions, whether open, closed or both, pay close attention to how questions are worded. Often, an unprepared interviewer will inadvertently ask questions that will be difficult to answer or produce unwanted answers. One example is the **double-barrelled question**. For example, 'Why do you want to leave our organisation?', 'Is there anything I can do to change your mind?', 'What are the pros and cons of using this system?', 'Do you think we should adopt this new insurance?', 'Have any of our competitors adopted it?'

Each of these questions contains at least two separate questions, and an unskilled interviewee really doesn't know which question to answer. A skilled interviewee may, however, choose the question to answer and unseat the interviewer. Avoid double-barrelled questions in all but the most informal situations.

Another potentially problematic question is the **bipolar question**. A bipolar question offers the interviewee two choices. For example, 'Did you vote yes or no on the union contract?' If what you want to know is whether or not the interviewee voted yes or no on the contract, this is a legitimate and appropriate question. However, suppose you asked this question: 'Do you approve or disapprove of overtime work?' Most people do not totally approve or totally disapprove of overtime work; yet this question forces interviewees to choose from limited options, neither of which is likely to represent their true stand on the issue. Thus, if you use bipolar questions, make sure that the options you offer are the only two possible

Table C.1 When to use open and closed questions

Use open questions when you want to:
- Discover the interviewee's priorities
- Discover the interviewee's frame of reference
- Let the interviewee talk through his or her opinions without constraint
- Ascertain the scope or depth of the interviewee's knowledge
- Ascertain how articulate the interviewee is
- Open an interview

Use closed questions when you want to:
- Save time, energy and money
- Maintain control over the interview situation
- Obtain very specific information from the interviewee
- Take generalisations to the specific and probe the depth of the interviewee's knowledge
- Encourage the interviewee to reconstruct a specific event
- Encourage a shy person to talk
- Avoid extensive explanations on the part of an interviewee
- Clarify a point made in answer to an open question
- Close an interview

options; otherwise, you will obtain inaccurate information and again open yourself up to the skilled interviewee.

One final category of problematic questions is the **leading question**, in which you let the interviewee know the answer you want to hear by how you phrase the question, for example, 'Don't you think that using this plan will alleviate the problems we've been having?', 'Are you in favour of this policy like all your co-workers?', 'Of course you want the best for your family, don't you?'

It would not take an astute interviewee very long to realise what you really wanted to hear, and so you are likely to get biased responses. Leading questions can be useful when a biased answer is intended and desired. For instance, the last question above would be useful in a sales interview as the interviewer tries to persuade a potential buyer to buy a set of encyclopaedias. However, if you do not realise that you have asked a leading question, you won't know whether you are receiving a biased answer, and this can create a serious problem.

Structure the interview using interviewing aids

After determining the purpose and agenda, and after formulating your questions, the next step in preparing for an interview is to develop a structure. To do this, you need to think about three things:

- The interview guide
- The questioning sequence
- Transitions

Table C.2 Rewording badly constructed questions

Double-barrelled question	*Problem*	*Better question*
1. Why do you want to leave our organisation and is there anything I can do about it?	Interviewee doesn't know which question to answer first and thus may not answer either one fully.	Why do you want to leave our organisation? (Let interviewee respond.) Is there anything I can do to change your mind?
2. What are the pros and cons of using this system?	The question could encourage the interviewee to only offer one pro and one con about the issue. It doesn't allow for a full answer to both parts.	What do you feel are the benefits of this system? (Let the interviewee respond.) What do you feel are the disadvantages of this system?
3. Do you think we should adopt this insurance? Is it of any real benefit? Have any of our offices adopted it? (Asked in succession, with no pauses for responses.)	Interviewee doesn't know which question to answer and is likely to become confused when faced with so many options.	Do you think we should adopt this insurance? (Let interviewee respond.) Do you think that it offers us new benefits? (Let interviewee respond.) Have any of our other offices adopted it?
Bipolar question	*Problem*	*Better question*
1. Do you prefer working with people or working alone?	The question assumes that there are only two possible choices.	Do you work well with other people? (Can be followed with appropriate probe.)
2. Do you approve or disapprove of the union contract?	The question assumes that there are only two ways to view the issue.	What are your feelings concerning the union contract?
Leading question	*Problem*	*Better question*
1. Don't you think that using this plan will alleviate the problems we've been having?	The question identifies the expected answer, making it difficult for the interviewee to disagree.	Do you think this plan will be useful in alleviating the problems we've been having?
2. Are you in favour of this policy like all your co-workers?	The question places interviewee in the position of siding with the 'right' side.	What is your attitude towards this policy?
3. Of course, you want the best for your family, don't you?	The question associates response with a desirable goal (getting the best for the family), making it difficult for the interviewee to say no.	This product offers you some real advantages. Could I take some of your time to tell you about them?

Table C.3 Funnel and inverted funnel question sequences

Funnel: from general to specific
- How do you feel about the new regulations concerning smoking in the building?
- How are these regulations curtailing smoking among employees?
- Are these regulations fair?

Inverted funnel: from specific to general
- Do you think the new smoking regulations are fair?
- How are these regulations curtailing smoking among employees?
- In general, how do you feel about these new regulations?

Use the funnel sequence when
- You want to discover the interviewee's frame of reference
- You want to avoid leading the interviewee
- You want to maximise your ability to probe issues
- The interviewee is willing to talk about the issues

Use the inverted funnel sequence when
- You want to get at specific facts before general reactions
- You want to motivate a reluctant interviewee
- You want to jog the interviewee's memory

Source: Adapted from Downs *et al.*, (1980)

The interview guide is an outline of the topics and sub-topics you want to cover, usually with specific questions listed under each heading. In other words, it is the finalised version of the agenda. Alternative interview guide formats will be discussed later.

While you are constructing the interview guide, you will also need to be concerned with the sequence of questions – how they will interconnect. The two most common types of question sequences are the **funnel sequence** and the inverted funnel sequence. The funnel sequence begins with general questions and then moves towards more and more specific questions. The **inverted funnel sequence** reverses this order, beginning with specific questions and moving towards more open questions towards the end. Table C.3 shows examples of these two sequences, and also summarises when you should use each of these sequences, depending on what you want to accomplish.

After establishing the sequence of your questions, you should consider what kinds of transitions you can use to help the interviewee flow. The transitions in an interview perform the same function as transitions in an oral presentation: They help listeners maintain focus and keep them aware of where the speaker is in terms of the overall organisation. Transitions are difficult to prepare ahead in unstructured interviews, yet a good interviewer will keep in mind that transitions should be used when a topic change occurs. A simple statement such as 'I hear what you're saying about that situation. Do you think you could help me with another issue?' allows you to move from one topic onto the next.

Plan the setting to enhance rapport

Where you hold the interview can have a large impact on the interview's atmosphere and outcome. If you hold the interview in your office or meeting room, you will create a formal atmosphere; if you conduct the interview in a more neutral area, such as a restaurant, the climate will be more relaxed. The choice of setting depends on what you want to accomplish in the interview. The most important point to remember is that, if at all possible, you should try to hold the interview in a setting that will be conducive to the kind of communication you seek.

Anticipate problems and prepare responses

As you prepare for an interview, you should spend some time considering what kinds of problems you might encounter. Imagine how the interviewee might respond to what you have to ask, and prepare for his or her objections and questions. Consider the personality of the interviewee and how you might have to adapt to draw the person out or to control his or her tendency to dominate. Anticipate how much time you will need to ask your questions and how much time your interviewee has to give you. Each interview will offer unique problems. If you can plan for some of these situations, you will be able to handle them better during the actual interview than if you had not considered them at all.

Conducting the interview

Thorough preparation must be coupled with sensitive implementation. In this section we will first briefly review the concept of supportive communication (introduced in Chapter 4) as it applies to interviews. Then we will look at the three stages of the interview – the introduction, body and conclusion – discuss the functions of each, and offer suggestions for developing the necessary skills to conduct an interview effectively. Finally, we will discuss ways of recording the interview information.

Establish and maintain a supportive communication climate. The 'climate' of the interview refers to the tone of the interview and the general atmosphere in which the interview occurs. An interview, like any other interpersonal communication event, should be a supportive interaction, one in which participants feel free to communicate accurately. As the interviewer, you set the climate of the interview in the introduction when you begin to build rapport with the interviewee. In general, you should seek to build a comfortable, open climate, free of stress and incongruence. Maintaining a supportive and productive climate requires that you constantly analyse and adapt to the interaction as it occurs. When you sense that the climate is no longer supportive, move away from the content level of the interview and address the relational level. Consider this excerpt from an information-gathering interview:

Interviewer: Thanks for taking the time to speak with me today.
Interviewee: Oh, it's no problem at all. What can I do for you?
Interviewer: Well, I was wondering if you could tell me a little about the incident that occurred on the shop floor last week. First, do you have any idea how it started?

Table C.4 Interview preparation checklist

---

1. Have I determined my general purpose?
2. Have I written out my specific purposes and agenda?
   (a) Do I know exactly what I want to accomplish in terms of content?
   (b) Do I know exactly what I want to accomplish in terms of the relationship with the interviewee?
3. Do my questions all relate to my purposes and agenda?
4. Are my questions clearly worded in language the interviewee can understand?
5. Are my questions worded in an unbiased manner?
6. Have I chosen an appropriate interview structure for the situation?
7. Have I chosen an appropriate question sequence for the interview situation?
8. Have I developed possible transitions to be used in the interview?
9. Have I chosen a physical setting properly suited to the topics and the interviewee?
10. Have I planned ways to deal with problems that could develop during the interview?

Interviewee: No, not really. I was doing my job and then, all of a sudden, the two of them were at it.

Interviewer: I see. You didn't hear them talking before they began to fight?

Interviewee: No. Like I said, it seemed to start out of the blue.

Interviewer: Weren't you paying attention?

Interviewee: How was I to know they were going to fight?!

By now, the questions are obviously beginning to irritate the interviewee. The interviewer has continued to probe an issue that the interviewee seems to think has already been covered sufficiently. The interviewer should move away from this point and attempt to ease the interviewee's discomfort before continuing.

Interviewer: You're right. You really weren't in a position to anticipate this situation. Perhaps, though, you could tell me what happened after the fight.

At this point, the interviewee may be hesitant to disclose fully. The interviewer may have to continue to be supportive until the interviewee appears to be comfortable in answering the questions.

Of course, a supportive climate is not maintained solely by verbal behaviour. Listening analytically is also essential to maintaining the climate of an interview. If you do not show that you are listening and responding to what the interviewee is saying, he or she will not want to continue talking with you. In general, you should listen for comprehension of the content of the interview, for empathy with the interviewee, and for evaluation of information and feelings (Stewart and Cash, 1985). Keep in mind the listening guidelines from Chapter 4. These will help you establish a productive and supportive climate in your interviews.

Introduce the interview

Supportive communication begins immediately in the introduction, where you establish the tone and set the climate of the interview. You should greet the interviewee in such a way as to build positive rapport. The impressions created in the initial minutes of an interview are crucial to its success (Stewart and Cash, 1985). You should try to convey a favourable impression as quickly as possible. After the greeting, you need to motivate the interviewee to participate willingly in the interview. Some common ways of doing this are to ask for the interviewee's help or tell the interviewee why he or she was chosen as a source of information. Finally, the introduction should contain an orientation to the total interview. You should tell an interviewee (1) the purpose of the interview, (2) how he or she will help meet that purpose, and (3) how the information obtained during the interview will be used. The introduction should end with a transition into the body of the interview. Using a transition statement, such as 'Now then, let me begin by asking . . .' or 'Now that you understand what's going to happen during the next few minutes, let's move on to the questions' tells the interviewee that the 'real' interview is about to begin.

Conduct the body of the interview

In general, the body of the interview will follow your interview guide, which is a predetermined sequence of questions. There are three types of guides: structured, semistructured and unstructured. If the interview guide is structured, you will simply read the questions on the guide and record the interviewee's answers. A semi-structured guide lists several recommended questions under each topic. The interviewer then selects the most appropriate questions for a specific candidate. A sample interview guide for a semi-structured employment interview is shown in Table C.5.

If the interview guide is unstructured, then you will use the guide only as an agenda. For example, an unstructured interview guide for a termination interview might simply list a few general topics for discussion, for example, 'What did he/she like/dislike about their work/the company?', 'Why is he/she leaving?', 'Any suggestions for improvement?' Particularly in an unstructured interview, an interviewee will need encouragement to answer your questions as fully as possible. In order to encourage complete answers, you will need to follow his or her initial responses with probing questions. Effective probing depends directly on your ability to listen and analyse the content and information the interviewee offers you. Probing questions are rarely planned ahead because you cannot predict how the interviewee will respond to your questions. You will want to probe when you feel that, for whatever reason, you are receiving an inadequate response to your question.

The kind of probing you do will depend on the responses given by your interviewee and the kind of information you are looking for. If you feel that the response is superficial or inadequate due to lack of information, you should use an **elaboration probe**, such as, 'Tell me more about that issue,' or 'Why do you suppose it happened that way?' or 'Was there anything else going on at the time?'

Table C.5 Sample interview question for an employment interview

Education
- What was it about your subject that appealed to you?
- What was your most rewarding experience in college?
- What subjects were the most difficult for you to master? Why?
- If you were starting college all over again, what courses would you take?
- What difficulties did you experience in getting along with fellow students and staff?
- What did you learn from your extra-curricular activities?

Work experience
- How did you obtain your current job?
- What duties occupy most of your time?
- What part of your work do you like the most/least?
- What has been your greatest frustration/joy?
- What thing about your supervisor did you like/dislike?
- What criticisms of your work have you received?

Self-evaluation
- What do you know about our industry/company?
- What interests you about our product/service?
- What is your long-term career objective?
- What are your greatest strengths/weaknesses?
- What have you done that has demonstrated intitiative and willingness to work hard?
- What do you think determines a person's progress in a good company?
- What are your plans for self-improvement during this year?
- What are the three most important things in your life?

If you need to clarify the information given by the interviewee, use a **clarification probe**, such as, 'What does job satisfaction mean to you?' or 'You said that you are unhappy with this policy. Can you tell me specifically what aspects make you feel this way?'

A **reflective probe** is also used when you want elaboration or clarification. It is non-directive in nature and generally mirrors or repeats some aspect of the answer the interviewee just gave you. For example, 'You think, then, that this policy will work?', 'Are you saying that your supervisor doesn't offer the kind of supervision you need?'

If the interviewee does not answer your question, you may need to use a **repetition probe**. Simply paraphrase the question or repeat it verbatim. If you want the interviewee to keep on talking freely, use silence to encourage him or her to do so. Silence tends to communicate that you expect more from the interviewee. Be careful not to wait too long, though; give an interviewee enough time to think but not enough time to become uncomfortable. Phrases like 'I see', 'Hmm mm', and 'OK, go on' are non-directive and non-evaluative ways of encouraging the interviewee to speak. Table C.6 summarises these probes and when to use them.

Table C.6 Types of probes and when to use them

Use an *elaboration* probe when an answer seems to be superficial or inadequate in some way:

Interviewer: How have you been able to adapt to your new job responsibilities?
Interviewee: Well, each day I find myself challenged by something new.
Interviewer: Oh really? Why don't you tell me more about a specific challenge.

Use a *clarification* probe when you need to clarify information given by the interviewee:

Interviewer: How do you feel about working overtime?
Interviewee: Well, it's okay some of the time.
Interviewer: Can you tell me specifically when you would be willing to work overtime?

Use a *reflective* probe when you want elaboration or clarification but want to obtain it in a non-directive manner:

Interviewer: So how are you adapting to your new responsibilities?
Interviewee: Well, each day I find myself challenged by something new.
Interviewer: Really, Something new each day?

Use a *repetition* probe when the interviewee doesn't answer your question:

Interviewer: What do you believe to be the most difficult aspect of your job?
Interviewee: Well, that's not an easy question. My supervisor says I have problems with meeting productivity quotas.
Interviewer: But what do *you* believe to be the most difficult aspect of your job?

Use *silence* when you want to encourage the interviewee to continue talking:

Interviewer: Do you think that we should continue our policy concerning absenteeism?
Interviewee: Yes, I do.
Interviewer: (*Pauses for 10–20 seconds*)

The effective use of probing questions is perhaps the most important skill an interviewer can develop. It is also the most difficult to develop. Too often, an interviewer leaves an interview and thinks about all the things that could have been discussed if only a topic had been followed up with appropriate probes. Or perhaps the interview was ineffective because the interviewer probed irrelevant topics and spent too much time gathering relatively useless information. An effective interviewer needs to learn when to probe and when to stop. If you have planned appropriately, you will be aware of the issues you want to cover and in what depth. Follow the cues given by your interviewee as well as your agenda in determining when and how much to probe issues.

Conclude the interview

The third stage of the interview is the conclusion. When you conclude an interview you should accomplish four purposes. First, be sure you indicate explicitly that the interview is about to end. Say something like, 'Well, that's all the questions I have' or 'You've been very helpful'. This helps the interviewee understand that if he or she has any questions, they should be asked now. Second, try to summarise the information you obtained. This serves as a check on the accuracy of the information: the interviewee can correct your impressions if they seem to be in error. Third, let the interviewee know what's going to happen next: Will you need to meet again? Will you make a report? Finally, make sure you continue to build the relationship by expressing appreciation for his or her time and thoughtful responses.

Record the information

While you may have planned the interview perfectly and asked all the right questions and probes, if you cannot remember accurately the information obtained, the interview cannot be considered a success. After all, you prepared and conducted the interview to get information, not simply because you wanted to have a conversation with someone. The first point that you need to recognise concerning remembering interview information is simple: memory alone will not work. Relying solely on memory leaves open the possibility of forgetting the information or readjusting it to meet your own needs. Even if you summarise the interview as soon as it is over, you run the risk of reinterpreting the information in ways that the interviewee did not intend you to. However, if summarising the interview is your preferred choice, make sure you write your summary immediately after the interview. Additionally, you might want to use your interview guide as a basis for summarising: review your questions and write out the interviewee's answers.

Perhaps a better way to remember information is to take notes during the interview. Make sure you ask the interviewee's permission to do this. If he or she agrees, take notes as unobtrusively as possible so as not to make the interviewee uncomfortable. Learn how to write notes while still maintaining eye contact with the interviewee. This is a difficult skill to master, but it can be done; journalists use this skill frequently with great success. Develop your own shorthand so that you are, in fact, taking notes and not recording the interview verbatim. If you need a verbatim account of the interview, then you should use a tape recorder. Again, first ask the interviewee if he or she minds being tape-recorded. Keep the recorder out of sight if possible so that neither you nor the interviewee feels threatened by it. One final way to help you remember the interview information is to have a second interviewer participate in the interview. After the interview, your discussion will function as a check on each other's memory of what occurred.

Specific types of organisational interviews

The information presented in the preceding sections will help you plan and conduct almost any type of interview. However, there are some special categories which may need extra consideration. In this section, we will briefly describe the most common types of organisational interview and apply the general principles presented earlier to specific issues and circumstances.

Information-gathering interviews

This type of interview is the one most frequently held in organisations, and is also the one that is most like a conversation. You might conduct this type of interview when you need to gather facts about an issue or to help in a problem-solving situation. If you treat these fact-finding missions as interviews, you will be in a better position to gather accurate, useful information because you will take the time to plan ahead. Clearly, you need to follow the planning steps discussed above, and decide on a general purpose and agenda; develop questions; develop the structure of the interview; plan the setting; and anticipate problems.

Furthermore, the information-gathering interview is the only interview for which you can choose your expert. In other organisational interviews, such as the selection interview or the performance appraisal interview, you have little choice of interviewee. In information-gathering interviews, however, the decision is based on two factors: who is capable of giving you the information you need and who is willing to give you this information (Stano and Reinsch, 1982). Too often, interviewers will talk to interviewees who are willing but who do not have the necessary information. For instance, suppose your organisation is considering the implementation of a flexible work schedule and you have been assigned to write a feasibility report. While you may get some interesting opinions from a colleague on the advantages of such a schedule, it would be better to find an expert on flexible time for your interview. On the other hand, if you wanted to find out how well received such a change would be, you would talk to colleagues rather than to an expert.

The nature of an information-gathering interview is such that the interviewee may not realise he or she is being interviewed at all. Thus it may be difficult to keep the interviewee on track and responsive to your questions. More so than in any other interview, you as the interviewer must remain flexible and adaptive to your interviewee. Choose a physical setting that will encourage talk and provide an appropriate climate. In general, the funnel sequence works well in information-gathering interviews because of its ability to immediately elicit general information and the interviewee's feelings on the subject. However, the inverted funnel may be a better choice if you will be interviewing a number of people on the same topic and you need to maintain consistency in evaluating their responses.

Selection interviews

The selection interview is used to help current organisational members choose new members. During the interview, the interviewer tries to assess whether job candidates will fit into the organisation and if they have the appropriate skills for the job. In addition, the interviewer often tries to sell the organisation itself to the interviewee. Questions asked during the selection interview address four general topics: work experience, education and training, personality characteristics, and related activities and interests. The nature of the job and the interviewee will dictate which topics will be emphasised.

As shown in Table C.7, there are three sources of information you should review when creating questions for a selection interview:

Table C.7   Bases for selection interview questions

- Use the *job description* to formulate questions concerning task-related skills and personality characteristics.
- Use the selection interview *evaluation form* to formulate questions that can help you assess the applicant on the basis of your organisation's general criteria for employees.
- Use the applicant's *resumé and cover letter* to formulate questions concerning the applicant's specific skills and previous work experience.

---

1. Review the job description to assess the technical skills and experience needed by the person. Also review the job environment to determine the desirable personal qualities required. Create your questions based on these reviews; avoid asking merely generic questions.

2. Look at the evaluation form your company uses to assess prospective employees. Make sure that some of your questions deal with the topics on this evaluation form. For instance, if one of the topics on this form is communication skills, create questions which specifically address this subject. In this case, you may want to ask the applicant about his or her writing skills and how he or she has used them in the past.

3. One final piece of information you should use for developing questions for a selection interview is the applicant's CV and covering letter. Read these documents carefully. If there are time gaps between jobs, ask the applicant about them. If the information on the CV is too general, develop questions to get at the specifics. Remember that most people create a CV with a very specific goal in mind: to obtain an interview. Therefore, the information tends to be a summary of all the good aspects of that person's career to date. Additionally, all information tends to be written in glowing language. Be prepared to reach beyond this language to obtain clarifying information. For example, suppose you came across this line in a cover letter: 'I've had years of experience in leadership positions'. Clearly, you would want to ask this applicant for more specific information: 'How many years?', 'What kinds of positions were these?', 'What were your specific leadership responsibilities?'

In constructing interview questions, be sure to include some that focus on specific experiences. For instance, you might want to ask something like 'Can you tell me about a time when you successfully met a goal you set?' The interviewee may be reluctant to be specific, but you should probe until the interviewee offers you useful, specific, behavioural information.

Why is behavioural information so important? Many experts believe that the best way to assess future job performance is to assess past behaviour: past behaviour predicts future performance. If you can find out how the interviewee behaved

Table C.8 Selection interview format (PEOPLE-oriented process)

P = Prepare
1. Review application, resumé, transcripts and other background information.
2. Prepare both general and individual-specific questions.
3. Prepare suitable physical arrangements.

E = Establish rapport
1. Try to make applicant comfortable.
2. Convey genuine interest.
3. Communicate supportive attitude with voice and manner.

O = Obtain information
1. Ask questions.
2. Probe.
3. Listen carefully.
4. Observe the person (dress, mannerisms, body language).

P = Provide information
1. Describe current and future job opportunities.
2. Sell positive features of firm.
3. Respond to applicant's questions.

L = Lead to close
1. Clarify responses.
2. Provide opportunity for final applicant input.
3. Explain what happens next.

E = Evaluate
1. Assess match between technical qualifications and job requirements.
2. Judge personal qualities (leadership, maturity, team orientation).
3. Make a recommendation.

in real situations in the past that are similar to those he or she is likely to face in your organisation, you can determine if his or her style will fit into your organisation and work well with other members.

Take care that you ask a balanced series of questions. Ask for negative information as well as positive. This will help you obtain a well-rounded picture of the interviewee and also expose hidden bias. For instance, you might want to follow the above question with something like 'Now tell me about a time when you failed to meet a goal you set'. Again, make sure the person gives you specific behavioural information.

In conclusion, remember that your primary purpose in a selection interview is to find a person who is qualified for a particular opening in your organisation. Table C.8 details a six-step process (using the acronym PEOPLE) used by a major firm to help interviewers accomplish this purpose. It follows the general interviewing model outlined in the first half of this supplement.

Appraisal interviews

The appraisal interview is usually part of a larger professional appraisal system. The goal of this system is to evaluate a member of an organisation and often provides a means of giving feedback to a subordinate concerning ways to improve job performance. While every organisation differs in the specifics of its appraisal system, there are some common aspects.

Generally, before the interview, written evaluations are prepared by the subordinate, the superior, or both people. There are any number of types of evaluation forms, including an essay form, where the manager writes a description of the subordinate's work, with no set format; forced-choice ratings, where the manager chooses a statement from many which might describe the subordinate in one area; a graphic rating scale, where the manager rates the subordinate in various areas on a 1–7 numerical scale. In most cases, though, you will be asked to back up your assessment of the subordinate with specific and concrete information. For instance, if you are using a graphic rating scale and indicate that the employee performed unsatisfactorily, you should write out in objective terms why you have made this assessment. The subordinate has a right to know, and you have the responsibility to back up your decisions with evidence.

It is the responsibility of the interviewer to prepare the structure of the appraisal interview. The interviewer should set a definite time and place for the interview, considering the effects these choices will have on the interview and the interviewee. The interviewer must decide on the general purpose of the interview and the agenda. Common topics that are often brought up in appraisal interviews include job knowledge, job performance, job goals, career goals and opportunities, and interpersonal skills.

The difficult aspect of the appraisal interview is that people tend to avoid evaluating others or being evaluated in face-to-face situations. Both participants in an appraisal interview may be apprehensive. As the interviewer, you need to reassure the interviewee that you are conducting the interview as a means of assisting in the interviewee's development. Keep in mind that people do not like to be criticised, and balance your criticisms with reassurances and commendations. As noted in Chapter 6, when you offer criticisms, work with the interviewee to develop ways to enhance performance in the future.

In conducting an appraisal interview, you must, as always, decide beforehand on your objectives. The objectives should then dictate the form of the interview. In general, three types of appraisal interviews seek to meet specific objectives (Maier, 1958), and a fourth type can be used to meet multiple objectives (Beer, 1987). These interview types are summarised in Table C.9.

The first type of appraisal interview is called the tell-and-sell interview. This approach is evaluative in nature. First, you tell the subordinate how you have evaluated him or her, and then you sell the subordinate on the ways you have chosen to improve his or her performance. This type of interview should be used when you must be very clear about your expectations. This format is also effective with young employees who find it difficult to evaluate themselves, with very loyal

Table C.9 Types of performance appraisal interviews

Tell-and-sell interview
Used for purely evaluative purposes. Manager tells the employee the evaluation and then persuades the employee to follow recommendations for improvement.

Tell-and-listen interview
Used for purely evaluative purposes. Manager tells the employee the evaluation and then listens to the employee's reactions to the evaluation in a non-judgemental manner.

Problem-solving interview
Used for employee-development purposes. Manager does not offer evaluation but lets employee decide his or her weak areas and works with employee to develop plan for improvement.

Mixed-model interview
Used for both evaluative and development purposes. Manager begins interview with problem-solving session and concludes with a more directive tell-and-sell approach.

employees or those who strongly identify with the organisation or the appraiser, and with employees who do not want to have a say in how to develop their job and role in the organisation (Downs *et al.*, 1980).

If, however, you want to let the subordinate respond to your evaluation, you would use the tell-and-listen appraisal format. In this interview, you first tell the employee your evaluation; then you listen to his or her reactions without displaying any agreement or disagreement. The objective of this interview is also evaluative, but you also want to hear the subordinate's viewpoints and work with the subordinate to help him or her accept your evaluation. Active listening directed at helping the subordinate work through his or her feelings about the evaluation and past performance will help you successfully complete a tell-and-listen appraisal. This type of interview works best with people who have a great need to participate in their jobs, with interviewees who are relatively close in status to the interviewer, and with subordinates who are highly educated (Downs *et al.*, 1980).

The third general type of appraisal interview is the problem-solving interview. In this interview, evaluating the person is no longer the goal. Rather, the appraiser's role is to help the employee develop a plan for improving his or her performance. The performance deficiencies are determined by the subordinate, not the supervisor. Your goal as the interviewer is to avoid judgements and evaluations; rather, you offer suggestions for solutions to the problems defined by the interviewee. You form a partnership with the subordinate to solve the problems he or she brings up.

Finally, if your objectives are to both perform an evaluation and offer developmental coaching, you could choose to use a mixed-model interview (Beer, 1987). In this type of appraisal interview, you begin with a problem-solving framework and end the interview with a more directive tell-and-sell approach. In this way, you can both help a subordinate meet the development goals as well as offer your own evaluation and plan for development.

No matter which type of interview you choose, an appraisal interview should contain all the elements of a general interview. Build rapport and orient the interviewee to the subject; conduct the body of the interview in a supportive manner; conclude by specifying what is going to happen. Additionally, the appraisal interview generally includes a discussion of a specific plan for improvement or change.

Summary and behavioural guidelines

While many people consider interviewing as a process that just happens, we have argued that effective interviewing requires planning and thought. The steps shown in Figure B.1 provide a framework for enhancing your interviewing skills. The first step, thorough preparation, is essential for a successful interview. Planning involves deciding on your purposes, questions, structure, setting, and responses to anticipated problems. During the actual interview, work towards establishing and maintaining a supportive and productive climate. Keep in mind that every interview should have an introduction, body and conclusion and that you need to develop ways to record the information you obtain during the interview.

There are a variety of organisational interviews, but the most common are the information-gathering interview, the selection interview and the performance interview. Each of these interviews has very different objectives and specific means to reach them. Be flexible in how you conduct these interviews. As in any communication activity, you should adapt to the situation, your personality, and the person with whom you are conversing.

Interviewing is a vital management skill. When done well, an interview can provide you with information not otherwise available. This information can then better inform the decisions you make as you act out your role in the organisation.

Following are general behavioural guidelines for planning and conducting interviews. Specific guidelines for specialised interviews are incorporated into the Observer's Feedback Form in the Skill Practice exercises.

Planning the interview

1. Specify your purposes and plan an agenda.
   - Determine your general purpose: to gather information, persuade, discipline or evaluate.
   - Compose an agenda, listing all topics by priority.
2. Formulate questions.
   - Determine the type of questions (closed or open) that are consistent with the objectives.

- Write specific questions for each topic on the agenda.
- Use appropriate language to word questions.
- Avoid biased or leading questions.

3. Develop the interview guide.

   - Select the appropriate format: structured, semi-structured or unstructured.
   - Use either the funnel or inverted-funnel question sequence.
   - Formulate transition statements between topics.

4. Plan the setting.

   - Select a setting that is consistent with your objectives.

5. Anticipate problems.

   - Identify potential complications that might occur during the interview and develop contingency plans.

Conducting the interview

6. Establish and maintain a supportive climate.

   - Greet interviewee and initiate a brief social conversation.
   - Foster a positive communications climate by constant analysis of, and adaptation to, the interview process.
   - Use effective listening skills and non-verbal language (eye contact, posture and gestures) to foster co-operation.

7. Introduce the interview.

   - State the purpose of the interview.
   - Clarify interviewee's and interviewer's roles.
   - Specify the time frame of the interview.
   - Indicate how the information will be used.
   - Use a transition to signal the beginning of the interview.

8. Conduct the interview.

   - Use interview guide to manage the flow of the interview.
   - Use probing questions when elaboration or clarification are required.
   - Be flexible and adapt to the flow of the interview.

9. Conclude the interview.

   - Signal that the interview is about to end.
   - Summarise the information you have collected.
   - Clarify details or technical information.
   - Review what will happen as a result of the interview.
   - Strengthen the relationship by expressing appreciation.

10. Record the interview content, using the appropriate format.

    - Write a summary immediately after the interview.
    - Take notes during the interview (sustaining eye contact).
    - Use a tape recorder (with the interviewee's permission).
    - Use a second interviewer to improve your recall.

Skill Practice

Exercises in conducting special-purpose interviews

EXERCISE **C.1**

EVALUATING THE NEW EMPLOYEE-ORIENTATION PROGRAMME

You work for a high-tech electronics firm that was recently purchased by a large, multi-business conglomerate. Your company produces components for highly sophisticated communications equipment used by the government. This is an exciting but somewhat confusing period in the company's history. The new parent company, Beta Products, is known as a Japanese-style firm. It emphasises high productivity, along with employee commitment and loyalty.

In two weeks time, Beta is sending a human resources management team to inspect your organisation. In advance, they have sent a list of programmes they want to review, including your new employee-orientation programme. Your boss, the director of Human Resources, has asked you to prepare a 30-minute briefing on this programme for the Beta task force. Specifically, she has asked you to interview representatives of various groups in your organisation to determine their perceptions of the programme's merits and shortcomings.

Currently, when a new employee enters your organisation, he or she goes through an extensive orientation session. During this session, the new employee meets a member of the Human Resources Department to learn about company policies and procedures and receive the Employee's Handbook. This session can last from two to three hours, depending on the participants. At the end of the session, the new employee is assigned a mentor, a member of the new employee's department who has been with the organisation for at least one year. The role of the mentor is to help the new employee become familiar with his or her new job and co-workers. The mentor is expected to meet the new employee on a semi-regular basis for at least six months. The relationship can continue if both parties agree. This orientation programme has been used for about three years but has never been formally evaluated.

Assignment

To complete this assignment, you have scheduled interviews with several department heads, mentors and current trainees. Prepare the interview you will conduct with the person who has been assigned to gather information about the orientation programme. (Before beginning this task, review the behavioural guidelines for planning an effective interview at the end of the Skill Learning section. You should also consult Tables C.1–C.3 and C.6.) In small groups, compare your questions with others. What did you leave out? What questions need to be reworded? What types of probes may be needed? After this discussion, split up into groups of three and take turns serving as the interviewer, interviewee and observer. Do not look at the following role descriptions while planning this exercise. Observers should give feedback using the Observer's Feedback Form in Appendix 1, page 642.

Role descriptions for interviewees

Trainee

You've just found out that you are going to be interviewed on the mentor programme with which you've been involved for three months. You've been quite happy with the programme and would like to see it continued; in fact, you would like to be a mentor to new employees one day.

Many of your friends have pointed out that you have a tendency to talk too quickly, talk a lot, and tend to dominate a conversation. You realise that when you get nervous or involved in an issue, you do talk a lot. You are certainly nervous about this interview because you are very involved in the programme and you've heard through the grapevine that the programme might be cut. You really want to let the interviewer know how much you've learned from your mentor and the whole orientation programme. What you have to say is important, and you want to make sure the interviewer hears all the good things you have to say about the programme.

You are particularly positive about the programme because it contrasts with your experience in your former job. In that organisation you were merely given a cursory overview of the company benefits via a videotape presentation. Furthermore, because there was no standardised mentoring programme, new employees were left to fend for themselves. They were given no clear picture of what the company expected of them, no encouragement, and no sense of involvement in a group effort. A great deal of confusion and misunderstanding resulted. Here, in contrast, you have appreciated being able to get answers to your questions from one person. Overall, you feel as though this approach enabled you to become proficient in your job very quickly.

Department head

You've just found out that you are going to be interviewed on the mentor programme, and it couldn't have come at a worse time. You've just lost one of your best employees, and you have been trying to find a replacement. You're really not interested in spending time to think about this interview or participate in it. You'd rather use the time on employment interviews to find a new assistant.

In fact, you tend to be uncomfortable in interviews of any kind. Because you are shy, this kind of one-to-one formal conversation always makes you feel uncomfortable. You don't mind it so much when you are the interviewer – at least then you have some control over the situation. But you don't feel you've ever been a really good interviewee. The direct questions always make you feel as if you are on trial; as a result, you withdraw and appear to be unco-operative, even defensive.

You feel that the interviewer should be talking to people more directly involved in the programme – you really don't have much to do with it anyway, except for matching up people. The programme seems to work well, but no doubt trainees would learn just as quickly if they sought out their own mentors. You know that many of your staff members feel the programme is worthwhile, so you'll back it up, albeit reluctantly. However, you would much rather write an evaluation of the programme than have to talk about it to a relative stranger.

Mentor

You've just found out that you are going to be interviewed on the mentor programme, a programme with which you've been involved for six months. When you first became a mentor, you were excited about the possibilities. Now, however, experience has shown that the programme is a waste of time. Too often the trainees use their mentors as a crutch, both at work and in their social lives. The programme inspires a dependency that you find counter-productive and time-wasting.

Too often you've found yourself in the position of practically taking over trainees' jobs because they got used to relying on your expertise. You've thought that this might simply be a result of your own personality – you are too willing to help, perhaps – but you've also noticed this behaviour in other mentors and trainees.

Furthermore, you haven't really noticed any difference in productivity between people who have gone through the programme and people who haven't. In fact, because of the development of social relationships, your feeling is that productivity has probably declined.

In general, you think the company ought to abandon the programme. While a brief orientation might be useful to new employees, you can no longer justify the amount of time you put into the programme, given the results. Even this evaluation of the programme is taking up your valuable time.

EXERCISE **C.2**

APPRAISAL INTERVIEW WITH CHRIS JACOBS

Background information for Pat Gleaves

You are Pat Gleaves, manager of the Commercial Loan Division at Firstbank. You have been with Firstbank for four years and have conducted a number of appraisal interviews. During your tenure, you have increased your division's profits by 45 per cent. Your goal is to increase them by another 15 per cent before the end of next year. In order to do so, you need to have aggressive, dynamic and dedicated loan officers working for you.

Chris Jacobs has been with Firstbank for three years. This is the first time you will be reviewing Chris's performance, because Chris was transferred to your department five months ago to take over as loan officer from Helen Smith, who had worked in the Personal Loan Division. You agreed to the transfer after reviewing Chris's credentials and past appraisal forms. Chris appeared to be qualified for the position, and the appraisal reports indicated that Chris's work was rated from above average to outstanding.

Unfortunately, you have been very disappointed with Chris's performance in your department. For a long-time bank employee, he seems surprisingly unfamiliar with standard procedures and protocol. Last week he told a customer there shouldn't be any problem getting approval for her loan application. She wanted to open a boutique in a renovated building in an inner-city area. However, the review committee turned it down because the building alterations haven't had planning approval yet.

There are several other deficiencies in Chris's performance. In contrast with Helen, Chris seems inattentive to detail. He has frequently left out important information on loan applications, causing needless delays in processing. Furthermore, he doesn't seem to be able to keep up with the workload. It takes him twice as long as it should to handle routine paperwork, and he seems totally ill-at-ease with your department's computerised information system. Due to a favourable investment environment and the recent opening of a local business park, your group's workload is up 50 per cent from last year. You simply can't tolerate having to take extra time to make sure Chris is doing things right the first time.

In Chris's favour, he is extremely punctual and his attendance has been perfect. He also keeps a very neat work area and takes pride in his own appearance. Furthermore, he was brought up in the area and is an active member of the Rotary Club which means he has very good contacts in the business community. Everyone likes Chris; he is jovial and easygoing and has a quick wit that livens up even the most routine and dull staff meeting. He loves treating co-workers during 'happy hour' after work. Unfortunately, he sometimes loses perspective and gets carried away. Indeed, you've wondered at times how this 'free spirit' ended up in a bank job. Certainly his attitude runs counter to your more formal and reserved personality, but it's hard to deny he has charm and class.

In general, Chris seems to have plenty of potential, but at best his current work performance is only average (an 'expected' rating on your company's form). He just hasn't applied himself to his new position. You wonder if this is the right work for him or if perhaps he hasn't had adequate training. You spent some time orienting Chris to the group and assigned Jim, a veteran of the department, to act as his mentor. But, in retrospect, the local business boom has made it difficult for you and Jim to help Chris 'learn the ropes'. Your days seem to be filled up with meetings with local investors and city planners. Still, it annoys you that he never asks questions. If he needs help with the technical aspects of the job, why doesn't he ever ask for assistance?

You have scheduled the interview with Chris for later in the day in your office. You know your review will make him very unhappy and probably put him on the defensive. He obviously has high aspirations for advancing in the bank and has received fairly positive feedback in the past. You must work out some way to improve his performance. Your department is short-handed, and everyone must contribute his or her share.

As you contemplate the unpleasant task ahead, you reflect, 'I certainly miss Helen. I never had to have this type of conversation with her.'

Assignment for Pat Gleaves

In preparation for this interview, complete a draft of the performance evaluation form in Exhibit 1, page 646 in Appendix 1. In keeping with standard practice, you have given a blank copy of the form to Chris and asked him to do a self-evaluation. He will bring his completed form to the interview.

After you have completed your draft, identify the type of appraisal interview you feel is most appropriate for this situation (see Table C.9, page 593). Also, review the behavioural guidelines at the end of the Skill Learning section, and the 3R's approach to shaping behaviour discussed in Chapter 5. Then formulate a series of questions consistent with your overall strategy. Finally, anticipate questions and objections Chris might initiate and prepare responses. Compare your plans in small groups and make revisions. Use the interview checklist in Table C.4, page 584, to guide your discussion.

Upon completion of your small-group discussion, prepare to conduct the interview with Chris. Do not look at the background information for Chris's role before the interview. An observer will use the Observer's Feedback Form on page 644 in Appendix 1 to give you feedback.

Background information for Chris Jacobs

You have been with Firstbank for three years. For most of that time, you worked in the Personal Loan Division as a Loan Officer. You liked your job, your clients, and the people with whom you worked. You had hoped that your first move at Firstbank would be a promotion within the Personal Loan Division. However, five months ago, you were transferred to the Commercial Loan Division to replace a loan officer who had worked in that position for 10 years. You did not really want the transfer, but you realised that the move would, in fact, put you in a better position for the next upward move. Your former supervisor indicated that you would not have to stay in this position very long if you kept receiving good ratings on your appraisal forms, and you have always received outstanding or above average ratings. He argued that you really needed to gain exposure to other departments in the bank as well as to other managers. And your new boss, Pat Gleaves, is a real 'rising star' in the bank.

However, this time you expect your new supervisor, Pat, is going to be pretty tough on you. You feel frustrated and upset because you don't feel there has been any change in your effort or commitment. Since you have been in the department, Pat's attitude towards you has seemed very distant and formal. You know that Pat thinks that the person you replaced was an excellent worker who contributed greatly to Pat's goal of achieving a 15 per cent increase in profits this year. But certainly she doesn't expect you to immediately pick up where a 10-year veteran left off.

And then there's the problem of training. She promised to give you a thorough orientation when you arrived, but instead you were 'shunted off' to Jim. He seemed sincere and interested in helping out, and he told you to come and ask questions whenever you needed help. However, when you asked about the department's loan application procedure, he made you feel like an idiot for asking such a basic question, and you've never gone back. Furthermore, Pat always seems to be in meetings. You realise that she is bringing in important business for the bank, so you feel it would be inappropriate to distract her with your basic questions.

This lack of assistance has caused you to make some mistakes. These have primarily been due to the change in procedures between the Personal and Commercial Loan departments. You had much more autonomy and authority over there, probably because the loans were much smaller. In addition, there are many more government regulations to worry about over here. Besides, you really miss the close contact with people that was built into your old job. That's why you took your first job in the bank. You have always been a very people-oriented person and received great satisfaction from helping them. Now, you just seem to be buried in paperwork and committee meetings. Some days you regret accepting the offer to transfer. You're not sure this 'stepping-stone' to advancement is worth the loss of the enjoyment you received in your former position.

Assignment for Chris Jacobs

Your interview with Pat is scheduled for her office. In preparation for the interview, Pat has asked you to complete a copy of the appraisal form as a self-evaluation. Prior to the interview, complete the form on pages 646 to 648. Do not review the background information for Pat's role.

EXERCISE **C.3**

SELECTION INTERVIEW AT SMITH FARLEY INSURANCE

Smith Farley is a rapidly growing insurance firm based in Peterborough. It offers general lines of insurance, including motor, fire, life and health. It prides itself on its competitive rates, excellent agent relations, and fast claim service. Employees of the firm appreciate its no-layoff policy, generous pay and benefits, and family oriented culture. It is one of the largest employers in the community, a source of employee pride.

Smith Farley has taken the lead in computerising the insurance business. Agents conduct much of their business using mini-computers in their offices, and claim handlers maintain all their records on local computer files. The agents' and claim handlers' offices are all networked with one another as well as with the regional offices. This permits rapid transfer of information, including rate changes, new applications and claims.

To support this massive computer system, the firm has installed state-of-the-art computer hardware in its ten regional office centres. In addition, the company has a large software development and maintenance department which has doubled in size in the past five years and now employs 800 programmers. These programmers are generally recruited directly from university. Although no previous experience is required of them, relevant experience can help new programmers move quickly into management or senior technical positions.

Programmer/analysts use typical programming languages to develop computer applications for the insurance business (e.g., new claim-handler and customer application forms), for the corporate headquarters staff (e.g., accounting and personnel records), and the computer system itself (internal procedures and controls). Data-processing positions range from extremely technical design of complex computer networks to routine maintenance of existing programmes.

All new programmers are put through a 16-week induction course in which they are oriented to the company and the data-processing department, brought up to date on the relevant programming languages and tools, and introduced to the corporate culture. To meet the heavy demand for computer applications, the data-processing department has been authorised to hire two cohorts of 60 programmers a year.

To attract programmers to the firm, Smith Farley offers above-average starting salaries and rapid promotions during the first five years. After that, individuals can continue to pursue the technical career option, which leads to a senior analyst's position that pays about £5,000 above industry average, or they can move into management. The consistently high performance of the firm and its ongoing expansion of data processing afford ample opportunity for promotion into senior positions.

You are Robert Henderson, a 20-year employee of Smith Farley. For the past 10 years you have been working in the personnel department, primarily interviewing job candidates for the data-processing department. You enjoy your work – the constant contact with young, enthusiastic university graduates is invigorating – but you find the constant travelling is making you tired.

For example, during next week you will be driving to Glasgow, then to Newcastle and finally to Bristol. In addition to the regular 'milk round' interviews you have scheduled in these areas, you have received several CVs in response to local newspaper adverts. In sifting through these inquiries, three CVs caught your interest. You have made arrangements to interview all three applicants during this trip.

Assignment

Review Exhibits 2 to 6, pages 649 to 654 in Appendix 1, and prepare a list of questions you would ask these three job candidates. Using the 'Interview guide' planning form on page 650, Appendix 1, review the general questions you should ask all three. In addition, identify several specific questions you would like to ask the candidate(s) you are assigned, based on their CVs and covering letters.

Review your proposed questions in small groups. What points did you overlook? What questions need to be reworded or discarded?

Using the questions you feel are most appropriate, be prepared to conduct selection interviews with these job candidates in class. Before each interview, think about the questions each candidate is likely to ask you about the company. In addition, identify your 'selling points' – the specific features of the company, the community, and the jobs that you think each candidate would find most attractive. Also review the general behavioural guidelines and the six-step PEOPLE approach to selection interviews (Table C.8, page 591). Remember, the interviewing process influences the content of the information exchanged.

Following the interview, take a few minutes and grade the interviewee on each of the seven criteria on the Interview guide (5 = high, 1 = low). Justify your grades with specific comments. Then make an oral report to the observer assigned to your interview; include a recommendation. (Assume the observer is the director of recruiting for your firm.) After your report, for those criteria related to the interview itself (as compared with the background of the assigned role) discuss your observations with the interviewee. Following this discussion, the observer will give you feedback on your performance as an interviewer using the Observer's Feedback Form in Appendix 1, page 645, as a guide.

Management of Information

Technology has transformed the way we find, and use, information. With the advent of the personal computer, the CD-ROM, the Internet and Intranets, has come a revolution in the 'information industry', and with it an increase in the number and variety of sources used to retrieve data and in the combination of skills needed to interpret the data. The work of information professionals has also changed beyond recognition to keep pace with the technology and to ensure that the best possible access is gained to the full range of material. If the work of these professionals has been so dramatically transformed, and their need to keep up-to-date with new developments had increased so much, we can imagine then how difficult it must be for the practising managers to try to keep apace of these changes, and not fall too far behind in the competitive world of information needed for their work.

In today's information-rich environment it may be helpful to give some guidance in the use of the variety of sources available, and the practices used in seeking out the most relevant and up-to-date sources. This supplement is therefore devoted to indicating the major providers of information, in a range of formats, which will be relevant to the subjects covered in this book.

This is not a comprehensive list of resources, but a selection of those which will be most readily available to companies for purchase or for individuals seeking information through libraries, where some of the resources listed should be available. New products are appearing all the time, and it is therefore very difficult to give an up-to-date picture of the resources available.

Printed sources

Indexes and **Abstracts** are used to find articles on specific topics, usually by key words, in a range of publications in subject areas, broad or narrow. Abstracts include summaries of the articles which help you to assess the relevance of an article to the topic you are searching for. Some of these are not only available in printed format, but can also be obtained as a CD-ROM, on-line databases or through the Internet. Some examples are:

Anbar Abstracts selected articles from more than 400 journals.

Aslib Index to Theses British theses accepted for higher degrees.

British Reports, Translations and Theses Lists research reports and doctoral theses.

Business Periodicals Index US-based indexing service (no abstracts).

Employee Relations International A bibliographical and abstracts journal; covers all topics relating to industrial relations.

Index to Business Reports Indexes over 800 reports in a range of newspapers and business journals.

Index to Conference Proceedings Indexes all conference publications held by the British Library Document Supply Centre.

Personnel Management Abstracts

Research Index Fortnightly index to company and industry information from a range of UK newspapers, journals and trade magazines.

Social Science Citation Index Citation indexing of over 1,000 leading social science journals.

CD-ROMs

The advent of CD-ROM technology has changed the way databases have been made available and are used. They are expensive, but once the subscription is paid they can be used as much and as often as required, whereas with on-line searching the costs are variable depending on the time taken and the amount of information retrieved. Searching on CD-ROM can more successfully be achieved by the end user without the need for trained professionals acting as intermediaries. Examples of CD-ROM databases:

ABI/INFORM Covers 1,000 business and management journals, abstracting every article from every issue of these journals. Covers both academic and practitioner titles, and there is a full-text CD-ROM option (available as BPO-Business Periodicals OnDisc).

Anbar Management Intelligence Covers 400 publications on all aspects of management.

European Business ASAP Covers over 900 titles in business, management, economics and industry, with full text of articles from 400 of the journals included.

FT McCarthy Company and market information from 50 leading international newspapers and business magazines.

HELECON International CD-ROM Comprises a number of databases covering books, dissertations, working papers, research reports, conference papers and journals, with abstracts from 1980 to date, on economics, business and finance.

IMID PLUS (Institute of Management International Databases) Six databases of references and abstracts to over 70,000 items, including books, reports, research papers, journal articles and training packages.

Management & Marketing Abstracts (PIRA) Abstracts of articles from over 200 management and marketing journals, including case studies and company profiles.

Quest Economics Economic and political profiles for 240 countries, including country risk data, forecasts and textual analysis, with over 21,000 full text articles.

Newspapers and Magazines All the major newspapers and some journals are now available in CD-ROM format, e.g., *The Guardian, Financial Times, The Times, The Independent, The Telegraph, The Economist, New Scientist, Business Week*, and there are numerous other subject or industry CD-ROMs available. A useful guide to the full range of business databases in all the formats is the Headland Business Information publication 'On-line/CD-ROM Business Sourcebook', which lists and evaluates the databases essential to business.

On-line databases

Databases allow the user greater flexibility in the way searches can be constructed, and are more precise and efficient in the results achieved. Most on-line databases are available to remote users all over the world, usually available through academic or corporate institutions who pay for their connection and use, and have traditionally been 'closed systems' based on their own network of service providers. Searching on-line databases can be very expensive, and they are therefore often conducted through an intermediary in the organisation, such as a librarian or information manager, so that the search strategy is conducted efficiently and economically, but at the same time achieving the best results.

Many databases are offered via the services of an on-line 'host' where all the information is held, and often this makes it possible to search across a combination of databases in one session. Examples of such hosts are **Dialog**, which was the first commercial on-line information service in the world, established in 1972, and which now has a global customer base of 200,000 users in over 150 countries, with millions of documents contained in over 450 databases.

Lexis/Nexis was launched in 1973, and provides access to more than 100 million documents covering international business, scientific and financial information, providing a service to more than a quarter of a million customers around the world.

FT Profile offers access to a wide range of information, much of it available full-text, on international news, business and finance, company and market data, science and technology topics.

The Internet

The Internet is a network of computer networks linked by global telecommunications systems, and joining together millions of computer networks around the world so that they can share their information electronically. There is no single owner or central controlling authority for the Net, nor is there any quality control over the information available, and it is therefore often very difficult to be sure of the reliability, currency or value of the contents. This introduction to some of the resources available is therefore not intended to be exhaustive, but may save you some of the frustration and time-wasting effort in finding your way around the maze.

The World Wide Web (WWW or the web)

The web is a navigational system used as an encyclopaedia of information and Internet resources. A Web site is a collection of web pages from a single Internet host. Each web site has a home page which is the starting point for information with links to other main sections or pages.

Search engines

Search engines are used to navigate the Internet. A search engine is a catalogue or index to a part of the Internet, but no single search engine covers the whole web. They index millions of web pages, and can help you to pinpoint the sites you want if you are very specific, but they may also produce thousands of hits if your search is too general or wide-ranging. Some of the best and most widely used search engines are:

ALTAVISTA	http://www.altavista.digital.com
EXCITE	http://www.excite.com
GLOBAL NETWORK NAVIGATE	http://www.gnn.com
HOTBOT	http://hotbot.com/index.html
INFOSEEK	http://guide.infoseek.com
YAHOO	http://www.yahoo.com

For more information on search engines, there is even a web page for search engine watch at: http://www.searchenginewatch.com.

Intranets

Intranets are internal corporate computer networks which can be used to distribute information within the organisation using Internet technologies and applications, and allowing access to Internet resources. There are now also available specific knowledge management tools which allow users to define more specifically their interests or needs, so that retrieved information is much more relevant. Examples of such tools are Hoover, Grapevine, for Notes, ReQUESTer for Lexis-Nexis, and there are several new products available for other systems.

Business information sources on the Net

1. Good directory of business information sources by University of Strathclyde:

   http://www.dis.strath.ac.uk/business/index.html

   General management information.

2. Academy of Management, Business Policy and Strategy Division:

   http://comsp.com.latrobe.edu.au/bps.html

   Gives links to many related sites and some information is directly available.

3. biz/ed – a dedicated gateway to business and economics on the Internet:

    http://www.bized.ac.uk

Includes an Internet Resources Catalogue with details about, and links to, many different kinds of quality resources in business and economics.

4. Benchmarking, re-engineering, quality – Benchmarking Exchange:

    http://www.benchnet.com

5. QualiNet – directory of information, resources and access to professionals:

    http://www.qualinet.com

6. Quality Resources On-line:

    http://Vector.casti.com/qc/

7. Economics & Business Education Association:

    http://www.bized.ac.uk/ebea

8. DTI Enterprise Zone:

    http://www.enterprisezone.org.uk

Gateway to over 70 other sites, selected for quality, objectivity, accuracy and relevance to small businesses.

9. The Training Net:

    http://www.trainingnet.com

On-line directory of training solutions, courses, magazine.

10. BRINT Research Initiative (Business Researchers' Interests):

    http://www.brint.com

Access to articles, case studies and other resources, some full-text, on business management and information technology.

Organisations

AMED – Association for Management Education and Development,
14–15 Belgrave Square, London SW1X 8PS
Tel.: +44-171-2353505   Fax: +44-171-2353505

ABS – Association of Business Schools,
344/345 Gray's Inn Road, London WC1X 8BP
Tel.: 0171 837 1899   Fax: 0171 837 8189
E-mail: abs@mailbox.ulcc.ac.uk   Website: http://www.leeds.ac.uk/bes/abs/

AMBA – Association of MBAs,
15 Duncan Terrace, London N1 8BZ
Tel.: 0171 837 3375   Website: http://www.mba.org.uk/

Academy of Management,
PO Box 3020, Briarcliff Manor, New York, 10510-3020, USA.
Tel.: (914) 923-2607   Fax: (914) 923-2615
E-mail: aom@academy.pace.edu/   Website: http://www.aom.pace.edu/
Leading professional association for management research and education in the US

American Society for Training & Development,
1640 King Street, Box 1443, Alexandria, Virginia 22313-2043, USA.
Tel.: 703/683-8100   Fax: 703/683-8103   Website: http://www.astd.org/
Information, research and analysis on training resources, products and services,
including access to on-line version of *Training & Development Magazine.*

AoM/IAoM – Association of Management and International Association of
Management,
Website: http://cob.isu.edu/Aom/
Non-profit US-based professional organisations – monitors new developments, con-
ducts research, disseminates information.

BCC – British Chambers of Commerce,
4th Floor, Manning House, 22 Carlisle Place, London SW1P 1JA
Tel.: 0171 565 2000   Fax: 0171 565 2049
Website: http://www.brainstorm.co.uk/BCC/Welcome.html

CBI – Confederation of British Industry,
103 New Oxford Street, London WC1A 1DU
Tel.: 0171 379 7400   Fax: 0171 836 5856
E-mail: cbi-information@geo2.poptel.org.uk   Website: http://www.cbi.org.uk

CEEMAN – Central and Eastern European Management Development Network,
Brdo pri kranju, SI-64000 Kranj, Slovenia
Tel.: +386-64-221761   Fax: +386-64-2220070   E-mail: misho@iedc-brd.si

EBEA – Economics and Business Education Association,
1a Keymer Road, Hassocks, West Sussex BN6 8AD
Tel.: 01273 846033   Fax: 01273 844646
E-mail: ebea@pavilion.co.uk   Website: http://www.bized.ac.uk/ebea/

ECLO – European Consortium for the Learning Organisation,
Venelle des Lauriers 8, B-1300 Wavre, Belgium
Tel./Fax: +32-10-241600   E-mail: ess-casteur-jack@msn.com

Efmd (European Foundation for Management Development)
Rue Washington 40, B 1050 Brussels, Belgium
Tel.: +32-2-6480385   Fax: +32-2-6460768   Website: http://wwwm.efmd.be

Foundation for Management Education,
Sun Alliance House, New Inn Hall Street, Oxford OX1 2QE
Tel.: 01865 251486   Fax: 01864 723488

IM – The Institute of Management,
2 Savoy Court, Strand, London WC2R 0EZ
Tel.: 0171 497 0580   Fax: 0171 497 0463
E-mail: institute@easynet.c.uk   Website: http://www.inst-mgt.org.uk

Institute of Administrative Management,
40 Chatsworth Parade, Petts Wood, Orpington, Kent BR5 1RW
Tel.: 01689 875555   Fax: 01689 870891
E-mail: iadmin@iadmin.netkonect.co.uk
Website: http://wwwm.electranet.com/iam

IMD – International Institute for Management Development,
Ch. de Bellerive 23, PO Box 915, CH-1001 Lausanne, Switzerland
Tel.: +41 21 618 0111   Fax: +41 21 618 0707
E-mail: info@imd.ch   Website: http://www.imd.ch/imd-home
Details of programmes, publications of this independent foundation.

IPD – Institute of Personnel and Development,
IPD House, Camp Road, London SW19 4UX
Tel.: 0181 971 9000   Fax: 0181 263 333
E-mail: ipd@ipd.co.uk   Website: http://www.ipd.co.uk

MCI – Management Charter Initiative,
Russell Square House, 10–12 Russell Square, London WC1B 5BZ
Tel.: 0171 872 9000   Fax: 0171 872 9099

RABE – Russian Association of Business Education,
Levoberezhnaya St. 32, Moscow 125475, Russia
Tel.: +7-095-4585786, 4586229   Fax: +7-095-4585786
E-mail: rabe@vksh.msk.su

Scoring Keys and Supplemental Materials

Introduction

Personal assessment of management skills (page 12)

You were asked to rate the various statements from 1 to 6.

Skill area	Items	Assessment Personal
Developing Self-awareness	**1–5**	
• Self-awareness and openness	1, 2	
• Awareness of self	3–5	
Managing Stress	**6–13**	
• Eliminating stressors	6, 7	
• Developing resilience	8, 9	
• Short-term coping	10, 11	
• Delegating	12, 13	
Effective Problem Solving	**14–25**	
• Rational problem solving	14–16	
Creative Problem Solving	**17–21**	
• Fostering innovation	22–25	
Constructive Communication	**26–34**	
• Coaching and counselling	26, 27	
• Effective negative feedback	28–30	
• Communicating supportively	31–34	

Skill area	Items	Assessment Personal
Effective Motivation	**35–43**	
Effective Conflict Management	**44–52**	
• Behaviour as initiator	44–46	
• Behaviour as respondent	47–49	
• Behaviour as mediator	50–52	
Effective Empowerment and Delegation	**53–60**	
• Empowerment skills	53–56	
• Delegation	57–60	
Teams, Leaders and Managers	**61–68**	
• Working in a team	61–62	
• Leading a team	63–68	
Management of Information	**69–72**	

TOTAL SCORE

The maximum you can get from the exercise is 428. Extrapolating from work with groups of managers we would see scores of above 350 as high, between 350 and 320 as good, 320 to 300 as moderate and below 300 as low. We suggest that you get colleagues to give their own views of your abilities.

SCORING KEY: CHAPTER 1

Developing Self-awareness

Survey 1.1: Self-awareness

Skill area	Items	Assessment Pre-	Post-
Self-disclosure and openness to feedback from others	1, 2, 3, 9, 11	_____	_____
Awareness of own values, cognitive style, change orientation, and interpersonal orientation	4, 5, 6, 7, 8, 10	_____	_____

TOTAL SCORE

To assess how well you scored on this instrument, compare your scores to three comparison standards: (1) Compare your scores with the maximum possible (66). (2) Compare your scores with the scores of other students in your class. (3) Compare your scores to a norm group consisting of 500 business school students. In comparison to the norm group, if you scored:

55 or above, you are in the top quartile;
52 to 54, you are in the second quartile;
48 to 51, you are in the third quartile;
47 or below, you are in the bottom quartile.

Survey 1.2: Defining Issues Test

The possibility of misusing and misinterpreting this instrument is high enough that its author, James Rest, maintains control over the scoring procedure associated with its use. Some people may interpret the results of this instrument to be an indication of inherent morality, honesty, or personal worth, none of which the instrument is intended to assess. A scoring manual may be obtained from James Rest, Minnesota Moral Research Center, Burton Hall, University of Minnesota, Minneapolis, MN 55455.

Our purpose is to help you become aware of the stage of moral development you rely on most when facing moral dilemmas. To help determine that, the following lists present the stage of moral development each statement associated with each story reflects. By looking at the four statements you selected as most important in deciding what action to take in each situation, you can determine which stage of development you use most often.

After you have done this, you should discuss which action you would take in each situation and why, and why you selected the statements you did as the most important ones to consider.

The escaped prisoner

1. Hasn't Mr Thompson proved that he is not really bad by being good for so long? (Stage 3)

2. Every time someone escapes punishment for a crime, doesn't that just encourage more crime? (Stage 4)

3. Wouldn't we be better off without prisons and the oppression of our legal system? (Indicates anti-authoritarian attitudes.)

4. Has Mr Thompson really paid his debt to society? (Stage 4)

5. Would society be failing if it did not deliver what Mr Thompson should fairly expect? (Stage 6)

6. What benefits would prison be apart from society, especially for a charitable man? (Nonsense alternative, designed to identify people picking high-sounding alternatives.)

7. How could anyone be so cruel and heartless as to send Mr Thompson back to prison? (Stage 3)

8. Would it be fair to all the prisoners who had to serve their full sentences if Mr Thompson was let off? (Stage 4)

9. Was Mrs Jones a good friend of Mr Thompson? (Stage 3)

10. Wouldn't it be a citizen's duty to report an escaped criminal, regardless of the circumstances? (Stage 4)

11. How would the will of the people and the public good best be served? (Stage 5)

12. Would going to prison do any good for Mr Thompson or protect anybody? (Stage 5)

The doctor's dilemma

1. Whether the woman's family is in favour of giving her an overdose or not. (Stage 3)

2. Does the doctor work to the same set of laws as everybody else if giving her an overdose would be the same as killing her? (Stage 4)

3. Whether people would be much better off without society regimenting their lives and even their deaths. (Indicates anti-authoritarian attitudes.)

4. Whether the doctor could make it appear like an accident. (Stage 2)

5. Does the government have the right to force continued existence on those who don't want to live? (Stage 5)

6. What is the value of death prior to society's perspective on personal values? (Nonsense alternative, designed to identify people picking high-sounding alternatives.)

7. Whether the doctor has sympathy for the woman's suffering or cares more about what society might think. (Stage 3)

8. Is helping to end another's life ever a responsible act of co-operation? (Stage 6)

9. Whether only God should decide when a person's life should end. (Stage 4)

10. What values the doctor has set for himself in his own personal code of behaviour. (Stage 5)

11. Can society afford to let everybody end their lives when they want to? (Stage 4)

12. Can society allow suicides or mercy killing and still protect the lives of individuals who want to live? (Stage 5)

The newspaper

1. Is the head more responsible to pupils or to the parents? (Stage 4)

2. Did the head give her word that the newspaper could be published for a long time, or did she promise to approve the newspaper one issue at a time? (Stage 4)

3. Would the pupils start protesting even more if the head stopped the newspaper? (Stage 2)

4. When the good name of the school is threatened, does the head have the right to tell the pupils what to do? (Stage 4)

5. Does the head have the freedom of speech to say 'no' in this case? (Nonsense alternative, designed to identify people picking high-sounding alternatives.)

6. If the head stopped the newspaper, would she be preventing full discussion of important problems? (Stage 5)

7. Would the head's order make Frank lose respect for her? (Stage 3)

8. Was Frank really loyal to his school? (Stage 3)

9. What effect would stopping the paper have on the pupils' education in critical thinking and judgements? (Stage 5)

10. Was Frank in any way violating the rights of others in publishing his own opinions? (Stage 5)

11. Should some angry parents be allowed to influence the head when she knows best what is going on in the school? (Stage 4)

12. Was Frank using the newspaper to stir up hatred and discontent. (Stage 3)

Survey 1.3: Learning Style Indicator

This survey has been scored in the text (see page 37).

Survey 1.4: Cognitive Style Instrument

To determine your score on the two dimensions of cognitive style, circle the items below that you checked on this instrument. Then count up the number of circled items and put your scores in the spaces below.

Gathering information		*Evaluating information*	
1a	1b	13a	13b
2a	2b	14b	14a
3b	3a	15a	15b
4b	4a	16b	16a
5a	5b	17b	17a
6b	6a	18a	18b
7b	7a	19a	19b
8a	8b	20a	20b
9a	9b	21b	21a
10b	10a	22a	22b
11a	11b	23b	23a
12a	12b	24a	24b
＿＿	＿＿	＿＿	＿＿
Intuitive score	Sensing score	Thinking score	Feeling score

Survey 1.5: Locus of Control Scale

Count up the number of items you selected of those listed below.

2a	9a	16a	23a
3b	10a	17a	25a
4b	11b	18a	26b
5b	12b	20a	28b
6a	13b	21a	29a
7a	15b	22b	TOTAL SCORE _____

Comparison data

Corporate business executives	Ave: 8.29	Sd: 3.57
Career military officers	Ave: 8.29	Sd: 3.86

Survey 1.6: Tolerance of Ambiguity Scale

Having intolerance of ambiguity means that an individual tends to perceive situations as threatening rather than promising. Lack of information or uncertainty, for example, would make such a person uncomfortable. Ambiguity arises from three main sources: novelty, complexity and insolubility. These three subscales exist within the instrument.

High scores indicate a greater *intolerance* for ambiguity. To score the instrument, the *even-numbered* items must be reverse-scored. That is, the 7s become 1s, 6s become 2s, 5s become 3s, and 4s remain the same. After reversing the even-numbered items, add the scores for all 16 items to get your total score.

The three subscales also can be computed to reveal the major source of intolerance of ambiguity – novelty (N), complexity (C) or insolubility (I). Here are the items associated with each subscale.

Item	Subscale	Item	Subscale
1	I	9	N
2	N	10	C
3	I	11	N
4	C	12	I
5	C	13	N
6	C	14	C
7	C	15	C
8	C	16	C

(N) Novelty score (2, 9, 11, 13)   ____
(C) Complexity score (4, 5, 6, 7, 8, 10, 14, 15, 16)   ____
(I) Insolubility score (1, 3, 12)   ____
TOTAL SCORE   ____

(Average range: 44–48)

Survey 1.7: Firo-B

Instructions for scoring

To derive your interpersonal orientation scores, refer to the table below. Note that there are six columns, each with *items* and *keys*. Each column refers to an interpersonal need listed in the chart at the bottom of the page. *Items* in the column refer to question numbers on the questionnaire; *keys* refer to answers on each of those items. If you answered an item using any of the alternatives in the corresponding key column, circle the item number on this sheet. When you have checked all of the items for a single column, count up the number on this sheet. When you have checked all of the items for a single column, count up the number of circled items and place that number in the corresponding box in the chart. These numbers will give you your strength of interpersonal need in each of the six areas. The highest possible score is 9. The lowest score is 0. Refer to the explanation in the chapter in order to interpret your scores and for some comparison data.

Expressed inclusion		Wanted inclusion		Expressed control		Wanted control		Expressed affection		Wanted affection	
Item	Key	Item	Key	Item	Key	Item	Key	Item	Key	Item	Key
1	1–2–3	28	1–2	30	1–2–3	2	1–2–3–4	4	1–2	29	1–2
3	1–2–3–4	31	1–2	33	1–2–3	6	1–2–3–4	8	1–2	32	1–2
5	1–2–3–4	34	1–2	36	1–2	10	1–2–3	12	1	35	5–6
7	1–2–3	37	1	41	1–2–3–4	14	1–2–3	17	1–2	38	1–2
9	1–2	39	1	44	1–2–3	18	1–2–3	19	4–5–6	40	5–6
11	1–2	42	1–2	47	1–2–3	20	1–2–3	21	1–2	43	1
13	1–2	45	1–2	50	1–2	22	1–2–3–4	23	1–2	46	5–6
15	1	48	1–2	53	1–2	24	1–2–3	25	4–5–6	49	1–2
16	1	51	1–2	54	1–2	26	1–2–3	27	1–2	52	5–6
SCORE		SCORE		SCORE		SCORE		SCORE		SCORE	

	Inclusion	Control	Affection	
Expressed behaviour toward others				Total E
Wanted behaviour from others				Total W
	Total Inclusion	Total Control	Total Affection	Social Interaction Index

SCORING KEY: CHAPTER 1

Managing Stress

Survey 2.1: Stress management

Skill area	Items	Assessment Pre-	Post-
Eliminating stressors	1, 5, 8, 9	____	____
Developing resilience	2, 3, 6, 7	____	____
Short-term coping	4, 10	____	____
Effective delegating	11, 12, 13, 14, 15	____	____

TOTAL SCORE

To assess how well you scored on this instrument, compare your scores to three comparison standards: (1) Compare your scores against the maximum possible (84). (2) Compare your scores with the scores of other students in your class. (3) Compare your scores to a norm group consisting of 500 business school students. In comparison to the norm group, if you scored:

70 or above, you are in the top quartile;
64 to 69, you are in the second quartile;
58 to 63, you are in the third quartile;
57 or below, you are in the bottom quartile.

Survey 2.2: Time management

To determine how effective you are as a manager of your time, give yourself the following number of points for the boxes you checked.

Points	Frequency
0	Never
1	Seldom
2	Sometimes
3	Usually
4	Always

If you completed only Section 1 of the instrument, double the scores for each category.

Add up your total points for the 40 items. If you scored 120 or above, you are an excellent manager of your time both personally and at work. If you scored between 100 and 120, you are doing a good job of managing your time and making a few refinements or implementing a few hints will help you achieve excellence. If you scored between 80 and 100, you should consider improving your time-management skills. If you scored below 80, training in time management will considerably enhance your efficiency.

Note: Sometimes people have markedly different scores in the two sections of this instrument. That is, they are better time managers at the office than in their personal lives, or vice versa. You may want to compute your scores for each section of the instrument and compare them.

Survey 2.3: Type A Personality Inventory

The Type A personality consists of four behavioural tendencies: extreme competitiveness, significant life imbalance (typically coupled with high work involvement), strong feelings of hostility and anger, and an extreme sense of urgency and impatience.

Scores above 12 in each area suggest this is a pronounced tendency.

Research suggests that the hostility aspect of the Type A personality is the most damaging to personal health.

Competitiveness		Life imbalance (work involvement)	
Item	Score	Item	Score
1	——	2	——
5	——	6	——
9	——	10	——
13	——	14	——
17	——	18	——
21	——	22	——
Total	——	Total	——

Hostility/Anger		Impatience/Urgency	
Item	Score	Item	Score
3	——	4	——
7	——	8	——
11	——	12	——
15	——	16	——
19	——	20	——
23	——	24	——
Total	——	Total	——

TOTAL SCORE

SCORING KEY: CHAPTER 3

Effective Problem Solving

Survey 3.1: Problem solving, creativity and innovation

		Assessment	
Skill area	Items	Pre-	Post-
Rational problem-solving	1, 2, 3, 4, 5	____	____
Creative problem-solving	6, 7, 8, 9, 10, 11, 12, 13, 14, 15	____	____
Fostering innovation	16, 17, 18, 19, 20, 21, 22	____	____

TOTAL SCORE

To assess how well you scored on this instrument, compare your scores to three comparison standards: (1) Compare your scores against the maximum possible (132). (2) Compare your scores with the scores of other students in your class. (3) Compare your scores to a norm group consisting of 500 business school students. In comparison to the norm group, if you scored:

105 or above, you are in the top quartile;
94 to 104, you are in the second quartile;
83 to 93, you are in the third quartile;
82 or below, you are in the bottom quartile.

Survey 3.2: How creative are you?

To compute your score, circle and add up the values assigned to each item. The values are as follows:

	A Agree	B Undecided or Don't know	C Disagree
1.	0	1	2
2.	0	1	2
3.	4	1	0
4.	−2	0	3
5.	2	1	0
6.	−1	0	3
7.	3	0	−1
8.	0	1	2

	A Agree	**B** Undecided or Don't know	**C** Disagree
9.	3	0	−1
10.	1	0	3
11.	4	1	0
12.	3	0	−1
13.	2	1	0
14.	4	0	−2
15.	−1	0	2
16.	2	1	0
17.	0	1	2
18.	3	0	−1
19.	0	1	2
20.	0	1	2
21.	0	1	2
22.	3	0	−1
23.	0	1	2
24.	−1	0	2
25.	0	1	3
26.	−1	0	2
27.	2	1	0
28.	2	0	−1
29.	0	1	2
30.	−2	0	3
31.	0	1	2
32.	0	1	2
33.	3	0	−1
34.	−1	0	2
35.	0	1	2
36.	1	2	3
37.	2	1	0
38.	0	1	2
39.	−1	0	2

Choice of words

The following have values of 2:

energetic	dynamic	perceptive	dedicated
resourceful	flexible	innovative	courageous
original	observant	self-demanding	curious
enthusiastic	independent	persevering	involved

The following have values of 1:

self-confident	determined	informal	forward-looking
thorough	restless	alert	open-minded

The rest have values of 0.
TOTAL SCORE

95–116	Exceptionally creative
65–94	Very creative
40–64	Above average
20–39	Average
10–19	Below average
Below 10	Noncreative

Survey 3.3: Innovative Attitude Scale

To determine your score for the Innovative Attitude Scale, add up the numbers associated with your responses to the 20 items. Then compare that score to the following norm group (consisting of graduate and undergraduate business school students, all of whom were employed full time).

Score	Percentile*
39	5
53	16
62	33
71	50
80	68
89	86
97	95

* Percentile indicates the percentage of the people who are expected to score below you.

Exercise 3.1: Applying conceptual blockbusting

The problem: The bleak future of knowledge

After the group has completed its problem-solving task, take the time to give the group feedback on its performance. Also provide feedback to each individual group member, either by means of written notes or verbal comments.

Group observation

1. Was the problem defined explicitly?

    a. To what extent was information sought from all group members?

    b. Did the group avoid defining the problem as a disguised solution?

    c. What techniques were used to expand or alter the definitions of the problem?

2. Were alternatives proposed before any solution was evaluated?
    a. Did all group members help generate alternative solutions without judging them one at a time?
    b. Did people build on the alternatives proposed by others?
    c. What techniques were used to generate more creative alternatives for solving the problem?
3. Was the optimal solution selected?
    a. Were alternatives evaluated systematically?
    b. Was consideration given to the realistic long-term effects of each alternative?
4. Was consideration given to how and when the solution could be implemented?
    a. Were obstacles to implementation discussed?
    b. Was the solution accepted because it solved the problem under consideration, or for some other reason?
5. How creative was the group in defining the problem?
6. What techniques of conceptual blockbusting did the group use?

Individual observation

1. What violations of the rational problem-solving process did you observe in this person?
2. What conceptual blocks were evident in this person?
3. What conceptual blockbusting efforts did this person make?
4. What was especially effective about the problem-solving attempts of this person?
5. What could this individual do to improve problem-solving skills?

Answers and solutions to problems

Solution to the Roman numeral problem on page 184.

'S'IX A more exotic answer we have been given uses a single line to erase the bottom half of the IX to make a VI. We often find that 'creative solutions' often annoy people who are not attached to them.

Solution to the matchstick problem on pages 184–5 (see Figure 3.2):

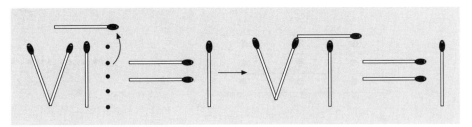

Answer to the Shakespeare problem on pages 186–7 (see Figure 3.3):
5 inches. (Be careful to note where page 1 of Volume 1 is and where the last page of Volume 4 is.)

Common terms applying to both water and finance (see question 1 on page 188):

banks	deposits	capital drain
currency	frozen assets	sinking fund
cash flow	float a loan	liquid assets
washed up	underwater pricing	slush fund

Answer to the Descartes story (question 2 on page 188): at the foundation of Descartes's philosophy was the statement, I think, therefore I am.

Solution to block of wood problem on page 188 (see Figure 3.4).

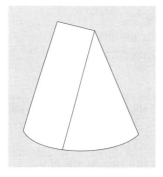

Exotic solutions to the nine-dot problem on page 189 (see Figures 3.5 and 3.6).

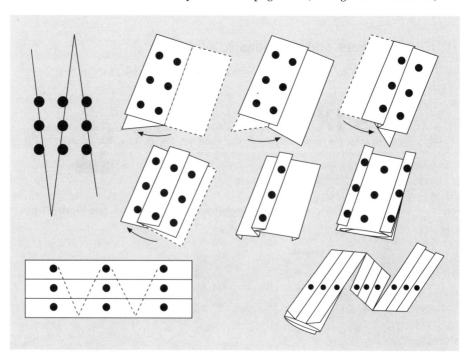

Solution to the fractionation problem on page 206 (see Figure 3.8).

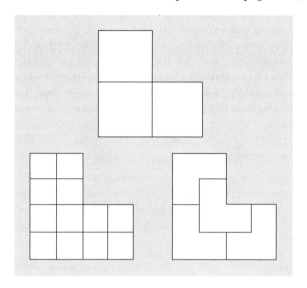

SCORING KEY: CHAPTER 4

Constructive Communication

Survey 4.1: Communicating constructively

Skill area	Items	Assessment Pre-	Post-
Knowledge of coaching and counselling	1, 2, 20	____	____
Providing effective negative feedback	3, 4, 5, 6, 7, 8	____	____
Communicating supportively	9, 10, 11, 12, 13, 14, 15, 16, 17, 18, 19	____	____

TOTAL SCORE

To assess how well you scored on this instrument, compare your scores to three comparison standards: (1) Compare your scores against the maximum possible (120). (2) Compare your scores with the scores of other students in your class. (3) Compare your scores to a norm group consisting of 500 business school students. In comparison to the norm group, if you scored:

99 or above, you are in the top quartile;
93 to 98, you are in the second quartile;
87 to 92, you are in the third quartile;
86 or below, you are in the bottom quartile.

Survey 4.2: Communication styles

Part 1   Identify the type of response pattern that you rely on most when required to be a coach or a counsellor by adding the numbers you gave to the response alternatives in Part 1. The chapter discusses the advantages and disadvantages of each of these response types. The most skilled supportive communicators score 9 or above on Reflecting responses and 6 or more on Probing responses. They score 2 or less on Advising responses and 4 or less on Deflecting responses.

Part 2   Circle the alternative that you chose. The most skilled communicators select alternatives 1a, 2d, 3e, 4h, and 5i.

Part 1

1. a. Deflecting response   ____
   b. Probing response   ____
   c. Advising response   ____
   d. Reflecting response   ____
   e. Deflecting response   ____

2. a. Reflecting response   ____
   b. Deflecting response   ____
   c. Advising response   ____
   d. Reflecting response   ____
   e. Probing response   ____

3. a. Probing response   ____
   b. Deflecting response   ____
   c. Advising response   ____
   d. Reflecting response   ____
   e. Probing response   ____

4. a. Reflecting response   ____
   b. Probing response   ____
   c. Deflecting response   ____
   d. Deflecting response   ____
   e. Advising response   ____

Part 2

1. a. Problem-oriented statement
   b. Person-oriented statement

2. a. Incongruent/minimising statement
   b. Congruent statement

3. a. Descriptive statement
   b. Evaluative statement

4. a. Invalidating statement
   b. Validating statement

5. a. Owned statement
   b. Disowned statement

OBSERVER'S FEEDBACK FORM

DIAGNOSING PROBLEMS AND FOSTERING UNDERSTANDING

Exercise 4.1: Vulcan Computers

Exercise 4.2: Brown vs Thomas

As the observer, rate the extent to which the role players performed the following behaviours effectively. Place the initials of each individual beside the number on the scale that best represents performance. Identify specific things that each person can do to improve his or her performance.

Action	Rating (1=low, 5=high)
1. Used problem-oriented communication.	_____
2. Communicated congruently.	_____
3. Used descriptive communication.	_____
4. Used validating communication.	_____
5. Used specific and qualified communication.	_____
6. Used conjunctive communication.	_____
7. Owned statements and used personal words.	_____
8. Listened attentively.	_____
9. Used a variety of response alternatives.	_____

Comments: _____

_____

_____

SCORING KEY: CHAPTER 5

Effective Motivation

Survey 5.1: Motivating others

Skill area	Item	Assessment Pre-	Post-
Diagnosing performance problems	1	____	____
	11	____	____
Establishing expectations and setting goals	2	____	____
	12	____	____
Facilitating performance (Enhancing ability)	3	____	____
	13	____	____
	20	____	____
Linking performance to rewards and discipline	5	____	____
	14	____	____
	6	____	____
	15	____	____
Using salient internal and external incentives	7	____	____
	16	____	____
	8	____	____
	17	____	____

Skill area	Item	Assessment Pre-	Post-
Distributing rewards equitably	9	___ ___	___
	18	___ ___	___
Provided timely and straightforward performance feedback	4	___ ___	___
	10	___ ___	___
	19	___ ___	___

TOTAL SCORE

To assess how well you scored on this instrument, compare your scores to three comparison standards: (1) Compare your scores against the maximum possible (120). (2) Compare your scores with the scores of other students in your class. (3) Compare your scores to a norm group consisting of 500 business school students. In comparison to the norm group, if you scored:

101 or above, you are in the top quartile;
94 to 101, you are in the second quartile;
85 to 93, you are in the third quartile;
84 or below, you are in the bottom quartile.

Survey 5.2: Work performance assessment

Step 1   Enter your score from each line below, as follows:
Regular scoring: Enter the number for your response on the survey.
Reverse scoring: Subtract the number of your response from 6 and enter the result.

Items	Score	Items	Score
1. Reverse	___	8. Regular	___
2. Reverse	___	9. Regular	___
3. Reverse	___	10. Regular	___
4. Reverse	___	11. Regular	___
5. Reverse	___	12. Regular	___
6. Reverse	___	13. Regular	___
7. Reverse	___	14. Regular	___

Step 2   Combine your scores according to the type of performance problem. Problems with scores higher than 7 are obstacles to high performance. Total scores over 50 suggest significant, broad-based motivational deficiencies.

Type of performance problem	Scores on items		Total of two items
Perception	1: ____	8: ____	____
Training	2: ____	9: ____	____
Aptitude	3: ____	10: ____	____
Resources	4: ____	11: ____	____
Expectations	5: ____	12: ____	____
Incentives	6: ____	13: ____	____
Reward salience	7: ____	14: ____	____

TOTAL SCORE

OBSERVER'S FEEDBACK FORM

Exercise 5.3: Reshaping unacceptable behaviours

Action	Rating (1=low, 5=high)
Reprimand	
1. Identified the specific inappropriate behaviour. Gave examples. Indicated that the action must stop.	_____
2. Pointed out the impact of the problem on the performance of others, the unit's mission, etc.	_____
3. Asked questions about causes and explored remedies.	_____

Action	Rating (1=low, 5=high)
Redirection	
4. Described the behaviours or standards expected. Made sure the individual understood and agreed that these are reasonable.	_____
5. Asked if the individual would comply.	_____
6. Was appropriately supportive. For example, praised other aspects of the person's work, identified personal and group benefits of compliance, and made sure there were no legitimate obstacles in the way of meeting stated expectations.	_____
Reward	
7. Identified rewards that were salient to the individual.	_____
8. Linked the attainment of desirable outcomes with incremental, continuous improvement.	_____
9. Rewarded (included using praise) all improvements in performance in a timely and honest manner.	_____

Comments: _____

_____

_____

_____

_____

SCORING KEY: CHAPTER 6

Constructive Conflict Management

Survey 6.1: Managing interpersonal conflict

Skill area	Item	Assessment Pre-	Post-
Initiating a complaint	1	____	____
	2	____	____
	3	____	____
	4	____	____
	5	____	____
	6	____	____
	7	____	____
	8	____	____
Responding to a criticism	9	____	____
	10	____	____
	11	____	____
	12	____	____
	13	____	____
	14	____	____
	15	____	____
	16	____	____
Mediating a conflict	17	____	____
	18	____	____
	19	____	____
	20	____	____
	21	____	____
	22	____	____
	23	____	____
	24	____	____

TOTAL SCORE

To assess how well you scored on this instrument, compare your scores to three comparison standards: (1) Compare your score with the maximum possible (144). (2) Compare your scores with the scores of other students in your class. (3) Compare your scores to a norm group consisting of 500 practising managers and business school students. In comparison to the norm group, if you scored:

120 or above, you are in the top quartile;
116 to 119, you are in the second quartile;
98 to 115, you are in the third quartile;
97 or below, you are in the bottom quartile.

Survey 6.2: Strategies for handling conflict

Forcing		Accommodating		Avoiding		Collaborating		Compromising	
Item	*Score*	*Item*	*Score*	*Item*	*Score*	*Item*	*Score*	*Item*	*Score*
1	___	4	___	2	___	5	___	3	___
6	___	9	___	7	___	10	___	8	___
11	___	14	___	12	___	15	___	13	___
16	___	19	___	17	___	20	___	18	___
Total	___	Total	___	Total	___	Total	___	Total	___

Primary conflict-management strategy: ___ (highest score)
Secondary conflict-management strategy: ___ (next highest score)

OBSERVER'S FEEDBACK FORM

RESOLVING INTERPERSONAL DISPUTES

Exercise 6.4: Where's my speech

Exercise 6.5: Can Harry fit in?

Exercise 6.6: Meeting at Hartford Manufacturing Co.

Action	Rating (1=low, 5=high)
Initiator	
Maintained personal ownership of the problem, including feelings	___
Avoided making accusations or attributing motives	___
Succinctly described the problem (behaviours, outcomes, feelings)	___
Specified expectations or standards violated	___

Action	Rating (1=low, 5=high)
Persisted until understood	_____
Encouraged two-way interaction	_____
Approached multiple issues incrementally (proceeded from simple to complex, easy to hard)	_____
Appealed to what the disputants had in common (goals, principles, constraints)	_____
Made a specific request for change	_____

Respondent

Showed genuine concern and interest	_____
Responded appropriately to the initiator's emotions	_____
Avoided becoming defensive or overreacting	_____
Sought additional information about the problem (shifted general to specific, evaluative to descriptive)	_____
Focused on one issue at a time, gradually broadening the scope of the discussion, searching for integrative solution	_____
Agreed with some aspect of the complaint (facts, perceptions, feelings or principles)	_____
Asked for suggestions for making changes	_____
Proposed a specific plan of action	_____

Mediator

Treated the conflict and disputants seriously	_____
Broke down complex issues, separated the critical from the peripheral. Began with a relatively easy problem	_____
Helped disputants avoid entrenched positions by exploring underlying interests	_____
Remained neutral (facilitator, not judge)	_____
Pointed out the effect of the conflict on performance	_____
Kept the interaction issue-oriented	_____
Made sure that neither party dominated conversation	_____
Kept conflict in perspective by emphasising areas of agreement	_____
Helped generate multiple alternatives	_____
Made sure that both parties were satisfied and committed to the proposed resolution	_____

Comments: _____

_____

_____

_____

_____

_____

_____

SCORING KEY: CHAPTER 7

Effective Empowerment and Delegation

Survey 7.1: Effective empowerment and delegation

		Assessment	
Skill area	Items	Pre-	Post-
Personal mastery experiences	1, 2	⎯⎯	⎯⎯
Modelling	3, 4	⎯⎯	⎯⎯
Providing support	5, 6	⎯⎯	⎯⎯
Arousing positive emotions	7, 8	⎯⎯	⎯⎯
Providing information	9, 10	⎯⎯	⎯⎯
Providing resources	11, 12	⎯⎯	⎯⎯
Organising teams	13, 14	⎯⎯	⎯⎯
Creating confidence	15, 16	⎯⎯	⎯⎯
Delegating work	17–26	⎯⎯	⎯⎯
TOTAL SCORE			

Comparison data

Compare your scores to three comparison standards: (1) Compare your score against the maximum possible (156). (2) Compare your scores with the scores of other students in your class. (3) Compare your scores to a norm group consisting of 500 business school students. In comparison to the norm group, if you scored

above 122	you are in the top quartile.
109 to 122	you are in the second quartile.
95 to 108	you are in the third quartile.
94 or below	you are in the bottom quartile.

Survey 7.2: Personal empowerment assessment

Skill area	Items	Mean (Total/4)
Self-efficacy (competence)	2, 7, 12, 17	⎯⎯⎯⎯⎯
Self-determination (choice)	3, 8, 13, 18	⎯⎯⎯⎯⎯
Personal control (impact)	4, 9, 14, 19	⎯⎯⎯⎯⎯
Meaningfulness (value)	1, 6, 11, 16	⎯⎯⎯⎯⎯
Trust (security)	5, 10, 15, 20	⎯⎯⎯⎯⎯

Comparison data

Scores from approximately 3,000 middle managers in manufacturing and service organisations.

	Mean	Top 1/3	Bottom 1/3
Self-efficacy	5.76	> 6.52	< 5.00
Self-determination	5.50	> 6.28	< 4.72
Personal control	5.49	> 6.34	< 4.64
Meaningfulness	5.88	> 6.65	< 5.12
Trust	5.33	> 6.03	< 4.73

CUSTOMER SCORING SHEET

EMPOWERING TEAM EXERCISE

Exercise 7.2: Satisfy the customer

Dimension	5	4	3	2	1
Innovativeness					
Excitement					
Probable effectiveness					
Number of commercials					
Overall quality					

Cost	Great bargain 5	4	3	2	Too high 1
Total scores Organisation 1 Organisation 2 Organisation 3 Organisation 4 Organisation 5 Organisation 6 Organisation 7					

SCORING KEY: CHAPTER 8

Teams, Leaders and Managers

Survey 8.1: Team development behaviour

Diagnosing team development	1, 16
Managing the Forming Stage	2/4
Managing the Storming Stage	10–12, 14, 15
Managing the Conforming Stage	6–9, 13
Managing the Performing Stage	5, 17, 18
Managing Team meetings	19–24

TOTAL SCORE

DISCUSSION ON THE CASE STUDIES

Case study 8.1: Charity Mission Statement

The external context in the UK had changed materially but most importantly, socially. The Victorian concept of institutional care had been replaced by concepts such as 'care in the community'. Also the family unit was seen as worth protecting – the image of protecting children by putting them in a health environment was seen now as 'taking them from their parents'. The cities were also multi-ethnic with Christianity sharing values with those of other faiths or indeed no faiths at all. The people engaged in the charity had probably not recognised or at least internalised these changes and still worked to the old Mission Statement.

The team, once the changes had been recognised, had reverted to the first stage of formation and individuals, neither accepted the new tasks nor the values upon which they were based. Control issues would be apparent.

The advice most relevant would be for the group to discuss the issues and accept that some individuals would be unlikely to adjust.

Case study 8.2: Harry Greenways

We leave the analysis to the group.

Case study 8.3: The hospital ward

The sister moved the issue from her own Circle of Concern or responsibility to that of the registrar suggesting outcomes that would have a dysfunctional impact on his internal context. The registrar's responsibility in theory was over the whole ward, its staff and its patients, but that was not the way he saw it when he was touring the wards. He was in a Circle of Concern of tasks involving repairs to people, surgical processes and recovery. His role was completely within this circle. The sister's Circle of Concern was her staff and patient care. Her tasks were concerned with getting the patients smoothly towards the recovery wards and her processes were more mundane – monitoring and servicing. The difficult patient impinged on both circles and provided an example of potential risk that could have easily escaped.

Case study 8.4: Bruddersford

The actions proposed were to separate the two divisions into business units and analyse the Circle of Concern for both.

The Cash Cow Division has been set tasks to reduce costs within its own potential profitability, while the Potential Star Division, freed from a cash drain, needs to adjust to the concerns of the holding company. The holding company, now seen for the first time as a major item in the external context, may well decide to float the Potential Star, having reached its potential, and close the Cash Cow. If this is so, the tasks of both divisions change completely.

Case study 8.5: The car parking problem

Many managers will remember interminable disputes on this and similar 'trivial' issues. Parkinson, of Parkinson's law fame, talked about the Bicycle Shed case when a board meeting spent hours on discussing the future of a cycle shed and minutes on the expense of an new atomic power plant. *What matters are that the issue is settled and that a decision sticks.*

The group of managers does not truly share the same goals as the manager and there is rivalry within the group. The manager COULD use all his or her clout to enforce a decision, but then would have to continue to monitor the result for ever: 'Yes of course I know the rules but I had a particularly important client, load of heavy material, bad weather conditions, working late . . .'

Case study 8.6: The R&D laboratory reorganisation

The R&D manager does not share the same goals as the team and although he could make a decision unaided, it is unlikely that such a decision would really work. There is also a new element – it is as if someone outside is watching over the decision and actually judging it – any decision will not do, the quality of the decision matters and a logical decision, given time, is probably possible. Looking at the process without any of the rules we will discuss later, we might see ourselves in either C1 or C11.

Consider C1 first. The manager has to act as a filter to the information coming from the subordinates and he or she does not really have the data to know who is lobbying from a genuine position.

He or she would feel at the time that THEY are either getting together behind closed doors or that there was a paranoid atmosphere being built up where trust was vanishing behind the door.

A C11 meeting could well be an experience that few managers would wish to share and one could well imagine entrenched positions becoming more entrenched and one's own leadership irrevocably challenged in public. Many managers given the choice have come up with a mixed style – A11 with a few 'supporters' allowing the complexity of the problem to be spread in the team followed by vigorous lobbying in C1. The climax would be a C11 after the manager had checked out on alternative employment prospects. Nobody ever said management was going to be easy.

Case study 8.7: The production manager's problem

In the automation problem, the manager has no expert knowledge, no hard data but the team does share the problem and will probably go with any solution proposed. The manager in a similar case tried a form of G11:

> 'Look I need your help and I have to have it for 12.00. Come to some form of consensus on what we have to do and I will present it to senior management. If you have nothing by the meeting I will simply toss a coin and good luck to all of us.'

He did not get a decision by 12.00 and made his threat of a guess again, this time increasing the time limit to 12.30. At 12.30 he was presented with a compromise potential answer which he presented to the Board. The compromise had the seeds of the full solution, which was in turn implemented.

SCORING KEY: SUPPLEMENT A

Conducting Meetings

OBSERVER'S FEEDBACK FORM

MEETING MANAGEMENT

Exercise A.1: Staff meeting at Thames Pump & Value

Action	Rating (1=low, 5=high)
1. Holding the meeting was appropriate because it satisfied at least one of the following purposes:	
a. A complex problem needed to be resolved drawing upon the expertise of multiple individuals.	_____
b. Group members' commitment to a decision needed to be enhanced.	_____
c. Group members' commitment to each other needed to be enhanced.	_____
d. Information needed to be shared among several people.	_____

Exercise A.2: Conducting a task force meeting

Planning Effective Meeting Processes

Possible group dynamics problems	*Preventive measures responses*

Meeting notice and agenda (see page 542)

MEMO

To:
From:
Date:

Meeting notification and agenda

Date:
Start time:
End time:
Location:
Agenda:

Topic	*Time*
1.	
2.	
3.	
4.	
5.	
6.	

Meeting objective:

Pre-meeting preparation:

Exercise A.3: Jim Lewis

WORKSHEET

	Personal preference	Group decision
1. Give Jimmy a warning that at the next sign of trouble a formal reprimand will be placed in his file.	_____	_____
2. Do nothing, as it is unclear that Jimmy has done anything seriously wrong. Give him a chance to prove himself.	_____	_____
3. Create strict controls (do's and don'ts) for Jimmy with immediate discipline for any misbehaviour.	_____	_____
4. Give Jimmy a great deal of warmth and personal attention (overlooking his annoying mannerisms) so he will feel accepted.	_____	_____
5. Fire him. It's not worth the time and effort spent for such a low-level position.	_____	_____
6. Treat Jimmy the same as everyone else, but provide an orderly routine so he can develop proper work habits.	_____	_____
7. Call Jimmy in and logically discuss the problem with him and ask what you can do to help.	_____	_____
8. Do nothing now, but watch him so you can reward him the next time he does something good.	_____	_____

Action	Rating (1=low, 5=high)
2. The appropriate **participants** were invited to the meeting, as reflected in the fact that:	
a. The size of the group was appropriate for the assigned task.	_____
b. Individuals likely to have a strong task-orientation and group-process-orientation were included.	_____
c. The group consisted of individuals with some common goal-orientations.	_____
d. All relevant expertise and knowledge was present.	_____
e. The group's composition reflected the goals of the meeting; homogeneity–solidarity and commitment; heterogeneity–creativity and innovation.	_____
3. Proper **preparations** were made for the meeting.	
a. Appropriate physical arrangements were provided.	_____
b. The agenda was prepared and distributed before or at the beginning of the meeting.	_____

Action	Rating (1=low, 5=high)
c. Priorities were established for the meeting's business and these were reflected in the sequence and length of time allotted to each item (more important business was discussed early in the meeting or for a longer time).	_____
d. The most appropriate decision-making structure was chosen for each business item (ordinary group decision or nominal group technique).	_____

4. The chairperson managed both the task and **process** aspects of the meeting effectively by:

a. Allowing members to become acquainted (if necessary) and making them feel comfortable.	_____
b. Reviewing the progress made to date and establishing the task for the meeting.	_____
c. Getting a report from each member with a pre-assigned task at the beginning of the meeting or as soon as possible.	_____
d. When critical thinking was important, playing a strong role in structuring the discussion, but refraining from expressing strong opinions.	_____
e. Sustaining the flow of the meeting using informational displays.	_____
f. Encouraging the group not to stray from assigned tasks.	_____
g. Managing the discussion to achieve equitable participation and discourage premature evaluation.	_____
h. Concluding the meeting by summarising what was accomplished and reviewing assignments.	_____

5. The participants in the meeting were effective group members because:

a. They were prepared for the meeting, and sought to understand the purposes of the meeting.	_____
b. They sought to accomplish the goals of the group, rather than serving their own personal goals.	_____
c. They listened to both the group leader and to other participants.	_____
d. They were supportive of others in the group, and sought to clarify and build on other's comments.	_____

Comments: _____

_____

_____

SCORING KEY: SUPPLEMENT B

Making Oral Presentations

OBSERVER'S FEEDBACK FORM

EFFECTIVE PRESENTATIONS

Exercise B.1: Speaking as a leader

Exercise B.2: Quality circles at Bradfield Foods

Action	Rating (1=low, 5=high)
Strategy	
1. Tailored message to audience. Message was concrete, specific, practical and relevant.	_____
2. Presented compelling case for proposal or point of view. Avoided logical fallacies.	_____
Structure	
3. Presented material in logically organised and easy-to-follow manner.	_____
4. Kept graphs, charts and other visual aids simple and straightforward.	_____
5. Prepared for contingencies and demonstrated flexibility in varying pace and approach to match audience interest and comprehension.	_____
Style	
6. Projected attitude of controlled enthusiasm, neither dull nor overbearing.	_____
7. Candidly discussed advantages and disadvantages.	_____
8. Used body movements, facial expressions, and tone of voice that enhanced presentation.	_____
9. Provided variety and relief. Alternated between speech and action, lecture and participation. Used humour well.	_____

Action	Rating (1=low, 5=high)

Supplement: questions and challenges

10. Handled questions and challenges thoughtfully, candidly and assertively. _____

11. Used questions from audience to point out advantages of proposal. Maintained generally positive atmosphere. _____

12. Maintained control of meeting. There was no question who was in charge during presentation. Presenter not easily intimidated by audience or caught off guard. _____

Comments: _____

_____

_____

_____

_____

_____

SCORING KEY: SUPPLEMENT C

Interviewing

OBSERVER'S FEEDBACK FORM

INFORMATION GATHERING INTERVIEW

Exercise C.1: Evaluating the new employee-orientation programme

Action	Rating (1=low, 5=high)

Introduction

Did interviewer

- use a friendly greeting? _____
- begin to build rapport? _____
- state purpose? _____
- orient interviewee _____
- ask to take notes or record interview? _____

Action	Rating (1=low, 5=high)

Body

Introduction

Did interviewer

- use internal summaries and transitions? _____
- use a variety of question types? _____
- use appropriate question sequence? _____
- respond to interviewee with good secondary questions (probes)? _____
- use silence when appropriate? _____
- maintain rapport with interviewee? _____
- handle problematic interviewee well? _____

Closing

Did interviewer

- thank interviewee? _____
- sum up? _____
- maintain/encourage good interpersonal relationship? _____
- indicate what would happen with information? _____
- set up another meeting, if appropriate? _____

Non-verbals

Did interviewer

- wear appropriate clothing? _____
- maintain eye contact with interviewee? _____
- use purposeful gestures? _____
- use appropriate tone of voice? _____
- maintain good posture? _____
- look enthused and interested in what interviewees had to say? _____
- take notes inconspicuously? _____
- avoid verbal pauses such as 'uh', 'uhm', etc.? _____

Comments:_____

_____

_____

_____

_____

_____

_____

OBSERVER'S FEEDBACK FORM

Exercise C.2: Appraisal interview with Chris Jacobs

Action	Rating (1=low, 5=high)

Introduction

Did interviewer

- use appropriate greeting? _____
- build rapport? _____
- orient interviewee to the interview? _____
- ask if he/she could take notes? _____

Body

Did interviewer

- praise individual's strengths? _____
- focus on specific concerns? _____
- compare perceptions of the problems? _____
- probe for underlying 'causes'? _____
- reach agreement on performance expectations/goals? _____
- discuss specific plans of action for improving deficiencies? _____
- make specific references to the appraisal form? _____

Conclusion

Did interviewer

- provide opportunity for interviewee to make suggestions and ask questions? _____
- specify when next appraisal interview will be held? _____
- summarise interview? _____

Non-verbals

Did interviewer

- use non-verbals to maintain open climate and good rapport? _____
- avoid use of 'uhs' and 'uhms'? _____
- maintain good posture? _____
- maintain eye contact? _____

Comments:_____

_____

_____

_____

_____

OBSERVER'S FEEDBACK FORM

Exercise C.3: Selection interview at Smith Farley Insurance

Action	*Rating* (1=low, 5=high)

Opening

Did interviewer

- use appropriate greeting?   _____
- build rapport?   _____
- orient interviewee to the interview?   _____
- use appropriate transition to body of interview?   _____

Body

Did interviewer

- clearly define structure of the interview?   _____
- use transitions between topics?   _____
- ask questions based on available information and needs?   _____
- probe when necessary?   _____
- solicit behavioural examples?   _____

Closing

Did interviewer

- offer organisational/job information?   _____
- invite questions?   _____
- answer interviewee's questions appropriately, specifically?   _____
- state when and how interviewer will be contacted?   _____

Non-verbal

Did interviewer

- act poised?   _____
- dress appropriately?   _____
- speak articulately?   _____
- act enthusiastic?   _____
- use appropriate language style?   _____
- maintain eye contact?   _____
- use purposeful gestures?   _____

Comments: _____

_____

_____

_____

Exhibits

Exhibit 1 (see page 600)

EMPLOYEE PERFORMANCE APPRAISAL FORM

DATE COMPLETED_____

NAME Chris Jacobs
DATE OF BIRTH 22/6/55
YEARS OF EMPLOYMENT 3
OFFICE LOCATION BRANCH 4 DEPARTMENTAL 9
DEPARTMENT Commercial

PRESENT JOB TITLE Loan Officer
CONVERSION CODE 32
YEARS IN PRESENT POSITION 6 months
SOC. SEG. NO. 555-33-9999
EDUCATION B.A. – Business

Select the statement under each of the following categories that best describes the individual.

Quality of work   General excellence of output with consideration to accuracy, thoroughness, dependability, without close supervision.

☐ Exceptionally high quality. Consistently accurate, precise, quick to detect errors in own and others' work.

☐ Work sometimes superior but usually accurate. Negligible amount needs to be redone. Work regularly meets standards.

☐ A careful worker. A small amount of work needs to be redone. Corrections made in reasonable time. Usually meets normal standards.

☐ Work frequently below acceptable quality. Inclined to be careless. Moderate amount of work needs to be redone. Excessive time to correct.

☐ Work often almost worthless. Seldom meets normal standards. Excessive amount needs to be redone.

Quantity of work   Consider the amount of useful work over the period of time since the last appraisal. Compare the output of work to the standard you have set for the job.

☐ Output consistently exceeds standard. Unusually fast worker. Exceptional amount of output.

☐ Maintains a high rate of production. Frequently exceeds standard. More than normal effort.

☐ Output is regular. Meets standard consistently. Works at steady average speed.

☐ Frequently turns out less than normal amount of work. A low producer.

☐ A consistently low producer. Excessively slow worker. Unacceptable output.

Exhibit 1 *(continued)*

Co-operation   Consider the employee's attitude towards the work, the employee's fellow workers, and supervisors. Does the employee appreciate the need to understand and help solve problems with others?

☐ Always congenial and co-operative. Enthusiastic and cheerfully helpful in emergencies. Well liked by associates.

☐ Co-operates well. Understands and complies with all rules. Usually demonstrates a good attitude. Liked by associates.

☐ Usually courteous and co-operative. Follows orders but at times needs reminding. Gets along well with associates.

☐ Does only what is specifically requested. Sometimes complains about following instructions. Reluctant to help others.

☐ Unfriendly and unco-operative. Refuses to help others.

Knowledge of the job   The degree to which the employee has learned and understands the various procedures of the job and their objectives.

☐ Exceptional understanding of all phases. Demonstrates unusual desire to acquire information.

☐ Thorough knowledge in most phases. Has interest and potential towards personal growth.

☐ Adequate knowledge for normal performance. Will not voluntarily seek development.

☐ Insufficient knowledge of job. Resists criticism and instruction.

☐ No comprehension of requirements of job.

Dependability   The reliability of the employee in performing assigned tasks accurately and within the allotted time.

☐ Exceptional. Can be left on own and will establish priorities to meet deadlines.

☐ Very reliable. Minimal supervision required to complete assignments.

☐ Dependable in most assignments. Normal supervision required. A profitable worker.

☐ Needs frequent follow-up. Excessive prodding necessary.

☐ Chronic procrastinator. Control required is out of all proportion.

Attendance and punctuality   Consider the employee's record, reliability and ability to conduct the job within the unit's work rules.

☐ Unusual compliance and understanding of work discipline. Routine usually exceeds normal.

☐ Excellent. Complete conformity with rules but cheerfully volunteers time during peak loads.

☐ Normally dependable. Rarely needs reminding of accepted rules.

☐ Needs close supervision in this area. Inclined to backslide without strict discipline.

☐ Unreliable. Resists normal rules. Frequently wants special privileges.

Exhibit 1 (continued)

Knowledge of company policy and objectives Acceptance, understanding, and promotion of company policies and objectives in the area of the employee's job responsibilities.

☐ Thorough appreciation and implementation of all policies. Extraordinary ability to project objectively.

☐ Reflects knowledge of almost all policies related to this position.

☐ Acceptable but fairly superficial understanding of job objectives.

☐ Limited insight into job or company goals. Mentally restricted.

☐ Not enough information or understanding to permit minimum efficiency.

Initiative and judgement The ability and interest to suggest and develop new ideas and methods; the degree to which these suggestions and normal decisions and actions are sound.

☐ Ingenious self-starter. Superior ability to think intelligently.

☐ Very resourceful. Clear thinker – usually makes thoughtful decisions.

☐ Fairly progressive, with normal sense. Often needs to be motivated.

☐ Rarely makes suggestions. Decisions need to be checked before implementation.

☐ Needs detailed instructions and close supervision. Tendency to assume and misinterpret.

Supervisory or technical potential Consider the employee's ability to teach and increase skills of others, to motivate and lead, to organise and assign work, and to communicate ideas.

☐ An accomplished leader who can earn respect and inspire others to perform. An articulate and artful communicator, planner and organiser.

☐ Has the ability to teach and will lead by example rather than technique. Speaks and writes well and can organise and plan with help.

☐ Fairly well informed on job-related subjects but has some difficulty communicating with others. Nothing distinctive about spoken or written word.

☐ Little ability to implement. Seems uninterested in teaching or helping others. Careless speech and writing habits.

☐ Unable to be objective or reason logically. Inarticulate and stilted in expression.

Overall rating There are five alternatives in each category. The first alternative is worth five points; the last alternative is worth one. Place a number from 1–5 by each of the selected alternatives and total the score for all nine categories. Then select the appropriate overall rating.

☐ Outstanding (45–39)

☐ Above expected (38–32)

☐ Expected (31–23)

☐ Below expected (22–16)

☐ Unsatisfactory (15–9)

Exhibit 2 (see page 602)

SMITH FARLEY INSURANCE

A. Positions open:

1. *Programmer/Analyst* – Car & Life Company Data Processing Trainee openings leading to Programmer/Analyst positions at the conclusion of *16-week* training programme. The DP Trainee is trained in the programming skills necessary to either develop new or to revise data-processing programmes that help administer over 10 million auto, life, fire and health insurance policies.

2. *Analyst* – Computer Operations Support Trainee opening leading to *Analyst* positions at conclusion of a *nine-month* training programme. Computer Operations Support is responsible for technical operations support for the Regional Data Processing Offices including: developing operator procedures, developing and administering training, problem resolution, and coordinating implementation of new systems and major changes for Regional Data Processing Offices.

B. Necessary qualifications:

We are recruiting for three Data Processing Departments (Car Insurance, Life Insurance and Computer Operations Support), each having different requirements, which are as follows:

1. *Car Insurance Data Processing*: Graduates in Applied Computer Science or Computer Technology, with specialisation in Management Information Systems (MIS), preferred. Logical analysis and problem-solving skills are essential as are good written and verbal communication skills. Working knowledge of COBOL and PL-1 essential.

2. *Life Insurance Data Processing*: Graduates in Mathematics or Business Studies will be preferred, but graduates in Science and the Arts may apply. Candidates must have an interest in computing and will be assessed on their aptitude for data processing.

3. *Computer Operations Support*: Most business majors are acceptable (i.e., Business, Business Administration, Finance, Economics, Accounting, etc. with 6–10 hours of Computer Science academic background).

C. Location:

The three positions will initially be located in Birmingham, but are likely to involve travel to other offices within the Group, including Continental Europe.

Exhibit 3 (see page 602)

INTERVIEW GUIDE FOR DATA PROCESSING (DP)

APPLICANT'S NAME _____   SCHOOL _____

INTERVIEW DATE _____   EXAMS _____

LOCATION _____ TIME _____   MAJOR _____

Criterion	Focus	General questions	Applicant-specific questions
Aptitude/Knowledge	Determine if exposure to and retention of a high-level computer language and development methods are adequate.	Of the DP courses you have taken which was the most beneficial, and why? Explain in detail the most difficult DP assignment you have undertaken. How do you rate yourself as a programmer? Why?	
Interest/Experience	Determine if interest and record of success in DP studies or work has been sustained (2+ years).	How did you first get interested in DP? What do you like about it the most? The least? Can you give me an example of a DP-related experience you have had that was satisfying? Not satisfying? What is your professional goal?	
Ability to work with others	Determine success of achieving results in team effort.	Do you feel you work more effectively on a one-to-one basis or in a group? Describe a situation in which you worked as a member of a team. What approach did you take to get people together and establish a common approach to the task?	
Commitment/ Initiative	Determine level of success in achieving task completion in light of task-complexity, adversity, load, level of knowledge, etc.	What approaches do you use to get people to accept your ideas or goals? What is a big obstacle you had to overcome to get where you are today? Do you consider yourself a self-starter or are you better at implementing the plans of others.	

Exhibit 3   (continued)

Criterion	Focus	General questions	Applicant-specific questions
Communication	Determine quality of written/spoken word.	Would you rather write a report or give a verbal report? Why? Do you think you are a good listener? What qualities do you need to be a good listener? How do you handle a situation when you are explaining something and the person doesn't understand?	
Problem solving/ Decision making	Determine if applicant has a record of addressing relatively complex projects.	In your opinion, what are the most difficult problems with which a programmer/analyst must deal? What particular strengths do you have that allow you to deal with these problems? What design methods do you use to create a program? Describe how you use them. Describe the most complex program you have ever written.	
Other	– Stability – Maturity – Leadership – Personal appearance		

Exhibit 4 (see page 602)

WILLIAM HENDERSON

ADDRESS:	68 West Avenue London SW18 8AR (081-605 6665)
POST APPLIED FOR:	Analyst/Data Processing.
EDUCATION:	Brighton High School 1975–85 A Levels: Physics (A), Mathematics (A), Computing (A), French (B).
	University of Sussex 1985–88 BSc Hons. Computer Science (2i).
	Warwick Business School 1988–90 Masters in Business Administration (Project: 'Computer Networks in the Office Environment').
EMPLOYMENT:	Vacation work with McDonald's 1986–88. Client liaison, Symonds Computer Bureau, summers 1988–89.
AVAILABILITY:	Immediate.
REFERENCES:	Available on request after passing initial selection.

Exhibit 5 (see page 602)

BRIAN JENSON
Peach Tree Cottage
West Lane
Leyburn
North Yorkshire
LB89 6DX
(Tel: 088-558890)

POST APPLIED FOR: Project Leader/Systems Analyst

BACKGROUND: Since leaving school I have worked for a variety of companies in the North of England, including Leyland Trucks and Royal Life Insurance. Under my first employer, Graham Industrial Hire Services, I was able to take a day-release course in computer science at Leeds Polytechnic. During that time, I also developed a data processing management information system for GIHS on a IBM 370. I would now like to specialise in data processing and use my leadership skills in running a department. I am highly motivated, versatile and happy to accept responsibility. My present domestic situation allows me to be mobile. I have O-Level qualifications in French and German.

HARDWARE: IBM 370 – Models 3090E, 3083, 3084, 4341; IBM PC/XT.

SOFTWARE: Case tools: Knowledgeware GAMMA
Databases: IMS-DL/1, DB11-SQL
Communications: IMS-MFS, TSO-ISPF
Languages: COBOL II, COBOL
Related: BTS, DDLTO, Datavantage, PFS File, Lotus 123, Freelance, Panvalet.

EMPLOYMENT: 1980–85: Graham Industrial Hire Services, systems administrator
1985–87: Leyland Trucks, systems support
1988–present: Royal Life Insurance, systems support and customer liaison leader supplying support and customer assistance to networked and standalone PC systems throughout the Group.

EDUCATION: Leeds School for Boys, Leeds
O-Levels: French, German, Geography, Computing, Mathematics.
Leeds Polytechnic, Leeds
Diploma in Computer Science

PERSONAL: Divorced, single parent with one son of six years. Clean driving licence.

Exhibit 6 (see page 602)

MARY DAVIES
234 West Parade
Birmingham
B56 3EF
(Tel. and Fax: 021-890345)

PERSONAL VISION:
To continue my academic research on catastrophe theory in industry.

EDUCATION:
Oxford University
Natural Sciences
Doctorate: 'Catastrophe Theory Simulations'. Awarded Brown Prize for Pure Mathematics and the Heinz Scholarship for Mathematical Logic.

EMPLOYMENT:
Summer 1988: Computer Services, verification and system supervision.
1988–92: National Computing Centre, developing advanced systems applications, in particular the application of Expert Systems to urban transport.
1992–present: Freelance consultant. Clients include several governmental departments, including the Cabinet Office, specialising in advanced networking facilities and security systems.

PUBLICATIONS:
See attached list.

INTERESTS:
Politics, discussion, food and dogs.

Glossary

360° degree appraisal One is 'judged' by one's manager, one's peers and one's subordinates.

Ability The product of aptitude and opportunity. The skills to perform.

Abstract conceptualisation With CONCRETE EXPERIENCE (cf.), a polarity used by Kolb to codify LEARNING STYLE (cf.). Abstract conceptualisation is a THINKING STRATEGY (cf.) based on the intellect where models are developed 'in the laboratory and not in the field'.

Achievement motivation Where one feels more able to perform because of what one has already achieved.

Active experimentation With REFLECTIVE OBSERVATION (cf.), a polarity used by Kolb to codify LEARNING STYLE (cf.). Active Experimentation is a method of learning that is based on trial and error – things have to be tried out.

Affection In the very specific sense of the Firo-B test, affection is about our need for one-to-one relationships. Our need to relate to individuals.

Annualised hours A system whereby employees have a contract to work a specific number of hours per year and not a set number of hours each day or week.

Anticipatory stress Stress arising from the anticipation of expected events.

Aptitude How well one is suited to the job.

Artificial constraints Arbitrary boundaries placed around a problem that restrict possible alternative approaches and make the problem difficult to solve creatively.

Autonomy The freedom to choose how and when to do a particular task.

Behaviour Actions that can be seen, felt and measured in other people.

Behavioural guideline The concept of providing direct advice on how to develop a particular skill is key to this book. The behavioural guidelines are often summaries of what has gone before without the background of justifications.

Bias against thinking The inclination to avoid mental work, one indication of the CONCEPTUAL BLOCK (cf.).

Brainstorming A technique designed to help problem solving by generating volumes of alternatives in a positive atmosphere.

Broken record A technique used in Assertiveness Training where a core objective is isolated and repeated until accepted by a respondent. (cf. FIELDING).

Chaos Chaos Theory sees chaos as a situation where the start point acutely effects the progressing situation. This has obvious connections with management. THEORY X (cf.) and COMMAND AND CONTROL ORGANISATIONS (cf.) lead to the wish to control 'everything, within reason'. Chaos, if accepted, is uncontrollable. The compromise is to allow staff and workers to work within a closely defined CIRCLE OF CONCERN (cf.) and control their own chaos within it.

Circle of concern Where you have authority and matched responsibility – your job.

Coaching A term used for the process whereby managers assist their people to perform their work by setting standards, providing training and support, and giving advice.

Cognitive style The manner in which an individual gathers and evaluates the information that he or she receives. An individual's characteristic and consistent manner of processing and organising what he or she sees and thinks about.

Command and control organisations The military model of organisations where there is a formal chain of command and orders come from the top.

Commitment The CONCEPTUAL BLOCK (cf.) that results when an individual commits himself or herself to a particular view, definition or solution.

Communication In the context of this book, communication is about the process of human interaction and not about the tools we may or may not use – the process by which individuals and groups influence each other.

Communication: egalitarian Communication which accepts that, on a particular issue, everyone has an equal claim to a valid opinion.

Communication: supportive communication (between managers and their subordinates) Communication that is effective in assisting the achievement of the task and allows each party top feel valued and develop.

Communication: validating communication Communication that confirms the value of the individual as a human being, regardless of the influence that individual finally achieves.

Communication: descriptive communication Communication involving an objective account of the event or behaviour that is a cause of your concern, developing the reaction or consequences of the event or behaviour and how it makes you feel, and suggestions for more acceptable alternatives while giving support to the individual concerned.

Competency The ability to perform effectively functions associated with management in a work-related situation.

Complacency The CONCEPTUAL BLOCK (cf.) that occurs not because of poor thinking habits or inappropriate assumptions but because of fear, ignorance, self-satisfaction or mental laziness.

Compression The CONCEPTUAL BLOCK (cf.) that results from an individual looking at a problem too narrowly, screening out too much relevant data or making assumptions that inhibit the solving of the problem.

Conceptual blocks Mental obstacles that restrict the way a problem is defined and limit the number of alternative solutions that might otherwise be considered.

Concrete experience With ABSTRACT CONCEPTUALISATION (cf.), a polarity used by Kolb to codify LEARNING STYLE (cf.). Concrete experience is a method of learning that is based on the senses – that which is based on actual personal measurement.

Conflict Disagreement between individuals, functional or dysfunctional at any level, from mild disapproval to 'open warfare'.

Congruence Matching one's own behaviour to what the other person is thinking or feeling – at its simplest, congruence is established by deciding the right place, time and context for communication.

Constancy The CONCEPTUAL BLOCK (cf.) that results from using a single approach to a problem.

Constructive conflict Much progress relies on challenges to the status quo and often such challenge involves conflict with those to jump to defend it. DYSFUNCTIONAL CONFLICT (cf.) is often personal and is inclined to produce a black and white analysis. Constructive conflict is not about personalities but about achieving some goal and often allows for the greys that assist us in a real world.

Consulting Once a subordinate has been allowed to develop his or her own work style to face a particular issue, then he or she is certainly in possession of more local and 'expert' information on what the task entails. In SUPPORTIVE COMMUNICATION (cf.) this is acknowledged by the manager and the subordinate's expertise is recognised – he or she is consulted when the work is being discussed.

Contingency planning The final stage of POTENTIAL PROBLEM ANALYSIS (cf.) and of the implementation process. Normally the implementation of contingency plans are NOT the responsibility of the application team or indeed the appointed problem owner, but should be referred to higher authority.

Control In the very specific sense of the Firo-B test, control is about our need to understand where we are in relation to other people. We may need to dominate or be dominated or simply to 'know where we are'.

Counselling In the management context, counselling is not associated with the psychiatrist's chair, but with frank one-to-one interviews where managers and subordinates discuss the personal issues faced in performing work effectively. Counselling is not about giving advice or direction but facing individual work-related issues.

Creative problem solving A process where issues are approached from directions not entirely dictated by precedent or logic.

Cross-functional teams Teams composed of the relevant disciplines to perform the task in hand. (cf. CUSTOMER-DIRECTED TEAMS and SELF-DIRECTED TEAMS.)

Customer-directed teams Self-contained teams with the relevant disciplines and skills to satisfy the needs of a specific customer or cluster of customers. (cf. CROSS-FUNCTIONAL TEAMS and SELF-DIRECTED TEAMS.)

Deep relaxation An approach for use in building psychological resilience in which both body and mind become completely relaxed.

Delegation Allocation of responsibilities to another – usually in business, to a subordinate.

Descriptive communication Objective description of the event of behaviour that needs modification: description of the reaction to the behaviour or its consequences and a possible suggestion of alternatives.

Diagnostic surveys In the world of psychology there is a clear distinction between questionnaires and tests. Tests have validity; they can be replicated and used to make comparisons between individuals and they have what we may call a provenance which may be checked by those who use them. Questionnaires are much less formal and, although useful, cannot be relied upon for comparisons between individuals and groups. Diagnostic surveys, as used in this book, are intended to assist individuals to gain an insight into their own behaviour, beliefs and capabilities. They do not have validity in any qualitative sense.

Direct analogies A SYNECTICS (cf.) problem-solving technique in which individuals are encouraged to apply facts, technology or previous experiences to a related (or indeed unrelated) problem.

Distributive negotiation strategy A PROCESS (cf.) that requires both parties to sacrifice self interests to resolve potential or real CONFLICT (cf.) by 'dividing a fixed cake'.

Downsizing Fitting the workforce to the tasks it has to accomplish and hopefully allowing a little slack for growth and eventualities.

Dysfunctional conflict Conflict that does not have a productive output.

Empowerment A process whereby people are given authority in balance with their responsibilities whereby they can accomplish their set objectives using their own balance of initiative and discretion.

Enabling The ultimate delegation. Trusting others to do a job after having made sure that the objectives and the ways and means are clear, while at the same time maintaining a monitoring role.

Encounter stress A type of stress that results from CONFLICT (cf.) with others.

Environmental stress A type of stress created by factors outside the control of the individual – forced change, reduced budgets, threats of redundancy.

Facilitation Helping others to have the materials and skills to do a job while NOT actually helping with the job itself.

Fantasy analogies A SYNECTICS (cf.) problem-solving technique in which individuals ask: 'In my wildest dreams, how would I wish the problem to be resolved?'

Feedback Information given regularly to individuals or groups about their performance.

Fielding A term used in Assertiveness Training, often coupled with BROKEN RECORD (cf.) where the respondent acknowledges the words of the initiator by repeating them in some form but not necessarily acknowledging their complete truth or relevance, thus 'I understand that you feel badly about your job, but that is not the point – you have been late ten times this month.'

Fixation A defence mechanism against stress in which an individual continues with a response regardless of its merit, e.g., repeatedly redialling the same telephone number.

Flatter organisations The COMMAND AND CONTROL ORGANISATIONS (cf.) worked by the rule of five – each manager had five subordinates. This set the hierarchy in stone – the number of layers was set by the numbers on the payroll. Multi-layered organisations are assumed to be slow in response to change. By various 'tricks', invariably involving teams, layers are removed.

Flexibility of thought The diversity of ideas or concepts generated.

Fluency of thought Used in our chapter on PROBLEM SOLVING (cf.) it refers to the ability of individuals or groups to come up with novel approaches to solving problems within a set period.

Followship A leader must have followers to be a leader. Following and sustaining a leaders is a skill like any other.

Force field analysis A system whereby one looks at what one wishes to achieve and the pressures that will help and impede your achieving it. Piece by piece way one then seeks to 'eliminate the negative and accentuate the positive'.

Forcing response An assertive, unco-operative response to a conflict situation that uses the exercise of authority to satisfy one's own needs at the expense of another's.

FRAME'd job descriptions the basic rules of motivational job descriptions with rules that are **F**ew, **R**ealisable, **A**greed, **M**easurable and **E**xplicit.

Goals Management jargon for the objectives set for workers.

Group shift The polarising effect that occurs during intensive group discussion when individuals tend to adopt a more extreme version of the position they held at the beginning of the meeting. The tendency is usually towards a risk-taking rather than a conservative stance.

Groupthink Jargon referring to a problem with groups. At particular times the pressure to reach consensus overrides individual critical faculties. Individuals may 'railroad' opinions and the effort to disagree with the 'groupthink' pseudo consensus can be very difficult.

Hardiness A combination of the three characteristics of a highly stress-resistant personality – control, commitment and challenge.

Holistic view Seen as an entity and not as parts of a whole.

Homogeneity/heterogeneity Groups composed of members with similar/dissimilar backgrounds, respectively.

Human resource management This title is a result of the newly perceived role of Director (HRM) personnel management' in organisations. The new status of HRM is that of an integrating and integrated function within an organisation.

Idea champion A person who is committed, often personally, to the implementation of particular solution.

Ignoring 'Ignoring' in CREATIVE PROBLEM SOLVING (cf.), is used a shorthand to indicate the failure to identify common features in apparently different things. A feature of the COMMITMENT BLOCK (cf.).

Illumination stage The Eureka moment, or the stage in the innovation cycle, when an insight is recognised and effectively articulated.

Imperviousness A barrier that excludes any argument or discussion from others.

Inclusion In the very specific sense of the Firo-B test, inclusion is the measure of our need to be gregarious.

Incubation stage An early stage in the thinking process or innovation cycle, sometimes known as 'sleeping on it', when unconscious mental activity combines and builds to produce a potential solution.

Integrative negotiation A negotiation in which the focus is on collaborative ways or strategies 'expanding the cake' by avoiding fixed, incompatible positions.

Internal and external context The boundaries of CIRCLE OF CONCERN (cf.).

Interpersonal competence The ability to manage conflict, to build and manage teams, to coach and council, to provide valuable feedback, to influence and to be otherwise effective as a human being with other human beings.

Interpersonal orientation A position or posture taken by individuals in relation to the external environment. Primary orientations are about physically meeting the environment – stance, posture. Secondary orientations are about the positions we take up with respect to achieving goals – reactive, aggressive, assertive.

Intervention When groups or individuals have been unable to do work effectively, the outsider (tutor or manager) may decide, through his or her monitoring function, that things are not going as planned and step in (intervening) to reset or review.

Invalidating communication – A process that denies not only the right for others to have opinions but also, in the extreme, the right of the individual to be worth consideration.

Kaisen A Japanese management philosophy of continuous improvement.

Lateral thinking A term coined by deBono for a thinking process that involves 'moving sideways' and not continuing in a sequential process. (cf. VERTICAL THINKING.) De Bono likens it to using the reverse gear on a car – not for use all the time, but essential when you need to get out of tight corners.

Leager A state between leader and manager.

Learning organisation A late 1990s concept with as many definitions as management gurus. The underlying concept is that to survive and prosper into the twenty-first century, organisations and individuals need to refresh their skills and knowledge on a continuous basis. This continuous learning can only come from the active participation of those within the organisation taking responsibility.

Learning strategies: intuitive, sensing and thinking We prefer certain ways of taking on new information or change in different ways. Some individuals are intuitive, others like to measure using their senses while others prefer to think about things and intellectualise. (cf. LEARNING STYLE and COGNITIVE STYLE.)

Learning style How we prefer to take on primary information.

Left hemisphere thinking A concept derived from a probable simplification of the way the human brain functions. It is implied that logical, analytical, linear or sequential thought comes from activity in the left hemisphere of the brain. (cf. RIGHT HEMISPHERE THINKING.)

Life balance The development of resilience in all areas of one's life in order to handle unavoidable stress.

Locus of control Events that occur as a result of one's own actions, behaviour or personality as opposed to those that can be attributed to luck, fate, chance or even THEM.

Management by Objectives (MBO) A mechanistic management tool whereby employees develop, with their managers, encompassing goals which are SMART – **S**pecific, **M**easurable, **A**greed, **R**ealistic and **T**imed. Management after the setting of the MBO goals is thus reduced to monitoring progress on these items.

Matrix organisation For convenience many organisations were designed along functions – marketing, finance, research. This has been called a silo organisation. The output of the organisation is concerned with projects or customers. In the matrix organisation, the silos of functions remain alongside a project management structure, individuals reporting to both.

Mentor Usually, and in management where a more mature or experienced colleague or manager acts as an adviser, giving help to a new and inexperienced worker.

Milestone reporting A job is structured so that, as opposed to one final point of success or failure, many steps towards the goals are recognised. At these points (milestones) interim reports are formalised.

Modelling Setting an example for others to copy. Thus managers wanting to spread an 'open door' policy in their organisations would have their own doors open for consultation.

Monitoring Watching and measuring and, if necessary, intervening in a project to ensure that norms and quality are maintained.

Morphology A technique which seeks to combine logical and creative thought processes. The process involves constructing a matrix, often having properties or attributes form as one dimension, and areas of use, the other. Each 'box' of the matrix is then tested for an 'idea' or 'application'. Thus, in looking for new uses of glass, the properties could be listed as transparency, softening under heat, light bending, brittleness and hardness, and the areas of use as home and industry. An 'empty box' from a process such as BRAINSTORMING (cf.) might well be 'softening under heat' and 'industry' – the use of glass as a heat fuse might be considered to fill the box.

Motivation A combination of desire and commitment demonstrated by effort.

Multiskilling New technology in particular has de-skilled many tasks so that for 80 per cent of the time, a trained generalist with motivation can accomplish them. An organisation undertaking a multiskilling programme will have looked at how the 20 per cent of the tasks can be tackled (cf. PARETO) and given training so that the 80 per cent can be achieved efficiently with a team.

Need The text has a very specific usage of a common word. A psychological need is that which is *necessary* for an individual's health or well-being.

Neuro Linguistic Programing (NLP) A codification of various theories of human communications by Richard Bandier and John Grinden.

Ocham's Razor A basic form of problem solving loved by Sherlock Holmes – 'Work on the most probable solutions first. When all these have been disposed of, what is left, however improbable, is the solution.' That is, of course, assuming you have ALL the solutions listed and that the problem is solvable without redefinition.

Outcomes What is actually accomplished.

Pareto's law A dignified way of saying that the first 20 per cent of virtually any sample produces 80 per cent of the 'important' effect. For example, we may find that 20 per cent of our customers generate 80 per cent of our profits.

Perceptual stereotyping Problem definition using unquestioned preconceptions.

Performance The product of ability and motivation. What people actually do.

Personal analogies A creative problem-solving technique used in SYNECTICS (cf.). New ways of solving problems are developed by asking individuals such questions as: 'If I was the machine performing this operation, how would I feel, what help would I need?' The answers to the questions are then used to develop a *better* machine.

Personality: altruistic-nurturing A type of personality that seeks gratification through the personality promotion of harmony and the enhancement of the welfare of others without expecting any reward.

Personality: analytic-autonomising A type of personality that seeks gratification through the personality achievement of self-sufficiency, self reliance and logical orderliness.

Personality: assertive-directing The type of personality that seeks gratification through self assertion and directs the activities of others with the expectation of reward.

Peter principle Promotion beyond the individual's level of competence – the good salesperson may well be a terrible sales manager.

Positive reinforcement Where good behaviour is praised or rewarded.

Potential problem analysis A technique developed by Kepner and Tregoe whereby BRAINSTORMING (cf.) is used to collect the problems that COULD occur in the implementation of a potential solution.

Preparation stage of problem solving The first stage in the thinking process or innovation cycle when data is being collected, the problem is being defined and the 'obvious' alternatives are being collected and evaluated.

Proactive strategy A method of managing stress that initiates action in order to resist the negative aspects.

Probes: clarification probe A request to make a statement more clear: 'Can you clarify what you have just said, I am not quite clear what you mean?'

Probes: elaboration probe A request for more detail in a discussion: 'Can you elaborate on what you have just said?'

Probes: reflection probe A method of getting further information by repeating the sense, if not the exact words, of the person being questioned: 'You say you were made to feel inferior by his response. How was that?'

Probes: repetition probe A return to a previous subject when the item has not been cleared up: 'Once again I must press the point. What did you actually do?'

Problem solving A term for dealing with unusual and different management issues. It implies a process of analysis, collecting alternatives, collating the alternatives and judging the most likely to succeed.

Process Management speak indicating how things are done as opposed to what is being done. In discussing interpersonal skills, process is seen as the way a task is performed by individuals and groups.

Push and pull strategies A 'push' strategy is based on changing the behaviour of others by some form of coercion whereas the 'pull' strategy uses influencing and consultative techniques and does not resort to coersion.

Rational problem solving A system of problem solving based on steps: 1. Defining the problem – constraints and standards to be achieved. 2. Generating alternatives. 3. Evaluating the alternatives against the constraints and standards. 4. Selecting a tentative solution. 5. Implementation, including contingency planning.

Reflective observation With ACTIVE EXPERIMENTATION (cf.), a polarity used by Kolb to codify LEARNING STYLE (cf.). Reflective observation involves, as it says, thinking on what has been observed.

Response: accommodating A response to conflict that tries to preserve a friendly approach interpersonal relationship by satisfying the other party's concerns while ignoring one's own. It generally produces a lose–lose situation to nobody's satisfaction.

Response: avoiding An unassertive, unco-operative reaction to conflict that neglects the interests of both parties by side-stepping the issue. The resultant frustration may cause a power struggle as others rush in to fill the vacuum.

Response: collaborating The co-operative, assertive, problem-solving way of resolving conflict. It focuses on finding solutions to the basic problems and issues that are acceptable to both parties, rather than on finding fault or allocating blame. Of the conflict management strategies, this is the only true WIN–WIN (cf.) approach.

Reversing the problem A tool for expanding problem definition by reversing the current way of thinking about a problem, e.g. 'The problem stated is to get the bones out of the fish. How about redefining the problem as getting the fish flesh off the bones?'

Right hemisphere thinking A concept derived from a probable simplification of the way the human brain functions. It is implied that holistic, intuitive, creative, qualitative thinking comes from activity in the right hemisphere of the brain.

Role Role has two heads. Firstly, there is the functional role based on skills, knowledge and aptitude – accountant, cook. Secondly, there is a social role based on who you are – your SHADOW (cf.) and your personality and needs. Together they make the role you prefer, but not necessarily the role demanded of you by the organisation.

Self-directed teams Teams which 'manage their own CHAOS' (cf.). Self-directed teams do not have hierarchical managers and are 'lead' in the organisation by someone who is responsible for proving the VISION (cf.) setting the task, providing resources and MONITORING (cf.) outputs but not, once it is agreed, the way things are done.

Self-actualisation In the Maslow Hierarchy of Needs the fulfilment of physiological needs is seen as the base and self-actualisation as the pinnacle. Perhaps with some reference to Zen, self-actualisation is seen as a state when personal fulfilment has been achieved.

Self-awareness The ability to understand one's own needs and VALUES (cf.).

Sensitive line The division between what is comfortable for the individual and that which is unknown, threatening or simply different.

Shadow In Jungian psychology, the shadow of an individual is considered as that person's 'dark side'. In the chapter on Effective Communication we take the word in a more metaphorical sense as being something that we unavoidably carry with us because of our role or calling. Thus the shadow of someone who is a policeman is the preconceptions that spring into other's minds when they meet someone who claims to be a policeman.

Shamrock organisations Charles Handy, among others, advocates organisations where only the key staff performing the core activities of the organisation are 'permanent staff'. Subsidiary staff performing core activities are under limited contracts and all other activities – canteens, maintenance, etc. – are contracted out.

Situational leadership A concept that leadership is contingent on the situation in which it finds itself. Hersey and Blanchard saw management/leadership style dependent of the maturity and motivation of the subordinates. Vroom and Yetton see the external context as compounding factors.

Skills The word 'skill' has a very definite meaning in management development. Three classifications – knowledge, skills and aptitude – need to be utilised to perform any effective task. We need to have knowledge of what has to be done, how it is to be done using our skills and willingness to do it – aptitude. *Background skills*: Heterogeneous groups are inclined to be better at solving complex or novel tasks than homogeneous groups (i.e. groups composed of members with similar backgrounds).

Small wins Using a 'small wins' strategy, the total 'project' or 'job' is divided into small steps and these are used as places for success or failure to be discussed.

SMART objectives see MANAGEMENT BY OBJECTIVES.

Stereotype An unevaluated view of another thing or person based on prejudice or previous experience.

Stress management: enactive strategy A method that creates a new environment by eliminating the stressors.

Stress management: reactive strategy A strategy that copes with the immediate stressors, temporarily reducing their ill effects but avoids any long-term considerations.

Stress management: regression strategy A strategy in which an individual adopts a behaviour pattern from the past, e.g. becomes childish.

Stress management: repression strategy A strategy in which an individual simply denies that the stress exists.

Stress management: small-wins strategy A strategy in which a large task is divided into small elements, so that a mini-victory celebration can be held at each small success. Alcoholics Anonymous use the small-wins strategy when they encourage drinkers to take each day as it comes and not plan for months or weeks ahead.

Stressors Stimuli that may cause physical and psychological reactions in individuals.

Subdivision of problems Breaking problems into a series of subproblems.

Symbolic analogies A problem-solving technique founded on SYNECTICS (cf.) where the problem is seen as though metaphor – thus a highly successful organisation is the Catholic Church: How would the Catholic Church deal with this problem? What in this solution can we adapt to the working of our organisation?

Supportive communication Communication that helps others share information accurately and honestly without putting in question medium- and long-term relationships.

Synectics A structured and effective system of creative problem solving using groups. Proposed by Gordon and later developed by Prince. The technique makes great play on the use of analogy.

Synergistic The whole is greater than the parts.

Task and process The task is what you have to do and the PROCESS (cf.) is how you do it.

Team development The process whereby a group of individuals progresses to a potential SELF-DIRECTED TEAM (cf.).

Teams Groups of people working together to perform a task.

Theories X, Y and Z The concept, due to McGregor, is that managers' views of why their subordinates work lie along two polarities. At one polarity – Theory X – they feel that people do not work without coercion. At the other polarity – Theory Y – they feel that, on the whole, given the right tools and conditions, people actually like working. Theory Z, also proposed by McGregor and developed later by others, allows us some middle ground – a view between X and Y.

Thinking languages The various ways in which a problem may be handled, probably reflecting the thinking process that makes an individual more confident. Words are the most obvious language but beyond words individuals think in images, pictures, sounds and feelings. By moving between the languages, problems can be solved more easily.

Thinking strategy The method followed by individuals for interpreting or judging data. In this text we see it as a systematic route that can be developed as a skill.

Threat rigidity A behaviour where the response to a threat of change is characterised by extreme conservatism. The ostrich's 'head in the sand' would be an extreme case.

Three-ring circus organisations Ricardo Semler advocates the ultimate FLATTER ORGANISATION (cf.). In the three-ring circus, the centre ring of 'Partners' is responsible for strategy, vision and direction; the inner ring for directing teams, 'Co-ordinators'; and the outer ring as the team members, 'Associates'. (cf. SELF-DIRECTED TEAMS.)

Time management A strategy for reducing stress caused by issues of insufficient or excess time.

Tolerance of ambiguity Freud discusses the human need to balance two Greek Gods – Thanatos, the God of synchronicity and order and Eros, the God of chaos. We all like to set our own balance. Those with a high acceptance of chaos – a high tolerance or ambiguity – are able to put the ordering or their universe on the back boiler longer than the lovers of order. We all worship both Gods at some time.

Transactional leadership The concept is that leadership is a fiction sustained by a contract between the leader and the led. The contract is about support, privilege, job satisfaction and material gain.

Transformational leadership The visionary leader is probably born and not made. These are the change masters. The transformational leadership is absolutely situationally dependent and provides, along with vision, modelling and the ability to create a legend. (cf. TRANSACTIONAL LEADERSHIP.)

Type A and Type B personalities Type A: hard driving, potentially hostile, intense and highly competitive personality. Type B is the opposite – able to be relaxed and 'listen without interrupting.'

Values That which individuals find good or beneficial to their well-being. Values provide the link between NEED (cf.) and action.

Verification The final stage in creative thought whereby standards are applied to potential solutions.

Vertical thinking A term used in the process of CREATIVE PROBLEM SOLVING (cf.), probably coined by deBono, implying a sequential thinking strategy which begins by defining a problem in a single way and continuing logically from that start point. Normally used in comparison with LATERAL THINKING (cf.)

Vision Having a vision – knowing the ultimate strategic purpose of one's actions.

Win–Win A jargon term often used in management speak for a situation where all the parties gain from a compromise and nobody has, or feels that they have 'lost', face or fact.

Response: compromising A response to conflict that attempts to find satisfaction for both parties by 'splitting the difference'. If over-used, it sends the message that settling disputes is more important than solving problems.

Work redesign A rethinking of the method of working to improve some measure – e.g., efficiency or sickness.

Work study A tool of 'scientific management' whereby jobs are reduced to elements. The elements are often allocated units of time and used for costing.

Working outside the square (a metaphor) The concept is that most of the time we work within the square assuming rules and regulations that may or may not apply to the exact situation in which we find ourselves. Sometimes we have to challenge the relevance of these assumptions to progress.

World class As a global market takes hold, organisations find that being a good company within their own national boundaries is not enough. They have to compare themselves – be benchmarked – against ALL relevant companies world wide.

References

3M Audio Visual Division (no date given) *Six secrets to hold a good meeting . . . every time*. 3M Corporation Pamphlet.

3M Meeting Management Team (1987) *How to run better business meetings*. New York: McGraw-Hill.

AACSB (1985) Preliminary report on the future of business education and development. St Louis, Mo.

Abrahams, P. (1993) Management: Creating cracks in the layers. *Financial Times*, 5 April 1993.

Adams, S. (1996) *Dogbert's management handbook*, London: Boxtree (imprint of Macmillian).

Adler, R.B. (1977) Satisfying personal needs: Managing conflicts, making requests, and saying no. *Confidence in communication: A guide to assertive and social skills*. New York: Holt, Rinehart & Winston.

Adler, V. (1989) Little control equals lots of stress. *Psychology Today*, **23**(4), 18–19.

Alday, R.J. and Brief, A.P. (1979) *Task design and employee motivation*. Glenview, Ill.: Scott Foresman.

Alinsky, S.D. (1971) *Rules for radicals: A pragmatic primer for realistic radicals*. New York: Vintage Books.

Allen, J.L. (1974) *Conceptual blockbusting*. San Francisco: W.H. Freeman.

Alloy, L.B., Peterson C., Abrahamson, L.Y. and Seligman, M.E.P. (1984) Attributional style and the generality of learned helplessness. *Journal of Personality and Social Psychology*, **46**, 681–7.

Allport, G., Gordon, R. and Vernon, P. (1931) *The study of values manual*. Boston: Houghton Mifflin.

Allport, G., Vernon, P. and Lindzey, G. (1960) *Study of values*. Boston: Houghton Mifflin.

Allred, B.B., Snow, C.C. and Miles, R.E. (1996) Characteristics of managerial education. *Academy of Management Executive*, **10**(4), 17–27.

AMA Report (1996) Taking the lid off leadership. *Management Review*, November, pp. 59–61.

Amabile, T.M. (1988) A model of creativity and innovation in organizations. In Cummings, L.L. and Staw, B.M. (eds), *Research in organizational behavior*, **10**, pp. 123–67.

Ambrose, S.E. (1985) *Pegasus Bridge June 6, 1944*, New York: Simon & Schuster.

Ancona, D.G. and Caldwell, D. (1992) Bridging the boundary: External activity and performance in organizational teams. *Administrative Science Quarterly*, **27**: 459–89.

Anderson, C.R. (1977) Locus of control, coping behaviors and performance in a stress setting: A longitudinal study. *Journal of Applied Psychology*, **62**, 446–51.

Anderson, C., Hellreigel, D. and Slocum, J. (1977) Managerial response to environmentally induced stress. *Academy of Management Journal*, **20**, 260–72.

Anderson, C. and Schneider, C. E. (1978) Locus of control, leader behavior, and leader performance among management students. *Academy of Management Journal*, **21**, 690–8.

Anderson, C., Hellreigel, D. and Slocum, J. (1977) Managerial response to environmentally induced stress. *Academy of Management Journal*, **20**, 260–72.

Anon. (1997) An interview with Warren Bennis. *Training*, August.

Antonovsky, A. (1979) *Health, stress and coping*. San Francisco: Jossey-Bass.

Argenti, J. (1976) *Corporate collapse: The causes and symptoms*. New York: Wiley.

Argyris, C. and Schon, D.A. (1978) *Organisational learning: A theory of action perspective*. Reading, Mass.: Addison Wesley.

Argyris, C. and Schon, D. (with Hedberg, B.) (1981) How organisations learn and unlearn. In Nysstrom, P.C. and Starbuck, W.H. (eds) *Handbook of organisational design*. London, pp. 8–27.

Ashby, R. (1956) *Design for the brain*. London: Science Paperbacks.

Ashridge College UK (1994) Business questionnaire – January 1994.

Athos, A. and Gabarro, J. (1978) *Interpersonal behavior*. Englewood Cliffs, NJ: Prentice Hall.

Atkinson, J.W. and Raynor, J.O. (1974) *Motivation and achievement*. Washington, DC: V.H. Winston.

Averill, J.R. (1973) Personal control over aversive stimuli and its relationship to stress. *Psychological Bulletin*, **80**, 286–303.

Baechler, M. (1996) I'm Mary, I'm a workaholic. *Incentive*, **18**(5), 29–30.

Bandler, R. and Grinder, J. (1979) Frogs into princes. *Maab*, Utah: Real People Press. *See also* Heather and Woods (1991).

Bandura, A. (1977a) *A social learning theory*. Englewood Cliffs, NJ: Prentice Hall.

Bandura, A. (1977b) Self-efficacy: Toward a unifying theory of behavioral change. *Psychological Review*, **84**, 191–215.

Bandura, A. (1986) *Social foundations of thought and action: A social cognitive theory.* Englewood Cliffs, NJ: Prentice Hall.

Bandura, A. (1989) Human agency in social cognition theory. *American Psychologist,* **44**, 1175–84.

Bannister, D. and Fransella, F. (1971) *Inquiring man.* Harmondsworth: Penguin.

Barber, B. *The logic and limits of trust.* New Brunswick, NJ: Rutgers University Press.

Barnett, A. (1998) *The Observer,* London, 16 August.

Barnlund, D.C. (1968) *Interpersonal communication: Survey and studies.* Boston: Houghton Mifflin.

Barrett, H. (1977) *Practical uses of speech communications* (4th edn). New York: Holt, Rinehart & Winston.

Barron, F.X. (1963) *Creativity and psychological health.* New York: Van Nostrand.

Basadur, M.S. (1979) Training in creative problem solving: Effects of deferred judgment and problem finding and solving in an industrial research organization. Unpublished doctoral dissertation, University of Cincinnati.

Bazerman, M. (1986) Why negotiations go wrong. *Psychology Today,* June, 54–8.

Beary, J.F. and Benson, H. (1977) A simple psychophysiological technique which elicits the hypometabolic changes in the relaxation response. *Psychosomatic Medicine,* **36**, 115–20.

Beehr, T.A. (1976) Perceived situational moderators of the relationship between subjective role ambiguity and role strain. *Journal of Applied Psychology,* **61**, 35–40.

Beer, M. (1987) Performance appraisal. In Lorsch, J.W. (ed.) *Handbook of organizational behavior.* Englewood Cliffs, NJ: Prentice Hall, pp. 286–300.

Belbin, M. (1981) and subsequent editions: *Why teams succeed or fail.* London: Heinemann. Building the Perfect Team (training film) Video Arts.

Benjamin, A. (1969) *The helping interview.* Boston: Houghton Mifflin.

Bennis, W. and Nanus, B. (1985) *Leaders: The strategies for taking charge.* New York: Harper & Row.

Bennis, W. (1984) Where have all the leaders gone?. In Rosenbasck, W.E. and Taylor, R.L. (eds) *Contemporary issues in leadership.* Boulder: Westview Press, pp. 42–60.

Benson, G. (1983) On the campus: How well do business schools prepare graduates for the business world? *Personnel,* **60**, 61–5.

Benson, H. (1975) *The relaxation response.* New York: William Morrow.

Berkowitz, L. (1953) Sharing leadership in small decision-making groups. *Journal of Abnormal and Social Psychology,* **53**(48), 231–8.

Bernard, C.I. (1938) *The functions of the executive.* Cambridge: Harvard University Press.

Berne, E. (1963) *The structure and dynamics of organizations.* New York: Grove Press.

Berryman-Fink, C. and Fink, C. (1996) Stress management strategies. *Incentive*, **170**(9), 59–60.

Beveridge, W. (1960) *The art of scientific investigation*. New York: Random House.

Bieri, J., Atkins, A.L., Bruar, S., Leaman, R.L., Miller, H. and Tripodi, T. (1966) *Clinical social judgment*. New York: Wiley.

Blanchard, K. and Peale, N.V. (1988) *The power of ethical management*. London: Cedar.

Blanchard, K.H. and Johnson, S. (1983) *The one minute manager*. London: Fontana.

Block, P. (1987) *The empowered manager: Positive political skills at work*. San Francisco: Jossey-Bass.

Bookman, A. and Morgan, S. (1988) *Women and the politics of empowerment*. Philadelphia: Temple University Press.

Boss, W.L. (1983) Team building and the problem of regression: The personal management interview as an intervention. *Journal of Applied Behavioral Science*, **19**, 67–83.

Bouchard, T.J. (1971) Whatever happened to brainstorming? *Journal of Creative Behavior*, **5**, 182–9.

Boulding, E. (1964) Further reflections on conflict management. In R.L. Kahn and E. Boulding (eds) *Power and conflict in organizations*. New York: Basic Books.

Bower, M. (1965) Nurturing innovation in an organization. In G.A. Steiner (ed.) *The creative organization*. Chicago: University of Chicago.

Bowers, D. (1983) What would make 11,500 people quit their jobs? *Organizational Dynamics*, **3**, 5–19.

Boyatzis, R.E. (1982) *The competent manager*. New York: Wiley.

Bradford, D.L. and Cohen, A.R. (1984) *Managing for excellence*. New York: Wiley.

Bramucci, R. (1977) A factorial examination of the self-empowerment construct. PhD dissertation, University of Oregon.

Bramwell, S.T., Masuda, M., Wagner, N.N. and Holmes, T.H. (1975) Psychosocial factors in athletic injuries. *Journal of Human Stress*, **1**, 6.

Brehm, J.W. (1966) Response to loss of freedom: A theory of psychological reactance. New York: Academic Press.

Broadwell, M.M. (1972) *The new supervisor*. Reading, Mass.: Addison Wesley.

Brouwer, P.J. (1964) The power to see ourselves. *Harvard Business Review*, **42**, 156–65.

Bruner, J.S. (1966) *On knowing: Essays for the left hand*. Cambridge: Harvard University Press.

Budner, S. (1962) Intolerance of ambiguity as a personality variable. *Journal of Personality*, **2**(30), 29–50.

Burnaska, R.F. (1976) The effects of behavioral modeling training upon managers' behavior and employees' perceptions. *Personnel Psychology*, **29**, 329–35.

Burnes, B. (1996) *Managing Change: Case study 5*. London: Pitman.

Burns, J.M. (1978) *Leadership*. New York: Harper & Row.

Business Week, 3 June 1985, 'Do mergers really work?', pp. 88–100.

Butler, S. (1996) Alternative ways to take out stress. *People Management*, **2**, pp. 43–4.

Buzan, T. (1974) *Use Your Head*. London: BBC Publications.

Byham, W.C. (1991) *Zapp! The lightning of empowerment*. London: Century Business.

Cameron, K.S. (1978) Measuring organizational effectiveness in institutions of higher education. *Administrative Science Quarterly*, **23**, 604–32.

Cameron, K.S., Freeman, S.J. and Mishra, A.K. (1991) *Best practices in white-collar downsizing: Managing contradictions*. Academy of Management Executive.

Cameron, K.S., Freeman, S.J. and Mishra, A.K. (1993) Organization downsizing and redesign. In G.P. Huber and W. Glick (eds) *Organizational change and design*. New York: Oxford University Press.

Cameron, K.S., Kim, M.U. and Whetten, D.A. (1987a) Organizational effects of decline and turbulence. *Administrative Science Quarterly*, **32**, 222–40.

Cameron, K.S., Whetten, D.A. and Kim, M.U. (1987b) Organizational dysfunctions of decline. *Academy of Management Journal*, **30**, 126–38.

Cameron, K.S., Whetten, D.A., Kim, M.U. and Chaffee, E.E. (1987c) The aftermath of decline. *Review of Higher Education*, **10**, 215–34.

Cameron, K. and Tschirhart, M. (1988) *Managerial competencies and organizational effectiveness*. Working paper, School of Business Administration, University of Michigan.

Cameron, K.S. and Ulrich, D.O. (1986) Transformational leadership in colleges and universities. In Smart, J. (ed.) *Higher education: Handbook of theory and research*, Vol. 2. New York: Agathon.

Cameron, K.S. and Whetten, D.A. (1984) A model for teaching management skills. *Organizational Behavior Teaching Journal*, **8**, 21–7.

Cameron, K.S., Freeman, S. and Mishra, A. (1990) Effective organizational downsizing: Paradoxical processes and best practices. *Academy of Management Executive*.

Cameron, K. (1988) Organizational downsizing and large-scale change. Working paper, School of Business Administration, University of Michigan.

Campbell, L. (1995) Stress litigation and training. *Management Development Review*, **8**(4), 21–2.

Campbell, N. (1952) *What is science?* New York: Dover.

Cannon, T. (1993) *How to get ahead in business*. London: Virgin Books.

Cannon Working Party Report (1994) *Progress and Change 1987–1994*. Corby: Institute of Management.

Carlson, S. (1951) *Executive behavior: A study of the work load and the working methods of managing directors*. Stockholm: Strombergs.

Carr, D. and Haldane, J. (1993) Centre for Philosophy and Public Affairs, University of St Andrews.

Catch a falling star. *The Economist*, 23 April 1988, pp. 88–90.

Cavanaugh, G.F. (1980) *American business values in transition*. Englewood Cliffs, NJ: Prentice Hall.

Chang, R. (1995) Core threads of continuous improvement. *Management Development Review*, **8**(4), 14–16.

Charlesworth, K. (1997) *Are managers under stress? A survey of management moral.* The Representation Unit, Institute of Management, 2 Savoy Court, Strand, London WC2R 0EZ, UK.

Cialdini, R.B. (1988) *Influence: Science and practice*. Glenview, Ill.: Scott Foresman.

Clare, D.A. and Sanford, D.G. (1979) Mapping personal value space: A study of managers in four organizations. *Human Relations*, **32**, 659–66.

Clark, R.D. III (1971) Group-induced shift toward risk: A critical appraisal. *Psychological Bulletin*, October, 251–70.

Coch, L. and French, J.R.P. (1948) Overcoming resistance to change. *Human Relations*, **11**, 512–32.

Colby, W. (1985) Motivation in motion. *Infosystems*, August, 81–3.

Collins, J. and Porras, J. (1995) How best to stay at the top. *Director*, **48**(11, June), 56–64.

Conger, J.A. and Kanungo, R.N. (1988) The empowerment process. *Academy of Management Review*, **13**, 471–82.

Conger, J.A. (1989) Leadership: The art of empowering others. *Academy of Management Executive*, **3**, 17–24.

Coonradt, C.A. (1985) *The game of work*. Salt Lake City: Shadow Mountain Press.

Cooper, C.L. and Davidson, M.J. (1982) The high cost of stress on women managers. *Organizational Dynamics*, **11**, 44–53.

Cooper, C.L., Cooper, R.D. and Eaker, L.H. (1988) *Living with stress*. London: Penguin.

Cooper, M.J. and Aygen, M.M. (1979) A relaxation technique in the management of hypocholesterolemia. *Journal of Human Stress*, **5**, 24–7.

Coulson-Thomas, C. (1992) Leadership and corporate transformation. *Leadership and Organisational Development Journal*, **13**(4), iv–vii.

Coulson-Thomas, C. and Coe, T. (1991) *The flat organisations, philosophy and practice*. Corby: British Institute of Management

Covey, S. (1989) *Seven habits of highly effective people*. New York: Wiley.

Cravens, R.W. and Worchel, P. (1977) The differential effects of rewarding and coercive leaders on group members differing in locus of control. *Journal of Personality*, **45**, 150–68.

Crocker, J. (1978) Speech communication instruction based on employers' perceptions of the importance of selected communication skills for employees on the job. Paper presented at the Speech Communication Association meeting, Minneapolis, Minn.

Crovitz, H.F. (1970) *Galton's walk*. New York: Harper & Row.

Cummings, L.L., Harnett, D.L. and Stevens, O.J. (1971) Risk, fate, conciliation and trust: An international study of attitudinal differences among executives. *Academy of Management Journal*, **14**, 285–304.

Curtis, D.B., Winsor, J.L. and Stephens, R.D. (1989) National preferences in business and communication education. *Communication Education*, **38**, 6–15.

Curtis, J.D. and Detert, R.A. (1981) *How to relax: A holistic approach to stress management*. Palo Alto: Mayfield Publishing, p. 134.

Cyert, R. and March, J. (1963) *A behavioral theory of the firm*. Englewood Cliffs, NJ: Prentice Hall.

Dalton, G., Lawrence, P. and Lorsch, J. (1970) *Organizational structure and design*. Homewood, Ill.: Irwin.

Davidson, M.S. and Sutherland, V. (1993) Using the Stress Audit. *Work & Stress*, **7**, No. 3, 273–86.

Davis, M., Eshelman, E. and McKay, M. (1980) *The relaxation and stress reduction workbook*. Richmond, Calif. New Harbinger Publications, p. 82.

Davis, T.W. and Luthans, F. (1980) A social learning approach to organizational behavior. *Academy of Management Review*, **5**, 281–90.

De Bono, E. (1971) *Lateral thinking for management*. New York and London: McGraw-Hill.

De Bono, E. (1968) *New think*. New York: Basic Books.

DeCharms, R. (1979) Personal causation and perceived control. In L.C. Perlmuter and R.A. Monty (eds) *Choice and perceived control*. Hillsdale, NJ: Erlbaum.

Deci, E.L. and Ryan, R.M. (1987) The support of autonomy and control of behavior. *Journal of Personality and Social Psychology*, **53**, 1024–37.

Deci, E.L., Connell, J.P. and Ryan, R.M. (1989) Self-determination in a work organization. *Journal of Applied Psychology*, **74**, 580–90.

Delbecq, A.L., Van de Ven, A.H. and Gustafson, D.H. (1976) *Group techniques for program planning: A guide to nominal group and Delphi processes*. Glenview, Ill.: Scott Foresman.

Dellas, M. and Gaier, E.L. (1970) Identification of creativity: The individual. *Psychological Bulletin*, **73**, 55–73.

Deutsch, M. (1973) *The resolution of conflict: Constructive and destructive processes*. New Haven: Yale University Press.

Dickson, A. (1982) A woman in your own right, Assertiveness and you. *Quartet*

DiClemente, C.C. (1985) Perceived efficacy in smoking cessation. Paper presented at the annual meeting of the American Association for the Advancement of Science, Los Angeles.

Dixon, N. (1994) *On the psychology of military incompetence*. London: Pimlico.

Downs, C.W., Smeyak, G.P. and Martin, E. (1980) *Professional interviewing*. New York: Harper & Row.

Drucker, P.F. (1988) The coming of the new organization. *Harvard Business Review* (January–February).

Drucker, P.F. (1974) *Management*. Oxford: Butterworth–Heinemann.

DuBrin, A.J. (1981) Human relations: A job oriented approach (2nd edn). Reston, Va: Reston Publishing.

Durand, D. and Shea, D. (1974) Entrepreneurial activity as a function of achievement motivation and reinforcement control. *Journal of Psychology*, **88**, 57–63.

Dyer, W.G. (1972) Congruence. In *The sensitive manipulator*. Provo, Utah: Brigham Young University Press.

Dyer, W.G. (1981) *Teambuilding*. Reading, Mass.: Addison Wesley.

Edwards, M. (1984) *Back from the brink*. London: Pan Books.

Einstein, A. (*c.* 1919, G. Holton) Fundamental ideas and methods of relativity theory, presented in their development. Unpublished manuscript.

Eisenhart, K.M. and Galunic, D.C. (1993) Renewing the strategy–structure–performance paradigm. *Research in Organizational Behavior*, **15**.

Elbing, A. (1978) *Behavioral decisions in organizations*. Glenview, Ill.: Scott Foresman.

Eliot, R.S. and Breo, D.L. (1984) *Is it worth dying for?* New York: Bantam Books.

Emery, F.E. and Trist, E.L. (1965) The casual texture of organisational environments. *Human Relations*, **18**, 21–2, (also in *Systems Thinking*, London: Penguin).

Ettlie, J.E. and O'Keefe, R.D. (1982) Innovative attitudes, values, and intentions in organizations. *Journal of Management Studies*, **19**, 163–82.

Fairholm, G.W. (1991) *Values leadership: Towards a new philosophy of leadership*. London: Praeger.

Farnham, A. (1991) Who beats stress best and how? *Fortune* (October 7), 71–86.

Festinger, L. (1957) *A theory of cognitive dissonance*. Stanford: Stanford University Press.

Filley, A.C. (1975) *Interpersonal conflict resolution*. Glenview, Ill.: Scott Foresman.

Filley, A. (1970) Committee management: Guidelines from social science research. *California Management Review*, **13**, 13–21.

Filley, A.C. (1978) Some normative issues in conflict management. *California Management Review*, **71**, 61–6.

Filley, A.C., House, R.J. and Kerr, S. (1976) *Managerial process and organizational behavior*. Glenview, Ill.: Scott Foresman.

Financial Times, London, 19 April 1985.

Finneston, M. (1980) *Engineering our future*. London: HMSO.

Fisher, R. and Brown, S. (1988) *Getting together: Building a relationship that gets to yes*. London: Hutchinson.

Fisher, R. and Ury, W. (1991) *Getting to yes*. London: Century Business.

Flanders, L.R. (1981) Report from the federal manager's job and role survey: Analysis of responses by SES and mid-management level executives and management development division. US Office of Personnel Management, Washington, DC.

Flexible benefits are spreading fast. *Dun's Business Month*, September 1981, pp. 82–5.

Flower, V., Hughes, C.I., Myers, M.S. and Myer, S.S. (1975) *Managerial values for working*. New York: American Management Association.

Fortune (1988) GM system is like a blanket of fog. 15 February 1988, pp. 48–9.

Freedman, R.D. and Stumpf, S.A. (1978) What can one learn from the Learning Style Inventory? *Academy of Management Review*, **5**, 445–7. (Kolb, D.A. (1981) Experiential learning theory and the learning style inventory: A reply to Freedman and Stumpf. *Academy of Management Review*, **6**(2), 289–96.)

Freedman, J.L. and Fraser, S.C. (1966) Compliance without pressure: The foot-in-the-door technique. *Journal of Personality and Social Psychology*, **4**, 195–202.

French, J.R.P. and Caplan, R.D. (1972) Organizational stress and individual strain. In A.J. Marrow (ed.) *The failure of success*. New York: AMACOM.

Freud, S. (1956) *Collected Papers* (Vols 3 and 4). London: Hogarth.

Friedman, M. and Rosenman, R.H. (1959) Association of a specific overt behavior pattern with blood and cardiovascular findings. *Journal of the American Medical Association*, **169**, 1286–96.

Friedman, M. and Rosenman, R.H. (1974) *Type A behavior and your heart*. New York: Knopf.

Friedman, M. and Ulmer, D. (1984) *Treating type A behavior and your heart*. New York: Knopf, pp. 84–5.

Friere, P. and Faundez, A. (1989) *Learning to question: A pedagogy of liberation*. New York: The Continuum Publishing Company.

Fromm, E. (1939) Selfishness and self love. *Psychiatry*, **2**, 507–23.

Galbraith, J.K. (1975) Are you Mark Epernay? The literary Galbraith on the art of writing. *Christian Science Monitor*, 9 December, p. 19.

Galbraith, J.R. (1982) Designing the innovating organization. *Organizational Dynamics*, Winter, 5–25.

Galloway, A. (1990) Maintenance of hierarchy. Doctoral thesis, University of Glasgow.

Gambetta, D. (1988) *Trust: Making and breaking cooperative relations*. Cambridge, Mass.: Basil Blackwell.

Gardner, J.W. (1965) *Self-renewal*. New York: Harper & Row.

Gassner, S.M. (1970) Relationship between patient–therapist compatibility and treatment effectiveness. *Journal of Counselling and Clinical Pychology*, **34**, 408–14.

Gerber, S.Z. (1996) Pulling the plug on stress. *HR Focus*, **73**(4), 12.

Gecas, V. (1989) The social psychology of self-efficacy. *Annual Review of Sociology*, **15**, 291–316.

Gecas, V., Seff, M.A. and Ray, M.P. (1988) Injury and depression: The mediating effects of self concept. Paper presented at the Pacific Sociological Association Meetings, Las Vegas.

Gennill, G.R. and Heisler, W.J. (1972) Fatalism as a factor in managerial job satisfaction. *Personnel Psychology*, **25**, 241–50.

Gennill, G.R. and Heisler, W.J. (1972) Fatalism as a factor in managerial job satisfaction, job strain, and mobility. *Personnel Psychology*, **25**, 241–50.

Geshka, H. Introduction and use of idea generation techniques in industry. *Creativity Network*, **3**(2), 3–6.

Ghiselli, E.E. (1963) *Managerial talent. American Psychologist*, **18**, 631–42.

Gibb, J.R. and Gibb, L.M. (1969) Role freedom in a TORI group. In A. Burton (ed.) *Encounter theory and practice of encounter groups*. San Francisco: Jossey-Bass.

Gibb, J.R. (1961) Defensive communication. *Journal of Communication*, **11**, 141–8.

Gill, L. (1987) Run ragged by the rat race. *The Times*, 5 January.

Gladstein, D.L. (1984) Groups in context: A model of task group effectiveness, *Administrative Science Quarterly*, **29**(4), 497–517.

Glasser, W. (1965) *Reality therapy: A new approach to psychiatry*. New York: Harper & Row.

Gleick, J. (1988) *Chaos, making a new science*. William Heinmann Ltd.

Goffman, E. (1955) On face-work: An analysis of ritual elements in social interaction. *Psychiatry*, **18**, 213–31.

Goldberg, H. (1978) *The hazards of being male*. New York: Nash.

Goldstein, A.P. and Sorcher, M. (1974) *Changing superior behavior*. New York: Pergamon.

Golembiewski, R.T. and McConkie, M. (1975) The centrality of trust in group processes. In C. Cooper (ed.) *Theories of group processes*. New York: Wiley.

Goodstadt, B.E. and Hjelle, L.A. (1973) Power to the powerless: Locus of control and the use of power. *Journal of Personality and Social Psychology*, **72**, 503–19.

Gordon, W.J.J. (1961) *Synectics: The development of creative capacity*. New York: Harper & Row.

Graves, C.W. (1970) Levels of existence: An open system theory of values. *Journal of Humanistic Psychology*, **10**, 131–55.

Greenberg, J. and Ornstein, S. (1984) Motivation in organizations. In R.G. Geen, W.W. Beatty and R.M. Arkin (eds) *Human motivation: Physiological, behavioral, and social approaches*. Boston: Allyn & Bacon.

Greenberg, J. (1982) Approaching equity and avoiding inequity in groups and organizations. In J. Greenberg and R.L. Cohen (eds) *Equity and justice in social behavior*. New York: Academic Press.

Greenberg, J. (1987) *Comprehensive stress management* (2nd edn). Dubuque, LA.: Wm. C. Brown Publishers.

Greenberger, D.B. and Stasser, S. (1991) The role of situational and dispositional factors in the enhancement of personal control in organizations. *Research in Organizational Behavior*, **13**, 111–45.

Greenberger, D.B., Stasser, S., Cummings, L. and Dunham, R.B. (1989) The impact of personal control on performance and satisfaction. *Organizational Behavior and Human Decision Processes*, **43**, 29–51.

Greene, C.N. (1972) The satisfaction-performance controversy. *Business Horizons*, **15**, 31–41.

Griest, J.H. *et al.* (1979) Running as treatment for depression. *Comparative Psychiatry*, **20**, 41–56.

Groves, A.S. (1983*) High output management*. New York: Random House.

Guardian, The (1994) London, 2 April, p. 21.

Guest, R.H. (1956) Of time and the foreman. *Personnel*, **32**, 478–86.

Guilford, J.P. (1962) Creativity: Its measurement and development. In S.J. Parnes and H.F. Harding (eds) *A sourcebook for creative thinking*. New York: Scribner.

Haan, N., Smith, M.B. and Block, J. (1968) Moral reasoning of young adults: Political–social behavior, family background, and personality correlates. *Journal of Personality and Social Psychology*, **10**, 183–201.

Haase, R.F., Lee, D.Y. and Banks, D.L. (1979) Cognitive correlates of polychronicity. *Perceptual and Motor Skills*, **49**, 271–82.

Hackman, J.R. (1980) *Work in groups*. Glenview, Ill.: Scott Foresman.

Hackman, J.R. (1990) *Teams and group failure (and those who don't)*. San Francisco: Jossey-Bass.

Hackman, J.R. (1993) *Teams and group failure*. Presentation to the Interdisciplinary College on Organizational Studies, University of Michigan, October.

Hackman, J.R. and Lawler, E.E. (1971) Employee reactions to job characteristics. *Journal of Applied Psychology*, **55**, 259–86.

Hackman, J.R. and Morris, C.G. (1975) Group tasks, group interaction processes, and group performance: A review and proposed integration. In L. Berkowitz (ed.) *Advances in experimental and social psychology*, Vol. 9. New York: Academic Press.

Hackman, J.R. and Oldham, G.R. (1975) Development of the job diagnostic survey. *Journal of Applied Psychology*, **60**, 159–70.

Hackman, J.R. and Oldham, G.R. (1980) *Work design*. Reading, Mass.: Addison Wesley.

Hackman, J.R. and Vidmar, N. (1970) Effects of size and task type on group performance and member reaction. *Sociometry*, **33**, 37–54.

Hackman, J.R., Oldham G.R., Janson, R. and Purdy, K. (1975) A new strategy for job enrichment. *California Management Review*, **17**, 57–71.

Haefele, J.W. (1962) *Creativity and innovation*. New York: Reinhold.

Hall, D.T. (1976) *Careers in organizations*. Santa Monica, California.: Goodyear.

Hambrick, D.C, Nadler, D.A. and Tushman, M.L. (eds) (1998) *Navigating change*. Boston, Mass.: Harvard Business School Press.

Hammer, H. and Champy, J. (1993) *Re-engineering the corporation*. London: Nicholas Brealey.

Hammer, T.H. and Vardi, Y. (1981) Locus of control and career self-management among nonsupervisory employees in industrial settings. *Journal of Vocational Behavior*, **18**, 13–29.

Hammer, T.H. and Vardi, Y. (1981) Locus of control and career self-management among non-supervisory employees in industrial settings. *Journal of Vocational Behavior*, **18**, 13–29.

Hamner, W.C. and Organ, D.W. (1978) *Organizational behavior: An applied psychological approach*. Dallas: Business Publications.

Hamner, W.C. (1974) Reinforcement theory and contingency management in organizational settings. In H.L. Yosi and W.C. Hamner (eds) *Organizational behavior and management: A contingency approach*. Chicago: St Clair Press.

Handy, C. (1993) *The age of unreason*. London: Hutchinson (and *Inside Organisations*, BBC Enterprises (Video)).

Handy, C. (1994) *The empty raincoat*. London: Hutchinson, Random House.

Handy, C. (1997) New language of organizing. *Executive Excellence*, May, pp. 13–14 – discussing his latest book *The Age of Paradox* (in preparation).

Haney, W.V. (1979) *Communication and interpersonal relations*. Homewood, Ill.: Irwin.

Hanson, G. (1986) Determinants of firm performance: An integration of economic and organizational factors. Unpublished doctoral dissertation, University of Michigan Business School.

Harris, R. (1995) *Enigma*. London: Hutchinson.

Harris, S. (1981) *Know yourself. It's a paradox*. Associated Press.

Harter, S. (1978) Effectance motivation reconsidered: Toward a developmental model. *Human Development*, **21**, 34–64.

Harvey, J.M. (1971) Locus of control shift in administrators. *Perceptual and Motor Skills*, **33**, 980–2.

Hawking, S.W. (1989) *A brief history of time*. London: Bantam.

Hayakawa, S.I. (1962) *The use and misuse of language*. New York: Fawcett World Library, Crest, Gold Medal, & Premier Books.

Heather, B. and Woods, M. (1991) *Training and management development methods*, **5**, 35–70. MCB University Press.

Heider, F. (1946) Attitudes and cognitive organization. *Journal of Psychology*, **21**, 107–12.

Henderson, J.C. and Nutt, P.C. (1980) The influence of decision style on decision-making behavior. *Management Science*, **26**, 371–86.

Hendricks, J.A. (1985) Locus of control: Implications for managers and accountants. *Cost and Management*, May–June, 25–9.

Henry, J. (1991) Making sense of creativity. In J. Henry (ed.) *Creative management.* London: Sage Publications.

Hermann, N. (1981) The creative brain. *Training and Development Journal.*

Herriot, P. and Pemberton, C. (1995a) *New Deals, The revolution in management careers.* Chichester: Wiley.

Herriot, P. and Pemberton, C. (1995b) *Competitive advantage through diversity.* London: Sage.

Hersey, P. and Blanchard, K. (1969 and 1982) *The management of organisational behaviour.* Englewood Cliffs, NJ: Prentice Hall.

Hersey, P. and Blanchard, K. (1986) *Leadership and the One Minute Manager.* London: William Collins.

Hill, S. and Gruner, L. (1973) A study of development in open and closed groups. *Small Group Behavior,* **4**, 355–81.

Hines, J.S. (1980) *Conflict and conflict management.* Athens, Ga.: University of Georgia Press.

Hingley, P. and Cooper, C.L. (1986) *Stress and the nurse manager.* London.

Ho, J. (1995) The Singapore executive: Stress, personality and well being. *Journal of Management Development,* **11**(4), 47–55.

Hoerr, J. (1989) The payoff for team work. *Business Week* (10 July), pp. 56–62.

Hollander, S. (1965) *The sources of increased efficiency.* Cambridge, Mass.: MIT Press.

Holmes, T.S. and Holmes, T.H. (1970) Short-term intrusions into the lifestyle routine. *Journal of Psychosomatic Research,* **14**, 121–32.

Holmes, T.H. and Masuda, M. (1974) Life change and illness susceptibility. In B.S. Dohnrenwend and B.P. Dohrenwend (eds) *Stressful life events: Their nature and effects.* New York: Wiley.

Holmes, T.H. and Rahe, R.H. (1967) The social readjustment scale. *Journal of Psychosomatic Research,* **11**, 213–18.

Holmes, T.H. and Rahe, R.H. (1970) The social reajustment rating scale. *Journal of Psychosomatic Research,* **14**, 121–32.

Holt, J. (1964) *How children fail.* New York: Pitman.

Hopfl, H. and Dawes, F. (1995) A whole can of worms. *Personnel Review,* **24**(6).

Hosmer, LaRue T. (1987) *The ethics of management.* Homewood, Ill.: Irwin.

Hosni, T. (1998) Empowerment and Staff. MBA Dissertation at Bradford University.

House, R.J. and Mitchell, T.R. (1974) Path-goal theory of leadership. *Journal of Contemporary Business,* **3**, 81–97.

How to make confrontation work for you. *Fortune,* 23 July 1984, pp. 73–5.

Huber, G.P. (1980) *Managerial decision making.* Glenview, Ill.: Scott Foresman. (Industrial Society Best Practice Report quoted in *Management development Review* (1995), **8**(4), 1.)

Huber, G. (1984) The nature and design of post-industrial environments. *Management Science,* **30**, 928–51.

Hudson, L. (1966) *Contrary imaginations*. Harmondsworth: Penguin.

Hunsicker, F.R. (1978) What successful managers say about their skills. *Personnel Journal*, November, 618–21.

Hunter, I.M.L. (1957) *Memory*. Harmondsworth: Penguin.

Huseman, R.C., Lahiff, J.M. and Hatfield, J.D. (1976) *Interpersonal communication in organizations*. Boston: Holbrook Press.

Interaction Associates. (1971) *Tools for change*. San Francisco: Interaction Associates.

Ivancevich, J.M. and McMahon, T.J. (1982) The effects of goal setting, external feedback and self-generated feedback on outcome variables: A field experiment. *Academy of Management Journal*, **23**, 359–72.

Ivancevich, J.M. and Matteson, M.T. (1980) *Stress and work. A managerial perspective*. Glenview, Ill.: Scott Foresman.

Jackson, D. and Humble, J. (1994) *Journal of Management Development*, **13**(3), 15–21.

Jackson, J. and Harkins, S.G. (1985) Equity in effort: An explanation of the social loafing effect. *Journal of Personality and Social Psychology*, November, 1199–1206.

Jacobs, M. (1973) Levels of confirmation and disconfirmation in interpersonal communications. Unpublished doctoral dissertation, University of Denver.

James, J. (1997) MBA Dissertation, University of Bradford.

James, W. (1965) [Cited in R.D. Laing (1965)] Mystification, confusion, and conflict. In I. Boszormenya-Nagy and J.L. Framo (eds) *Intensive family therapy*. New York: Harper & Row.

Janis, I.L. (1971) *Groupthink*. New York: Free Press.

Janis, I. (1972) *Victims of groupthink*. Boston: Houghton Mifflin.

Jay, A. (1967) *Management and Machiavelli, an inquiry into the politics of corporate life*. New York: Holt, Rinehart & Winston.

Jebb, F. (1996) Sumantra Ghoshal. *Management Today*, December, 70–1.

Jenkins, C.D. (1976) Recent evidence supporting psychological and social risk factors in coronary disease. *New England Journal of Medicine*, **294**, 1033–4.

Jewell, L.N. and Reitz, H.J. (1981) *Group effectiveness in organizations*. Glenview, Ill.: Scott Foresman.

Johnston, G. (1997) *Monkey business*. London: Gower.

Jordan, P.C. (1986) Effects of extrinsic rewards on intrinsic motivation: A field experiment. *Academy of Management Journal*, **27**, 405–12.

Jourard, S.M. (1964) *The transparent self*. Princeton, N.J.: Van Nostrand.

Jung, K. (1971) *Psychological types*. London: Routledge & Kegan Paul.

Kahn, W.A. (1990) Psychological conditions of personal engagement and disengagement at work. *Academy of Management Journal*, **33**, 692–724.

Kamiya, J. (1978) Conscious control of brain power. *Psychology Today*, **1**, 57–60.

Kanter, R.M. (1968) Commitment and social organization: A study of commitment mechanisms in utopian communities. *American Sociological Review*, **33**, 499–517.

Kanter, R.M. (1983) *The change masters*. London: Routledge.

Katz, R.L. (1974) Skills of an effective administrator. *Harvard Business Review*, **51**, 90–102.

Katzenbach, J.R. (1998) *Teams at the top*. Harvard Business School Press.

Katzenbach, J.R. and Smith, D.K. (1993) *The wisdom of teams*. Cambridge, Mass.: Harvard Business Press.

Kearns, J. (1986) *Stress at work: The challenge of change*. BUPA.

Kellogg, M.S. (1979) *Putting management theories to work*. Englewood Cliffs, NJ: Prentice Hall.

Kelly, J. (1970) Make conflict work for you. *Harvard Business Review*, July–August, **48**, 103–13.

Kepner, C.H. and Tregoe, B.B. (1965) *The rational manager*. Maidenhead: McGraw-Hill.

Kerr, S. (1975) On the folly of rewarding A, while hoping for B. *Academy of Management Review*, **19**, 769–83.

Kezsbom, D.S. (1994) Team-based organizations and the changing role of the project manager. *Transactions of the American Association of Cost Engineers*, p. HF11–HF15.

Kilmann, R. and Taylor, V.A. (1974) Contingency approach to laboratory learning: Psychological type versus learning norms. *Human Relations*, **27**, 891–909.

King, D. (1981) Three cheers for conflict. *Personnel*, **48**, 13–22.

Kipnis, D. and Schmidt, S. (1983) An influence perspective in bargaining within organizations. In M.H. Bazerman and R.J. Lewicki (eds) *Bargaining inside organizations*. Beverly Hills, Calif.: Sage Publications.

Kipnis, D. (1976) *The power holders*. Chicago, Ill.: University of Chicago Press.

Kobasa, S.C. (1979) Stressful life events, personality, and health: An inquiry into hardiness. *Journal of Personality and Social Psychology*, **37**, 1–12.

Kobasa, S.C. (1982) Commitment and coping in stress resistance among lawyers. *Journal of Personality and Social Psychology*, **42**, 707–17.

Koestler, A. (1967) *The act of creation*. New York: Dell.

Kohlberg, L. (1969) The cognitive-developmental approach to socialization. In D.A. Goslin (ed.) *Handbook of socialization theory and research*. Chicago: Rand McNally.

Kohlberg, L. (1976) Moral stages and moralization, the cognitive-developmental approach. In T. Lickona (ed.) *Moral development and behaviour*. New York: Holt, Rinehart & Winston.

Kolb, D.A. (1971) Individual learning styles and the learning process. Working Paper 535-71. MIT Sloan School of Management.

Kolb, D.A. (1974) On management and the learning process. In D. Kolb, I. Rubin and J. McIntyre (eds) *Organizational psychology: A book of readings* (2nd edn). Englewood Cliffs, NJ: Prentice Hall.

Kolb, D.A. (1984) *Experiential learning: Experience as the source of learning and development*. Englewood Cliffs, NJ: Prentice Hall.

Kolb, D.A. (1986) *Experiential Learning*. New York: Prentice Hall.

Kolb, D.A., Rubin, I.M. and McIntyre, J.M. (1971) *Organisational psychology*. Englewood Cliffs, NJ: Prentice Hall.

Kolb, D.A. (1978) *The learning style inventory. Technical manual*. McBer & Co.

Kolb, D.A. and Fry, R. (1975) Towards an applied theory of experiential learning. In C.L. Cooper (ed.) *Theories of group processes*. Chichester: Wiley.

Kolb, D.A. *et al.* (1979) *Organisational psychology: A book of readings* (3rd edn). Prentice Hall.

Kolb, D.A. *et al.* (1984) *Organisational psychology: An experiential approach to organisational behaviour* (4th edn). Prentice Hall.

Kolb, D.A. and Plovnik, M.S. (1977) The experiential learning theory of career development. In J. Van Maanen (ed.) *Organisational careers: Some new perspectives*. Chichester: Wiley.

Kopelman, R.E. (1985) Job redesign and productivity: A review of evidence. *National Productivity Review*, Summer, 237–55.

Korac-Kakabadse, A. and Korac-Kakabadse, N. (1997) Best practice in the Australian Public Service (APS): An examination of discretionary leadership. *Journal of Managerial Psychology*, **12**(7).

Kotter, J. (1987) *The general managers*. New York: Free Press.

Kram, K. (1985) *Mentoring at work*. Glenview, Ill.: Scott Foresman.

Kuhn, A. and Beam, R.D. (1982) *The logic of organizations*. San Francisco: Jossey-Bass.

Langer, E.J. and Rodin, J. (1976) The effects of choice and enhanced personal responsibility. *Journal of Personality and Social Psychology*, **34**, 191–8.

Langer, E.J. (1983) *The psychology of control*. Beverly Hills: Sage.

Latane, B., Williams, K. and Harkins, S. (1979) Many hands make light of the work: The causes and consequences of social loafing. *Journal of Personality and Social Psychology*, June, 822–32.

Latham, G. and Locke, E. (1979) Goal setting: A motivational technique that works. *Organizational Dynamics*, **8**, 68–80.

Latham, G. and Wexley, K. (1981) *Increasing productivity through performance appraisal*. Reading, Mass.: Addison Wesley.

Latham, G.P. and Saari, L.P. (1979) Application of social learning theory to training supervisors through behavioural modelling. *Journal of Applied Psychology*, **64**, 239–46.

Latham, G.P., Cummings, L.L. and Mitchell, T.R. (1981) Behavioral strategies to improve productivity. *Organizational Dynamics*, **10**, 5–23.

Latham, G., Erez, M. and Locke, E. (1988) Resolving scientific disputes by the joint design of crucial experiments by the antagonists: Application to the Erez–Latham disputes regarding participation in goal setting. *Journal of Applied Psychology*, **73**, 753–72.

Lawler, E.E., Mohrman, S.A. and Ledford, G.E. (1992) *Employee involvement and total quality management*. San Francisco: Jossey-Bass.

Lawler, E.E. (1971) *Pay and organizational effectiveness*. New York: McGraw-Hill.

Lawler, E.E. (1992) *The ultimate advantage: Creating the high involvement organization*. San Francisco: Jossey-Bass.

Lawler, E.E. (1973) *Motivation in work organizations*. Belmont, Calif.: Brooks/Cole.

Lawrence, P. and Lorsch, J. (1967) *Organizations and environments*. Homewood, Ill.: Irwin.

Leana, C.R. (1987) Power relinquishment versus power sharing: Theoretical clarification and empirical comparison on delegation and participation. *Journal of Applied Psychology*, **72**, 228–33.

Leavett, H.J. (1987) *Corporate pathfinders: Building visions and values into organizations*. New York: Penguin.

LeDue, A.I., Jr (1980) Motivation of programmers. *Data Base*, **3**, 5.

Levering, R., Moskovitz, M. and Katz, M. (1984) *The 100 best companies to work for in America*. Reading, Mass.: Addison Wesley.

Levinson, J.D. (1978) *Seasons of a man's life*. New York: Knopf.

Lewin, K. (1951) *Field theory in social science*. New York: Harper & Row.

Lewis, R. and Margerison, C. (1979) Working and learning: Identifying your preferred ways of doing things. *Personnel Review*, **8**(2).

Lickona, T. (1976) Critical issues in the study of moral development and behavior. In T. Lickona (ed.) *Moral development and behavior: Theory, research, and social issues*. New York: Holt, Rinehart & Winston.

Likert, R. (1967) *The human organization*. New York: McGraw-Hill.

Lindenield, G. (1986) *Assert yourself*. England: Thorson.

Livingston, S.W. (1971) The myth of the well-educated manager. *Harvard Business Review*, **49**, 79–89.

Locke, E. and Latham, G. (1984) *Goal setting: A motivational technique that works*. Englewood Cliffs, NJ: Prentice Hall.

Locke, E.A., Shaw, K., Saari, L. and Latham, G. (1981) Goal setting and task performance: 1969–1980. *Psychological Bulletin*, **90**, 125–52.

Locke, E.A. and Schweiger, D.M. (1979) Participation in decision making: One more look. *Research in Organizational Behavior*, **1**, 265–340.

Loomis, F. (1939) *The consultation room*. New York: Knopf.

Lopez, F.M. (1975) *Personnel interviewing*. New York: McGraw-Hill.

Lord, R.G. (1977) Functional leadership behavior: Measurement and relation to social power and leadership perceptions. *Administrative Science Quarterly*, **22**, 114–33.

Luhmann, N. (1979) *Trust and power*. New York: Wiley.

Luthans, F. and Kreitner, R. (1975) *Organizational behavior modification*. Glenview, Ill.: Scott Foresman.

Luthans, F., Rosenkrantz, S.A. and Hennessey, H.W. (1985) What do successful managers really do? An observation study of managerial activities. *Journal of Applied Behavioral Science*, **21**, 255–70.

Luthe, W. (1962) Method, research and application of autogenic training. *American Journal of Clinical Hypnosis*, **5**, 17–23.

Macdonald, C. (1996) Frayed to breaking point. *Credit Union Management*, **19**(6), 30–1.

McGrath, J.E. and Kravitz, D.A. (1982) Group research. *Annual Review of Psychology*, **33**, 195–230.

Macy, B.A., Norton, J.J., Bliese, P.O. and Izumi, H. (1990) The bottom line impact of new design: North America from 1961–90. Paper presented to the Conference on Self-Managing Workteams, Denton, Texas, September.

Maddi, S. and Kobasa, S.C. (1984) The *hardy executive: Health under stress*. Homewood, Ill.: Dow Jones–Irwin.

Maier, N.R.F. (1958) Three types of appraisal interviews. *Personnel*, March/April.

Maier, N.R.F. (1967) Assets and liabilities in group problem solving: The need for an integrative function. *Psychological Review*, **74**, 239–49.

Maier, N.R.F. (1970) *Problem solving and creativity in individuals and groups*. Belmont, Calif.: Brooks/Cole.

Maier, N.R.F. (1973) *Psychology in industrial organizations* (4th edn). New York: Houghton Mifflin.

Maier, N.R.F., Solem, A.R. and Maier, A.A. (1973) Counselling, interviewing, and job contacts. In N.R.F. Maier (ed.) *Psychology of industrial organizations*. Boston: Houghton Mifflin.

Management Today, London, June 1988.

Manz, C.C. and Sims, H. (1989) *Super-leadership: Teaching others to lead themselves*. Englewood Cliffs, NJ: Prentice Hall.

Manz, C.C. and Sims, H.P. Jr (1990) *Superleadership: Leading others to lead themselves*. Berkeley, CA: Prentice Hall.

March, J.G. and Simon, H.A. (1958) *Organizations*. New York: Wiley.

Margerison, C. and Kakabadse, A. (1984) *How American chief executives succeed*. New York: AMA Publications.

Markoff, J. (1988) For scientists using supercomputers, visual imagery speeds discoveries. New York Times News Service, Ann Arbor News, 2 November.

Martindale, C. (1975) What makes creative people different. *Psychology Today*, **9**, 44–50.

Marx, K. *Early Writings*. Edited and translated by T.B. Bottomore. New York: McGraw-Hill.

Maslow, A. (1965) *Eupsychian management*. Homewood, Ill.: Irwin.

Maslow, A.H. (1962) *Toward a psychology of being*. Princeton, NJ.: D. Van Nostrand Company.

McAller, N. (1991) The roots of inspiration. In J. Henry (ed.) *Creative Management*. London: Sage.

McCarthy, B. (1987) *The 4MAT System. Teaching to learning styles with right/left mode techniques*. Barrington, Ill.: Excel Inc.

McClelland, D. (1975) *Power: The inner experience*. New York: Irvington.

McDonald, A.P. (1970) Internal–external locus of control and the practice of birth control. *Psychological Reports*, **27**, 206.

McGregor, R. (1960) *The human side of enterprise*. New York: McGraw-Hill.

McKenney, J.L. and Keen, P.G.W. (1974) How managers' minds work. *Harvard Business Review*, **51**, 79–90.

McKim, R.H. (1972) *Experiences in visual thinking*. Monterey, Calif.: Brooks/Cole.

McMillan, I. (1985) Progress in research on corporate venturing. Working paper, Center for Entrepreneurial Studies, New York University.

Medawar, P.B. (1967) *The art of the soluble*. London: Methuen.

Mednick, M.T. (1982) Woman and the psychology of achievement: Implications for personal and social change. In H.J. Bernardin (ed.) *Women in the work-force*. New York: Praeger.

Mambert, W.A. (1976) *Effective presentation*. New York: Wiley.

Mendelsohn, G.A. and Rankin, N.O. (1969) Client–counselor compatibility and the outcome of counseling. *Journal of Abnormal Psychology*, **74**, 157–63.

Michener, H.A., Fleishman, J.A. and Vaske, J.J. (1976) A test of the bargaining theory of coalition formulation in four-person groups. *Journal of Personality and Social Psychology*, **34**, 1114–26.

Middlebrook, M. (1983) *The Kaiser's War*. London: Penguin, p. 54.

Milgram, S. (1963) Behavioral study of obedience. *Journal of Abnormal and Social Psychology*, **67**, 371–8.

Miller, D., Kets de Vries, Manfred, F.R. and Toulouse, J.-M. (1982) Top executive locus of control and its relationship to strategy-making, structure, and environment. *Academy of Management Journal*, **25**, 237–53.

Miller, M.A. and Rahe, R.H. (1997) Life changes scaling for the 1990s Social Readjustment Rating Scale. *Journal of Psychosomatic Research*, **43**(3), 279–92.

Miner, J.B. (1984) The validity and usefulness of theories in an emerging organizational science. *Academy of Management Review*, **9**, 296–306.

Miner, J.B. (1973) The real crunch in managerial manpower. *Harvard Business Review*, **51**, 146–58.

Mintzberg, H. (1973) *The nature of managerial work*. New York: Harper & Row.

Mintzberg, H. (1975) The manager's job: Folklore and fact. *Harvard Business Review*, **53**, 49–71.

Mintzberg, H. (1987) Training managers, not MBAs. Paper presented at the Macro Organizational Behavior Society meetings. Northwestern University, September.

Mishra, A.K. (1993) Organizational response to crisis: The role of mutual trust and top management teams. PhD dissertation, University of Michigan.

Mitchell, T.R. (1975) Expectancy models of job satisfaction, occupational preference, and effort: A theoretical, empirical, and methodological appraisal. *Administrative Science Quarterly*, **22**, 264–80.

Mitchell, T., Smyser, C.M. and Weed, S. (1975) Locus of control: Supervision and work satisfaction. *Academy of Management Journal*, **18**, 623–30.

Mitroff, L.I. and Emshoff, J.R. (1979) On strategic assumption making: A dialectical approach to policy and planning. *Academy of Management Review*, **4**, 5.

Mitroff, L.L. and Kilmann, R. (1974) On evaluating scientific research: The contributions of the philosophy of science. *Technological Forecasting and Social Change*, **8**, 163–74.

Modlin, H. and Faris, M. (1956) Group adaptation and interaction in psychiatric team practice. *Psychiatry*, **19**, 97–103.

Monsarrat, N. (1951) *The Cruel Sea*. Harmondsworth: Penguin.

Moore, T. (1987) Personality tests are back. *Fortune*, 30 March, pp. 74–82.

Morris, W. and Sashkin, M. (1976) *Organizational behavior in action*. St Paul, Minn.: West Publishing.

Moses, J.L. and Ritchie, R.J. (1976) Supervisory relationships training: A behavioral evaluation of a behavioral modeling program. *Personnel Psychology*, **29**, 337–43.

Moskal, B.A. (1991) Is industry ready for adult relationships? *Industry Week* (21 January), 19–27.

Mulkowsky, G.P. and Freeman, M.J. (1980) The impact of managerial orientation on implementing decisions. *Human Resource Management*, **18**, 6–14.

Murnighan, K. (1981) Group decision: What strategies to use? *Management Review*, **70**, 55–61.

Myers, I.B. (1980) *Introduction to type*. Palo Alto, Calif.: Consulting Psychologists Press.

Nadler, D.E. and Lawler, E.E. (1977) Motivation: A diagnostic approach. In J.R. Hackman, E.E. Lawler and L.W. Porter (eds) *Perspective behavior in organizations*. New York: McGraw-Hill.

Nayak, P.R. and Ketteringham, J.M. (1986) *Breakthroughs!* New York: Rawson Associates.

Near, R. and Weckler, D. (1990) Organizational and job characteristics related to self-managing teams. Paper presented to the Conference on Self-Managing Workteams, Denton, Texas, September.

Nemeth, C.J. (1986) Differential contributions of majority and minority influence. *Psychological Review*, **93**, 23–32.

Neufeld, R.W.J. and Thomas, P. (1977) Effects of perceived efficacy of a prophylactic controlling mechanism on self-control under painful stimulation. *Canadian Journal of Behavioral Science*, **9**, 224–32.

Newcomb, T. (1954) An approach to the study of communicative acts. *Psychological Review*, **60**, 393–404.

Newman, W.H. and Warren, K. (1977) The process of management. Englewood Cliffs, NJ: Prentice Hall.

Newton, R. and Wilkinson, M. (1995) Critical success in management development. *Management Development Review*, **8**(1), 16–24.

Nielson, E.H. (1986) Empowerment strategies: Balancing authority and responsibility. In S. Scrivastiva *et al.* (eds) *Executive power*, San Francisco: Jossey-Bass.

Nord, W.R. (1975) Some issues in the application of operant conditioning to the management of organizations. *Organization and Administrative Sciences*, **6**, 55–62.

Northcraft, G. and Neale, M. (1990) *Organization behavior*. Chicago: Dryden Press.

Nunney, D.N. (1978) Cognitive style mapping. *Training and Development Journal*, **32**, 50–7.

O'Connell, A. (1995) Boost self-esteem. *Executive Excellence*, **12**(1), 8.

Oakland, J.S. (1994) *Total quality management*. Oxford: Butterworth-Heinemann.

Oakland, S. (1997) PhD, University of Bradford, and papers on stress in Head Teachers.

Okanlawon, A. (1989) Management education and learning styles in Nigeria. PhD Bradford University.

Organ, D. and Greene, C.N. (1974) Role ambiguity, locus of control, and work satisfaction. *Journal of Applied Psychology*, **59**, 101–12.

Orme-Johnson, D.W. (1973) Autonomic stability and transcendental meditation. *Psychosomatic Medicine*, **35**, 341–9.

Osborn, A. (1953) *Applied imagination*. New York: Scribner.

Ouchi, W. (1981) *Theory Z*. Reading, Mass.: Addison Wesley.

Ozer, E.M. and Bandura, A. (1990) Mechanisms governing empowerment effects: A self-efficacy analysis. *Journal of Personality and Social Psychology*, **58**, 472–86.

Parnes, S.J. (1962) Can creativity be increased? In S.J. Parnes and H.F. Harding (eds) *A source book for creative thinking*. New York: Scribner.

Peoples, D.A. (1988) *Presentations plus*. New York: Wiley.

Perl, L. (1980) *Junk food, fast food, health food*. New York: Clarion Books.

Peters, T. (1988) *Thriving on chaos*. New York: Knopf.

Peters, T. (1992) *Liberation management*. Basingstoke: Macmillan.

Peters, T.J. and Waterman R.H. (1982), *In search of excellence: Lessons from America's Best-Run Companies*. London: HarperCollins.

Phillips, E. and Cheston, R. (1979) Conflict resolution: What works. *California Management Review*, **21**, 76–83.

Plovnick, M.S. (1971) A cognitive ability theory of occupational roles. Working paper #524–71, Massachusetts Institute of Technology, Sloan School of Management, Spring.

Porras, J.I. and Anderson, B. (1981) Improving managerial effectiveness through modeling-based training. *Organizational Dynamics*, **9**, 60–77.

Porter, E.H. (1973) *Manual of administration and interpretation for strength deployment inventory*. LaJolla, Calif.: Personal Strengths Assessment Service.

Porter, L.W. and McKibbin, L.E. (1988) *Management education and development: Drift or thrust into the 21st century?* New York: McGraw-Hill.

Poza, E. and Markus, M. (1980) Success story: the team approach to work restructuring. *Organisational Dynamics*, Winter, 2–25.

Prentice, M.G. (1984) An empirical search for a relevant management curriculum. *Collegiate News and Views*, Winter, 25–9.

Preston, P. and Zimmerer, T.W. (1978) *Management for supervisors*. Englewood Cliffs, NJ: Prentice Hall.

Prince, G.M. (1969) How to be a better meeting chairman. *Harvard Business Review*, **47**, 98–108.

Probst, G. and Buchel B. (1997) *Organizational learning*. London: Prentice Hall.

Pruitt, D.G. (1983) Integrative agreements: Nature and consequences. In M.H. Bazerman and R.J. Lewicki (eds) *Negotiating in organizations*. Beverly Hills, Calif.: Sage Publishing.

Pryer, M.W. and Distefano, M.K. (1971) Perception of leadership behavior, job satisfaction, and interexternal locus of control across three nursing levels. *Nursing Research*, 534–537. Psychology, 63, 371–78.

Quick, T.L. (1977) *Person to person managing*. New York: St Martin's Press.

Rahe, R.H. (1974) The pathway between subjects' recent life change and their near future illness reports: Representative results and methodological issues. In B.S. Dohrenwend and B.P. Dohrenwend (eds) *Stressful life events: Their nature and effects*. New York: Wiley.

Rahe, R.H., Ryman, D.H. and Ward, H.W. (1980) Simplified scaling for life change events. *Journal of Human Stress*, **6**, 22–7.

Rappaport, J., Swift, C. and Hess, R. (1984) *Studies in empowerment: Steps toward understanding and action*. New York: Haworth Press.

Raudsepp, E. (1981) *How creative are you?* New York: Putnam.

Raymont, K.W. (1988) *Kolb's experiential learning theory*. MBA, University of Bradford.

Reid, M.H. (1987) *The Learning Style Inventory as a tool to study management*. MBA, University of Bradford.

Rest, J.R. (1979) Revised manual for the Defining Issues Test: an objective test of moral judgement development. Minneapolis Moral Research Papers.

Rickards, T. (1974) *Problem solving through creative analysis*. London: Gower.

Rickards, T. (1988) *Creativity and problem solving at work*. London: Gower.

Robbins, S.P. (1974) *Managing organizational conflict: A nontraditional approach*. Englewood Cliffs, NJ: Prentice Hall.

Robbins, S.P. (1978) Conflict management and conflict resolution are not synonymous terms. *California Management Review*, **21**, 67–75.

Roethlisberger, F.J. and Dickson, W.J. (1939) *Management and the worker*. An account of a research program conducted by the Western Electric Company (Hawthorne Works). Chicago, Cambridge, Mass.: Harvard University Press.

Rogers, C. (1961) *On becoming a person*. Boston: Houghton Mifflin.

Rogers, C. and Farson, R. (1976) *Active listening*. Chicago: Industrial Relations Center.

Rokeach, M. (1973) *The nature of human values*. New York: Free Press.

Rose, S.D., Crayner, J.J. and Edleson, J.L. (1977) Measuring interpersonal competence. *Social Work*, **22**, 125–9.

Rose, S.M. and Black, B.L. (1985) *Advocacy and empowerment: Mental health care in the community*. Boston: Routledge & Kegan Paul.

Ross, D. (1986) Coaching and counseling. Unpublished manuscript, University of Michigan Executive Education Center.

Rossiter, R. (1995) MBA Dissertation. Bradford University.

Rothbaum, F., Weisz, J.R. and Snyder, S.S. (1982) Changing the world and changing the self: A two-process model of perceived control. *Journal of Personality and Social Psychology*, **42**, 5–37.

Rothenberg, D.L. (1980) Professional achievement and locus of control: A tenuous relationship reconsidered. *Psychological Reports*, **46**, 183–8.

Rothenberg, A. (1979) Creative contradictions. *Psychology Today*, **13**, 55–62.

Rotter, J.B. (1966) Generalized expectancies for internal versus external control of reinforcement. *Psychological Monographs*, **80**, 1–28.

Ruble, T. and Thomas, K. (1976) Support for a two-dimensional model of conflict behavior. *Organizational Behavior and Human Performance*, **16**, 145.

Runyon, K.E. (1973) Some interaction between personality variables and management style. *Journal of Applied Psychology*, **57**, 288–94.

Ryan, L.R. (1970) *Clinical interpretation of the FIRO-B*. Palo Alto, Calif.: Consulting Psychologists Press.

Sailer, H.R., Schlacter, J. and Edwards, M.R. (1982) Stress: Causes, consequences, and coping strategies. *Personnel*, **59**, 35–48.

Salisbury, D.L. (1982) *America in transition: Implications for employee benefits*. Washington DC.: Employee Benefits Research Institute.

Samaritans, The (1996) *The Cost of Stress*.

Sanford, W.P. and Yeager, W.H. (1963) *Principles of effective speaking* (6th edn). New York: Ronald Press.

Sashkin, M. (1982) *A manager's guide to participative management*. New York: American Management Association.

Sashkin, M. (1984) Participative management is an ethical imperative. *Organizational Dynamics*, **12**, 4–22.

Savage, G.T., Blair, J.D. and Sorenson, R.L. (1989) Consider both relationships and substance when negotiating strategically. *Academy of Management Executive*, **3**, 37–48.

Sayles, L. (1964) *Managerial behavior: Administration in complex organizations*. New York: McGraw-Hill.

Schachter, S. (1959) *The psychology of affiliation: Experimental studies of the sources of gregariousness*. Stanford, Calif.: Stanford University Press.

Schein, E.H. (1960) Interpersonal communication, group solidarity, and social influence. *Sociometry*, **23**, 148–61.

Schere, J.L. (1982) Tolerance of ambiguity as a discriminating variable between entrepreneurs and managers. *Academy of Management Proceedings*, pp. 404–409.

Schmidt, S. (1991) Der Diskurs des Radikalen Konstruktivism. Suhrkamp, Frankfurt-Schlapfer company document 1993 quoted in Probst *loc. cit.*

Schmidt, W.H. and Tannenbaum, R. (1965) Management of differences. *Harvard Business Review*, **38**, 107–15.

Schmidt, W.H. and Posner, B.Z. (1982) *Managerial values and expectations*. New York: American Management Association.

Schneider, J.A. and Agras, W.W. (1985) A cognitive behavioural treatment of bulimia. *British Journal of Psychiatry*, **146**, 66–9.

Schneier, C. (1979) Measuring cognitive complexity: Developing reliability, validity, and norm tables for a personality instrument. *Educational and Psychological Measurement*, **39**, 599–612.

Schriesheim, C. and Von Glinow, M. (1977) The path-goal theory of leadership: A theoretical and empirical analysis. *Academy of Management Journal*, **20**, 398–405.

Schumacher, E.F. (1977) *A guide for the perplexed*. New York: Harper & Row.

Schutz, W.C. (1958) *FIRO: A three-dimensional theory of interpersonal behavior*. New York: Holt, Rinehart and Winston.

Schutz, W.C. (1984) *The Truth Option*. 10 Speed Press, PO Box 7123, Berkeley, Calif.

Schwalbe, M.L. and Gecas, V. (1988) Social psychological consequences of job-related disabilities. In J.T. Mortimer and K.M. Borman (eds) *Work experience and psychological development through life span*. Boulder, Colo.: Westview.

Scott, O.J. (1974) *The creative ordeal: The story of Raytheon*. New York: Atheneum.

Scott-Morgan, P. (1994) *Unwritten rules of the game*. McGraw-Hill.

Sculley, J. and Byrne, J.A. (1989) *Odyssey: Pepsi to Apple*. London: Fontana.

Seeman, M. and Anderson, C.S. (1983) Alienation and alcohol. *American Sociological Review*, **48**, 60–77.

Seeman, M. (1982) On the personal consequences of alienation in work. *American Sociological Review*, **32**, 273–85.

Seibold, D.R. (1979) Making meetings more successful: Plans, formats, and procedures for group problem solving. *Journal of Business Communications*, **16**, 3–20.

Seligman, M.E.P. (1975) *Helplessness: On depression, development, and death.* San Francisco: Freeman.

Selye, H. (1976) *The stress of life* (2nd edn). New York: McGraw-Hill.

Selznick, P. (1957) *Leadership in administration.* New York: Harper & Row.

Semler, R. (1993) *Maverick.* London: Century.

Senge, P. (1991) *The fifth disciple.* New York: Doubleday.

Sewell, C. (1990) *Customers for life.* New York: Pocket Books.

Shalinsky, W. (1969) Group composition as a factor in assembly effects. *Human Relations*, **22**, 457–64.

Sharman, C. (1997) Looking for tomorrow's leaders. *Management Today*, August, p. 5.

Shaw, M.E. (1976) *Group dynamics: The psychology of small group behavior* (2nd edn). New York: McGraw-Hill.

Shea, G.P. and Guzzo, R.A. (1987) Group effectiveness: What really matters? *Sloan Management Review*, **28**, 25–31.

Sieburg, E. (1969) Dysfunctional communication and interpersonal responsiveness in small groups. Unpublished doctoral dissertation, University of Denver.

Sieburg, E. (1978) Confirming and disconfirming organizational communication. Working paper, University of Denver.

Simon, H.A. (1973) Applying information technology to organization design. *Public Administration Review*, **34**, 268–78.

Simon, S.B. (1974) *Meeting yourself halfway: 31 value clarification strategies for daily living.* Niles, Ill.: Argus Communications.

Sincoff, M.Z. and Goyer, R.S. (1984) *Interviewing.* New York: Macmillan.

Singleton, W.T., Spurgeon, P. and Stammers, R.B. (1980) *The analysis of social skill.* New York: Plenum.

Skinner, B.F. (1953) *Science and human behavior.* New York: Macmillan.

Smith, P.E. (1976) Management modeling training to improve morale and customer satisfaction. *Personnel Psychology*, **29**, 351–9.

Smith, S. and Haythorn, W.W. (1973) Effects of compatibility, crowding, group size, and leadership seniority on stress, anxiety, hostility, and annoyance in isolated groups. *Journal of Personality and Social Psychology*, **22**, 67–79.

Smith, S. and Leach, C. (1972) A hierarchical measure of cognitive complexity. *British Journal of Psychology*, **63**, 561–8.

Smith, W.P. (1987) Conflict and negotiation: Trends and emerging issues. *Journal of Applied Social Psychology*, **17**, 631–77.

Snyder, M., Stephen, W. and Rosenfield, D. (1978) Attributional egotism. In J. Harvey, W. Ickes and R. Kidds (eds) *New directions in attributional research*, Vol. 2. Hillsdale, NJ: Erlbaum.

Solomon, B.B. (1976) *Black empowerment: Social work in oppressed communities*. New York: Columbia University Press.

Spector, P.E. (1982) Behavior in organizations as a function of employee's locus of control. *Psychological Bulletin*, May, 487–9.

Spreitzer, G.M. (1992) When organizations dare: The dynamics of individual empowerment in the workplace. PhD dissertation, University of Michigan.

Stabell, C. (1973) The impact of a conversational computer system on human problem solving behavior. Working paper, Massachusetts Institute of Technology, Sloan School of Management.

Stano, M.E. and Reinsch, N.L. Jr (1982) *Communication in interviews*. Englewood Cliffs, NJ: Prentice Hall.

Staples, L.H. (1990) Powerful ideas about empowerment. *Administration on Social Work*, **14**, 29–42.

Staw, B.M., McKechnie, P. and Puffer, S. (1983) The justification of organizational performance. *Administrative Science Quarterly*, **28**, 582–600.

Staw, B.M., Sandelands, L. and Dutton, J. (1981) Threat-rigidity effects in organizational behavior: A multi-level analysis. *Administrative Science Quarterly*, **26**, 501–24.

Steil, L.K. (1980) *Your listening profile*. Minneapolis: Sperry Corporation.

Steiner, G. (1978) *The creative organization*. Chicago: University of Chicago Press.

Stewart, C.J. and Cash, W.B. Jn (1985) *Interviewing: Principles and practice* (4th edn). Dubuque, Iowa: Wm. C. Brown Publishers.

Stewart, I. and Joines, V. (1987) *TA today*. Nottingham: Lifespace Publishing.

Stone, R.A. and Deleo, J. (1976) Psychotherapeutic control of hypertension. *New Journal of Medicine*, **294**, 80–4.

Strauss, G. (1963) Some notes on power equalization. In H. Levitt (ed.) *The social science of organizations*. Englewood Cliffs, NJ: Prentice Hall.

Summers, D. (1990) Testing for stress in the workplace. *Financial Times*, 6 December

Susman, G.I. (1990) Work groups, technology and choice. In P.S. Goodman and L.S. Sprout (eds) *Technology and organisations*. San Francisco: Jossey-Bass.

Syer, J. and Connolly, C. (1984) *Sporting body, sporting mind*. Cambridge: Cambridge University Press.

Syer, J. (1986) *Team spirit*. London: Simon & Schuster.

Szilagyi, A.D. and Wallace, M.J. (1983) *Organizational Behavior and Performance*, 3rd edn. Glenview, Ill.: Foresman, pp. 204–5.

Tannenbaum, R. and Schmidt, W.H. (1958) How to choose a leadership pattern. *Harvard Business Review*, **3**, 95–101.

Taylor, C.W. and Barron, F.X. (1963) *Scientific creativity: Its recognition and development*. New York: Wiley.

Taylor, F.W. (1911) *The principle of scientific management* (1947 edn). New York: Harper.

Terborg, J.R., Castore, C. and DeNinno, J.A. (1976) A longitudinal field investigation of the impact of group composition on group performance and cohesion. *Journal of Personality and Social Psychology*, **34**, 782–90.

Thamia, S.A. and Woods, M.F. (1984) A small group approach to creativity and innovation. *R&D Management*, **14**(1).

Thomas, K. (1976) Conflict and conflict management. In M.D. Dunnette (ed.) *Handbook of industrial and organizational psychology*. London: Routledge & Kegan Paul.

Thomas, K.W. and Velthouse, B.A. (1990) Cognitive elements of empowerment: An interpretive model of intrinsic task motivation. *Academy of Management Review*, **15**, 666–81.

Thomas, K.W. (1977) Toward multi-dimensional values in teaching: The example of conflict behavior. *Academy of Management Review*, **2**, 487.

Thomas, E. and Woods, M. (1994) *The manager's casebook*. London: Penguin.

Thompson, D.W. (1978) *Managing people: Influencing behavior*. St Louis: C.V. Mosby Co.

Thompson, J.D. and Tuden, A. (1959) Strategies, structures, and processes or organizational decision. In J.D. Thompson and A. Tuden (eds) *Comparative studies in administration*. Pittsburgh: University of Pittsburgh Press.

Thorton, B.B. (1966) As you were saying – The number one problem. *Personnel Journal*, **45**, 237–8.

Thurber, J. (1945) *The Thurber Carnival*. Harmondsworth: Penguin.

Tichy, N. (1983) *Strategic human resource management*. New York: Wiley.

Toffler, A. (1980) *The third wave*. New York: Morrow.

Topping, P.A. On being a leader. *Business and Economic Review*, **43**(3), 14–16.

Torrance, E.P. (1965) Scientific views of creativity and factors affecting its growth. *Daedalus*, **94**, 663–82.

Trist, E. (1969) On sociotechnical systems. In W.G. Bennis, K. Benne and R. Chin (eds) *The planning of change*. London: Penguin.

Tuckman, B.W. (1965) Development sequence in small groups. *Psychological Bulletin*, **63**, 384–99.

Twiss, B. (1980) *Managing technological innovation*. London: Longman.

Urwick, L. (1944) *Elements of administration*. New York: Harper & Brothers.

Vernon, P.E. (ed.) (1970) *Creativity*. New York: Penguin Books.

Vertinsky, I. (1976) Implementation II. A multi-paradigm approach. Working paper presented at International Conference on the Implementation of Management Science in Social Organizations. University of Pittsburgh.

Vogt, J.F. and Murrell, K.L. (1990) *Empowerment in organizations*. San Diego: University Associates.

von Occh, R. (1986) *A kick in the seat of the pants*. New York: Harper & Row.

Vroom, V.H. and Jago, A.G. (1974) Decision making as social process: Normative and descriptive models of leader behavior. *Decision Sciences*, **5**, 743–69.

Vroom, V.H. and Yetton, P.W. (1973) *Leadership and decision making*. Pittsburgh: University of Pittsburgh Press.

Vygotsky, L. (1962) *Thought and language*. Cambridge, Mass.: MIT Press.

Walsh, J. and Ungson, G. (1991) Organisational Memory. *Academy of Management Review*, **16**(1), 57–91.

Walton, R. (1969) *Interpersonal peacekeeping: Confrontations and third party consultation*. Reading, Mass.: Addison Wesley.

Walton, R.E. (1965) Two strategies for social change and their dilemmas. *Journal of Applied Behavioural Science*, **1**, 167–79

Wanous, J.P. and Youtz, A. (1986) Solution diversity and the quality of group decisions. *Academy of Management Journal*, **1**, 149–59.

Wanous, J.P. (1980) *Organizational entry*. Reading, Mass.: Addison Wesley.

Wanous, J.P., Richers, A.E. and Malik, S.D. (1984) Organizational development – towards an integrated perspective. *Journal of Management review*, **9**(4), 670–83.

Warburton, F.E. (1993) Enhancing competitiveness through leadership in management. *Business Council Bulletin*, Oct., pp. 28–30.

Watson, J.: Cannon Working Party Report, *Progress and Change 1987–1994*.

Weick, K. (1979) The *social psychology of organizing*. Reading, Mass.: Addison Wesley.

Weick, K. (1984) Small wins. *American Psychologist*, **39**, 40–9.

Weick, K. (1993) The collapse of sensemaking in organizations. *Admistrative Science Quarterly*, **38**(4), 52–62.

Wellins, R.P., Bynam, W.C. and Wilson, J.M. (1991) *Empowered teams*. San Francisco: Jossey-Bass.

Wheeler, R.W. and Davis, J.M. (1979) Decision making as a function of locus of control and cognitive dissonance. *Psychological Reports*, **44**, 499–502.

Whetten, D.A. and Cameron, K.S. (1983) Management skill training; A needed addition to the management curriculum. *Organizational Behavior Teaching Journal*, **8**, 10–15.

White, M. and Trevor, M. (1983) *Under Japanese management: The experience of British workers*. PSI Heinemann.

White, R.W. (1959) Motivation reconsidered: The concept of competence. *Psychological Review*, **66**, 297–333.

Whittaker, J. (1970) Models of group development. *Social Services Review*, **44**(3), 308–22.

Wickens, P. (1987) *The Road to Nissan Flexibility, Quality, Teamwork*. Basingstoke: Macmillan Press.

Wilcox, R.P. (1967) *Oral reporting in business and industry.* Englewood Cliffs, NJ: Prentice Hall.

Wilsons D.K. (1986) An investigation of the properties of Kolb's Learning Style Inventory. *Leadership and Organisational Development Journal,* **7**(3).

Wolf, R.N. (1972) Effects of economic threat on autonomy and perceived locus of control. *Journal of Social Psychology,* **86**, 233–40.

Wolff, H.G., Wolf, S.G. and Hare, C.C. (eds) (1950) *Life stress and bodily disease.* Baltimore: Williams & Wilkins.

Wolman, B.B. (ed.) (1982) *Psychological aspects of obesity: A handbook.* New York: Van Nostrand Reinhold.

Woods, M. (1987) *The New Manager.* Shaftsbury, UK: Element Books.

Woods, M. (1989) *Aware Manager!!!.* London: Element/Penguin.

Woods, M. (1997a) Empowerment and culture. *Training and Management Development Methods,* **11**, 8.19–8.36.

Woods, M. (1997b) Leadership in the new organisation. *Training and Management Development Methods,* **11**, 4.01–4.32.

Woods, M. (1998) Making change happen. *Training and Management Development Methods,* **12**, 8.01–8.21.

Woods, M. and Davies, G.B. (1973) Potential Problem Analysis: a systematic approach to problem prediction and contingency planning. *R&D Management,* **4**(1), October.

Woods, M., Fedorkow, M. and Smith, M. (1998) Modelling the Learning Organisation. University of Bradford Occasional Papers 9805.

Woods, M. and Okanlawon, A. (1991) *Training and Management Development Methods,* **5**, 2.01–2.15 MCB University Press.

Woods, M. and Thomas, E. (1992) The Belbin Interplace III. Training and Management Development Methods, **6**, 2.01–2.18.

Woods, M. and Whitehead, J. (1993) *Working alone.* London: Pitman.

Zaleznik, A. (1977) Managers and leaders: Are they different? *Harvard Business Review,* **55**(3), 67.

Zand, D.E. (1972) Trust and managerial problem solving. *Administrative Science Quarterly,* **17**, 229–39.

Zimmerman, M.A. and Rappaport, J. (1988) Citizen participation, perceived control, and psychological empowerment. *American Journal of Community Psychology,* **16**, 725–50.

Zimmerman, M.A. (1990) Taking aim on empowerment research: On the distinction between individual and psychological conceptions. *American Journal of Community Psychology,* **18**, 169–77.

Index